Nurturing Creativity in the Classroom is a groundbreaking collection of essays by leading scholars who examine and respond to the tension that many educators face in valuing student creativity while believing they cannot support creativity given the curricular constraints of the classroom. Is it possible for teachers to nurture creative development and expression without drifting into curricular chaos? Do curricular constraints necessarily lead to choosing conformity over creativity? This book combines the perspectives of top educators and psychologists to generate practical advice for considering and addressing the challenges of supporting creativity within the classroom. It is unique in its balance of practical recommendations for nurturing creativity and thoughtful appreciation of curricular constraints. This approach helps ensure that the insights and advice found in this collection will take root in educators' practice, rather than being construed as yet another demand placed on their overflowing plate of responsibilities.

Ronald A. Beghetto, PhD, is Associate Professor of Education Studies at the University of Oregon. His scholarship focuses on promoting creativity in K-12 classrooms and the influence of past schooling experience on K-12 teacher development. His recent publications on creativity and teacher development appear in a wide variety of scholarly journals – including *Creativity Research Journal, Journal of Creative Behavior, Creativity and Thinking Skills, Educational Psychologist, Journal of Advanced Academics, Journal of Research in Science Teaching*, and *Journal of Educational Research* – and edited volumes – *Creativity and Reason in Cognitive Development, Creativity: From Potential to Realization, Creativity: A Handbook for Teachers, Critical Issues and Practices in Gifted Education*, and *Rethinking Gifted Education*. He serves on the editorial boards of *Psychology of Aesthetics, Creativity, and the Arts; Journal of Creative Behavior;* and *Journal of Educational Research* and is Associate Editor for the *International Journal of Creativity and Problem Solving*. He is the 2008 recipient of the Daniel E. Berlyne Award from the American Psychological Association's Division 10. He has also received awards for excellence in teaching, including the 2005–2006 Crystal Apple Ersted Award for Outstanding Teaching from the University of Oregon.

James C. Kaufman, PhD, is Associate Professor of Psychology at the California State University at San Bernardino, where he directs the Learning Research Institute. His research broadly focuses on nurturing and encouraging creativity. He is specifically interested in creativity's role in fairness, everyday creativity, increasing creativity in the classroom, and the structure and assessment of creativity. He is also interested in related topics such as intelligence, personality, motivation, and thinking styles. Kaufman is the author or editor of sixteen books, either published or in press, including *Creativity 101, Essentials of Creativity Assessment* (with Jonathan Plucker and John Baer), *International Handbook of Creativity* (with Robert Sternberg), and *Applied Intelligence* (with Robert Sternberg and Elena Grigorenko). His research has been featured and discussed in the articles or broadcasts of CNN, NPR, *The New York Times, Los Angeles Times, The New Yorker*, and the BBC. Kaufman is a founding coeditor of the official journal for the APA's Division 10, *Psychology of Aesthetics, Creativity, and the Arts*, and edits the *International Journal for Creativity and Problem Solving*. He also is Associate Editor of *Psychological Assessment* and the *Journal of Creative Behavior*. He received the 2003 Daniel E. Berlyne Award from APA's Division 10, the 2008 E. Paul Torrance Award from the National Association of Gifted Children, and the 2009 Early Career Research Award from the Western Psychological Association.

Nurturing Creativity in the Classroom

Edited by

Ronald A. Beghetto
University of Oregon

James C. Kaufman
California State University at San Bernardino

CAMBRIDGE UNIVERSITY PRESS
Cambridge, New York, Melbourne, Madrid, Cape Town, Singapore,
São Paulo, Delhi, Dubai, Tokyo

Cambridge University Press
32 Avenue of the Americas, New York, NY 10013-2473, USA

www.cambridge.org
Information on this title: www.cambridge.org/9780521715201

© Cambridge University Press 2010

This publication is in copyright. Subject to statutory exception
and to the provisions of relevant collective licensing agreements,
no reproduction of any part may take place without the written
permission of Cambridge University Press.

First published 2010

Printed in the United States of America

A catalog record for this publication is available from the British Library.

Library of Congress Cataloging in Publication data

Nurturing creativity in the classroom / edited by Ronald A. Beghetto,
James C. Kaufman.
    p.   cm.
Includes bibliographical references and index.
ISBN 978-0-521-88727-4 (hardback)
1. Creative thinking.   2. Creative ability.   I. Beghetto, Ronald A., 1969–
II. Kaufman, James C.   III. Title.
LB1062.N87   2010
370.15′2 – dc22   2009047359

ISBN 978-0-521-88727-4 Hardback
ISBN 978-0-521-71520-1 Paperback

Cambridge University Press has no responsibility for the persistence or
accuracy of URLs for external or third-party Internet Web sites referred to in
this publication and does not guarantee that any content on such Web sites is,
or will remain, accurate or appropriate.

This book is dedicated, with much love, to Jeralynn — my wife, best friend, and most ardent supporter.

— RAB

To my wife's parents, fellow university educators
Joseph and Jean Katz,
with love and gratitude for welcoming me into their family,
and to her sister, Cynthia,
as she begins her own journey as a classroom teacher.

— JCK

CONTENTS

CONTRIBUTORS

JOHN BAER
Rider University, USA

ALEXINIA YOUNG BALDWIN
University of Connecticut, USA

RONALD A. BEGHETTO
University of Oregon, USA

ANNA CRAFT
University of Exeter, UK
The Open University, UK

BONNIE CRAMOND
University of Georgia, USA

SUSAN DANIELS
California State University
at San Bernardino, USA

CATHARINA F. DE WET
University of Alabama, USA

GAYLE T. DOW
Christopher Newport University, USA

ELIZABETH FAIRWEATHER
University of Georgia, USA

TRACEY GARRETT
Rider University, USA

ELENA L. GRIGORENKO
Yale University, USA
Moscow State University, Russia

DIANE F. HALPERN
Claremont McKenna College, USA

BETH A. HENNESSEY
Wellesley College, USA

JAMES C. KAUFMAN
California State University at
San Bernardino, USA

RAYMOND S. NICKERSON
Tufts University, USA

WEIHUA NIU
Pace University, USA

MICHAEL M. PIECHOWSKI
Institute for Educational
Advancement, USA
Northland College, USA

JANE PIIRTO
Ashland University, USA

JONATHAN A. PLUCKER
Indiana University, USA

JOSEPH S. RENZULLI
University of Connecticut, USA

RUTH RICHARDS
Saybrook University, USA
McLean Hospital and
Harvard Medical School, USA

MARK A. RUNCO
University of Georgia, USA

R. KEITH SAWYER
*Washington University
  in St. Louis, USA*

THOMAS SKIBA
Yale University, USA

ROBERT J. STERNBERG
Tufts University, USA

PATRICIA D. STOKES
*Barnard College, USA
Columbia University, USA*

MEI TAN
Yale University, USA

ZHENG ZHOU
St. John's University, USA

PREFACE

In addition to being creativity researchers, both of us are fathers of young children. As we watched Olivia and Jacob develop, the importance of an educational system that values creativity has become increasingly salient. Our children have an advantage in that their fathers value creativity (perhaps too much!). Like so many other parents, we are committed to providing diverse learning opportunities for our children. However, this commitment is not enough.

As college professors, both of us have seen many types of students. We see the student who is utterly convinced she is not creative and yet surprises herself by sharing a profoundly creative idea in class or on an assignment. Another student believes he is not creative and initially has no interest in cultivating his creativity. Yet another sees herself as a creative musician but fails to see any creativity in science or mathematics. It takes time and effort for these students to shake off their (mis)conceptions about creativity.

Then, there are the students we never see, those who have had limited opportunities to develop their creative potential. Not only do these students fail to find success in school, often for capricious and unjust reasons, but they may also believe that they lost what little spark of creativity and curiosity they had before entering formal schooling.

Finally, there are those students who have been mentored, supported by inspirational teachers, and (when appropriate) left alone to develop their creative potential. We are not too worried about these students; however, they, too, should not be forgotten. It is our hope that this book inspires educators, parents, and researchers to ensure that all students have an opportunity to find, nurture, and sustain their creative potential.

Such a goal is ambitious and one that we cannot hope to accomplish alone. We therefore selected contributors who we not only respected and admired but who we thought could most directly address the challenge of supporting creativity in the classroom. We hope that you will enjoy and draw as much insight and inspiration from these essays as we have. We close the book with a coda that highlights twenty key points and repeated motifs across the chapters.

ACKNOWLEDGMENTS

The authors would like to thank Simina Calin and Eric Schwartz of Cambridge University Press for their assistance in seeing this book through to publication. They also would like to thank Ryan Holt and Tessy Pumaccahua for their help with manuscript preparation.

The authors thank Jonathan Plucker and Robert Sternberg, who were both wonderful mentors.

Ron would like to thank his colleagues in the University of Oregon's Department of Education Studies for their collegiality and support – in particular, his chair Jerry Rosiek and his dean Mike Bullis for their leadership and encouragement and all his students who hold great potential for transforming the future of education through their own commitments to creative and inspiring teaching. He would also like to thank his family, in particular, his mother Teresa, his sister Christina and her family, and his wife Jeralynn and daughter Olivia for the love and support they provide on a daily basis.

James would like to thank his CSUSB family for consistent and meaningful support – colleagues Mark Agars, Allen Butt, Susan Daniels, and Mihaela Popescu; his chair Robert Cramer, his dean Jamal Nassar, and his president Al Karnig; Stacy Brooks, Stephanie Loera, Jane Rowland, and the rest of the unfathomably good administrative support staff; and his students, whose many pathways to excellence inspire him every day. He also would like to thank his family for their love and support, especially his parents Alan and Nadeen, his sister Jennie and her family, his wife Allison, and his son Jacob.

1

How to Discourage Creative Thinking in the Classroom

RAYMOND S. NICKERSON

One would like to know how to teach students to think creatively. There are numerous proposals on the subject and a small amount of encouraging data (Cropley, 1992; Finke, Ward, & Smith, 1992; Nickerson, 1999; Stein, 1974, 1975; Sternberg & Lubart, 1991). I am becoming increasingly convinced that attitudes and beliefs play a much greater role in determining the quality of one's thinking – creative or critical – than is generally recognized. This is not to suggest that skills and knowledge are unimportant but rather that they are only part of the equation, and by themselves are insufficient to ensure that creative thinking will occur.

The idea that attitudes and beliefs are important to creative thinking – as well as to critical thinking – is not novel; many researchers have expressed it (Andrews & Debus, 1978; Baron, 1991; Deci & Ryan, 1985; Dweck, 1975; Reid, 1987). Unfortunately, research has not yet yielded a reliable prescription for promoting the attitudes and beliefs on which creative or critical thinking depends. It occurred to me that it might be easier to specify how to instill attitudes and beliefs that tend to stifle thinking, because, if the conclusions from numerous assessments of the thinking abilities of many students are to be believed, we collectively seem to know how to do this rather well.

While not wishing to claim to be an expert on how to stifle creativity, I know how I would go about it if that were my purpose. The following is a proposed set of rules for fostering attitudes and beliefs that will almost surely inhibit creative thinking by a large majority of nearly any group of students – at least that is my conjecture. The reader may see ways to improve the list.

- Perpetuate the idea that there is one correct way to do any particular task and that there is one and only one correct answer to every question. Emphasize the overriding importance of being right. Insist that students give back on tests precisely what they have been given in class. Tolerate no deviations. Promote the belief that all errors and mistakes are bad – causes for embarrassment. Waste no time in trying to figure out the basis (often

1

rational [Ben-Zeev, 1998; VanLehn, 1990]) behind incorrect solutions to problems, and make sure that students do not get the idea that errors sometimes give evidence of ingenuity and highly creative thinking, and almost always can be opportunities for learning.

- Cultivate an unquestioning submission to, and preferably a fear of, authority, especially the teacher's. Fear is recognized as a major determinant of conformity of behavior, if not of thought (Crutchfield, 1962; Freeman, 1983). And even if it does not ensure conformity of thought, it lessens the likelihood that unconventional ideas will be expressed. Remind students often of who is in charge and never admit to being wrong. Impress upon them the belief that questioning authority is disrespectful. Reinforce the idea that if something is written in a book, it must be true. Present your own views as the truth – never as opinions – and tolerate no challenges of them. Permit no discussion in class of ideas that you do not thoroughly understand. Never say "I don't know" out loud. Remind students from time to time that you have lived much longer than they and therefore are infinitely more knowledgeable and wise.

- Insist on adhering to the lesson plan at all costs. Let students work only on problems that are prescribed either by you or by their textbooks. Many researchers have stressed the importance of problem finding – as distinct from problem solving – as an aspect of creativity (Campbell, 1960; Getzels & Csikszentmihalyi, 1975, 1976; Mackworth, 1965; Okuda, Runco, & Berger, 1991; Runco, 1994; Runco & Nemiro, 1994; Starko, 1989). Creative students are very likely to want, occasionally, to explore problems other than those that someone else has laid out for them to solve. One may not be able to keep them from doing this on their own time outside the classroom, but one can make sure they understand that they are to work on prescribed tasks while at school, and their own interests are irrelevant.

- Disabuse students of the notion that they should aspire to have original thoughts. Such a notion is dangerous; *creativity* sometimes is defined as a tendency to have original and daring ideas (Cropley, 1992; Feldhusen & Treffinger, 1986). Promote the belief that genius is a rare quality, that few people are born with it, and the rest – the vast majority – must be content with thinking other people's thoughts and should not aspire to originate any of their own. Dismiss any temptation to believe that those researchers who contend that nearly anyone can be creative in one way or another could be right (Amabile, 1983; Cropley, 1992; Treffinger, Isaksen, & Dorval, 1994). When a student tries to express an original idea in class, be quick to point out what is wrong with it. If finding a specific fault is not easy, simply declare it to be incorrect, impractical, or bizarre. The teacher is in charge and not obliged to justify, or even explain, his or her assertions.

- Promote belief in the compartmentalization of knowledge. Be sure students see no connection between what is taught in English class and what is taught in history or physics. Try to prevent them from getting the idea that the problem-solving approaches that are useful in one domain might have some applicability in another. This is very important, especially in view of Koestler's (1964) warning that a sure sign of creativity is a capacity to make connections that most people overlook.

- Use slogans to prove points. It matters little what point one wants to prove; one can always find a slogan that will fit. If you want to justify increasing the size of a working group, point out that "Many hands make light work"; if you want to decrease the size, use "Too many cooks spoil the broth"; if you want to hurry the class up, note that "He who hesitates is lost"; and if you want to slow it down, point out that "Haste makes waste." The important thing to get across, by illustration, is the idea that if one has an adequate stockpile of such handy maxims, one need never give much thought to one's behavior, because one can almost always find a pithy saying with which to justify it.

- Discourage curiosity and inquisitiveness. One might think this would be difficult because children seem to be naturally curious and inquisitive about all manner of things, but the evidence is quite compelling that it can be done fairly easily. When a persistent child insists on asking questions for which you do not know the answers, take the opportunity to point out their absurdity. "What a silly question" should suffice to do the trick in most cases; ridicule is a devastatingly effective tool. Make it clear that awe and amazement at anything are childish reactions and need to be outgrown. Persistence in the entertaining of questions that generally only children entertain has been credited with the formulation of Einstein's theory of relativity, one of the most impressively creative scientific theories of all time (Holton, 1973). The sooner that children are disabused of wondering about unanswerable questions, the better. Never admit to being amazed or to wondering "why" about anything yourself. Promote the idea that science is a catalog of facts. Be sure the students do not have a chance to come to think of it as a quest, as a dynamic process of information seeking, or as an exciting intellectual adventure.

- Promote beliefs that are antithetical to the development of creative thinking. Researchers have identified many of these. The belief that intelligence is a genetically determined and unchanging property of an individual, for example, can demotivate children from making an effort to excel at intellectually demanding tasks (Dweck, 1975; Dweck & Bempechat, 1983; Elliot & Dweck, 1988; Stevenson, Cheng, & Lee, 1993). A closely related and equally destructive belief is that if one is sufficiently gifted, one need not learn a lot about a domain to be creative in that domain, and if one is not gifted, any effort to be creative in that domain will be futile. One wants to guard diligently against the belief that creativity is determined to a large degree by commitment and hard work.

- Above all, never permit learning or problem solving to be fun. Be sure students understand that one cannot work hard and have fun at the same time, that one cannot expect to enjoy the effort of trying to accomplish something of intellectual value. If children are encouraged to think, especially about problems in which they are genuinely interested, there is a real risk that they will experience the deep satisfaction that Csikszentmihalyi (1996), among others, has written about that can come from being engaged in creative work. Be very sure they never have the opportunity to make a real discovery; this can give a boost to the creative instinct from which they might not recover (Finke et al., 1992). Here, again, it is important to set a proper example. Intellectual enthusiasm is contagious; treat it like a disease. It is risky to show enthusiasm or excitement about anything!

I do not claim that this list is exhaustive or even that it is the best one that could be generated. I believe, however, that if one wishes to stifle creative thinking in the classroom – or elsewhere – the application of these rules with a modicum of consistency will accomplish that goal. Usually it should not be necessary to apply all of them; often one or two will suffice. My favorite is the last; it alone should do the trick in many cases.

Of course, there will always be the occasional child who will think creatively, despite one's best efforts to discourage it. There is little to be done in such cases except to insulate the rest of the class, insofar as possible, from the influence of such a child. One can be sure that if one applies these methods, such children will be rare; moreover, one or two here or there can be used to advantage. They will provide many opportunities to point out to the class forms of behavior that are not to be tolerated.

None of these suggestions requires the expenditure of extra time by the teacher or the introduction of additional or nonstandard subject matter. They all are matters of projecting and reinforcing beliefs and attitudes in the normal course of events in the classroom.

REFERENCES

Amabile, T. M. (1983). *The social psychology of creativity.* New York: Springer-Verlag.
Andrews, G. R., & Debus, R. I. (1978). Persistence and the causal perception of failure: Modifying cognitive attributions. *Journal of Educational Psychology, 70,* 154–166.
Baron, J. (1991). Beliefs about thinking. In J. F. Voss, D. N. Perkins, & J. W. Segal (Eds.), *Informal reasoning and education* (pp. 169–186). Hillsdale, NJ: Erlbaum.
Ben-Zeev, T. (1998). Rational errors and the mathematical mind. *Review of General Psychology, 2,* 366–383.
Campbell, D. (1960). Blind variation and selective retention in creative thought as in other knowledge processes. *Psychological Review, 67,* 380–400.
Cropley, A. J. (1992). *More ways than one: Fostering creativity.* Norwood, NJ: Ablex.
Crutchfield, R. S. (1962). Conformity and creative thinking. In H. Gruber, G. Terrell, & M. Wertheimer (Eds.), *Contemporary approaches to creative thinking* (pp. 120–140). New York: Atherton Press.

Csikszentmihalyi, M. (1996). *Creativity: Flow and the psychology of discovery and invention.* New York: Harper Collins.

Deci, E. L., & Ryan, R. M. (1985). *Intrinsic motivation and self-determination in human behavior.* New York: Plenum Press.

Dweck, C. S. (1975). The role of expectations and attributions in the alleviation of learned helplessness. *Journal of Personality and Social Psychology, 45,* 165–171.

Dweck, C. S., & Bempechat, J. (1983). Children's theories of intelligence. In S. Paris, G. Olsen, & H. Stevenson (Eds.), *Learning and motivation in the classroom* (pp. 239–256). Hillsdale, NJ: Erlbaum.

Elliott, E. S., & Dweck, C. S. (1988). Goals: An approach to motivation and achievement. *Journal of Personality and Social Psychology, 54,* 5–12.

Feldhusen, J. F., & Treffinger, D. J. (1986). *Creative thinking and problem solving in gifted education.* Dubuque, IO: Kendall/Hunt.

Finke, R. A., Ward, T. B., & Smith, S. M. (1992). *Creative cognition: Theory, research, and applications.* Cambridge, MA: MIT Press.

Freeman, J. (1983). Emotional problems of the gifted child. *Journal of Child Psychology and Psychiatry, 24,* 481–485.

Getzels, J. W. & Csikszentmihalyi, M. (1975). From problem solving to problem finding. In I. A Taylor & J. W. Getzels (Eds.), *Perspectives in creativity* (pp. 90–116). Chicago: Aldine.

Getzels, J. W. & Csikszentmihalyi, M. (1976). *The creative vision: A longitudinal study of problem finding in art.* New York: Wiley.

Holton, G. (1973). *Thematic origins of scientific thought.* Cambridge, MA: Harvard University Press.

Koestler, A. (1964). *The act of creation.* New York: Dell.

Mackworth, N. H. (1965). Originality. *The American Psychologist, 20,* 51–66.

Nickerson, R. S. (1999). Enhancing creativity. In R. J. Sternberg (Ed.), *Handbook of creativity* (pp. 392–430). New York: Cambridge University Press.

Okuda, S. M., Runco, M. A., & Berger, D. E. (1991). Creativity and the finding and solving of real-world problems. *Journal of Psychoeducational Assessment, 9,* 45–53.

Reid, W. A. (1987). Institutions and practices: Professional education reports and the language of reform. *Educational Researcher, 16*(8), 10–15.

Runco, M. A. (Ed.) (1994). *Problem finding, problem solving, and creativity.* Norwood, NJ: Ablex.

Runco, M. A., & Nemiro, J. (1994). Problem finding, creativity, and giftedness. *Roeper Review, 16,* 235–241.

Starko, A. J. (1989). Problem finding in creative writing: An exploratory study. *Journal for the Education of the Gifted, 12,* 172–186.

Stein, M. I. (1974). *Stimulating creativity,* Vol. 1. New York: Academic Press.

Stein, M. I. (1975). *Stimulating creativity,* Vol. 2. New York: Academic Press.

Sternberg, R. J, & Lubart, T. I. (1991). An investment theory of creativity and its development. *Human Development, 34,* 1–31.

Stevenson, H. W., Chen, C., & Lee, S.-Y. (1993). Mathematics achievement of Chinese, Japanese, and American children: Ten years later. *Science, 259,* 53–58.

Treffinger, D. J., Isaksen, S. G., & Dorval, K. B. (1994). Creative problem solving: An overview. In M. A. Runco (Ed.), *Problem finding, problem solving, and creativity* (pp. 223–256). Norwood, NJ: Ablex.

VanLehn, K. (1990). *Mind bugs: The origins of procedural misconceptions.* Cambridge, MA: MIT Press.

2

Teaching for Creativity in an Era of Content Standards and Accountability

JOHN BAER AND TRACEY GARRETT

INTRODUCTION

Teaching for creativity and teaching specific content knowledge need not be in opposition, as is often feared by educators. Creative thinking actually *requires* significant content knowledge, and thinking creatively about a topic helps deepen one's knowledge of that topic. Many creativity-relevant skills, such as divergent thinking, can be used in ways that increase both creativity and knowledge of specific content. There are also ways to make use of rewards and evaluations judiciously that will allow teachers to help students become more creative thinkers and also acquire important domain-specific skills and content knowledge. This chapter summarizes relevant research to provide a theoretical framework and describes specific classroom techniques that promote both creativity and the acquisition of content knowledge.

MUST CONTENT STANDARDS AND ACCOUNTABILITY BE IN CONFLICT WITH CREATIVITY?

The past two decades have seen a major and unrelenting call for more testing of students and more explicit and more detailed content standards that form the framework for such assessment. Although No Child Left Behind legislation has played a prominent role in recent educational policy formulations, federal mandates have not been the only force pushing for greater accountability (Fuhrman, 2001; Ladd, 1996). This movement includes both state initiatives and nongovernment, nationwide efforts like the Core Knowledge Foundation's Core Knowledge Sequence (Core Knowledge Foundation, 1998; Hirsch, 1987, 1991–1997, 1996). We will not argue the merit (or lack of merit) of an increasing reliance on standardized testing or the wisdom of fine-grained, grade-by-grade content standards. That debate is ongoing, and for the moment we will take the current situation, and a near-term future that seems to be heading toward ever more explicit content standards, as a given that any educational goals or activities must acknowledge and, to some extent at least, accommodate. We will argue that these initiatives (both the focus on explicit and detailed content standards and the standardized test-based accountability to which these standards are often closely linked) need not doom the teaching and promotion of creativity in the classroom. Teaching for creativity and detailed required content standards can coexist quite comfortably and, although they may seem at times to be working at cross purposes (and, indeed, this is sometimes the case), they just as often work synergistically, such that teaching for creativity helps meet content standards goals and teaching detailed content knowledge can reinforce and enhance student creativity.

At first glance, creativity and accountability do appear to be at odds. Most educators readily associate creativity with divergent thinking (coming up with many possible ideas in response to an open-ended prompt). For example, Woolfolk (2001) noted that "encouraging creativity in a classroom means to accept and encourage divergent thinking" (p. 102). They may also associate accountability with convergent thinking (finding a single correct or best answer to a problem) and/or evaluative thinking (judging whether an answer is accurate, consistent, or valid). The concepts of divergent, convergent, and evaluative thinking originated in Guilford's Structure of the Intellect Model, and because divergent thinking is widely believed to be an important component of creative thinking, the improvement of divergent thinking skills has often been the goal of creativity training (Baer, 1997a; Guilford, 1956; Woolfolk, 2007). In addition, the most widely used tests of creativity – the Torrance Tests of Creative Thinking – are actually not tests of creativity but rather tests of divergent thinking (Kim, 2006; Torrance, 1966, 1974, 1998; Torrance & Presbury, 1984). So these common associations are not unexpected.

But creativity is not just about divergent thinking; it also requires evaluative and convergent thinking, as well as a great deal of domain knowledge and skills (Kaufman & Baer, 2006; Runco, 2003; Simonton, 1999, 2006). For example, one of the best studied and most influential models of creativity, Campbell's blind-variation and selective-retention model, requires a combination of chance variation to produce new ideas (divergent thinking) and selective retention of more workable ideas (evaluative and convergent thinking) to produce creative breakthroughs (Campbell, 1960; see Simonton, 1994, 1998, and 2004 for more recent versions of this model). The Creative Problem Solving (CPS) model, which may be the most well-validated practical approach to creativity enhancement on the level of more everyday creativity and problem solving, also requires both divergent thinking and evaluative judgment as part of each and every step in the process (Baer, 1987a, 1997a; Isaksen & Treffinger, 1985; Puccio, Murdock, & Mance, 2007; Treffinger, Isaksen, & Dorval, 2006). So, although divergent thinking might be the first thing to come to mind when one thinks of creative thinking, it is not all there is to creativity; judgment, evaluation, skills, and knowledge all play important roles.

Creativity and content knowledge and skills are not (or need not be) orthogonal variables. They interact, and creativity is dependent on domain knowledge and skills. Nonetheless, the pressures of accountability and testing naturally affect the ways teachers teach, and one common fear is that creativity may be lost in the shuffle (Baer, 1999, 2002; Beghetto & Plucker, 2006; Fasko, 2001).

The effort to devise and implement detailed content standards has had many critics, many of whom have charged that attention to such content standards will detract from student thinking and creativity. Several have suggested that adherence to content standards like those exemplified by the Core Knowledge Sequence will result in the unthinking, uncritical, and uncreative absorption of knowledge (Orwin & Forbes, 1994; Schear, 1992; Vail, 1997). One critic called students in Core Knowledge schools "informational blotters" (Paul, 1990, p. 431) and claimed that these students would be able to do very little interesting or productive thinking with the knowledge that they obtained in Core Knowledge schools. There is a sense among many educators that the push for stricter content standards will decrease the amount of time teachers can allocate to the teaching of thinking skills. There is also a concern that content standards will encourage teachers to limit their instruction to that which will be tested (Jones, Jones, & Hargrove, 2003; Olson, 2000, 2001; Tucker, 2002).

We cannot deny that this happens. But there is significant evidence that the introduction of explicit content standards does not lessen students' creativity; in fact, it may do just the opposite. In the one large study ($N = 540$) to date that has looked directly at this issue (Baer, 2003), students in Core Knowledge middle schools had as high or higher creativity ratings than matched students in non–Core Knowledge middle schools. This study looked at actual performances of students on creativity-relevant tasks (such as writing stories and poems), not simply scores on divergent thinking tests. Contrary to the predictions of critics like Paul (1990), students in schools with detailed content standards and a strong focus on teaching to those content standards were not less creative than similar students in schools with less-detailed content standards. They were several creativity measures in this study, and on some of the measures, the Core Knowledge students were judged to be more creative, while on others, there was no statistically significant difference between the two groups. In none of the creativity assessments was the Core Knowledge group judged to have lower creativity than the matched non–Core Knowledge group.

The possibility that teaching for creativity and emphasizing content knowledge may be in conflict is part of the larger question about the relationship between learning content and learning to think more effectively (see, e.g., Chi, Glaser, & Farr, 1988; Feldhusen, 2006; Glass & Holyoak, 1986; Hirsch, 1996; Johnson-Laird, 1983; Karmiloff-Smith, 1992; Kaufman & Baer, 2006; Mayer,

2006; Paul, 1990; Chase & Simon, 1973; Woolfolk, 2007). It is also related to questions about the possibilities of transfer of learning and of teaching to promote such transfer (see, e.g., Gage & Berliner, 1992; Mayer, 1987; Perkins & Salomon, 1988; Salomon & Perkins, 1989; Woolfolk, 2007). It has become increasingly clear that thinking depends quite heavily on knowledge, that mistakes in everyday critical thinking are more often the result of faulty premises (i.e., incorrect factual knowledge) than a lack of general problem-solving skills, and that teaching for transfer requires a great deal of context-specific training or practice in any domain to which transfer is desired (Ashcraft, 1989; Baer, 1993, 1996; Kaufman & Baer, 2006; Weisberg, 1988, 1999, 2006; Willingham, 2001; Woolfolk, 2007). It seems that content knowledge is essential to serious thinking, that teaching content-free thinking skills is not possible, that higher-level thinking requires the automatization of lower-level skills, and that to improve students' thinking in a given domain, students must acquire an understanding of much factual content about that domain as well as a variety of domain-specific cognitive skills.

So we must teach students content knowledge if we want to improve their thinking. Conversely, often the best way to teach content knowledge is to get students to think about it in some way – to become actively engaged with the content to be learned (Ashcraft, 1989; Craik & Lockhart, 1972; Hirsch, 1987, 1996; Lockhart & Craik, 1990; Mayer, 1987; Woolfolk, 2007; Zimbardo & Gerrig, 1999). Being actively engaged with the content to be learned means being actively engaged *cognitively*, of course. Simply being physically active or emotionally engaged is not what is required (and may even get in the way of meaningful cognitive engagement). An emphasis on the acquisition of content knowledge does not conflict with an emphasis on active processing of information; in fact, the former requires the latter.

For these reasons, an emphasis on content standards need not hinder those who wish to emphasize the development of students' thinking skills, and this is true for creativity just as it is for other kinds of thinking. Having richer and more extensive content knowledge and skills should support, not detract from, creative thinking, just as such knowledge and skills support other kinds of thinking. There is a consensus among creativity researchers and theorists that creative genius in particular requires extensive content knowledge (Gruber, 1981; Gruber & Davis, 1988; Simonton, 1994, 1998, 1999, 2004, 2006; Weisberg, 1988, 1999, 2006), and there is much evidence to support what has come to be known as the "ten-year rule," which claims that it generally takes at least ten years of extensive work and/or study in a field before truly creative work is even possible (see, e.g., Chase & Simon, 1973; Hayes, 1989; Kaufman & Baer, 2002; Weisberg, 1999).

This is not to suggest that all is well and that there is no conflict between content standards (and test-based accountability) and teaching for creativity. There are very real problems, problems that are in most cases avoidable, but very real problems because they are often not avoided. In fact, teachers' misperceptions of how best to meet accountability standards often result in the worst possible outcomes: lower test scores and lessened creativity. Teachers who feel pressured to raise test scores may drop anything resembling divergent thinking from their lesson plans. They may also emphasize rote memorization at the expense of thinking about and understanding the content they are teaching. But dropping divergent thinking activities and focusing on memorization is not only bad for creativity – it is also bad for the acquisition of skills and content knowledge. As will be argued later, the most effective ways to teach skills and content knowledge often involve the very same activities one would emphasize to promote creative thinking. When teachers banish divergent thinking and replace it with rote memorization, they are creating the worst of all possible educational worlds, one in which both creativity and content knowledge suffer. Although there are situations in which these two goals are at odds, they are more often synergistically linked. More creativity will often lead to more content knowledge, and more content knowledge will generally lead to more creativity. But there are a few bumps on the road to this educational nirvana, which we will explain.

HOW TO EMPHASIZE ACQUISITION OF SKILLS AND CONTENT KNOWLEDGE *AND* ENHANCE CREATIVITY

Teaching Divergent Thinking

The most widely used teaching techniques for improving student creativity are brainstorming activities (e.g., "List as many different possible uses for a brick as you can" or "How many different ways can you think of to get people to use less petroleum?"). The rules of brainstorming are fairly simple:

- *Defer judgment.* The goal of brainstorming is to come up with unusual and original ideas. When ideas are being judged, most people will take fewer risks and self-censor many ideas. Judgment can come later, after all the ideas are on the table. This includes both negative judgments and positive ones.
- *Avoid ownership of ideas.* When people feel that an idea is "theirs," egos sometimes get in the way of creative thinking. They are likely to be more defensive later when ideas are critiqued, and they are less willing to allow their ideas to be modified.
- *Feel free to "hitchhike" on other ideas.* This means that it is okay to borrow elements from ideas already on the table or to make slight modifications of ideas already suggested.
- *Wild ideas are encouraged.* Impossible, totally unworkable ideas may lead someone to think of other, more possible, more workable ideas. It is easier

to take a wildly imaginative bad idea and tone it down to fit the constraints of reality than to take a boring bad idea and make it interesting enough to be worth thinking about. (Baer, 1997a, p. 43)

There are many programs designed to enhance creativity that are used in schools, such as Synectics (Gordon, 1961), Talents Unlimited (2009), CPS (Eberle & Stanish, 1980), and the Odyssey of the Mind creative problem-solving competition (formerly known as the Olympics of the Mind; Micklus, 1986; Micklus & Micklus, 1986). In all these programs, the development of divergent thinking skills is paramount and brainstorming (or a variant of brainstorming) is used as a primary tool for encouraging and improving divergent thinking. Brainstorming can be used as part of a broader program of creativity training (as in CPS), or it can stand alone as a way to improve divergent thinking.

For many teachers, these kinds of divergent thinking activities are both fun and worthwhile, but not essential – and there certainly are not going to be any divergent thinking questions on the state's standardized assessments of student learning. When accountability push comes to testing shove, therefore, teachers may be quick to stop asking students to "think of many varied and unusual ways to do X" and use that time to drill math facts or practice reading comprehension strategies.

It is hard to argue with the reasoning behind such a decision. Helping children improve their divergent thinking skills may have long-term value – it may help them become more creative thinkers – but it is hard to see how listing 100 interesting and unusual ways to use egg cartons will help Johnny improve his scores on state-mandated achievement tests.

We agree that daily brainstorming activities using "How many uses can you think of for X?" kinds of questions are probably not a good use of class time. In fact, it is not even clear that such activities will have much impact on students' creativity, because "unusual uses" kinds of brainstorming activities exercise only a very limited number of divergent thinking muscles. Divergent thinking, like creativity more generally, varies from domain to domain, and even from task to task within a given domain. Doing the same kind of brainstorming activity every day would be rather like going to the gym every day and doing a single exercise, the same exercise, every day. One set of muscles would get stronger, but the rest would atrophy (Baer, 1993, 1996, 1997a, 1998a; Baer & Kaufman, 2005; Kaufman & Baer, 2005).

Using brainstorming only in response to unusual uses kinds of prompts, while perhaps a good way to improve one's score on a divergent thinking test, is nonetheless a very unimaginative and unproductive way to use brainstorming in the classroom. Even if improving students' creative thinking were a teacher's only goal, she or he would still be well advised to use brainstorming in a wide range of contexts and with as diverse a set of prompts as possible. But the benefits of brainstorming need not be limited to improving divergent thinking skills; they can also be used to help students acquire content knowledge and develop skills. (It is perhaps worth noting that unusual uses kinds of prompts *can* be an excellent choice the very first time a group is introduced to brainstorming, because they are very easy to understand. But after that, one needs to branch out.)

Here is a very simple example of a way to use brainstorming in class to help students learn content knowledge. At the beginning of a lesson, teachers can ask students to brainstorm what they already know about the topic the class is about to study. Let's say a third-grade class is about to read a book about Abraham Lincoln. Students might be asked to brainstorm everything they know about Lincoln, with the teacher recording their responses on the board. (Remember in doing this the *Defer Judgment* rule – If someone says that Lincoln was the first president, the teacher should just write it down, and if another student tries to correct this, she might remind him that time for judging or commenting on the ideas will come later. Judging ideas in the middle of brainstorming will short-circuit the process, because if students worry that their ideas might be criticized they will hold back and take fewer risks expressing ideas about which they might not be fully confident.) Soon the board will be filled with ideas – some correct, some incorrect, some important, some tangential – about Lincoln. What has been accomplished?

1. The students have activated their own background knowledge about Lincoln. It is therefore more likely that the new information they are about to learn will be encoded in long-term memory and linked in a propositional network with other things they know about Lincoln, making it much easier to recall the information later (even on a test!).
2. The students will be learning new things about Lincoln from the ideas offered by other students.
3. The teacher will get a quick reading of what students know about Lincoln, a kind of formative assessment that can help guide the lesson that will follow.
4. The teacher will quickly become aware of misconceptions students may have about Lincoln and have an opportunity to correct these mistaken ideas. Getting those incorrect ideas (such as Lincoln being the first president) on the board provides an opportunity to deal with those misconceptions straightforwardly (but only *after* brainstorming ends). Some such mistaken notions can be corrected easily (e.g., in response to a brainstorming response that Lincoln was the first president, the teacher might explain that "Sometimes students confuse Lincoln, who was president during the Civil War, with George Washington, who was our leader during the Revolutionary War and who later became our first president"). Other misconceptions may be more subtle and better dealt with later in the lesson

(e.g., it might take a while to explain why the claim that "Lincoln started the Civil War to free the slaves" is not exactly true).
5. Students will get practice doing divergent thinking.

Brainstorming can be used in many other ways to help students develop skills and acquire content knowledge that meet state content standards. Here is an example taken from the New Jersey Core Curriculum Content Standards (New Jersey Department of Education, 2004). Standard 6 states (among other things) that students will be able to "Analyze the impact of various human activities and social policies on the natural environment and describe how humans have attempted to solve environmental problems through adaptation and modification"; "Apply spatial thinking to understand the interrelationship of history, geography, economics, and the environment, including domestic and international migrations, changing environmental preferences and settlement patterns, and frictions between population groups"; and "Analyze why places and regions are important factors to individual and social identity."

One of us designed a middle-school social studies project some time ago that is directly related to this standard and that uses divergent thinking as a way to learn skills and content while at the same time developing creative thinking skills. Students were asked to create a new continent somewhere on the globe and to explain how this continent might have developed culturally. This was a project that lasted about two weeks with several lessons on different topics along the way, but the general goal was to help students understand how geography and human history interact (e.g., how such things as climate, landforms, and natural resources influence how people live and how the ways people live are adapted to their differing geographical settings).

The unit started off with some exercises designed to improve some divergent thinking skills that students might find useful as they worked on the project. Here are three abilities that were thought to be important and that would help them make their projects more creative:

1. Ability to think of specific cultural elements that might be influenced by geography
2. Ability to think of ways that geography might influence general features of a culture
3. Ability to think of ways that a society's culture might lead them to adapt different geographical elements to a given purpose

Each of these provided the content for a brainstorming exercise. For example, after learning what the expression "specific cultural elements" means, students brainstormed and created lists of things that might count as cultural elements. Later, they brainstormed cultural elements that might be influenced by geography. Evaluation of their ideas can follow these brainstorming sessions, providing another chance to grapple with important knowledge and skills. These activities – and similar activities related to abilities 2 and 3 above – were designed to increase students' divergent thinking skills in these particular social studies content areas. Development of these particular divergent thinking skills supported the larger create-a-continent activity, and it also addressed New Jersey Core Curriculum Content Standard 6.9. (For more information on other divergent thinking activities that support various curricular objectives, see Baer, 1997a.)

Balancing Intrinsic and Extrinsic Motivation

Teaching for creativity and teaching for content tend to go in opposite directions when it comes to motivation. (Recall that at the beginning of this paper we acknowledged that at times creativity and content standards really *do* work at cross purposes.) Student motivation is one place where that is particularly true, as will be explained. But the situation is not hopeless.

Amabile's (1983, 1996) intrinsic motivation theory has been one of the most powerful and productive ideas to come out of the last quarter century of creativity research. This theory states that people are more creative when they do something simply because they find it intrinsically interesting – because it is something they have chosen to do just because they derive pleasure, or even joy, from doing it – and they are less creative when they do something because they are extrinsically motivated, such as to earn a reward.

This idea probably seems pretty harmless, but it is not just saying that being intrinsically motivated leads to more creative behavior. It is also saying that when people do things to earn rewards, or when they expect that their work will be evaluated, they become *less* creative; and when they do things primarily to please someone else, they also become less creative. It is somewhat distressing to many teachers to hear that the things they do everyday – offer rewards to students (that is, bribe students to do things they might not do otherwise) and evaluate their work – tend to decrease students' creativity. But troubling though it may be, it is nonetheless true.

Intrinsic and extrinsic motivation tend to compete with each other, and when we experience both at the same time, extrinsic motivation tends to drive out intrinsic motivation. When a teacher offers students rewards for doing things, or when they evaluate their students' work, they do indeed increase their motivation – their extrinsic motivation – but at the same time they are diminishing their students' intrinsic motivation for those activities. And by reducing intrinsic motivation, they are also causing their students to be less creative. (For more information about this theory and the evidence supporting it, see Amabile, 1993, 1996; Hennessey & Amabile, 1988; Hennessey & Zbikowski, 1993. The negative impact of extrinsic motivation on creativity is especially powerful for girls; see Baer, 1997b, 1998b.) But we must evaluate students' work – if for no other reason (and there are other and better reasons, to be discussed later) because we must give grades of some kind. And sometimes if we could not offer rewards – if we could not bribe students – we simply would not be able to get them to do some things that they really need to do. For better or worse, some of the same things that we know tend to diminish creativity are the very things that tend to increase competence. Students *need* feedback (a.k.a. evaluation) on their performance if they are to improve their skills, and they sometimes need some kind of extrinsic motivation – rewards – to keep working when they would otherwise simply stop. They need extrinsic motivation to learn, and teachers need extrinsic motivation (bribes and evaluations) to teach them. And so teaching for creativity and teaching to learn content do seem to part company when it comes to motivation. This sometimes forces us to make difficult choices.

One way out of this fix would be to argue that even though doing something for a reward, or working harder because one wants to earn a better evaluation, may lower one's creativity in the short run, it is this extrinsically motivated learning that makes it possible to acquire the skills and knowledge that one will need in the future to do something in a more creative way than would be possible at present. The skills and knowledge that our students are acquiring (with the help of evaluation and occasional rewards) will allow them to be more creative in the future, because they will need considerable amounts of both skills and knowledge to do anything truly creative. And this is true. But it is only one part of the story. The other part – the intrinsic motivation–reducing effects of evaluation and rewards – does not just go away because they may also have some other positive effects. And if students lose their intrinsic motivation, they may have the skills and knowledge they need to be creative, but they may no longer have any interest in doing anything creative with those skills and that knowledge. And if you do not do anything, you do not do anything that is creative.

Teachers thus find themselves between a rock and a hard place, needing evaluations and rewards but knowing they also have negative effects. The way out of this dilemma is first to keep in mind one's goals for a given lesson. If one's focus is on skill development or knowledge acquisition, then one needs to use extrinsic motivation and (at least temporarily) risk depressing creativity. To the extent that evaluation is viewed by students as empowering, there is even some evidence that it may not negatively affect creativity at all (Eisenberger, Pierce, & Cameron, 1999; Eisenberger & Rhoades, 2001; Eisenberger & Shanock, 2003); if the focus is on the student's work (rather than on the student's abilities), this should also lessen the negative impact (Amabile, 1983, 1996). But the fact that under some conditions and for some students the creativity-dampening, intrinsic motivation–killing effects of rewards and evaluations might be mitigated does not mean there are no negative effects. They are real and they should not be ignored.

Sometimes a teacher's goal is not skill development, however. For some lessons or activities, the primary goal may well be to encourage both intrinsic motivation and creativity, and in those cases one needs to avoid doing things that will increase extrinsic motivation and try to do whatever one can to increase intrinsic motivation. For example, when teaching writing, we want students to learn a number of skills, and sometimes we want them to write imaginatively. These goals are sadly at odds because one requires an emphasis on extrinsic motivation – evaluative feedback, in this case – and the other just the opposite (a focus on intrinsic motivation, which would require one to avoid evaluation). If one tries to do a little of each, it will not work, because extrinsic motivation will win – it will tend to drive out students' intrinsic motivation. But a teacher can do both if she does them at *different times*. When working on skill development in writing, she can let students know the criteria or rubric she will use to evaluate their work (to promote skill development), and at other times she can tell them that although they must do the writing assignment, they will get credit simply for doing it and there will be no further evaluation (to promote intrinsic motivation and creativity). Teachers often evaluate work in different ways for different purposes (and may evaluate the same piece of writing in different ways, depending on the stage of the writing process), and it is appropriate to evaluate different aspects of students' performance when emphasizing different goals. Consider, for example, how for very young writers it may be helpful at some times to ignore spelling errors and have students use invented spelling rather than have them completely shut down every time they need a word they cannot spell, while at other times it is better to teach spelling directly and expect students to learn to spell the words that they have studied correctly. Teachers using this strategy can emphasize both correct spelling and fluency in writing, but at different times, with the long-term goal of both fluent and correct writing (Bank Street College, 1997; Burns, Griffin, & Snow, 2000).

Some teachers object that this is unrealistic and students will not believe it anyway, but if one actually follows through on the promise not to evaluate, students will (gradually) come to believe this promise. This will allow them to concentrate on skills and focus on doing things "right" when they expect evaluation and it will free them up to write more imaginatively (albeit often with less technical correctness) when the no-evaluation promise is in effect. One cannot simultaneously make extrinsic and intrinsic motivation salient (because extrinsic motivation will win and drive out intrinsic motivation), but one can do both at different times. This allows both skill development and a nurturing of interest in creative writing.

Will some kids abuse the license that a no-evaluation promise provides? Of course they will. But sometimes we need to allow the students who want to do as little as possible to get away with it, in order not to punish those students who do have the kind of intrinsic motivation that we wish all our students had.

But what about content standards and accountability? Will this take time away from learning content? Probably so. (Remember, sometimes content standards and accountability *do* come into conflict with creativity. There is no free lunch here.) But probably not as much as one might fear. If students spend a few hours each week doing activities that will not be evaluated but which will be likely to increase students' intrinsic motivation, it will not take a huge amount of time away from learning the content knowledge on which they will be tested, and these activities may help students acquire important content knowledge and skills, even without evaluations or rewards, simply because they allow and encourage students to think about that content knowledge and apply those skills in different, and sometimes even original, ways. Thinking deeply about content is a highly effective way to retain it – more effective in the long term than many short-term strategies like flashcards – so teachers might think of divergent thinking or other creativity-relevant activities as investments in their students' long-term acquisition of content knowledge (Woolfolk, 2007). In addition, these kinds of activities may simply help getting students to show up in class – psychologically as well as physically. And without that, all the great content knowledge and skill-focused lessons cannot do them any good anyway.

Using Both Teacher-Centered and Student-Centered Learning

There are many continua on which different teaching approaches can be located, such as constructionist/transmissive, progressive/traditional, and teacher-centered/student-centered. These are at best fuzzy guides because it is often on the most extreme cases that are easy to classify, but they are often used to describe different teaching approaches.

Schuh (2003), an advocate of student-centered and constructivist teaching, defines the teacher-centered/student-centered distinction in a way that also encompasses the constructivist-transmissive and progressive-traditional continua:

> In a teacher-centered model of instruction, the instructor's role is seen as imparting knowledge to students, and instruction proceeds from the instructor's point of view.... The teacher decides for the learner what is required ... by defining characteristics of instruction, curriculum, assessment, and management ... in which the information ... is moved into the learner.... In contrast, learner-centered instruction (LCI) fosters opportunities for learners to draw on their own experiences and interpretations.... LCI proposes that teachers need to understand the learner's perspective and must support capacities already existing in the learner to accomplish desired learning outcomes. Learning goals are then achieved by active collaboration between the teacher and learners who together determine what learning means and how it can be enhanced within each

individual learner by drawing on the learner's own unique talents, capacities, and experiences . . . (p. 427, quoted in Beghetto & Plucker, 2006,
pp. 319–320)

Student-centered (also known as learner-centered) approaches have been
associated with creativity (Beghetto & Plucker, 2006; Fasko, 2001), although
this is a prediction, not a tested empirical claim. It is not difficult to see
why teaching for creativity seems to fall into the student-centered side of this
continuum. How can an idea be new or original – how can it be creative? –
if it has been "moved into the learner" by an outside force (the teacher)? It
is perhaps almost as obvious why teaching students content knowledge – the
stuff of state content standards and the stuff that will be on the state-mandated
tests – seems to fall on the teacher-centered instructional side (certainly it is
the state, and its employee, the teacher, who "decides for the learner what is
required").

What often gets lost when thinking about student- and teacher-centered
instruction (and similar schemes for comparing modes of instruction) is that
this is a continuum, not a dichotomy. Most teachers do not use exclusively the
rote memorization strategies that are typically invoked when teacher-centered
instruction is attacked (see, e.g., Jones, Jones, & Hargrove, 2003, who argue that
high-stakes testing leads to more teaching via rote memorization in schools
serving low-scoring, disadvantaged populations, but see also the review by
Pletka, 2005, of their book, which contends that they provide no statistics to
support this assertion). Similarly, most teachers do not use the pure discovery, unguided, or minimally guided instructional approaches that Kirschner,
Sweller, and Clark (2006) have shown to be significantly "less effective and
less efficient than instructional approaches that place a strong emphasis on
guidance of the student learning" (p. 75) – that is, more teacher-centered
approaches.

Teachers are more likely to use techniques that fall at neither extreme of this
continuum but rather use approaches that fall closer to the middle (or to use a
mix of approaches). There is a conservatism in teaching that results in teachers
rarely adopting the more extreme stances of reformers (Kennedy, 2006). There
is certainly reason for the concerns raised by Jones, Jones, and Hargrove (2003)
that accountability concerns may lead teachers to adopt ineffective teaching
methods, because rote memorization is not only bad for creativity – it is also
a poor way to learn content (Woolfolk, 2007). As Beghetto and Plucker (2006)
contend in their plea that creativity not be forgotten in our schools:

We argue that student understanding develops from a balance between the
pursuit of efficient methods to attain viable solutions *and* opportunities
to engage in the creative process of developing the personal knowledge of
when, why and how to arrive at those solutions. This includes allowing

students the time and experiences necessary to develop an understanding of what those solutions mean in the context of the particular problem as well as a more general set of problems. Conversely, when teachers simply teach the most efficient method they may actually short-circuit the creative process necessary for the development of meaningful understanding. Again, this is not to say that students should never be taught the most efficient method, but rather they should be given opportunities to work through the problems in their own way such that they develop an accurate yet personally meaningful understanding. (p. 324)

As with divergent thinking, so it is with teacher-centered versus student-centered learning. The most effective way to teach for the knowledge and understanding that will result in good scores on state accountability measures dovetails quite nicely with effective methods for teaching for creativity. Misunderstanding how students learn (and going to either extreme of the teacher- or student-centered continuum) will result in both less skill and knowledge acquisition and less student creativity.

Teaching for creativity in an era of content standards does, at times, force teachers to make difficult choices, as the section on intrinsic and extrinsic motivation described. But if teachers avoid (1) mistaken notions that teaching academic skills and content knowledge requires them to abandon creativity-relevant skills like divergent thinking or (2) retreating into rote memorization strategies that drain learning of meaning, they can successfully meet both accountability standards and promote creativity in their classrooms.

REFERENCES

Amabile, T. M. (1983). *The social psychology of creativity*. New York: Springer-Verlag.
Amabile, T. M. (1996). *Creativity in context: Update to the social psychology of creativity*. Boulder, CO: Westview.
Ashcraft, M. H. (1989). *Human memory and cognition*. New York: Harper Collins.
Baer, J. (1993). *Creativity and divergent thinking: A task-specific approach*. Hillsdale, NJ: Lawrence Erlbaum Associates.
Baer, J. (1996). The effects of task-specific divergent thinking training. *Journal of Creative Behavior*, **30**, 183–187.
Baer. J. (1997a). *Creative teachers, creative students*. Boston: Allyn and Bacon.
Baer, J. (1997b). Gender differences in the effects of anticipated evaluation on creativity. *Creativity Research Journal*, **10**, 25–31.
Baer, J. (1998a). The case for domain specificity in creativity. *Creativity Research Journal*, **11**, 173–177.
Baer, J. (1998b). Gender differences in the effects of extrinsic motivation on creativity. *Journal of Creative Behavior*, **32**, 18–37.
Baer, J. (1999). Creativity in a climate of standards. *Focus on Education*, **43**, 16–21.
Baer, J. (2002). Are creativity and content standards allies or enemies? *Research in the Schools*, **9**(2), 35–42.
Baer, J. (2003). Impact of the Core Knowledge Curriculum on creativity. *Creativity Research Journal*, **15**, 297–300.

Baer, J., & Kaufman, J. C. (2005). Bridging generality and specificity: The Amusement Park Theoretical (APT) model of creativity. *Roeper Review, 27*, 158–163.

Bank Street College. (1997). America reads: Bank Street College's approach to early literacy acquisition [online]. Retrieved on April 28, 2008, from: http://www.paec. org/david/reading/amreads.pdf.

Beghetto, R. A., & Plucker, J. A. (2006). The relationship among schooling, learning, and creativity. In J. C. Kaufman & J. Baer (Eds.), *Reason and creativity in development* (pp. 316–332). New York: Cambridge University Press.

Burns, M. S., Griffin, P., & Snow, C. E. (Eds.). (2000). *Starting out right: A guide to promoting children's reading success.* Washington, DC: National Academies Press.

Campbell, D. T. (1960). Blind variation and selective retention in creative thought as in other knowledge processes. *Psychological Review, 67*, 380–400.

Chase, W. G., & Simon, H. A. (1973). The mind's eye in chess. In W. G. Chase (Ed.), *Visual information processing* (pp. 215–281). New York: Academic Press.

Chi, M. T. H., Glaser, R., & Farr, M. (Eds.). (1988). *The nature of expertise.* Hillsdale, NJ: Erlbaum.

Core Knowledge Foundation. (1998). *Core Knowledge sequence: Content guidelines for grades K–8.* Charlottesville, VA: Core Knowledge Foundation.

Craik, F. I. M., & Lockhart, R. S. (1972). Levels of processing: A framework for memory research. *Journal of Verbal Learning and Verbal Behavior, 11*, 671–684.

Eberle, B., & Stanish, B. (1980). *CPS for kids: A resource book for teaching creative problem-solving to children.* Buffalo, NY: D.O.K. Publishers.

Eisenberger, R., Pierce, W. D., & Cameron, J. (1999). Effects of reward on intrinsic motivation: Negative, neutral, and positive. *Psychological Bulletin, 125*, 677–691.

Eisenberger, R., & Rhoades, L. (2001). Incremental effects of reward on creativity. *Journal of Personality and Social Psychology, 81*, 728–741 (Award for the Best Paper on Organizational Behavior at the 2001 Academy of Management Conference).

Eisenberger, R., & Shanock, L. (2003). Rewards, intrinsic motivation, and creativity: A case study of conceptual and methodological isolation. *Creativity Research Journal, 15*, 121–130.

Fasko, D. (2001). Education and creativity. *Creativity Research Journal, 13*, 317–327.

Feldhusen, J. F. (2006). The role of the knowledge base in creative thinking. In J. C. Kaufman & J. Baer (Eds.), *Reason and creativity in development* (pp. 137–144). New York: Cambridge University Press.

Fuhrman, S. H. (Ed.). (2001). *From the capital to the classroom: Standards-based reform in the states.* Chicago, IL: National Society for the Study of Education.

Gage, N. L., & Berliner, D. C. *Educational psychology* (5th ed.). Boston: Houghton Mifflin.

Glass, A. L., & Holyoak, K. J. (1986). *Cognition* (2nd ed.). New York: Random House.

Gordon, W. J. J. (1961). *Synectics.* New York: Harper & Row.

Gruber, H. E. (1981). *Darwin on man: A psychological study of scientific creativity* (2nd ed.). Chicago: University of Chicago Press.

Gruber, H. E., & Davis, S. N. (1988). Inching our way up Mt. Olympus: The evolving-systems approach to creative thinking. In R. J. Sternberg (Ed.), *The nature of creativity* (pp. 243–270). New York: Cambridge University Press.

Guilford, J. P. (1956). The structure of intellect. *Psychological Bulletin, 53*, 267–293.

Hayes, J. R. (1989). Cognitive processes in creativity. In J. A. Glover, R. R. Ronning, & C. R. Reynolds (Eds.), *Handbook of creativity* (pp. 135–145). New York: Plenum.

Hennessey, B. A., & Amabile, T. M. (1988). Conditions of creativity. In R. J. Sternberg (Ed.), *The nature of creativity* (pp. 11–38). New York: Cambridge University Press.

Hennessey, B. A., & Zbikowski, S. (1993). Immunizing children against the negative effects of reward: A further examination of intrinsic motivation techniques. *Creativity Research Journal, 6*, 297–308.

Hirsch, E. D., Jr. (1987). *Cultural literacy: What every American needs to know.* Boston: Houghton Mifflin.

Hirsch, E. D., Jr. (Ed.). (1991–1997). *The Core Knowledge Series: Resource books for kindergarten through six.* New York: Doubleday.

Hirsch, E. D., Jr. (1996). *The schools we need and why we don't have them.* New York: Doubleday.

Isaksen, S. G., & Treffinger, D. J. (1985). *Creative problem solving: The basic course.* Buffalo, NY: Bearly Limited Press.

Johnson-Laird, P. N. (1983). *Mental models.* Cambridge, MA: Harvard University Press.

Jones, G., Jones, B., & Hargrove, T. (2003). *The unintended consequences of high-stakes testing.* Lanham, MD: Rowman & Littlefield.

Karmiloff-Smith, A. (1992). *Beyond modularity: A developmental perspective on cognitive science.* Cambridge, MA: MIT Press.

Kaufman, J. C., & Baer, J. (2002). Could Steven Spielberg manage the Yankees? Creative thinking in different domains. *Korean Journal of Thinking and Problem Solving, 12,* 5–14.

Kaufman, J. C., & Baer, J. (2005). The amusement park theory of creativity. In J. C. Kaufman & J. Baer (Eds.), *Creativity across domains: Faces of the muse* (pp. 321–328). Hillsdale, NJ: Lawrence Erlbaum Associates.

Kaufman, J. C., & Baer, J. (Eds.). (2006). *Reason and creativity in development.* New York: Cambridge University Press.

Kennedy, M. M. (2006). *Inside teaching: How classroom life undermines reform.* Cambridge, MA: Harvard University Press.

Kim, K. H. (2006). Can we trust creativity tests? A review of the Torrance Tests of Creative Thinking. *Creativity Research Journal, 18,* 3–14.

Kirschner, P. A., Sweller, J., and Clark, R. E. (2006). Why minimal guidance during instruction does not work: An analysis of the failure of constructivist, discovery, problem-based, experiential, and inquiry-based teaching. *Educational Psychologist 41*(2), 75–86.

Ladd, H. F. (1996). *Holding schools accountable: Performance-based reform in education.* Washington, DC: Brookings Institution Press.

Lockhart, R. S., & Craik, F. I. M. (1990). Levels of processing: A retrospective commentary on a framework for memory research. *Canadian Journal of Psychology, 44,* 87–122.

Mayer, R. E. (1987). *Educational psychology: A cognitive approach.* Boston: Little, Brown and Company.

Mayer, R. E. (2006). The role of domain knowledge in creative problem solving. In J. C. Kaufman & J. Baer (Eds.), *Reason and creativity in development* (pp. 145–158). New York: Cambridge University Press.

Micklus, C. S. (1986). *OM-AHA! Problems to develop creative thinking skills.* Glassboro, NJ: Creative Competitions.

Micklus, C. S., & Micklus, C. (1986). *OM program handbook.* Glassboro, NJ: Creative Competitions.

New Jersey Department of Education. (2004). New Jersey Core Curriculum Content Standards [On-line]. Retrieved on May 10, 2007, from http://www.state.nj.us/njded/cccs/index.html.

Olson, L. (2000). Worries of a standards 'backlash' grow. *Education Week,* **19**(30), **1,** 12–13.

Olson, L. (2001). Education alliance calls for corrections to standards-based systems. *Education Week,* **20**(19), 6.

Orwin, C., & Forbes, H. D. (1994). Cultural literacy: A Canadian perspective. *International Journal of Social Education,* **9**(1), 15–30.

Paul, R. W. (1990). Critical thinking and cultural literacy: Where E. D. Hirsch goes wrong. In R. W. Paul (Ed.), *Critical thinking: What every person needs to survive in a rapidly changing world* (pp. 429–435). Rohnert Park, CA: Center for Critical Thinking and Moral Critique (Sonoma State University).

Perkins, D. N., & Salomon, G. (1988). Teaching for transfer. *Educational Leadership,* **46**(1), 22–32.

Pletka, B. (2005, March 26). Review of the unintended consequences of high-stakes testing. *Education Review.* Retrieved on May 12, 2007, from http://edrev.asu.edu/reviews/rev369.htm.

Puccio, G. J., Murdock, M. C., & Mance, M. (2007). *Creative leadership: Skills that drive change.* San Diego, CA: Sage Publications.

Runco, M. A. (Ed.). (2003). *Critical creative processes.* Cresskill, NJ: Hampton Press.

Salomon, G., & Perkins, D. N. (1989). Rocky roads to transfer: Rethinking mechanisms of a neglected phenomenon. *Educational Psychologist,* **24**(2), 113–142.

Schear, E. L. (1992). Cultural literacy and the developmental student: Whose culture and what kind of literacy? *Research and Teaching in Developmental Education,* **8**(2), 5–14.

Schuh, K. L. (2003). Knowledge construction in the learner-centered classroom. *Journal of Educational Psychology,* **95,** 426–442.

Simonton, D. K. (1994). *Greatness: Who makes history and why.* New York: Guilford Press.

Simonton, D. K. (1998). *Scientific genius: A psychology of science.* New York: Cambridge University Press.

Simonton, D. K. (1999). *Origins of genius: Darwinian perspectives on creativity.* New York: Oxford University Press.

Simonton, D. K. (2004). *Creativity in science: Chance, logic, genius, and zeitgeist.* New York: Cambridge University Press.

Simonton, D. K. (2006). Creative genius, knowledge, and reason. In J. C. Kaufman & J. Baer (Eds.), *Reason and creativity in development* (pp. 43–59). New York: Cambridge University Press.

Talents Unlimited, Inc. (2009). Talents Unlimited. Retrieved on Dec. 28, 2009, from the Talents Unlimited, Inc. website: http://www.mcpss.com/?DivisionID=2142&DepartmentID=2004&ToggleSideNav=ShowAll.

Torrance, E. P. (1966). *The Torrance Tests of Creative Thinking – Norms-Technical Manual Research Edition – Verbal Tests, Forms A and B – Figural Tests, Forms A and B.* Princeton, NJ: Personnel Press.

Torrance, E. P. (1974). *The Torrance Tests of Creative Thinking – Norms-Technical Manual Research Edition – Verbal Tests, Forms A and B – Figural Tests, Forms A and B.* Princeton, NJ: Personnel Press.

Torrance, E. P. (1998). *The Torrance Tests of Creative Thinking Norms-Technical Manual Figural (Streamlined) Forms A & B.* Bensenville, IL: Scholastic Testing Service, Inc.

Torrance, E. P., & Presbury, J. (1984). The criteria of success used in 242 recent experimental studies of creativity. *Creative Child & Adult Quarterly, 9*, 238–243.

Treffinger, D. J., Isaksen, S. G., & Dorval, K. B. (2006). *Creative problem solving: An introduction* (4th ed.). Waco, TX: Prufrock Press.

Tucker, M. S. (2002). The roots of backlash. *Education Week, 21*(16), 76, 42–43.

Vail, K. (1997). Core comes to Crooksville. *American School Board Journal, 184*(3), 14–18.

Weisberg, R. W. (1988). Problem solving and creativity. In R. J. Sternberg (Ed.), *The nature of creativity* (pp. 148–176). New York: Cambridge University Press.

Weisberg, R. W. (1999). Creativity and knowledge: A challenge to theories. In R. J. Sternberg (Ed.), *Handbook of creativity* (pp. 226–250). New York: Cambridge University Press.

Weisberg, R. W. (2006). Expertise and reason in creative thinking. In J. C. Kaufman & J. Baer (Eds.), *Reason and creativity in development* (pp. 7–42). New York: Cambridge University Press.

Willingham, D. B. (2001). *Cognition: The thinking animal.* Upper Saddle River, NJ: Prentice-Hall.

Woolfolk, A. (2001). *Educational psychology* (8th ed.). Boston: Allyn and Bacon.

Woolfolk, A. (2007). *Educational psychology* (10th ed.). Boston: Allyn and Bacon.

Zimbardo, P. G., & Gerrig, R. J. (1999). *Psychology and life* (15th ed.). New York: Addison Wesley Longman.

3

Developing Creative Productivity in Young People through the Pursuit of Ideal Acts of Learning

JOSEPH S. RENZULLI AND CATHARINA F. DE WET

INTRODUCTION

The September 2007 issue of *Smithsonian Magazine* was dedicated to "America's Young Innovators in the Arts and Sciences" – 37 people under the age of 36 who are making names for themselves and are well on their way to eminence in their fields. Most of them can trace their passion and career focus to a few key experiences. Cristián Samper, for example, Acting Secretary of the Smithsonian Institution, says in his editorial introduction,

> My own love of science came from a love of nature. As a Boy Scout, I camped and hiked in Colombian rain forests, returning home eager to organize my collections of plants and animals. . . . At 15, I joined ornithologist Jorge Orejuela on a World Wildlife Fund (WWF) summer expedition to the remote rain forests in the Choco region of Colombia. This was my first experience in hands-on fieldwork, and as I saw scientific data, field observation, conservation biology and environmental policy all coming together, I was hooked. (*Smithsonian Magazine*, 2007, p. 3)

The unfortunate truth is that schools are not places where youngsters gain these kinds of experiences nor places where creativity thrives, especially in the current educational climate where the emphasis is on increasing the academic achievement of underperforming students (Renzulli, 2005; Robinson, 2001). Academic achievement has become the focus of most of the thought, finances, and energy expended in education, and yet, we have an ambiguous relationship with academic achievement. Academic ability is believed to be essential for individual success and societal advancement, but anything impractical or not worthwhile is easily dismissed as being "academic" (Robinson, 2001).

Formal and Informal Education

Dewey (1916) divided educational activities in society into two distinct arenas: the informal and the formal. While all education is a social renewal process

24

of "transmission by communication" (p. 11), and all social interactions have some educative effect, informal education occurs when children learn the skills, habits, and customs of their society by participating in activities with their elders. In other words, they learn by experience and by watching and doing. Lisa Sanditz, a landscape painter whose first museum show was presented by the Kemper Museum of Contemporary Art in Kansas City in 2006, was looking at paintings from the time she could walk – her mother and grandmother both were museum docents (Lubow, 2007). Lisa says, "My greatest professional influence is my grandmother's knowledge and insight about contemporary art" (see http://www.smithsonianmag.com/specialsections/innovators/sanditz-lw.html for a quick questionnaire with Ms. Sanditz).

Formal education, by contrast, is purposeful or intentional teaching of the younger members of society by older and more experienced members of that society. Formal education has been dominated since the Enlightenment by the desire for knowledge and the emphasis on intelligence, deductive reason, and "objective" scientific evidence. In the process, the role of creativity in learning and thinking has been reduced, and rationalist tradition has dominated our education system. Dewey states that the need for intentional, formal education increases as society becomes more complex but that the increase of formal education brings with it the danger of an "undesirable split" between the (informal) experience gained in more direct associations and the (formal) education that is acquired in school. "This danger was never greater than at the present time," says Dewey (1916), "on account of the rapid growth in the last few centuries of knowledge and technical modes of skill" (p. 11).

This "rapid growth of knowledge and technical modes of skill" is nowhere better exemplified than by the actions of Joshua Schachter (Rogers, 2007). All he wanted to do in 1998 was keep track of those sites on the Internet that interested him and that he thought he might want to revisit. He devised a simple way of tagging sites with one key word in his bookmark folder. Today, his Web site is called "del.icio.us," and 2.5 million visitors a day use it to search the Web. He had the knowledge he needed to build a website from studying electrical and computer engineering at Carnegie Mellon University. (Mr. Schachter publishes a blog on http://joshua.schachter.org/.) What was it that set him apart from his classmates (and earned him a reputed $30 million buyout from Yahoo)?

Renzulli has written extensively about two kinds of giftedness or ability (1978a). The first category is referred to as "schoolhouse ability," or test-taking or lesson-learning ability. It is the kind most easily measured by intelligence quotient (IQ) or other cognitive ability tests and, for this reason, it is also the type most often used for selecting students for entrance into special programs. The abilities that people display on IQ and aptitude tests are exactly the kinds of abilities most valued in traditional school learning situations. In other words, the games people play on ability tests are similar in nature to the games that teachers require in most lesson-learning situations. Research tells us that students who score high on IQ tests are also likely to get high grades in school. Research also has shown that these test-taking and lesson-learning abilities generally remain stable over time. The results of this research should lead us to some very obvious conclusions about schoolhouse giftedness: It exists in varying degrees; it can be identified through standardized assessment techniques; and we should therefore do everything in our power to make appropriate modifications for students who have the ability to cover regular curricular material at advanced rates and levels of understanding (Renzulli, 1978a). Terence Tao is an excellent example of a person with this kind of ability (Mackenzie, 2007). He taught himself arithmetic at age 2 and excelled in mathematics at school. He was the youngest competitor ever (at age 10) in the International Mathematical Olympiad and won its gold medal at 12, outshining high school competitors. Earning his doctorate in mathematics at 20, four years later at 24, Tao became the youngest full professor in University of California Los Angeles history. Today, after a decade of work in mathematics, he has 140 papers to his credit. Dr. Tao has a website at http://www.math.ucla.edu/~tao/.

This is not the end of the Terence Tao story, though. He is an excellent example of a person who combines academic ability with Renzulli's second kind of ability – creative productivity. Tao is described by colleagues as unusually open-minded and exceedingly tenacious. "The heart of Tao's gift may simply be his ability to let his thinking roam freely toward an unseen horizon" (Mackenzie, 2007, p. 75). He works with pure mathematics, yes, but he also loves practical math. For example, he tried to improve the data acquisition of digital cameras. Present-day cameras acquire a vast amount of data, and then computers use a compression algorithm to reduce the data in a picture to manageable amounts. Tao's question was, Why not design a camera that would acquire only a fraction of the data to begin with? His work created a new field of mathematics called compressive sampling. This is an excellent example of the second kind of ability. Creative productive ability describes those aspects of human activity and involvement in which a premium is placed on the development of original material and products that are purposefully designed to have an impact on one or more target audiences.

IDEAL ACTS OF LEARNING

What sets Terence Tao apart from other mathematicians is his ability to apply his vast knowledge of the principles and methodologies of mathematics to the solution of practical, real problems. What sets Joshua Schachter apart from his classmates is the ability to ask a simple question arising from a personal need (a need many people have, as evidenced by the millions who use his Web tool, including the present authors) and devise a stunningly simple answer. They are innovators – creative producers rather than replicators. We value creative producers, as opposed to replicators, because they are the persons who go beyond our current levels of knowledge and understanding to bring about new ideas, questions, solutions to problems, and new products and services that did not exist prior to their application of the creative process. It is the creative producers who, in effect, create thousands of jobs for replicators. One creative idea, such as a book, a symphony, a new device, or a software program for a computer, starts the wheels of production turning, thereby creating thousands of jobs in manufacturing and a host of other areas, such as finance, advertising, marketing, packaging, transportation, and sales. Thomas Edison's invention of the storage battery gave rise to an entire industry that still prospers today and that has the added benefit to society of being a vehicle for the multitude of modifications and improvements made on this innovative product over the years.

Both Tao and Schachter are illustrative of important truths with regard to the two kinds of giftedness:

1. Both types are important.
2. There is usually an interaction between the two types.
3. Our education programs should make appropriate provisions for encouraging the development of both types of ability, as well as providing numerous occasions when the two types can interact with each other.

Components of Ideal Acts of Learning

Learning situations that are designed to promote creative productive giftedness emphasize the use and application of information (content) and thinking processes in an integrated, inductive, and real-problem–oriented manner. The role of the student is transformed from that of a learner of prescribed lessons to one in which she or he uses the modus operandi of a firsthand inquirer. This approach is quite different from the development of lesson-learning ability, which tends to emphasize deductive learning, structured training in the development of thinking processes, and the acquisition, storage, and retrieval of information. Creative productivity is simply putting one's abilities to work on problems and areas of study that have personal relevance to the student and that can be escalated to appropriately challenging levels of investigative activity. Within an educational setting, the learner is not, however, solely responsible for this kind of activity. Two other components are critically important – the teacher and the curriculum.

When these three components – the *learner*, the *teacher*, and the *curriculum* – are present in a particular manner, ideal acts of learning occur, often with creative productivity as the result. The relationships between and among these components are represented in Figure 3.1. The diagram emphasizes the dynamic nature of the interactions between the components and is not meant

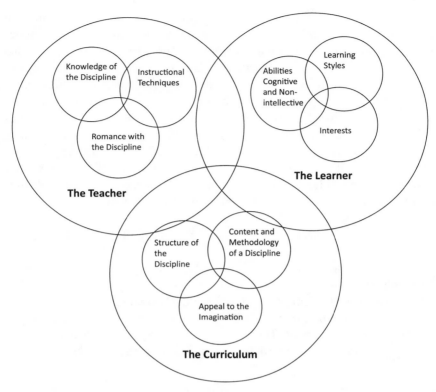

Figure 3.1. An ideal act of learning.

to represent equity among the components and subcomponents. The circles may vary in size from one learning situation to another, and even within a single learning situation. However, all components have to be present to some degree for ideal acts of learning to occur.

The Learner

Abilities
Learner abilities include both cognitive and noncognitive traits. Moral courage, optimism, vision, charisma, hope, absorption, personal choice, tolerance for ambiguity, risk taking, and perseverance are noncognitive traits that may influence what creative work a person chooses to do and how that person chooses to go about his or her creative activities. In an ideal learning situation, environmental variables, the domains in which youngsters work, and the contexts in which they pursue their work are considered.

Interests
Interests play a crucial role in learning and in high levels of creative productivity. The degree of interest that is present in an act of learning enhances all cognitive

behavior, wherever that cognitive behavior may be on the continuum from basic skill learning to higher levels of creative productivity. Personal interests are often motivators for youngsters to commit to the hard work involved in creative productivity. Piaget (1981), Albert and Runco (1986), and Gruber (1986) all emphasize the importance of personal interest in constructing a person's activities. Renninger and Wozniak (1985) examined children between 2.9 and 4.2 years of age and found that as young as they were, they had strong, stable, and relatively focused individual interests that were powerful determinants of their attention, recognition, and recall. Renninger (1989, 1990) also found that fifth- and sixth-graders were more competent in both reading and mathematical performance when the content involved material with both high levels of knowledge and high levels of value (as measured by interest) compared to similar levels of knowledge with low levels of value. The best indicator of college majors and expressions of career choice on the part of young adults has been intensive involvement in projects (Hébert, 1993; Renzulli, 1977b). Interest is a fundamental part of ideal learning situations.

Learning Styles
An area of major importance in which students differ is their style of learning. Learning styles have been variously defined according to psychological types:

1. Introversion versus extraversion (Myers, 1980)
2. Preference for varying degrees of structure in the learning process (Hunt, 1975)
3. Concrete to abstract and from sequential to random (Gregorc, 1985; Kolb, Rubin, & McIntyre, 1971)
4. Various physical characteristics of the learning environment (e.g., auditory and mobility preferences, comfort requirements, and preferences for individual versus group work; Dunn, Dunn, & Price, 1975)
5. Sensory modality preference (visual, auditory, tactile, and kinesthetic; Barbe & Swassing, 1979)

Learning styles have also been typified as preferences for function (Sternberg, 1988): legislative (creation, formulation, and planning); executive (the execution of plans and ideas); and judicial (monitoring, judging, and evaluating). Furthermore, Renzulli and Smith (1978) developed an instrument called *The Learning Styles Inventory* which assesses styles in correspondence with the following instructional techniques: projects, drill and recitation, peer teaching, discussion, simulation and teaching games, independent study, programmed instruction, and lecture.

Most of the persons who have contributed to the literature on learning styles agree on certain issues. First, there may be "natural" preferences for a particular style that are a function of personality variables; however, styles are also a function of socialization, and therefore several styles can be developed.

Second, there is a complexity of interactions between and among styles, and styles further interact with abilities and interests. Third, certain curricular or environmental situations favor the applicability of some styles over others. Ideally, we should attempt to match students with teachers and learning environments that capitalize on their preferred style, but a more realistic approach to capitalizing on differences in learning style is to begin in the early years of schooling to provide young students with a broad range of experiences that expose them to various styles. We should be exposing students to carefully planned ways of using various instructional styles. The collective experiences in learning styles should provide: (1) exposure to many styles, (2) an understanding of which styles are the most personally applicable to particular subjects, and (3) experience in how to blend styles to maximize both the effectiveness and satisfaction of learning.

Curriculum

Much has been written on what characterizes effective curriculum. A good deal of this material may best be described as ordinary lists of curricular principles or "should lists" that focus on thinking skills, abstract concepts, advanced level content, interdisciplinary studies, thematic approaches, and a blending of content, process, and product. Three major components of curriculum that prepare young people for creative productivity are discussed here: structure of the discipline, content and methodology of the discipline, and appeal to the imagination.

Structure of the Discipline

The predominant value of a discipline lies not so much in its accumulated facts and principles as in its systematic way of thinking about a body of knowledge – its forms and connections, its unsolved problems, its methods of inquiry, its aspirations for improving mankind, and the special way it looks at phenomena. A concern for structure even includes the folklore, humor, personalities, gossip, and insider's knowledge that cause a person to be a member of the discipline rather than merely a student studying about the discipline. Curricular emphasis on the structure or "psychology" of a discipline is recommended because *advanced* involvement in any area of study requires that the interested novitiate learn how to think *in* the discipline. An example will clarify what thinking in a discipline means. Some people can communicate in a non-native language, but they do not know how to think in that language. They communicate by simply translating words they hear or read into their native language, formulating a mental response in their native language, and then translating that response into written or spoken words in the non-native language. Similarly, in mathematics, some people can solve standard problems, even very complex ones, by using replicative thinking – simply "plugging" information into a formula and performing customary calculations. But without being able to think *mathematically*, it is unlikely that this person will be able to deal with nonstandard problems, let alone make contributions that will lead to the advancement of the discipline.

To promote within-discipline thinking, curricular experiences should be developed in a way that places the learner in the role of a professional or firsthand inquirer in a field rather than as a mere assimilator of information. Within-discipline information is usually based on the following questions:

1. What is the overall purpose or mission of this field of study?
2. What are the major areas of concentration of the field and its subdivisions?
3. What kinds of questions are asked in the subdivisions?
4. What are the major sources of data in each subdivision?
5. How is knowledge organized and classified in this field or subdivision?
6. What are the basic reference books in the field or subdivision?
7. What are the major professional journals?
8. What are the major databases? How can we gain access to them?
9. Is there a history or chronology of events that will lead to a better understanding of the field or subdivision?
10. Are there any major events, persons, places, or beliefs that are predominant concerns of the field or best-case examples of what the field is all about?
11. What are some selected examples of "insiders' knowledge," such as field-specific humor, trivia, abbreviations and acronyms, "meccas," scandals, hidden realities, or unspoken beliefs?

Every experience should be viewed as a *confrontation* with knowledge, and students should be empowered to believe that they have the license to question, criticize, and, most important, add their own interpretations and contributions to existing knowledge. The concept of validation of knowledge and the direct teaching of epistemology (i.e., different ways of knowing, such as authoritarianism, empiricism, revelation, etc.) is another kind of confrontation that teaches students the meta-cognitive procedures for examining critically their own interpretations and creative contributions. A confrontation with knowledge means that everything that is already known, or that we hope students will acquire, is secondary to the development of mind in general and within-discipline thinking in particular.

Content and Methodology of a Discipline
Phenix (1964) recommends that a focus on representative concepts and ideas is the best way to capture the essence of a discipline. Representative ideas or concepts consist of themes, patterns, main features, sequences, organizing principles and structures, and the logic that defines a discipline and distinguishes it from other disciplines. Representative ideas and concepts can also be used as the bases for interdisciplinary or multidisciplinary studies.

When we select content, the level of advancement or complexity of material must first and foremost take into consideration the age and ability, maturity, previous study, and experiential background of the students. Beyond these considerations, three principles of content selection are recommended.

(1) Curricular material should escalate along a hierarchy of the following dimensions of knowledge: facts, conventions, trends and sequences, classifications and categories, criteria, principles and generalizations, and theories and structures.

(2) Movement toward the highest level, theories and structures, should involve continuous recycling to lower levels so that facts, trends and sequences, and so on can be understood in relation to a more integrated whole rather than isolated bits of irrelevant information.

(3) The cluster of diverse procedures that surround the acquisition of knowledge – that dimension of learning commonly referred to as "process" or thinking skills – should themselves be viewed as a form of content. It is these more enduring skills that form the cognitive structures and problem-solving strategies that have the greatest transfer value. When we view process *as* content, we avoid the artificial dichotomy and the endless arguments about whether content or process should be the primary goal of learning. Combining content and process leads to a goal that is larger than the sum of the respective parts. Simply stated, this goal is the acquisition of a scheme for acquiring, managing, and producing information in an organized and systematic fashion. A focus on methodology is the most direct way to prepare young people for their roles as contributors in future fields of professional involvement.

A focus on methodology means more than just teaching students methods of inquiry as content. Rather, it is designed to promote an understanding of and appreciation for the *application* of methods to the kinds of problems that are the essence of particular fields of knowledge. The goal of a focus on methodology is to cast the young person in the role of a firsthand inquirer rather than a mere learner-of-lessons, even if this role is carried out at a more junior level than the adult professional. This role encourages young learners to engage in the kinds of thinking, feeling, and doing that characterize the work of the practicing professional because it automatically creates the kind of confrontations with knowledge described earlier. It is this kind of work that mimics that of a practicing professional that is encouraged in creative productivity.

Appeal to the Imagination
In selecting curricular materials, a component often disregarded completely is how the material to be learned can be structured in a way that will appeal to the imagination of the learner (Phenix, 1964). Phenix argues very persuasively for the selection of curricular material that will lift students to new planes of experience and meaning. Material drawn from the extraordinary should

allow students to "see more deeply, feel more intensely, and comprehend more fully" (p. 346). He sets forth three conditions that should guide our thinking with regard to this concept and the role that teachers play in the pursuit of imaginative teaching. First, the means for stimulating the imagination differ according to the individual, his or her level of maturity, and the cultural context in which the individual is located. Second, the teacher must exemplify the imaginative qualities of the mind we are trying to develop in students and be able to enter sympathetically into the lives of students. Finally, imaginative teaching requires faith in the possibility of awakening imagination in any and every student, regardless of the kinds of constraints that may be placed on the learning process. This kind of content represents powerful and controversial manifestations of basic ideas and concepts. Thus, for example, the concepts of loyalty versus betrayal might be examined and compared in political, literary, military, or family perspectives but always in ways that bring intensity, debate, and personal involvement to the concepts. An adversarial approach to ideas and concepts (i.e., loyalty *versus* betrayal) also guarantees that the essential element of confrontations with knowledge will be present in selected curricular topics. In a certain sense, the history of creative productivity can be written as a chronicle of men and women who confronted existing ideas and concepts in an adversarial fashion and who used existing information only as counterpoints to what eventually became their own unique contributions to the growth of knowledge.

The Teacher

In any formal learning situation, the role of the teacher is well recognized and is probably the most important ingredient in any model of learning. Teachers make curricular and instructional decisions that directly affect the learner and his or her environment. When Walberg, Rasher, and Parkerson (1980) examined the biographical antecedents of persons of accomplishment, they found that almost two-thirds of their subjects were exposed to creatively productive persons at a very early age. Bloom (1985) reported that demanding teachers and mentors played an important role in the development of high-achieving youth, and Goertzel, Goertzel, and Goertzel (1978) concluded in their biographical study of eminent persons that mentors were especially important in evoking motivation. When we view teachers in an expanded role as mentors and models, a compendious biographical and autobiographical literature also points to the significant roles that dedicated teachers-as-mentors have played in the development of persons who have made important contributions to their respective areas of study.

The kinds of teachers who promote high levels of creative productivity in their students have certain characteristics in common. They tend to allow students greater choice in the selection of topics, welcome unorthodox views, reward divergent thinking, express enthusiasm for teaching, interact with their students outside of class, and generally conduct classes in an informal manner (Chambers, 1973). They establish positive relationships with their students by always working in close proximity with them; they engage in frequent verbal interaction of high-quality with their students, including verbal motivation, higher-level questioning skills, and a reciprocal sense of humor; are flexible about their use of time and scheduling, spending more time with students as it becomes necessary; and recognize that their students' creative productivity is an ultimate goal. These teachers provide human and physical resources to help students realize this goal (Story, 1985). In a study by Torrance (1981) that examined follow-up data of adolescent and adult creative behavior, 220 subjects provided anecdotal reflections about "teachers that made a difference." The findings support Chambers' conclusions and point out teacher attitudes and techniques that helped young learners "fall in love" with a topic or subject to such an extent that it became the center of their future career image.

Three major components constitute the ideal teacher for the development of creative productivity: knowledge of the discipline, instructional technique, and a teacher's romance with the discipline.

Knowledge of the Discipline

Arguments go back and forth about the degree to which teachers should be masters of the content area(s) in which they teach. The position we take here is that advanced competency in at least one discipline is important because it is through such content mastery and personal involvement that teachers, even if they are dealing with topics outside of their major area, develop the kinds of appreciations for within-discipline thinking that improves the guidance of learning in other areas. This is one area where we are in agreement with No Child Left Behind legislation, in the requirement for highly qualified teachers. Equally important for teachers of high-potential young children is an understanding of general research methodologies[1] and a repertoire of managerial skills that allow them to guide students through investigative activities (Renzulli & Reis, 1988). But advanced competency, in and of itself, is no guarantee that high-quality teaching will take place. Knowledge of the discipline means far more than merely knowing the facts, principles, and theories that define an area of knowledge. It also means knowing and understanding the role of methodology and being able to guide students through the application of methodology in real problem situations. It is this level of involvement – the

---

[1]   At the University of Connecticut and the University of Alabama, all persons enrolled in our programs for teachers of the gifted are required to take at least one course in research methods. Additionally, persons enrolled in a course dealing with curriculum development for the gifted are required to gain at least introductory college-level familiarity with an academic area in which they are planning to prepare curricular materials.

application of authentic investigative methods to self-selected and personally meaningful problems that we believe represents true differentiation in learning and is the goal of creative productivity.

Instructional Technique

The essential issue regarding instructional technique, and especially technique that fosters creative productivity, is best phrased as questions. To what extent is effective technique a "natural" characteristic of the individual teacher, and to what extent can it be taught? Both personality and training contribute to the development of teachers who encourage and facilitate creativity. Years of training teachers of the gifted have led us to believe that certain personality characteristics are necessary for highly effective teaching of creative students. These characteristics, which are generally found in confident but nonauthoritative persons, include flexibility, openness to experience and new ideas, a high energy level, optimism, commitment to excellence, and enthusiasm for living. These characteristics are viewed as "starting material," and they are important enough for us to recommend that *teacher selection should be a consideration that precedes teacher training.*

But training in pedagogy also plays an important role, and we have attempted to describe the areas on which teacher training should focus in the four menus subsumed under Instructional Technique in Figure 3.2. These menus are taken from The Multiple Menu Model guide for developing curriculum (Renzulli, Leppien, & Hays, 2000). The Instructional Objectives and Student Activities Menu addresses the following hierarchy of thinking processes: Information Pick-up (assimilation and retention), Information Analysis (higher order processing), Information Output (synthesis and application), and Evaluation (review and critique). The Instructional Strategies Menu identifies fourteen teaching strategies that range along a continuum from structured to unstructured patterns for organizing learning. The Instructional Sequence Menu deals mainly with organizational and management techniques, and the Artistic Modification Menu focuses on techniques that personalize the teaching process and encourage teachers to put themselves *into* the material rather than merely teaching about it. Although teachers undoubtedly have "natural" preferences for specific techniques within the several categories that constitute each instructional menu, the broad range of student differences that will be encountered when focusing on nurturing creativity in students requires that a repertoire of techniques be developed. Ideal acts of learning will obviously be enhanced if there is a perfect match between teacher and learner styles. Perfect matches, however, are the exception rather than the rule; therefore, teacher training should be geared toward developing a range of teaching styles and encouraging a flexible use of styles to accommodate individual abilities, interests, and learning styles.

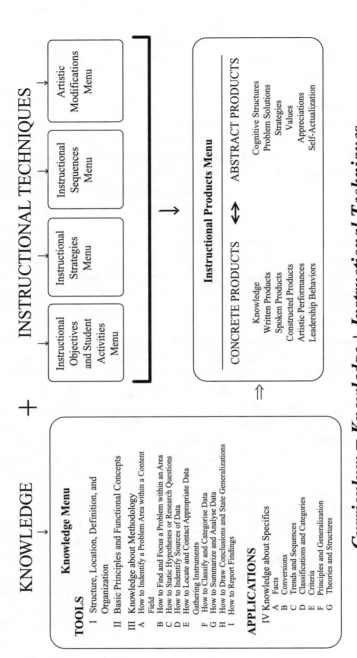

KNOWLEDGE + **INSTRUCTIONAL TECHNIQUES**

Knowledge Menu

TOOLS

I Structure, Location, Definition, and Organization

II Basic Principles and Functional Concepts

III Knowledge about Methodology
A How to Indentify a Problem Area within a Content Field
B How to Find and Focus a Problem within an Area
C How to Static Hypotheses or Research Questions
D How to Indentify Sources of Data
E How to Locate and Contact Appropriate Data Gathering Instruments
F How to Classify and Categorise Data
G How to Summarize and Analyse Data
H How to Draw Conclusions and State Generalizations
I How to Report Findings

APPLICATIONS

IV Knowledge about Specifics
A Facts
B Conversions
C Trends and Sequences
D Classifications and Categories
E Criteria
F Principles and Generalization
G Theories and Structures

Instructional Objectives and Student Activities Menu

Instructional Strategies Menu

Instructional Sequences Menu

Artistic Modifications Menu

Instructional Products Menu

CONCRETE PRODUCTS ⟷ ABSTRACT PRODUCTS

Knowledge
Written Products
Spoken Products
Constructed Products
Artistic Performances
Leadership Behaviors

Cognitive Structures
Problem Solutions
Strategies
Values
Appreciations
Self-Actualization

Curriculum = Knowledge + Instructional Techniques

Figure 3.2. The Multiple Menu Model.

Romance with the Discipline

One of the characteristics that distinguish truly inspiring teachers is their love for the material they are teaching. Most of what we know about teachers who possess this romance with their discipline comes from biographical and auto-biographical accounts of well-known persons who were inspired and guided by an outstanding teacher. A book edited by John C. Board entitled *A Special Relationship: Our Teachers and How We Learned* (1991) consists of the memoirs of eminent persons from all walks of life who describe the important roles that outstanding teachers played in their early development. In analyzing the common themes that existed between teachers and learners, Board comments:

> These teachers, almost without exception, displayed masterful command of their subject matter. All were caring. All were possessed of an uncanny ability to unleash youthful potential. All were demanding, all relentless in their determination to ignite in every student the will to excel. And all were, to borrow Louis Nizer's words, "alike in their boundless energy." (p. 19)

Board goes on to describe what he calls "an uncommon characteristic that great teachers hold in common," and that characteristic is their own passion for knowledge and learning. They view themselves as a part of the discipline, rather than as a person who merely studies about it or teaches it to others. We believe that it is this romantic relationship with a discipline that causes certain teachers to seek out and nurture students of remarkable potential. In much the same way that the owner of a successful business or *object d'art* wants to ensure that a prized possession is passed on to someone who is a trustworthy recipient, so also is it feasible to postulate that the kinds of ownership and involvement that cause a romantic relationship with a discipline will result in similar concerns about the intellectual heirs of one's beloved field of study. Although the teacher's technique and romance with a discipline may not be as objectively verifiable as the extent of knowledge and methodology that the teacher possesses, the importance of these characteristics in the development of creative productivity in young people should cause us to examine them more carefully.

Ideal acts of learning can be described as action learning (Revans, 1982) – a situation where student, teacher, and curriculum function together in a way that encourages the acquisition of knowledge and skills, the asking of deep questions of interest to the student, the search for solutions and generation of new ideas, and the application of acquired knowledge and skills to the asked questions. Revans suggested that action learning is a reiterative cycle of acting, gathering data, reflecting, designing, and taking new action. Action learning and ideal acts of learning are not linear but require constantly revisiting and redefining the goals and objectives of learning. How can this be practically applied in the classroom?

NURTURING CREATIVE PRODUCTIVITY THROUGH ENRICHMENT LEARNING AND TEACHING

Enrichment learning and teaching represent a particular way of applying the essential components of ideal acts of learning described earlier. Enrichment learning and teaching have also been called high-end learning (Renzulli, 1978b). High-end learning can be defined in terms of the following four principles:

1. Each learner is unique, and therefore all learning experiences must be examined in ways that take into account the abilities, interests, and learning styles of the individual.
2. Learning is more effective when students enjoy what they are doing, and therefore learning experiences should be constructed and assessed with as much concern for enjoyment as for other goals.
3. Learning is more meaningful and enjoyable when content (knowledge) and process (thinking skills and methods of inquiry) are learned within the context of a real and present problem, and therefore attention should be given to opportunities to personalize student choice in problem selection, the relevance of the problem for individuals and for students who share common interests in the problem, and strategies for assisting students in personalizing problems they might choose to study.
4. Some formal instruction may be used in high-end learning, but a major goal of this approach to learning is to enhance knowledge and thinking skills acquisition gained through teacher instruction with applications of knowledge and skills that result from students' construction of meaningfulness.

The ultimate goal of learning that is guided by these principles is to replace dependence and passive learning with independence and engaged learning. The most difficult part of enrichment learning and teaching is getting teachers to stop teaching and to become facilitators of learning – the proverbial "guide-on-the-side" rather than the disseminator of information. The teacher's role is to assist in problem finding and problem focusing and in the procurement of content and methodological resources and to help students understand how to use the resources. The only time that direct instruction should take place is when the instruction is necessary to help produce and improve the product or service.

For high-end learning or enrichment learning and teaching to be systematically applied to the learning process in the regular classroom, it must be organized in a way that makes sense to students and teachers. An organizational pattern called the Enrichment Triad Model (Renzulli, 1987b) is used for this

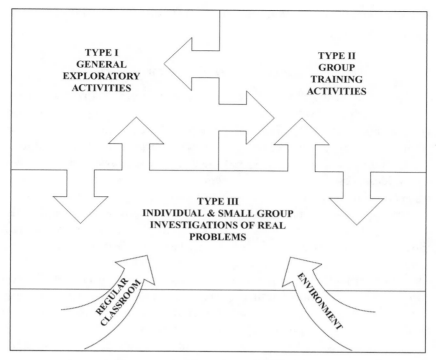

Figure 3.3. The Enrichment Triad Model.

purpose. The three types of enrichment in the model are depicted in Figure 3.3. Type I enrichment consists of general exploratory experiences that are designed to expose students to topics in areas of study not ordinarily covered in the regular curriculum. Type II enrichment consists of group training in thinking and feeling processes, learning-to-learn skills, research and reference skills, and written, oral, and visual communications skills. Type III enrichment consists of firsthand investigations of real problems. Problem solving in real life almost always results in a product or service that has a functional, artistic, or humanitarian value. The learning that takes place in real problem situations is collateral learning that results from attacking the problem to produce a product or service, what we previously called "action learning." As an example, consider a group of engineering students who want to build a bridge across a stream. They examine the scope of the problem, what they already know, and what they need to know and do to build the bridge. In the process, they may learn about geometry, strength of materials, planning and sequencing, cooperativeness, structural design, spatial relationships, aesthetics, mechanics, and a host of other things necessary to get the job done. This kind of learning that focuses on the interaction between product and process results in learning experiences that nurture creativity.

Type I Enrichment: General Exploratory Experiences

One of the enduring problems of teaching to nurture creativity is how to motivate students to act on their interests in a creative and productive way. The major purpose of Type I enrichment is to include within the overall school program carefully selected experiences that are purposefully developed to be highly motivational and to expose students to a wide variety of disciplines, topics, ideas, concepts, issues, and events that are not ordinarily covered in the general curriculum. Students may not know whether they will develop a sustained interest in a particular topic if they have not been exposed to the topic. Type I experiences should be selected and planned to be exciting and appealing to students and might be presented to all students in the classroom, grade level, or cross-grade group. A good menu of Type I experiences should be diversified across many topics and curricular categories. Such diversification improves the probability of influencing broader ranges of student interest and, accordingly, of increasing the number of students who will select an area in which they may like to pursue follow-up activities.

To qualify as a bona fide Type I experience, any and all planned activities in this category have to be purposefully designed to stimulate new or present interests that may lead to more intensive follow-up on the parts of individual students and small groups of students and that may lead to creative productive activity. An activity can be called a Type I experience only if it meets the following three conditions:

1. Students are aware that the activities invite them to various kinds and levels of follow-up.
2. There is a systematic debriefing of the experience to learn who might want to explore further involvement and the ways in which follow-up on the activity might be pursued.
3. There are many opportunities, resources, and encouragement for diverse kinds of follow-up. An experience is not a Type I if every student is required to follow-up on an activity in the same or similar way. Required follow-up is a regular curricular practice and it almost always fails to capitalize on differences in students' interests and learning styles. Type I activities that encourage maximum student involvement and hands-on problem solving, or activities that require discussion, debate, and confrontations with topics and issues, are much more effective in prompting the kind of affective reactions that help students to personalize a topic and to make a commitment to more intense follow-up.

Type II Enrichment: Group Training Activities

Type II enrichment consists of instructional methods and materials that are purposefully designed to develop a broad range of process skills in the following five general categories:

> (1) Cognitive training, (2) affective training, (3) learning how to learn training, (4) research and reference procedures, and (5) written, oral, and visual communication procedures. The term "process skills" includes all of these categories. Specific skills within each of these general categories can be found in a taxonomy of Type II thinking skills at http://www.gifted.uconn.edu/sem/typeiips.html. (Renzulli, 1977b)

Within each category of Type II enrichment, the targeted skills exist along a continuum ranging from very basic manifestations of a given skill to higher and more complex applications of any given process. Skills such as conditional reasoning or recording data from original sources can be taught to students at any grade, but the level and complexity of the specific activities will vary according to the students' developmental levels. Primary-grade students, for instance, can learn observational and data-gathering skills by counting and recording the number of times different kinds of birds come to a bird feeder during a given period of time. These data might be presented by using simple tallies or pictograms. Older students can develop the same skills on higher levels by observing and recording pulse and blood pressure measures while controlling for factors such as age, height/weight ratios, and specified periods of exercise. The advanced mathematics and computer skills of older students might enable them to engage in more sophisticated statistical analyses of their data. As an example, a group of fourth- and fifth-grade students from an elementary school in Western Australia engaged in a long-distance race with another group of students in a different state using the Nike Plus System. The system consists of a measurement device that connects to the runner's shoe and to an iPod, which then downloads information on speed and distance run by a student to a calculator on the Nike Web site. The calculator gives information about energy expended. These students were able to calculate how far they had to run to burn the calories consumed when eating different kinds of food. A podcast made by these students telling of this "Race around Australia" is available at http://www.teachertube.com/view_video.php?viewkey=13d65899f9d0522a893f.

There are three different methods for presenting Type II enrichment. The first method consists of planned systematic activities that can be organized in advance for any unit of instruction within the general curriculum. These kinds of Type II activities are planned in advance and form a part of an ongoing framework to develop a comprehensive "scope and sequence" of process-oriented activities that parallel regular curriculum topics. The "Race around Australia" is one of this type of enrichment that was integrated into physical education and science. The main criterion for selecting Type II activities in this category is that the activity bears a direct or indirect relationship to the subject matter being taught.

The second method for presenting Type II enrichment consists of activities that cannot be planned in advance because they grow out of students' reactions to school or nonschool experiences. In other words, this dimension is characterized by responsiveness to student interests rather than preplanning. Enrichment in this dimension can also fill the motivational goal of the model by stimulating interests that may lead to more intensive follow-up in the form of Type III enrichment. An example of this kind of Type II enrichment is given by middle-school teacher Jennifer Winslett from Birmingham, Alabama. She tells her story in Figure 3.4. Student and teacher interest drove the skills instruction in this unit developed by Jennifer and her students.

My fellow colleagues and I decided to implement a student driven interest study program as a part of our pull-out program. We felt it was vital to student success. Our desire was to instill the value of life-long learning in our students. We began by revisiting the existing pull-out program schedule and making appropriate revisions. The new schedule allowed each student to attend a one hour interest study class once a week in addition to attending a three hour curriculum based class once a week.

Students were given an interest inventory which drove class instruction. Students were placed in classes according to their interests. We also felt it was very important for the teacher to not only express an interest in the class, but have a passion for the topic as well. It was important for the students to see our enthusiasm for learning and as a result motivate their own learning.

As a young adult, I aspired to become a nurse anesthetist. I began my college career as a nursing major, thus taking many biology and physiology classes. Naturally, I took on the role of facilitating learning in the interest area of the human body. My class, Doctor Doctor, began with an introduction to the human body. Students were introduced to the different body systems and took a superficial look at the function of each. I noticed during this introduction that my students were extremely interested in the heart.

During the next class, I showed students how to check vital signs, including pulse rates, blood pressures, and respiratory rates and allowed students to practice with each other using actual instruments used in the medical field. I then posed the question, "How does exercise affect your vital signs?" Various answers were yelled out and I could see their wheels turning. After a few minutes of intense conversation, students stood and participated in various exercises such as jumping jacks for five minutes.

They then rechecked their vital signs and compared them to initial vital signs taken at rest. I extended this lesson beyond the classroom by asking students to complete the same exercises over the course of the next week on a daily basis, check their pulses, and record their findings.

The next week during classes they again exercised for five minutes, checked vitals, and compared their findings. Students concluded that exercise increased vital signs, yet after a week of exercising vital signs decreased after exercise. They also began asking questions about the effects of smoking on exercise, resulting in a conversation about the effect smoking as well as other unhealthy practices have on vital signs and overall health. As a result of their interest, a video clip was viewed. The video clip explained the effects of unhealthy practices and heart disease. Students were able to see inside blood vessels, plaque residue, build-up and how a heart attack resulted.

The clip prompted more questions and more research. To conclude the study, I partnered with St. Louis University School of Medicine via Distance Learning and Virtual Field Trips. The program, Adventures in Medicine and Science: Pig Heart Dissection, focused on teaching students not only the anatomy of the heart, but also the flow of blood through the heart. We were able to see an instructor at St. Louis University and dialogue with him as he guided us through the process. Each pair of students had a pig heart to dissect and study. The instructor was also able to see us and students were able to converse with him as well. Students were able to see an actual human heart; one that was healthy and one that was enlarged due to heart disease.

Hands-on learning as well as expert exposure allowed my students a once in-a-lifetime experience. It is my belief that students were not only inspired to learn more and dig deeper, but also inspired to lead healthy lives. The impact of this program was phenomenal. My students have already begun to inquire about this type of learning experience in the future.

Jennifer Winslett – Birmingham

Figure 3.4. Doctor, doctor – Story of interest-driven skills instruction.

The third method for presenting Type II enrichment consists of the activities that are used within the context of already initiated Type III investigations. Activities used in this way represent the best application of inductive learning. Simply put, an individual or a group learns a process skill because they need the skill to solve real and present problems. Traci Ingleright is an elementary enrichment teacher in Birmingham, Alabama. In 2007, Traci had 86 elementary students in grades 3 through 5 who completed Type III experiences. For these young students to be successful, Traci had to teach them certain process skills as a group. Some of the skills they learned were how to refine a research question from a wide variety of interests, how to conduct research and gather data, how to use the school copier and fax machine, how to properly answer a telephone, how to prepare for a telephone interview and to interview adults, and many more similar skills. Individual children also had to learn skills specific to their projects. One girl learned how to sew for her dress designing project. A boy learned to make flyers to spread the word about his project – gathering diapers for babies in foster care. Another boy had to learn how to speak to public meetings because he was asked to be the spokesperson for Operation Lifesaver (read about him at http://www.oli.org/enewsletter/FromTheStates.html).

Type III Enrichment: Individual and Small Group Investigations of Real Problems

Type III enrichment leads to creative productive activity on the part of youngsters. It consists of investigative activities and the development of creative products in which students pursue roles as firsthand investigators, writers, artists, or other types of practicing professionals. Although students pursue these kinds of involvement at the more junior level than adult professionals, the overriding purpose of Type III enrichment is to create situations in which young people are thinking, feeling, and doing what practicing professionals do in the delivery of products and services. Type III enrichment experiences should be viewed as vehicles in which students can apply their interests, knowledge, thinking skills, creative ideas, and task commitment to self-selected problems or areas of study. In addition to this general goal, there are four objectives of Type III enrichment:

1. To acquire advanced-level understanding of the knowledge and methodology used within particular disciplines, artistic areas of expressions, and interdisciplinary studies
2. To develop authentic products or services that are primarily directed toward bringing about the desired impact on one or more specified audiences
3. To develop self-directed learning skills in the areas of planning, problem finding and focusing, organizational skills, resources utilization, time management, cooperativeness, decision making, and self-evaluation
4. To develop task commitment, self-confidence, feelings of creative accomplishment, and the ability to interact effectively with other students and adults who share common goals and interests

This type of enrichment is defined in terms of the pursuit of real problems. Real problems have four characteristics. (1) It must have a personal frame of reference for the individual or group pursuing the problem. For example, we knew a student named Davis who became interested in train crossing safety because three of his friends died in an accident on a train crossing. (2) Real problems do not have existing or unique solutions for the people addressing the problem. If there is an agreed-on or correct solution or set of strategies for solving the problem, it is more appropriately classified as a training exercise. Even simulations that are based on approximations of real-world events are considered to be training exercises if their main purpose is to teach content or thinking skills. (3) A problem is "real" because people want to bring about some form of change in actions, attitudes, or beliefs on the parts of a targeted audience or they want to contribute something new to the sciences, arts, or humanities. By "new," we mean new in the local rather than global sense. We do not expect young people to make contributions that are new "for all mankind." For example, if a group of young people gather data about their running as in the "Race around Australia" example given earlier, the data and resulting analysis would be new in the sense that they never existed before and the insights would be new for these youngsters. (4) Real problems are directed toward a real audience. "Real audiences" are defined as persons who voluntarily attend to information, events, services, or objects. Consider, for example, a student who works to have novelty cigarette lighters banned because of safety concerns. He could present his research findings to his classmates to rehearse his presentation and get feedback, but an authentic audience might be the fire marshals and city council members, who are able to enact regulations that would ban the sale of these unsafe items.

While there is nothing inherently wrong with using simulated problems for training and learning, there are benefits to encouraging students to pursue real problems of particular interest to them in which they can learn real-life skills. Alane Starko (1986) studied students who participated in Triad programs for at least four years. They were compared to students who qualified for such programs but received no services. Results indicated that students who became involved in independent study projects of the type suggested here more often initiated their own creative products both *in and outside of school* than did students in the comparison group. The group in the Enrichment Triad Program reported more than twice as many creative projects per student as the comparison group and reported doing more than twice as many creative products outside of school on their own time (1.03) than the comparison group (0.50). Hébert (1993) also showed that experiences with Type III activities in elementary school laid a solid foundation for continued creative productivity in later years; even when students were not encouraged to engage in these kinds of activities in middle and high school, they continued to pursue creative independent projects outside of school. The young people Hébert interviewed discussed how their Type III experiences helped them later in school. The planning, research, and time management skills they learned stood them in good stead in middle and high school. These young people also talked about the life-shaping effects their early independent projects had on them. Their early Type III projects had a significant impact on their later career choices.

Brianne Burrowes, now a journalism major at the University of Montana, was such a student – a teenager intrigued by magazines. Encouraged by her enrichment teacher, and given the appropriate training and opportunity, she started her own e-zine and was featured in the national *ELLEgirl* magazine. We interviewed Ms. Burrowes for this chapter, and the full interview is given in Appendix A.

Five Essential Elements of Type III Enrichment

Five essential elements that typify Type III enrichment are focus on individual or group interests, focus on advanced-level knowledge, focus on methodology, a sense of audience, and authentic evaluation.

A Focus on Individual or Group Interests

Problems being pursued through this type of learning experience must be based on individual or group interests. In the spirit of acting as facilitators of learning, teachers and other adults can provide guidance toward the formulation of a problem, but they must avoid at all costs crossing the line from suggestion to prescription. The role of adults is primarily that of assisting students in problem finding and focusing. Some Type III problems will be specific to individual students. Other Type III problems will be of more general interest to a group of students. It is possible to guide students in this situation to become involved in different ways with the same problem or problem area. In most cases, the division of labor that takes place in group Type III situations causes a broader range of talents to be developed and promotes the kind of real-world cooperativeness and mutual respect that we are attempting to achieve in high-end learning. Problems that require a diversity of specialties also create opportunities for more personalization on the parts of individuals in the group. When each person feels that she or he owns a part of the problem, the first characteristic of a real problem is met.

The Focus on Advanced-Level Knowledge

Type III enrichment should draw on authentic, advanced-level knowledge. If we want young people to approximate the roles of practicing professionals, then it is important to examine the characteristics of persons who have displayed high levels of expertise in their respective domains of knowledge. During the past three decades, cognitive psychologists have devoted much research to the topic of experts and expertise and the role of knowledge in attaining expert performance. Glaser (1988) summarized some of the key characteristics of expert performance, and these characteristics can be used to provide guidance for this dimension of the Enrichment Triad Model:

- Experts mainly excel in their own domain and spend much more time than novices analyzing information within their respective fields of study.
- Experts also perceive large, meaningful patterns in their domain and they have an understanding of how knowledge is organized in their domain.

- They tend to represent problems at deeper levels by creating conceptual categories rather than categories based on surface or superficial features.
- They are goal oriented, and they access knowledge mainly for its applicability to present problems.
- Finally, experts develop self-regulatory skills such as judging problem difficulty, apportioning time, asking questions, revealing their knowledge, and predicting outcomes.

For students to gain higher levels of expertise in a topic or domain, time spent on independent projects has to increase significantly and the amount and complexity of knowledge available to students pursuing advanced studies and investigations must also be expanded. While the amount of advanced level of knowledge that teachers possess is a major determinant of the level of courses they teach, technology has made access to experts relatively easy. Consider again the example of Jennifer Winslett, who was able to partner with an instructor at St. Louis University through distance education technology to teach her students about the heart. She did not need to be an expert herself but could tap into another person's expertise for her students.

A Focus on Methodology
The use of authentic methodology is an essential element of Type III enrichment. Because one of the goals of Type III enrichment is to help young people extend their work beyond the usual kinds of reporting often resulting from student research (read "looking up information"), the end result of a Type III investigation should be a creative contribution that goes beyond already existing information that is typically found in encyclopedias and other "all-about" books. *Methodology* often defines a field of organized knowledge, and the methodology of most fields can be found in certain kinds of guidebooks or how-to manuals. These how-to books are the key to escalating studies beyond the traditional report approach that often passes for research. Furthermore, every field of knowledge can also be partly defined by the kinds of data that represent the raw material of the field. New contributions to a field result from one of two types of occurrences: (1) investigators may apply well-defined methods of the field to the process of making sense out of random bits and pieces of information – in other words, synthesizing information in a new way as in the example of Joshua Schachter's development of del.icio.us, or (2) investigators may develop new methods to work with well-known pieces of information, such as in the example of Terence Tao's development of more efficient digital cameras.

Some investigations require levels of sophistication and equipment that are far beyond the reach of young investigators, but all fields of knowledge have entry-level and junior-level data-gathering opportunities. We have seen scientifically respectable questionnaire studies on food and television preferences carried out by primary-grade students. A group of middle-grade students gathered and analyzed water samples as part of a large regional study on the extent and effects of acid rain. This work was so thoroughly and carefully done that the students' findings were requested for use by a state environmental agency. A fifth-grade student wrote a guide book that was adopted by his city's government as the official historical walking tour of the city; another elementary student convinced all the fire marshals in the State of Alabama to ban the sale of novelty cigarette lighters, which posed a safety risk to children and adults alike. In a small town in Alabama, a group of students decided to interview elderly citizens before "they were all gone" and were instrumental in establishing a museum for their town with priceless historical objects garnered from the senior citizens. These examples reflect the success and high levels of product development attributed to the proper use of authentic methods and techniques, even when the techniques are carried out at a somewhat junior level compared with the techniques used by adult inquirers. The facilitating teacher's role in providing methodological assistance is to help students identify, locate, and obtain resource materials and/or persons to provide assistance in the appropriate use of investigative techniques.

A Sense of Audience

Products and services resulting from this kind of involvement have to be targeted to real audiences. This sense of audience that students develop in connection with their work is an essential element in the success of many Type III projects. This sense of audience gives students a reason to improve the quality of their products and to develop effective ways of communicating their results with interested others. The sense of audience is also a primary contributor to the creation of task commitment and concern for excellence and quality that have to characterize Type III investigations. A large part of the facilitating teacher's effort must be focused on helping students find appropriate outlets and audiences for their most creative efforts. In real life, creative and productive individuals have the same concern. The reason most creative and productive people create and produce is their intended impact on the audience. Type III investigations provide the same kind of personal satisfaction and self-expression that result from bringing an important piece of work to fruition. Placing an emphasis on outlets and audiences helps students take one small but often neglected first step in the overall process of product development – to consider what people in a particular field produce and how they typically communicate their results to other interested persons. We can look to the activities of practicing professionals and the how-to books for guidance in this instance. In many cases, young artists and scholars will be restricted to local outlets and audiences, but there will be occasions when products of unusual excellence can be shared with larger audiences. Jane Newman, now professor in gifted and talented education at the University of Alabama, started her teaching career years ago as a teacher of gifted students in Albertville, Alabama. She tells

Some of the projects that I facilitated lasted 2 years. In the early 1980s I had a group of students who were interested in the history of their town – it was a small town, my town, and they wanted to read about the history of Albertville, but there was nothing. They went to the library, but there was nothing. So they said, "Well, we need to write a history!" We got involved, we got a grant, and we got a consultant from the University of Alabama to come down and teach us how to collect oral history from the senior citizens. This project was a 2 year project and it gave the students something to do after school. We lived in a rural area and there was not really a lot to do after school and on weekends. It turned into a nice project. We published a hardbound book with illustrations and pictures. It was adopted by the school system as a textbook for 3rd and 4th grade students, and it still is one of the textbooks.

Also aside from that, as the students were interviewing these older citizens from the area, they would say, "Well, I have this old plough back there in the shed that I don't have a use for. If you want it, you can have it." Or they'd say, "I have this mortar and pestle that we used to grind corn on and we don't use it anymore." So our kids got the mayor of the town to donate this caboose that was just sitting around and we turned it into a museum and it is still there. And people donated things. My husband and I cleaned out my parents' house. My grandparents had lived there, and we had all these pieces of old farm equipment. I would have kept them, but my husband said, "No, we can't take those to Birmingham." So we donated those to the museum, and people can go and see what the settlers from that area used and what life was like.

Jane Newman, Birmingham

Figure 3.5. Interview with Jane Newman.

the story of how her students created a history book about their town that was adopted by the local school district as an elementary history textbook (Figure 3.5).

An important role Jane played was to find a funding source and to find a knowledgeable person to teach her students how to do the things they wanted to do. Teachers should always help students gain a perspective for more comprehensive outlet vehicles and audiences beyond local communities. Many organizations, for example, prepare newsletters and journals at state and national levels, and virtually every interest group has a broader array of Web sites and other means for electronic communications. A youngster from Alabama was featured in the newsletter of a state organization that deals with foster children and orphans, and another became a spokesperson for a national organization. Exploring external audiences will help young people develop standards of quality and will also provide them with real-world experiences about the rigors and challenges of reaching out to wider audiences.

Authentic Evaluation

Work carried out using a Type III enrichment approach should be evaluated in an authentic rather than an artificial manner. The ultimate test of quality in the world outside of school is whether products and services achieve the desired impact on clients or selected audiences. It is for this reason that Type III products should never be graded or scored. This traditional school practice is antithetical to the ways in which work is evaluated in the real world. A guide such as the Student Product Assessment Form (Renzulli & Reis, 1997; available at http://www.gifted.uconn.edu/sem/pdf/spaf.pdf) can be used to provide students with categorical feedback, but even this instrument should only be used to help students refine and improve their work. Teachers and other adults should take the role in the feedback process of a "resident escalator." Sensitive and specific recommendations about how particular aspects of the work can be improved will help students move slowly but surely toward higher and higher levels of product excellence. Feedback should be specific and encouraging to avoid student discouragement and to reconfirm a belief in the overall value of their endeavors.

Teachers as Facilitators of Type III Investigations

Teachers who facilitate Type III activities fulfill a range of duties, such as project manager, facilities supervisor, supply clerk, coach, secretary, production manager, caterer, transportation manager, and cheerleader. Few students, especially young ones, naturally have the deep interest and task commitment to sustain them through a semester or year-long investigation without help. Without help and proper support, students may start a project and fail to carry it to completion. Completing a high-quality product does not automatically occur; it requires interest, self-motivation, and direction, as well as the acquisition of critical thinking and planning skills (Newman, 2006).

There are a variety of ways to accomplish this objective. Schlichter (1986, 2009) proposed using the Talents Unlimited Model as a Type II skills training model. The Talents Unlimited Model consists of the following work-related thought processes: productive thinking, communication, forecasting, decision making, and planning (Schlichter & Palmer, 2002). These processes help improve students' critical and creative thinking skills in the classroom context and provide a framework for improving the chances of success of independent projects. According to several research studies (Burns, 1987; Gubbins, 1982; Schack, 1986; Starko, 1986), personal variables such as locus of control, self-concept, self-efficacy, grade, gender, learning style preferences, achievement, and Type II orientation lessons have a significant impact on students' decisions to start an independent project. Newman (2005, 2006) found that students who used the Talents Unlimited Model model to focus and plan their investigations were significantly more likely to complete projects successfully than were students who had not received such training (100% versus 79%). The talents most helpful, according to these students, were productive thinking (for interest finding), decision making (for narrowing the topic to a single research question), and planning.

Case Study: The Lightbulb Expo

Traci Ingleright, an enrichment teacher in Hoover, Alabama, is an excellent example of a teacher who nurtures creative productivity in her classroom. She has perfected the process over several years, and in spring 2007, 86 of her third-, fourth-, and fifth-grade students completed independent projects (T. Ingleright, personal communication, October 16, 2007). Ms. Ingleright encourages her students to read the newspapers and watch the news. They regularly talk about current events. She takes this approach a step further, however. She encourages her students to think of a situation or problem in their lives or their community that they can change. The first step in the development of Type III investigations is a process she calls "Ten Questions." She has the youngsters write down as many topics as possible that they might wish to investigate. She then has a conference with each student to get to that one topic that most interests them, and for which they can find resources and information. After they have identified their topic of interest, she asks them to write down ten questions: ten things they want to know about their topic. In finding resources, students search the school and community libraries, and then make copies of the pages containing pertinent information, as well as the bibliographical information of the resources. These pages are stored in the three-ring binder that each student has so they can easily find the information later when they create their bibliography. The process is fluid, and students sometimes have to change topics when they cannot find enough information. They also search the Internet for information and resources.

A requirement of the project is that each student should gather as many sources of information as possible, including real people who might be interviewed. The school has installed a telephone in the enrichment room for the purpose of allowing students to place and receive telephone calls connected to their projects. These students have to learn many process skills to complete their investigations successfully – research skills, data-gathering skills, telephone etiquette, how to keep accurate records, how to keep journals of their progress, and how to handle multiple pieces of mail and email that come in response to their queries.

To simplify the process, Ms. Ingleright has developed a system for communicating with students and their parents through regular meetings and emails.

She also has two mail areas – one for students to leave her mail, which often consists of questions or requests for help, and one where students can pick up their mail. Each student has a basket where they keep their supplies and a three-ring binder for keeping track of research materials, journal entries, activity logs, and mail.

When students have gathered enough information to start formulating answers to their ten questions, they create their first product – a research paper based on the ten questions. The paper includes a bibliography. Students also prepare for a public event where their projects are displayed. This event is called the Lightbulb Expo, and for the Expo each student prepares a display board in three parts: the middle part portrays their research question and research findings. On one side they portray what action they have taken to solve their problem, and on the other side they put information under the heading "What can you do?" Each student is available to answer questions about their project. Several students also prepare interest development centers to be donated to the school library for the use of teachers and students. What is most interesting, though, are the out-of-school results of the projects. The student activities do not just revolve around research, a paper, and an exhibition.

The following examples of creative productivity come from the Spring 2007 Lightbulb Expo. One third-grader, Collin, became aware of the large foster children population in Birmingham. His research question was "What can I do to reduce the number of foster children?" His first solution was that Ms. Ingleright should adopt some children. When she gently declined, he had to find other solutions. He contacted 14 foster care agencies in the Birmingham area, and through his research realized that adoption of all the children in these homes would not be possible. He had to change his research question, and then became aware of an urgent need for diapers and baby formula for the many babies in the foster care system. Also being a baseball player, he decided to involve his friends in the junior baseball leagues in collecting products for foster babies. He found a ready audience. Coaches and parents of boys in the baseball league contributed generously. A former professional baseball player visited the school for an unrelated reason and was promptly introduced to this young boy. The upshot was that the Birmingham Barons baseball team held a benefit game for foster children, and the Atlanta Braves contributed to his campaign. Collin's B.A.B.I.E.S. campaign (Baseball Assisting Babies In Emergency Situations) collected over 5,000 boxes of diapers that he donated to Birmingham Area children's homes. The Alabama Baptist Children's Homes published a story about Collin's help in their Spring 2007 *LifePrints* newsletter available at http://www.abchome.org/publications.html.

Another boy, a fourth-grader called David, discovered that many novelty cigarette lighters sold at gas stations were actually illegal, because they have no safety mechanisms. He mounted a campaign to get these lighters banned in his town. With the help of the Hoover fire chief, he has spoken with every fire marshal in the state of Alabama, and they have all agreed to help this now 10-year-old boy do what he needs to do to get these lighters banned.

Katy is a young lady who became concerned about homeless women and discovered a charity called Clara's Closet in nearby Tuscaloosa. This charity was founded by a lawyer in Tuscaloosa, who was Mrs. America 2005 and also happened to be a friend of Ms. Ingleright. With this woman's help, Katy collected professional clothes for women in need and donated a truckload of clothes to Clara's Closet.

Many of the students in this program were able to achieve real-world results with their projects, and you can read a newspaper story about them in the April 26, 2007, edition of the *Birmingham News*. Not all the projects were as spectacular as these examples, but all these students gained immeasurably in skills, knowledge, and self-confidence. Many of the adults who had mentored and helped the youngsters with their projects, including the Hoover fire chief and Mrs. America 2005, attended the final Lightbulb Expo evening to pledge their continued support.

APPLYING IDEAL LEARNING SITUATIONS WITHIN SCHOOL STRUCTURES

There are a variety of school structures within which these kinds of ideal acts of learning can be accommodated. These structures range from opportunities classroom teachers can make for creative work on the part of their students within their regular curriculum, to special grouping strategies and elective or pullout classes.

Regular Classroom and Curriculum Opportunities

Classroom teachers can create opportunities for independent and semi-independent projects that stem from the regular curriculum by giving students choices in exhibiting what they have learned. Instead of requiring a research paper or a written exam, teachers may give students the choice of a wide variety of products. Some possible product choices are suggested in Table 3.1.

Some classroom activity may be used as training for creative productivity and may not result in real-world problem solving, products, and services. The second author of this chapter taught sixth-grade students for several years in a school that integrated social studies and literature. Part of the regular curriculum was studying Greek and Roman history and geography and integrating literature studies consisting of Greek and Roman myths, as well as the works of Homer. This curriculum was usually taught in the second quarter, before the winter holidays. As a culminating activity, students were given a 3 × 3 grid containing nine possible products, of which they had to complete three (Table 3.2). Beyond these nine products, students always had an open

Table 3.1. *Product planning guide*

Artistic Products

Architecture	Batik	Landscaping	Puzzles
Murals	Exhibits	Terrariums	Car design
Decoration	Cartoons	Mosaic	Sewing
Sculpture	Book cover/designs	Collage	Puppets
Filmstrips	Fabric design	Silk screens	Set design
Slide shows	Maps	Movies	Tin ware
Comic strips	Mobiles	Videos	Pottery
Yearbook	Fashion design	Aquariums	Iron work
Advertisements	Jewelry	Painting	Weaving
Drawing	Diorama	Web pages	Calligraphy
Graphic design	Furniture design	Package design	Tessellations
Photography	Wood carvings	Postcards	Multimedia presentations
Engraving	Political cartoons	Posters	
Etching	Horticultural design	Computer graphics	

Performance Products

Skits	Dance	Films/videos	Interpretive song
Role playing	Mime	Reader's theater	Composition
Simulations	Puppet shows	Poetry readings	Chorale
Theatrical performance	Dramatic dialogues	Improvisations	Concerts
Vocal	Comic performances	Musical performance	Parades
Athletic events	Demonstrations	Experiments	Reenactments

Spoken Products

Debates	Lecture	DJ shows	Book talks
Speeches	Mock trials	Panel discussions	Chronicles
Radio plays/podcasts	Songs	Celebrity roasts	Forums
Advertisements	Sales promotions	Narrations	Sign language
Poetry readings	Simulations	Sermons	Puppet shows
Storytelling	Demonstrations	Dedication ceremonies	Book reviews
Poetry for two voices	Telephone conversations	Weather reports	Audiotapes
Interviews	Eulogies	Rap songs	Infomercials
Oral histories	Announcements	Town crier	Master of ceremony
Newscasts	Comedy routines	Guided tours	Oral reports

Visual Products

Videos	Layouts	Ice sculptures	Maps
Slide/digital photo shows	Models	Demonstrations	Diagrams
Computer printouts	Pottery	Cartoons	Mobiles
Sculptures	Proclamations	Travel brochures	Set design
Table settings	Computer programs	Athletic skills	Experiments
Advertisements	Timelines	Blueprints	Caricatures
Puppets	Diagrams/charts	Lists	Silk screening
Calendars	Sketches	Multimedia presentations	Graphic organizer
Musical scores	Graphs	Graphic design	Photography
Book jackets	Collages	Painting	Fashion design

Table 3.2. *Activity grid for Homer's Odyssey*

Design a coin	Mapping Odysseus' travels	Timeline
Choose any character from the book to honor with a coin. Design a coin and create it. Present it with a plaque containing an address explaining why the character was worthy of this honor.	Create a map of ancient Greece. Indicate on the map the route Odysseus traveled. You may represent the map any way you choose. You may use Google Maps, you may make a three-dimensional map, or any other type of map you wish.	Create an illustrated timeline for the travels of Odysseus from the time he left Troy until the time he is reunited with his family in peace. You may present the timeline in table form or graphically.
Greektionary Choose five word roots from the accompanying list. Use each as the trunk of your tree and find as many English words that contain the Greek root as you can to form branches of the tree. You may present the tree in any form.	**Holiday Tree Ornament** Choose a character, object, or symbol from the Odyssey. Create a Christmas tree ornament depicting this character, object, or symbol. Write an entry for the *Ithaca Trading Company Holiday Catalogue* describing your ornament.	**Create Your Own Odyssey** Create a fictitious character. Write of his/her odyssey and all the adventures along the way. Also tell how he/she overcame adversity.
Write a Poem Look at the accompanying example of an hexameter poem. Write your own hexameter poem about Odysseus. You may put it to music to create a song.	**Write Your Own Myth** Study the attributes of a myth. Use this knowledge to create your own myth. You can place it in any time or place. You may present your myth any way you like. You may present it in written form, or as a play, or as a one person show, or any other way that will highlight the activity.	**Create a Board Game** Use the facts in the story of Odysseus' travels to create a board game. See the accompanying rules and examples page to help you.

choice – they could decide to pursue any project of their choice. The grid is reproduced in Figure 3.6. All students were required to complete the center activity – creating a holiday ornament symbolizing an idea, person, or object from Homer's *Odyssey*. The teacher brought into class a four-foot-high holiday tree, and students could hang their ornaments as they completed them, making a presentation on the meaning of the ornament, and what it symbolized in Homer's tale. Students also wrote a description of the ornament suitable for a catalogue, and all the descriptions with illustrations were collected into the *Ithaca Trading Company Holiday Catalogue*. The catalogues were reproduced and each student took home a catalogue. The annual Odyssey holiday tree was put on display in the school foyer two weeks before school closed for the holidays.

Other activities were designed to tap into student's interests and style preferences and still present an opportunity for students to showcase what they had learned. It gave ample opportunity for creativity. Students who chose to create a game had the pleasure of playing their games with classmates. In the process, they learned how to refine rules and make the game as user-friendly as possible.

If we had to do it again, we would invite the sixth-graders to put together a presentation of Homer's *Odyssey* consisting of the best examples of each activity. This presentation could then quite easily be presented as a podcast. The teacher would certainly have a Web site where the podcast could be posted. Students could be presenters or filmographers or recorders or the technicians transferring and editing videotape and audiotape into podcast format. Another student might be in charge of lighting or sound or even the Web master.

The same class of fourth- and fifth-grade students showcased in "Race around Australia" regularly produces class podcasts viewable on www.podkids .com.au. These podcasts cover a wide variety of curriculum-related topics. Episode 14 posted in August 2007, for example, features an interview with Elaine Forrestal, the author of a book read all over Australia for National Reading Day. The students also created a Web page about the book, *Someone Like Me*. With podcasting and blogging technology freely available today, teachers and students can be endlessly creative in extending their regular curriculum. This podcast is an excellent example of a Type I enrichment opportunity that evolved into a Type III enrichment situation. In the process, students had to learn many Type II skills – how to record a speaker, how to ask good questions, how to prepare the podcast, and how to post it.

Even without the addition of technology to record the visit, students can have the benefit of an author visit, whether in person or via video. A third-grade teacher in New Orleans regularly invites her graduate professor, who is a well-known children's author of Louisiana tales, to visit her classroom to read her books to students and answer student questions. There are also author interviews available online. Many authors have Web sites, and bookstores will often host podcasts of author interviews.

This is not the only way to incorporate the Enrichment Triad Model into the literature classroom. There are a variety of ways student writing can be published. With the advent of computers and printers and a wide variety of software, self-publishing has become as easy as putting the work together and printing it out. There are many competitions for student authors, and specialized works, such as the Albertville history that Jane Newman's students wrote, will always be in demand.

Gretchen Anderson of Middlebury, Massachusetts, was 9 years old when she began adapting recipes found in Louisa May Alcott's books to include modern ingredients and cooking methods with the encouragement of her classroom teacher. Her book, *The Louisa May Alcott Cookbook,* was published in 1985 and was sold by the Louisa May Alcott Museum for several years. Gretchen went on to earn a doctorate in literature.

Every classroom teacher has to deal with those students who complete their work before their peers. Some students will quietly sit and read while they wait for the rest of the class to finish, but there are always those students who get in trouble while they wait. One solution is to encourage those students to pursue an independent investigation.

Curriculum Compacting

Curriculum compacting (Reis, Burns, & Renzulli, 1992) is a relatively simple procedure whereby teachers can allow students to buy time for independent projects. Through curriculum compacting, a teacher can streamline the regular curriculum for students who are capable of mastering it at a faster pace. It is defined as "the process of identifying learning objectives, pretesting students for prior mastery of these objectives, and eliminating needless teaching or practice of mastery that can be documented. The time saved through this process may be used to provide either acceleration or enrichment for students" (Reis et al., 1992, p. 10). The compacting process occurs in eight steps:

1. Identify the relevant learning objectives in the subject area or grade level.
2. Find or develop a means of pretesting students on one or more of these objectives before instruction.
3. Identify students who may benefit from curriculum compacting and should be pretested.
4. Pretest students to determine mastery levels of the chosen objectives.
5. Eliminate practice, drill, or instructional time for students who have demonstrated prior mastery of these objectives.
6. Streamline instructions of those objectives students have not yet mastered but are capable of mastering more quickly than their classmates.
7. Offer enrichment or acceleration options for students whose curriculum has been compacted.
8. Keep records of this process and the instructional options available to compacted students.

Tannenbaum (1986) called a similar process "telescoping," which he describes in the following way: students "complete the basics in the least amount of time, thereby sparing themselves the tedium of dwelling on content that they either know already or can absorb in short order" (p. 409).

Many students can benefit from curriculum compacting because they already know much of the curriculum before they study it in school. Recent studies have shown that 78–88% of fifth- and sixth-graders who read at the average–to–above average reading level could pass pretests on basal comprehension skills at about 92–93% accuracy before these were covered in the basal curriculum. Reis et al. (1993) found that as much as 40–50% of the basal curriculum could be eliminated for 10–15% of all students with no deterioration in grades and test performance.

Compacting is not enrichment but provides opportunity or time in the school day for students to engage in enriching activities. Think of compacting as diagnosis and prescription. This is an educational technique used for decades in remedial education. The difference is, however, that we are not identifying objectives that students have not mastered, but we are identifying objectives and skills that students have already mastered. Curriculum compacting provides time for a variety of activities: accelerated instruction of content and enrichment of regular content through the pursuit of the depth and complexity, self-selected reading, or interest-based independent investigations. Detailed information on curriculum compacting and how to do it can be found at http://www.gifted.uconn.edu/sem/semart08.html and in the book *Curriculum Compacting* (Reis et al., 1992).

Enrichment Clusters

Inserting a block of time into the school week during which inductive learning is the major focus of all student activity is an excellent way of making a time for highly engaging learning activities. One way to structure such a block of time is to create an enrichment cluster program (Renzulli, Gentry, & Reis, 2003). In an enrichment cluster program, educators focus on student-driven learning, turning students' attention toward authentic learning applied to real-world problems. Enrichment clusters allow groups of students who share a common interest to come together each week during a specially designed time to produce a product or targeted service based on that common interest. Activities in the clusters center around six key questions:

1. What do people with an interest in this topic or area of study do?
2. What products do they create and/or what services do they provide?
3. What methods do they use to carry out their work?
4. What resources and materials are needed to produce high-quality products and services?
5. How and with whom do they communicate the results of their work?
6. What steps need to be taken to have an impact on intended audiences?

Eight guidelines differentiate an enrichment cluster from a traditional course, mini-course, or unit of instruction.

Focus on application of content and process. The golden rule of enrichment clusters is that all cluster activity be directed toward the production of a product, performance, or service for an authentic audience.

Allow students and teachers to select the clusters in which they wish to participate. In most formal schooling situations, students have few choices.

Enrichment clusters emphasize product or service development, so it is worthwhile to help students examine their preferences and interests. There are many interest surveys and style preference surveys available to help teachers and students accomplish this. The family of *Interest-A-Lyzers* (Renzulli, 1977a) helps students get in touch with potential interests through a series of open-ended questions. A self-assessment instrument entitled *Inspiration* (Gentry & Renzulli, 1995) fulfills a similar purpose for teachers.

Group students across grade levels by interest areas. In the out-of-school world, people are most often grouped by interest or common tasks, and not by age or grades. Enrichment clusters aim to follow a real-world pattern of organization and learning, and therefore we recommend that cluster enrollment range across two or three grade levels. Age becomes imperceptible when there are strong commonalities of interest, and many benefits result when a younger student's unpolished but creative idea is teamed up with an older student's know-how or extended experience in a certain segment of the task.

Do not use predetermined unit or lesson plans. This is perhaps the most difficult guideline for beginning cluster facilitators to deal with. It is crucial that facilitators and students work together to develop the scope and sequence of the cluster. Start-up activities can be selected and developed by facilitators, but how a cluster develops from there depends on the interests and skills of the students involved. This development takes place through discussion and the cluster facilitator takes the role of resource person, finding resources and know-how needed to produce the product or deliver this service agreed on through discussion. Not having predetermined lesson plans does not mean the cluster will involve fun and games only.

Guide clusters with authentic methods and advanced content and materials that investigators and creative professionals use. Manuals or how-to books can be called "mentors in print" because they supply information about how professionals in a particular field of study go about carrying out investigative, creative, or action oriented work. The Internet is a vast storehouse of how-to information. Cluster facilitators can also ask professionals in various fields for recommendations of resources.

Provide opportunities to develop multiple talents with in an enrichment cluster through division of labor. Not all students in a cluster should do the same task. In real-world productivity, there is a division of labor and everyone contributes in his or her own area of interest and developing expertise. What connects the group is a common purpose, but each member makes a unique contribution to the overall enterprise. The division of labor concept is valuable in cluster planning because it encourages teachers to help young people explore multidimensional products. It is also possible to have several different outcomes within a single cluster. Individuals or small groups of students may choose to move in divergent directions within the general topic area, thereby creating several different products and services within a single cluster.

Set aside designated time blocks for enrichment clusters. Student-driven learning can take place in any classroom, but the pressures imposed by top-down curricular requirements and today's emphasis on preparation for standardized tests place limits on the amount of inductive learning that can take place in most classrooms. We recommend that schools set aside specially designated time blocks during the week when inductive learning becomes part of all students' learning experiences. A block of time ranging from one hour to one half-day per week provides ample time for effective clusters. To allow for total faculty availability and opportunity to create the critical mass of interested students in each cluster, schedule all of the clusters at the same time for the whole school. If it is not possible for the whole school to participate, or if not all faculty value student-driven learning, grade-level teams may agree on the time for clusters. Individual teachers can also schedule time for clusters if no one else wants to participate. This is not an optimum situation. The fewer participating teachers there are, the fewer choices are available for students, unless the teacher can prevail upon parent and community support to facilitate clusters.

Suspend the customs of regular schooling. Many regulations and traditions guide schools and classrooms. Cluster time, however, has to be different from the regular school environment. We would like to see across-grade grouping by interest, focus on products and services rather than the acquisition of predetermined knowledge, and facilitation instead of teaching that follows traditional lessons or unit plans. Also be aware that group size may vary considerably from one cluster to another. Cluster size should depend on how many students are interested and how many students a teacher feels comfortable accommodating. Cluster work should not be graded and should mimic real-life work situations as best as possible.

School of Design – Metairie Academy

A magnet school in Louisiana, Metairie Academy, has embraced the concept of enrichment clusters. Three times a week during the last hour of the school day, students and teachers come together for cluster time. Clusters range from art clusters for primary students to a cooking cluster for older students that incorporates mathematics and chemistry in the development and testing of recipes. Of course, it has the added bonus that students and teachers can sample the results of the cluster!

One of the clusters was featured in a local magazine, *New Orleans Homes and Lifestyles* (January, 2007). A group of 15 third-, fourth-, and fifth-grade students participated in an interior design cluster presented by Ms. Watson, a language arts teacher who also holds an interior design degree. After the devastating floods in New Orleans, many students were dealing with the loss of possessions and personal space. These students chose to design new bedrooms

---

The Quilting Bee

Pictures in fabric, family stories, expressions of beauty, geometric shapes. All these things are quilts!

Do you want to know the history of quilts, help design quilts, find out how they are made, how they have been used? Come to Mrs. De Wet's quilting bee and try your hand at FABRIC ART!

Figure 3.6. The quilting bee advertisement.

for themselves. Since this was the first time many of the students had ever chosen fabric and paint colors, Ms. Watson spent time explaining the color wheel, dividing the color spectrum into summer, fall, winter, and spring tones. A parent of one of the boys in the cluster manages an interior design store in the neighborhood. He came to speak to the cluster and showed them how to draft their rooms in quarter-inch scale on graph paper. He donated wallpaper and fabric sample books and invited students on a field trip to his store where they could look at fabric samples and experiment with furniture and fabric on the store's computers. Students had to learn and use many academic skills in executing the products, such as measuring, calculating price per yard of fabric, and creating scale drawings of their bedrooms. They then created colored boards and shoebox dioramas of their dream bedrooms. At last report, several of these students have been able to execute their designs in their own homes.

The Quilting Bee

As an example for those interested in facilitating an enrichment cluster, an outline of possible activities for a sample enrichment cluster is given here. The first step in organizing a cluster is making it known to the student body. For this purpose, an advertisement is created that gives some indication of the topic and scope of the cluster. An advertisement for a quilting bee cluster is given in Figure 3.6.

The facilitator might choose to emphasize any feature of the topic in the introductory meeting. For our example, the facilitator brings in several quilts from her home. The first one she shows is the first quilt she ever made. Another is a quilt her grandmother made from scraps left over from family clothing. Each piece of fabric has a history and connects closely to her family history. Another quilt is a memory quilt made by students as a birthday gift to her. She tells the story of each quilt and invites students to touch and examine the quilts. She elicits a discussion on colors, patterns, and fabrics found in the quilts, as well as the construction of each quilt. She then draws students' attention to a variety of books she has brought to the meeting that covers many aspects

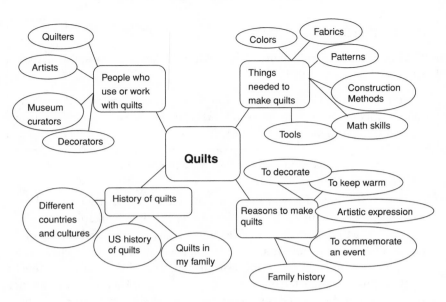

Figure 3.7. Concept web for the quilting bee.

of quilt making. She gives students ample time to page through the books and comment on what interests them. She then spends time with the students brainstorming possible topics for investigation using a concept web. A sample concept web is given in Figure 3.7.

Once this web is created, the facilitator surveys students to see which aspect of quilting interests them. She might discover that one student is particularly interested in her own family history as expressed by quilts. Several other students are interested in the preservation of quilts and old fabric. Another set of students would love to make baby quilts to donate to the local homeless shelter. She asks students to gather in their interest groups and come up with a list of ideas and resources they would need to accomplish their goal. She ends the session by informing the students that they would receive a visit at the next cluster meeting from a group of ladies who form the neighborhood quilting bee.

The teacher functions as a facilitator in this cluster. She does not necessarily have to know much about quilting to facilitate the cluster. She needs to prepare introductory materials and information and lead the discussion on possible directions for this quilting cluster. After the first meeting, she would need to contact a museum employee or find another person knowledgeable in the preservation of fabrics. She will also need to guide students in planning their activities, help them find the necessary resources, and gain the necessary skills to complete the projects. The student interested in her family history might need to learn oral history data-gathering skills to record interviews with family members. They may decide to publish a little family history book complete with family trees and family photographs. The students wishing to make quilts may need a mentor from the visiting quilting bee to help them in the construction of quilts. An exhibition of the students' quilts may be arranged at a local fabric or quilting store before donating them to the homeless shelter.

A large number of ideas and guidelines for enrichment clusters may be found at www.gifted.uconn.edu/clusters/.

Electives and Pullout Programs

Student-driven learning with the goal of creative productivity is especially suited to electives and pullout programs. These school structures are often not subject to the same rigid requirements for "covering the material" or preparing for standardized tests as are regular classrooms. Creative teachers who are willing to forego control over every aspect of learning can profitably use these learning situations to allow students to pursue their own interests.

An international school in Ecuador has instituted an elective program for their middle-school students called *Choose Your Own Adventure!* These classes meet twice weekly and have the expressed purpose of providing students with the opportunity to further advance exploration of their topic of interest into Type III investigations. As a first step, teachers in the middle school survey students by means of an interest survey created by the teachers, and they survey the parents using the *Things My Child Likes to Do* instrument (http://www.gifted.uconn.edu/sem/pdf/thingsdo.pdf). The teachers then come up with a list of possible topics; these have included Fun With Dance, Animal Dissections, Rock of Ages (focusing on rock music), Sounds and Images Short Film Workshop, Girls Rock (a cluster for girls only to select their own interest topic), Moviemaker (focusing on how to use Microsoft Moviemaker software), Study Skills, and First Edition (focusing on creating a student newspaper).

Another example of electives mimicking real-world working situations is described on the Web site *Epistemic Games* (www.epistemicgames.org). Shaffer (2006) describes epistemic games as games that help players learn the ways of thinking – the epistemologies – of the digital age. Epistemic games, he says, "can help players learn to think like engineers, urban planners, journalists, lawyers, and other innovative professionals, giving them the tools they need to survive in a changing world" (p. 59). These epistemic games allow students to participate in simulations of real-world work and help them develop ways of thinking and knowing that are valued in the real world. This is another way of saying that students engage in a personalized act of ideal learning, creating an authentic product for an authentic audience, using real-world professional methodologies and ways of organizing knowledge. One of these games that classroom teachers may be able to replicate is called *Journalism.net*. Middle-school students have played the roles of science reporters, writing for the *Wisconsin Science Journal,* and high school students have worked as civic reporters for the *South Madison Times.* Editions of these publications containing student work can be seen at http://epistemicgames.org/eg/?category_name=journalism-game. Researchers at the University of Wisconsin-Madison have seen the following results of this game:

1. Science.Net players developed the epistemic frame, the skills, knowledge, values, identity, and epistemology of journalists.
2. The process of revising to editor copyedits helped the reporters to develop this frame through their story writing.
3. This binding of skills, knowledge, and values support players' new community-based understanding of science (Magnifico & Shaffer, in preparation).

Working with professional journalists and editors of a newspaper or other publication helps students gain professional skills and mindset. Collateral learning occurs as they research science subjects in the community. Similar games have been developed for students to work as urban planners (*Urban Science*), animators designing creatures for an animated movie (*Digital Zoo*), and working as negotiators on the ethics of transplanting animal organs into humans (*The Pandora Project*). There are many computer simulations and games available on the Internet and for sale commercially. While the educational quality of some of these games are suspect, many educators and researchers are developing high-quality games and platforms that will support the kind of student-centered learning we are advocating in this chapter.

Renzulli Learning Systems

Remarkable advances in instructional communication technology (ICT) have now made it possible to provide high levels of enrichment and the kinds of standards-based differentiation with academic rigor that facilitates powerful learning services to students who have access to a computer and the Internet. The Renzulli Learning System (RLS) is a strength-oriented Internet-based enrichment program that is built on a high-end learning theory that focuses on the development of creative productivity through the *application* of knowledge rather than the mere acquisition and storage of knowledge. The RLS goes beyond the popular "worksheets-online" or courses online that, by and large, have represented the early applications of ICT in most school situations. These early applications have been based on the same pedagogy that is regularly practiced in most traditional teaching situations, thereby minimizing the full capacity of ICT, and in many cases simply turning the Internet into a gigantic encyclopedia rather than a source of information for the application of knowledge in powerful learning situations.

The RLS is a comprehensive program that begins by providing a computer-generated profile of each student's academic strengths, interests, learning styles, preferred modes of expression, as well as academic challenge level. A search engine then matches Internet resources to the student's profile from fourteen carefully screened databases that are categorized by subject area, grade level, state curricular standards, and degree of complexity. A management system called the Wizard Project Maker guides students in the application of knowledge to teacher- or student-selected assignments, independent research studies, or creative projects that individuals or small groups would like to pursue. Students and teachers can evaluate the quality of students' products using a rubric called the Student Product Assessment Form, as mentioned earlier. Students can evaluate each site visited, conduct a self-assessment of what they have gained from the site, and place resources in their own Total Talent Portfolio for future use. RLS also includes a curriculum acceleration management system for high achieving students that is based on the many years of research and widespread use of the curricular modification process called curriculum compacting, also discussed earlier.

Teacher functions allow downloading of hundreds of reproducible creativity and critical thinking activities as well as numerous offline resources for lesson planning and curricular integration. Management functions allow teachers to group students by interests and learning styles. The management tools also allow teachers to place teacher-selected resources in individual, whole class, or selected students' portfolios for classroom or special project use. Teachers can oversee all students' activity including where and when students have been online using the RLS, projects or assignments under way or completed, and areas where curriculum has been compacted. The system can be used at home and during summer, and parents can view their son's or daughter's work on the system. The principal or designated project manager can also examine all activity taking place in a given building or program. This feature allows for accountability, system assessment, and guidance in staff development and program planning needs. The RLS also provides individual differentiation, with appropriate levels of academic challenge for every student in a way that honors differences and ensures that true differentiated learning occurs for each child with engaging, challenging work in areas of interest.

In research on the RLS, Dr. Gara Field of the University of Georgia investigated the use of RLS to increase students' reading fluency and comprehension when they were able to use RLS for three hours per week. In this study (2007), quantitative procedures were used to investigate the use of the RLS on reading fluency and comprehension in two schools, an urban middle school where a majority of students are placed at risk due to poverty or other factors, and a suburban elementary school in a middle-class neighborhood. The sample included 385 students from two schools with administrators who volunteered to have students in both schools participate in the study. An experimental design was used with random assignment of students to treatment and control groups, and recommended follow-up procedures to explore specific group and individual differences were used. After only 16 weeks, students who participated in the RLS demonstrated significantly higher growth in reading comprehension, significantly higher growth in oral reading fluency, and significantly higher growth in social studies achievement than those students who did not participate in the RLS. Persons interested in examining the RLS can tour the Web site at www.renzullilearning.com, and further descriptive information can be obtained at info@renzullilearning.com.

CONCLUSION

What causes some people to use their intellectual and creative abilities to generate concrete creative products while others do not? What is it that motivates people like Edison and Curie, Bill Gates, and Jane Goodall to be creative producers where others might have similar talents but fail to turn their creative ideas into useful products? Is it possible to educate youngsters to become creative producers? It is our contention that it is indeed possible and in fact urgently necessary to provide youngsters the opportunities to develop skills, learn how to put creativity theory into practice, and prepare for the challenges they will face in the twenty-first century.

To achieve this goal, we must create opportunities for students to pursue questions of personal interest to them. Teachers have to facilitate this kind of learning intentionally, helping students find resources and mentors, whether in person or in print, and find audiences and outlets and, above all, help them to put their abilities to work on problems and areas of study that have personal relevance to the student and that can be escalated to appropriately challenging levels of investigative activity while emphasizing the use and application of information (content) and thinking processes in an integrated, inductive, and real-problem–oriented manner.

APPENDIX A
INTERVIEW WITH BRIANNE BURROWES

DE WET: Where did your interest in magazines start? Did you have a school experience (elementary through high) that helped with that?

BURROWES: My interest in magazines began in sixth grade. My Mom bought me my very first grown up magazine and I was beyond excited. It was the *Seventeen* Back-to-School issue and it featured the girls from Clueless. I walked around reading that magazine and I felt so cool. Then, the more I read the magazine the more I craved another, and then another. Suddenly I was begging my mom to read Cosmo at 12 years old! (She wouldn't allow it – so I sneaked issues into my room once I was in eighth grade.) I found something in magazines that I had been craving in my life. I always was a "dorky" girl. I was very smart and popular among my group of friends, but I had to face the reality that guys just weren't that interested in a girl with curly hair and glasses who loved to wear bright pink Bonne Bell lip gloss.

Anyway, as I read these magazines I started becoming obsessed with the advice from all of these teens and young women who just had it all. They got along with their parents, had a great boyfriend, wore amazing clothes, and I started to want that life. I never had an older sister that I could go to for advice, so Seventeen magazine became that older sister for me.

Shortly after my magazine obsession began, just reading magazines wasn't good enough for me any more. I always knew I wanted to be a writer, only up until that point I thought I wanted to write books. One day I was sitting in class bored out of my mind and the thought came to me, "Why don't I just create my own magazine?" This was around the same time that my family got the Internet for the first time and I had a wealth of information at my fingertips. So, I created an eight-page magazine called "Limited," ran off 20 copies on my computer's printer, and distributed them to my friends.

Then, in seventh grade I was taking a Gifted and Talented class from Tamara Fisher at Polson Middle School. In this class she said something that would forever change my life. She wanted us to think about what job we could do—if we could do anything in the world that we wanted to—and she then wanted us to use her class as an opportunity to do that. I realized then that this was my opportunity to create my own magazine, with the assistance and guidance of a really amazing teacher. I created the second issue of *Limited* that year. This time it had about thirty pages, and was more like a real magazine.

The following year, when I was in eighth grade, I took that same class and Miss Fisher presented us with that same question. I chose to stick with the same project, and create *Limited* again, but this time I had a new goal in mind. I wanted it to be even more like a real magazine—complete with a celebrity on the cover who had been interviewed by me. Through my Mom's connections, I was able to interview Kellie Martin (who, at the time, was playing Lucy Knight alongside Noah Wylie on "ER"). Martin also has appeared in "Christie," "As Life Goes On," etc.

When I entered high school I met another great teacher, Judie Woodhouse, who opened my eyes to the world of journalism. Through her, I learned that my passion for writing could be put to the most fulfilling use yet – through journalism. I quickly rose the ranks on the Polson High School newspaper, the *Salishian*. By my sophomore year, I was co-editor. I was editor-in-chief my junior and senior years.

Then, my junior year in high school, Fisher's Gifted and Talented course was offered at PHS. I re-arranged my schedule the second I heard because I just had to get in. It was there that I made my fourth magazine, this time titled *UnLimited*. I realized I wanted to communicate to girls that their potential is unlimited, and I wanted a title to reflect that. With my newly acquired knowledge from the high school paper and yearbook of Adobe Pagemaker, I created, wrote, edited, designed, and published *UnLimited*. I printed 500 copies on our self-publishing yearbook printer. It was the same quality as our yearbook. Then, I sent my magazine to various magazines that I loved – *Seventeen, CosmoGIRL!* and *ELLEgirl. ELLEgirl* loved it so much, that they included a blurb on it in their magazine that told readers where they could check out my magazine. After that, I received more than 300 requests for magazines, which I filled and sent. In total, I printed 800 copies of that issue in high school, not to mention it was posted on the Web, and has received numerous viewings since then.

DE WET: How did you develop the skills to publish a magazine online?

BURROWES: I actually didn't publish the magazine online. My distribution process is detailed above. The magazine was converted into an Adobe pdf and the computer technician at Polson High School posted the pdf to our school Web site for me.

DE WET: Did you have any adults who were particularly encouraging or instrumental in developing your interest and/or skills?

BURROWES: Yes–there are five people, who I all consider to be mentors, who have been crucial in helping me grow and become a better writer and editor. First, Tamara Fisher, who I discussed above, was the first one to see a spark in me and give me the opportunity to make my dream happen. Second, Judie Woodhouse, who I talked about above as well, was crucial in teaching me everything I know about the media. Woodhouse shaped me when I was green and her touch will continue to affect everything I do for the rest of my life. Third, is my mentor Autumn Madrano. I met her through *CosmoGIRL!* While in high school, I applied to be a *CosmoGIRL!* reader contributor. Autumn, an editorial assistant at the time, immediately bonded with me (we were both West Coast girls) and to this day we keep in touch. She still is at CG!, now as copy chief. I had the opportunity to meet her for the first time in person two years ago when traveling to New York City for the MTV reality show, "Miss Seventeen." She also was the person who helped me get my first national magazine appearance – a written blurb rating the "hotness" of a guy in their "Boy-O-Meter" section. Fourth, is a journalism professor who now works for the University of Maryland, named Michael Downs. He helped me hone my craft and was always a believer in my dreams and passions. The School of Journalism at UM is one of the top ten journalism schools in the country, according to reviews by Hearst. The only thing is that they used to focus more on newspapers – not magazines. He helped me fight against the "glass ceiling" of old-school journalism, by allowing me to change assignments and make them "magazine friendly." Finally, Rita Munzenrider, who currently serves as my boss (she is the director of University Relations here at UM), has believed in me and given me opportunity after opportunity. She is the one who believed in me enough to promote me to the position of Editor-in-Chief of the Montanan, UM's alumni magazine, at the age of 22.

DE WET: What drove your decision to pursue journalism?

BURROWES: Passion–I've always had a voice inside of me that's told me I was born to be a writer. As cheesy as it sounds, writing is as critical to me as eating and breathing. I truly believe I would die if I could never write.

Ultimately the reason I pursue journalism is because I want to tell the stories of those who don't have the means to speak for themselves–either because they can't, they're not allowed to or because they don't have a platform for doing so. I want to weave my words to tell their story and share their experience with the world. I am someone who craves feeling connected, and journalism provides that opportunity for me.

DE WET: What did you learn from your magazine experience?

BURROWES: Making *UnLimited* magazine in high school taught me that even though I was in a small town in Montana with a population of 4,500 people, I could still break into the magazine industry. Whenever life discourages me I can always look at that magazine and know that I did it–on my own. It's an incredibly empowering feeling and it helps me to believe that I really can do whatever I set my mind to–whatever it happens to be. I'm very fortunate to have had amazing parents and a lot of great mentors in my life who have always told me that I can do anything my heart desires. It's now my goal to share that message with people everywhere–especially young women.

DE WET: How are those experiences driving what you do today?

BURROWES: These experiences are driving what I do today in every way. *UnLimited* opened so many doors for me. It brought me the mention in *ELLEgirl*, it helped me establish new and important connections in the magazine industry and it helped the producers choose me for Miss Seventeen. I can say that *UnLimited* has affected my job in every way, even to this day.

DE WET: Have your experiences at college changed your future plans and dreams in anyway?

BURROWES: My experiences at college have not dramatically changed my future or my dreams in anyway. If anything, it has helped reaffirm that I am on the right path and that creating magazines is what I want to spend my life doing. Since graduating in January of 2007, I have worked on the *Montanan*. Up until the end of June I was an editorial assistant. I now am the editor-in-chief. In July I went to New York City and Los Angeles to interview for jobs, but my boss missed my work so much, that she then offered me the editor-in-chief position. Obviously, this was something I couldn't pass up. I am currently in love with my job and doing everything I can to grow and learn more about the magazine industry every day. My plan is to be here for the next year or so, and then I want to move to New York City or Los Angeles and write for women's magazines. I one day hope to be editor-in-chief of a major national magazine for women–such as *In Style* or *Glamour*.

REFERENCES

Albert, R. S., & Runco, M. A. (1986). The achievement of eminence: A model on a longitudinal study of exceptionally gifted boys and their families. In R. J. Sternberg & J. E. Davidson (Eds.), *Conceptions of giftedness* (pp. 332–357). New York: Cambridge University Press.

Barbe, W. B., & Swassing, R. H. (1979). *Teaching through modality strengths: Concept and practices.* Columbus, OH: Zaner-Bloser, Inc.

Bloom, B. S. (Ed.). (1985). *Developing talent in young people.* New York: Ballantine Books.

Board, J. (1991). *A special relationship: Our teachers and how we learned.* Wainscott, NY: Pushcart Press.

Burns, D. E. (1987). *The effects of group training activities on students' creative productivity* (doctoral dissertation, University of Connecticut, 1982). *Dissertation Abstracts International*, **48**, 3072A.

Dewey, J. (1916). *Democracy and education.* New York: MacMillan.

Dunn, R., Dunn, K., & Price, G. E. (1975). *Learning style inventory.* Chappaqua, NY: Rita Dunn & Associates.

Field, G. B. (2007). *The effect of using Renzulli Learning on student achievement: An investigation of Internet technology on reading fluency and comprehension.* Unpublished doctoral dissertation, University of Connecticut.

Gentry, M., & Renzulli, J. S. (1995). *Inspiration: Targeting my ideal teaching and learning situation.* (Interest Inventory). Storrs, CT: The National Research Center on the Gifted and Talented.

Glaser, R. (1988). Thoughts on expertise. In C. Schooler & W. Schaie (Eds.), *Cognitive functioning and social structure over the life course* (pp. 81–94). Norwood, NJ: Ablex.

Goertzel, M. C., Goertzel, V., & Goertzel, T. G. (1978). *Three hundred eminent personalities.* San Francisco, CA: Jossey Bass.

Gregorc, A. (1985). *Inside style: Beyond the basics.* Maynard, MA: Gabriel Systems, Inc.

Gruber, H. E. (1986). The self-construction of the extraordinary. In R. J. Sternberg & J. E. Davidson, J. (Eds.), *Conceptions of giftedness* (pp. 247–263). New York: Cambridge University Press.

Gubbins, E. J. (1982). Revolving door identification model: Characteristics of talent pool students (doctoral dissertation, University of Connecticut, 1982). *Dissertation Abstracts International*, **43**, 2630A.

Hébert, T. P. (1993). Reflections at graduation: The long-term impact of elementary school experiences in creative productivity. *Roeper Review*, **16**, 22.

Hunt, D. E. (1975). Person-environment interaction: A challenge found wanting before it was tried. *Review of Educational Psychology*, **45**, 209–230.

Kolb, D., Rubin, I., & McIntyre, J. (1971). *Organizational psychology: An experimental approach.* Englewood Cliffs, NJ: Prentice Hall.

Lubow, A. (2007). Painting the edge. *Smithsonian Magazine*, October 2007.

Mackenzie, D. (2007). Primed for success. *Smithsonian Magazine*, October 2007.

Magnifico, A. M. & Shaffer, D. W. (in preparation). Writing beyond the curriculum. Retrieved on November 27, 2007, from http://epistemicgames.org/eg/?p=382.

Myers, I. B. (1980). *Gifts differing.* Palo Alto, CA: Consulting Psychologists Press.

Newman, J. (2005). Talents and Type IIIs: The effects of the Talents Unlimited Model on creative productivity in gifted youngsters. *Roeper Review*, **27**(2), 84–90.

Newman, J. L. (2006). *Talents and type III's: A guide for becoming a better creator, decision maker, planner, forecaster, and communicator.* Mansfield, CT: Creative Learning Press.

New Orleans Homes and Lifestyles, January 2007. Retrieved on January 21, 2008, from http://neworleanshomesandlifestyles.com/in-this-issue/articles/news/school-of-design-1715.html.

Phenix, P. H. (1964). *Realms of meaning.* New York: McGraw-Hill.

Piaget, J. (Ed. and Trans.). (1981). *Intelligence and affectivity. Their relationship during child development.* Annual Reviews Monograph. Palo Alto, CA: Annual Review.

Reis, S. M., & Renzulli, J. S. (in preparation). A follow-up study of high creative producers who participated in an Enrichment Triad based program.

Reis, S. M., Burns, D. E., & Renzulli, J. S. (1992). *Curriculum compacting: The complete guide to modifying the curriculum for high ability students.* Mansfield Center, CT: Creative Learning Press.

Reis, S. M., Westberg, K. L., Kulikowich, J., Caillard, F., Hébert, T., Plucker, J., Purcell, J. H., Rogers, J. B., & Smith, J. M. (1993). *Why not let high ability students start school in January? The curriculum compacting study* (Research Monograph 93106). Storrs, CT: The National Research Center on the Gifted and Talented, University of Connecticut.

Renninger, K. A. (1989). Individual patterns in children's play interests. In L. T. Winegar (Ed.), *Social interaction and the development of children's understanding* (pp. 147–172). Norwood, NJ: Ablex.

Renninger, K. A. (1990). Children's play interests, representation, and activity. In R. Fivush & J. Hudson (Eds.), *Knowing and remembering in young children* (pp. 127–165). Emory Cognition Series (Vol. III). Cambridge, MA: Cambridge University Press.

Renninger, K., & Wozniak, R. H. (1985). Effect of interest on attentional shift recognition and recall in young children. *Developmental Psychology, 21,* 624–632.

Renzulli, J. S. (1977a). *The interest-a-lyzer.* Mansfield Center, CT: Creative Learning Press.

Renzulli, J. S. (1977b). *The enrichment triad model: A guide for developing defensible programs for the gifted.* Mansfield Center, CT: Creative Learning Press.

Renzulli, J. S. (1978a). What makes giftedness? Re-examining a definition. *Phi Delta Kappan, 60,* 180–184, 261.

Renzulli, J. S. (1978b). What makes a problem real? Stalking the illusive meaning of qualitative difference in gifted education. *Gifted Child Quarterly, 26,* 148–156.

Renzulli, J. S. (2005). A quiet crisis is clouding the future of R&D. *Education Week, 24*(38), 32–33, 40.

Renzulli, J. S., & Reis, S. M. (1997). *The schoolwide enrichment model: A how-to guide for educational excellence* (2nd ed.). Mansfield Center, CT: Creative Learning Press.

Renzulli, J. S., & Smith, L. H. (1978). *The learning style inventory: A measure of student preference for instructional techniques.* Mansfield Center, CT: Creative Learning Press.

Renzulli, J. S., Gentry, M. & Reis, S. M. (2003). *Enrichment clusters: A practical plan for real-world, student-driven learning.* Mansfield Center, CT: Creative Learning Press.

Renzulli, J. S., Leppien, J. H., & Hays, T. S. (2000). *The Multiple Menu Model: A practical guide for developing differentiated curriculum.* Mansfield Center, CT: Creative Learning Press.

Revans, R. (1982). *The origins and growth of action learning.* Bikley, UK: Chartwewll-Bratt.

Robinson, K. (2001). *Out of our minds: Learning to be creative.* Oxford, UK: Capstone Publishing.

Rogers, A. (2007). Site seer. *Smithsonian Magazine,* October 2007.

Schack, G. (1986). Creative productivity and self-efficacy in children (doctoral dissertation, University of Connecticut, 1986). *Dissertation Abstracts International, 47,* 905B.

Schlichter, C. L. (1986). Talents unlimited: Applying the multiple talent approach in mainstream and gifted programs. In J. S. Renzulli (Ed.), *Systems and models for developing programs for gifted and talented* (pp. 352–390). Mansfield Center, CT: Creative Learning Press.

Schlichter, C. L. (2009). Talents unlimited: Thinking skills instruction for all students. In J. S. Renzulli, E. J. Gubbins, K. S. McMillen, R. D. Eckert, & C. A. Little (Eds.), *Systems and models for developing programs for the gifted and talented* (2nd ed., pp. 433–457). Mansfield Center, CT: Creative Learning Press.

Schlichter, C. L., & Palmer, W. R. (2002). Talents unlimited: Thinking skills instruction as enrichment for all students. *Research in Schools, 9*(2), 53–60.

Shaffer, D. W. (2006). *How computer games help children learn.* New York: Macmillan.

Starko, A. J. (1986). The effects of the revolving door identification model on creative productivity and self-efficacy (doctoral dissertation: University of Connecticut, 1986). *Dissertation Abstracts International, 47*, 339A.

Sternberg, R. J. (1988). Mental self-government: A theory of intellectual styles and their development. *Human Development, 31*, 197–224.

Story, C. M. (1985). Facilitator of learning: A micro-ethnographic study of the teacher of the gifted. *Gifted Child Quarterly, 29*(4), 155–159.

Tannenbaum, A. J. (1986). Giftedness: A psychological approach. In R. J. Sternberg & J. E. Davidson (Eds.), *Conceptions of giftedness.* New York: Cambridge University Press.

Torrance, E. P. (1981). Predicting the creativity of elementary school children (1958–80) – and the teacher who "made a difference." *Gifted Child Quarterly, 25*, 55–62.

Walberg, H. J., Rasher, S. P., & Parkerson, J. (1980). Childhood and eminence. *Journal of Behavior, 13*, 225–231.

4

Creativity: A Look Outside the Box in Classrooms

ALEXINIA YOUNG BALDWIN

The concept of creativity is often dependent on the ideas of the person presenting the concept, thereby generating both positive and negative responses that often confuse teachers who try to use creative skills within the classroom to enhance out-of-the-box thinking.

Creativity has become a major buzzword among scholars in the arts, psychology, business, education, and science and in many corporate offices where unique designs are a basic commodity. Although this is the current buzzword, as John Baer (2003, p. 37) has said:

> Of all the things that it is hard to understand – and this would be a very long list – creativity is certainly one of the hardest, and most mysterious, even when considered within the confines of a single culture.

DEFINING *CREATIVITY:* WHAT IT IS AND IS NOT

Three decades ago, Treffinger, Renzulli, and Feldhusen (1971) argued that as a result of the lack of a unified widely accepted theory of creativity, researchers and educators have been confronted with several difficulties: establishing a useful operational definition, understanding the implications of differences among tests and test administration procedures, and understanding the relationship of creativity to other human abilities (p. 107).

Three decades later, there remains uncertainty and lack of reliability and acceptance of the existence of and the value of creative planning in the teaching of various subjects in the classroom.

Amabile (2001), who heads the Entrepreneurial Management Unit at the Harvard Business School, has devoted her research program to the study of creativity. She has been the foremost explorer of business innovation. The literature is replete with the research she has done and, although related to business, it is relevant to educational programs. For business purposes, she has culled from her research six basic myths:

- *Creativity comes from creative types.* Amabile says the fact is that any-one with normal intelligence is capable of doing some degree of creative work.
- *Money is a creativity motivator.* Bonuses and pay-for performance plans can even be problematic when people believe that every move they make is going to affect their compensation.
- *Time pressure fuels creativity.* Her research data showed that time pressure causes a person's creativity to go down for some period of time.
- *Fear forces breakthroughs.* She found that creativity is highly correlated with joy and love and negatively associated with anger, fear, and anxiety.
- *Competition beats collaboration.* She found that creativity gets lost when there is competition instead of confidence and working together in the company.
- *A streamlined organization is a creative organization.* Although in many instances, "downsizing" is said to make a company lean and creative, she found that it cuts creativity because of the uncertainties of the workforce.

These are myths that help managers of business groups understand that creative activities are important for business growth if one allows this creativity to grow. Her six myths are very close in concept to those that have been stated by researchers noted later. As Treffinger indicated in his *Roeper Review* interview (Henshon, 2006), the Creative Problem Solving (CPS) model emerged out of the influence of the work of Alex Osborne who had been an advertising professional in a New York Agency. Osborne's work with Sid Parnes and Ruth Noller brought together business managers and education professionals to explore how creativity could develop better work in their businesses and school environments as well.

Michael Michalko (2001), who has been an outspoken proponent of cre-ative thinking, has also used his arguments for businesses, which to me indi-cates that educators should take heed and start early to allow and encourage creative thinking. Michalko indicated, when asked about common myths in an interview by Management Consulting News (MCN), that it is a myth that creativity cannot be learned and that you are either born creative or you are not. Creativity is not genetically determined (MCN, 2008, para. 4).

These concepts that are expressed as useful in businesses are the same as those expressed in educational circles although they are worded differently. In their research with the Structure of Intellect (SOI) Model, J. Paul Guilford (1962) and Mary Meeker (1978) referred to *divergent production* as important in creative activity. Divergent production is based on the ability to elaborate and think of many diverse ideas through brainstorming. This concept merges with Guilford's *convergent production*. Divergent production and convergent production work together to produce a diversity of ideas and then narrow and define what the product will be. Problem solving is a large part of the combination of divergent and convergent thinking.

Sternberg and Williams (1996) have shared their ideas with teachers through their book *How to Develop Student Creativity*. It is thought that their ideas could be bridged with planning in the workplace. Their suggestions have contained some of the earlier concepts of Torrance and others and have been framed around Sternberg's theory that creative work consists of the application and melding of three types of thinking:

- **Synthetic ability**, which includes divergent thinking and requires a flow of ideas. In this area, the student would create, invent, discover, imagine if, suppose that, and predict.
- **Analytical ability**, which requires critical thinking, which in turn brings into play convergent thinking. Ideas are sorted out, and the best conclusions are reached. Students are drawn into analyzing, critiquing, judging, comparing and contrasting, evaluating, and assessing.
- **Practical ability**, which refers to the ability to translate abstraction and theories into realistic applications. Students in this area would be led to apply use, put into practice, implement, employ, and render practical ideas. In this area, Sternberg also believes that persistence is important. (Renzulli [1999] calls this *task commitment*.)

Education Imperatives

For experienced teachers and especially preservice teachers, it is important to shed their monocultural orientations. Both teachers and students need to go through stages of development. This is especially relevant to understand the ways in which creativity can be shown in different cultures and environments.

Within every culture of our increasingly global community, the evidence of different forms of creativity and the acceptance of this concept of creativity vary. Vygotsky (1978) has written about the manner in which people in the most primitive areas use their innate skills to create an environment to accommodate their needs. Daugherty and White (2008) attempted in their research to determine whether Vygotsky's notion of private speech among children was related to the creativity measures of fluency, originality, and imagination. They found in their study that "originality creativity was related to self-direction private speech.... As self-directed private speech increased ... originality measures also increased." They also found that "fluency creativity was associated with self-directed math private speech." Their findings suggested that there is a "need for early intervention to nurture and enhance creative ability in children from different cultural and economic backgrounds" (pp. 37–38). As with Vygotsky, Csikszentmihalyi (1997) has expressed his ideas about creativity. He views creativity as the achievement of something remarkable and new, something that transforms and changes a field of endeavor in a significant way.

Torrance (1979), who spent time in Japan exploring the view of creativity there, explains in his book *The Search for Satori and Creativity* that *Satori* is the highest point attainable, a sudden flash of enlightenment. In America, it could be called an "aha" moment. *Satori* requires persistence (as stated previously by Sternberg), self-discipline, diligence, and energy. These are all ideas of creativity with which most researchers agree.

TEACHER AWARENESS OF CREATIVITY

Fredericks (2005) has pointed to Torrance's suggestions as skills that can be taught to children. Even though the labels are different, there is a definite relationship to listings of Guilford and Sternberg. Fredericks' list includes:

- *Fluency* – the ability to produce a large number of ideas (*divergent production, synectics*)
- *Flexibility* – the ability to make connections between unrelated concepts (*convergent production, analytic*)
- *Originality* – the ability to make unique ideas (*divergent production, synectics*)
- *Elaboration* – the ability to manipulate an idea and work on it until it is well formed (*practical*)

For teachers in the classroom, teaching skills can become a daunting task since there has been increased pressure in the United States from the No Child Left Behind legislation to test the success of each child in the classroom with a battery of imposed test protocols that set guidelines and subsequent consequences. This pressure has caused many teachers to abandon the creative activities that would cause children to "think outside of the box" and instead prepare them for the evaluative processes that will judge not only the children but also the teachers.

The work of E. Paul Torrance, with his Torrance Tests of Creative Thinking (TTCT), has remained the stellar contribution in the area of creativity. He had a keen interest in minority children and their ability to succeed in creative areas while failing in some academic areas. In one of his speeches, he referred to a little black boy's cry of concern with his classroom activities. The youngster said to Dr. Torrance (1971), "I was a block and nobody builded me."

Among children of different ethnic groups, language or experiential barriers have caused them to bury their creative instincts to fit into the expected mold or to express their creativity in ways that are not acceptable to the teacher. Baldwin (1985) listed some common characteristics and indicators that reflect creative traits that could be found among African American students:

- Language rich in imagery, humor, symbolism, and persuasion
- Logical reasoning, planning ability, and pragmatic problem-solving ability

- Sensitivity and alertness to movement
- Resiliency to hardships encountered in the environment

Very often, students from minority populations or low economic situations find that their creative problem-solving methods are the only things that keep them from giving up on their education. These types of coping skills can be channeled into effective academic skills in the classroom through creative processes.

Many teachers do not capitalize on these problem-solving qualities to develop appropriate classroom activities that can:

- Develop new ideas through many mediums.
- Become a catalyst for enhancing academic weaknesses.
- Be a means for developing leadership skills.
- Promote a positive self-concept (Baldwin, 1985).

As noted by Baldwin (1985), Torrance (1965), and others, children of ethnic backgrounds, especially African Americans and those with language differences, are often relegated to special tutoring classes because they have responded to classroom situations creatively or "outside of the box" when teachers were not accepting of this behavior. Very often, the assessment strategies have been inadequate for noting their creative abilities.

Writers such as Scott, Deul, Jean-Francois, and Urbano (1996) reported from their research the following ideas that can help design protocols and/or assess diverse students earlier and thus capture these creative abilities to better direct the learning strategies for the students. In many instances, these children are gifted.

- Ethnic minority gifted can be located through kindergarten screening programs.
- Open-ended tasks, which encourage fluency, are the most promising.
- Verbal tasks that use familiar concepts and vocabulary do not necessarily discriminate against young ethnic minority gifted students (p. 147).

EXTENDING CREATIVE IDEAS

Very often, creativity is thought to be games and strategies that are done in isolation of core subject matter, but this is a misconception. As Augustus de Morgan said (1866), "The moving power of mathematical invention is not reasoning but imagination" (as cited in Mann, 2006, p. 236).

Mann (2006), in his article *Creativity: the Essence of Mathematics*, stated that unlike math classes of the past, time should not be spent in learning from the master but rather in experimenting with the various math concepts. Mann says that solutions to real problems entail problem solving, which is a very important aspect of creative thinking. "Teaching practices need to shift to a more balanced application of Whitcombe's [as cited in Mann, 2006, p. 252] model of the mathematical mind that recognizes creativity and the beauty of mathematics as well as the rule-based algorithms that dominate most mathematics classrooms."

Amabile (2001) has proposed that testing for creativity be done by *consensual assessment*. This research was done to test the reliability of the use of consensual assessment in determining which of the set of judges were more reliable in their ratings of creativity in the music compositions of fourth- and fifth-grade students. It was found that there were significant correlations between the music teachers and music theorist. It is interesting that there was a very weak or negative correlation between the composers' scores and the scores of the other groups. Could it be that composers were more set in what they considered "good" compositions without looking further for creative output?

In a language classroom, Houston (2007) outlined how the four major creative skills can be used. For **fluency,** students need to come up with a wide range of options from which they can choose ideas for their creative work. **Flexibility** will help them expand their ability to produce metaphors and analogies that will expand their thinking. **Originality** is used in helping students produce or think of something new or different. **Elaboration** is the skill used to bring together the ideas that have come forth and organize them in a finished product that can be shared with others.

These are just three examples of the role that creativity can play in the teaching of traditional subjects such as math and language, plus the in-depth creative assessment of abilities that can occur in the arts, or the big "C" creative as referred to in the Baldwin Identification Matrix (Baldwin, 1984). The little "c" in the matrix represents the creative problem solving that can be used within the classroom with basic or core activities.

ASSESSMENT IMPERATIVES

Kerr and Gagliaradi (n.d.) have given a detailed outline of the use of creativity assessment in counseling. They have warned that when using different tests to assess creativity, problems arise when one measure is inappropriately compared against another.

As early as 1962, J. Paul Guilford developed his Structure of Intellect theory that differentiated 180 kinds of thinking. As mentioned earlier in this chapter, divergent thinking could be used in combinations with any of the 180 different areas of his three faces of intellect. For instance, there could be divergent production of figural classes (DFC) or divergent production of semantic transformation (DMT). In each of these, Guilford's battery of tests used questions or request such as, What to do with it? Make something out of it. The premise of Guilford's concept of divergent thinking has had a great impact on the planning and ideas of creativity, although the subsequent assessment protocols are not as useful as they once were in pinpointing creative behavior or potential.

The TTCT are the tests that are most widely used to assess creativity. Their use is supported by more evidence of validity than other tests of creativity. The Baldwin Identification Matrix (1984) includes these tests as a part of its total profile of a student's strengths, with creativity being an important aspect of this profile. The requirement of expert training and scoring in the use of the TTCT makes it burdensome for school districts that would like to use it on large populations.

There have been several lists of traits that are said to be indicative of creativity such as personality inventories, interest and attitude measures, self- and peer nominations, interviews, and personality inventories. As Feist (as cited in Kerr & Gagliardi, n.d., p. 14) wrote, "One of the most distinguishing characteristics of creative people is their desire and preference to be somewhat removed from regular social-contact, to spend time alone working on their craft . . . to be autonomous and independent of the influence of a group." Perhaps preference for time to be alone should be included in the list of characteristics of creative people.

This report by Kerr and Gagliardi outlines the use of creativity assessment in counseling because often certain behaviors or personality traits require counseling for the student as well as the parent and teacher so there can be an understanding of any behaviors that appear be aberrant.

Thinking and Acting Outside of the Box in the Classroom

There are several lists of how creativity can be killed. The methods are centered around too much interference, competition, and the process of evaluation and rewards.

The following list indicates some of the ways creativity can be killed (Taylor, 1972, p. 8):

Twelve Golden Rules on How to Kill Creativity

1. Assume there is only one academic type of talent.
2. Ignore scientific research results about creative talents.
3. Teach the best and shoot the rest!
4. Keep doing what was done to your ideas – and even do it more.
5. Be very human – react quickly and negatively to new ideas.
6. If you do not understand it – oppose it!
7. Keep the rule going: "The more creative the idea, the more likely in trouble."
8. Have a deadly negative incentive system for creative persons and ideas.

9. Fail to try opportunities (which is better than to try opportunities and fail).
10. Organize creatives in (under your control) – or organize them out.
11. Design all possible features into organizations that stifle or kill creativity.
12. Jealously guard and keep prerogatives only to yourself to plan, think, and create.

Thinking positively, we must do all we can to boost creativity. Some suggestions follow.

Get out of a rut. Serve as a model for the students by trying new ways to teach the lesson. Engage the students in giving ideas. Encourage them to question.

Try different techniques such as Scamper to stimulate creative thinking (Mishalko, 2001):

S = Substitute something.
C = Combine your subject with something else.
A = Adapt something to your subject.
M = Magnify or modify – add to it or change it in some fashion.
P = Put it to some other use.
E = Eliminate something from it.
R = Rearrange or reverse it.

Produce situations that can **encourage different answers**

Use "outside-of-the-box activities" such as music, new resources, special guests, and different classroom arrangements to stimulate different and creative thinking.

Houston (2007) has outlined a sample lesson that can be used to stimulate creative thinking. This example is among several that can help teachers plan outside-of-the-box activities. Each of the following actions includes examples of their use within a class activity. This example can be used as a stimulus for even more exciting and fun activities. Action items are input, humor, random input, metaphors and similes, opposites challenge, different perspectives, imagine, maps and diagrams, combinations, and brainstorming.

Input – Bring interesting and unusual things to class to keep students involved. Examples include pictures, artwork, music, and fragrances, among others.

Humor – One great resource of linguistic ingenuity is humor.

Random input – Here the emphasis is on choosing something randomly and responding to it, such as a page from a magazine, dictionary, encyclopedia, classic novel, etc.

Metaphors and similes – Thinking in metaphors and similes is great for improving thinking skills. Metaphors encourage making connections between two very different things.

Opposites challenge – Get students to think of the opposite of a word, a thing, or a situation.

Different perspectives – Tell students to think about things from several different points of view.

Imagine – Students can close their eyes and enter a fantasy world.

Maps and diagrams – Mind mapping, Venn diagrams, and fishbone diagrams are just a few examples of how students can organize their thoughts on paper.

Combinations – Students can combine ideas, images, or words to produce new creations.

Brainstorming – This well-known activity has students working in a group, thinking of ideas or solutions based on a problem statement.

The following is an example of the use of these ideas (Houston, 2007, http://www.hallhouston.com.

Unit Title: Having a Job Interview

Input – Bring in a short film clip of someone having a job interview. Ask students to respond to the film clip, either orally or in writing.

Humor – Organize students into groups and ask them to create a humorous skit about a job interview.

Random input – Call a student to the front of the class. The student opens up a dictionary at random and points to a word. Ask the class to make some connection between this word and the subject of job interviews.

Metaphors and similes – Write the following on the board:
A JOB INTERVIEW IS LIKE_____
Call on a student to say the first noun he or she thinks of. Ask another student to explain the simile [assuming students know what metaphors and similes are].

Opposites – Read out an interview-related sentence. Ask students to write down the opposite of the sentence (they will most likely come up with very different ideas of what is the opposite of the sentence).

Different perspectives – After studying a sample job interview (see Houston, 2007), get students to write about the interview from two different perspectives: that of the interviewer and that of the job applicant.

Imagine – Turn off the lights. Tell students to be quiet and close their eyes. Narrate the story of a job interview (see Houston, 2007) Do not describe everything but give them a chance to speculate how the interviewer is dressed, how the room looks, what are the job applicant's facial expressions, etc. Turn on the lights and ask students some of the interesting details they remember.

Maps and diagrams – Have students create their own mind maps on the subject of job interviews. Have them compare their mind maps in groups of four. Ask each group to send the student with the best mind map to draw it on the board.

Combinations – Choose two pictures from the book, show them to the class, and invite students to combine them mentally and then to describe this combination.

Brainstorming – Put students into small groups and ask them to brainstorm ten things everyone should do before a job interview.

Houston's example gives teachers some idea of how his suggestions can be used with a unit; however, one important part that is not included is the convergent portion of the complete cycle of creative thinking, which is the presentation of the final project in some fashion.

Frank Williams (1970) included in his book *Classroom Ideas for Encouraging Thinking and Feeling* several examples of his teacher behaviors for helping students to develop cognitive (intellective) and affective (feeling) strengths through the use of creative activities for teachers and students. He listed *fluent thinking, flexible thinking, original thinking,* and *elaborative thinking* under "cognitive-intellective behaviors" and *risk taking, complexity, curiosity,* and *imagination* under "affective-feeling."

It is easy to see that the themes of creativity are repeated over and over again by various authors. For teachers, he listed eighteen different behaviors that were important for teachers to apply to all of the subject matter content usually found in school curricula (Table 4.1).

Some sample activities that incorporate the three dimensions (curriculum, pupil behaviors, and teachers' strategies) are shown next (Williams, 1970).

Example No. 1

To encourage:	Curiosity and Imagination
Through:	Social studies and art
Using strategies:	Paradoxes, organized random search, and visualization skill
Activity:	After learning about a number of political people and events in history, the pupils in this class were given the opportunity to create their own political cartoon with a humorous caption. The theme of the cartoon was to be a hypothetical meeting of two paradoxical characters. The class was to explore and wonder what kind of conversation might have taken place between such two characters as:

Nathan Hall and Benedict Arnold; Eisenhower and Khuchev; Lyndon Johnson and Robert Kennedy; Richard Nixon and Eugene McCarthy; Martin Luther King and Eldridge Cleaver

Table 4.1. *Dimension 2 teacher behaviors (strategies)*

1.	Paradoxes	Common notion not necessarily true in fact. Self-contradictory statement or observation
2.	Attributes	Inherent properties; ascribing properties
3.	Analogies	Situation of likeness; comparing one thing to another
4.	Discrepancies	Gaps of limitations in knowledge; missing links
5.	Provocative question	Inquiry to bring forth meaning
6.	Examples of change	Provide opportunities for making alterations
7.	Examples of habit	Effects of habit-bound thinking; against rigidity in ideas
8.	Organized random search	Using familiar structure to build another structure
9.	Skills of search	Search for the current status of something
10.	Tolerance for ambiguity	Provide situations which puzzle, intrigue, or challenge
11.	Intuitive expression	Feeling about things through all the senses; nudges and hunches
12.	Adjustment to development	Develop many options or possibilities
13.	Study creative people	Analyze traits of eminently creative people, invention, incubation
14.	Evaluate situations	Decide upon possibilities; look at implications
15.	Creative reading skill	Generating new ideas by reading
16.	Creative listening skill	Generating ideas through listening
17.	Creative writing skill	Communicating ideas in writing
18.	Visualization skill	Illustrating thoughts and feelings

As the children recalled previously acquired information about these characters, they transformed this into an imaginative oral conversation. This technique is most effective as a review about people and events in history (p. 159).

Example No. 2

To encourage: Original thinking and complexity

Through: Language arts

Using Strategies: Analogies, organized random search, evaluate situations

Activity: Crossword puzzles were used effectively to teach spelling and word meaning. Children were divided into groups of three, and *each group was asked to design its own crossword puzzle using 10 to 12 of the words from the weekly spelling list in some clever or unusual way.* Working in groups seemed to generate a great deal of enthusiasm. The groups then exchanged puzzles and solved them by using the appropriate words. This challenged each group to use words in unique ways for the design of their crossword puzzle and to see if they could stump other groups by their originality (p. 134).

Adams (1979) suggested classroom activities that can serve as conceptual blockbusting. This type of "blockbusting" helps to release creative ideas. The next example is one of many listed in his book.

Morphological Forced Connections

1. List the attributes of the situation.
2. Below each attribute, place as many alternates as you can think of.
3. When completed, make many random runs through the alternates, picking up a different one from each column and assembling the combinations into entirely new forms of your original subject.

After all, inventions are merely new ways of combining old bits and pieces (Adams, 1979, p. 110).

Example:
Subject: Improve a ball-point pen.
Attributes:

Cylindrical	Plastic	Separate Cap	Steel Cartridge
		Alternatives	
Faceted	Metal	Attached cap	No cartridge
Square	Glass	No cap	Permanent
Beaded wood	Wood	Retracts	Paper cartridge
Sculptured	Paper	Cleaning cap	Cartridge made of ink

Personal Reflections and Conclusions

As a beginning teacher, I discovered that reaching the students of my classes required me to engage them and myself in creative thinking. At the time I did not attach a name to the many "outside of the box" activities that occurred in the class, but experience through the years helped me understand that creativity was important in helping students draw upon their inner strengths and apply those strengths to the academic challenges they faced.

The students that I had the first opportunity to teach were from an ethnic/minority group in a segregated environment. Appropriate supplies and equipment to assist in learning were not always available for them. New ways of dealing with these disadvantaging situations brought into play one of the important hallmarks of creativity, that is, *improvising*. Problem solving, for example, came into play when students experimented with different kinds of wood and the dimensions necessary for replacing the missing black and white keys of the piano in the music room.

This is just one example of the many incidents of creative problem solving that turned into lessons of mathematical frequencies and timbre and many other lessons of cooperative brainstorming and problem solving.

Intelligence tests and the more standardized academic assessment protocols would not have measured the strategies and mental operations used to solve the problem of the missing piano keys; however, as a teacher I was able to capitalize upon the teachable moment for math and science teaching.

Very often, students who use creative methods to express their ideas are ignored because their ideas are not the expected or traditional responses required. In the new era of No Child Left Behind, creativity has taken a back seat due to the inability of teachers to allow time to be spent incubating, brainstorming, and collaborating with each other in class to solve problems.

The Future

Businesses are embracing the ideas of creative problem solving even within the financial arena. Places like General Electric need highly qualified scientists but they also need these scientists to use their knowledge creatively in solving problems and inventing new products. Technology and its new applications allow for creative ventures and inventions. Creativity is critical to social progress at the social and societal levels and is evidenced, for example, in the development of ways to produce energy without depending on oil. New ways to communicate and connect with others through social networking services (e.g., *Facebook* and *Twitter*) are examples of bubbling creativity in society. Research and recommendations in this area are being carried out. Scientific collaboration is an important aspect of the future of creativity and of its future as a viable psychological area of study.

In one sense, the story of Michael Faraday could be reassuring to parents who are concerned about the child who has dyslexia. New research is focusing on one of the great scientists of the nineteenth century, who had all of the symptoms of a dyslexic individual. He had trouble with spelling and punctuation and could not handle mathematics. He had a powerful visual sense, though, which he used to build a mental image of lines of force. He had the ability to see things holistically and had verbal retention. It was something like a "second sight," which is often hard to display to others. He looked at the whole and broke it down into parts. James Maxwell, who was a great mathematician, found this difficult to do but set aside his mathematical thoughts and then was able to understand and see the brilliance of Faraday's conception of electrical force fields. Together, the creative visionary and the mathematician were able to provide a graph of a magnetic field. Although there is evidence that Einstein was also having language disorder and math problems, the research that provides a correlation with some mental disorders is not proved. Researchers at Georgia Tech are, however, delving into this research, which will have its affect on educational planning. West (1991) explores some of these theories in his book.

Many of the assumptions about the connection of creativity to intelligence have been based on case studies and observations by alert professionals.

Technology and enhanced scientific analyses will provide a more definitive verification of these assumptions.

CONCLUDING THOUGHTS

Helping students during this twenty-first century to venture outside of the box and become more creative in their thinking is crucial because of the speed with which the environment and knowledge is changing. The ideas for encouraging students to participate in outside-of-the-box activities are limitless. Those listed here only begin to show how in-class activities can encourage creative thinking. Teachers must also be willing to take a risk because modeling creative behaviors gives students the feeling of security while trying new things themselves. To paraphrase Torrance's conference report, **teachers must build the blocks of creativity**.

REFERENCES

Adams, J. L. (1979). *Conceptual blockbusting: A guide to better ideas* (2nd ed.). New York: W.W. Norton & Company.

Amabile, T. M. (2001). Beyond talent: John Irving and the passionate craft of creativity. *The American Psychologist*, **56**, 333–336.

Baer, J. (2003). Double dividends: Cross-cultural creativity studies teach us about creativity and cultures. *Inquiry: Critical Thinking across the Disciplines*, **22**(3) 37–39.

Baldwin, A. Y. (1984). *Baldwin identification matrix 2 for the identification of gifted and talented*. New York: Royal Fireworks.

Baldwin, A. Y. (1985). Programs for the gifted and talented: issues concerning minority populations. In F. Horowitz & M. O'Brien (Eds.), *The gifted and talented: Developmental perspectives* (pp. 223–249). Washington, DC: American Psychological Association.

Csikszentmihalyi, M. (1997). *Creativity*. New York: Harper Collins.

Daugherty, M., & White, C. S. (2008). Relationships among private speech and creativity in Head Start and low-socioeconomic status preschool children. *Gifted Child Quarterly*, **52**, 31–39.

Fredericks, A. D. (2005). *The complete idiot's guide to success as a teacher*. New York: Alpha.

Guilford, J. P. (1962). Potentiality for creativity. *Gifted Child Quarterly*, **6**, 87–90.

Henshon, S. (2006). Creative exploration: An interview with Don Treffinger. *Roeper Review*, **29**, 119–121.

Houston, H. (2007). *The creative classroom: Teaching languages outside the box*. Vancouver, BC: Lynx Publishing.

Kerr, B., & Gagliardi, C. (n.d.). *Measuring creativity in research and practice*. Retrieved on January 8, 2008, from the University of Arizona Web site: http://courses.ed.asu.edu/kerr/measuring_creativity.rtf.

Management Consulting News (MCN). (2008). Retrieved on January 7, 2008, from http://www.managementconsultingnews.com/interviews/michalko_interview.php

Mann, E. (2006). Creativity: The essence of mathematics. *Journal for the Education of the Gifted*, **30**, 236–260.

Meeker, M. (1978). Measuring creativity from the child's point of view. *Journal of Creative Behavior*, **12**, 52–62.

Michalko, M. (2001). *Cracking creativity.* Berkeley, CA: Ten Speed Press.

Renzulli, J. S. (1999). What is this thing called giftedness, and how do we develop it? A twenty-five year perspective. *Journal for the Education of the Gifted*, **23**, 3–54.

Scott, M. S., Duel, L. S., Jean-Francois, B., & Urbano, R. C. (1996). Identifying cognitively gifted ethnic minority children. *Gifted Child Quarterly*, **40**, 147–153.

Sternberg, R., & Williams, W. (1996). *How to develop student creativity.* Alexandria, VA: Association for Supervision and Curriculum Development.

Taylor, C. (1972). A climate of creativity. In *Report on the Seventh National Research Conference on Creativity* (pp. 22–23). Salt Lake City, UT: University of Utah.

Torrance, E. P. (1965). *Rewarding creative behavior: Experiments in classroom activity.* Englewood Cliffs, NJ: Prentice-Hall.

Torrance, E. P. (1971). *I was a block and nobody builded me!* Paper presented at the meeting of the Council on Exceptional Children, Miami Beach, FL.

Torrance, E. P. (1979). *The search for Satori and creativity.* Great Neck, NY: Creative Synergetics Association, Ltd.

Treffinger, D. J., Renzulli, J. S., & Feldhusen, J. F. (1971). Problems in the assessment of creative thinking. *The Journal of Creative Behavior*, **5**, 104–111.

Vygotsky, L. (1978). *Mind in society: The development of higher mental processes.* Cambridge, MA: Harvard University Press.

West, T. G. (1991). *In the mind's eye: Visual thinkers, gifted people with learning difficulties, computer images, and the ironies of creativity.* Buffalo, NY: Prometheus Books.

Whitcombe, A. (1988). Mathematics: Creativity, imagination, beauty. *Mathematics in School*, **17**, 13–15.

Williams, F. E. (1970). *Classroom ideas for encouraging thinking and feeling* (rev. ed.). Buffalo, NY: D.O.K Publishers.

5

Using Constraints to Develop Creativity in the Classroom

PATRICIA D. STOKES

Creativity is a commendation given to responses that are new and appropriate, generative, or influential (Csikszentmihalyi, 1996; Simonton, 1999). Appropriate means that the novelty solves a problem; generative, that it leads to other new things; influential, that it expands a domain. Children, like other novices, are capable of creativity at the appropriateness level. Generativity and domain change require far greater expertise. (Stokes, 2005).

Creativity at the classroom level can be characterized by two things, novelty and appropriateness. Novelty depends upon variability; appropriateness, on expertise. This chapter introduces a constraint-based model of problem solving to establish these two important precursors of creativity. Before introducing the problem-solving model and applying it to the classroom, we briefly discuss the critical connections between variability, novelty, and learning.

VARIABILITY, NOVELTY, AND EXPERTISE

Variability is defined as how differently something is done. As Figure 5.1 shows, variability can be pictured as a continuum with high and low levels at its extremes.

High Variability and Novelty

Expected (reliable, repeated) behaviors lie closer to the low end of the continuum, while surprising (novel, unanticipated) behaviors lie closer to the higher end (Stokes, 1999). The reason for the placements is simple: reliability is rewarded, reinforced. As a result of operant conditioning, responses that were successful in particular situations in the past will be tried before new ones are attempted. Since familiar solutions surface sooner than novel ones (Maltzman, 1960; Runco, 1986; Ward, 1969), variability is a precondition for novelty. It is also a precondition for acquiring expertise.

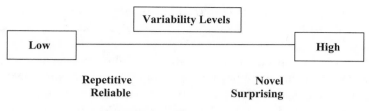

Figure 5.1. Variability continuum.

High Variability and Expertise

Classic developmental theories (Piaget, 1955; Vygotsky, 1987) posit that learn-ing occurs during periods of increased variability. The periods are temporary and transitory; they appear when children are expanding their spatial/motor (Adolph, 1997; Kerr & Booth, 1978; Manoel & Connelly, 1995) and cognitive (Alibabli & Goldin-Meadow, 1993; Fujimara, 2001; Siegler & Jenkins, 1989) skills. These skills range from scientific reasoning (Schauble, 1996) and spelling (Rittle-Johnson & Siegler, 1999) to conservation (Goldin-Meadow, Alibali, & Church, 1993).

For example, imagine a child attempting to solve a classic Piagetian prob-lem: liquid conservation. Water is poured from a tall, thin glass into a short, squat bowl. Is there more, less, or the same amount? The child widens and nar-rows her grasp to indicate that the bowl is fatter than the glass; at the same time, she says there is more water in the glass because it is taller (i.e., the water level is higher). The mismatch between her gestures and words suggests the simulta-neous activation of multiple solution strategies. Transitory mismatches of this sort have also been observed when children begin to solve number conserva-tion (Church & Goldin-Meadow, 1986) or mathematical equivalence (Perry, Church, & Goldin-Meadow, 1988) problems correctly.[1]

Importantly, greater initial variability leads to greater learning (Fujimara, 2001; Goldin-Meadow & Alibali, 2002; Siegler, 1996). Students who use many procedures benefit more from teaching than those who use few (Coyle & Bjorkland, 1977). In mastering number conservation, children who generate more gesture–speech mismatches acquire the correct strategies sooner (Church & Goldin-Meadow, 1986); children who offer more explanations (correct or incorrect) during pretesting produce higher percentages of correct explana-tions during training (Siegler, 1995). Early motor training that requires high variability responding enhances later performance and, significantly, gener-alization (Manoel & Connelly, 1995; Schmidt & Bjork, 1992). Children who

---

[1] Similar increases in variability are seen earlier – when infants are acquiring postural control (Hadders-Algra, 2002) and later – when adults are acquiring expertise in radiology (Lesgold et al., 1988).

practice tossing shuttlecocks to several different locations perform more accurately on a set of transfer tasks than those who practice with one location (Moxley, 1979).

These positive effects of initially high variability on later learning have been variously attributed to having a large number of interconnected, accessible strategies (Siegler, 1996); to sensitivity to changes in condition (Joyce & Chase, 1990; Stokes, Lai, Holtz, Rigsbee, & Cherrick, 2008b) or flexibility in recombining elements of a skilled repertoire (Lee & McGill, 1983); to more elaborate search strategies (Doane, Sohn, & Schreiber, 1999) or richer sets of retrieval cues (Shea & Morgan, 1979); to persistence (Eisenberger, 1992) or openness to exploration (Simon & Bjork, 2002). Dramatically, Darwinian models of learning (Holland, Holyoak, Nisbett, & Thagard, 1987; Palmer & Donahoe, 1992) and dynamic systems theory (Thelen & Smith, 1994) assume that neither exploration nor selection is possible without variation. In these views, "no variability" would mean "no learning."

How (and when) constraints can help children become habitually more variable in the classroom will be covered in the section on *Variability Constraints*.

PROBLEM SOLVING AND CREATIVITY

In order to study how solutions are arrived at, a structural model that divides a problem into its constituent parts was created by Newell and Simon (1972). This basic model will be expanded and applied to all problems discussed in the remainder of the chapter.

The Problem Space Model

According to Newell and Simon, a problem space is a representation of a problem by its solver. The definition captures the difference between novice and expert (Chi, Glaser, & Farr, 1986): the way a given problem is represented, structured, and solved depends on one's knowledge and experience.[2] A problem space has three parts:

- An initial state: the problem, the situation to be altered, changed, or resolved.
- A goal state: the solution, along with a criterion for knowing that you have, indeed, reached the goal.
- A search space in which a solution path from initial to goal state is to be constructed. The meaning of "search" is straightforward: to explore alternatives, to seek for the solution path. The path itself is a sequence of

---

[2] Good teachers are well aware of this discrepancy and adjust their demonstrations and explanations to the level of their students.

Table 5.1. *Problem space for paint-by-number*

Initial State
Numbered cartoon on unpainted canvas.
Operators
1. If filling in area numbered 1, use paint numbered 1.
2. If filling in area numbered 2, use paint numbered 2.
3. Continue until all areas are filled in.
Goal State
Match picture on the cover of paint-by-number set.

operators, condition-action rules of the form, "If the condition is X, then do Y."[3]

Problem spaces may be completely or incompletely specified. Those that are completely specified are called "well-structured"; those that are incompletely specified are called "ill-structured."

Well-Structured Problems

In a well-structured or well-defined problem, all the information needed to construct a solution path is given. An example of a well-structured problem, outlined in Table 5.1, is paint-by-number.

The initial state is an unpainted canvas with a numbered cartoon. There is one basic operator: if the number on the canvas is *n*, then fill that area with the paint numbered *n*. Applied recursively (repeated until all the numbers have been used), it will reliably generate a solution path to the goal, completing the canvas so that the painting matches the picture (the criterion) on the cover of the paint-by-number kit. Since little, if any, search is required to follow the single, correct solution path, creativity is precluded (Stokes & Fisher, 2005). This is true of all well-structured problems.

Ill-Structured Problems

Creativity is only possible with incompletely defined, ill-structured problems. Ill-structured means that some of the information needed to solve the problem is missing (Reitman, 1965; Voss & Post, 1988). For example, in 1865, Monet did not know what "light breaking up on things" (the goal, a yet-to-be-developed style) should look like. Table 5.2 shows a simplified version of this problem space with its incomplete operators. The process of selecting operators to solve Monet's stylistic problem involved precluding specific aspects of chiaroscuro-style painting[4] and promoting their opposites. In other words, using paired constraints which are the bases of our expanded model.

---

[3] In the expanded model, the constraint pairs that generate the operators will take their places.
[4] Think of value (dark-light) contrasts, an illusion of three-dimensionality, and of course, brown shadows.

Table 5.2. *Problem space with unspecified operators for Impressionism*

Initial State
    Existing Style: Chiaroscuro.
Operators
    1. If choosing colors, select . . .
    2. If applying paint, use . . .
    3. If painting shadows, make them . . .
Goal State
    New Style: How light breaks up on things.

The Constraint-Pair Model

In common usage, constraints are seen as one-sided, defined solely as limitations or restrictions. In problem solving, they are dually defined, two-sided, paired. One of the pair retains its restrictive function, *precluding* search in some parts of the problem space while the other *directs* search in other (Reitman, 1965), often opposite (Stokes, 2007), parts.

In Table 5.3, the operators shown in Table 5.2 are replaced by constraint pairs. The pairings reveal the process, that is, ***how*** Monet arrived at his solution. For example, to show light breaking up (into primary and secondary hues), the first constraint pair precludes value contrasts between darks and lights and promotes contrasts between colors/hues of like value.

We now explore how using this model can help children arrive at their solutions variably and expertly.

CONSTRAINTS IN THE CLASSROOM

Five kinds of constraints are found in the classroom: *cognitive* constraints, which determine how many things a child's brain can process and how quickly; *talent* constraints, which direct interest in the area of a gift; *curricular*

Table 5.3. *Problem space with constraint pairs for Impressionism*

Initial State
    Existing Style: Chiaroscuro.

Constraint Pairs

Preclude		Promote
1. Dark-light contrasts	→	Contrasting hues
2. Continuous paint application	→	Mosaic of separate strokes
3. Brown shadows	→	Blue shadows

Goal State
    New Style: How light breaks up on things.

---

constraints, which involve standards and standardized testing; *domain* constraints, which define areas of expertise; and *variability* constraints, which specify how differently something must be done. We consider each in turn.

Cognitive Constraints

Cognitive constraints, based on development of the prefrontal cortex (PFC), can also be considered in pairs, with the child's current capacity promoting some things and precluding others. Maturation of the PFC, which continues into early adulthood, influences problem-solving in multiple, noticeable ways.

- Memory span increases: older children can hold more items in working memory than younger ones (Henry & Miller, 1991; Huizinga, Dolan, & van der Molen, 2006; Siegler, 1996).[5]
- Processing speed increases: older children perform faster on cognitive tasks (Bjorklund & Green, 1992; Kail, 1986, 1991).
- Off-task and inefficient responses are more easily inhibited (Williams, Ponesse, Schachar, Logan, & Tannock, 1999).
- Shifting between tasks or mental sets improves (Lehto, Juujarvi, Kooistra, & Pulkinen, 2003).

As a result of maturation, strategy generation (Bjorklund & Harnishfeger, 1987; Kee, 1994) and execution (Baker-Ward, Ornstein, & Holden, 1984; Miller, Woody-Ramsey, & Aloise, 1991) become less effortful, and strategy selection (Siegler, 1996) becomes more sophisticated.

Talent Constraints

Talent constraints are related to neural plasticity in brain areas other than the pre-frontal cortex. Plastic means moldable, flexible, variable. Plasticity at the neural level refers to the relative ease with which the brain adapts to different contexts (visual, vocal, spatial, mathematical), establishing or reorganizing associative networks (Garlick, 2002) in ways that facilitate further adaptation to new experience (Nelson, 1999) in specific areas (Trainor, 2005; Werker & Tees, 2005). The most adaptable areas in the child's brain are the bases of a talent or gift.

Like all constraints, talents are two-sided. They simultaneously promote and preclude interest and skill acquisition in different domains. For example, a child born with perfect pitch, who easily recognizes and remembers specific sounds, can play with those sounds in her head. Her "pre-tuned" brain will motivate her to sing or play an instrument. It will allow earlier entry and

---

[5] Experience also expands capacity: experts group or chunk items into larger units.

earlier mastery of her domain (Winner, 1996). However, even with early entry, mastery takes a minimum of ten years (Gardner, 1993).

Curricular Constraints

Constraints here include standards and – the area we focus on – standardized testing. The *No Child Left Behind* program has often left teachers feeling caught between promoting reliability ("teaching the test") and promoting variability in their classrooms. The paired constraint model proffers a solution to this problem: rethinking test prep as a way to increase variability.

First, consider why doing well on a standardized test requires practice. Standardization, which makes tests reliable, is the reason. A student who takes one version of the test usually gets similar scores on another version. Practice, although it may not make perfect, improves performance by making students familiar with the test's content (what it covers) and the form (how to take it).[6] Familiarity reduces cognitive load.

Now, try to see standardized testing this way. Variability is a measure of how differently something is done. Teaching/practicing the test is doing math or reading differently from the way it is usually done in the classroom. In this sense, it precludes presenting material in familiar ways and promotes using it in unfamiliar ways. Familiar and unfamiliar refer to both teacher and student. Taking the constraint pair perspective, teaching the test might make both (teacher and student) more variable.

Domain Constraints

Constraints define domains, well-developed areas of knowledge (e.g., math and music) with agreed-upon performance criteria (Abuhamedeh & Csik-szentmihali, 2004; Chi, 1997; Johnson-Laird, 1988; Simonton, 2004). *Goal constraints* are overall criteria. If accepted by a domain, they become stylistic conventions, approved ways to paint (Impressionism), build (Post-Modern), calculate (geometry), or sing (a capella). Goal constraints are primary because other constraints are chosen to realize them. These include *source constraints*, existing elements that the creator works with or against. Source constraints include *subject constraints*, which determine content or motif, and *task constraints*, which govern materials and their application (Stokes, 2001, 2005).

Again using Impressionism as an example, Monet's goal constraint was painting how light broke up on things. One source constraint that Monet worked with to reach this goal was the color wheel (a diagram of primary and secondary colors); another was a familiar subject (water) that provided

---

6   This is also known as procedural knowledge. With practice, the test can become a stimulus for automatic, algorithmic responding.

Table 5.4. *Subject and task constraints for learning to draw*

Steps	Subject constraints	Task constraints
1. Scribbles	Abstract	Practice making marks
2. Geometric forms	Abstract	Preclude open marks → promote closed forms Preclude the random → promote the repetitive
3. Combined forms	Preclude completely abstract → promote the "identifiable" (potato head figures)	Preclude single forms → promote forms inside other forms Preclude simplicity → promote complexity
4. Conceptual perspective	Preclude the ideographic → promote the canonical	Preclude ambiguity → promote correct, complete Preclude overlapping → promote separation Preclude side or back views → promote frontal views Preclude single viewpoint → promote multiple perspectives

multiple armatures (things and their reflections) for showing the unfamiliar (how light broke up). Sources that Monet worked against included technical aspects of the then-dominant style. These were the task constraints that he precluded: dark-light contrasts, brown shadows, etc.

Becoming expert means mastering a domain's constraints (Ericcson, 1996; 2007). Attainable skills are practiced, promoted, and then precluded when more complex ones become accessible. A simple example involves the acquisition of representational drawing skills in young children. The steps from scribbles to conceptual perspective (Gardner, 1980), with some relevant constraint pairs, are shown in Table 5.4.

The geometric forms practiced during the second step include circles, triangles, squares, and rectangles. Once mastered (at least to some degree), the forms become elements for recombination in the following, more sophisticated steps. "Identifiable" in the third step means that the drawing is differentiated enough *for the child* to discern who or what it is supposed to be. "Canonical" in the fourth step means that the drawing captures the definitive features of the concept it represents. For example, a house is a large vertically oriented rectangle with a triangle for a roof and smaller rectangles for door and windows.

Children at this stage are drawing what they know, not what they see. Since what they know expands during these stages, conceptually based drawings can become more variable as details are added. For example, a simple frontal figure (with head, torso, arms, and legs) may suddenly sprout fingers, sometimes even toes; straight arms will bend (usually at a right angle).

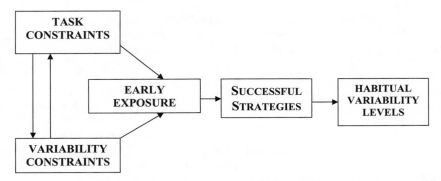

Figure 5.2 Habitual variability model.

We will return to, and complete, this progression in the section on art.

Variability Constraints

As we saw in Figure 5.1, reliability and novelty are opposite ends of the variability continuum. In general, variability constraints preclude expected, existing responses and promote unexpected, novel ones. They can also be more specific – for example, precluding reliability by promoting originality, fluency, or flexibility.[7]

Such constraints are particularly important when children are first introduced to new areas of learning. This is because learning *how* to do something involves learning *how differently* to do it (Stokes, 1999; Stokes & Harrison, 2002). The *how* is the skill; the *how differently* is the **habitual variability level**, a preferred performance range within which responses differ from each other (Stokes & Balsam, 2001). These are the two things (expertise and variability) on which creativity depends.

Figure 5.2 presents the elements involved in establishing a habitual variability level. Task constraints are specific to a domain; they determine *how* something can be done; variability constraints specify the *how differently*. More difficult tasks or variability constraints, ones that require greater search among lower probability responses, generate higher variability than less difficult ones. Encountered early in skill acquisition, the combined constraints contribute to the acquisition of successful strategies that establish and maintain habitual variability levels in a domain. The words "mastery" and "early" are equally important. Early variability levels that are associated with success are maintained; those that lead to failure are not.

---

[7]   These are aspects of divergent thinking: originality refers to how infrequent a response is in a given population; fluency measures number of different responses in a domain; flexibility, number of different domains included in one's responding.

Although not focused on habitual variability levels per se, multiple cognitive development studies (Carpenter & Moser, 1982; Fuson, 1982; Lamaire & Siegler, 1995; Siegler, 1996) demonstrate their stability. Variability here is measured as the number of strategies a child uses to solve a set of problems. The basic finding is that the number does not diminish when more sophisticated, efficient strategies are acquired. Rather, variability is maintained by shifts in the distribution. For example, a child who habitually uses three strategies in addition may begin a school year by switching between guessing, retrieving, and counting all the digits involved. By the end of the year, the same child could be switching between retrieving, counting from the higher addend, and decomposing ($9 + 3 = 10 + 2 = 12$).

Since these levels are learned early in exposure to a domain, the examples that follow focus on early learning.

USING CONSTRAINTS IN THE CLASSROOM: MATH

The more speculative ideas at the start of this section stem from three years of working in Japan. I had to calculate using the Japanese count. Surprisingly, the count was not difficult: only ten number-names are needed to go from 1 to 99. The count in turn simplified the calculating. I am convinced that the count and the kind of calculating it allows make math far more accessible, easier to understand, and simpler to problem solve in, for a Japanese child[8] than it is for an American.

The less speculative, more easily applicable, ideas that follow come from my own research on learned variability levels.

LEARNING IN JAPANESE AND AMERICAN CLASSROOMS

Task Constraints

Table 5.5 shows the Japanese count from one through twenty-nine.

Notice how the numbers 1 to 10 recombine in regular, reiterative patterns as the count progresses. One is *ichi,* two is *ni,* ten is *ju:* eleven is *ju-ichi* (ten-one); twenty-one is *ni-ju-ichi* (two-ten-one). It's simple to figure out that thirty-one is *san-ju-ichi* (three-ten-one). The count offers several **cognitive economies.**

- There is no need to "translate" name to quantity; the names are quantitative. The difference in the English and Japanese counts appears with the number 11. Coincidentally, this is where American children begin to have difficulty counting. "Eleven," the English name for the number "11" may as well be "Sam"; the name has no transparent quantitative meaning, no

---

8   The same applies to Korean and Chinese classrooms where the count (albeit in Korean and Chinese) has the same structure as the Japanese.

Table 5.5. *Japanese count*

Ones		Tens		Twenties	
		10	ju	20	**ni**-ju
1	**ichi**	11	ju-**ichi**	21	**ni**-ju-**ichi**
2	**ni**	12	ju-**ni**	22	**ni**-ju-**ni**
3	**san**	13	ju-**san**	23	**ni**-ju-**san**
4	**shi**	14	ju-**shi**	24	**ni**-ju-**shi**
5	**go**	15	ju-**go**	25	**ni**-ju-**go**
6	**roku**	16	ju-**roku**	26	**ni**-ju-**roku**
7	**shichi**	17	ju-**shichi**	27	**ni**-ju-**shichi**
8	**hachi**	18	ju-**hachi**	28	**ni**-ju-**hachi**
9	**kyu**	19	ju-**kyu**	29	**ni**-ju-**kyu**

apparent relationship to the count that precedes it, and no reference to its place value (e.g., the first 1 = 10, the second 1 = 1). In Japanese, the name for "11" is "ten-one." This clearly articulates its quantity, its connection to the number that precedes it, and the place value of each digit. In short, the count precludes translation and promotes immersion, the basis of fluency in any language.

- The count provides an easy introduction to both addition and multiplication. For example, the number 20 is called "two-ten." What does two-ten mean? Either "10 and 10" or "two times ten."
- The recombination algorithm reveals large meaningful patterns. Experts differ from novices in their ability to perceive and solve problems using these kinds of patterns in their domains. The patterns are the product of a well-organized knowledge base (Ericcson, 1996; Chase & Simon, 1973), provided here by the reorganization algorithm itself.
- The combinations clarify place value. For example, twenty-three is *ni-ju-san* (two-ten-three). To a Japanese child, the "two" obviously has a greater value than the "three" because it indicates how many "tens." Clarifying place value also simplifies application: when asked to choose blocks that represented the number 42, Japanese first graders choose four tens blocks and two unit blocks; American first graders count out 42 unit blocks (Miura, Okamoto, Kim, Steere, & Fayol, 1993).

Variability Constraints

There is always a "new" math in the United States. One current version, with "discovery" as its goal, uses many different media and tasks. For example, a first grade *Everyday Mathematics* class includes mental math exercises, filling in math boxes, explorations, and games. Paradoxically, a profusion of projects can produce low variability levels. One reason is that children vary by switching *between tasks* instead of *between strategies* on the same task. Another is that many do not discover the required algorithms. Sans mastery, high variability is punished, not rewarded. The result is that low variability levels – which do not facilitate learning or creativity – are acquired in the domain. (Rote, repetitive learning errs in the opposite direction, with much the same results. In this case, products, not processes, are rewarded. Low variability is maintained because it is associated with success).

In contrast, the Japanese curriculum precludes switching between tasks and promotes switching between strategies.[9] Teachers focus on one problem or topic per class. Children are expected to come up with different solution paths based on their already acquired knowledge. That is, they are not expected to "discover" a set of algorithms, but to apply and combine or recombine (this is where creativity is possible) ones already mastered into novel solution paths. In like manner, one set of manipulatives is used in successive grades, on successively harder problems (Uttal, Schudder, & DeLoache, 1997). Associated with multiple applications, the set itself becomes a conditioned stimulus for highly variable responding.

The early levels of acquired knowledge with a count like the Japanese are impressive. Base-10 decomposition is the primary backup strategy (used when children cannot retrieve a correct answer from memory) for Korean (Fuson & Kwon, 1992) and Chinese children – the latter using it as early as kindergarten (Geary, Bow-Thomas, Liu, & Siegler, 1996). Fluency in the language of mathematics makes this kind of acceleration possible.

Assuming, however, that a Japanese-style count will not be next year's "new" math, a set of basic learning principles and a way to easily incorporate them into current curricula are considered next.

LEARNING TO BE RELIABLE AND VARIABLE

Basic Principles

Given our goal – expertise and variability, the two bases of creativity in the classroom – there are three important things to be learned about learning.

- *Understanding and expertise are domain-specific.* In mathematics, knowledge is primarily numerical, not verbal. It requires fluency in numbers, signs, relations, and transformations, not words. One learns by doing (Anzai & Simon, 1979); the doing should be domain-centered. One consequence of such an approach would preclude (or at least postpone) word problems until children master the structure of the mathematical solutions

---

[9] For a review, see Grow-Maienza, Hahn, & Joo, 2001.

Table 5.6. *Paired constraints for the basic
alternation problem*

Steps	Task and variability constraints
1. Exit only	Preclude trial and error → promote reliability/mastery Preclude multiple exits → promote single correct exit
2. Exit + variability	Preclude repetition → promote multiple paths to single exit

on which words can be mapped.[10] This is particularly important in view of cognitive constraints: very young children cannot hold, much less manipulate, multiple items in working memory.

- *High variability should be required earlier than later.* Habitual variability levels are acquired soon after students are introduced to new domains. The goal is to teach students to be reliably masterful and reliably variable. This means that early problems should be *difficult enough* to require trying several things to solve them. This will promote and reward both high variability and persistence (Eisenberger, 1992). Problems that are too simple, requiring little search for solution, will reward low variability (and, in addition, induce boredom, which in itself is punishing). Problems that are too difficult, resulting in frustration or failure, will punish high variability.
- *The variability requirements should be very clear.* As we will see in the section on art, Eisenberger and Cameron (1996) have convincingly argued that reliability is rewarded far more often than creativity in a classroom context. As a result, low variability must be specifically precluded in order to promote higher levels.

Applications

The Alternation Problem

Since I am not a mathematics teacher, I cannot provide a sample lesson plan. What I can do is describe a simple and promising procedure. The procedure involves systematic switching between mastery of a new procedure/strategy and varying its application. It was developed using a set of computer maze games that alternatively rewarded task and combined task/variability constraints.

Table 5.6 shows the basic alternation requirements as paired constraints.

---

[10]   Children do not like word problems and, in the current view, are correct in their dislike. Siegler and Robinson (1982) reported that 4- and 5-year-olds wanted problems presented in number (i.e., "How much is 3 + 5?") rather than word (e.g., "You have 3 apples and I give you 5 more. How many apples do you have?") format.

Table 5.7. *Paired constraints for addition-alternation problems*

Steps	Task and variability constraints
1. Single strategy + variability	Preclude repetition → promote variation in procedure (fingers, manipulatives, marks, etc.) → Promote variation in terms (plus, and, one more, etc.)
2. Multiple strategies + variability	Preclude single strategy → promote multiple strategies on single problem or type of problem

The game display was a triangular maze with eight exits at its base. The basic task constraint required ending a path through the maze at a specific exit: the combined constraint – that each path to that exit differ from the immediately prior path. During the game, the number of rewarded exits decreased (from 3 to 2 to 1), while the number of different paths increased (from 1 to 2 to 5). There were three important results.

- First, high variability levels were maintained after both kinds of constraints were relaxed. This was even the case with students who knew when any path to any exit would be rewarded (Stokes et. al, 2008b).
- Second, high variability facilitated transfer to different spatial problems.
- Third, task constraints could be repeated (to promote expertise in students who needed more practice) without compromising the results so long as variability constraints were introduced early enough in training.[11] How early depends on the domain. However, variability constraints introduced late in learning only raised variability levels for their duration (Stokes & Balsam, 2001).

Addition as an Alternation Problem

This procedure could easily be applied to teaching single-digit addition. Table 5.7 suggests constraints for alternations in addition.

Following the principle that high variability be introduced earlier rather than later, a child could first learn several ways to apply a procedure. At the very start, the simplest strategy (count all) could be practiced in three ways: counting with fingers, with manipulatives, or with marks. Practice could also include varying the way the child describes what they are doing: one *plus* one, one *and* one, one and *one more*.

---

[11] For example, the training sequence might look like this: **Task A** → Vary Task A → **Task A** → Vary Task A → **Task B**, etc.

Table 5.8. *Subject and task constraints for perceptual perspective*

Step	Subject constraints	Task constraints
Perceptual perspective	Preclude the canonical → promote the naturalistic	Preclude frontal and flat → promote foreshortened Preclude separation → promote overlapping Preclude multiple viewpoints →promote single viewpoint

Once the child masters three different addition strategies (there are at least eight),[12] a variability constraint might require that the third problem in a set be solved using a strategy different from any used on the two prior problems. In the series $1 + 2, 4 + 5, 3 + 2$, a child could retrieve the first answer (3), decompose $(5 + 5 = 10 - 1 = 9)$ for the second, and count all $(1, 2, 3; 1, 2; 1, 2, 3, 4, 5)$ for the third. As the child masters more strategies, the variability requirement could rise proportionally. Since the requirement does not specify that all solutions be different from each other, a student could simply repeat one strategy and then switch. However, since neither grade school (Stokes et al, 2002a) or college students have done this on our tasks, I wouldn't expect it to happen.

USING CONSTRAINTS IN THE CLASSROOM: ART

This section actually started earlier, with the first four steps in learning to draw (Table 5.4). Children climb those steps themselves; gifted children climb faster, elaborating as they accelerate (Milbraith, 1998; Winner, 1996). For all children, the next step signals the start of apprenticeship, the acquisition and mastery of the skills that define a domain under the tutelage of an expert.[13] That step, shown in Table 5.8, is called perceptual perspective.

Its subject constraint precludes drawing what you know (the canonical) and promotes drawing what you see (the naturalistic). Its task constraints preclude flat, frontal, separated objects seen from multiple perspectives and promote in their place partial, overlapping, foreshortened objects seen from a single vantage point.

Three learning principles outlined in the previous section apply here as well. (1) Expertise is domain-specific: skill acquisition precedes creativity. (2) High variability in a domain facilitates skill acquisition. "Early" should not mean "easy": this is very important since habitual variability levels (how differently a child applies her skills) are acquired when novel domains are first

---

[12] For a complete description of the strategies, see Siegler & Jenkins (1989).
[13] The start of the apprenticeship is usually marked by a noticeable slip in spontaneity and of what adults think of as "creativity" in children's drawings. The children however are correct in precluding spontaneity in order to concentrate on skill acquisition.

encountered. (3) High variability should be normative, built into lesson plans, and clearly communicated as criteria to the children.

COMBINED CONSTRAINTS

In art, multiple constraints are always in effect. Since projects involve materials, they call for task constraints. Since materials and skills in applying them are more or less malleable, there are variability constraints as well. Rather than ignore obvious combinations, I will point out as many as matter in the examples that follow.

Source and Subject Constraints

Larry Rivers (1987), painter and jazz musician, called art history the "first chorus" on which a painter improvises. The first chorus is another name for source constraints, the styles that constitute and define a domain. Very sophisticated styles (Fauvism, Expressionism, Minimalism) and painters (Derain, Marc, Kelly) are magically accessible to young children, who should be exposed not simply to the wonderful illustrations in their books, but to all sorts of sources.[14]

What could be a better place to see sources than at an art museum? As a child, I went to "Saturday school" at the Brooklyn Art Museum. It was wonderful. As an adult, going back to observe, it is still wonderful. The class that impressed me most was about wings – angels' not birds'. The children (7- and 8-year-olds) walked around the galleries, looking at realistically rendered wings (saturated in color and sparking in stained glass) and at highly stylized ones (gilded in Siennese paintings, starker in Assyrian sculptures). Sitting in front of each example, the children participated in the discussion, naming the colors, explaining the textures, describing the shapes.

Back in the studio, they made "snow angel" wings to fit their own bodies and began using markers and tempera paints to fill in the outlines. A few did just that, filled in the outlines; others improvised in ways that showed the sources. One spattered paint to make her wings "glitter-y" like the gold paintings; another carefully lay down sections to make the "feathers" overlap like the sculpted ones; a third separated her colored areas to replicate the richness of stained glass.

While this example might not be replicated in a classroom, the learning principles embedded in it can and should be. These principles are:

- *Explanations by the children.* Explaining is an important learning tool. It precludes lack of focus and promotes attention. It also precludes simpler,

---

[14] My daughter's first favorite painting was an Fauve portrait of a diva in profile: her body is bright yellow, the shadow falling on her face is orange; there is a bright green feather on her pink hat. The painting is by Kees Van Dongen: Amy stood wide-eyed in front of it.

surface- level processing and promotes deeper, associatively based processing, which in turn augments memory and facilitates further learning.[15]

- *Multiple examples.* These make variability normative. There is no one
  goal criterion; rather, there are many; some accessible, others, not yet.
  Accessibility, of course, depends on mastery of task constraints.

Task and Variability Constraints

Monet's Series

A great example of a task-variability combination is Monet's serial strategy. In
mid-career, Monet's goal became showing how light broke up between things.
The "between" is what he called the *enveloppe*, what we call the atmosphere. To
teach himself how to do this, Monet turned repetition into variation. Setting
his easel in a field, he painted twenty-three canvases of the same two grain
stacks, at different times of day, in different weather conditions. No two look
the same. The critical constraint pair precluded shifts in subject in order to
promote concentration on, and change in, how the subject was seen.[16]

The serial strategy, with one change, is easily adopted in the classroom. The
basic constraint is the same: preclude changing the subject, promote different
ways of realizing it. The change involves materials. Since students are not
as skilled as Monet (paint is not as malleable in their hands), a number of
materials are used, separately and successively. For example, a simple still life
can be rendered in pencil, marker, or tempera, with scissors, paste, and paper.
Each version will promote a different way of looking (at outlines, as color
blocks, as shapes to be rearranged), as well as a different way of making. Source
constraints could be introduced into the project as well. For example, cut or
torn papers are used to quite different effect in Cubist collages and Matisse's
large, late decorations.

Notice how Monet's series-strategy is similar to, analogous to, solving a
single math problem in multiple ways. The commonality is the paired constraint that keeps something constant (the subject, the problem) in order to
systematically vary some other things.

An Experimental Series

Many studies have children's creativity as their subject. The three in this section
demonstrate the differences between, as well as the effectiveness, of implicit,
explicit, and in-between variability constraints on an assortment of tasks. My
research assistants (Barnard and Columbia College undergraduates) are the
experimenters in the first study.

---

[15] For a summary of cognitive studies on the benefits of explanation, see Siegler (2006)
[16] For a complete discussion and description of Monet's constraints, see Stokes (2005).

Implicit

High or low variability can be implied simply by the examples provided for a project. In this on-going study, first, third, and fifth grade students are given a sheet with twelve empty circles and asked to make drawings (supposedly for my office) using the circles.[17] There is no suggestion that the drawings differ from each other. After the children are done, the experimenters ask them to label their drawings. This is to make sure we know what each is meant to represent.

Half the children get a sheet with a common example (a smiley face) inside one circle. The other half get two unusual examples: a fish bowl (mostly inside) one circle, and a bicycle joining two circles for its wheels. Preliminary results are confirming our prediction: the two examples implicitly preclude repetition and promote differences both in subject and style. One of my favorite drawings is a fried egg with its white indicated by a squiggly line drawn outside and around the circular yoke.

Explicit

These constraints, which make their criteria very clear, promote either a general level (high or low) or specific kind (novelty, originality) of variability. The reason for clarity in criteria is important. Remember operant conditioning: when children are rewarded (by praise, prizes, or good grades), they learn what kind of performance counts in a particular context. In the classroom, reliability is rewarded more often than creativity; as a result, children perform in conventional ways unless cued to be creative[18] (Eisenberger & Rhoades, 2001).

The good news is that explicit criteria can create a context for variability. For example, rewarding novel performance in one task (multiple words from letter strings or unusual uses for common objects) not only increased novelty in that task (compared to nonspecific instructions), but, also in a subsequent different (drawing), unrewarded task (Eisenberger & Armeli, 1998; Eisenberger & Selbst, 1994). In these studies, the initial task criterion created a performance context for an immediately following but unrelated task. The next set of studies show more lasting effects in rewarded and related (not unrelated) domains.

In-Between

I'm not sure if Holman, Goetz, & Baer (1977) would agree with my characterization of their constraint, but I think it's a hybrid. The task was easel painting. Paint applications and effects (forms) were coded for recognition and reinforcement by the experimenters. Examples of two codes are: "Blended Color: any hue formed by mixing two or more pure or available hues onto the

---

[17]   We will also be comparing the effect of materials: magic markers in two colors versus crayons in eight.

[18]   The other antidote is acquiring habitually high variability levels in a particular domain.

paper," and "Mass: any combination of strokes in a manner that results in a solid colored area of at least 2″ square." Individual children were not instructed to make new forms when they painted, but every instance of novelty in a session was immediately praised. Over multiple sessions,[19] novelty (new forms in a session) and variability (number of different, not necessarily new, forms) increased. After all experimental sessions were over, novelty and variability were maintained in the original domain (easel painting) and generalized to a related (felt-pen drawing), but not an unrelated (block-building) one.

Basic Principles

In addition to showing how different kinds of variability constraints can be used in the classroom, the experiments demonstrate four more things to be learned about learning.

- *Instructions matter.* Make them as clear as possible. Young children are novices. Your instructions should make a problem relatively well-structured, indicating appropriate task constraints and, of course, your goal criterion.[20]
- *Examples matter.* Use them to communicate your criteria. The first experiment used a simple show (the drawings) and tell (the spoken instructions) procedure. Given the combination, the children could process the information in two different ways. This is important: the more ways information is presented and processed, the greater the number of neural connections made and the easier it becomes both to retrieve the new information and to build on it.
- *Consequences matter.* Make them as immediate as possible. Remember operant conditioning: responses that are reinforced increase in frequency.
- *Contexts matter.* Instructions, examples, and consequences matter most when habitual variability levels are first acquired. However, since many skill areas will not be new, they can be used to create contexts that *temporarily increase* and sometimes even *sustain* variability. In the short-term (single) session, instructions and reward can create an immediate context for novelty in a different domain. You saw this in the second experimental example. In the longer-term (multiple) sessions or lessons, they can create

---

[19] The design called for seven reinforced sessions, followed by four non-reinforced ones, and then seven more reinforced sessions.

[20] An example of a great assignment with not-so-great instructions was given to a nephew in fifth grade. The assignment was: write a book to be read out loud to a first grade class. An adult could be "commissioned" to illustrate the book. I was the illustrator. Anthony's first draft was written in perfectly grammatical sentences, appropriately punctuated, but too long and too complicated to read well aloud. What the teacher should have done, and what I did, was tell the class to look at first-grade level books to see how they were written. Anthony did that. His second draft was much better because the criteria (task and goal) had been clarified.

a continued context for novelty in the rewarded one. You saw this in the third example. You can do it in the classroom.

- *In art, materials matter.* They matter for mature artists. In mid-career, Matisse eschewed color for black ink and concentrated on contours, outlines that altered the ways he subsequently organized color. They matter for fledgling artists. Children can only give shape to their ideas in ways that materials allow. For example, wide brushes and markers lead to large and loose pseudo–Abstract Expressionist compositions; colored pencils, or thin-tipped markers shape smaller, more tightly controlled forms.[21]

ARTISTIC FREEDOM

After all this talk about constraints, someone must be thinking, "What about artistic freedom?" One answer can be found in any introductory textbook (and also in the introduction to variability constraints). Free to do anything, most of us do whatever worked best in the past. This is the definition of an operant: a behavior with a frequency proportional to its payoff. This is also why most experts get "stuck" in successful solutions (Stokes & Fisher, 2005).

The other answer is that artistic freedom means choosing one's own constraints. Novices don't do that: their constraints are chosen by their teachers. Experts earn that freedom by mastering the constraints that define their domains. Remember Larry Rivers' remark about history being the "first chorus" on which the painter improvises? He also said that for improvisation to be possible, aspiring painters needed to paint their way through that history. In other words, to master its constraints.

Talent without teaching gets a novice nowhere.

CONCLUDING THOUGHTS AND A CONCLUDING CAVEAT

The Thoughts

Thinking about what I'd like to leave you with, I came up with a list, a short one. I left some spaces so you can add to.

- Think of problems as opportunities for solutions.
- Think of paired constraints as ways to construct creative solution paths.
- Think of teaching students what constraints are and what they do.
- Think about applying the learning principles in the classroom.
- Think of the classroom as a context for creativity.
- Think of making high variability normative in the classroom.
- Think of new subject areas as opportunities to establish high habitual variability levels.

[21] For an expanded discussion of materials and teaching methods, see Korzenik (1995).

- Think about standardized testing as a venue for varying how you teach.
- Think about an existing lesson plan. Preclude one part of it and promote its opposite.
-
-
-

The Caveat

Most children – gifted or not – will become productive as adults in some areas of expertise. Many will produce novelties that are useful or even generative (i.e., lead to further discoveries). A very few will change their domains. Knowing how constraints can be used to develop creativity (yours and your students) in the classroom will help keep all those options open.

REFERENCES

Abuhamdeh, S., & Csikszentmihalyi, M. (2004). The artistic personality: A systems perspective. In R. J. Sternberg, E. L. Grigorenko, & J. L. Singer (Eds.), *Creativity: From potential to realization* (pp. 31–42). Washington, D.C.: American Psychological Association.

Adolph, K. E. (1997). Learning in the development of infant location. *Monographs of the Society for Research in Child Development, 62*(3, Serial No. 251).

Alibali, M. W., & Goldin-Meadow, S. (1993). Gesture-speech mismatch and mechanisms of learning: What the hands reveal about a child's state of mind. *Cognitive Psychology, 26,* 147–279.

Anzai, Y., & Simon, H. A. (1979). The theory of learning by doing. *Psychological Review, 86,* 124–140.

Baker-Ward, L., Ornstein, P. A., & Holden, D. J. (1984). The expression of memorization in early childhood. *Journal of Experimental Child Psychology, 37,* 555–575.

Bjorklund, D. F., & Green, B. L. (1992). The adaptive nature of cognitive immaturity. *American Psychologist, 47,* 46–54.

Bjorklund, D. F., & Harnishfeger, K. K. (1987). Developmental differences in the acquisition and maintenance of an organizational strategy: Evidence for the utilization deficiency hypothesis. *Journal of Experimental Child Psychology, 44,* 109–125.

Carpenter, T. P, & Moser, J. M. (1982). The development of addition and subtraction problem-solving skills. In T. P. Carpenter, J. M. Moser, & T. A. Romberg (Eds.), *Addition and subtraction: A cognitive perspective* (pp. 9–24). Hillsdale, NJ: Erlbaum.

Chase, W. G., & Simon, H. A. (1973). Perception in chess. *Cognitive Psychology, 4,* 55–81.

Chi, M. T. H. (1997). Creativity: Shifting across ontological categories flexibly. In T. B. Ward, S. M. Smith, & J. Vaud (Eds.), *Creative thought: An investigation of conceptual structures and processes* (pp. 209–234). Washington, DC: American Psychological Association.

Chi, M. T. H., Glaser, R., & Farr, M. J. (1986). *The nature of expertise.* Hillsdale, NJ: Erlbaum.

Church, R. B., & Goldin-Meadow, S. (1986). The mismatch between gesture and speech as an index of transitional knowledge. *Cognition, 23*, 43–71.

Coyle, T. R., & Bjorklund, D. F. (1997). Age differences in, and consequences of, multiple- and variable-strategy use on a multiple sort-recall task. *Developmental Psychology, 33*, 372–380.

Csikszentmihalyi, M. (1996). *Creativity: Flow and the psychology of invention.* NY: Harper Collins.

Doane, S. M., Sohn, Y. W., & Schreiber, B. (1999). The role of processing strategies in the acquisition and transfer of a cognitive skill. *Journal of Experimental Psychology: Human Perception and Performance, 25*, 1390–1410.

Eisenberger, R. (1992). Learned industriousness. *Psychological Review, 99*, 248–267.

Eisenberger, R., & Armeli, A. (1998). Can salient reward increase creative performance without reducing intrinsic creative interest? *Journal of Personality and Social Psychology, 72*, 704–714.

Eisenberger, R., & Cameron, J. (1996). Detrimental effects of reward: Reality or myth? *American Psychologist, 51*, 1153–1166.

Eisenberger, R., & Rhoades, L. (2001). Incremental effects of reward on creativity. *Journal of Personality and Social Psychology, 81*, 728–741.

Eisenberger, R., & Selbst, M. (1994). Does reward increase or decrease creativity? *Journal of Personality and Social Psychology, 66*, 1116–1127.

Ericcson, K. A. (1996). The acquisition of expert performance: An introduction to some of the issues. In K. A. Ericcson (Ed.), *The road to excellence: The acquisition of expert performance in the arts and sciences, sports and games* (pp. 1–50). Mahwah, NJ: Erlbaum.

Ericcson, K. A. (2007). An introduction to Cambridge handbook of expertise and expert performance: Its development, organization, and content. In K. A. Ericcson, N. Charness, P. J. Feltovich, & R. R. Hoffman (Eds.), *The Cambridge handbook of expertise and expert performance* (pp. 3–20). NY: Cambridge University Press.

Fujimura, N. (2001). Facilitating children's proportional reasoning: A model of reasoning processes and effects of intervention on strategy change. *Journal of Educational Psychology, 93*, 589–603.

Fuson, K. C. (1982). An analysis of the counting-on solution procedure in addition. In T. P. Carpenter, J. M. Moser, & T. A. Romberg (Eds.), *Addition and subtraction: A cognitive perspective* (pp. 67–81). Hillsdale, NJ: Erlbaum.

Fuson, K. C., & Kwon, Y. (1992). Korean children's single-digit addition and subtraction: Numbers structured by ten. *Journal for Research in Mathmatics Education, 23*, 148–165.

Gardner, H. (1980). *Artful scribbles: The significance of children's drawings.* NY: Basic Books.

Gardner, H. (1993). *Creating minds.* NY: Basic Books.

Garlick, D. (2002). Understanding the nature of the general factor of intelligence: The role of individual differences in neural plasticity as an explanatory mechanism. *Psychological Review, 109*, 116–136.

Geary, D. C., Bow-Thomas, C. C., Liu, F., & Siegler, R. S. (1996). Development of arithmetic competencies in Chinese and American children: Influence of age, language, and schooling. *Child Development, 67*, 2022–2044.

Goldin-Meadow, S., & Alibali, M. W. (2002). Looking at the hands through time: A microgenetic perspective on learning and instruction. In N. Granott & J. Parsiale (Eds.), *Microdevelopment: Transition processes in development and learning* (pp. 80–105). Cambridge, UK: Cambridge University Press.

Goldin-Meadow, S., Alibali, M. W., & Church, R. B. (1993). Transitions in concept acquisition: Using the hand to read the mind. *Psychological Review*, 10, 279–297.

Grow-Maienza, J., Hahn, D., & Joo, C. (2001). Mathematics instruction in Korean primary schools: Structures, processes, and a linguistic analysis of questioning. *Journal of Educational Psychology*, 93, 363–376.

Henry, L. A., & Miller, S. (1991). Memory span increases with age: A test of two hypotheses. *Journal of Experimental Child Psychology*, 51, 459–484.

Holland, J. H., Holyoak, K. J., Nisbett, R. E., & Thagard, P. R. (1987). *Induction: Processes of inference, learning, and discovery*. Cambridge, MA: MIT Press.

Holman, J., Goetz, E. M., & Baer, D. M. (1977). The training of creativity as an operant and an examination of its generalization characteristics. In B. C. Etzel, J. M. LeBlanc, & D. M. Baer (Eds.), *New developments in behavioral research: Theory, methods and applications* (pp. 441–471). Hillsdale, NJ: Erlbaum.

Huizinga, M., Dolan, C. V., & van der Molen, M. W. (2006). Age-related changes in executive function: Developmental trends and a latent variable analysis. *Neuropsychologica*, 44, 2017–2036.

Johnson-Laird, P. N. (1988). Freedom and constraint in creativity. In R. J. Sternberg (Ed.), *The nature of creativity: Contemporary psychological perspectives* (pp. 202–219). NY: Cambridge University Press.

Joyce, J. H., & Chase, P. N. (1990). Effects of response variability on the sensitivity of rule-governed behavior. *Journal of the Experimental Analysis of Behavior*, 54, 251–262.

Kail, R. (1986). Sources of age differences in speed of processing. *Child Development*, 57, 969–987.

Kail, R. (1991). Processing time declines exponentially during childhood and adolescence. *Developmental Psychology*, 27, 259–266.

Kee, D. W. (1994). Developmental differences in associative memory: Strategy use, mental effort, and knowledge-access interactions. In H. E. Reese (Ed.), *Advances in child development and behavior*. Vol. 25 (pp. 7–32). NY: Academic Press.

Kerr, R., & Booth, B. (1978). Specific and varied practice of motor skill. *Perceptual and Motor Skills*, 46, 395–401.

Korenzek, D. (1995). The changing concept of artistic giftedness. In C. Golumb (Ed.), *The development of artistically gifted children* (pp. 1–30). Hillsdale, NJ: Erlbaum.

Lamaire, P., & Siegler, R. S. (1995). Four aspects of strategic choice: Contributions to children's learning of multiplication. *Journal of Experimental Psychology: General*, 83–97.

Lee, T. D., & Magill, R. A. (1983). The locus of contextural interference in motor-skill acquisition. *Journal of Experimental Psychology: Learning, Memory, & Cognition*, 9, 730–746.

Lehto, J. E., Juujarvi, P., Kooistra, L., & Pulkkinen, L. (2003). Dimensions of executive functioning: Evidence from children. *British Journal of Developmental Psychology*, 21, 59–80.

Maltzman, I. (1960). On the training of originality. *Psychological Review*, 67, 229–242.

Manoel, E. de J., & Connolly, K. J. (1995). Variability and the development of skilled actions. *International Journal of Psychophysiology*, 19, 129–147.

Milbrath, C. (1998). Patterns of artistic development in children: Comparative studies of talent. Cambridge, UK: Cambridge University Press.

Miller, P. H., Woody-Ramsey, J., & Aloise, P. A. (1991). The role of strategy effortfulness in strategy effectiveness. *Developmental Psychology*, 27, 738–745.

Miura, I. T., Okamoto, Y., Kim, C. C., Steere, M., & Fayol, M. (1993). First graders' cognitive representation of number and understanding of place value: Cross-national comparisons – France, Japan, Korea, Sweeden, and the United States. *Journal of Educational Psychology*, **85**, 24–30.

Moxley, S. E. (1979). Schema: The variability of practice hypothesis. *Journal of Motor Behavior*, **11**, 65–70.

Nelson, C. A. (1999). Neural plasticity and human development. *Current Directions in Psychological Science*, **8**, 42–45.

Newell, A., & Simon, H. A. (1972). *Human problem solving*. Englewood Cliffs, NJ: Prentice Hall.

Palmer, D. C., & Donahoe, J. W. (1992). Essentialism and selectionism in cognitive science and behavior analysis. *American Psychologist*, **47**, 1344–1358.

Perry, M., Church, R. B., & Goldin-Meadow, S. (1988). Transitional knowledge in the acquisition of concepts. *Cognitive Development*, **3**, 359–400.

Piaget, J. (1955/1977). The stages of intellectual development in childhood and adolescence. In H. E. Gruber & J. J. Voneche (Eds.), *The essential Piaget* (pp. 814–819). London: Routledge & Kegal Paul.

Reitman, E. (1965). *Cognition and thought*. NY: Wiley.

Rivers, L. (1987, March 31). *Improvisation and the creative process in jazz and the visual arts*. Presentation given at Barnard College, Columbia University, NY.

Rittle-Johnson, B., & Siegler, R. S. (1999). Learning to spell: Variability, choice, and change in children's strategy use. *Child Development*, **70**, 332–348.

Runco, M. A. (1986). Flexibility and originality in children's divergent thinking. *Journal of Psychology*, **120**, 345–352.

Schauble, L. (1996). The development of scientific reasoning in knowledge-rich contexts. *Developmental Psychology*, **32**, 102–119.

Schmidt, R. A., & Bjork, R. A. (1992). New conceptualizations of practice: Common principles in three paradigms suggest new concepts for training. *Psychological Science*, **3**, 207–217.

Shea, J. B., & Morgan, R. L. (1979). Contextural interference effects on the acquisition, retention, and transfer of a motor skill. *Journal of Experimental Psychology: Human Learning and Memory*, **5**, 179–187.

Siegler, R. S. (1995). How does change occur? A microgenetic study of number conservation. *Cognitive Psychology*, **28**, 225–273.

Siegler, R. S. (1996). *Emerging minds: The process of change in children's thinking*. NY: Oxford University Press.

Siegler, R. S. (2006). Microgenetic analyses of learning. In W. Damon & R. M. Lerner (Series Eds.) & D. Kuhn & R. Sieger (Vol. Eds.), *Handbook of child psychology: Vol. 2: Cognition, perception, and language* (6th ed., pp. 464–510). Hoboken, NJ: Wiley.

Siegler, R. S., & Jenkins, E. (1989). *How children discover new strategies*. Hillsdale, NJ: Erlbaum.

Simon, D. A., & Bjork, R. A. (2002). Models of performance in learning multisegment movement tasks: Consequences for acquisition, retention, and judgments of learning. *Journal of Experimental Psychology: Applied*, **8**, 222–232.

Simonton, D. K. (1999). *Origins of genius: Darwinian perspectives on creativity*. NY: Oxford University Press.

Simonton, D. K. (2004). Creativity as a constrained stochastic process. In R. J. Sternberg, E. L. Grigorenko, & J. L. Singer (Eds.), *Creativity: From potential to realization* (pp. 83–101). Washington, D.C.: American Psychological Association.

Stokes, P. D. (1999). Learned variability levels: Implications for creativity. *Creativity Research Journal,* **12,** 37–45.

Stokes, P. D. (2001). Variability, constraints, and creativity: Shedding light on Claude Monet. *American Psychologist,* **56,** 355–359.

Stokes, P. D. (2005). *Creativity from constraints: The psychology of breakthrough.* NY: Springer.

Stokes, P. D. (2007). Using constraints to generate and sustain novelty. *Psychology of Aesthetics, Creativity, and the Arts,* **1,** 107–113.

Stokes, P. D., & Balsam, P. (2001). An optimal period for setting sustained variability levels. *Psychonomic Bulletin and Review,* **8,** 177–184.

Stokes, P. D., & Fisher, D. (2005). Selection, constraints, and creativity case studies: Maz Beckmann and Philip Guston. *Creativity Research Journal,* **17,** 283–291.

Stokes, P. D., & Harrison, H. (2002). Constraints have different concurrent and after-effects on variability. *Journal of Experimental Psychology: General,* **131,** 552–566.

Stokes, P. D., Holtz, D., Massel, T., Carlis, A. & Eisenberg, J. (2008a). Sources of variability in children's problem solving. *Korean Journal of Thinking and Problem Solving,* **18,** 49–68.

Stokes, P. D., Lai, B., Holtz, D., Rigsbee, E., & Cherrick, D. (2008b). Effects of practice on variability, effects of variability on transfer. *Journal of Experimental Psychology: Human Perception and Performance,* **18,** 49–67.

Thelan, E., & Smith, L. B. (1994). *A dynamic systems approach to the development of cognition and action.* Cambridge, MA: MIT Press.

Trainor, L. J. (2005). Are there critical periods for musical development? *Developmental Psychobiology,* **46,** 262–278.

Uttal, D. H., Schudder, K. V., & DeLoache, J. S. (1997) Manipulatives as symbols: A new perspective on the use of concrete objects to teach mathematics. *Journal of Applied Developmental Psychology,* **18,** 37–54.

Voss, J. F., & Post, T. A. (1988). On the solving of ill-structured problems. In M.T.H. Chi, R. Glaser, & M. J. Farr (Eds.), *The nature of expertise* (pp. 261–285). Hillsdale, NJ: Erlbaum.

Vygotsky, L. S. (1987). *The collected works of L.S. Vygotsky.* NY: Plenum.

Ward, W. C. (1969). Rate and uniqueness in children's creative responding. *Child Development,* **40,** 869–878.

Werker, J. F., & Tees, R. C. (2005). Speech perception as a window for understanding plasticity and commitment in language systems of the brain. *Developmental Psychobiology,* **46,** 233–251.

Williams, B. R., Ponesse, J. S., Schachar, R. J., Logan, G. D., & Tannock, R. (1999). Development of inhibitory control over the life span. *Developmental Psychology,* **35,** 205–213.

Winner, E. (1996). *Gifted children: Myths and realities.* NY: Basic Books.

6

Infusing Creative and Critical Thinking into the Curriculum Together

ELIZABETH FAIRWEATHER AND BONNIE CRAMOND

1907 "Children, please have your parents sign or put their X on your graded papers and return them to me tomorrow, or else I'll have to speak to your parents about it at services Sunday. Now, fifth-year children, take out your science books and turn to page 141 so we can read about the eight planets."

1957 "Kids, please have your mother sign the graded papers and send them back as soon as possible so you don't get a demerit. Now, take out your science books and turn to page 141 so we can read about the nine planets."

2007 "Please remember to get your parent or guardian to log in to the class home page so that I know that someone has seen your posted assignments. Now, take out your science books and turn to page 141 so we can read about the eight planets."

THINKING CREATIVELY ABOUT CRITICAL THINKING: INFUSING CREATIVITY AND CRITICAL THINKING INTO THE CURRICULUM TOGETHER

Many things have changed in schools in this country, but curriculum has been resistant to change. If you could go back in time and sit in a classroom with your great-grandparents when they were children, or with your grandparents or parents, you would notice some very distinct differences from the classroom you were in, or that of your children. Today you would see smaller class sizes, more diversity, less order and respect for teachers, more technology, and, if you are lucky, some changes in the methods that the teachers use to teach the students. Some of the content would reflect more recent events, advances, and understandings, and the reading level of the textbooks would get easier as you move forward in time (Chall & Conrad, 1991; Reis, 2003). However, it is likely that the curriculum would be divided in pretty much the same way that it has been divided forever. Some of the names have changed. We now teach *mathematics* instead of arithmetic and *language arts* instead of reading and

English. Gym has morphed into *P.E.*, and history and geography have become *social studies*. However, by and large, the content divisions remain the same. The world has changed dramatically in the past 100 years, but education has not kept pace. According to a recent report from the New Commission on the Skills of the American Workforce (2006), the curriculum has not changed significantly in a century.

For example, Doll (1993) argued that our curriculum is based on an outmoded factory system whereby curriculum is seen as discrete bits of information that must be taught in a linear manner and mastered by the student. He posited that the traditional three Rs of Reading, Writing, and Arithmetic be replaced by the new four Rs of Richness, Recursion, Relations, and Rigor. Broadly defined, the new four Rs refer to the learner's explorations of topics in depth, while looking at multiple meanings and their relations to the learner as well as the environment, culture, and the larger context of the world. Instead of mastering content, students would be led to critically examine knowledge and regard it as transitory. There would be emphasis on larger ideas and the interconnections among them. Written in 1993, the grand curriculum revolution that Doll suggested has not come to pass.

Recent reports on education have reemphasized the need for infusing higher-level thinking skills into the curriculum. In Great Britain, the National Advisory Committee on Creative and Cultural Education (1999) warned that the curriculum not only did not nurture creativity, it actually stymied it. In the United States, the groundbreaking 2006 report *Tough Choices or Tough Times* (National Center on Education and the Economy, 2006) advised a systematic change in the curriculum:

> Strong skills in English, mathematics, technology, and science, as well as literature, history, and the arts, will be essential for many; beyond this, candidates will have to be comfortable with ideas and abstractions, good at both analysis and synthesis, creative and innovative, self-disciplined and well organized, able to learn very quickly and work well as a member of a team and have the flexibility to adapt quickly to frequent changes in the labor market as the shifts in the economy become ever faster and more dramatic. (p. 8, Executive Summary)

Many educators blame the emphasis on basic skills and high stakes testing for the lack of emphasis on critical and creative thinking in the classroom. They claim that they do not have time to teach to the standards and add higher-level thinking skills, too. Yet, such a choice is untenable. Robinson (2001) argued that educators cannot continue to debate between "traditional or progressive methods, creativity or rigour" and prepare students for the demands of the twenty-first century (p. 5). We must learn that creativity is not something to be taught as an add-on, as "fluff," or between other activities. Creativity is vital for individuals' well-being and for the well-being of our world. Using Beyer's (1995) simple definition of critical thinking as making reasoned judgments about the value or validity of something, one can see that this type of thinking is also necessary in the development of creative or innovative products, including ideas.

Think back to the classroom you were in as a child. How much of what you learned is no longer true? How much new information and technology has the world acquired since you were in that classroom? Depending on your age, when you were in elementary school, there may have been only 48 states in the United States. Man had not walked on the moon; even airplane trips were reserved for the wealthy, but travel was easy. Our food was not zapped, and our files were not zipped. The idea of a black man or a woman running for president was unthinkable. (In 1960, the idea of a Catholic running for president was controversial.) YouTube, iPods, cell phones, Skype, Blue Tooth, email, eBay, and Facebook had no meaning. Amazon, chats, and MySpace had different meanings, and "text" was not a verb. People, not machines, got viruses.

R. Buckminster Fuller (1981), inventor, architect, engineer, mathematician, poet, and cosmologist, recalled that during his childhood at the turn of the century, people tried to predict the future and could not begin to conceive of automobiles, electrons, travel to the moon, or even air wars as reality. At that time, only about 1% of the world was literate, and fewer still thought of humanity in world terms. We, too, are poised on the brink of change in this new millennium, and the situation is the same: successful adaptation to world change and enrichment of our world depend on creative endeavors. As Hoffer (2006), a self-educated social writer and philosopher, once said, "In a time of drastic change, it is the learners who inherit the future. The learned find themselves equipped to live only in a world that no longer exists" (p. 32).

If we will not accept the Solomon-like choice between higher-order skills like creativity and critical thinking, on the one hand, and academic rigor, on the other, how do we teach both in the limited class time we have? It should be clear that they must be taught together. We must *infuse* these higher-order skills into the teaching of academics to ensure that they are not easily eliminated and to increase the chances that they are transferred to other situations (Lipman, 2003). The purpose of this chapter is to demonstrate for teachers how to infuse these thinking skills into the curriculum together, beginning with the classroom environment and extending to specific examples of creative strategies applied in content lessons.

CLASSROOM ENVIRONMENT

Before designing lessons that integrate creativity and critical thinking into the curriculum, teachers should address classroom environment as specific characteristics are associated with classrooms that engender creativity development among students. Many of these characteristics are related to teacher behavior. Torrance (1965, 1987) stressed the importance of teachers' expression of their own creative qualities as well as their open valuing of creativity as a means of influencing children's creativity. Flexibility, optimism, and spontaneity are other qualities of teachers who are effective in developing creativity in their students, as is not taking oneself too seriously (Fryer, 1996). According to Amabile (1996, p. 230), children who "perceive warmth from their teachers" showed greater intrinsic motivation related to creativity, and "likeability, enthusiasm, and courteousness" in teachers were all positively correlated with children's motivation.

Teachers also affect creativity development through the atmosphere they create in the classroom. Teachers advance creativity when they ensure a climate of psychological safety. In such a climate, students feel safe from ridicule by teachers and peers, accepted for who they are, willing to take risks, and free from excessive pressure (Rogers, [1900] 1976). Psychological safety is achieved by accepting and valuing all children's contributions, stressing cooperation among students, and limiting time constraints, competition, and punitive evaluation. It is very important that an atmosphere of respect is prioritized in the classroom with zero tolerance for taunting, name-calling, bullying, or put-downs of any kind.

Creating environments in which students have autonomy also boosts creativity (Amabile, 1989). To bring about a sense of autonomy in students, teachers can allow students to self-select specific content for independent study, encourage them to participate in determining criteria used for assessment, engage students in self-evaluation of work, and task them with setting their own pace for accomplishing subgoals during long-term projects. At the same time, some structure and guidance are necessary for creativity. The teacher can provide this structure by articulating consistent and high expectations in a nonthreatening manner (Damico & Purkey, 1978; Ziff, 1983). Feedback is an important vehicle for articulating expectations. Teachers should take care to provide specific feedback rather than nebulous comments such as "Great sentence" and refrain from using it to dominate students (Amabile, 1989). In this way, feedback is used to convey standards and promote learning while maintaining an atmosphere in which students feel free to continue to stretch their limits.

A helpful guide for structuring such tasks and providing feedback was developed by Treffinger (1995). In his model for teaching for self-directed learning, he has delineated three levels of contracts that teachers can use with their students depending on each student's ability to handle independence. The first-level contract has students choose from a limited list of topics and a limited list of methods to carry out the research. The student is given specific steps and specific times to report to the teacher on progress. The teacher meets with the student regularly to confer about progress and give specific feedback. The second level is the lengthiest contract because the student chooses a specific topic of study within a general topic, then outlines, with help from the teacher, how and when each step will be done to complete the project. The teacher meets with the student at the predetermined times to confer on progress, and the student participates in evaluating strengths, weaknesses, and progress. The final-level contract is brief because it is the most open-ended. The student chooses a topic of study, outlines the steps she will take, and develops a timeline for completion as well as the criteria for evaluation of the product. The teacher meets periodically with the student to confer, answer questions, and offer help as needed.

Physically, the ideal environment for fostering creativity would be one rich in a variety of resources, with room for movement and varying workspaces, and places for active as well as quiet learning. In a classroom, this might mean that there is a loft, quiet corner, or study carrel as well as tables and desks for students to work in groups. However, teachers often have limited control over the physical environment; the psychological environment is more important and malleable by the teacher.

Why the areas for quiet? So many people believe that creativity is fostered through stimulation. Stimulating environments do spark ideas, but individuals usually need some down time to reflect upon, develop, and transform the ideas. In the 1960s, when so much groundbreaking work on curriculum was done, Hilda Taba (1962) exhorted educators to design curriculum that emphasized major concepts, focused on people, and involved the students in thinking. She also reminded teachers that a lesson should have a rhythm. There should be both stimulation and quiet reflection. More recent theories of cognitive processing seem to validate Taba's advice; students need time to process information. A teacher may not be able to provide a physical space for quiet thought, but he or she can pace the lesson to provide students with some time for processing rather than being bombarded with new information.

WHY CRITICAL AND CREATIVE THINKING TOGETHER?

After establishing an appropriate atmosphere, teachers can shift their focus to integrating creative and critical thinking into the curriculum. Although claims are made that critical and creative thinking are disparate sets of skills and are difficult to put into the same context, these important skills are really complementary, often actually coincidental, and are both needed for problem solving, decision making, and many other important life functions.

For the purposes of this chapter, we will use simple definitions of creative and critical thinking. A commonly accepted and well-published definition of *creative thinking* is thought that results in an idea that is novel and useful. If the idea is not novel, it is banal; if it is not useful, it may just be bizarre, whereas "critical thinking is reasonable reflective thinking focused on deciding what to believe or do" (Ennis, 2002). So, the key component of creative thought is the generation of ideas, and the key component of critical thought is the judgment of ideas. It should be apparent that one must use some judgment in determining if the new idea is useful or appropriate. Also, in critically analyzing and comparing ideas, the resulting gaps provide the impetus for creative thought. The processes are undoubtedly recursive, parallel, coincidental, and idiosyncratic to the situation and the person. We separate them for study and teaching, as we dissect a frog to study its anatomy, but the living frog's systems operate interdependently, as do our thoughts.

Using both critical and creative thinking skills to accomplish creative goals is much like using a pair of glasses with bifocal lenses while driving to a distant location for the first time. The distance viewing portion of the lens is used to see far away and to take in the entirety of the surroundings as when a person is driving on an uncrowded highway, far away from her final destination, taking in the scenery and keeping a casual eye on the landmarks indicating proximity to the final destination. In the same way, creativity skills are used at the beginning of the process when an individual is thinking in general terms about his or her creative goals. At this point, creative thinking skills allow individuals to see the big picture, take in all of the options, and "see" and explore all of the possibilities. On the other hand, there is the portion of the lens intended for close-up viewing. The driver making her way along her trip uses this portion of the lens to focus on closer and smaller portions of the environment when she exits from the highway and stops the car to scrutinize the details of the map and the directions given to her by a friend, as well as to take in the constraints on the voyage (one-way streets, traffic, etc.). This portion of the lens is similar to the critical thinking skills used during the creative process, which allow individuals to narrow their sights on a smaller portion of the whole situation, gather and discriminate information that will be valuable for the process, and scrutinize the details of this information and the context in which it will be used. Finally, as the driver takes off again, through city streets, closing in on her destination, she uses both lenses to take in the overall environment and the situation of important landmarks within it while carefully checking street signs and numbers to be sure she is indeed meeting her short-term goals so that she will eventually reach her destination. Likewise, individuals engaged in a creative task use creative and critical thinking skills simultaneously toward the end of their tasks to keep one eye on the goal and move forward by expanding and elaborating on ideas while continually monitoring and making decisions about these ideas to be sure they are appropriate and will result in goal attainment.

As early as 1950, J. P. Guilford theorized that creativity is a process that involves reasoning and other "thinking factors" (p. 451) including problem finding (ability to recognize problems), fluency (ability to produce many ideas), originality, (ability to produce novel ideas), flexibility (ability to produce varied

Table 6.1. *Gubbins' matrix of thinking skills*

Problem Solving	**Divergent Thinking Skills**
Identifying general problem	Listing attributes of objects situations
Clarifying problem	Generating multiple ideas (fluency)
Formulating hypothesis	Generating different ideas (flexibility)
Formulating appropriate questions	Generating unique ideas (originality)
Generating related ideas	Generating detailed ideas (elaboration)
Formulating alternative solutions	Synthesizing information
Choosing best solutions	**Evaluative Thinking Skills**
Applying the solution	Distinguishing between facts and opinions
Monitoring acceptance of the solution	Judging credibility of a source
Drawing conclusions	Observing and judging observation reports
Decision Making	Identifying central issues and problems
Stating desired goal/condition	Recognizing underlying assumptions
Stating obstacles to goal/condition	Detecting bias stereotypes clichés
Identifying alternatives	Recognizing loaded language
Examining alternatives	Evaluating hypotheses
Ranking alternatives	Clarifying data
Choosing best alternatives	Predicting consequences
Evaluating actions	Demonstrating sequential synthesis of information
Inferences (Inductive and Deductive)	Planning alternative strategies
Inductive	Recognizing alternative strategies
Determining cause and effect	Recognizing inconsistencies in information
Analyzing open-ended problems	Identifying stated and unstated reasons
Reasoning by analogy	Comparing similarities and differences
Making inferences	Evaluating arguments
Determining relevant information	**Philosophy and Reasoning**
Recognizing relationships	Using dialogical/dialectical approaches
Solving insight problems	
Deductive	
Using logic	
Spotting contradictory statements	
Analyzing syllogisms	
Solving spatial problems	

ideas), categorizing ability (ability to group ideas together or to separate them), and evaluation ability (the ability to delay selection of an idea until appropriate evaluation has been made). Next to Guilford's framework one might compare Gubbins' (1985; cited in Sternberg, 1985, p. 54) matrix of critical thinking skills and dispositions. Gubbins surveyed critical thinking theories and models as well as various measures of critical thinking, and then developed a matrix of skills and dispositions associated with critical thinking. The matrix is shown in full in Table 6.1 (Sternberg, 1985, pp. 33–35).

As suggested in the bifocal metaphor, even a quick glance at Gubbins' matrix reveals that the two constructs share many skills. Independent components of creativity are found in different parts of the Gubbins matrix. Fluency, for example, is found in problem solving (generating related ideas, formulating alternative solutions), making inferences (reasoning by, or coming up with, analogies), and divergent thinking skills. Another illustration of the concurrence of creative and critical thinking skills lies in Guilford's evaluation aspect of creativity. This aspect of creativity in which individuals select appropriate ideas and solutions involves many of the skills included in Gubbins' "Evaluative Thinking Skills" section, including planning alternative strategies, recognizing inconsistencies in information, comparing similarities and differences, and evaluating hypotheses and arguments. Even the classic four stage model of creativity as described by Wallas (1926) – preparation, incubation, illumination, and verification – includes processes that involve critical thinking. Certainly, the preparation phase involves critical choices about what to study, and the verification phase invokes judgment about the quality and fitness of the idea.

One example that illustrates this alternation between thinking modes is the Osborn-Parnes Creative Problem Solving Model (Isaksen & Treffinger, 1985; Osborn, 1953; Parnes, 1967). Figure 6.1 demonstrates one way to visualize the interaction of creative and critical thinking skills, although the processes are not always so orderly when used outside of a structured model. One thing that is notable about this problem-solving model is that each step first involves a divergent, or creative, thinking phase in which many ideas are generated and then a convergent, or critical, thinking phase in which only the best ideas are selected for further exploration.

For example, during the mess-finding stage, the participants first use divergent thinking to seek all possible problems to work on and then converge in choosing one general topic. During fact finding, participants diverge in finding facts, questions, information, and feelings about the topic and then converge in choosing the substantiated and most relevant ones. The problem-finding stage is marked by generation of many possible specific problems to work on followed by a selection of the most pertinent problem to attack. During idea finding, they brainstorm possible ideas (divergent thinking) and then select the best ten or so to consider (convergent thinking). During solution finding, the participants consider many criteria by which to judge their solutions and then choose the most pertinent ten or so, which are applied to the top ten solutions, to choose the best solution. Finally, in acceptance finding, the participants think of many ways to sell the solution to stakeholders and then choose the best one to apply. It is helpful when learning the model to use it in sequence as illustrated but, like the scientific process, it is really iterative, so that steps may be skipped or repeated, and the process can restart at any point.

A classroom application might clarify things. A teacher with a creative disposition trying out new methods and ideas in the classroom recognizes that she has desire to foster creativity in her classroom by allowing students time

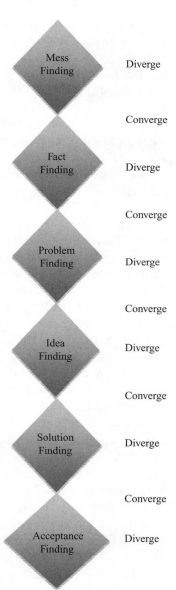

Figure 6.1. Illustration of divergent and convergent thinking through creative problem solving.

to work on independent projects. Unfortunately, whenever she tries to do so, chaos ensues. She cannot discern why this is the case. Critical thinking skills are necessary for the second step, fact finding, to determine what information is needed as a background for developing ideas related to these tensions and desires and what information will ultimately feed the ideas likely to spring from those tensions and desires and be helpful for elaborating on them. The teacher in the example searches for information related to the general situation she has identified as one in which a breakthrough could be made. Then she methodically pours through all of this information about fostering creativity in the classroom, classroom management, content suited for independent projects, developing autonomy in students, etc. and narrows it down to pertinent information to study as a source for ideas of how to reach her goal.

During the problem-finding step, individuals use both types of thinking skills to sift through the information and find inconsistencies that, when addressed, will relieve their tensions or help them fulfill their desires. After narrowing the literature about teaching and creativity, the teacher reviews and reflects on it to identify the source of difficulty in implementing strategies that foster creativity. Creative thinking skills take the primary role during the next step, idea finding, as individuals use divergent thinking to come up with many different ways to solve their problem or associational skills in putting together ideas. The teacher who wishes to try something new to enhance the creative output of her students would use creative thinking skills to synthesize the information at hand and generate strategies that might be used in her classroom to accomplish her goal. A return to critical thinking skills is necessary for the next step, evaluation of ideas. Here, individuals focus on the details of each idea and compare the ideas to the constraints that exist in the context in which they will be used to decide which idea will provide the best solution. For the teacher under discussion, this means using decision-making skills to judge various possible teaching strategies and methods against important criteria, such as "Will the strategy really allow students to work independently? Result in work time that is productive? Actually foster creativity? And, perhaps most important, will the strategy be easy enough to introduce and use on a regular basis?" Finally, the two sets of skills are used together once again in the final step, implementing solutions. During the implementation process, individuals use critical thinking skills to judge the effectiveness of the solution and creative skills to adapt the solution as necessary. Using the same criteria used to select a solution to implement, the teacher would evaluate the effectiveness of the solution she chose and reflect on how well it worked in relation to her goal. Then she would make changes to the solution so she can address any unanticipated problems related to implementing it and make it more appropriate for her needs.

In their own way, creativity strategies, such as making analogies, attribute listing, visual imagery, and role playing, involve the use of critical thinking or complement critical thinking skills in the formulation of a product or meeting an objective. On the other hand, the production of a creative product requires solving many problems that require critical thinking, as, for example, in the evaluation of the product. As the Root-Bernsteins (1999) noted, scientists and artists at the highest levels of accomplishment recognize the combination of thought processes in their accomplishments. They quoted some of these eminent individuals, many of whom were Nobel Prize winners, but the French physician Armand Trousseau seemed to sum it up well in the following quote, "All science touches on art; all art has its scientific side. The worst scientist is he who is not an artist; the worst artist is he who is no scientist" (p. 11).

INFUSING CREATIVE AND CRITICAL THINKING INTO THE CLASSROOM

As a result of the interconnectedness of creative and critical thinking, it is natural, and necessary, in the process of meeting the various objectives mandated within the curriculum to engage students in both critical and creative thinking. Think of the following questions you might pose to students. How many different ways can you find the perimeter of a rectangle? Which is the best way? What are all of the possible ways to get ten? These are questions that stimulate creative and critical thinking while helping students meet curricular objectives. Take, for example, the task "Name all of the possible ways to reach ten." The objective of this task is for students to learn the sets of numbers that add to ten. While teachers might simply have students memorize the pairs or triads of numbers that sum to ten (assuming the objective refers to positive whole numbers), integrating critical and creative thinking skills into the learning process by having students explore the concept of ten allows students to develop a greater understanding of addition and the concept of "ten." Approaching the objective this way involves critical thinking because the students must come up with an exact, correct answer – ten. And it involves creativity because students are trying to be flexible to think of as many different ways as they can. The students use divergent thinking skills when they start with a known equation $(5 + 5)$ and then alter it to get a different one that also produces a sum of ten. (It also allows students to work at their own level as they might think to add numbers that result in a sum greater than ten and subtract to get back to ten – a form of creative thinking based on extra knowledge about numbers.)

Thinking more broadly about the curriculum, and given the illustrations of the integrated nature of creative and critical thinking skills, it is clear that there are many ways to infuse critical and creative thinking skills into the classroom by engaging students at various times in several well-known and easily used creative processes such the creative problem-solving process, creating analogies, using attributes/characteristics of objects or concepts, and viewing ideas from other perspectives. Below are some steps for matching curriculum standards with these creative processes to develop successful activities ranging from lessons that incorporate strategies as simple as presenting questions like those given earlier to units that embrace an interdisciplinary approach and provide extended opportunities for skill development.

When integrating creativity/critical thinking development into the curriculum, an easy and efficient approach is to adapt the creative strategy (which has critical thinking skills embedded in it) around the curricular standards because creativity strategies are broad and applicable across the disciplines. The following four simple steps help teachers match a creative strategy with a curriculum objective and design instructional activities that promote creative and critical thinking while meeting curricular objectives. (The steps are given here and then several examples follow for implementing the steps.)

1. Start with the *curriculum goal.* Choose a curriculum goal or objective that lends itself to a mixture of creative and critical thinking. Choose broad goals and standards that leave room for exploration. Within these, goals/objectives with words such as "analyze," "evaluate," "recognize," "distinguish," "explore," and "shape" are good candidates into which to integrate creative/critical thinking because they will automatically involve the higher-order thinking skills necessary for critical thinking development. Of course, even if the goal/objective uses words like "describe" or "explain," which many do, the level of thinking can be raised to develop important critical thinking skills through the creative strategy that is chosen.

2. Determine the *nature of the thinking skills* related to or that could be incorporated into the concepts or skills involved in the goal/objective. Does the goal/objective require identifying attributes? Would making analogies best suit the objectives? Would problem finding or solving bring about greater insight than other methods? Would analyzing and evaluating a structure or system bring about greater understanding? Do students need to generate various ideas about the topic covered in the lesson? Do students need to make connections between things to generate these ideas, or do they need to be flexible? Answering these questions leads to choosing the best creativity-enhancing strategy embedded with the appropriate critical thinking skills. Make a note of the creative objectives that would fit best with the curricular objectives.

3. *Select a creativity strategy* that matches answers to your questions and ultimately allows students to demonstrate proficiency in the expected assessment mode. To do so, creativity-developing activities should engage students in the type of thinking that is at at least the same level that is expected in the curriculum output based on the goal/objective.

4. *Design instructional activities* that achieve curricular and creativity objectives while simultaneously allowing opportunities for students to obtain feedback.

The following lesson ideas were developed using the steps just articulated. An explanation of how each step was completed for each goal/objective is provided.

Example No. 1: English/Language Arts

1. **Objective:** "Students apply a wide range of strategies to comprehend, interpret, evaluate, and appreciate texts. They draw on their prior experience, their interactions with other readers and writers, their knowledge of word meaning and of other texts, their word identification strategies, and their understanding of textual features (e.g., sound-letter correspondence, sentence structure, context, graphics)" (Education World, 2008, Evaluation Strategies Section a).

2. **Nature of thinking:** Looking at the questions in the second step earlier, it seems that students will need to analyze and evaluate the structure of something – in this case the setting, characters, and events in the text they are reading – to make judgments and inferences that help them to interpret the text. Being able to view the text from different perspectives would also be helpful to students. A creative strategy that helps them step outside of their own "box" and analyze and evaluate a situation from several perspectives would be appropriate here.

3. **Strategy:** The Six Thinking Hats strategy developed by de Bono (1985) fits perfectly here. As students put on the different "hats," they see the setting, characters, and events in the story from different perspectives and can analyze and evaluate them more effectively.

4. **Instructional activity:** After students read *To Kill a Mockingbird*, put them into groups of six and assign each student a hat color. Tell each group that they are going to decide whether Boo Radley should be arrested for the murder of Bob Ewell. Each group will look at the situation from the perspective of a different character in the story – Atticus Finch, the sheriff, and Bob Ewell himself. Students should use the text as a source when making their arguments. To be more closely in line with de Bono's Six Thinking Hats approach, students can assign each of the perspectives (white hat – information/factual perspective, yellow hat – positive perspective, black hat – judgment/critical perspective, red hat – emotional perspective, green hat – creative perspective, blue hat – facilitator perspective) to the appropriate character in the book and then discuss using these specific perspectives.

Example No. 2: English/Language Arts

1. **Objective:** The students demonstrate competence in a variety of genres by producing a narrative that engages the reader by establishing setting, conflict, characters, and significant events (Georgia Department of Education, 2006, ELA seventh-grade GPS).

2. **Nature of thinking:** To put together a story, students must understand the elements that make up a story. This suggests that identifying attributes is a part of this objective. Also, to have an idea to use, you need many ideas. Brainstorming, then, seems to be in order.
3. **Strategy:** Morphological synthesis is a strategy in which attributes are used to stimulate brainstorming, so it would be very useful here. SCAMPER, an acronym for a strategy in which the basic idea is adjusted in different ways, also makes use of attributes to inspire thinking of new ideas (Eberle, 1996).
4. **Instructional activity:**
   a. Morphological synthesis: Provide students with a chart that has columns with the following headings – Setting, Conflict, Characters, Events. The rows are numbered 1, 2, 3, 4, and 5 down the left side. Students place one- or two-word responses in each of the columns without any intention of the responses being related. For example, students might put responses like "haunted house," "ranch," "Florida," "Mars," and "deserted island" for their five settings (rows 1 through 5) and then "brothers fighting," "man vs. nature," and "nuclear war" and so on for the five conflicts, filling in the five rows for each of the four headings. Students should not end up with, for example, "ranch," "cattle rustling," "cowboys and rustlers," and "round-up" in one row under the four columns because these are immediately related concepts. Then, each student pairs up with another student and chooses one number from each column from the other student's chart and writes down each of the resulting responses. The student uses this combination of words to think of an idea for a story.
   b. SCAMPER: Students can discuss the conflict, characters, significant events, and setting of a book (or books) that the class has read as a group. Students can go through the SCAMPER process to make alterations to the original story to create a new story idea. For example, they can "substitute" different settings and conflicts in the book they have read to inspire them to think of a new story. Or, they can "combine" plots from two or more books as fodder for their own story. Used this way, the strategy should allow students to generate several different ideas for writing a story.

Examples No. 3 and 4 are based on levels 5 through 8 life science standards from the National Science Education Standards (1996, Table 6.3), which set the expectation that students should achieve an understanding of the "diversity and adaptations of organisms."

Example No. 3: Science

1. **Objective:** Students will become aware of the effects on living organisms of changes in the environment.
2. **Nature of thinking skills:** A change in environmental conditions that affects organisms sounds like a problem. A strategy focusing on problem solving is just what is needed here.
3. **Strategies:** Creative Problem Solving (CPS) is a strategy that is a perfect fit here of course. Students will need to recognize problems related to environmental conditions. Because students will need to come up with different possible solutions to find the right one as they solve their problem, SCAMPER (Eberle, 1996) can be incorporated as well.
4. **Instructional activity:** Students use the CPS steps (sense a need, gather information, define the problem, generate solutions, evaluate and refine solutions, implement solution) to choose a system they believe is currently in danger and work to produce a solution. Students can incorporate SCAMPER into their problem solving. Students use any or all of the processes in SCAMPER to modify successful solutions to other environmental problems or alter conditions within the system they are studying to solve their problem. If students are investigating the sea turtle situation in Florida, they might research how DDT affected the bald eagle population and the steps that were taken to ban DDT to increase the bald eagle population. Or, they might "eliminate" humans from the sea turtle habitat by restricting further building near the beach. Or, they might "modify" the environment by having residents near the beach put red light bulbs in their outdoor fixtures so turtles are not attracted away from the water by the white light. Teachers can have students implement their solutions in some meaningful way such as writing letters to public officials, sponsoring a public awareness campaign, or starting a fund-raising organization.

Example No. 4: Science

1. **Objective:** Students will appreciate the interconnectedness of organisms and how much organisms rely on their environments (National Science Education Standards, 1996, Table 6.3).
2. **Nature of thinking:** In examining the dependence of organisms on one another and their environments, students will need to look at the structure of these relationships, make inferences about them, and ultimately evaluate how well they might work under different circumstances. Consequently, a creative strategy that helps students analyze

and evaluate relationships between organisms and allows them to gain greater awareness of the environment would be helpful.

3. **Strategy:** The encounter lesson is a good strategy to use in this situation. Through the encounter lesson, students can use questions and visualization to investigate relationships between organisms and between organisms and their environment.

4. **Instructional Activity:** Teachers use the five steps of the encounter lesson structure to have students imagine themselves as an organism – for example, a prairie dog. This process begins when teachers ask students to close their eyes and sit quietly to consider the following:

   1. What kind of prairie dog are you – male or female, adult or pup? (identity)
   2. Where do you live? (identity)
   3. What do you hear . . . see . . . feel . . . smell . . . taste? (awareness)
   4. You are away from the rest of the colony. How do you feel? (isolation)
   5. You've spotted a predator. How do you feel? (danger)
   6. What have you learned from these experiences? What would you like to tell the other prairie dogs? (wisdom)

   Then, students can take turns telling about their experiences or write journal entries about themselves as the organisms.

The next two examples relate to understanding the "structure and function in living systems," level 5 through 8 life science standards from the National Science Education Standards (1996, Table 6.3).

Example No. 5: Science

1. **Objective:** Students will be able to describe the major organ systems of the human body.
2. **Nature of thinking**: The process of describing the organ systems naturally incorporates an understanding of the attributes of the different organs and organ systems.
3. **Strategy:** Morphological synthesis, discussed earlier, is a strategy that helps students focus on attributes and then synthesize what they have learned about them. Using morphological synthesis in this case, students would identify the attributes of the major organ systems and then use them to create new ideas about the human body.
4. **Instructional activity:** The goal of this activity is for students to use attribute listing to create hybrid organs that would conduct several human body processes simultaneously. Here, students should make a chart of the attributes of the major organs in the human body (shape, size, parts, functions, problems) and fill in the attributes for each organ.

Then students put together attributes from various columns to design hybrid organs. Students finish up by drawing and naming their hybrid organs, labeling the parts, and explaining the functions.

Example No. 6: Science

1. **Objectives:** Students will explain the composition of organ systems including the structure and function of cells and how cells are organized into subsequently larger and larger systems (tissue, organs, organ systems).
2. **Nature of thinking:** To meet these objectives, it would help students to identify attributes of organisms. Because there are many different relationships, including small–large and part–whole relationships, making analogies might also be a way for students to gain greater understanding.
3. **Strategy:** Attribute listing will help students identify all of the elements with which they have to work in making their analogies, not to mention help the students learn about the elements better and understand how they relate to each other. Creating analogies will strengthen this understanding.
4. **Instructional activity** (This activity is a sample performance task from the Georgia Performance Standards Web site – Georgia Department of Education, 2006): Students think of a theme as a context for developing an analogy that helps to show the cell structures, functions, needs, and the cell's place in other systems. Students will list the attributes of the cell and the attributes of the theme to observe any connections. For example, students can use "grocery store," "house," "factory," etc. as themes for their analogies. Students should make representations of their analogies (drawings, skits, etc.) and share them with other students.

Example No. 7: Math

1. **Objective:** Students will "develop meaning for integers and represent and compare quantities with them" (National Council of Teachers of Mathematics, 2004, Number and Operations Standard for Grades 6–8).
2. **Nature of thinking:** Relationships are at the heart of an objective that calls for making comparisons. As a result, analogies might be most appropriate, especially analogies that help students understand the structure of the number system.

3. **Strategies:** Making a direct analogy as directed in the Synectics model can be applied in this lesson (Gordon, 1961). Students might benefit from analogies that are fairly personal in nature, so personal analogy, also from the Synectics model, is also appropriate.

4. **Instructional activities:**
    a. Direct analogy: To engage students in a direct analogy, teachers might have students think of a set of items – for example, animals. Then students should place groups of the items on a number line above the rational numbers (whole numbers if it works better) and explain why they placed the items where they did. For example, they might put dinosaurs above negative ten (-10) because they do not exist anymore but they used to exist in large numbers. They might put ants at positive twenty ($+20$) because they do exist and there are at least twice as many ants as there were dinosaurs. They might put whales at positive one ($+1$) because their numbers are dwindling. Allow students opportunities to explain their work to other students.
    b. Personal analogy: To create a personal analogy, students imagine they are a particular rational number – for example, negative seven and three eighths ($-7\frac{3}{8}$). Then students write a short travel journal about their experiences on the number line, including the following considerations: What am I worth? How do I feel about my worth? How "long" would it take me to get to zero? What number did I visit first? Why? How long did the journey take? What was it like? Where else did I go? Who are my relatives on the number line? Why? What is your relationship?

Example No. 8: Math

1. **Objectives:**
    a. The students will "examine the congruence, similarity, and line or rotational symmetry of objects using transformations" (NCTM, 2004, Geometry Standards for Grades 6–8).
    b. The students will "describe sizes, positions, and orientations of shapes under informal transformations such as flips, turns, slides, and scaling" (NCTM, 2004, Geometry Standards for Grades 6–8).

2. **Nature of thinking:** To raise the thinking level of these objectives, students could be expected to demonstrate their capacities vís-a-vís these skills by creating different objects while making similar geometric shapes and putting them together in different ways. This suggests generating various ideas.

3. **Strategy:** Several strategies present themselves for generating ideas to solve problems, but because students are looking at ways to manipulate specific objects to solve their problem – namely, make a new object with their geometric pieces – SCAMPER, which incorporates such ideas as magnify and minify, is a good choice for this situation (Gordon, 1961).

4. **Instructional activity:** Teachers might give each student a set of geometric pieces – a square, rectangle, triangle, etc. and ask students to arrange the pieces into an object. Then, they can challenge students to make a different object using the SCAMPER method with one of the pieces to change the object into something else. (When students magnify and minify the piece, they must use the properties of similarity expected in the objective.)

Example No. 9: Social Studies

1. **Objective:** The students will understand how "people's cultural beliefs, such as religion or political ideals, influence other parts of a culture" (National Council for the Social Studies, Revised Standard Draft, 2008, p. 26).

2. **Nature of thinking:** Students enrich their understanding of the effects of cultural beliefs by being able to elaborate on many different aspects of them. So, the more categories of religious practices, customs, and traditions of which students are aware, the more they will take in and the fuller their descriptions will be.

3. **Strategy:** Brainstorming is a good strategy for helping students elaborate on their descriptions.

4. **Instructional activity:** The teacher selects a picture of a religious or cultural event from one of the countries about which students have been learning that does not indicate the country in which it occurs. Students look at the picture to try to determine the country in which it occurs. Students play a form of "twenty questions" in which they ask yes-or-no questions trying to get information about what is happening in the event and the cultural clues surrounding it to deduce which country is represented in the picture. (Of course, students may not try to determine the country in question by asking "Is this China?" "Is this India?" etc.). They might ask questions like "Is that a Buddhist temple?" "Are the men and women separated in that picture?" "Is that man reading from the Koran?" After a suitable period of time, students make an argument for what country they think it is based on the answers they heard to the questions that were asked. (This is an activity that is modified from one presented in *Creativity in the Classroom* [Starko, 2005].)

MANAGING A CREATIVE CLASSROOM

Integrating critical thinking and creativity in the classroom takes more than just planning individual lessons. Effective classroom management is necessary to ensure that students will embrace autonomy and have access to appropriate feedback as well as opportunities to explore their interests and find their strengths. The backbone of a classroom management program that provides teachers with time to supply feedback to students while helping them develop the self-discipline necessary for successful autonomy is a system in which students have clear, consistent expectations about the use of their time. In such a system, students know what to do, how they should be doing it, and how to deal with any problems that arise that prevent them from doing it. This provides the teacher with time to conference with students to provide appropriate feedback.

Such a system will differ depending on the students' maturity and previous experiences with independence, so a class of immature learners might have to start slowly. Treffinger (1975) has illustrated the levels of a learning contract, for example, that might be used with students of varying levels of readiness for independence, even in the same class. The first contracts are very simple with few tasks and short checkup times that are primarily decided by the teacher with student input. At each step, the student takes more responsibility for determining what tasks need to be accomplished and when. The final learning contract is again very simple, with the student just indicating what the final product will be, what resources will be used, and when it will be completed. For primary grade children, learning centers are more appropriate for management, and they provide good preparation for the independence of learning contracts.

In addition to learning centers and contracts, the management system might include providing students with the following:

1. A daily agenda with "back-up" activities
2. Sticky notes on which students can write any questions they have and place them in a designated spot for the teacher to address when it is appropriate
3. A "plan for the period" that contains an ordered list of activities to be completed
4. The name of a partner or facilitator who can provide assistance if needed
5. Any special instructions such as "do not have writing conferences today as we need it to be very quiet for extra concentration"

Getting students to use the system effectively takes training and ownership. Students will need to practice independent work sessions several times to "work out the bugs" before the teacher begins using independent work sessions for opportunities to conference with students and provide feedback.

During the practice sessions, the teacher can serve as a model for the students by working on a creative activity while surreptitiously noting any kinks in the system. After practice sessions, the teacher and student can engage students in a class discussion about what worked and did not work, and students can offer suggestions of ways to alter the environment and the instructional structure. In this way, teachers prompt students to think of what they think will work best for them at times when they do not have access to the teacher. For example, students might consider where to situate materials to facilitate easy access, how to structure the room to minimize movement and noise, and what learning aids (such as "tips for using reference materials" or "steps for logging on to the computer") can be provided for students so they can solve problems that arise when the teacher is involved with other students. Allowing students to discuss these concerns with each other after they have practiced independent work sessions may stimulate better solutions for addressing these issues.

The Guided Discovery method (Denton, 2005), a method for introducing, or reintroducing, students to materials they are likely to use regularly in the classroom, might also be useful in preparing students to be successful in a classroom that supports creativity. In Guided Discovery, teachers present materials to students and help them discover the best ways to use the materials to meet their needs. One aspect of the Guided Discovery process is encouraging students to use materials in new ways and then giving them ample time to share their ideas. For example, when conducting a Guided Discovery of construction paper, a teacher might have students simply do anything they want with the paper. After finishing, students might be asked to reflect on how well the construction paper was suited to meet their needs or how their ideas were inspired by the paper itself. Then, students might be paired and asked to share with each other what they have done and what they learned during the process about how they might use construction paper in the future. Finally, the whole class might gather together to look at each others' products and make comments and final reflections. Through the sharing students learn from each other ways to use materials and even build on each others' ideas. Thus, this method is especially suited for developing creativity because it expands the backgrounds from which students pull their ideas and helps them look flexibly at the materials they might use in creative endeavors.

Management of time is also important in terms of providing students the space they need for coming up with original ideas and evaluating ideas for satisfaction, applicability, and potential success (Vosburg & Kaufmann, 1999). This is especially true to provide for the critical thinking aspects of the creative process. Many students may need long periods of time to pore over details as they gather information related to their creative endeavors as well as long-term and involved methods to evaluate their ideas and products. Deadlines can be difficult for these students. Prepping them for what is coming along so they can start thinking about it might be a way to give them lead time. Allowing them to work at their own schedule may be important as well.

INTERDISCIPLINARY APPROACH

An interdisciplinary approach can provide an effective structure for incorporating creativity and critical thinking into the curriculum. An interdisciplinary approach is one in which teachers focus instruction on broad themes, either for the year or for a unit of study, that allow them to bring together several disciplines of study (VanTassel-Baska & Stambaugh, 2005). For example, fifth-graders often study European exploration and settlement of America, the westward movement, space, and classification of organisms. Therefore, an appropriate interdisciplinary theme for the fifth-grade year might be "Exploring New Worlds," in which all of these "worlds" are explored using math and language arts as vehicles for discovery.

Interdisciplinary teaching is important for creativity and critical thinking development for many reasons. First, an interdisciplinary approach inherently promotes many of the skills that are components of the creativity strategies mentioned above, including "formation of analogies, building up of chains of ideas . . . and looking at existing information in new ways" (Cropley, 1992, p. 93). It is easier for students to construct analogies when disciplines are tied together by a theme. In the fifth-grade unit, students make many analogies between sixteenth-century exploration and space exploration. Students use analogical thinking to compare the reasons for New World exploration and space exploration, the types of navigation equipment and transportation vehicles, and the outcomes of exploration in both situations. The same is true of chains of ideas. With an interdisciplinary theme, students can lay side by side the structures of the various disciplines they are studying to gain greater understanding of how each of the structures has been developed. This leaves them with a greater chance of viewing information and situations from a new vantage point.

Also, background knowledge is an important component of being able to think creatively and critically (Cropley, 1992; Sternberg, 1996; Weisberg, 1999). Interdisciplinary teaching enables teachers to maximize the use of time in providing students access to more background information. On the other hand, because creative ideation often comes from making unusual connections or novel associations – creativity blossoms when background knowledge is diverse. Interdisciplinary teaching shows students how a diverse collection of knowledge can be linked together. Using the fifth-grade example, students develop the capacity to think metaphorically when they compare exploration of America with that of space exploration and use what they have learned about

American history to suggest ways space exploration might solve current problems on earth. They further develop these capacities when they evaluate the attributes used to classify organisms, countries, and locations for settlements or when they see space exploration as a metaphor for their exploration into their unknown futures when learning about careers.

Thinking in metaphors can easily be framed as a critical thinking skill as well. The diverse background knowledge provided by an interdisciplinary approach aids in developing other critical thinking skills. In such a wide context, students can find many examples of cause and effect and reasoning as well as a good foundation for making inferences. Because diverse background knowledge gives students many points of view from which to look at the world, it also provides a greater context for evaluative thinking skills such as recognizing underlying assumptions, detecting bias, distinguishing between fact and opinion, and judging credibility of a source.

Another feature of an interdisciplinary approach that enhances creative and critical thinking is that it is more likely to fuel intrinsic motivation because it enables students to focus on their strengths. This is particularly true if assessment is developed thematically. Although students are responsible for all content and skills, they can focus any performance tasks or culmination products on their areas of strength. Another closely related reason is that interdisciplinary teaching appeals to the interests of a wider range of students. Also, the interdisciplinary approach readily lends itself to independent study in big picture projects that develop autonomy among students.

TEACHING FOR TRANSFER

Teacher to student: "Why did you misspell 'oxygen' in your science essay? That was one of our spelling words last week, and you got 100% on the spelling test."
Student: "The essay wasn't for spelling class."

This exact scenario may not have occurred in your class, but if you are like most teachers, something similar has occurred. It can be frustrating and puzzling for teachers to realize that students often do not generalize learning outside of the specific instructional situation. Of course, we hope and expect that students will use knowledge and skills that they learn in appropriate situations outside of the training. Fortunately, there are several things that we can do while teaching to facilitate such transfer.

On the basis of empirical evidence, Halpern (1998) recommended four components for training in critical thinking to increase the probability of transfer of learned strategies to appropriate problem situations. Although she was referring specifically to critical thinking, there does not seem to be any reason why these components should not facilitate transfer of any type of thinking skill. The components include:

> (a) a dispositional component to prepare learners for effortful cognitive work, (b) instruction in the skills of critical thinking, (c) training in the structural aspects of problems and arguments to promote transcontextual transfer of critical-thinking skills, and (d) a metacognitive component that includes checking for accuracy and monitoring progress toward the goal. (p. 449, abstract)

We have already discussed the instruction in the skills of thinking, so the remainder of this section will refer to the other three components.

Mark Twain has often been quoted as saying, "A person who won't read has no advantage over one who can't read." The same might be said about a person who will not think. Thinking is hard work, and most of us avoid hard work unless it is necessary. The key is deciding when it is necessary. As Halpern (1998) pointed out, not all intellectual endeavors require equal amounts of effort. For example, it usually requires less effort to read a comic book, romance novel, or simple novel than a complex poem, sophisticated text, or multilevel novel with multiple meanings. Likewise, if one encounters a problem for which there is an easy, known, successful solution, there is no reason to think of a creative solution. Part of teaching thinking is teaching students how to decide when a task requires effort and when a large amount of effort is not necessary.

On the other hand, part of the teaching of thinking includes fostering problem-solving dispositions and habits. These include curiosity, openness to new information, willingness to engage in complex thinking, persistence in problem solving, and appreciation for alternative ideas, among others (Halpern, 1998; Tishman, & Andrade, 1995). Many of the same dispositions may be necessary for both critical and creative thinking, although there are some differences in how they relate to each type of thinking. Perhaps the differences in the two types of thinking observed by Beyer (1987) also explain the predominant dispositions for the two types of thinking:

> Whereas creative thinking is divergent, critical thinking is convergent; whereas creative thinking tries to create something new, critical thinking seeks to assess worth or validity in something that exists; whereas creative thinking is carried on by violating accepted principles, critical thinking is carried on by applying accepted principles. Although creative and critical thinking may very well be different sides of the same coin, they are not identical. (p. 35)

Perhaps the difference in creative and critical thinking dispositions is a preference for one type of thinking over another. However, the effective thinker will be aware of and able to apply the appropriate skills to the situation.

How does one teach such dispositions? Tishman and Andrade (1995) argued that thinking dispositions are best taught through immersion in a culture that models, discusses, values, and reinforces thinking. Such a culture in a classroom would include modeling of good thinking, opportunities and rewards for thinking critically and creatively, discussions about strategies and rationales for effective thinking, and reinforcement for effective thinking. Of course, this teaching requires teachers who have the dispositions and skills themselves.

The last two components of Halpern's (1998) model for facilitating transfer refer to components of the task itself and the learner's awareness of how well s/he is performing in solving the problem or completing the task. Of these, the first, which Halpern calls structure training (p. 452), refers to teaching students how to analyze the properties of a problem or task in order to make a strategic judgment about how to approach the task. The evidence from expert-novice studies in psychology reinforces the notion that experts spend more time analyzing a problem before beginning to solve it, whereas, novices are more likely to jump in and start the trial and error process (c.f. Gick, 1986; Holyoak, 1995). Teaching students how to recognize the common structural properties of problem types enables them to recognize new problems as variations of problems they have solved before and to systematically choose the most appropriate method for attempting a solution. On the other hand, the student might realize that the problem is one for which there is no known solution, thus a creative solution is required. This is the source of Torrance's simple definition of creativity: "Whenever people confront a problem for which they have no learned and practiced solution, some degree of creativity is required" (Torrance, 1988, p. 57; 1999, p. 1).

Finally, successful application of thinking requires that the individual constantly monitor the effects of the thinking and make decisions about proceeding or changing course based on the feedback. Such meta-cognitive monitoring, according to Halpern (1998), needs to be made "explicit and public" so that students learn to effectively "monitor their thinking process, checking whether progress is being made toward an appropriate goal, ensuring accuracy, and making decisions about the use of time and mental effort" (p. 454). She added that students learn to do this with guided questions before, during and after solving a problem. Before solving the problem, they should be asked questions such as ones about the problem, the strategy for solving the problem, how difficult they assess the problem to be, how much time and effort they expect the problem to take, and how they will know when they have solved it correctly. During problem solving, they might be asked to determine their progress toward the goal, and when finished, they might reflect upon how well they feel they solved the problem and what they have learned to apply to problems in the future (p. 454).

While conducting a study with colleagues on teaching gifted middle school students about problem solving (Cramond, Martin, & Shaw, 1990), I was surprised to observe how little these very bright and high achieving students knew about the structure of different types of problems, strategies for solving problems, and their own relative abilities and preferences for different types of problem solving. They expressed surprise when asked to study a set of very different problems and decide how to solve them without giving an answer. It was very clear that they were unused to examining the structure of a problem before determining how to proceed. They depended more upon the problem context for clues to solutions – in math class the problems require mathematical heuristics; in catechism class, they might deal with moral or ethical concerns; in the gifted class, they might apply future problem solving, etc. They were clearly unprepared for the complex nature of real problems in the real world. In the intervening years, I have observed that this is true of many students at all levels of education and at all ability levels. They may have learned effective thinking skills and strategies, but no one ever taught them how to apply those strategies systematically. Yet, it is something that most students want and need.

CONCLUSION

Creative and critical thinking can and should be taught to students throughout their school years. Students of all ability levels can be taught to think critically and creatively, and the teaching should be infused into the curriculum. To be effective, the teaching of thinking must be systematic, intentional, and accompanied by the modeling and reinforcement of the dispositions and habits of thinking. In addition, there must be real opportunities to apply the skills to meaningful problems with an emphasis on the structure of problems across contexts. Students should be encouraged to practice meta-cognitive monitoring through direct questioning and discussions of the thought processes applied and to engage in personal assessments of strengths and preferences. In short, there must be an overt emphasis on thinking. The creation of a cultural milieu for thinking requires that the teacher value and be skilled at thinking, can create a conducive environment, develop tasks, and teach strategies for thinking effectively. It seems like a tall order, but it is a worthy goal to work toward by adding components in (small) steps whenever possible.

REFERENCES

Amabile, T. M. (1989). *Growing up creative: Nurturing a lifetime of creativity.* New York: Crown Publishers, Inc.

Amabile, T. M. (1996). *Creativity in context.* Boulder, CO: Westview Press.

America's Inventor Online Edition (2007). *1940's Film goddess Hedy Lamarr responsible for pioneering spread spectrum: Hedy Lamarr.* Retrieved on April 1, 2007, from http://inventors.about.com/gi/dynamic/offsite.htm?site=http://inventionconvention.com/americasinventor/dec97issue/section2.html. *American Heritage of Invention and Technology*, 1997, **12**(4).

Beyer, B. K. (1987). *Practical strategies for the teaching of thinking.* Boston: Allyn and Bacon.

Beyer, B. K. (1995). *Critical thinking.* Bloomington, IN: Phi Delta Kappa Educational Foundation.

Chall, J. S., & Conard, S. S. (1991). *Should textbooks challenge students? The case for easier or harder textbooks.* New York: Teachers College Press.

Cramond, B., Martin, C. E., & Shaw, E. (1990). Generalizability of the creative problem solving process to real-life problems. *Journal for the Education of the Gifted*, **13**, 86–98.

Cropley, A. J. (1992). *More ways than one, fostering creativity.* Norwood, NJ: Ablex Publishing.

Damico, S. B., & Purkey, W. W. (1978). Class clowns: A study of middle school students. *American Educational Research Journal*, **15**, 391–398.

de Bono, E. (1985). *Six thinking hats.* New York: Little, Brown and Co.

Denton, P. (2005). *Learning through academic choice.* Portland, ME: Stenhouse.

Doll, W. E., Jr. (1993). *A Post-Modern perspective on curriculum.* New York: Teachers College Press.

Eberle, B. (1996). *SCAMPER: Games for imagination development.* Waco, TX: Prufrock Press.

Education World. (2008). National Standards: Language Arts. Retrieved on January 12, 2009, from http://www.education-world.com/standards/national/lang_arts/english/k_12.shtml.

Ennis, R. H. (June 20, 2002). *A super-streamlined conception of critical thinking.* Retrieved on December 28, 2002 from http://www.criticalthinking.com/articles.html.

Fryer, M. (1996). *Creative teaching and learning.* London: Paul Chapman Publishing, Ltd.

Georgia Department of Education. (2006). *Georgia standards.org: Science standards.* Retrieved on March 18, 2007, from http://www.georgiastandards.org/science.aspx.

Gick, M. L. (1986). Problem-solving strategies. *Educational Psychologist*, **21**, 99–120.

Gordon, W. J. (1961). *Synectics: The development of creative capacity.* New York: Harper and Row.

Gubbins, E. J. (1986). Gubbins' matrix of thinking skills, in R. J. Sternberg (Ed.), *Critical thinking: its nature, measurement and improvement* (Eric Document Reproduction Service No. 272882). Retrieved on December 28, 2008, from http://eric.ed.gov:80/ERICDocs/data/ericdocs2sql/content_storage_01/0000019b/80/2f/64/fe.pdf.

Guilford, J. P. (1950). Creativity. *American Psychologist*, **5**, 444–454.

Halpern, D. (1998). Teaching critical thinking for transfer across domains: Dispositions, skills, structure training, and metacognitive monitoring. *American Psychologist*, **53**, 449–455.

Hoffer, E. (2006). *Reflections on the human condition.* New York: Hopewell Publications. (original work published 1932).

Holyoak, K. J. (1995). Problem solving. In D. E. Smith & D. N. Osherson (Eds.), *An invitation to cognitive science* (Vol. 3, 2nd ed., pp. 267–296). Cambridge, MA: MIT Press.

Isaksen, S. G., & Treffinger, D. J. (1985). *Creative problem solving: The basic course.* Buffalo, NY; Bearly Limited.

Lipman, M. (2003). *Thinking in education.* New York: Cambridge University Press.

National Advisory Committee on Creative and Cultural Education. (1999). *All our futures: Creativity, culture, and education.* London, UK: Department of Education and Employment. Retrieved on March 1, 2007, from http://www.dfes.gov.uk/naccce/.

National Center on Education and the Economy. (2006). Tough choices or tough times: The report of the new commission on the skills of the American workforce. New York: Jossey-Bass. Also available from www.skillscommission.org.

National Council for the Social Studies. (2008). Expectations of excellence: Curriculum standards for social studies, draft revision. Retrieved on January 12, 2009, from http://www.socialstudies.org/system/files/StandardsDraft10_08.pdf.

National Council of Teachers of Mathematics. (2004). Principles and standards for school mathematics. Retrieved on January 12, 2009, from http://standards.nctm.org/document/chapter6/geom.htm.

National Science Education Standards. (1996). Center for Science, Mathematics, and Engineering Education. Retrieved on January 12, 2009, from http://www.nap.edu/openbook.php?record_id/4962.

Osborn, A. F. (1953). *Applied imagination.* New York: Scribner.

Parnes, S. J. (1967). *Creative behavior guidebook.* New York: Scribner.

Reis, S. M. (2003). Reconsidering regular curriculum for high achieving students, gifted underachievers, and the relationship between gifted and regular education. In J. H. Borland (Ed.), *Rethinking gifted education* (pp. 186–200). New York: Teacher's College Press.

Robinson, K. (2001). Mind the gap: The creative conundrum. *Critical Quarterly,* **43**(1), 41–45.

Rogers, C. ([1900] 1976). Toward a theory of creativity. In A. Rothenberg & C. Hausman (Eds.), *The creativity question* (pp. 296–304). Durham, NC: Duke University Press.

Root-Bernstein, R. S., & Root-Bernstein, M. M. (1999). *Sparks of genius: The thirteen thinking tools of the world's most creative people.* New York: Houghton Mifflin.

Starko, A. J. (2005). *Creativity in the classroom: Schools of curious delight* (3rd ed.). Mahwah, NJ: Lawrence Erlbaum Associates.

Sternberg, R. J. (1985). Critical thinking: Its nature, measurement and improvement. In F. Link (Ed.), *Essays on the intellect* (pp. 45–66). Washington, DC: Curriculum Development Associates/Association for Supervision and Curriculum Development.

Taba, H. (1962). *Curriculum development: Theory and practice.* New York: Harcourt, Brace & World.

Tishman, S., & Andrade, A. (1995). *Thinking dispositions: A review of current theories, practices, and issues.* ACCTION Report 1. Washington, DC: ACCTION. Retrieved on December 23, 2008, from http://learnweb.harvard.edu/alps/thinking/docs/Dispositions.htm.

Torrance, E. P. (1965). *Rewarding creative behavior, experiments in classroom creativity.* Englewood Cliffs, NJ: Prentice-Hall.

Torrance, E. P. (1987). Teaching for creativity. In S. G. Isaksen (Ed.), *Frontiers of creative research: Beyond the basics* (pp. 189–215). Buffalo, NY: Bearly Limited.

Torrance, E. P. (1988). The nature of creativity as manifest in its testing. In R. J. Sternberg (Ed.), *The nature of creativity* (pp. 43–75). New York: Cambridge University Press.

Torrance, E. P. (1999). Test developer profiles: E. Paul Torrance, Ph.D. In *Psychological Testing and Assessment* (4th ed.) New York: McGraw Hill. Retrieved on December 30, 2008, from http://www.mhhe.com/mayfieldpub/psychtesting/profiles/torrance.htm.

Treffinger, D. (1995). Self directed learning. In J. Maker (Ed.), *Teaching models in education of the gifted* (2nd ed., pp. 327–370). Austin, TX: PRO-EDUCATION.

VanTassel-Baska, J., & Stambaugh, T. (2005). *Comprehensive curriculum for gifted learners* (3rd ed.). Boston: Allyn & Bacon.

Wallas, G. (1926). *The art of thought.* New York: Harcourt Brace.

Weisberg, R. W. (1999). Creativity and knowledge: A challenge to theories. In R. J. Sternberg (Ed.), *Handbook of creativity* (pp. 226–250). Cambridge: Cambridge University Press.

Ziff, S. S. (1983). An investigation of the written expression of humor by sixth-grade gifted children. Unpublished doctoral dissertation, Virginia Polytechnic Institute and State University, 1983.

7

The Five Core Attitudes, Seven I's, and General Concepts of the Creative Process

JANE PIIRTO

When I began working in the field of the education of the gifted and talented, as a county coordinator in Ohio, in 1977, I looked at the categories of giftedness as described in the Marland Report of 1971. These categories were superior cognitive ability, specific academic ability, creative thinking, visual and performing arts ability, and psychomotor ability. I asked myself, "Aren't smart people creative? Aren't people good at academic subjects creative? Aren't visual and performing artists creative? Aren't athletes creative? Why is there a separate category for creativity?" Over the next thirteen years, I was a county coordinator in two states and the principal of New York City's Hunter College Elementary School, the oldest U.S. school for gifted children. I am now a college professor who runs a graduate program for certification for teachers of the gifted and talented. I am unusual, I suspect, because in my inner life, my real life, I am and have been an artist – a published novelist and a poet – and I see the world not only through the eyes of a researcher in education and psychology but also through an artist's eyes (e.g., Piirto, 2008b; Piirto & Reynolds, 2007). I have also been what is called a *teaching artist* (Oreck & Piirto, 2004), as I also worked for four years as a Poet in the Schools in the National Endowment for the Arts "Artist in the Schools" program during the late 1970s and early 1980s.

I was trained in many of the current (and still ongoing – not much has changed since the 1970s) creativity training programs: Creative Problem-Solving, Future Problem-Solving, Odyssey of the Mind. I began to think about my own creative process. I learned firsthand from California's Mary Meeker about the Structure of the Intellect (Meeker, 1977), and I became one of her first advanced trainers, going around the country giving workshops on Guilford's theory of intellect and on divergent production – fluency, flexibility, and elaboration, synthesis and the like (Guilford, 1950, 1967). After giving a workshop, I would go home and write my literary works, send them

This article's precepts and concepts have been published in various iterations (see Piirto, 1998, 1999, 2004, 2006, 2007, 2008a, 2009).

out for possible publication, and receive many rejections and enough acceptances to keep me going. My own creative life contained little brainstorming, SCAMPERing, generating of alternative solutions, or creative problem-solving, as described by the flow chart handouts I had been given at the many workshops I attended.

I began to offer a course in interdisciplinary studies for undergraduate students at the small Midwestern comprehensive university where I teach, and I constructed exercises and activities that reflected the creative process of the eminent creators that I was discovering in my reading and reflection. Most creative adults talked about their creative process in more organic terms. One of the most influential essays on that topic was written by poet Brewster Ghiselin in 1952, as an introduction to his anthology, *The Creative Process*, in which he had collected essays by creative people describing what they do before, during, and after they create.[1] My artistic self gravitated toward accounts such as Ghiselin's, even though cognitive psychologists have disparaged such accounts, which they call anecdotal and retrospective, and therefore untrustworthy, saying that you cannot trust what people say about their creative processes, because how can they know what is really happening inside? (c.f. Perkins, 1981; Sternberg & Lubart, 1999). Such disparaging of the biographical is a common practice for scientifically oriented psychologists who distrust any findings that are not made with double-blind experiments. But my literary background, which dwelt on the poetic way of knowing that embraces the psychoanalytic and the depth psychological viewpoints of Freud ([1908] 1976), Jung ([1923] 1976), and Hillman (1975), caused me to doubt the psychologically scientific and to search for the experiential, the affective, and the artistic in these biographical descriptions.

I found no mention of the words *creative problem-solving, fluency, flexibility, brainstorming,* or *elaboration* in the essays, memoirs, biographies, and interviews I used to formulate the theory I am elucidating in this chapter, even though the creative process as practiced by creative productive adults has engaged thinkers of the world from prehistoric times. For example, mythological and classical perspectives on the creative process have viewed inspiration as the visitation of the Muse (Calame, 1995; Plato, *Dialogues*). Historically, the creative process has been tied with desire for spiritual unity, and with the desire for personal expression. The creative process can be viewed in the context of a person's life and the historical milieu. Contemporary psychological and religious thought have emphasized that the creative process has universal implications. What is popularly called "right-brain thinking," as well as visualization, metaphorization, and imagery, seems to help people in the creative process. The concept of two sides of the brain – one for creativity and one for plodding intellect – continues (cf. Pink, 2006), although we need the whole

---

[1]   Ghiselin was Calvin Taylor's colleague at the University of Utah. Taylor was a psychologist who was a pioneer in creativity studies who held seminal conferences on creativity in the early 1950s. Ghiselin came to creativity studies through his friendship with Taylor.

brain for creative production. The creative process is a concern of humanists as well as of scientists. While scientific experimentation has sought to demystify many popular creative process beliefs, even the most recent biographical accounts described experiences similar to those of yore. I reluctantly concluded that the repertoires of those who teach about creativity in the classroom, who often use only the Creative Problem Solving (CPS) and Guilford's cognitive aspect of divergent production in enhancing creativity, should be expanded.

Many of the creative and productive adults whose lives I read about seemed to have creative processes that could be divided into three themes, with several subthemes. (1) They seemed to have certain core attitudes toward creativity; (2) they experienced what I came to call the Seven I's (Inspiration, Insight, Intuition, Incubation, Improvisation, Imagery, Imagination); and (3) they engaged in certain general practices – a need for solitude and for rituals, they had formally studied their domains, they liked meditative practices, they were part of a community of people working in the same domain, and their creativity was part of a lifestyle, a lifelong process. I collapsed these into what I have called the Five Core Attitudes for Creativity, the Seven I's for Creativity, and the General Practices for Creativity, and I began to translate these concepts into lessons. One caveat is that all of these have not been found in all creators, but many of them have been found in most creators.

By now, I have assembled a full course – nay, more than that – of activities that tap into the mysterious, nebulous, dreamy, solitary, quietness of the creative process as it has been written about and talked about by adult creators (Table 7.1). My graduate students, teachers training to achieve a 20-semester hour endorsement for teaching the gifted in our state, have translated these principles into their own practices. In the course we used my books as primary texts (Piirto, 2004, 2007b). Over fifteen years, students have completed biographical studies seeking to confirm or deny my findings; at this date, over a thousand biographical studies have been conducted, and those findings have been mostly confirmatory.

However, although the exercises can enhance and direct the students to the creative process as creators practice it, the creators have what is absolutely necessary and nonnegotiable to creative production – they have a desire, a motivation, a passion to do the work in the domain they have chosen. And so in the beginning of the course, we focus on my notion of the thorn of fiery passion as explicated in my model of the Pyramid of Talent Development (Figure 7.1). In describing the Piirto Pyramid of Talent Development, I (1994, 1995a, 1995b, 1998a, 1999, 2000, 2002, 2004, 2006, 2007a, 2007b; Reynolds & Piirto, 2007) used the image of the thorn as a metaphor for the motivation to develop one's inborn talent. Although absolutely necessary, the presence of talent for work in the chosen domain is not sufficient. Many people have more than one talent and wonder what to do with their talents. What is the impetus and what is the reason for one talent taking over and capturing the passion and

Table 7.1. *Piirto model for creativity course for five core attitudes,*
Seven I's, and general concepts

Concept	Subconcept	Type	Exercise
Five core attitudes	Naiveté		• Raisin meditation (taste, touch, and smell) • Draw a detail (sight) • Listen closely (hearing)
	Risk-taking		• Princess and the Pea
	Self-discipline		• Thoughtlogs
	Group trust		• Field trips – bonding • Caveat about confidentiality and respect • Storytelling
	Tolerance for ambiguity		• Janusian
			• Escher • Mock debate
Seven I's	Inspiration		
		Muse	• Write a sonnet • Sculpt a holder
		Nature	• Nature walk
		Substances	• Focus question
		Travel	• Field trips–bookstore/library, a museum, a concert, a play, a movie, a reading or lecture, a place
		Dreams	• Dream interpretation
	Insight		• Grasping the Gestalt • Aha! • Zen sketching
	Incubation		• Individual creativity project
	Imagination		• Myth creation with costumes
	Imagery		• Ten-minute movie • Guided imagery
	Imagination		• Acting • Fingerpainting • Clay • Poetry • Fiction
	Intuition		• Intuition probe • Psychic intuition • Dream work
	Improvisation		• Jazz • Theater • Word rivers • Writing practice • Creative movement

(*continued*)

Table 7.1 *(continued)*

General	Creativity rituals	• Rhythm and drumming • Scat singing • Doodling • Thoughtlogs • Biographical study
	Meditation	• Meditate on beauty (15 minutes before a work of art; aesthetics; archetypes) • Meditate on the dark side (a visit to a cemetery; the shadow) • Meditate on God (bring a sacred text class; literature) • Meditate on nature (I am a naturalist; this is the day which the Lord hath made; Gaia)
	Knowledge about demands/training in the domain	• Noticing oceanic consciousness (flow)
	Salon	• Biographical study • Field trip
	Exercise	• Biographical study • Run, walk, exercise, swim, noticing when creative thoughts come
	Process of a life	• Whole course • Biographical study

commitment of the person with the talent? Which talent a person with multiple talents will choose is evident by its insistence and its continuous presence.

Much evidence exists to show that the creative person decides to pursue the development of his or her talent after some catalyst reveals what must and can happen. It may be winning a contest, receiving praise, or becoming so pleasantly engrossed in what is being created that the person realizes that it is what he or she must do at all costs. It may be a depression that is assuaged by making or creating, such that the self-healing that occurs when one is creative warns the person that he or she must create in order to prevent illness. It may come after a long period of thought and meditation. The creative person recognizes that the thorn is pricking and the call must be answered. Reynolds and Piirto (2005, 2007) and Reynolds (1990, 1997) presented a philosophical and theoretical rationale and many activities that can be used by teachers to identify and nurture the thorn.

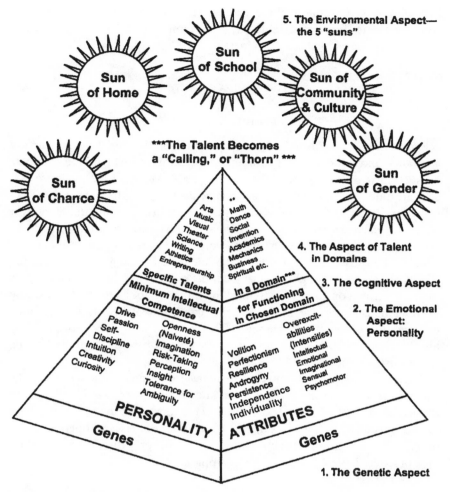

Figure 7.1. The Piirto Pyramid of Talent Development. (©Jane Piirto, 2002. All rights reserved.)

In the creativity class, students are encouraged to honor their domains of passion – that which they can't *not* do.

My students who are becoming teachers of the gifted and talented tell me that yes, indeed, the K-12 students that they work with can begin to see the creative process as something that is, at base, more a transformational journey than a cognitive one. Every week they try out the activities I created, modifying them for their own use. For a student to devise an activity at the application level that is suitable for the students one teaches is where the true creativity of the teacher is shown, and that is my goal as a professor. After each exercise, I ask the students to tell about a way this concept could be applied. The sections that follow are organized as follows: First the concept is defined; then biographical examples are given; and, finally, a class activity is described. An outline of the course activities is given in Table 7.1, and examples of a few of the activities teachers have developed are given in Table 7.2.

Core Attitude of Naiveté

Naiveté means "openness." Openness is one of the Big Five personality attributes, and some studies are finding that creators score highest in openness on such instruments as the NEO PI-R (Costa & McRae, 1992). Naiveté as a core attitude refers to the fact that creative people pay attention to the small things and are able to view their fields and domains by seeing the old as if it were new. Naiveté is an attitude of acceptance and curiosity about the odd and strange. Naiveté includes the ability to notice and to remark on differences in details. The artists Arshile Gorky and Willem de Kooning used to walk the streets of New York at night, pointing out the reflections of the few neon lights in paper thrown on the streets, remarking on the shapes and shadows, seeing the obvious as if new (Spender, 1999). Composer Igor Stravinsky (1990) called it "the gift of observation." He said, "The true creator may be recognized by his ability always to find about him, in the commonest and humblest thing, items worthy of note" (p. 11).

The raisin meditation is an exercise in taste and smell. Students eat, slowly, two raisins, noticing the taste, texture, and smell. Other exercises follow, in the senses of sight (draw a detail of this classroom), hearing (listen carefully to this music and to this noise), etc. After initial exercises in openness, and observation, students wrote about how they would apply this principle to their own practice. Table 7.2 shows some examples.

Core Attitude of Self-Discipline

When one studies the lives of creators, one often finds they have created many, many works, even though they are only known for one, two, or a few (Simonton, 1995). This self-discipline leads to the great productivity of creators. Van Gogh (1937) wrote to Theo, "I am daily working on drawing figures. I shall make a hundred of them before I paint them" (p. 45). Choreographer Agnes de Mille, noted that "all artists – indeed all great careerists – submit themselves, as well as their friends, to lifelong, relentless discipline, largely self-imposed and never for any reason relinquished" (deMille, 1991, p. 124). Most well-known creators are known for only a few of their voluminous numbers of creative works, produced through great self-discipline over a period of years. Expertise research says that one cannot contribute anything new to a domain unless one has been working in the domain for at least ten years (Ericsson, 1996).

Table 7.2. *Examples from teachers of five core attitudes, Seven I's*

Naiveté (openness to experience)	1. Do not provide an example; share an experience using sensory details.
	2. Because some children rush through things to move onto something else, I would perform the relaxation technique and then have them draw an object and commit them to a time (20 or 30 minutes) during which only that activity can be worked on.
	3. Bring in objects that are unfamiliar to the students. Play "twenty questions" on the purpose of the object, such as old kitchen utensils.
	4. Students who test out of a math unit can look at the concept through "new" eyes and create a game that would require a demonstrated mastery of the skill/concept.
	5. Taste the hardtack in simulation of a Civil War soldier's life.
Inspiration of love	1. For middle-schoolers, we would focus on a variety of choices with a gentle push in the direction of love for mankind, friends, schoolmates, teachers, etc.
	2. Share meaningful picture books about love: *Thank you Mr. Falker* (Patricia Polacco books – she uses family tales). Have students share meanings or do a write-off of an idea. Relate text to self, to other text, to world. Pose: How would the world change with love of all cultures?
	3. Teach your students about the types of love (agape, eros, filios). Teach them (especially boys) that it is OK to tell someone you love them, whether it is a family member, a friend, or a significant other.
	4. With fourth-, fifth-, and sixth-graders, the poetry, the music, the clay sculpture would all work. They have strong feelings of love at their young ages. I know this from reading their journals. Some have a passion for animals, some for young children, many for a parent, grandparent, aunt, or uncle. One has a strong bond with a neighbor.
	5. When teaching Shakespeare, love always pops up. Write sonnets when studying Shakespeare.
Imagery	1. Imagery could be used to set the stage for an event in history. Students would close their eyes and listen as the teacher painted a word picture of the scene. Descriptions of the place, the people, the emotion, the action gives a clear sense of what it was like to be there.
	2. My students always write better and more naturally after I show them video excerpts concerning the historical facts and commentary from the time and place that we are studying. This is partly due to them acquiring background knowledge, but more because the images in the film connect with the images in their own minds and blend to form new images in their writing.

(*continued*)

Table 7.2 *(continued)*

	3. Use imagery when studying bees. By using cups with different scents the students will explore how bees use their senses to find the pollen that needs to be collected. By using their sense of sound, students will listen to the flight of the bumblebee to imagine the sounds of a busy beehive. Connections made from human to nature help understand life.
	4. Before reading Susan B. Anthony's speech, "Are Women Persons?" create an imagery exercise about women and men coming to hear her speak. Maybe a woman with her child in arms. Jeers in the background. Loud noise. Posters on both sides of issue. After giving a chance to imagine setting, I will read the speech.
	5. Forming the semiregular polyhedra from the regular polyhedra; imagine the truncation of the vertices – see the new faces. Using images to predict and then concretely verify those images.
Intuition	1. First, have a discussion of intuition and then have students generate examples to spur awareness. Have students make predictions about the rest of the day (phrases they may hear, what they expect for dinner, etc.). Then they can watch and listen. This might heighten awareness of what is going on around them: 1) make connections with one another throughout the year; 2) share of experience; 3) discuss intuition: has it affected them in any way? 4) relate historical events to being intuitive; 5) conduct beginning-of-year versus end-of-year exercise with kids regarding how they have developed; and 6) relate to subjects: history/math with problem solving.
	2. Recognize hunches. Help with hunches, allow hunches, allow exploration of hunches. The I of Intuition wonders. The I of Intuition thinks this might happen . . . for academic situations. For social situations: follow your gut; go with what seems right. Allow them to give intuition a shot. Talk about times they followed/did not follow their intuition. What can we learn from this? Expose them to intuition as a part of themselves; they may not realize it.
	3. Play Battleship.
	4. Working with intuition with the kids could include work with the invention process. If they go with their gut instinct rather than try to overthink everything, what will solve this problem? How will it work?
	5. In my gifted pullout program, we study art pieces. I could have them study a painting before reading about a period of history and ask them to use their intuition to read the artist's message before. I could use a representative piece of music in the background as my intuition about the piece.

In creativity class, the thought logs are solitary creative practice, as well as practice in the core attitude of self-discipline. The students must make marks for 10 minutes a day. "Making marks" means anything – not only writing; sometimes, literally, the page for the day has consisted of one pencil slash. These are not judged or commented on. For example, this is not a dialogue between teacher and student as journals often are but rather an attempt to imitate the creative practice of creators, who all make marks about their products. They do not hold them in their heads and produce them full blown, as Venus rises from the sea, from the sperm of Zeus. It takes about 21 days to 2 months to form a habit, according to popular Internet sources. This requirement has had various results – one student used the sketches in her thoughtlog for her senior art show; others have not continued the practice but have looked back on the 15 weeks of creativity class and find there a portrait of their lives at that time.

Core Attitude of Risk-Taking

Risk-taking in creative people has been noticed since creativity began to be studied at the Institute of Personality Assessment and Research in the 1950s (Barron, 1968; Mackinnon, 1978). Risk-taking enables one to try new things. While introverted and shy creators may eschew physical risk-taking, profes-sional risk-taking in creators may be manifested in trying new forms, styles, or subjects. The kind of courage they have is the courage to stumble, fail, and, after rejection, try again. May (1975) called it *creative courage*, which is finding the new, providing the vanguard's warning of what is about to happen in the culture and showing in image and symbol, through their imaginations, what is possible. The creative artists and scientists threaten what is. That is why, in repressive societies, those creators who speak out in image and in sym-bol are jailed or exiled. Courage is required in the presence of censure and rejection.

For example, take the case of Nikola Tesla, the inventor of alternating current. He fought and won, fought and lost, trusted and was betrayed, and still remained steadfast to his principle that alternating current would eventually be preferred over direct current (Cheney, 1981). The biographical literature is rife with examples of how creators stepped into the river of their domains and became, through the years, the leader through ground-breaking risk-taking work.

The exercise used for illustrating risk-taking is called "The Princess and the Pea." Students list about five personal acts that would be risk-taking for them. They then fold this into a "pea" and place it upon their body (in a shoe, in a pocket, in a bra), where it will bother them and where they will notice it. They then take a vow to try ("I will try, Jane") to do one of the risks this semester. One student, whom I had the year before, came to me at a conference and said, "I took my risk. I finished a quilt and entered it into a quilt show. I didn't win, but I did it." This is a common result. Each class period has a time set aside to discuss progress on risk-taking.

Core Attitude of Tolerance for Ambiguity

The term *tolerance for ambiguity* comes from the research done by the IPAR (Institute for Personality Assessment and Research) group in the 1950s, especially that of the late Frank Barron. Likewise, psychiatrist Albert Rothenberg (1979), in his research, thought that creators used a Janusian process in creating, referring to the two-faced god Janus, who was able to face in opposite directions. In fact, few research findings are cut and dried – true without any doubt. The researcher must set out the study's method, participants, and findings according to a prescribed way and then must take into account the arguments that would be opposing. Albert Einstein was described by biographer Isaacson thus: "He retained the ability to hold two thoughts in his mind simultaneously, to be puzzled when they conflicted, and to marvel when he could smell an underlying unity" (Isaacson, 2007, location 536, Kindle).

Tolerance for ambiguity is necessary to not focus on one solution too soon. It is related to the "I" of Incubation. Abstract expressionist Mark Rothko would lie on a couch in his studio for hours and days, contemplating the placement of the shades and stripes and colors of his mammoth abstract paintings, rising occasionally to make a dab or two, mulling over the implications of these ambiguous forms (Breslin, 1993).

Tolerance for ambiguity is illustrated in the creativity class through a discussion of critical thinking, and its various forms. We conduct a mock debate about current issues, for example, the response to the New Orleans hurricane fiasco, with some people taking the role of Homeland Security and others taking the roles of the politicians and mayor of the city.

Core Attitude of Group Trust

In collaborative creativity, which is the kind that is usually encouraged in business and manufacturing, theater, dance, athletics, and music, the members of the group who is creating have to trust each other. Leaders make sure that the people in the group feel comfortable taking risks, are open and naïve, have acceptance for differing views and for incomplete answers, and do the work with regularity and discipline. From the raucous team in a closed room writing the jokes for a talk show or situation comedy, to the football team studying the game mistakes after losing the big one, members of a group must be confident enough and have enough trust in the process and in the group to be able to move on, to take criticism, and to do more. Working in a group creates interdependency, as each member has a role to play, and a job to do, and they cannot be egotistical or selfish, or the whole project will suffer. One person cannot dominate; everyone must play and experience together. Trust is necessary among the members of the group. Each team or ensemble has its own culture. One must look for a "good fit." Sawyer (2007) called it "group genius," and he chronicled studies where the creative community had more juice than the individual. However, even when the creator creates alone, he or she is really not alone, for what I have called the "Sun of Community and Culture" on my Pyramid of Talent Development (see Figure 7.1) is operative; the work is judged by peers and connoisseurs of the domain, and the creator socializes with and learns from other creators in the domain. No creator is isolated from the domain's rules, laws, and members.

The American Abstract Artists group in the 1930s gave each other problems at their meetings, as they experienced rivalry as to who would be the best teacher of abstract art, and who was the best abstract artist:

> Gorky suggested that they all go off and produce a painting restricted to the colors black and red. At the next meeting they would decide whose was the best. Or else they could produce a communal painting, choosing from among themselves who was the beset draftsman, who is the best colorist, who the best in textures, and so forth. They would produce a masterpiece in which each would set his hand to a different task, and they would exhibit the result, naturally, unsigned. Or – craziest idea of all – they should go home to their studios and come back next week with an object made from a light bulb and a piece of string. That would surely determine who was best qualified to teach abstraction. (Spender, 1999, p. 159)

Group trust in the creativity course is developed through affective activities, whereby students feel that they can take risks without being ridiculed or teased. The class begins with a caveat based on the advertisement for Las Vegas – "What is said in creativity class stays in creativity class," to encourage confidentiality and no gossip about what people said. At each course meeting, students must read their essays about focus questions aloud. I also take students on field trips, where they see and meet each other outside of the classroom and travel together, sharing personal experiences. It is called *meditation day* – we visit a nature preserve early in the morning in the dew and colored leaves, to meditate on nature and its inspiration for creative work; we go to a cemetery, where we reverently and quietly contemplate the dark side and its inspiration for creativity; we lunch at the art museum, where we practice "salon conversation," about the news, the arts, books read, and issues about the world; we then visit the museum, with the rule for the day being that students must simulate solitude – that is, they do the activities alone, writing notes in their thoughtlogs, with a time for sharing afterward. Students realize the difficulty of organizing field trips, with fund raising, permissions, and the like, but this activity inspires them to try and to develop group trust among their own students through the affective.

THE SEVEN I'S

Here are some further aspects of the creative process as really practiced by real creators in the arts, sciences, and business (Piirto, 2004). I have called them the Seven I's – several types of (1) Inspiration, (2) Imagery, (3) Imagination, (4) Intuition, (5) Insight, (6) Incubation, and (7) Improvisation. I have developed exercises for each of these aspects so that my students can teach them in their classes and practice them in their lives.

Inspiration

All creators talk about inspiration. Literally, inspiration is a taking in of breath. In terms of creativity, inspiration provides the motivation to create. Inspiration is a breathing or infusion into the mind or soul of an exaltation. Creators in domains discuss several types of inspiration, including the inspiration of love, of nature, through substances, by others' works, from dreams, from travel, etc.

The Visitation of the Muse: The Inspiration of Love

Being inspired by regard for another – by the gaze of desire – has been called the visitation of the muse. Muse originally meant "reminder." The Muses were inspirations for creators in various domains. Each muse had her own province in music, literature, art, and science. Calliope was the muse of epic poetry; lyric poetry had Clio (as portrayed in *The Allegory of Painting* by Vermeer); and Euterpe, Thalia, Melpomene, Terspichore, Polyhymnia, and Thalia inspired tragedy, comedy, choral singing, dance, and poetry celebrating the divine, respectively. Erato was the muse of love poetry.

The person experiencing the inspiration of the muse is inspired by that feeling and seeks to impress the object of desire, by making something or showing something. The whole industry of greetings related to February 14 is an example of the pervasive inspiration of love. One need only study art history to see the myriads of works dedicated to desire. The paintings of Gerome (the Pygmalion and Galatea series), Tura, Poussin, Chagall (*Apparition: Self Portrait with Muse*), Picasso's many models and several wives, Dali – the list is infinite. Listening to popular radio songs also illustrates the power of desire and erotic love to inspire songwriters. The desire inspires longing and the longing leads to the creative work.

Inspiration by the muse also has a mystical aspect. The people who are inspired often say that they are possessed. This idea is an ancient one, with a broad literature that is seldom referred to by psychologists working on the creative process. The Platonic view puts forth that the work comes from elsewhere than the intellect. The surrealists elaborated on this idea to theorize that the inspiration is from the unconscious, the unknown within (Maritain, 1953; Plato, *Dialogues*) – thus, "visitation" of the Muse. Creators often speak as if what they write was sent from something within yet afar. Inspirations "come." Some creators feel as if they are go-betweens, mediums. Some mysterious force impels them, works through their hands, wiggles through them, shoots from them. This type of inspiration also applies in theater. For example, some actors speak of being receptacles for their characters' souls, of being possessed. Today actors talk about "getting into" character. Athletes talk of putting on their "game face," an oblique reference to the mask, echoing the masks of Greek theater. They often have pre-performance rituals for entering the state of mind necessary. This might include putting on their makeup, meditating, or being alone for a period of time.

When I teach about the inspiration of love for creativity, I discuss the Greek terms for love – *agape* (love of God), *storge* (love of family), *filios* (brotherly love), *eros* (sexual love), and *patrios* (love of country or tribe). After I speak about how the 14-line sonnet imitates human breath through the meter of iambic pentameter, students write a love sonnet. Students sculpt a holder for this powerful love, out of clay. Clay is ground, earth, a way to contain strong emotion. Students have shared ideas about the influence of love and how to include it into their practice as teachers. Some of their ideas are given in Table 7.1.

The Inspiration of Nature

The inspiration of the natural world, from mountains, plains, animals, landscapes, insects, snakes, and all things natural, pervades much creative work, and creators are frank in their gratitude to nature. One of the most telling differences between scientists and mathematicians is that scientists are inspired by the opportunity to solve mysteries of nature, whereas mathematicians seek to solve theorems and abstract problems. Mathematics is a tool for scientists, a tool that helps them understand nature. The inspiration of nature was particularly pervasive in the works of the nineteenth-century British and American transcendentalists and romantics, writers such as Wordsworth, Coleridge, Shelly, Byron, Emerson, Dickinson, and Thoreau. They decried the industrial revolution and sought to return to simpler times when nature was preeminent, and not the conquering of nature.

The meditation day field trip mentioned earlier crystallizes the influence of nature on human beings, as we silently walk in a park in solitude, with only a camera, drawing materials, and Thoughtlog, thinking about things. During the opening exercise, I read poetry by nature poets, and an adjunct professor with a guitar plays a song about meditation on nature. The mood is set, and the instructions given. "This is your day to be selfish. You are busy mothers, fathers, people with demands upon your time, people and duties pulling you in different directions. This is your day to be alone with yourself, to be selfish. Enjoy it. Put away all thoughts of home, still all cell phones, and just take a walk in the woods." This is often the favorite part of meditation day for the students, and they in turn take their own students out of the school buildings, to meditate on nature.

Inspiration through Substances

The use of substances – alcohol, drugs, herbs – has a long and respectable reputation within the literature on the creative process in writers, artists, musicians, and others. Aldous Huxley wrote about the influence of mescaline; Samuel Taylor Coleridge about the influence of opium; Jack Kerouac about amphetamines; Edgar Allen Poe about absinthe; the seventh-century Chinese Zen poet Li Po about wine; Fyodor Dostoevsky about whiskey; Allen Ginsberg about LSD; Michael McClure about mushrooms – peyote – and also about heroin and cocaine:

The list of substances used could go on and on. The altered mental state brought about by substances has been thought to enhance creativity – to a certain extent. The partaker must have enough wits about self to descend into the abyss to reap what is learned there, but to also be able to return and put it aside. The danger of turning from creative messenger to addicted body is great, and many creators have succumbed, especially to the siren song of alcohol.

After taking drugs, Allen Ginsberg had a vision of William Blake. "I had the impression of the entire universe as poetry filled with light and intelligence and communication and signals. Kind of like the top of my head coming off, letting in the rest of the universe connected to my own brain" (Miles, 1989, p. 79). Ginsberg viewed the initial vision as the most important, most genuine experience he ever had, and he spent many years trying to recapture it through drugs and, after he gave up drugs, through meditation.

This is a difficult and often illegal way to illustrate inspiration, so I just mention it in my book (Piirto, 2004), and many students choose this focus question ["Discuss the role of substances (alcohol, drugs, hormones for sports, etc.) in the creative process" (Piirto, 2004, p. 456)], but we all know our duty about substances in the school setting. Nevertheless, the presence of substances in the creative process is duly noted.

Inspiration by Others' Creativity, Especially Works of Art and Music

Many creators are inspired by others' creativity, especially by works of art and music produced by other artists. Art inspires. Music also inspires. Friendships between artists of different genres abound in biographical literature.

The Canadian artists called The Group of Seven made history by creating an art that was truly Canadian, of the Canadian landscapes. They were Tom

Thomson, Arthur Lismer, F. H. Varley, A. Y. Jackson, Arthur Lismer, Franklin Carmichael, and Lawren Harris. Harris had studied in Berlin early in the twentieth century and then returned to Toronto, where his family was prominent. His return enabled him to re-view the Canadian landscape with naiveté, with new eyes and a sense of openness. A traveling exhibit of Scandinavian art firmed up his resolve to paint Canada (Harris, 1964). He was also influenced by the postimpressionists being exhibited at Stieglitz's Gallery 291 in New York. An art movement called synchromism (Chilvers, 1990), which was founded by American artists McDonald-Wright and Russell, whereby colors were treated like sounds (similar to synaesthesia), also influenced Harris' work. The onset of World War I and his brother's death led Harris to a nervous breakdown and early discharge from the army. While recovering, he traveled to the Algoma region north of Sault Ste. Marie, Ontario, where he experienced a spiritual reawakening that led him to paint local landscapes, unique to Canada and the north (Murray, 2003).

They later admitted one woman to their number, Emily Carr of British Columbia, who also had a passion for painting and writing about the natural world of western Canada (Carr, 1971; Crean, 2001; Walker, 1990). Carr had previously felt isolated and persecuted. Harris called Carr "one of us," and although she was very frank and independent, he encouraged her in her solitary attempts to paint what she saw in the West.

In physics, the Manhattan Project put scientists Neils Bohr, Joseph Carter, Enrico Fermi, Richard Feynman, Hans Bethe, and J. Robert Oppenheimer, among others, together in a remote location in New Mexico, where they inspired each other to perfect the atomic bomb that was later dropped on Hiroshima and Nagasaki. Bird and Sherwin (2005), biographers of Oppenheimer, said, "Wartime compelled some mild-mannered men to contemplate what was once unthinkable" (p. 222).

Singer/songwriter and poet F. Christopher Reynolds (Reynolds, 1997) has founded a movement called the ur-realist movement, where creators in various domains are encouraged to "answer art with art." When one artist, for example, writes a song, an artist friend responds with a sculpture, a poet responds with a poem, a playwright writes a scene, and the inspiration is continued through the symbolic and artistic work of friend for friend. In creativity class, this movement is mentioned, and such artistic responses of one student to another's work are common. Some of the more ambitious teachers have translated this "art with art" into their classrooms, especially teachers in the arts and creative writing.

Inspiration from Dreams

Dreams have inspired many creative works. Dreams often have personal meanings that solve problems that the dreamers are incubating. Dreams can also present images that entice creators to make their works. The Surrealists encouraged creators to use their dreams as inspiration. Freudian psychology had a great influence on the Surrealists. Both Freud and Jung wrote extensively on the significance of dreams. Freud believed that dreams are wish fulfillment and Jung asserted that dreams capture the collective unconscious – the primitive archetypes lost to us in our waking state. The Indian-born and wholly naturally talented mathematical genius Ramanujan said that his genius came in dreams from a goddess named Namagiri (Hoffman, 1998). Sculptor David Smith said that dream images were "exchange" images – that is, even though he did not "consciously use either signs or symbols . . . they've arrived in my mind as exchange images," that is "dream images, subconscious images, afterimages" (Kuh, 1990, p. 219). Einstein received an image for field theory from his dreams; Ingmar Bergman's films are notoriously based on dreams; the prophets of the Old and New Testaments were inspired by dreams (cf. the story of Joseph and the seven plagues of Egypt); the list goes on and on.

In creativity class, students are encouraged to begin to write down their dreams in their daily thoughtlogs, and several dream interpretation sessions are held, where a student shares a dream and we all use techniques from dream psychologists Reed (1988) and Aizenstadt (2004).

The Inspiration of Novel Surroundings: Travel

Travel makes it easy to maintain openness and naiveté. Being in a new setting, seeing new places makes everyone burn with the fire of apprehending what is new, novel. Often, the traveler awakens to deep insight about his or her own reality, his or her own life. Oftentimes, the subject of the creative work is the creator's homeland. Picasso and Miró traveled to Paris and painted Spain. The presence of American writers and artists in Paris in the 1920s is another example. Students are encouraged to recall how they felt when they first saw and apprehended the strange wonders of new places. I read poems from my own work in this area of inspiration (Piirto & Reynolds, 2007).

Other types of inspiration that are not elaborated on here but are experienced in creativity class form the inspiration of the dark side (of tragedy, death, mysterious goings-on), of the "I'll show you" or personal, of just plain curiosity about a phenomenon. Others are possible, but time is limited, even during a semester course.

Imagery

Imagery is also part of the creative process. The term *imagery* is psychological, the ability to mentally represent imagined or previously perceived objects accurately and vividly. Imagery is an attribute of imagination. Imagery is not only visual but also auditory, tactile, olfactory, and gustatory. Three types of studies of creativity and imagery have been done – (1) biographical and anecdotal studies of creators telling about their personal imagery and how it inspired them; (2) studies that compared people's ability to create imagery and their scores on certain tests of creative potential; and (3) studies about creative imagery and creative productivity (Houtz & Patricola, 1999).

Guided imagery training goes on in schools, in athletics, and in business and industry. This training attempts to help people learn to manipulate images in their minds. Imagery is essentially spatial, and as such, concrete evidence of the mind's power to construct. Coaches teach athletes to image their performances before they do them – they visualize the ski run, the football play, or the course for the marathon. Studies have shown that athletes who use imagery perform better (Murphy & Martin, 2002).

In creativity class, an example of guided imagery from the seminal book on classroom imagery (Bagley & Hess, 1983) is practiced. Students then think of ways they could use imagery in their own practice (see Table 7.2). One student wrote,

> I love the imagery exercise. It feels so real – helps create so much in my mind. It also makes me feel so calm and centered. I would like to do more with my students in this area. Setting a scene is a great way to make students think visually. I also might have my students take turns describing a place while the other students draw that place. I also like closing my eyes. Using the mind's eye is a great skill. I think we should all develop the ability to create in our heads.

Another imagery exercise encourages students to teach where their own students are most competent; in the apprehension of images. I have an exercise called "Ten Minute Movie," in which students are randomly given a time and a place, and must create a storyboard for a movie based in that time and place.

Imagination

Imagination in the creative process refers to a mental faculty whereby one can create concepts or representations of objects not immediately present or seen. The philosopher Aristotle considered works of the imagination such as poetry, drama, and fiction more true than history because the artist could fabricate truth from the elements of history rather than exhaustively tell all the facts. The artist is able to tell the truth on a deep level, being able to see the patterns, and the overarching themes, using the imagination. Working from the imagination is both stimulating and entertaining. Visual imagination is not the only kind that creators use. Composers imagine works in their "mind's ear," and mechanics imagine problems in their physical, spatial, array. Imaginative thought is also called daydreaming and may be called night dreaming, as well as fantasy.

Inventor Nicoli Tesla had, from his childhood, an imagination that could create images of inventions, without the help of drawings (Cheney, 1981). Tesla wrote in a 1919 essay about his inventions,

> When I get an idea I start at once building it up in my imagination. I change the construction, make improvements and operate the device in my mind. It is absolutely immaterial to me whether I run my turbine in my thought or test it in my shop. I even note if it is out of balance. (p. 12)

In creativity class, the students rummage through my costume trunk, choose a costume, and form teams whereby they imagine a myth of creation for a mask I randomly hand out. They then act out the myth. This exercise ends up in hilarity, as well as profundity, and illustrates, in a short concrete way, how the imagination, when permitted, is used in creating literary works and works of the body such as theater and dance.

Intuition

Intuition is having a hunch. "Just knowing," having a gut feeling. Creative people trust and prefer to use their intuition. Everyone has intuition, but many do not trust intuition. Intuition is ambiguous, nebulous. Biographical information, testing, historical and archival research, and experimental studies have shown that creative people use intuition [as operationally defined in instruments such as the Myers-Briggs Type Indicator (MBTI), which is based on Jung's work on types] in doing their work. For example, skipping steps in mathematics is an indicator that intuition is being used. Paul Erdös frustrated even fellow mathematicians with his tendency to skip steps and then expect that people understood him (Hoffman, 1998). Those who prefer the intuitive often prefer not to read technical manuals but rather jump straight to the tasks, using trial and error to solve the problems.

Intuition is not verifiable by scientific or empirical means. Intuition seems to be a personality preference on the MBTI for artists, scientists, and writers, entrepreneurs, mathematicians, actors, inventors, and composers (Barron, 1968; MacKinnon, 1978; Myers & McCaulley, 1985). The place of intuition in creating has long been honored. Jung (1971) thought that intuition was a message from the collective unconscious of the archetypes of the deep human experience. He defined *intuition* as "neither sense nor perception . . . a content presents itself whole and complete, without our being able to explain or discover how this content came into existence" (p. 453). Jung wrote, about introverted intuition, that it makes mystical dreamers, creative artists, or cranks: "If he is an artist, he reveals strange, far-off things in his art, shimmering in all colours, at once portentous and banal, beautiful and grotesque, sublime and whimsical. If not an artist, he is frequently a misunderstood genius . . . (Jung, 1971, p. 401).

The importance of intuitive perception of the world, of a nonconcrete but still tangible apprehension of underlying truth, informs the creator's view of life. Adapting an exercise from Reed (1988), I instruct the students to sit back to back and try to send a message, one at a time, to the person behind them. They then give each other feedback. It is sometimes amazing what people are able to intuit. Another exercise that we do in class is Zen sketching, after Franck (1983). I project a series of artworks on the screen in a darkened room, and students quickly sketch the outlines. This helps them see the big picture, a characteristic of the intuitive perceiver. This is the exercise I also use to illustrate insight, as they must immediately see the negative and positive spaces in the illustrations. One of the teachers said, about intuition:

> Intuition is something that children recognize. They already know it and are comfortable with whatever it is that they know. Therefore, they should be allowed to explore it fully. Intuition will be the base, and from it will extend elaboration, fluency, and the development of their gifts.

Another teacher said, after the evidence of how many talented and gifted people prefer intuition was presented (see Piirto, 1998b; Piirto & Johnson, 2004), "This is perplexing to me, as I am definitely a Sensing person. It's a skill I need to work on – especially making students feel comfortable with expressing such things."

Examples of how teachers would use intuition in their teaching practice are given in Table 7.2.

Insight

Insight in the creative process is the ability to see and understand clearly the inner nature of things, especially by intuition. Cognitive psychologists have researched several types of insight. The studies have shown that insight has the appearance of suddenness, requires preparatory hard work, relies on reconceptualization, involves old and new information, and applies to ill-structured problems.

Insight involves restructuring the problem so that it can be seen in a different way. Many notable creative works have originated from insights. When insight happens, we just have to say, "Aha! So that's how it works. So that's the answer. So that's what it's all about. So that's what the pattern is." The most famous image of insight is that of Archimedes rising from the bathtub, saying "Aha!" and running down the street, after he discovered the principle of the displacement of water. The "Aha!" comes after knowing the field really well, and after incubation.

Physicist J. Robert Oppenheimer was known as an idea man. He would have the insight and publish a small paper about black holes before anyone, just ahead of the scientists who would develop the elegant solutions to the problems. He published but then moved on to another insight and another, having no patience for developing the problem further (Bird & Sherwin, 2005).

Insight is demonstrated in the creativity class with the drawing exercise, after Franck, as explained earlier. Students also record their creative process in their thoughtlogs, as they decide on their individual creativity project, which is the culminating activity of the course. They cite their dreams, their walks, their drives, and such, as the moments when it all came together – their "Aha!" experiences. (Author's note: My own experiences of insight come from all of those, and also from the long swims I make several times a week.)

Incubation

Incubation as a part of the creative process occurs when the mind is at rest. The body is at rest. The creator has gone on to something else. The problem is percolating silently through the mind and body. But somewhere, inside, down there below the surface, the dormant problem is arising. A solution is sifting. Incubation was one of the steps in Wallas' four-part description of problem solving (1926). Psychologists speak of an "incubation effect," which may be caused by conscious work on the problem, and afterward, overwhelming fatigue, where what does not work has been forgotten (Navarre, 1979; Smith & Dodds, 1999). While resting, the mind works on putting unlike things together. All the ideas may be assimilated through this time period. Then awareness comes and the answer is there. Experiments have shown that if people are given a problem and told to solve it right away, they solve it less successfully than if they are given the problem and told to go away and think about it. People often incubate while driving, sleeping, exercising, even showering. Kary Mullis, a Nobel Prize winner, formulated polymerase chain reaction while driving (Mullis, 1997).

In creativity class, incubation is illustrated by the individual creativity project, which is the final product. Students spend days (some who prefer Judging and Sensing on the MBTI know instantly what they will do, but others take time), weeks, and months thinking of what they will do for this project. "Let it incubate," I say. "You'll know what you will do when you know what you will do." I must approve this project, and so I have ongoing discussions with each student, as they incubate about it. Then, when they choose their product, they incubate about how to present it, and what to make.

Improvisation

The importance of improvisation in the creative process cannot be understated. To play your musical instrument without music in front of you is frightening to some who have learned to trust in their reading ability and not in their intuition and musical memory. The idea of "play" in improvisation is a necessity. Think of children making up the game as they go along, lost in imagination, forming teams and sides in a fluid all-day motion generated by the discourse of the moment.

Improvisation seems to be a key part of the creative process. Although improvisation is a key skill in the domains of music and theater, other creators also use it. Visual artist Edward Hopper relied on improvisation as he painted: "More of me comes out when I improvise" (Kuh, 1990, p. 131). The poet James Merrill used automatic writing as an improvisational technique; William Butler Yeats used automatic writing as inspiration for work. Improvisation underlies all creativity, but in music and theater, the performer cannot revise the work as can writers or painters. Improvisation in theater and music is almost always collaborative and requires instant communication between people in the improvisation group. Improvisation reveals inner truth. Dance choreographers rely almost universally on improvisation to begin to form a dance. Martha Graham would begin to dance, outlining the pattern she wanted, and her dancers would imitate her. Then she would work on fixing the gestures so that the dancers would be moving together.

In creativity class, the exercise on imagination cited earlier also relies on improvisation. We also do several exercises from improvisational theater, such as "What Are You Doing?" and others (Newton, 1998). One class half-hour is spent dancing to a video by dancer Gabrielle Roth (1992), who is a teacher of dance as creative practice. Improvisation on several rhythms – largo, staccato, etc. – are demonstrated and the students follow.

GENERAL ASPECTS OF THE CREATIVE PROCESS

In the studies, biographies, and memoirs, several other aspects of the creative process seem apparent (Piirto, 2002, 2004): (1) the need for solitude, (2) creativity rituals, (3) meditation, (4) the need for community and culture, and (5) creativity as the process of a life.

The Need for Solitude

The core of the creative process in domains such as creative writing, music composition, mathematics, and visual arts is solitude. Solitude is not loneliness but rather a fertile state where the creator can think and work freely. Poet Amy Clampitt said, "I think the happiest times in my childhood were spent in solitude – reading ... Socially, I was a misfit" (Hosmer, 1993, p. 80). Today, those who seek solitude are often looked at askance, for people are supposed to be in society, and to crave companionship. The Internet abounds with dating sites, comradeship sites, chat rooms, and gaming sites, where for a minimal sum, people can connect with each other. People who do not have human relationships, who are not married or in love or in a family, are viewed as somehow sick. In creative people's lives, their work is often the most important thing. The iPod may be playing, for the need for broadcast noise seems to be omnipresent, but the work is often done while in solitude. Creative people may be solitary but that does not make them neurotic or unhappy. There is something transcendental about such experiences. When the person is suddenly alone and able to concentrate, she is able to decipher what may have seemed too puzzling and to unite ideas that may have seemed too different. Not being able to achieve solitude frustrates for many creative people. Loneliness often ensues after the solitude; the creator seeks society.

Solitude induces reverie. The state between sleeping and waking is relaxed, allowing images and ideas to come so that attention can be paid. What is important is a state of passivity and receptivity. Some people achieve this while cooking, cleaning, or sewing alone, walking in the woods, or during a long, boring drive. It is here, in solitude that, as Buber (1985), said, "We listen to our inmost selves – and do not know which sea we hear murmuring" (p. 11).

The thoughtlogs are companions on meditation day – the full-day field trip – as well. During each visit (woods, cemetery, museum), students must do the activity alone, reflecting on themselves and their thoughts. They are not permitted to speak to their classmates, and as they pass each other silently, in solitude, they just nod in acknowledgement to their classmates, without other communication. This is simulated solitude, and student evaluations have said, "I am such a busy person; mother, teacher, student; this day gave me a chance to reflect within, in solitude. I am grateful." Others said, "The thoughtlogs made me realize what a creative person I really am; as I made my marks each day for 10 minutes, the alone time really made me focus. I thought about things I hadn't thought about for years." Students have translated the thoughtlog experience for their students of various ages.

Creativity Rituals

Ritual is repetitive practice. Ritual involves special places, special procedures, and special repetitive acts during or before creating. Rituals are sometimes personal. The artist Arshile Gorky would, every week, scrub the parquet floor of his studio with lye and keep his hallway dark so he could see who was knocking without being observed. His biographer, Spender, said, "His working day was governed by ritual. A certain state of dreamy exhaustion was necessary, he used to say, to create freely and spontaneously" (1999, p. 83).

Ritual serves to remove the creator from the outer and propel her to the inner. Some people walk or exercise before creating, and they often get their best ideas while doing it. Some people go for a long drive. Some arrange their rooms or desks a certain way. Some like to work at a certain time of day. The approach to the work is ritualistic, and the work itself could be called, perhaps, the ceremony. Rituals are individually prescribed and performed. No one can impose a ritual on another that will be sure to prepare the creator to create.

In creativity class, students are encouraged to write in their thoughtlogs about their own rituals. They also speak of instilling certain rituals in their classrooms; for example, having everyone clean their desks before they do finger painting or having everyone breathe silently with eyes closed before writing.

Meditation

Meditation is a part of the creative process in all domains. Whether it is formal, tied to a religion like Buddhism, or informal, tied to a need for inner quiet, creators meditate. Visual artist Morris Graves said of painting, "The act is a meditation in itself" (Kuh, 1990, p. 116). A 1991 anthology of poetry contained works by contemporary poets who practice Buddhism (Johnson & Paulenich, 1991). In his introduction, poet Gary Snyder stated:

> In this world of onrushing events the act of meditation – even just a "one-breath" meditation – straightening the back, clearing the mind for a moment – is a refreshing island in the stream . . . it is a simple and plain activity. Attention; deliberate stillness and silence . . . the quieted mind has many paths, most of them tedious and ordinary. Then, right in the midst of meditation, totally unexpected images or feelings may suddenly erupt, and there is a way into a vivid transparency. (p. 1)

The vehicles for discovering one's self are breathing, sitting still, and waiting. Often the creative work follows the meditation, and the meditation is a preparatory ritual for the creative work. Others have embraced the contemplative life of the Christian monastery – for example, the poets Kathleen Norris and Daniel Berrigan.

Wonder. Beauty. Dissolving. Disintegrating. Ecstasy. What "unscientific" words these are! What language used by those who treasure precision in language. In more prosaic terms, the experimental research psychologists have categorized such responses and examples as the "mystical" approach (Sternberg & Lubart, 1999, p. 3).

In creativity class, the Meditation Day field trip is one way in which meditation is honored; the exercises mentioned here are also often preceded by closed eye, attentive posture, and deep breathing.

Creativity as Defined by Community and Culture

Recent television reality shows such as *American Idol, So You Think You Can Dance, Can You Duet, Project Runway, Top Chef,* and the like, have featured excruciatingly embarrassing auditions by people who consider themselves to be singers or dancers with enough talent and background to become professionals. These people lack experience of having received feedback and the criticism of the professional community, and are often unable to take the rejection of the judges, as they stumble, sing off-key, and blindly assume they are able to jump into the field without, as they say, "paying their dues." In fact, no domain exists where higher and higher level practice is not required. Each domain has its rules that are enforced by the domain's gatekeepers. Even those visual artists known as "primitive" (unschooled) are judged and admitted to critical acclaim and higher prices for their works by schooled and influential critics and connoisseurs. For creators who want to enter a domain not to become aware and to follow the prescribed rules of the domain is folly, for their chances of reaching a place of respect and influence are almost nil. Space does not permit an explication of the rules for proceeding in the various domains, but prospective creators must know these rules, which are almost always tacit. Creativity class is but an attitudinal, emotional, and illustrational venue; if a student wants to achieve in a domain, the thorn must pierce, and the schooling must be undertaken.

The "sun" of community and culture in the Piirto pyramid is an environmental necessity in the development of talent. Almost all creators formally belong to professional associations and groups dedicated to the pursuit of creativity in their domain of choice. That said, the creativity can also be what Csikszentmihalyi (1995) called "little c" creativity; creativity as an enjoyable way to live life.

Creativity as the Process of a Life

The creative process is viewed these days as the province of every human being, and not just of the Einsteins, O'Keeffes, or Darwins of the world, or of those who make creative products such as music or poems or mathematical formulas. People's lives are their creative products. In the past few years, the creative process has gained cachet. Best-selling books have detailed how creativity is The Way. Florida (2003) described a "creative class," which is predicted to provide the most growth in jobs and salaries for the future.

In enhancing people's creativity, teachers sometimes use methods such as visualization, imagery, metaphorization, chanting, and the formulation of affirmations. People hold sacred objects such as quartz crystals and sit beneath pyramids. They go on vision quests and bang drums, chant in tones and dance like dervishes, seeking inner peace and the guidance for living a creative life. Creativity is intertwined in the feeling of awe, of closeness to the essential that results.

Other, less exotic methods such as writing in journals (Cameron, 1992; Goldberg, 1986; Progoff, 1980), drawing (Edwards, 1979), crooning and engaging with the Mozart effect (Campbell, 1997), or dancing (Roth, 1992) are also used in teaching people to be more creative, and thus to enhance the process of their lives. Again, the educational psychology of divergent production is notably absent.

An outgrowth of the humanistic psychology movement and of the work of such humanistic psychologists as Rogers (1976), Maslow (1968), and Perls (Amendt-Lyon, 2001), this quest for inner meaning has even made it to public television stations, where fund-raising is led by former Detroit parochial high school guidance counselor, Wayne Dyer (2006), who recently talked about inspiration. Public television has also hosted the Bill Moyers *Creativity* series (1982) and the series called *The Creative Spirit* (Goleman, Kaufman, & Ray, 1992), both of which spoke to creativity as the process of a life. The Open Center and the Omega Institute in New York offer creativity-focused sessions such as intensive journal workshops, dream, singing, empowerment, improvisational theater, and dance workshops. Almost all the teachers of these workshops have written books that tell us how to enhance our creativity. All have in common the probing of the inner psyche, making one's life a work of art, and the attainment of inner peace through autotherapy done by making creative products.

Thus, the nurturing of creativity in the classroom is a partnership between the professor and the students, with the professor providing concepts and theories and the students providing the practical applications to their own practices. Along the way, the students might also make the core attitudes, seven I's, and general practices part of their own lives.

REFERENCES

Adorno, T., Frenkel-Brunwik, E., Levinson, D., & Sanford, N. (1950). *The authoritarian personality: Studies in prejudice series*, Vol. 1. New York: W. W. Norton.

Aizenstadt, S. (2004, August 25). Dream tending: Techniques for uncovering the hidden intelligence of your dreams. Workshop handout. Pacifica Graduate Institute, Santa Barbara, CA.

Amendt-Lyon, N. (2001). Art and creativity in gestalt therapy. *The Gestalt Review*, **5**, 225–248.

Bagley, M., & Hess, K. (1983). *200 Ways of using imagery in the classroom*. New York: Trillium.

Barron, F. X. (1968). *Creativity and personal freedom*. New York: Van Nostrand.

Bird, K., & Sherwin, M. J. (2005). *American Prometheus: The triumph and tragedy of J. Robert Oppenheimer*. New York: Vintage Books.

Breslin, J. E. B. (1993). *Mark Rothko: A biography*. Chicago: University of Chicago Press.

Buber, M. (1985). *Ecstatic confessions*, trans. by Paul Mendes-Flohr. New York: Harper & Row. Original published in German as *Ekstatische Konvessionen* (1909).

Calame, C. (1995). *The craft of poetic speech in ancient Greece*. Trans. by Janice Orion. Ithaca, NY: Cornell University Press.

Cameron, J. (1992). *The artist's way: A spiritual path to higher creativity*. Los Angeles, CA: Jeremy Tarcher.

Campbell, D. (1997). *The Mozart effect: Tapping the power of music to heal the body, strengthen the mind, and unlock the creative spirit*. New York: Avon.

Carr, E. (1971). *Klee Wyck.* Toronto: Clark Irwin.

Chency, M. (1981). *Tesla: Man of our time.* New York: Barnes & Noble Books.

Chilvers, I. (Ed.). (1990). *The concise Oxford dictionary of art and artists.* Oxford: Oxford University Press.

Costa, P. T., Jr., & McCrae, R. R. (1992). *NEO PI-R professional manual.* Odessa, FL: Psychological Assessment Resources, Inc.

Crean, S. (2001). *The laughing one: A journey to Emily Carr.* Toronto: HarperCollins Canada.

Csikszentmihalyi, M. (1990). *Flow.* New York: Cambridge.

Csikszentmihalyi, M. (1995). *Creativity.* New York: HarperCollins.

deMille, A. (1991). *Martha: The life and work of Martha Graham.* New York: Random House.

Dyer, W. (2006). *Inspiration: Your ultimate calling.* Carlsbad, CA: Hay House.

Eberle, B. (1996). *SCAMPER.* Waco, TX: Prufrock Press.

Edwards, B. (1979). *Drawing on the right side of the brain.* Los Angeles: Tarcher.

Ericsson, K. A. (1996). *The road to excellence: The acquisition of expert performance in the arts and sciences, sports, and games.* Mahwah, NJ: Erlbaum.

Florida, R. (2003). *Rise of the creative class.* New York: Basic Books.

Franck, F. (1983). *The Zen of seeing: Drawing as meditation.* New York: Random House.

Freud, S. ([1908] 1976). Creative writers and daydreaming. In A. Rothenberg & C. Hausman (Eds.), *The creativity question* (pp. 48–52). Durham, NC: Duke University Press.

Ghiselin, B. (Ed.). (1952). *The creative process.* New York: Mentor.

Goldberg, N (1986). *Writing down the bones.* New York: Quality Paperbacks.

Goleman, D., Kaufman, P., & Ray, M. (1992). *The creative spirit.* New York: Dutton.

Guilford, J. P. (1950). Creativity. *American Psychologist, 5,* 444–454.

Guilford, J. P. (1967). *The nature of human intelligence.* New York: McGraw-Hill.

Harris, L. (1964). *The story of the Group of Seven.* Toronto: Rous & Mann Press Limited.

Harrison, J. (1991b). *Just before dark: Collected nonfiction.* New York: Houghton Mifflin.

Hillman, J. (1975). *Re-visioning psychology.* New York: Harper Colophon Books.

Hoffman, P. (1998). *The man who loved only numbers: The story of Paul Erdös and the search for mathematical truth.* New York: Hyperion.

Hogan, J. (2001). *The woman who watches over the world: A native memoir.* New York: W. W. Norton.

Hosmer, R. (1993). The art of poetry: Interview with Amy Clampitt. *The Paris Review, 126,* 76–109.

Houtz, J. C., & Patricola, C. (1999). Imagery. In M. Runco & S. Pritzer (Eds.), *The encyclopedia of creativity,* II. (pp. 1–11). San Diego, CA: Academic Press.

Isaacson, W. (2007). *Einstein.* New York: Simon and Schuster.

Johnson, K., & Paulenich, C. (Eds.). (1991). *Beneath a single moon: Buddhism in contemporary American poetry.* Boston: Shambhala.

Jung, C. G. (1971). *Psychological types,* trans. by R. F. C. Hull. Bollingen Series XX. Princeton, NJ: Princeton University Press.

Jung, C. G. ([1923] 1976). On the relation of analytical psychology to poetic art. In A. Rothenberg & C. Hausman (Eds.), *The creativity question* (pp. 120–126.) Durham, NC: Duke University Press.

Kaufman, J., & Baer, J. (Eds.) (2004). *Creativity in domains: Faces of the muse.* Parsippany, NJ: Lawrence Erlbaum.

Kuh, K. (1990). *The artist's voice: Talks with seventeen modern artists.* Cambridge, MA: DaCapo Press.

MacKinnon, D. (1978). *In search of human effectiveness: Identifying and developing creativity.* Buffalo, NY: Bearly Limited.

Maritain, J (1953). *Creative intuition in art and poetry.* Trustees of the National Gallery of Art, Washington, DC. The A.W. Mellon Lectures in the Fine Arts. Bollingen series XXXV. Princeton, NJ: Princeton University Press.

Marland, S. (1971). *Education of the gifted and talented: Report to the Congress of the United States by the U.S. Commissioner of Education.* Washington, DC: U.S. Government Printing Office.

Maslow, A. (1968). *Creativity in self-actualizing people. Toward a psychology of being.* New York: Van Nostrand Reinhold Company.

May, R. (1975). *The courage to create.* New York: Bantam.

Meeker, M. (1977). *The structure of intellect.* Columbus, OH: Merrill.

Miles, B. (1989). *Ginsberg.* New York: Simon and Schuster.

Moyers, B. (1982). *Creativity.* Television series. Public Broadcasting Service.

Moyers, B. (1995). *The language of life: A festival of poets.* New York: Doubleday.

Mullis, K. (1997). The screwdriver. In F. Barron, A. Montuori, & A. Barron (Eds.), *Creators on creating* (pp. 68–73). Los Angeles: Jeremy P. Tarcher/Putnam.

Murphy, S. M., & Martin, K. A. (2002). The use of imagery in sport. In T. S. Horn (Ed.)., *Advances in sport psychology* (2nd ed.). pp. 405–439. Champaign, IL: Human Kinetics.

Murray, J. (1984). *The best of the Group of Seven.* Toronto: McClelland and Stewart, Ltd.

Murray, J. (2003). *Lawren Harris: An introduction to his life and art.* Toronto: Firefly Books.

Myers, I. B., & McCaulley, M. H. (1985). *Manual: A guide to the development and use of the Myers-Briggs type indicator.* Palo Alto, CA: Consulting Psychologists Press.

Navarre, J. P. (1979). Incubation as fostering the creative process. *Gifted Child Quarterly,* **23**, 792–800.

Newton, B. (1998). *Improvisation: Use what you know – make up what you don't.* Scottsdale, AZ: Great Potential Press.

Oreck, B. A., & Piirto, J. (2004, April). *Teaching artists identifying talents in the arts.* Presented at the American Educational Research Association meeting, San Diego, CA.

Perkins, D. (1981). *The mind's best work.* Boston: Harvard University Press.

Piirto, J. (1992). *Understanding those who create.* Dayton, OH: Ohio Psychology Press.

Piirto, J. (1994). *Talented children and adults: Their development and education.* New York: Macmillan.

Piirto, J. (1995a). Deeper and broader: The Pyramid of Talent Development in the context of the giftedness construct. *Educational Forum,* **59**(4), 363–371.

Piirto, J. (1995b). The Pyramid of Talent Development in the context of the giftedness construct. Talent Development. Proceedings of the European Council for High Ability Conference. University of Nijmegen, The Netherlands.

Piirto, J. (1998a). *Understanding those who create,* 2nd ed. Tempe, AZ: Gifted Psychology Press.

Piirto, J. (1998b). *Feeling boys and thinking girls: Talented adolescents and their teachers.* Proceedings of the CAPT Conference, Orlando, Florida.

Piirto, J. (1999). A different approach to creativity enhancement. *Tempo,* **XIX**, 3, 1, ff.

Piirto, J. (2000). How parents and teachers can enhance creativity in children. In M. D. Gold & C. R. Harris (Eds.), *Fostering creativity in children, K-8: Theory and practice* (pp. 49–68). Needham Heights, MA: Allyn & Bacon.

Piirto, J. (2001, Winter). The Piirto pyramid of talent development: A conceptual framework. *Gifted Children Today*, **23**(6), 22–29.

Piirto, J. (2002). *"My teeming brain": Understanding creative writers*. Cresskill, NJ: Hampton Press.

Piirto, J. (2004). *Understanding creativity*. Scottsdale, AZ: Great Potential Press.

Piirto, J. (2005). Rethinking the creativity curriculum. *Gifted Education Communicator*, **36**(2), 12–19 [*Journal of the California Association for the Gifted*].

Piirto, J. (2007a). A postmodern view of the creative process. In J. Kincheloe & R. Horn (Eds.), *Educational Psychology Handbook*. Greenwood Press.

Piirto, J. (2007b). *Talented children and adults: Their development and education*, 3rd ed. Waco, TX: Prufrock Press.

Piirto, J. (2008a). Rethinking the creativity curriculum: An organic approach to creativity enhancement. *Mensa Research Journal*, **39**(1), 85–94.

Piirto, J. (2008b). *Saunas: Poetry*. Bay City, MI: Mayapple Press.

Piirto, J. (2009. The creative process as creators practice it: A view of creativity with emphasis on what creators really do. *Perspective in Gifted Education: Creativity*. Vol. 5(pp. 42–67). Institute for the Development of Gifted Children. Ricks Center for Gifted Children, University of Denver.

Piirto, J., & Johnson, G. (2004). *Personality attributes of talented adolescents*. Presented at the National Association for Gifted Children conference, Salt Lake City, UT; at the Wallace Research Symposium, in Iowa City, IA; and at the European Council for High Ability conference, Pamplona, Spain.

Piirto, J., & Reynolds, F. C. (2007). *Journeys to sacred places: Places sacred: Poems and songs*, 2nd ed. Ashland, OH: Sisu Press.

Pink, D. (2006). *A whole new mind: Why right-brainers will rule the future*. New York: Riverhead Books.

Plato. The republic. In R. Ulrich (Ed.). (1954). *Three thousand years of educational wisdom: Selections from great documents* (pp. 31–62), trans. by P. Shorey. Cambridge, MA: Harvard University Press.

Plato. The ion. In *Great Books of the Western World*, Vol. 7. (1952). Chicago: Encyclopedia Britannica.

Progoff, I. (1980). *The practice of process meditation: The intensive journal way to spiritual experience*. New York: Dialogue House Library.

Reed, H. (1988). *Getting help from your dreams*. New York: Ballantine.

Reynolds, F. C. (1990). Mentoring artistic adolescents through expressive therapy. *Clearing House*, **64**, 83–86.

Reynolds, F. C. (1997). *Reifying creativity during the adolescent passage*. Presented at Ashland University Ohio Summer Honors Institute, July 13, 1997.

Reynolds, F. C., & Piirto, J. (2005). Depth psychology and giftedness: Bringing soul to the field of talent development education. *Roeper Review*, **27**, 164–171.

Reynolds, F. C., & Piirto, J. (2007). Honoring and suffering the thorn: Marking, naming, and eldering: Depth psychology, II. *Roeper Review*, **29**, 48–53.

Rogers, C. (1976). Toward a theory of creativity. In A. Rothenberg & C. Hausman (Eds.), *The creativity question* (pp. 296–305). Durham, NC: Duke University Press.

Roth, G. (1992). *The wave* [videotape]. Boston: Shambhala.

Rothenberg, A. (1979). *The emerging goddess: The creative process in art, science, and other fields*. Chicago: University of Chicago Press.

Sawyer, K. (2007). *Group genius: The creative power of collaboration.* New York: Basic Books.

Simonton, D. (1995). *Greatness: Who makes history and why?* New York: Guilford.

Smith, S. M., & Dodds, R. A. (1999). *Incubation.* In M. Runco & S. Pritzker (Eds.), *Encyclopedia of creativity,* Vol. 2 (pp. 39–43). San Diego, CA: Academic Press.

Spender, M. (1999). *From a high place: A life of Arshile Gorky.* Berkeley: University of California Press.

Sternberg, R., & Lubart, T. (1999). The concept of creativity: Prospects and paradigms. In R. Sternberg (Ed.), *Handbook of creativity* (pp. 3–15). London: Oxford University Press.

Stravinsky, I. (1990). On conductors and conducting. *Journal of the Conductors' Guild,* 11(1 & 2), 9–18.

Van Gogh, V. (1937). *Dear Theo.* I. Stone (Ed.). New York: Doubleday.

Walker, D. (Ed.). (1990). *Dear Nan: Letters of Emily Carr, Nan Chency, and Humphrey Toms.* Vancouver, BC: University of British Columbia Press.

Wallas, G. (1926). *The art of thought.* New York: Harcourt Brace Jovanovich.

8

Learning for Creativity

R. KEITH SAWYER

Most educators believe that creativity and the arts should be an important part of the school day. But the arts have been struggling to hold their place in the curriculum. The No Child Left Behind Act of 2001, with its mandatory annual testing on math and reading, has increased pressure on schools to demonstrate that their students are proficient in math and reading. Low math and reading scores in some school districts have led to an increasing emphasis on teaching these basic skills. When these pressures are combined with tight budgets, as is often the case in districts with high percentages of underprivileged students, administrators often choose to dedicate a larger percentage of the budget to math and literacy instruction. In exchange, the amount invested in arts education is reduced or removed completely.

It is ironic that the arts are losing their place in school curricula while creativity is increasingly in demand around the globe. In the last several decades, many of the world's most developed countries have shifted from an industrial economy to a knowledge economy (e.g., Bell, 1973; Drucker, 1993). Scholars of the knowledge age have argued that creativity, innovation, and ingenuity are more important today than ever before. Florida (2002) argued that "we now have an economy powered by human creativity" (pp. 5–6) and that human creativity is "the defining feature of economic life" (p. 21). Two recent best-selling books have extended Florida's argument to the international arena. Dan Pink, in *A Whole New Mind* (2005), argued that any activity that does not involve creativity will someday be automated; ultimately, the only jobs remaining will be those requiring creativity. Tom Friedman, in *The World Is Flat* (2005), argued that creativity is becoming increasingly important due to increasing global competitiveness.

Early in this new century, educators began to realize that if the economy was no longer an industrial-age factory economy, then our schools were designed for a quickly vanishing world (Bereiter, 2002; Hargreaves, 2003; Sawyer, 2006c). To determine how schools should respond, many major government and international bodies commissioned research efforts that resulted in reports containing policy recommendations; these reports include the Organisation for Economic Co-operation and Development (OECD)'s *Innovation in the Knowledge Economy: Implications for Education and Learning* (2004) and two high-profile 2005 reports in the United States (Business Roundtable, 2005; Council on Competitiveness, 2005). These reports, and many others, recommended transforming education to emphasize innovation. (The Council on Competitiveness report led directly to the America Competes Act of 2007, with bills introduced into both houses of Congress; the bill never became law.)

Why are schools reducing their investments in arts education, at the same time that creativity and innovation are more important than ever? In conversations with colleagues, I have discovered that there are two widespread explanations for this paradox – one is depressing and one is hopeful. I think the depressing explanation is incorrect, and I side with the hopeful explanation.

THE DEPRESSING EXPLANATION: SCHOOLS AS BUREAUCRATIC INSTITUTIONS

The depressing explanation is that schools as institutions are fundamentally incapable of incorporating innovation. There is a long tradition in the sociology of education of arguing that schools function as institutions that reproduce the social order; the social order does not really want innovative graduates, because they might use their innovation to challenge the social order. Creative thinking might be desirable within the ruling elites but not among the working classes. This neo-Marxist critique, common in the sociology of education in the 1960s and 1970s, emphasizes institutional structures such as tracking – arguing that the ultimate function of tracking is to reproduce social class. This critique has also emphasized the unwritten or informal curriculum – the subconscious and often unexamined actions taken by teachers, and the interaction patterns that become established in classrooms – and has concluded that these aspects of schools function to reproduce power structures. The logic of these largely leftist scholars is that knowledge is power; thus, those in power would attempt to preserve their knowledge advantage and deliver no more education to the masses than is absolutely necessary for them to fulfill their role at the bottom of the economic order.

I do not think the depressing explanation is tenable any longer, given the rising chorus of business and government leaders calling for more creativity and innovation. The Marxist arguments increasingly sound dated, like a distant echo from an earlier time – a time when we were still an industrial economy. The chorus of high-profile reports emanating from business leaders and government leaders makes it clear that they genuinely believe that the pressures of global competitiveness require all U.S. citizens to realize their full potential and that no country can be successful if substantial segments of the population are poorly educated and thereby incapable of playing a role in the creative age.

I accept one component of the depressing explanation: I believe that schools as institutions are organizationally structured in ways that block the spread of innovation. In most sectors of the economy, organizations have transformed away from a Weberian bureaucracy toward flatter organizational structures, with looser relationships among organizational units – the terms used by management scholars are "organic" or "loosely coupled" or "agile." Apart from government agencies, schools are the only large human institutions that still have an industrial era structure. This structure blocks innovation, and I believe that schools will have to be redesigned organizationally before education will become more creative (see Sawyer, 2006c).

Although assessment has always been a central component of schools as modern institutions, one effect of the No Child Left Behind Act of 2001 has been an increasing use of assessments to measure student, teacher, and institutional performance. I support accountability in general, but the tests in use today are largely focused on the assessment of superficial knowledge, rather than the deeper conceptual understanding that supports innovative performance. As long as schools and teachers are held accountable to industrial-age tests, they will find it difficult to shift away from industrial-age teaching methods and begin to educate for innovation. I argue that we need to develop new and fundamentally different assessments before creativity will be fully integrated into the curriculum.

THE HOPEFUL EXPLANATION: TRANSFORMING SCHOOLS BASED ON LEARNING SCIENCES RESEARCH

Just because the arts are disappearing from the curriculum does not mean that creativity is disappearing, too. What schools ultimately need is for creativity to be spread throughout the curriculum. Math, science, literacy – the learning sciences are providing research showing how all subjects could be taught to foster innovation. If creativity were introduced throughout the curriculum, the arts would no longer stand out as the one time during the school day when creativity was welcomed and fostered. Our schools are not there yet, but learning sciences research is pointing the way toward a new type of learning environment, one that helps learners master deeper conceptual understanding, problem solving, and critical thinking.

Many advocates of arts education implicitly assume that classroom instruction in other subjects follows a traditional model that I call *instructionism* (following Papert, 1993). Creativity is rarely found in instructionist classrooms, and as a result, arts educators have been able to argue that only in arts classes do students have an opportunity to be creative. This model of classroom instruction, which emerged late in the nineteenth century, is based on common-sense assumptions:

- Knowledge is a collection of *facts* about the world and *procedures* for how to solve problems. Facts are statements like "The earth is tilted on its axis by 23.45 degrees" and procedures are step-by-step instructions like how to do multidigit addition by carrying to the next column.
- The goal of schooling is to get these facts and procedures into the student's head. People are considered to be educated when they possess a large collection of these facts and procedures.
- Teachers know these facts and procedures, and their job is to transmit them to students.
- Simpler facts and procedures should be learned first, followed by progressively more complex facts and procedures. The definitions of "simplicity" and "complexity" and the proper sequencing of material were determined either by teachers, by textbook authors, or by asking expert adults like mathematicians, scientists, or historians – not by studying how children actually learn.
- The way to determine the success of schooling is to test students to see how many of these facts and procedures they have acquired.

Because this traditional vision of schooling has been taken for granted for so long, it has not been explicitly named until recently. Within the OECD/Centre for Education Research and Innovation (CERI) program "Alternative Models of Learning" project, this traditional model is referred to as *the standard model*. Along with other learning scientists, I refer to the traditional model as instructionism, because it assumes that the core activity of the classroom is instruction by the teacher. Other education researchers have called this a *transmission and acquisition* model of schooling (e.g., Rogoff, 1990), because it emphasizes that a knowledgeable teacher transmits knowledge, and a learner then acquires that knowledge.

Instructionist schools were designed to prepare students for the industrialized economy of the early twentieth century; schools based on this model have been effective at transmitting a standard body of facts and procedures to students. The goals of instructionist classrooms were to ensure standardization – all students were to memorize and master the same core curriculum – and instructionism has been reasonably effective at accomplishing these goals. Traditional schools were structured, scheduled, and regimented in a fashion that was explicitly designed by analogy with the industrial-age factory (Callahan, 1962), and this structural alignment facilitated the ease of transition from school student to factory worker.

It is extremely difficult to incorporate creativity into instructionist classrooms. Consequently, as long as instructionism continues to be the dominant form of schooling, arts educators can argue that arts classes are the only time during the school day when students can engage in creative thinking and practice. But we are now at the beginning of a historic transformation in schools – a shift away from the commonsense but unscientific instructionism of Industrial Age schooling, toward a more creative form of instruction that is based in learning sciences research. In the future, in new schools based on learning sciences research, creativity will be suffused throughout the curriculum. As a result, arts classes will no longer have a monopoly on creativity.

The learning sciences are grounded in cognitive science research of the 1970s and 1980s. By the 1980s, cognitive scientists had discovered that children retain material better, and are able to generalize it to a broader range of contexts, when they learn deep knowledge rather than surface knowledge, and when they learn how to use that knowledge in real-world social and practical settings. Studies of creative workers show that they almost always apply their expertise in complex social settings, with a wide array of technologically advanced tools along with old-fashioned pencil, paper, chalk, and blackboards. These observations have led learning sciences researchers to a *situated* view of knowledge (Greeno, 2006). "Situated" means that knowledge is not just a static mental structure inside the learner's head; instead, knowing is a process that involves the person, the tools and other people in the environment, and the activities in which that knowledge is being applied. This perspective moves beyond instructionism; in addition to acquiring content, what happens during learning is that patterns of participation in collaborative activity change over time (Rogoff, 1990, 1998).

In the creative age, memorization of facts and procedures is not enough for success. Educated graduates need a deep conceptual understanding of complex concepts and the ability to work with them creatively to generate new ideas, new theories, new products, and new knowledge. They need to be able to critically evaluate what they read, to be able to express themselves clearly both verbally and in writing, and to be able to understand scientific and mathematical thinking. They need to learn integrated and usable knowledge, rather than the sets of compartmentalized and decontextualized facts emphasized by instructionism. They need to be able to take responsibility for their own continuing, life-long learning. These abilities are important to the economy, to the continued success of participatory democracy, and to living a fulfilling, meaningful life. Instructionism is particularly ill-suited to the education of creative professionals who can develop new knowledge and continually further their own understanding.

Many of today's schools are not teaching the deep knowledge that underlies innovative activity. But it is not just a matter of asking teachers to teach different curricula, because the structural configurations of instructionist classrooms make it very hard to create learning environments that result in deeper understanding. One of the central underlying themes of the learning sciences is that students learn deeper knowledge when they engage in activities that are similar to the everyday activities of professionals who work in a discipline. This focus on authentic practice is based on a new conception of the expert knowledge that underlies knowledge work in today's economy. In the 1980s and 1990s, scientists began to study science itself, and they began to discover that newcomers become members of a discipline by learning how to participate in all of the practices that are central to professional life in that discipline. And increasingly, cutting-edge work in the sciences is done at the boundaries of disciplines; for this reason, students need to learn the underlying models, mechanisms, and practices that apply across many scientific disciplines, rather than learning in the disconnected and isolated six-week units that are found in many instructionist classrooms – moving from studying the solar system to studying photosynthesis to studying force and motion, without ever learning about connections among these units.

The implication of learning sciences research is that instruction in all subjects must undergo a dramatic transformation – a shift from instructionist delivery of facts and procedures, to the creation of learning environments that scaffold active learning and creative knowledge building. This changes the debate about how best to introduce creativity into schools. No longer is the argument about the number of arts classes or whether the arts should be integrated into other content areas; no longer is the argument about whether to add a weekly class on creativity techniques. It is now a much more profound argument about how to transform classrooms across content areas. As we engage in this argument moving forward, we will benefit from the perspective provided by the history of attempts to introduce the arts and creativity into the curriculum.

The next two sections consider, in turn, the arts and education, and creativity and education, before I turn to my recommendation – schools should use ensemble performance to foster collaborative creative learning.

ARTS AND EDUCATION

The first scholars arguing for creativity in the classroom were arts educators, because in instructionist schools, creativity is rarely found outside of arts, music, and drama classes. There are three basic arguments in support of arts education. The first argument is that the arts are important in and of themselves, and that all educated citizens should have a solid grounding in the arts, as a part of our shared cultural heritage. This argument is open to various criticisms, from the instrumental (critics argue that schools should focus on learning that is useful to graduates in the economy) to the political (Whose cultural heritage should be emphasized? What arts traditions are worthy of being taught to all students?). The argument of "art for art's sake" tends to lose in the face of tight budgets and hard choices.

When financial pressures first began to impact arts programs in schools, in the 1970s and increasingly in the 1980s, arts education researchers developed a second and a third argument in defense of arts education, both based on the argument that arts education provided unique cognitive benefits to the learner, and that these benefits would transfer to other content areas (including math, science, and literacy) and would result in enhanced learning across the curriculum.

The second argument is that education in the arts results in enhanced cognitive skills that would then transfer to other content areas, resulting in enhanced learning of all content areas. One of the hypothesized benefits of arts education was enhanced creativity. These new arguments emerged at the same time that the cognitive revolution spread through psychology and education research more generally (Eisner, 1982, 2002a; Gardner, 1973). Among the most influential cognition and arts research was that done at Harvard University's Project Zero and that written in the several books about arts, education, and development by Howard Gardner during the 1970s (e.g., Gardner, 1973). The primary impact of Gardner's 1983 book, *Frames of Mind*, was to provide academic support for educators who wanted to prevent schools from being narrowly focused on the "rationalist" content areas of math, science, and literacy. (Ironically, *Frames of Mind* was published in the same year as the "Nation at Risk" report; the latter publication contributed to a subsequent emphasis on math and science education and increased cuts in arts education.) Gardner's 2007 book, *Five Minds for the Future*, argues even more explicitly that schools should provide a broad education that incorporates not only disciplinary knowledge but also creativity, ethics, and integrative knowledge.

Many general cognitive skills have been hypothesized to result from arts education. For example, it has been hypothesized that music listening enhances spatial reasoning, that classroom drama enhances verbal achievement, and that music enhances mathematic ability. Elliot Eisner (2002b) proposed six distinctive "artistically rooted forms of intelligence": (1) experiencing qualitative relationships and making judgments; (2) working with flexible goals that emerge from the work; (3) working with form and content as inseparable; (4) working with forms of knowledge that cannot be represented propositionally; (5) thinking with a medium that has unique constraints and affordances; (6) thinking and work that results in satisfaction and flow that are inherently engaging. The question of whether the arts provide unique cognitive benefits that transfer to other content areas is controversial, with education researchers divided (see Burnaford, 2007 in support and Hetland & Winner, 2004, and Moga, Burger, Hetland, & Winner, 2000, for a critique). Yet even the strongest critics of transferable cognitive benefits argue that arts education results in unique "habits of mind" or dispositions that are valuable in learning other content areas (Hetland, Winner, Veenema, & Sheridan, 2007) – the dispositions to observe, envision, express, reflect, stretch and explore, engage and persist, develop craft, and understand the art world.

The third argument in defense of arts education is that when the arts are integrated with instruction in another content area, such as math or science, that knowledge is learned more effectively. Arguments to integrate the arts throughout the curriculum began in the progressivist era of the 1930s (Efland, p. 104); the arts as a mode of experience was a central component of John Dewey's framework (Dewey, 1934). This line of thought led to the founding of the Waldorf schools in Germany and Switzerland in the 1920s, based on the ideas of Rudolf Steiner. During this era, perhaps the strongest advocate of arts integration was Leon Winslow (1939). Winslow argued that art teachers should relate the arts to the full range of content areas.

In recent decades, arts educators use the term "interdisciplinary" or "arts integration" to refer to curricula that integrate the arts with other subjects (e.g., Burnaford, 2007; Cornett, 1999; Schramm, 2002; Strokrocki, 2005). Eisner (2002a) identified four possible curricular structures for arts integration: (1) in a unit focusing on a particular historical period or culture; (2) a unit that focuses on similarities and differences among art forms; (3) a unit that is centered on a major theme or idea that can be explored through the arts and other fields, too; and (4) a unit in which students are asked to solve a problem that has roots in both the arts and another content area. The claim is that when the arts are integrated with instruction in other content areas, learners achieve a deeper understanding, acquire an ability to think more flexibly using content knowledge, and develop enhanced critical thinking and creativity – the arts help teachers engage students more deeply and reach a broader range of learning styles (Burnaford, 2007).

It has proved to be exceedingly difficult to design studies that support these second and third arguments. The most exhaustive survey of research in support of transfer (argument 2) and arts integration (argument 3) is found in a 2007 report from the Arts Education Partnership (Burnaford, 2007). The most extensive critique of research in support of transfer is a meta-analysis by Lois Hetland, Ellen Winner, and colleagues (Hetland & Winner, 2004; Moga et al., 2000). My reading of this debate is that the jury is still out on whether arts education enhances creativity in general. In fact, the general consensus among creativity researchers is that creativity is domain-specific – that the ability to be creative in any given domain, whether physics, painting, or musical performance, is based on long years of study and mastery of a domain-specific set of cognitive structures (Sawyer, 2006b). If so, then learning how to be creative in one of the arts would not transfer to being creative in other content areas.

In the last section, I argue that a unique benefit of arts education, one that has been neglected in this research tradition, is in the enhancement of social interaction and collaboration – collective benefits that improve the learning environment by helping to create a community of learners.

CREATIVITY EDUCATION

The modern era of creativity research in psychology can be dated to 1949, when J. P. Guilford gave his legendary presidential address to the American Psychological Association (Guilford, 1950). In this address, Guilford noted that psychologists had neglected creativity, and he advocated increased funding and effort. After Guilford's stamp of approval at the national psychology conference, studies of creativity blossomed. During the years that followed Guilford's address, there were almost as many studies of creativity published in each year as there were for the entire twenty-three years prior to his address (Getzels, 1987; Sternberg & Dess, 2001).

During the 1950s, creativity became associated with *divergent thinking* – the ability to come up with many potential answers or solutions. During the 1960s, many researchers developed tests of divergent thinking. One of the most widely used measures of divergent thinking was developed by Paul Torrance and is known as the Torrance Tests of Creative Thinking, or TTCT (Torrance, 1974). Torrance's tests were designed to satisfy one of the key goals of 1960s creativity research: to identify children with high creative potential so that they could be steered into careers requiring creativity and to transform education to fully realize the creative potential of every student. The TTCT is still widely used, particularly for admission to gifted programs in schools.

Educational programs to teach creative thinking first emerged during the 1960s; Torrance (1965) developed one of the most influential programs. A series of studies has shown that participation in Torrance's creativity curriculum results in increased scores on the TTCT. But these studies have a weakness: because the students were told the course would enhance their creativity and because the students knew their divergent thinking was supposed to go up, they might have provided more answers on the post-test in a desire to conform to teacher expectations (Wallach, 1988). An even greater problem with measures of divergent thinking is that high scores on these tests do not correlate highly with real-life creative output (Guilford, 1970, 1971; also see Baer, 1993, Cattell, 1971, Wallach, 1971). Barron and Harrington (1981) reviewed hundreds of studies; in some, divergent thinking was correlated with other measures of creative achievement but in others they were not (pp. 447–448). Most psychologists now agree that divergent thinking tests do not predict creative ability and that divergent thinking is not the same thing as creativity. Creative achievement requires a complex combination of both divergent and convergent thinking, and creative people are good at switching back and forth at different points in the creative process.

Torrance's work is the model for what any advocate of creativity in schools will have to do in the future – to propose both a curriculum and an outcome assessment (because standardized assessments in use today do not reflect creative potential or ability). If divergent thinking tests are not an adequate measure of creative potential (or of "creative thinking" or "creativity"), then a high priority for researchers should be the development of a new assessment, one that is correlated with real-world creative achievement, and one that could be used to demonstrate the desired outcomes of a more creative curriculum.

LEARNING HOW TO CREATE IN GROUPS

Ensemble performances – musical groups like jazz ensembles and European orchestras, or stage performances like traditional Western theater or the performative rituals found in cultures throughout the world – require collaborative ability and interactional skill. But the form of ensemble performance that enhances collaborative ability most greatly is improvisational group performance. In improvisational theater, a group of actors creates a performance without using a script. Some groups specialize in short skits only a few minutes long, and others specialize in fully improvised one- or two-act plays of an hour or longer. These performances emerge from unpredictable and unscripted dialogue, on stage and in front of an audience. In a similar way, an effective classroom discussion emerges from classroom discourse and is not scripted by the lesson plan or by the teacher's predetermined agenda. In a study of improvised theater dialogues, Sawyer (2003b) referred to this type of discourse as *collaborative emergence*. Both classroom discussion and theater improvisations are *emergent* because the outcome cannot be predicted in advance, and they are *collaborative* because no single participant can control what emerges – the outcome is collectively determined by all participants.

Unfortunately, arts education has neglected the performing arts. For example, Arthur Efland's 2002 book *Art and Cognition* is about visual arts only. Ellen Winner's book *Invented Worlds: The Psychology of the Arts* (1982) has chapters on writing, music, and painting but omits performance. Scholars on both sides of the debate about whether arts education transfers to other content areas have almost completely omitted the performing arts (including the "pro" camp, Burnaford, 2007, and the "con" camp, Hetland et al., 2007). Instead, arts educators have emphasized solitary activities like painting and creative writing, activities that are consistent with a "lone genius" myth that creativity research dispelled long ago. This tendency is reinforced by the desire of many arts educators to teach creative traditions that have been historically important in European cultures – fine art painting, literature and poetry, and music composition or play-writing. Unfortunately, all of these "high art" activities can be engaged in as solo endeavors.

Psychologists who study creativity have reinforced this tendency in arts education with their focus on activities that result in objective, ostensible products, which remain after the creative act is complete. In scientific disciplines, these creative products include theories, experimental results, and journal articles; in the arts, products include paintings, sculptures, and musical scores. While focusing on creative products, and the psychological processes that generate them, creativity researchers have tended to neglect the creativity of performance (Sawyer, 1998). In Western cultures, creative individuals often choose to enter the sciences or the arts, where they will generate creative products such as journal articles, books, paintings, and orchestral scores.

In my 2006 book *Explaining Creativity*, I described a historical debate about the creative process as a debate between *idealist theories* and *action theories* of creativity. Idealist theorists argue that once you have the creative idea, your creative process is done. Creativity does not involve execution of the idea, and it does not require an audience. The creative work is done when the idea is fully formed in the head. This idea is often called the "Croce-Collingwood" theory, after two philosophers who promoted it in the twentieth century (see Sawyer, 2000). Those who associate creativity with divergent thought – having lots of ideas – implicitly accept the idealist theory.

Action theorists, in contrast, argue that the execution of the creative work is essential to the creative process. Action theorists point out that in real life, creative ideas often happen while the creator is working with discipline-specific materials. Once the creator begins to execute an idea, he or she often realizes that it is not working out as expected, and he or she often changes the original idea. Sometimes the final product that results is nothing like the beginning idea. Perhaps the purest example of action creativity is jazz improvisation. Because it is improvised, musicians do not know what they will play in advance; the notes emerge in the moment, from the complex give-and-take among the members of the ensemble. In improvisation, performers start playing with essentially no ideas at all.

As I argue in *Explaining Creativity*, scientific studies of creativity have shown that the idealist theory is false. Creativity takes place over time, and most of the creativity occurs while doing the work. The medium of the artwork is an essential part of the creative process, and creators often get ideas while working with their materials. However, our creativity myths align better with idealist theory than with action theory. We tend to think that ideas emerge spontaneously, fully formed, from the unconscious mind of a solitary creator. And we tend to think that executing the idea – generating the finished work – does not involve creativity. Craft, yes; talent, yes; but creativity, we associate with the moment of inspiration.

Although product creativity dominates in Western cultures, cross-cultural study indicates that performance genres may be a much more common form of creativity worldwide. Unlike product creativity, which involves a long period of creative work leading up to the creative product, in performance creativity, the creative process and the resulting product are co-occurring. This is particularly true of improvisational performance. Although most Western performance genres are scripted or composed, most non-Western performances incorporate improvisational elements.

Even though performance has rarely been a subject for creativity research, it may actually represent a more common, more accessible form of creativity than privileged domains such as the arts and sciences. If one recognizes that all social interactions display improvisational elements, then everyday activities such as conversation also become relevant to creativity theory. Creativity in interactional domains, including teaching, parenting, leadership, and mentoring, is recognized to be important to our lives and our culture (Sawyer, 2001).

Psychological studies of performance creativity are rare. Partly this is because acting is an ensemble art form, and it is hard to isolate the creative contribution of any one actor (Sawyer, 2003b). But it is also due to an implication of idealist theory – that performance is not creative but is just execution and interpretation (Kogan, 2002). For example, creativity researchers have usually separated ideation, divergent thought, and insight, on the one hand, and execution, implementation, and performance, on the other. But with performance creativity, it is particularly difficult to separate individual creativity from social and contextual factors. Perhaps this in part explains why creativity researchers have almost completely neglected performance. It is fundamentally public, interactional, and social, making it problematic for psychology's focus on the individual.

Even with solitary product creativity, the creativity does not occur all in the head, as idealist theory would have it; it occurs during the hard work of execution. Thus, explaining creativity requires a focus on the creative process. No creative process is ever completely predictable; there is always some improvisation. A painter constantly responds to his canvas and oils as he is painting. Each step of the painting changes the artist's conception of what he is doing – the first part of a painting often leads to a new insight about what to do next. Fiction writers constantly interact with the story as they write. A character or a plot line frequently emerges from the pen unexpectedly, and an experienced writer will respond and follow that new thread, in an essentially improvisational fashion. Improvisation is most essential in stage performance, because unlike the painter or the writer, performers have no opportunity to revise their work. The improvisations of the painter can be painted over or discarded, and the writer has the power of a word processor to generate the next draft. But the improvisations that occur on stage are exposed to the audience. Even the most famous artists often destroy or paint over a significant number of their canvases, and these aborted attempts are generally lost to history. But actors can never take back a bad night.

I believe that ensemble performing arts can teach creativity better than solitary product-focused art forms, and I believe that ensemble performance is more likely to result in transferable skills that are useful in learning other content areas. I base this belief, first, on the above observations that ensemble performance is more similar to real-world creativity than our mythical belief in the solitary genius artist. But to provide additional support for my claim, there is a large body of research showing that collaborative learning is more likely to result in deeper conceptual understanding and greater creative potential in math and science (Sawyer, 2006a). Much learning sciences research recommends that groups of students work together: a recommendation grounded in social constructivist findings that clashes of views and argumentation result in greater learning, and in sociocultural findings that social interaction is often a "zone of proximal development."

However, research also shows that many students do not know how to collaborate effectively (e.g., Azmitia, 1996). Participation in group musical performance or in theater could result in transferable improvements in collaborative ability. The basic insight of constructivism is that learning is a creative improvisational process (Sawyer, 2003a). Recent work that extends constructivist theory to classroom collaboration conceives of learning as *co-construction*. Both neo-Piagetian social constructivists and Vygotskian-inspired socioculturalists focus on how knowledge is learned in and by groups (see Sawyer, 2006a). Sociocultural studies have demonstrated the importance of social interaction in groups and have shown that a microgenetic focus on improvised interactional process can reveal many insights into how learning takes place. A central theme in the sociocultural tradition is the focus on the group rather than the individual. Socioculturalists analyze the entire group as their unit of analysis; cognition is "an aspect of human sociocultural activity" rather than "a property of individuals" (Rogoff, 1998, p. 68). As a result of this emphasis, these scholars examine how groups collectively learn and develop; in Rogoff's terms, learning is reconceptualized as a "transformation of participation in sociocultural activity" (1998, p. 687). Socioculturalists hold that groups can be said to "learn" as collectives, and that knowledge can be a possession or property of a group, not only of the individual participants in the group (Rogoff, 1998).

In sociocultural and social constructivist theory, effective teaching must be improvisational, because if the classroom is scripted and directed by the teacher, the students cannot co-construct their own knowledge (Sawyer, 2004). Such talk is open-ended, is not structured in advance, and is an interaction among peers, where any participant can contribute equally to the flow of the interaction.

The sociocultural perspective implies that the entire classroom is improvising together; and it holds that the most effective learning results when the classroom proceeds in an open, improvisational fashion – as children are allowed to experiment, interact, and actively participate in the collaborative construction of their own knowledge. In improvisational teaching, learning is a shared social activity and is collectively managed by all participants, not only the teacher. In improvising, the teacher creates a dialogue with the students, giving them freedom to creatively construct their own knowledge, while providing the elements of structure that effectively scaffold that co-constructive process.

Collaboration is increasingly important in professions that require creativity (Sawyer, 2007). Creative products in today's economy are not the result of isolated work; they result from collaborative teams and geographically dispersed social networks (as in open source communities). Ask any older scientist today and you will hear that science has become dramatically more collaborative in recent decades. When Dan Pink or Tom Freidman argue that the United States is losing ground because our graduates are not capable of creative work, they are not talking about isolated individuals. They are talking about the need for creative teams. Creative teaching and learning must be fundamentally collaborative and improvisational.

RECOMMENDATIONS

Conceiving of creative teaching and learning as an improvisational performance emphasizes the interactional and responsive creativity of a teacher working together with a unique group of students. In particular, effective classroom discussion is improvisational, because the flow of the class is unpredictable and emerges from the actions of all participants, both teachers and students. Several studies have found that as teachers become more experienced, they improvise more (Berliner & Tikunoff, 1976; Borko & Livingston, 1989; Moore, 1993). Creative teaching is *disciplined* improvisation because it always occurs within broad structures and frameworks. Expert teachers use routines and activity structures more than novice teachers, but they are able to invoke and apply these routines in a creative, improvisational fashion (Berliner, 1987; Leinhardt & Greeno, 1986). Several researchers have noted that the most effective classroom interaction balances structure and script with flexibility and improvisation (Borko & Livingston, 1989; Brown & Edelson, 2001; Erickson, 1982).

There is a national consensus developing that we need math and science curricula that result in cognitive outcomes that support creative performance. Our economy needs workers who can use math and science creatively, not workers who have simply memorized decontextualized facts and procedures. If math and science continue to be taught in the instructionist style, then no amount of creativity training or arts education can help redress the problem. The problem is deeper and more foundational than that, and this is why learning sciences research can be invaluable. Learning scientists emphasize the importance of deeper conceptual understanding, problem solving, and thinking – the cognitive structures that support innovative work. And learning scientists are developing innovative new curricula that are aimed at transforming classrooms, particularly in math and science.

In today's climate of accountability, what is not assessed does not count. Any benefits we claim accrue from creativity in the classroom must be demonstrated using a standardized test. No good tests for creative learning exist right now. Existing tests are inadequate, because students in many of the new learning sciences–based classrooms perform at comparable levels on existing tests to students in traditional, instructionist classrooms. However, on newer experimental tests that assess deeper conceptual understanding, students in learning sciences–based classrooms score substantially higher than students in traditional classrooms.

The most widely used test of creativity, the TTCT, is inadequate in its focus on divergent thinking. It is also inadequate because it does not assess for creative learning in specific content areas; we need new tests in both math and in the sciences. The first step in developing an assessment is to identify the claimed cognitive benefits of educating for creativity. They must be those for which there is a consensus that they are essential to graduates, to the workforce, and to the economy.

Thus, the way for schools to generate more creative graduates is not to add a new course to the curriculum called "being creative," and not necessarily to add more arts courses. No amount of such instruction can help, if the cognitive outcomes of math and science instruction are not the deeper conceptual understanding that underlies creative work. If we want creative scientists and engineers, we have to start by reforming math and science education.

To some extent, arts educators have been able to argue that the arts are essential for creative learning simply because math and science education has been so bereft of teaching for creativity. A line of reasoning that was common in the past was "the arts are creative, therefore the best way to make students more creative is to give them more arts classes." But when the discussion about school reform is reframed as a discussion about which learning environments result in the deeper conceptual understanding that supports innovative work, it changes the discussion about creativity and arts education, because in this future school all content areas would be taught in a creative manner. My argument is that all content area classrooms need to educate for innovation— when math and science education are reformed, and creativity is embedded throughout the curriculum and in all content areas, then what place is left for the arts? We can no longer easily argue that the provision of arts education is the best way to help students develop creativity-linked outcomes, whether personal expression, creativity, or flexible thinking.

CONCLUSION

Historically, discussions about creativity in school have been compartmentalized. Advocates of creativity have either argued for more arts (or for arts integration) or have argued for dedicated creativity training. Consequently, math educators and science educators have, for the most part, ignored research on creativity. But in this edited volume, we are concerned with creativity throughout the curriculum. Although much of the volume focuses on the creativity of teachers, I focused on fostering creativity in learners. I claimed that the latest findings in learning sciences research argue for a fundamental transformation of schooling, a shift to a form of teaching and learning, in all content areas, that would result in creative learners. If so, then creativity in the classroom becomes central to all content areas – not just the arts but also math, science, language arts, and social studies.

As schools transform in this direction, research on creativity and learning will become diverse. One key finding to emerge from learning sciences research is that learning trajectories are discipline specific. Designing a learning environment that leads to creative learning of one body of knowledge requires deep understanding of that body of knowledge. Research on the best ways to teach math in a creative fashion will not necessarily apply to teaching other content areas. Consequently, creativity research per se will not be the academic home of this research. It will be conducted by math educators, science educators, and other content area experts.

If the depressing explanation is correct, then schools will never change along the lines suggested by learning sciences research. Or, perhaps a few elite schools will change, so that the children of the rich and powerful acquire creative understanding. But this is not a very satisfying future for arts education – to be a tool to reproduce social inequities.

If my hopeful explanation turns out to be the right one, it will be a happier situation for arts education but also a challenging one. Once all content areas are transformed along learning sciences principles, the arts can no longer claim to be unique among all school subjects. The cognitive benefits claimed to accrue from arts education would now be acquired across the curriculum. Advocates for arts education will need to become experts in learning sciences research and will need to craft increasingly sophisticated arguments about what unique educational benefits are provided by the arts. I am impressed with the work done in the United Kingdom in connection with their current national curriculum; researchers there have shifted from talking about "arts education" to talking about "creative learning" and "possibility thinking" (Craft, Cremin, & Burnard, 2008; Craft, Jeffrey, & Leibling, 2001).

The jury is still out on whether the solitary product arts contribute to cognitive development. However, we have not concentrated enough on the performing arts and on the ensemble arts. There are almost no studies of the transferable benefits of participating in ensemble performance. I recommend future studies along these lines. I predict that participation in group improvisational arts will be shown to lead to a form of sociocultural learning – learning at a group level of analysis, not only at an individual level of analysis. Learning that can result in collective knowledge building. Learning that can contribute to the formation of a community of learners.

REFERENCES

Azmitia, M. (1996). Peer interactive minds: Developmental, theoretical, and methodological issues. In P. B. Baltes & U. M. Staudinger (Eds.), *Interactive minds: Lifespan perspectives on the social foundation of cognition* (pp. 133–162). New York: Cambridge.

Baer, J. (1993). *Creativity and divergent thinking: A task-specific approach.* Hillsdale, NJ: Erlbaum.

Barron, F., & Harrington, D. M. (1981). Creativity, intelligence, and personality. *Annual Review of Psychology, 32,* 439–476.

Bell, D. (1973). *The coming of the post-industrial society: A venture in social forecasting.* New York: Basic Books.

Bereiter, C. (2002). *Education and mind in the knowledge age.* Mahwah, NJ: Erlbaum.

Berliner, D. C. (1987). Ways of thinking about students and classrooms by more and less experienced teachers. In J. Calderhead (Ed.), *Exploring teachers' thinking* (pp. 60–83). London: Cassell Education Limited.

Berliner, D. C., & Tikunoff, W. J. (1976). The California beginning teacher study. *Journal of Teacher Education, 27*(1), 24–30.

Borko, H., & Livingston, C. (1989). Cognition and improvisation: Differences in mathematics instruction by expert and novice teachers. *American Educational Research Journal, 26*(4), 473–498.

Brown, M., & Edelson, D. C. (2001, April). *Teaching by design: Curriculum design as a lens on instructional practice.* Presented at the Annual meeting of the American Educational Research Association, Seattle, WA.

Burnaford, G. (2007). *Arts integration frameworks, research, & practice: A literature review.* Washington, DC: Arts Education Partnership.

Business Roundtable. (2005). *Tapping America's potential: The education for innovation initiative.* Washington, DC: Business Roundtable.

Callahan, R. E. (1962). *Education and the cult of efficiency: A study of the social forces that have shaped the administration of the public schools.* Chicago: University of Chicago Press.

Cattell, R. B. (1971). *Abilities: Their structure, growth, and action.* Boston: Houghton Mifflin.

Cornett, C. E. (1999). *The arts as meaning makers: Integrating literature and the arts throughout the curriculum.* Upper Saddle River, NJ: Merrill.

Council on Competitiveness. (2005). *Innovate America: National innovation initiative summit and report.* Washington, DC: Council on Competitiveness.

Craft, A., Cremin, T., & Burnard, P. (Eds.). (2008). *Creative learning 3–11: And how we document it.* Stoke-on-Trent, UK: Trentham Books.

Craft, A., Jeffrey, B., & Leibling, M. (Eds.). (2001). *Creativity in education.* London: Continuum.

Dewey, J. (1934). *Art as experience.* New York: Perigree Books.

Drucker, P. F. (1993). *Post-capitalist society.* New York: HarperBusiness.

Efland, A. D. (2002). *Art and cognition: Integrating the visual arts in the curriculum.* New York: Teachers College Press.

Eisner, E. W. (1982). *Cognition and curriculum: A basis for deciding what to teach.* New York: Longman.

Eisner, E. W. (2002a). *The arts and the creation of mind.* New Haven, CT: Yale University Press.

Eisner, E. W. (2002b). What can education learn from the arts about the practice of education? In *The encyclopedia of informal education.* Retrieved from http://www. infed.org/biblio/eisner_arts_and_the_practice_or_education.htm.

Erickson, F. (1982). Classroom discourse as improvisation: Relationships between academic task structure and social participation structure in lessons. In L. C. Wilkinson (Ed.), *Communicating in the classroom* (pp. 153–181). New York: Academic Press.

Florida, R. (2002). *The rise of the creative class and how it's transforming work, life, community and everyday life.* New York: Basic Books.

Friedman, T. L. (2005). *The world is flat: A brief history of the twenty-first century.* New York: Farrar, Straus, and Giroux.

Gardner, H. (1973). *The arts and human development: A psychological study of the artistic process.* New York: Wiley.

Gardner, H. (1983). *Frames of mind: The theory of multiple intelligences.* New York: Basic Books.

Gardner, H. (2007). *Five minds for the future.* Boston, MA: Harvard Business School Press.

Getzels, J. W. (1987). Creativity, intelligence, and problem finding: Retrospect and prospect. In S. G. Isaksen (Ed.), *Frontiers of creativity research* (pp. 88–102). Buffalo, NY: Bearly Limited.

Greeno, J. G. (2006). Learning in activity. In R. K. Sawyer (Ed.), *Cambridge handbook of the learning sciences* (pp. 79–96). New York: Cambridge.

Guilford, J. P. (1950). Creativity. *The American Psychologist,* **5**(9), 444–454.

Guilford, J. P. (1970). Creativity: Retrospect and prospect. *The Journal of Creative Behavior,* **4**(3), 149–168.

Guilford, J. P. (1971). Some misconceptions regarding measurement of creative talents. *The Journal of Creative Behavior,* **5**, 77–87.

Hargreaves, A. (2003). *Teaching in the knowledge society: Education in the age of insecurity.* New York: Teacher's College Press.

Hetland, L., & Winner, E. (2004). Cognitive transfer from arts education to non-arts outcomes: Research evidence and policy implications. In E. W. Eisner & M. D. Day (Eds.), *Handbook of research and policy in art education* (pp. 135–162). Mahwah, NJ: Erlbaum.

Hetland, L., Winner, E., Veenema, S., & Sheridan, K. M. (2007). *Studio thinking: The real benefits of visual arts education.* New York: Teachers College Press.

Kogan, N. (2002). Careers in the performing arts: A psychological perspective. *Creativity Research Journal,* **14**(1), 1–16.

Leinhardt, G., & Greeno, J. G. (1986). The cognitive skill of teaching. *Journal of Educational Psychology,* **78**(2), 75–95.

Moga, E., Burger, K., Hetland, L., & Winner, E. (2000). Does studying the arts engender creative thinking? Evidence for near but not far transfer. *Journal of Aesthetic Education,* **34**(3/4), 91–104.

Moore, M. T. (1993). Implications of problem finding on teaching and learning. In S. G. Isaksen, M. C. Murdock, R. L. Firestien, & D. J. Treffinger (Eds.), *Nurturing and developing creativity: The emergence of a discipline* (pp. 51–69). Norwood, NJ: Ablex.

OECD. (2004). *Innovation in the knowledge economy: Implications for education and learning.* Paris: OECD Publications.

Papert, S. (1993). *The children's machine: Rethinking school in the age of the computer.* New York: Basic Books.

Pink, D. H. (2005). *A whole new mind: Why right-brainers will rule the future.* New York: Riverhead Books.

Rogoff, B. (1990). *Apprenticeship in thinking: Cognitive development in social context.* New York: Oxford University Press.

Rogoff, B. (1998). Cognition as a collaborative process. In D. Kuhn & R. S. Siegler (Eds.), *Handbook of child psychology,* 5th ed., Vol. 2: *Cognition, perception, and language* (pp. 679–744). New York: Wiley.

Sawyer, R. K. (1998). The interdisciplinary study of creativity in performance. *Creativity Research Journal,* **11**(1), 11–19.

Sawyer, R. K. (2000). Improvisation and the creative process: Dewey, Collingwood, and the aesthetics of spontaneity. *Journal of Aesthetics and Art Criticism,* **58**(2), 149–161.

Sawyer, R. K. (2001). *Creating conversations: Improvisation in everyday discourse.* Cresskill, NJ: Hampton Press.

Sawyer, R. K. (2003a). Emergence in creativity and development. In R. K. Sawyer, V. John-Steiner, S. Moran, R. Sternberg, D. H. Feldman, M. Csikszentmihalyi, & J. Nakamura (Eds.), *Creativity and development* (pp. 12–60). New York: Oxford University Press.

Sawyer, R. K. (2003b). *Improvised dialogues: Emergence and creativity in conversation.* Westport, CT: Greenwood.

Sawyer, R. K. (2004). Creative teaching: Collaborative discussion as disciplined improvisation. *Educational Researcher,* **33**(2), 12–20.

Sawyer, R. K. (2006a). Analyzing collaborative discourse. In R. K. Sawyer (Ed.), *Cambridge handbook of the learning sciences* (pp. 187–204). New York: Cambridge University Press.

Sawyer, R. K. (2006b). *Explaining creativity: The science of human innovation.* New York: Oxford.

Sawyer, R. K. (2006c). The schools of the future. In R. K. Sawyer (Ed.), *Cambridge handbook of the learning sciences* (pp. 567–580). New York: Cambridge.

Sawyer, R. K. (2007). *Group genius: The creative power of collaboration.* New York: Basic Books.

Schramm, S. L. (2002). *Transforming the curriculum: Thinking outside the box.* Lanham, MD: Scarecrow Education.

Sternberg, R. J., & Dess, N. K. (2001). Creativity for the new millennium. *American Psychologist,* **56**(4), 332.

Strokrocki, M. (Ed.). (2005). *Interdisciplinary art education: Building bridges to connect disciplines and cultures.* Reston, VA: National Art Education Association.

Torrance, E. P. (1965). *Rewarding creative behavior: Experiments in classroom creativity.* Englewood Cliffs, NJ: Prentice-Hall.

Torrance, E. P. (1974). *Torrance tests of creative thinking: Norms-technical manual.* Princeton, NJ: Personnel Press/Ginn.

Wallach, M. A. (1971). *The intelligence/creativity distinction.* New York: General Learning Press.

Wallach, M. A. (1988). Creativity and talent. In K. Grønhaug & G. Kaufmann (Eds.), *Innovation: A cross-disciplinary perspective* (pp. 13–27). Oslo: Norwegian University Press.

Winner, E. (1982). *Invented worlds: The psychology of the arts.* Cambridge, MA: Harvard University Press.

Winslow, L. (1939). *The integrated school art program.* New York: McGraw-Hill.

9

Broadening Conceptions of Creativity in the Classroom

RONALD A. BEGHETTO AND JAMES C. KAUFMAN

Over the past decade, we have watched with growing concern as creativity has been squeezed out of many educational arenas. Whether it is the increasingly narrow educational outcomes that policy makers and educational leaders emphasize in their curricular policies and school improvement plans (such as marshaling scarce resources to nudge reading and math scores a fraction of a point higher) or the belief, held by some educators, that the unexpected nature of creativity is nothing more than a distracting tangent, something to be explored "later," or even a behavior problem – creativity seems to belong on the endangered species list (next to the mantled howler monkey).

The severity of this situation is even more pronounced for high-poverty and traditionally "underperforming" schools that have turned to scripted, "teacher-proof" curricula (Sawyer, 2004) in hopes of boosting performance on standardized learning assessments. It is doubtful that without opportunities to also develop creative and divergent thought that such hollow standardization efforts will boost anything – except, perhaps, longstanding educational inequalities experienced by students who attend these "standardized" schools (McNeal, 2000).

For once, however, we are addressing people who are committed to creativity in the classroom – not those who consistently find ways to resist it (as we realize they likely would only pick up this book to put it back in the mailbox of the person who misplaced it). We are writing to the reader who has bought, borrowed, or stolen this book because they are interested in the topic. We are speaking to you, frankly, because you share both our passion and our concern. We are writing to the teacher who wants to inspire his or her students' creative potential, the graduate student interested in researching how to promote creativity in the classroom, and anyone who is nodding along right now. We want to briefly share some of our ideas about how together we might aspire to help, nurture, and develop creativity in all students.

Many educators, even those who are committed to creativity, still often wonder: Is it really possible to infuse creativity in an already overpacked curriculum – yet still adhere to the curricular standards and constraints? In this chapter we hope to address this question by discussing how a broader conception of creativity can support educators in nurturing student creativity and, at the same time, allow them to fulfill curricular requirements.

DO CURRICULAR CONSTRAINTS SUPPRESS TEACHERS' ABILITY TO SUPPORT CREATIVITY?

Teachers commonly find themselves caught between contradictory demands of externally imposed mandates and supporting the needs of their students (Ingersoll, 2003). In a time of heightened school accountability (largely propelled by the No Child Left Behind Act of 2001), teachers may feel that they cannot nurture student creativity within the constraints of the required curriculum – particularly when they feel increased pressure to cover standardized curricula and prepare students for standardized learning assessments.

Indeed, as Aljughaiman and Mowrer-Reynolds have reported (2005), many teachers feel "overwhelmed" with curricular pressures and, consequently, nurturing creativity takes a backseat to more convergent, skill-and-drill approaches to the teaching the curriculum. Even prospective teachers seem to feel this pressure. For instance, Beghetto (2007a) found that prospective middle and secondary teachers generally preferred more expected (and less unique) student responses during class discussions. This preference was frequently underwritten by a concern that unexpected student responses, while potentially promising, would take class discussions "off-task."

When creativity is viewed as an "add-on" to the curriculum or expression of unconstrained originality, it makes sense that teachers might feel ambivalent about supporting creativity in their classroom. This may help explain why so many teachers, from around the globe, have been found to hold negative views about creative students. For instance, researchers (e.g., Cropley, 1992; Dawson, 1997; Scott, 1999) have found that teachers sometimes prefer less creative students in their classroom, in part because they associate creativity with nonconformity, impulsivity, and disruptive behavior. Similar findings have been reported by researchers outside of the United States. Tan (2003) found that prospective teachers in Singapore favored students who had pleasant dispositions (e.g., kind, friendly, etc.) over students who they viewed as more creative and risk-taking. Chan and Chan (1999) found that Chinese teachers associated socially undesirable traits with student creativity – explaining that in Chinese culture, nonconforming or expressive behavior can be interpreted as arrogant or rebellious. Güncer and Oral (1993) reported similar beliefs held by Turkish teachers.

Not all studies have found that teachers hold negative views about creative students (e.g., Runco, Johnson, & Bear, 1993). However, subsequent studies have indicated that teachers who hold more favorable views about creativity are not fully clear on what creativity actually means. For example, in one study (Westby & Dawson, 1995), teachers reported that they enjoyed working with creative students, yet when given adjectives that are typically used to describe creative people, they rated students who possessed those adjectives as their least favorite type of student (see also Aljughaiman & Mowrer-Reynolds, 2005). In another study, teachers and parents in America and India reported favorable views of creativity but also linked several words associated with mental illness (emotional, impulsive) with creativity (Runco & Johnson, 2002).

When teachers develop negative or conflicted views about creativity, it can result in missed opportunities for teachers to develop students' creative potential and even result in the systematic suppression of students' creative expression in the classroom (Beghetto, 2009a). This need not be the case. Teachers who successfully support creativity in their classroom recognize the complementary (and necessary) relationship between creativity and curricular constraints. This recognition is underwritten by an understanding that in order for an idea, a product, or a behavior to be considered creative it must combine originality *and* appropriateness (see Plucker, Beghetto & Dow, 2004, for a review). A few hypothetical (yet representative) examples might help clarify.

Tessa teaches mathematics, and she assigns her students a series of algebraic equations. She looks for originality in how a student chooses different strategies to get to the solution, but she also considers appropriateness (do the strategies reach the correct solutions?). Markus is a poetry teacher, and he asks his class to write Haikus. His goals for originality revolve around the students' use of language, word choice, imagery, and metaphor – but he also expects students to be appropriate and follow the specific rules for writing a Haiku. A student who hands in a free verse poem would not be considered creative in this instance (because the poem does not meet the conventions of Haiku or task constraints of the assignment). Laura is a creative shop teacher who asks her students to construct wooden birdhouses. She expects originality in their designs and decorations (students use a variety of unique architectural designs and decorate them with a variety of novel materials, including shells and beads), but the appropriateness (can a bird roost there?) is key.

When teachers recognize that creativity is not simply unconstrained originality – but actually requires a combination of originality and task appropriateness – they can see the value of curricular standards and conventions. Indeed, curricular constraints provide necessary evaluative criteria for judging whether student's original ideas, novel products, and unique accomplishments are appropriate (and therefore creative) within the constraints of particular curricular task, activity, or assignment.

Teachers who have a clear understanding of the nature of creativity – particularly with respect to the necessary combination of originality and task appropriateness – are able to avoid negative stereotypes and myths about creativity and, thereby, make room in for creativity in their curriculum

(Beghetto & Plucker, 2006). Even with this understanding it is sometimes still difficult to image how creativity might be supported as part of everyday curriculum.

WHAT ROLE CAN CREATIVITY PLAY
IN THE DAY-TO-DAY CURRICULUM?

When most people think of creative individuals, two types of images generally come to mind. The first image includes legendary pathfinders who have produced amazingly novel accomplishments (e.g., the jazz of John Coltrane, the poems of Emily Dickenson, the scientific brilliance of J. Robert Oppenheimer, or the social justice of Martin Luther King, Jr.). The other type of image is that of the more everyday creative person (e.g., the teacher down the hall who always has the most unique classroom decorations and bulletin boards, the front office secretary who makes original woven baskets, or the facilities crew member who consistently comes up with novel solutions to broken classroom equipment).

These two types of images are often described as Big-C (legendary) and little-c (everyday) creativity. This Big-C/little-c dichotomy, on first blush, seems to offer broad enough categories for classifying creativity. However, as with most dichotomies, these categories are too restrictive – particularly in the context of the classroom. Consider, for instance, a junior high student who has several unique and personally meaningful insights about how she might arrange graphics and text for her school's yearbook. If the little-c category is the only alternative to Big-C, this student's creative insights might be overlooked or unfairly compared to those of a college student enrolled in a graphic arts degree program or even a professional graphic artist who is giving a guest lecture on graphic design at a local university. Or consider the veteran teacher who has been consistently creative in her approach to teaching – it would be somewhat insulting to equate this teacher's creativity with a student-teacher who has developed one or two creative ideas about how he would like to teach a lesson. It seems equally unhelpful to compare her teaching with the transformative pedagogical approaches pioneered by Maria Montessori. If there is no middle ground between Big-C and little-c creativity, then where does this teacher's creativity fit? Neither category seems appropriate.

In an effort to address the limitations of the Big-C/little-c dichotomy, we recently proposed the Four-c Model of Creativity (Kaufman & Beghetto, 2009), which includes interpretive (mini-c) creativity (Beghetto & Kaufman, 2007) and professional (pro-c) creativity. We believe that this model better clarifies different levels of creative expression and can help teachers consider how different levels of creativity may (or may not) be appropriate for their classroom and curriculum. In the following we briefly discuss each category from smallest to largest and highlight classroom implications for each level of creativity.

INTERPRETIVE (MINI-C) CREATIVITY

Although the Big-C and little-c categories offer some level of distinction in creative expression, both conceptions tend to focus on clear-cut creative products and accomplishments – the difference pertains to level of contribution (legendary versus everyday). With respect to creativity in the classroom, this product-oriented focus is problematic for at least two reasons. First, as Runco (2005) has pointed out, the "extremely product-orientated" conceptualizations of creativity can result in educators failing to recognize the creative potential and personal creative efforts of individuals who have not yet "impressed some qualified audience" (p. 616). Even when compared among peers, the creative insights of students who currently lack the experience or knowledge necessary to fully express their ideas may be overlooked in favor of the few students who can more effectively communicate their ideas. Although producing products and persuasively communicating one's ideas are important aspects of creativity (Sternberg & Lubart, 1996), judging creative potential by the products students' produce confuses potential with accomplishment.

Second, product-only conceptualizations of creativity minimize the more dynamic and developmental nature of creativity (Cohen, 1989) – placing too great an emphasis on the more static or "fossilized" outcomes of creativity (Moran & John-Steiner, 2003). Consequently, teachers may fail to recognize that students' unique insights and interpretations might be developed into larger-c creative products and accomplishments. This failure to recognize creative potential is why some creativity researchers have worked to broaden traditional descriptions of creativity to include more "personal" (Runco, 1996), "universal" (Cohen, 1989), and "developmental" (Moran & John-Steiner, 2003) conceptions of creativity – what we have called mini-c creativity (Beghetto & Kaufman, 2007).

Mini-c creativity focuses on the *novel and personally meaningful interpretation of experiences, actions, and events* (Beghetto & Kaufman, 2007) that often occur during the process of learning (e.g., a student having a new and personally meaningful insight about how to incorporate design principles she learned in art class in her PowerPoint presentation on the Civil War). Our conception of mini-c creativity is informed by a Vygotskian (or sociocultural) view of knowledge that stresses the transactional relationship between the individual and social world. This sociocultural emphasis underscores how internal (mini-c) insights and interpretations are influenced by interactions and experiences with domain-relevant knowledge and how, under the right conditions, those internal (mini-c) insights can potentially develop into external (larger-C) contributions.

A real-life example (as reported by Lofing, 2009) may help illustrate this process. Navel orangeworms are a major pest of almond and pistachio growers. Growers commonly use bait made with almonds to attempt to control this pest. However, Gabriel Leal, a sixth-grade student and son of an entomol-ogy professor at University of California at Davis, had the mini-c insight that orangeworms might actually prefer pistachios over almonds. This insight was based on his own experiences (pistachios tasted better to him) and interpre-tation of the problem (if he preferred the taste of pistachios, then perhaps the orangeworms would also prefer pistachios). Although Gabriel's mini-c insight ran counter to prior research (and the practice of growers), he was supported in testing this idea in a controlled experiment, using his dad's University of California at Davis lab, under the supervision of one of his father's colleagues. The results of the experiment shocked researchers and confirmed Gabriel's mini-c insight. The findings have subsequently been reported at a professional conference by his father, thereby influencing the work of researchers and impacting professional knowledge and practice.

The above example illustrates how mini-c creativity can, under the right conditions, lead to larger-c contributions. Of course, most students do not have access to the kinds of supports, domain-relevant knowledge, and resources to take their mini-c ideas directly to real-world contributions (as Gabriel, the sixth-grader, did). Still, with respect to creativity in the classroom, awareness of mini-c creativity can help educators recognize that not only do students' mini-c insights have the potential to develop into external expressions of creativity but also such insights and interpretations can (and should) be considered creative in their own right.

As Vygotsky ([1967] 2004) argued, "Any human act that gives rise to some-thing new is referred to as a creative act, regardless of whether what is created is a physical object or some mental or emotional construct that lives within the person who created it and is known only to him" (p. 7). Thus, whatever the creative product (be it an idea, paintings, or performance) or the magnitude of that product (be it little-c or Big-C), it all starts with the imaginative and personal interpretations of mini-c.

Recognizing mini-c Insights

Teachers can go a long way in supporting students' creative potential by recog-nizing the mini-c insights that students have as part of their everyday learning of academic subject matter. Instead of dismissing students' unexpected (yet potentially creative) ideas, teachers who support creative expression will help their students clarify, re-voice, and, when necessary, reconsider their novel ideas and interpretations.

Recognizing and encouraging the expression of students' mini-c insights serve at least three purposes. First, it helps students develop confidence in their own creative potential. For instance, Beghetto (2006) found that positive teacher feedback about students' creativity was the strongest unique predictor of students' confidence in their own creativity. Such confidence is critical as it increases the likelihood that students will take the intellectual risks necessary to share their mini-c insights, interpretations, and ideas (Beghetto, 2009a; Nickerson, 1999).

Second, encouraging students to share their unique ideas is necessary if teachers want to help students develop their mini-c (personal) interpretations into socially vetted ideas and understandings. Teachers who support the development of students' creative potential do so, in part, by helping their students become aware of academic subject matter conventions and constraints, teaching students how to articulate the relevance of their mini-c ideas in light of those conventions and constraints and, when necessary, helping them realize that it is sometimes necessary to let go of some ideas in search of more generative ones.

Finally, encouraging students to share their mini-c insights – and providing informative feedback on those insights – can enrich other students' learning and understanding. When students have an opportunity to share their unique and meaningful strategies for solving problems in mathematics, for instance, other students can develop a more nuanced understanding of the nature of mathematical reasoning. The same can be said for most any subject area (be it unique interpretations of an historical event, novel insights about a scientific phenomenon, or a new way of interpreting the meaning of a poem). Providing students with opportunities to find their own path through problems and share their unique ideas is a sign of a powerful learning environment (Duckworth, 1996) – a learning environment that supports the development of creative potential.

In sum, teachers who support the creative potential of their students welcome and work with – rather than dismiss and suppress– students' unexpected interpretations and insights. This involves taking the time to hear and attempt to understand students' mini-c interpretations, helping students recognize when their contributions are not making sense given the curricular constraints of a particular activity or task and providing multiple opportunities for students to practice developing the skills of a particular domain or task (Beghetto, 2007b). These strategies, like other practical suggestions for supporting creativity (highlighted in various chapters throughout this book), stress the importance of teachers recognizing students' creative potential while at the same time introducing students to the conventions, standards, and existing knowledge of the various academic subject areas. As a result, students can develop the requisite academic subject matter knowledge necessary for moving from mini-c interpretations to little-c expressions of creativity.

EVERYDAY (LITTLE-C) CREATIVITY

Everyday, or little-c, creativity refers to the creativity accessible to most anyone (Richards, 2007). Examples of little-c creativity include a fourth-grader's drawing displayed at the local grocery store, a group of high-school actors' unique interpretation of *The Crucible*, and a middle-school teacher's original way of teaching grammar. Little-c creativity rarely garners the same level of pop culture attention as Big-C creativity, with the exception of sometimes highlighting cute and clever comments of a young child being interviewed on a televised talk show or the unique twist put on classic recipes submitted by readers of a popular cooking magazine.

Although pop culture pays only passing attention to little-c creativity, several theories of creativity have focused on this more everyday level of creative accomplishment. Ruth Richards' theoretical conception of everyday creativity, for instance, underscores the vital importance of not over-looking or denying the expression of little-c creativity (see Richards, 2007). Amabile's (1996) Componential Model of Creativity is another example of a theory that has relevance for more everyday or classroom level creativity. This theory highlights three components that seem necessary for creative accomplishments to occur: domain-relevant skills (e.g., learning how to play a musical instrument), creativity-relevant skills (i.e., the ability to synthesize and combine musical notes and scales in unique ways), and task motivation (i.e., the requisite commitment to put in the hard work and sustain that effort in the face of challenges).

Little-c Expectations

The little-c category is a reminder that creative expression is possible for most any student, in almost any curricular subject area, on almost any given day. Teachers who support little-c creativity in their classroom recognize that creative expression is not a distal goal or extracurricular activity but rather a seamless part of their everyday curriculum.

Elena Grigorenko and her colleagues (Grigorenko, Jarvin, Tan, & Sternberg, 2008), for instance, demonstrated how little-c creativity can be "naturally integrated into teaching and assessing domain-specific knowledge" (p. 304). Their work is particularly compelling because it focuses on the use of curriculum based assessments of creativity, which offer teachers ways to monitor and support creative thinking proficiency as part of their regular teaching of the academic curriculum.

Teachers who integrate creativity into their regular curriculum do so by including little-c expectations in their everyday learning activities, assignments and assessments. As Grigorenko and her colleagues (2008) have explained:

> The learning of new content in all areas lends itself to creative exercises. For example, when learning new math applications, students can be asked to imagine new, futuristic, or fantastical uses of such an application. Facts learned in a science exercise can be employed in visual creations (pictures and illustrations, e.g., Draw a scenario in which some typical behaviors of a sea anemone are included); in verbal creations (sentences or stories,

e.g., Write a sentence or story about sea anemones employing some facts that you have learned); as well as in numerical creations (mathematical equations or relationships, e.g., Come up with some equations that describe quantitative relationships that are important in the life cycle or in the environment of a sea anemone). (p. 305)

In addition to integrating expectations for creative expression in everyday assignments and assessments, creativity researchers have also stressed the importance of monitoring the motivational messages sent by common teaching and assessment practices. Recommendations based on a summary of this work (see Beghetto, 2005) include (1) focusing students' attention on interesting and personally meaningful aspects of tasks; (2) providing students with opportunities to generate a wide array of novel ideas and then helping them focus their attention on selecting the most promising and appropriate ideas for a given task; (3) minimizing the pressures of assessments, grades, and other forms of evaluation; (4) encouraging students to focus on self-improvement, increased effort, and seeking help from others when necessary; (5) helping students frame mistakes as a natural and necessary part of learning; and (6) helping students focus on what grades mean with respect to what they did well and how they might improve in the future.

In this way, little-c creative expression becomes part of (rather than an add-on to) the curriculum. Teachers who include little-c expectations as part of the regular curriculum not only provide students with an opportunity to develop confidence and competence in their creative expression but also help to debunk entrenched myths and stereotypes about creativity (such as, only certain people can be creative, creativity is only appropriate in the arts, and so on – see Plucker et al., 2004, for an overview).

PRO-C CREATIVITY

Pro-c creativity represents developmental and effortful progression beyond little-c that has not yet attained Big-C status. Consider the hypothetical case of Wanda, who earned her doctorate in science education. Her dissertation explored methods for teaching aquatic science to youth attending high-poverty schools along the Pacific Coast. She later received a small grant and conducted a study on how science teachers used both in-class activities and out-door excursions to reach their students. After publishing this research in a peer reviewed journal, her next project (on scientific reasoning in elementary classrooms) won an award for the best paper published that year on that topic.

If we stick to little-c/Big-C distinction, where do we place Wanda? Categorizing her efforts in the little-c category diminishes everything she has accomplished. Yet placing Wanda in the Big-C category is equally inappropriate. Her work is creative and has attained a level of creative acumen in a professional field, but she has not made the kind of contribution that will place her in the history books. The Pro-c category offers accomplished creative individuals, like Wanda, their own category.

Anyone who attains professional-level expertise in any creative area is likely to have attained Pro-c status. Not all working professionals in creative fields will necessarily reach Pro-c (a street artist at *Disneyland* who draws quick caricatures of tourists, for example, may make a good living but may not necessarily be Pro-c level creative in his or her craft). Similarly, some people may reach Pro-c level without being able to quit their day jobs. Some areas of creative expression may not provide enough monetary sustenance to allow financial freedom from other responsibilities. Yet many "amateur" artists are being creative at the Pro-c level, even if it is not their primary means of support. Most poets, for example, earn the majority of their income from teaching (or other work). A poet who has published in many top literary magazines may be highly respected yet unable to make a living solely from writing.

Although many creativity theories have focused on Big-C or little-c, there is at least one that seems more suited for Pro-c levels of creativity: the Propulsion Theory of Creative Contributions (Sternberg, Kaufman, & Pretz, 2002). Sternberg's theory highlights eight different types of creative contributions. The first type, *replication*, primarily keeps the status quo of earlier creations by reproducing past work (e.g., movie sequels, such as the seemingly endless, yet slightly different, string of *Friday the 13th* horror movies). The remaining seven types of creativity, in contrast, highlight more profound contributions. *Reinitiation*, for instance, represents contributions that move some field to a new starting point and then progresses from there (e.g., the development and progression of American jazz music). And *creative integration*, which merges two diverse domains, can result in new genres and transformative paradigms (e.g., George Lucas combining samurai movies, ancient myths, and science fiction to create *Star Wars*). Pro-c is often seen in and across these various types of creative contributions.

Of the eight types of contributions in the theory, *replication* is perhaps most relevant for the classroom (e.g., a high school student writing a sonnet in the style of Shakespeare). The other types of contributions speak to large scale innovations that usually take many years of intensive study and expert skill development and, therefore, are not feasible or directly relevant for the typical classroom.

The concept of Pro-c is consistent with the expertise acquisition approach of creativity (Ericsson, 1996), which stresses that creative expertise results from many years of deliberate practice in a particular domain. Typically a decade (or more) of intensive preparation is necessary to become an international performer in a broader range of domains including chess, sports, the arts, and science (Hayes, 1989). These years are not necessarily spent simply learning and following standard protocol but rather actively experimenting and exploring (Gardner, 1993). There is also evidence that it may take even longer than ten years of active acquisition. For example, Kaufman and Kaufman

(2007) analyzed contemporary fiction writers and found that there was a further time lag (also approximately ten years) between an author's first publication and a peak publication. This finding is consistent with Simonton's (2000) work with classical composers, which suggests that although it does take about ten years to learn a field, it may take additional time to reach a level of eminence. Some domains that focus more on consistent strong performance (such as chess, sports, and medicine) may only need ten years, whereas domains that require a variety of styles and ranges may take longer (Martindale, 1990).

Pro-c Goals

Although most K-12 students will not be in a position to produce Pro-c creations, including examples of Pro-c level creativity in the curriculum can still offer long-range goals for which students can strive. Teachers can support the development and students' movement toward attaining such goals by developing assignments and activities that highlight the specific skills, knowledge, dispositions, and strategies necessary for creative work in and across various academic disciplines (see also Piirto, 2004).

Science teachers, for instance, can have their students investigate the types of knowledge, training, and creative aspects of developing and conducting scientific inquiry. Students in language arts classes might be asked to consider the creative and imaginative aspects involved in writing (including everything from novel uses of language and grammar to how story ideas are generated and represented in various types of narratives). Math teachers might help their students explore the more creative and imaginative aspects of mathematics – everything from how mathematicians work with highly abstract concepts to the aesthetics of visual representations of quantitative data.

Teachers can also support students' understanding of creativity in the professions by inviting visits from local Pro-c professionals (e.g., architects, scientists, professional artists, novelists, and so on) who can help youngsters understand what it takes to be creative in various professions and academic disciplines. This might include everything from the type and amount of professional training required to how creativity is judged in that particular profession (e.g., peer review, critics, connoisseurs, etc.). Providing students opportunities to hear from and ask questions of Pro-c professionals can go a long way in sparking (and sustaining) students' interest in how creativity might be expressed in and across various professions.

LEGENDARY (BIG-C) CREATIVITY

As we have already mentioned, legendary creative accomplishments occupy a great deal of attention – both in the scholarly literature and pop culture representations. Indeed, many of the iconic images of creators come from television, film, and other sources of media. Consider for instance, the *A&E Biography* television program, which highlights well-known creators from history, or movies such as *Pollack, Amadeus,* or *Capote,* which offer fictionalized portrayals of genius-level creators. Big-C creativity has also garnered a great deal of attention among creativity scholars, including Simonton's (1994) work on greatness; Gruber's (1981) compelling case study of Darwin's notebooks; Gardner's (1993) case histories of Freud, Einstein, Picasso, Stravinsky, Eliot, Graham, and Gandhi; and Nandy's (1995) studies of creative scientists and mathematicians, including the great Srinivasa Ramanujan. Many of the most prominent theories of creativity focus on the most highly accomplished creators but also highlight how creativity can differ both by domain (e.g., artistic versus scientific) and type of contribution (incremental versus transformative).

Csikszentmihalyi's (1999) Systems Model, for instance, describes how accomplishments in a particular domain (such as art) are judged to be creative by gatekeepers of that domain (critics, curators, collectors, and fellow artists). This theory highlights how eminent levels of creativity are different across domains (partly because accomplishments are being judged by different criteria, conventions, and constraints).

Big-C Exemplars

Although nurturing students' smaller-c creativity is what teachers can most readily incorporate into their curriculum, legendary creators can serve as important illustrations of the highest levels of creative achievement that have occurred in various disciplines. Such Big-C exemplars can serve as particularly powerful illustrations for students when they are considered in light of the full trajectory of creative development – exploring not only how these creators progressed from having mini-c insights to producing Big-C breakthroughs, but what kinds of supports, setbacks, and chance occurrences were involved along the way. Including Big-C biographies in the curriculum can help capture students' imagination, raise important questions, and even dispel misconceptions about major creative contributions in particular fields and professions.

When sharing legendary biographies, educators need to be careful that they are not reinforcing persistent and pernicious myths about creativity (e.g., only certain people have creative potential) but rather use these biographies to illustrate the domain knowledge, access to resources, confidence, effort, and chance opportunities necessary to go from mini-c insights to trend setting breakthroughs (see also Simonton, 2004).

MAKING ROOM FOR CREATIVITY IN THE CLASSROOM: NOW AND FOR THE FUTURE

As we finish this chapter, the United States stands at a potential crossroads in many arenas – including educational policy and practice. During the past ten years or so, increased pressures have been placed on teachers to meet content standards (often at the expense of creative teaching and learning). It is unclear whether the years to come will result in more balanced educational policies (which recognize the importance of nurturing student creativity) or further exacerbate the creativity and curricular divide.

Although the future is uncertain, we remain optimistic and confident that whatever the future holds there will always be creative teachers who are committed to finding ways to integrate creativity in their curriculum. We hope that the ideas presented in this chapter help current and future educators develop new and more powerful ways to support the development of students' creative potential within the curricular constraints of the various academic disciplines.

We recognize that such work can be as challenging as it is exhilarating – particularly in the face of ever-increasing external curricular demands and constraints. Fortunately, the authors in this volume provide a variety of insights into how to navigate and work within such constraints as a means for nurturing the creative potential of all students.

Perhaps most important, in a classroom context, are the caring teachers and their allies (be they parents, researchers, or fellow educators) who are truly committed to providing opportunities for students to develop their creative potential – from the mini-c level upward. We admire all teachers who are committed to this effort and hope that our ideas can in some way further inspire and support your important work.

REFERENCES

Aljughaiman, A., & Mowrer-Reynolds, E. (2005). Teachers' conceptions of creativity and creative students. *Journal of Creative Behavior, 39*, 17–34.

Amabile, T. M. (1996). *Creativity in context: Update to the social psychology of creativity.* Boulder, CO: Westview.

Beghetto, R. A. (2005). Does assessment kill student creativity? *The Educational Forum, 69*, 254–263.

Beghetto, R. A. (2006). Creative self-efficacy: Correlates in middle and secondary students. *Creativity Research Journal, 18*, 447–457.

Beghetto, R. A. (2007a). Does creativity have a place in classroom discussions? Prospective teachers' response preferences. *Thinking Skills and Creativity, 2*, 1–9.

Beghetto, R. A. (2007b). Ideational code-switching: Walking the talk about supporting student creativity in the classroom. *Roeper Review, 29*, 265–270.

Beghetto, R. A. (2009a). In search of the unexpected: Finding creativity in the micro-moments of the classroom. *Psychology of Aesthetics, Creativity, and the Arts, 3*, 2–5.

Beghetto, R. A. (2009b). Correlates of intellectual risk taking in elementary school science. *Journal of Research in Science Teaching, 46*, 210–223.

Beghetto, R. A., & Kaufman, J. C. (2007). Toward a broader conception of creativity: A case for "mini-c" creativity. *Psychology of Aesthetics, Creativity, and the Arts, 1*, 13–79.

Beghetto, R. A., & Plucker, J. A. (2006). The relationship among schooling, learning, and creativity: "All roads lead to creativity" or "You can't get there from here?" In J. C. Kaufman & J. Bear (Eds.), *Creativity and reason in cognitive development* (pp. 316–332). Cambridge, UK: Cambridge University Press.

Chan, D. W., & Chan, L. K. (1999). Implicit theories of creativity: Teachers' perception of student characteristics in Hong Kong. *Creativity Research Journal*, **12**, 185–195.

Cohen, L. M. (1989). A continuum of adaptive creative behaviors. *Creativity Research Journal*, **2**, 169–183.

Cropley, A. J. (1992). *More ways than one: Fostering creativity*. Norwood, NJ: Ablex.

Csikszentmihalyi, M. (1999). Implications of a systems perspective for the study of creativity. In R. J. Sternberg (Ed.), *Handbook of human creativity* (pp. 313–338). New York: Cambridge University Press.

Dawson, V. L. (1997). In search of the wild Bohemian: Challenges in the identification of the creatively gifted. *Roeper Review*, **19**, 148–152.

Duckworth, E. (1996). *The having of wonderful ideas and other essays on teaching and learning* (2nd ed.). New York: Teachers College Press.

Ericsson, K. A. (Ed.). (1996). *The road to expert performance: Empirical evidence from the arts and sciences, sports, and games*. Mahwah, NJ: Erlbaum.

Gardner, H. (1993). *Creating minds*. New York: Basic Books.

Grigorenko, E. L., Jarvin, L., Tan, M., & Sternberg, R. J. (2008). Something new in the garden: Assessing creativity in academic domains. *Psychology Science Quarterly*, **50**, 295–307.

Gruber, H. (1981). *Darwin on man*. Chicago: University of Chicago Press.

Güncer, B., & Oral, G. (1993). Relationship between creativity and nonconformity to school discipline as perceived by teachers of Turkish elementary school children, by controlling for their grade and sex. *Journal of Instructional Psychology*, **20**, 208–214.

Hayes, J. R. (1989). *The complete problem solver* (2nd ed.). Hillsdale, NJ: Erlbaum.

Ingersoll, R. M. (2003). *Who controls teachers' work? Power and accountability in America's schools*. Cambridge, MA: Harvard University Press.

Kaufman, J. C., & Beghetto, R. A. (2009). Beyond big and little: The Four C Model of creativity, *Review of General Psychology*, **13**, 1–12.

Kaufman, S. B., & Kaufman, J. C. (2007). Ten years to expertise, many more to greatness: An investigation of modern writers. *Journal of Creative Behavior*, **41**, 114–124.

Lofing, N. (2009, January 10). Davis sixth-grader's science experiment breaks new ground. *Sacramento Bee* (Sacramento, CA). Retrieved January 13, 2009, from http://www.sacbee.com/education/v-print/story/1530953.html.

Martindale, C. (1990). *The clockwork muse: The predictability of artistic change*. New York: Basic Books.

McNeil, L. M. (2000). Contradictions of school reform: Educational costs of standardized testing. New York: Routledge.

Moran, S., & John-Steiner, V. (2003). Creativity in the making: Vygotsky's contemporary contribution to the dialectic of development and creativity. In R. K. Sawyer, V. John-Steiner, S. Moran, R. J. Sternberg, D. H. Feldman, J. Nakamura, et al. (Eds.), *Creativity and development* (pp. 61–90). New York: Oxford University Press.

Nandy, A. (1995). Alternative sciences: Creativity and authenticity in two Indian scientists. Delhi: Oxford University Press.

Nickerson, R. S. (1999). Enhancing creativity. In R. J. Sternberg (Ed.), *Handbook of human creativity* (pp. 392–430). New York: Cambridge University Press.

No Child Left Behind Act of 2001, Pub. 1, No. 107–110, 115 Stat. 1425 (2002).

Piirto, J. (2004). *Understanding creativity*. Scottsdale, AZ: Great Potential Press.

Plucker, J. A., Beghetto, R. A., & Dow, G. T. (2004). Why isn't creativity more important to educational psychologists? Potentials, pitfalls, and future directions in creativity research. *Educational Psychologist*, **39**, 83–96.

Richards, R. (2007). Everyday creativity: Our hidden potential. In R. Richards (Ed.), *Everyday creativity and new views of human nature* (pp. 25–54). Washington, DC: American Psychological Association.

Runco, M. A. (1996). Personal creativity: Definition and developmental issues. *New Directions for Child Development*, **72**, 3–30.

Runco, M. A. (2005). Motivation, competence, and creativity. In A. Elliott & C. Dweck (Eds.), *Handbook of achievement motivation and competence* (pp. 609–623). New York: Guilford.

Runco, M. A., & Johnson, D. J. (2002). Parents' and teachers' implicit theories of children's creativity: A cross-cultural perspective. *Creativity Research Journal*, **14**, 427–439.

Runco, M. A., Johnson, D. J., & Bear, P. K. (1993). Parents' and teachers' implicit theories of children's creativity. *Child Study Journal*, **23**, 91–113.

Sawyer, R. K. (2004). Creative teaching: Collaborative discussion as disciplined improvisation. *Educational Researcher*, **33**, 12–20.

Scott, C. L. (1999). Teachers' biases toward creative children. *Creativity Research Journal*, **12**, 321–337.

Simonton, D. K. (1994). *Greatness: Who makes history and why*. New York: Guilford Press.

Simonton, D. K. (2000). Creative development as acquired expertise: Theoretical issues and an empirical test. *Developmental Review*, **20**, 283–318.

Simonton, D. K. (2004). *Creativity in science: Chance, logic, genius, and zeitgeist*. Cambridge, UK: Cambridge University Press.

Sternberg, R. J., Kaufman, J. C., & Pretz, J. E. (2002). *The creativity conundrum*. New York: Psychology Press.

Sternberg, R. J., & Lubart, T. I. (1996). Investing in creativity. *American Psychologist*, **51**, 677–688.

Tan, A. G. (2003). Teaching the Chinese learner: Psychological and pedagogical perspectives. *International Journal of Educational Development*, **23**, 233–240.

Vygotsky, L. S. (2004). Imagination and creativity in childhood. (M. E. Sharpe, Inc., Trans.). *Journal of Russian and East European Psychology*, **42**, 7–97. (Original work published 1967).

Westby, E. L., & Dawson, V. L. (1995). Creativity: Asset or burden in the classroom? *Creativity Research Journal*, **8**, 1–10.

10

Everyday Creativity in the Classroom: A Trip through Time with Seven Suggestions

RUTH RICHARDS

Years ago, while a secondary-level student teacher (I was getting a teaching credential in physics and math, and also in visual arts), a friend asked me if I would visit the fourth- through six-grade class at a small and quite charming three-room schoolhouse – truly a little wooden house – in a quaint rural California town, to teach a guest science lesson. I was learning some good things and wanted to try them out, so I said, "Sure!"

There were three schoolrooms: My friend's personally designed classroom (K–3), the upper elementary room (4–6), and finally what was at that time called a junior high school (7–8) – here the junior high school *room*. My friend's K-3 room had the distinction of red and white-checkered curtains, special areas, and clustered furniture, a very homey feel, and she often played music, especially classical, for the kids. As I recall, there was a lot of time for reading and thinking, and I can picture them happily scattered on the floor with their books, on large cushions. They also got to ask lots of questions.

I was encouraged – surely my own creative lesson plan would be welcome. I was training to work with secondary-level kids, not with fourth- through six-graders. But I was bringing challenging activities for any age, I thought; surely my attempts would be appreciated. Yet, as it turned out, they were not appreciated by everyone. This experience has actually motivated me for years.

TEACHING "DISCOVERY SCIENCE"

Thanks to my gifted professor at the University of California, Berkeley, School of Education, the late John David Miller, I had been doing "discovery science," as a student teacher in two different high school classrooms, and had also assisted Dr. Miller in a "discovery science" workshop for junior high school teachers. Let me add, in honor of Dr. Miller, that he was a role model

---

Some parts of this chapter were adapted from a paper presented at the 2006 annual meeting of the American Psychological Association.

extraordinaire, joyous at the marvels of science, and sharing infectious enthusiasm with us as we learned to discover scientific wonders for ourselves and help others do likewise.

Discovery science was designed, of course, to help secondary-level students come up with ideas and conclusions on their own. Certainly, the students might memorize an equation or two. But this was often done after they had discovered – or at least validated – the equation for themselves. It was not quite as hard as for Sir Isaac Newton, discovering gravity, after the fabled apple fell on his head, but our students did discover that "gravity works." And they discovered just *how* it works, too.

What happened on my visit? I arrived as visitor at the fourth- through six-grade classroom complete with a couple of dozen "C" batteries, small light bulbs, and wires. This was not like my friend's classroom. At fourth grade, it seems, one gets serious. There were dark wooden desks set in rows, with a portion of the writing desk that curves out in front so you can put your paper on it.

The kids got in pairs, clustering around one desk or another, on their feet instead of sitting. Each pair got one of three things: battery, wire, and bulb. The assignment? Try to make the light bulb light up!

The kids were fascinated, totally engaged. How would one do this? They would touch the bulb stem to the end of the battery. Just sitting there, bulb on battery. Nothing. No luck.

They struggled, they worked. The kids knew the wire had something to do with it. How do you attach a wire to a bare bulb? Don't you have to have two wires? Why does the battery have another metal end? Is that important? What is it that makes a bulb light up anyway?

Suddenly, one pair got it! They'd made a circuit! The electricity flowed from battery to bulb, from another bulb part to the other end of the battery. The bulb lit up brightly!

There were whoops and screams of delight and joy. Other fourth- through six-graders were running around the room to see for themselves and then racing back to their own desks to try it with their own equipment. Another bulb lit up. And another! A room full of light bulbs were shining, and the kids were just delighted. They were truly jumping for joy!

Then, back to the desks, a quieter time, discussion, electrons, currents, wire conductors, energy in batteries, plugs in the wall – why does the cord have two parts, anyway? There was a whole lot of interest, until finally, the time was up. Out of the room went the kids, chattering, and still, themselves, energized.

NOT EVERY TEACHER WANTS THE SAME RESULT

Now, as calm settled, and the room cleared, the regular teacher came up to me. She looked very embarrassed.

"I'm so sorry!" she said.

"Sorry about what?" From my end, I thought things had gone very well.

"About the way they acted!" she said. "The kids have never done *anything*
   like that before."
What?! I suddenly had a picture of the kids sitting quietly in long rows,
   raising their hands and speaking when they were called on. Never had they
   run around the room, at least not until now, or whooped, or shouted or
   spoken out of turn.

To be fair, I was fresh and green, and used to older kids. Perhaps I could
have kept this group a little quieter. A little more in line. But on the other hand,
wasn't this was the joy of creative discovery?

I reassured the teacher. I told her this was the "discovery" method and a
certain amount of disorder and enthusiasm were allowed. I said I had even
allowed and encouraged this to happen. Somehow, though, she was reluctant
to blame it on me and saw this as kids getting "out of control" and forgetting
their classroom discipline.

I came away from this experience chastened. At least, I knew one
thing – these kids would go home and look at lamps and cords in their
homes in an entirely new way. They would also wonder what was going on
behind their walls to make the ceiling fixture light up when a wall switch was
flipped.

These kids would not soon forget how they had lit up their own little bulbs
at school. Nor would they forget that they (to varying degrees) had figured it
out for themselves. Furthermore, they had found new evidence that they, and
their own experience, could be an important source of knowledge. As part of
this, they had seen that they could initiate a reasoned trial and error process,
that they could make mistakes – and that this was even a good thing that
helped them narrow in on a solution. Finally, they had seen that doing science
can be fun. *Whatever the teacher's response had been, I knew that the students
had learned – had really learned.*

CREATIVITY – WHO WANTS IT AND WHY?

Creativity had supposedly already become key in education, or at least in my
progressive part of the woods. The light bulb experiment was a well-tried part
of an experimental curriculum. I had done it with success with urban high-
schoolers but in a setting that had fully bought in to the "discovery" method.
What was "creativity"? After Barron (1969), we asked for only two criteria, in
whatever domain one might choose: *originality* and *meaningfulness.*

This was quite a few years ago, actually, and twelve years after Sputnik,
the Russian satellite, had circled the globe, leaving Americans gazing up at the
heavens, worrying about the "Cold War" and whether America was losing the
"space race." We were still in the wake of that event; and we, the USA, needed
more creativity in science! The call had gone out. The young people were
to be stimulated. The video *October Sky,* with Jake Gyllenhaal as the talented

rocket-building high school science student, captures the era rather well. Interestingly, the town I visited was a little closer to that kind of setting than was my urban student teaching site. If you recall, what set Jake's character on the road to a new life was an extraordinary teacher.

The American reaction to Sputnik over a couple of decades did, at least, stimulate (1) a period of greater focus on, and funding for, creativity in education – creativity that, significantly, was *not* defined in terms of arts, the way I had first learned it, but rather in terms of originality more generally and of science in particular. This led to what my colleague Dennis Kinney and I later came to call it *everyday creativity* (Richards, Kinney, Benet, & Merzel, 1988a; Richards, 2007), defined as per Frank Barron (1969). There was also (2) a specific emphasis on, and funding for, science education with a healthy subtheme of creative thinking. Alas, those international tensions just morphed into others, still ever so painful today. Where is our creativity in self-understanding and international relations?

There was also a felt sense, back then, an enthusiasm, that creativity could be more general, or hold more general aspects, than special capabilities found in one domain or another. No longer was it just about arts! We as educators were lighting that general creative fire. A burning light of enthusiasm, new ideas, risk-taking, adventure, and fun – so badly needed across the curriculum. The debate still goes on today about whether creativity is domain-specific or crosses domains (e.g., Plucker & Beghetto, 2004). Both aspects seem valid (Gardner, 1983; Sternberg, Grigorenko, & Singer, 2004), and we do find core personality traits that seem to cross fields (Barron & Harrington, 1981). Regarding generality, we have also seen patterns of creativity that are dense within certain families but that come out in different domains for one and another relative (e.g., Andreasen, 1987; Richards et al., 1988b, see Richards, 2007a). Unlike the extended Bach Family, the relatives are not all musicians.

Some of us graduate students were intrigued by the psychometrics of creativity. I remember exploring a "Guilford divergent production test" (see Guilford, 1968) in a teaching methods class, along the lines of giving "multiple uses for a tin can." What an eye opener this was! We, the teachers-in-training, were *fluent*, were *flexible*, and were coming up with many *original* ideas – three of the ways of scoring this semantic "divergent production" test of Guilford's – and weren't we the creative ones! In fact, Frank Barron had proposed that originality was "habitual" with highly creative people (Barron, 1969, 1995; Barron & Harrington, 1981; Richards, 2006); surely we could do it too. Uses for a can? How about a cup, a hat, a bell, a lid, two cans for a walkie-talkie – and what about several cans for a musical instrument?

As student teachers, we had begun to think of creativity as a more universal capability, involving "originality" in the population at large, in science and in many other areas, too, at both work and at leisure – and not just among the elect in the arts, or maybe sciences, or among a rarefied group of so-called creative geniuses (see Richards, 2006). Creativity is found across diverse subject areas and naturally should be stressed in the public schools.

The 1960s were merging into the 1970s, with many graduate students less into the space race than into the Age of Aquarius. Far from building rockets (and perhaps bombs), they wanted to empower young people toward a better and less war-traumatized future. How little has changed since then. It was time then (and now) to ask some new questions. Why is it, we teachers-in-training wondered, that we are all too often helping kids learn to "get 100%" on someone else's test and not to ask questions of their own?

We also had the advantage of an academic center. Psychologists, including Frank Barron (e.g., 1969) and Ravenna Helson (1970), and others at Berkeley, Sarnoff Mednick (1962), E. Paul Torrance (1965), and Wallach and Kogan (1965), with young people, were all assessing creativity, and we encountered it. Remarkable. One could conceptualize creativity, assess it psychometrically, study it, and encourage it in everyone. Attention to the affective domain was growing as well, including nonintellective correlates of creative thinking, although there was less emphasis than there is today (Barron, 1969; Russ, 1999).

Some of us became especially interested in the study of creativity – in my case, it was originally due to my interest in art, but I got really hooked when I saw it applied to science, social science, and everything else. In the longer run, I ended up getting a PhD in education, and my dissertation was on modes and measures of creative thinking. Others also turned to this new educational area. There were happy and idealistic dreams of new worlds.

OBSTACLES TO CREATIVITY THEN AND NOW

There I was, high on creativity, seeing it as an educational necessity, and fresh from teaching classes already primed for doing "discovery science." I had heard it but not believed it – creative learning was not as welcome elsewhere in the country as it seemed to be at the University of California, Berkeley. Now I became aware of the following, at least as hypotheses:

- That creative disinhibition and enthusiasm will not be accepted by everyone.
- That to some teachers, these enthusiastic reactions in kids, even when tied to learning, can be seen as bad behavior or misbehavior.
- That some creative kids who may show high spirits, enthusiasm, and a raucous independence as they do their work may even end up getting in trouble.
- That there is a lot of valuing in classrooms of sitting quietly at one's desk in long straight rows of attentive (or at least quiet) students, who then get the "right answer."

- That kids, from a more hesitant group by nature, may not dare to go the creative route (and the dangerous route) that they have witnessed with their outspoken peers, and they may stick to quiet and "safe" behaviors.
- Particularly interesting was that, despite my protests, this student energy and activity were seen as problems of the kids, not the teacher.
- There was perhaps an implicit assumption that a teacher would never want a child to get out of line; teachers should be quietly listened to and respected, so that "real" learning can take place.

Clearly, we as educators would deliberately need to introduce (1) new teaching-learning methods, along with (2) different values and norms for what a creatively active schoolroom might look like. There was need for an entire culture change.

BETTER TODAY?

Things would surely be better today? Unfortunately, schools can fall into their own mentality of "getting the right answer on the test," particularly with objective and standardized measures linked to student progress, teacher advancement, or school and district ratings. Take No Child Left Behind. Objective standardized assessment can be fine in its place. But what is its place? And how can assessment honor creativity (Beghetto, 2005; Cramond, 2005; Smith, Smith, & Delisi, 2001)? For that matter, how many schools are choosing the gifted and talented from some of those same standardized test scores (Cropley, 1992; Winner, 1996)? It took years to show that intelligence quotient (IQ) and creativity were not the same thing (Barron, 1969, Guilford, 1968, Richards, 1981), but today many still do not believe it.

Where is the creativity we need as we face a rapidly shrinking globe, expanding information culture, widespread domestic violence and international conflict, poverty, starvation, disease, population expansion, environmental degradation, youth alienation, new levels of depression, substance abuse, and despair? More than ever, we need creative thinking at all levels, both individually and together. In an information culture, talent and innovation are increasingly sought at all levels of the workforce. There is even concern in the United States that we may lose our innovators to other countries (e.g., Clark, 2002; Florida, 2005). When is it time to do something?

After a section on definitions and related issues for education, we shall turn to seven suggestions for enhancing everyday creativity in the schools. Table 10.1 provides a preview. The suggestions involve both the educational setting and the personal abilities and qualities that can enhance creative outcomes. They also involve features that can help change the norms of a society so that human creativity will be more valued.

Table 10.1. *Seven suggestions for creative learning*

We need greater valuing and conscious development of our:

Outer space	Creating a rich environment, safe. and accepting of divergence, errors, novelty, surprise; making room for innovation
Inner space	Valuing our fullest experience and ways of knowing including unconscious modes and the curious revelations they may force upon us, even when we do not want them
Bravery – within oneself	Taking creative risks, conscious of inner pressures and fears, and doing what is needed even when it is uncomfortable
Bravery – in the world	Awareness of social constraints and pressures, yet able to follow what is creatively necessary to produce and share one's creative activity
Cherishing of creativity	Recognizing, valuing, and taking care not to devalue creative qualities in self and others including multiple modes of life experience and knowing
Ability to relate creatively to each other	Practicing and valuing interpersonal creativity including the revelations and mutual growth that can result
Knowing of the joy	Embracing the glowing moments that can result while turning creative talents toward personal growth and social good

WHAT IS EVERYDAY CREATIVITY AND DO THE SCHOOLS REALLY WANT IT?

Definition

To what extent is this definition intuitive for us? *Everyday creativity,* after Barron (1969), refers to outcomes (products, actions, ideas) that are new or unusual [as Torrance (1966) put it] or characterized by relative *originality* and *meaningfulness* [as Barron (1969) put it]. We speak of relative *originality* so as to include most people and creative acts, and not only those few that are unequivocally unique innovations. The *meaningfulness* criterion is to exclude fully random and accidental acts. We do not care if the outcome is valuable or useful, as some others do in their definitions. Value may not show up for years. Nor do we require that someone become famous or socially recognized, for the same reason. In addition, people become quickly notorious for reasons that time shows to be less creative than just attention grabbing. Everyday creativity is about the present moment and holds highest the distinctiveness of the work itself.

In my research with Dennis Kinney and others at McLean Hospital and Harvard Medical School, *everyday creativity* has been operationally defined by our *Lifetime Creativity Scales* (Kinney, Richards, & Southam, in press; Richards et al., 1988a; Shansis, et al., 2003). It is interesting that these scales ended up making *The New York Times* (Goleman, 1988), even sparking a Tuesday Science News feature. Why should that even have happened?

Do Some People Still Link Creativity Only with the Arts?

Could it have been that creativity outside of the arts was still news? The arts are marvelous, and that is how I got into the field. But such a narrow view, for creativity as a whole, if it persists today, cannot help us position broader creative curricula in schools. Even now I run into people who say, "I can't draw a face – I'm not creative!" Is that all it is about? Some Saybrook graduate students are still amazed to learn they have been everyday creative themselves, repeatedly, and for a long time, in raising their child, repairing their home, teaching their classes, or making do on a tight budget. They needed their consciousness raised about their own flexible improvisations, adaptability, and real-life ingenuity. One subject in our research was a mechanic who invented his own tools. So what if someone cannot paint a proper portrait? Everyday creativity is about *how one does things,* much more than *what* one does. It is our originality of everyday life.

Or did our *Lifetime Creativity Scales* make the news because we were looking in depth at real-life activities, at work and leisure (Richards et al., 1988). Was there hope we could now put everyone's creative activities on a ruler? Some R&D departments thought so and actually called to see if the scales would show who to hire. Sorry, we said, they were experimental scales, much too rough for such a purpose.

Actually, one reason we made the news, mentioned later in the same *Times* article, is because our scales allowed us to turn a time-honored mental health question around, and thus find a very different, and healthier, answer (Richards et al., 1988a, 1988b; Kinney et al., in press; see Runco & Richards, 1998), as noted later. This information, too, is relevant to creativity in the schools.

Issues of Creativity and Mental Health

When real-life creativity is the dependent variable, when participants are not being chosen for homogeneous types of creativity – such as, say, creative writers, or artists, or inventors – but are chosen instead for other features, such as belonging to a family at risk for mood disorders or schizophrenia or for attention-deficit/hyperactivity disorder, or for attending rural versus urban schools, or trying curriculum A versus curriculum B, then the assessment requirements change. One chooses one's groups or families or classes in the most valid way and then must be there to assess real-life everyday creativity, wherever and in whatever form that originality may ultimately come out. If it is home repairs or childrearing or perhaps brilliant golf or tennis, and you only look at endeavors at paid work, you may miss a key relationship. On the other hand, you cannot leave out a family member if he or she is famous. They are still everyday creative.

Note the different research questions, and designs, when creativity is the dependent variable. Have you heard the phrase "creativity and madness"? Alas for this saying, which dates to antiquity – with a different meaning, actually: "divine madness" (Becker, 1978). It is more recently due to dramatizations of findings for eminent creators in the arts. There are a lot of mood disorders. But the saying has likely done harm, and perhaps helped some people pathologize creativity and what they fear for themselves should they dare to create (Richards, 1998).

Never mind that the fear may really have been of their own unconscious mind, their Freudian id, their irrationality, projected onto someone else who happens to carry a diagnosis (see Barron, 1969; Richards, 2006). It is hard to inject creativity into the schools if this same creativity is unconsciously feared as destabilizing (Richards, 2007b) – and almost in confirmation, if it becomes linked with offbeat and disruptive and far too enthusiastic kids who challenge authority and do not follow the rules. Yet, ironically, even for these eminent writers with mood disorders, it is possible that creativity may have been working in the service of health.

Consider the subpopulation of eminent creative writers [many of whom do have a history of mood disorders, see Andreasen (1987), Jamison (1993), and Richards (1998)]. These writers are already unusual among depressed or bipolar people. They are much more successful; they have gotten an education, finished school (often), and found a job (hopefully) and a publisher (most likely). They have written, revised, edited, and corrected their page proofs. Many do work that is magical and awe-inspiring, but it is a Psychology 101 error to assume that is *because* of their full-blown mood disorder. In fact, the highest creativity appears to occur during milder mood states (e.g., Jamison, 1993; Richards & Kinney, 1989; Runco & Richards, 1998). They may indeed have had their challenges, but we do not know how they would have done *without* their craft, their creative, and perhaps, vital means of coping. I have heard it said that Virginia Woolf believed her writing helped keep her stable.

Compensatory Advantage

There does seem to be a *creative advantage*, based on our work and that of others (e.g., Jamison, 1993; Ludwig, 1995; Richards et al., 1988b; Schuldberg, 2000–2001; see Runco & Richards, 1998, for key papers and an integrative summary) linked to *risk* of, or *genetic liability for*, bipolar mood disorders. Even the *risk* by itself may carry a subclinical advantage because psychiatrically *normal* relatives of bipolar individuals may also benefit from this family history (Richards et al.,

1988b). In fact, the highest creativity does not correspond to the most severe illness at all but, rather, occurs in better *functioning relatives* (such as persons with cyclothymia), consistent with a "compensatory advantage" and a proposed "inverted-U" effect.

What type of study reveals this? One that looks at real-life everyday creativity as a *dependent variable,* drawing subjects from a more representative population, and which, in addition, rules out rater bias by using separate raters for creativity and for psychopathology, masking out all but the information to be rated. Other studies indeed support this one (see Runco & Richards, 1998). The conclusion even makes one wonder if creative activity might be *preventative* for young people at genetic risk for bipolar disorder (Richards, 1998), something else the schools might consider addressing.

Defining Other Subtypes of Creativity

Mini-c. Everyday creativity, then, is found widely in the general population, and its operational measure can open new research doors. There are other valuable subtypes of creativity being proposed, such as what Beghetto and Kaufman (2007) call "mini-c" and Runco (2007) calls "personal creativity." This important type represents a personal best and assesses how a young person does with self as baseline, a crucial educational perspective complementing that offered by the norm-referenced *everyday creativity.* This new subtype is of clear value in the schools, and an operational measure of it would be valuable.

Problem of social recognition. To some researchers, the relative exclusion of fame or social recognition as primary criterion for *everyday creativity* may seem refreshing. At the eminent level, recognition is sometimes given as one of the primary requirements for creativity, a decision that poses its own logical and assessment problems (e.g., Runco, 2007).

We (Richards & Kinney, 1989) suggested instead that a socially recognized aspect of creative success might be ascribed to certain "extracreativity" factors operating beyond *everyday creativity.* Kaufman and Beghetto (in press) have another approach, proposing two additional measures for creativity at professionally relevant levels: (1) creativity-in-training while developing standing and impact in an domain, although not yet achieved, and (2) successful creativity that wins major public acclaim. Such differentiation could be valuable for schools and universities. Do note, however, that *everyday creativity* is broader, has major overlap with both of these, and serves a different and more general function.

With *everyday creativity,* for our purposes here, we stick with the present moment, the creative act, what product emerges, and how relatively unusual it is, as long as it is nonrandom (no matter whether one likes it), and we leave the rest to other work and investigators.

The "Four P's" of Creativity

Did you notice? The discussion earlier has been mainly about creative *product* or outcome. What about the others of the "Four P's" of creativity, originally developed by Rhodes (1961). We discuss them soon, particularly the second P, creative *process*, for individuals and groups, a major focus in my recent book (Richards, 2007), as well as the third P, creative *person*, which helps us identify qualities of these young creators. The "fourth P," *press of the environment*, can make or break some people's creative opportunities (Amabile, 1996) and hopefully is one that educators can affect.

This following section integrates several perspectives with these Seven Suggestions for Enhancing Everyday Creativity. This includes (1) "twelve potential benefits of everyday creativity," the twelve integrating themes from chapters on individual and social creativity in *Everyday Creativity and New Views of Human Nature* (Richards, 2007a), (2) Cramond's (2005) prescriptions for each of the "Four P's" in *Fostering Creativity in Gifted Students,* and (3) Gardner's (2007) latest prescription for future education and human development, in the form of his *Five Minds for the Future.*

SEVEN SUGGESTIONS FOR ENHANCING EVERYDAY CREATIVITY

These seven suggestions are not trivial. They all involve some degree of honoring activities, qualities, resources, and responses that lie outside of the norm, may be completely unexpected, and may sometimes be fiercely resisted, by ourselves or others. This is what everyday creativity is sometimes about – changing the status quo, and sometimes changing ourselves in turn. The seven suggestions are somewhat arbitrary, in that they could have been framed differently, and the reader might wish to do so. But they do take advantage of several schemes developed through extensive effort of multiple people, schemes with evident benefits for our students. If these suggestions stimulate thought, they will have done their job.

Recommendation: A Greater Valuing and Conscious Development of Our . . .

I – OUTER SPACE: WE NEED GREATER ATTENTION TO OUR STUDENTS' OUTER SURROUNDS AND INFLUENCES. This is about a rich, and safe, environment to stimulate young people and their creativity. Think about popcorn. You heat up the pan, and the popcorn starts popping. First a short wait, then a few isolated pops, and then a sudden staccato of many of these pops, reaching a crescendo.

You never know exactly when a pop will come. But you know how to make the popcorn's popping more likely. It is easy; you can heat up the pan! Creative insight is a bit like this. It has been explained with an "edge of chaos" model (Abraham, 1996; Richards, 1996, 2000–2001), where being closer to the edge increases the odds of innovation. Creativity of course tends to thrive more in rich and fertile environments with stimulation and many resources (e.g., Albert & Runco, 1986; Amabile, 1996; Richards, 1981) including ones allowing stimulation plus safety for intrinsic creative activity. Mentors and role models are also very important and, of course, supportive teachers. These and various other conditions correspond to "heating up the pan," providing the setting that lets insights pop into being!

We can heighten awareness of the *dynamic* of creativity, specifically, including its nonlinear and recursive interdependence of many factors, as well as our *conscious* presence in the place and the moment as part of our creative process. We can also stimulate *integrative* thought, and rich understandings. These are three of the themes or "twelve benefits" of living more creatively derived from *Everyday Creativity and New Views of Human Nature* (Richards, 2007c; Table 2). Certainly being involved in *flow* (Csikszentmihalyi, 1990) involves challenge and awareness in an environment that is stimulating but just stimulating enough. The environment also involves what seem to be more "passive" resources, say books or films, but encountered in a way that spurs active inner work and contemplation, even what Pritzker (2007) has called "audience flow."

Observing actively and being *brave* are two others of the twelve benefits (Table 10.2). The classroom atmosphere is such that each child is encouraged to be mindful of what they are doing, and are not passively following a routine. Can they be *brave* enough to be themselves, ask their questions, show their quirks, and tolerate others in turn – valuing a "broader acceptable range of normality" (Richards, 1998)? Abnormality is not the same thing as pathology. It is just a departure from the norm. Sometimes it is about being highly and uniquely creative.

Gardner's (2007) "five minds for the future" include, first, the (1) mastery of a discipline, then the (2) synthesizing, and then (3) creating minds, followed by (4) the mind respectful of differences in views and background and culture, and finally, the mind so badly needed in education, the (5) ethical mind that asks what we are doing, and why, what ethical voices we attend to, and how we are benefitting ourselves and our discipline and our world. Let's not keep reinventing the wheel – or the weapon. To encourage creativity (No. 3), which is hopefully a given, one would include in an environment disciplinary resources for gaining expertise in a field (mind No. 1) for synthesizing richly, and respectfully, across fields and persons and worldviews (Nos. 2 and 4), and as one learns creatively, reflecting across cultures and history as to why one is creative and contributes in the first place (No. 5).

Cramond's (2005) suggestions are also useful, based on the Four P's (Table 10.3). She stresses not only the need for safety in the classroom, under the fourth P, *Press of the environment,* and for spurring intrinsic motivation, but environments that allow both *stimulation* and times for *quiet reflection.* Safety, of course, includes letting kids be themselves, get involved, take a chance, be wrong, act a little strange without censure (definitely not always a given – see

Table 10.2. *When I am creative, I am . . .*

Dynamic	Seeing change, aware of dynamic interacting systems, and of *oneself* as process.
Conscious	Attentive and responsive to the present moment, to immediate experience, and to the environs.
Healthy	With a lifestyle that furthers sound, sustainable integrated physical and psychological functioning.
Nondefensive	Alert to and relatively less affected by unconscious, conscious, and environmental forces that restrict awareness.
Open	Welcoming of new experiences without and within, aware, intuitive, sensitive, bypassing preconceptions.
Integrating	Functioning across multiple sensory modalities, states of consciousness, multiperspectival, enjoying complexity.
Observing actively	With conscious and active mental participation, whether attention is focused or diffuse, involved and not mindless or blindly habit-driven.
Caring	Guided by values and concerns rooted in love, compassion, and a greater good or meaning.
Collaborative	Working with others toward broader goals, honoring uniqueness along with the larger and co-created picture.
Androgynous	Bridging false dichotomies, beyond limits and stereotypes, e.g., sensitive and assertive, intuitive and logical, gentle and strong, able to be most fully oneself.
Developing	Aware that personal development and species evolution (biopsychosocial, technological, spiritual) can be ongoing, progressive, and in part conscious.
Brave	Accepting and welcoming of the risks of exploring the unknown with trust in the creative process and oneself.

Note: The table is adapted from Richards (2007c), p. 2.

Table 10.3. *Four areas for educational focus based on the "Four P's" of Creativity and Cramond's (2007) program*

Environmental press	Offer psychological safety, chance to access intrinsic motivation, chance to pursue interests, with space for stimulation and quiet reflection.
Person	Recognize characteristics consistent with creativity and nurture them. Resist negative stereotyping, make room for deviance.
Process	Encourage open ended approaches, and strategies for warm-up and stretching of one's creative mind and possibilities.
Product	Use rubrics that honor creative intentions, outcomes, harmonious with the nature of creative work, even generated *with* students. Resist ready-made, standardized templates.

Cramond, 2005. Richards, 2006; Torrance, 1965), and at times display their all-too-eager enthusiasm. Giving kids time for *quiet reflection* means they are not always sitting quietly in rows listening to the next lesson but might behave more like my friend's class, at times, sprawled on cushions on the floor, reading and dreaming and asking questions. We might hope *stimulation* includes kids engaged in doing projects, and at times jumping up and down, for instance in the electrical circuit experiment when they suddenly find a solution.

The teacher needs to know where each child is, so as to recognize what represents a new step for him or her, consistent with focus on *personal creativity* or *mini-c* (Beghetto & Kaufman, 2007; Runco, 2007). Here, each young person's fully exuberant enthusiasm at learning and discovery needs to be valued (even if loud! Even if many others already knew the answer!) and be celebrated. The light bulb goes on! Talk about an "Aha!" moment.

Recommendation: A Greater Valuing and Conscious Development of Our...
II – INNER SPACE: THIS IS ABOUT FULLER DEVELOPMENT AND *ACCEPTANCE* OF ALL OUR MENTAL PROCESSES, INCLUDING IRRATIONAL OR UNCONSCIOUS CONTENT. This is, after all, what "regressing in the service of the ego" (Kris, in Richards, 1981, 2006) is all about. Letting all that mental content in, in an adaptive way, and then sorting it out.

Whatever the creative environment, insights will not come our way if our minds are set and closed, if we are sure the world works a certain way. If we are *conscious* of our limitations and *open* to alternatives, *actively listening*, questioning and *integrating* other viewpoints, we will be vastly more apt to find new solutions. Openness and integrative thought in this context (Richards, 2007c) also mean openness to altered states – states that may indeed be quite natural to creativity (see Martindale, 1999). We also acknowledge structures of consciousness (Combs & Krippner, 2007) that filter and actually construct our reality. We need the humility to deeply realize that we really appreciate only the tiniest slice of our manifest world – this already skewed by personal structures, perspectives, needs, and mind-sets, and by schemas and deep-seated stories, of which we may be unaware, that structure our lives and even our day-to-day perceptions (e.g., Combs and Krippner, 2007; Feinstein & Krippner, 1997; Richards, 2007c).

What does this mean in the classroom? For one thing, humility. Here is where an open-minded teacher and role model, authentic and disclosing, who also promotes divergent thinking and rewards unusual perspectives (and does this whether or not they always "work") can make a difference. An important part of this is helping kids develop the patience and the sense of adventure inherent in a puzzle unsolved – including traits such as *tolerance of ambiguity* and *preference for complexity* that are related to the deferred gratification (or alternative gratification) of ultimate creative discovery (e.g., Barron, 1969, 1995; Richards, 2007c).

Cramond (2005), discussing the creative *person,* points out what I saw so clearly in the light bulb experiment – how some students' traits may be seen as negative. In addition, openness may be seen as as a failure to finish things, curiosity as nosiness, risk-taking as thrill seeking, and so on. Sometimes this is bias on the teacher's part. Sometimes it speaks to a need to see more clearly the developmental path for creativity. A child, for example, with too much unharnessed energy in childhood may be able to direct this to a creative accomplishment.

Turning to Gardner's (2007) five future minds, his *creating mind* and *respectful mind* (and hence ever open mind) are very much what we are talking about. Gardner focuses more on large-C or eminent creativity. But he also points out that, for a creation to be distinguished, and take root, it must affect culture, and human creativity, at all levels (also see Richards, 1998).

This section is also about students learning to value *process,* creative thinking for its own sake, and as a skill like riding a bicycle. They need to know the power of their own creativity. Think about *flow* (Csikszentmihalyi, 1990), for example, which students can not only engage but also learn to know along with its conditions. It is also, interestingly, about knowing when to *play. Play* is anything but frivolous, and it is one way that we truly – and delightfully – learn (Nachmanovitch, 1990; Golinkoff, et al., 2006). The wise teacher will teach *process* and sensitivity and choice in how to use one's creative mind. This invokes a different value system.

Needless to say, there is more individualization of instruction required for this type of learning. There may also be a wide variation in outcome. Here is where we may attend particularly to a student's own personal best (Beghetto & Kaufman, 2007; Runco, 2007). A more traditional attitude of "get the 'right answer' as quickly as possible" can of course shut down all these processes (Amabile, 1996). The wise teacher learns when to let loose and when to reconvene and reorganize (what I was at least trying to do with the light bulb experiment). The student can learn to "trust the process," his or her own intuition, and deeper self (Nachmanovitch, 1990). How thrilling this can be – at least usually. At other times, an answer may elude us. But this is really OK, too; it is how it sometimes goes in life. Here is where we have the chance truly to launch our youth into the future. To show them the road as yet untraveled. To point out where they can do better than we have.

Recommendation: A Greater Valuing and Conscious Development of Our . . .

III – BRAVERY WITHIN: WE AND OUR STUDENTS NEED TO BE BRAVE AND FEARLESS IN KNOWING OURSELVES. Why, someone might ask, is this such a problem? In fact, we have already alluded to various reasons. One can come to devalue one's creative mind, particularly if it (1) seems out of control and/or (2) is devalued or pathologized by others. And creative kids have many challenges in classrooms (Cropley, 1992; Torrance, 1965; Westby & Dawson,

1995). What has been called "regression in the service of the ego," as well as other process-oriented signatures of creative functioning, do indeed depart from our "ordinary mind" and from a strong ideal of control. Are we able to teach students about this – and explain why we are doing this to their parents?

What is particularly interesting here is how *healthy* this process can sometimes be. For instance, Pennebaker and various associates (e.g., Lepore & Smythe, 2002; Pennebaker, Kiecolt-Glaser, & Glaser, 1988), working with expressive writing that brings up long-buried and traumatic material, have found actual advantages for psychological health, physical health, and even *immune function*. There are also increases in, for example, working memory (see Richards, 2007b). Kaufman's (2006 work on poets actually supports this, because poetry may involve less of the working through than expressive prose, a finding also supported by Sundararajan and Richards (2005, cited in Richards, 2007). There is less psychological work going on.

With expressive writing, then, are mental blocks coming down, and greater psychological integration resulting? It could be. With immune function being enhanced, Mother Nature seems to be telling us that such creative activity might be very good for us indeed. We might even live longer. Here are, from the twelve benefits in Table 10.2, references to themes including *nondefensive, healthy, open,* and *brave.* And with *openness,* let us not forget its current status, as one member of the Five Factor Theory of Personality (e.g., Costa & Widiger, 1994). Let it indeed have its classroom time.

If health is the outcome, how does one integrate a literature on the "creativity and madness" issue? As noted, we see it differently, and especially for everyday creativity. Design factors and results can vary when creativity is the *dependent variable.* Not the same design at all when one selects people for diagnosis, compared to studies of famous people, selected for their creativity, where one looks at diagnosis. First, they are in no way typical of the larger cohort of people with that disorder. Second, it is wrong to assume, because there are mental health issues, that creativity involves pathology, rather than, for example, a "compensatory advantage."

Dennis Kinney at Harvard Medical School and I and others (e.g., Kinney, Richards, Lowing, LeBlanc, Zimbalist, & Harlan, 2000–2001; Richards et al., 1988a, b, Richards, 1998; Sass, 2000–2001; Schuldberg, 1990) see a valid creativity-psychopathology connection, perhaps even including subtle schizophrenia spectrum pictures, and one that may weigh in on the side of health, or "compensatory advantage" (see also Richards, 2000–2001, and this whole special issue on the "schizophrenia spectrum" of *The Creativity Research Journal*).

In fact, it is particularly interesting how *extraordinarily healthy* those individuals can be who are said to manifest *self-actualizing creativity* in the studies of Abraham Maslow (1970, 1971). Here, creativity even emerges as part of a developmental path! Here are individuals showing many features reminiscent of everyday creativity, along with childlike joy, spontaneity, and presence in the moment. In addition, they seemed to be at a higher ("being" rather than "deficiency") level in the principles that guide their lives, with concern for "being values," such as truth or justice, goodness or beauty (see Richards, 2007b, c).

This in interesting indeed. Gardner (2007) suggests we include emphasis on *the ethical mind* (his No. 5) in our education of the future. Maslow's self-actualizers are doing this as a matter of course. Should creativity with, in the best case, its potential for psychological openness and integration, have this potential, we should the more quickly honor these benefits of a more fully developed creative process. There is not a moment to lose in our troubled globe with its many escalating threats.

Do such recommendations enter the thorny realm of religious belief, where public schools do not enter or show preference? Not a problem, says His Holiness the Dalai Lama (1999). The way to true happiness, and to serving each other (these are connected), shows many ethical similarities across the world's wisdom traditions. Yet one does not need a religious or spiritual orientation to value these. Compassion and caring can speak for themselves.

Yet, with all this good press for creativity, it is poignant indeed how some teachers, even those who say they value creativity, in fact do not recognize those students who are creative in their classrooms (e.g., Westby & Dawson, 1995). They find instead, as Cramond (2007) indicated, some creative traits to be problematic. They may select some of the less creative students as their poster child for creativity. Clearly, some teacher education is needed. The focus can include (1) what a creative orientation involves and (2) the ways it may manifest, as well as (3) how one can help shape it in the most prosocial and useful way. Again, let's actively counteract a tendency to reject our less rational (if sometimes brilliantly original) parts of our minds. This will require personal and social reevaluations of attitudes and beliefs. That is another place where *bravery* may be needed.

Recommendation: A Greater Valuing and Conscious Development of Our...

IV. BRAVERY IN THE WORLD: WE NEED TO BRING CREATIVITY FEARLESSLY INTO THE WORLD. To begin, it helps if we have a peer group, support, mentors, or role models and an environment that values creativity (Amabile, 1996; Richards, 1981; Torrance, 1965). If one doubts the power of the peer group to shape opinion and control behavior, just think about our teenagers and prevailing norms in dress, music, and the like. For a much greater worry, recall Zimbardo's Stanford Prison experiment in the 1970s (in Zimbardo, Johnson, & Weber, 2006) or, for more real-life chills, think about Abu Ghraib. In the Stanford University research, some screened and healthy students became prisoners, chosen by lots, with others becoming the jailers. This was intended to be a two-week experiment. We educators and readers would not abuse *our power*, though, correct? Well, consider what happened. The jailers became so intoxicated by power, the prisoners so frightened and abused – in this make-believe setting – that the study needed to be terminated after six days and some participants had already been released with stress-related complaints.

If one really thinks about the pressures of conformity, one realizes all the more the power, the importance, and the incredible preciousness of the creative mind and spirit. We can cultivate citizens who can go against unfair norms, discover new truths, and create (we hope) better ways of being and living in the world. It is of interest, for many reasons, that meditators have shown higher creativity (Krippner, 1999). One aspect of the practice, across traditions, is detachment from the usual sets, memories, emotions, and expectations that may carry us along, with often a questioning of mind itself, as well as the forces we may let guide us mindlessly. Why are we so sure? In fact, who are we anyway? [See Hanh (1997) and Tulku (1978).]

Are we so immune to social pressures in our "objective" practices of science? Richards (2007a) presents scary cases that suggest that not only can creativity be suppressed in obvious and conscious ways, involving scientific discovery, but there can be *unconscious, group,* and *self-organizing* forces that can drive out a new idea, or finding, or even an individual. Along perhaps with scientific learning that could save lives. Here is where the benefits (Table 10.2) of being *conscious, nondefensive, open,* and *brave,* as well as *caring,* can really pay off. We may lose knowledge that can perhaps save lives. We may also lose our ethical selves. Remember Gardner's Fifth Mind for the Future.

Gruber and Barrett (1981) and Loye (2007) show another problem, a reporting error, and this too can serve subtle social ends. The work of Charles Darwin, no less, was subject to selective transmission, with relative celebration of "survival of the fittest" compared to some of his other – and more humanistically aware – work. The latter celebrated the uniquely human capacities for ethical behavior, empathy, and caring. (Yes, this *too* was Darwin. And part of our creative power for *development* and evolution.)

We have already dealt with self-censure of creative people from the inside out, self-pathologizing, doubting, devaluing. But now consider the pressures from without at a young and tender age, before the child has developed, censure that can squash a creative spirit. Can't we do better than this? A few may "make it through" by adopting one defense or another, but how many more kids gave up and have fallen by the wayside? Ten times the number? A hundred (Richards, 1998)?

To save our youth's creativity, we need a different *culture,* incorporating teachers, parents, employers, and all of us who value divergence (with all its trappings of disagreement and troublesomeness) that will *expand the usual limits of normality* (Richards, 1998). It is fine to be a little weird, a little offbeat, to dress in a nonconformist way, or it should be, to be who we are, and to have the space to learn about this. Very different than having a few eminent creators do all the work for us (Richards, 2008). If we overidealize these creators, we can give up our own creative birthright (Richards, 2007d). Plus, we are all needed, every one.

We also need more skills taught in conflict resolution, and in creative dialogue (e.g., Rosenberg, 2005), so as to work better with our interesting kids, and help them work better with each other, without losing their creative spark – to value the unique and shiny pieces of the mosaic they represent, while also developing the overall picture. This is presumably why we have diversity among a faculty (and such disagreements at times in faculty meetings!). Thus, our creativity goes hand in hand with the *respectful and ethical* minds of Gardner (2007) and our need for *integration* and *collaboration*.

This is about learning particular skills so we can co-create in groups as well as individually. We need these cultures of creativity (see Eisler, 2007; Goerner, 2007) for a forthcoming paradigm shift (if we are to save our environment, for example) and perhaps for our very survival as a species. This will require its own form of *bravery* from educators who facilitate change in the schools. It should make life less scary for the students of the future.

It is worth mentioning again, specifically, our culture of competition, which can make us afraid to take risks or be wrong, never mind hesitate to celebrate each others' creative strengths. Evaluation using criterion-referenced rubrics that respect creativity (Cramond, 2007) and that fit seamlessly into ongoing activity (Smith et al., 2001) will surely help, as will "personal best" types of evaluation and ones that honor group efforts. In fact, at times, people, given the chance, are hard pressed *not* to be collaborative (Gruber, in Runco & Richards, 1998). We are the most socially interdependent creatures on the planet (Brewer, 2007). We need to make more of our potential for co-creation in the schools; the changes this requires may also take some faculty bravery.

Recommendation: A Greater Valuing and Conscious Development of Our...

V. CHERISHING OF CREATIVITY – SEEING THE DEEP VALUE OF CREATIVE FUNCTIONING. Why are the arts so wondrous? They open new doors of mind and life, to truths we may not have even suspected, to beauty, awe, and wonder that we may have missed (e.g., Richards, 2001; Schneider, 2004; Zausner, 2007) to new ways of being and nondiscursive ways of knowing (Richards, 2007d; Zausner. 2007). But this realm was not always the purview of special eminent creators, while others stood by respectfully or went to the museum (Richards, 2007d). In ancient Greece, for example, music did not even have a special word. It was intertwined with dance and poetry (Storr, 1992). And everyone joined in the expression.

We may cherish creative results, but let us also cherish the creative *process* and the *dynamic* engagement it gives us in life (Csikzentmihalyi, 1990; Richards, 2007c. As Martindale (1999), Richards (2007c), Zausner (2007), and others suggest, a creative orientation can lead to other *states of consciousness.*

Altered states can occur as part of normal waking life, without alteration through artificial means. It's all part of our normal creative palette. A more *integrative* (Richards, 2007d) way of being, including multiple and nondiscursive ways of knowing (Richards, 2007d) could be offered more in the schools. As one important result, we may become more fully human.

Let us also cherish our creative peers. Consider among conformist norms for kids, the example of gender stereotyping. Compare to this the relative *androgyny* of creative kids, which is not about being any less one's gender, female or male, but about being more fully alive within the bounds of one's humanity, without being boxed in by "gender polarization" (Bem, 1993) and other constraints. As Barron (1967) and others (Eisler, 2007; Montuori et al., 2004; Richards, 2007c) have noted, creative people are more expressive, fully experiencing, open, unrestrained. Hence, they may be both logical and intuitive, strong and sensitive. Big boys do cry – and without being weak. Big girls can be assertive and dominant, even speaker of the house – without being called a nasty B word. Recalling Maslow's (1970) self-actualizing people, one recalls their fuller emotional integration and fuller comfort with themselves.

These examples are again about cherishing our diversity and what it can offer creatively, about considering our differences as precious as the ways we go lockstep together in certain social groups. Human groups are typically distinguished by similarities. But unlike the conventional wisdom, positivity about these in-group features does not need to imply "out-group derogation" (Brewer, 2007). We can be more inclusive than exclusive, more open to, and respectful of, each other, our creativity – and even the parts we may not, at present, like about ourselves.

Recommendation: A Greater Valuing and Conscious Development of Our...

VI. RELATING TO EACH OTHER CREATIVELY – This is about more than conflict resolution, or getting along with each other, when we must. It is about harmony and pleasure as we relate as partners, or co-create in schools, at work, and in life. As mentioned, creators will need new skills to work more smoothly and frequently in groups.

But there is more, and it is empathy, mutuality, deep connection. It is about creative relating. Empathy is not only found in other creatures than humans, but in humans at all ages, across culture and gender. Even young babies will cry in sympathy with their neighbor (Jordan et al., 1991). New research on mirror neurons (e.g., Goleman, 2006) shows we physically, and biologically, "light up" some of the same neurons as that person we are becoming attuned to. But can we do a more creative job of this (Richards, 2007e)?

We have probably all been with someone at the breakfast table, when we wanted to share something important. They were reading the paper. "Uh huh, uh huh," they said, distractedly, while their attention was miles away. Creative relating is much the opposite. We are truly *conscious*, aware, attuned, and on many different levels. We not only attend, we *listen actively* (Pritzker, 2007). We are *nondefensive,* hopefully, and *open* to what is said. Hence our conversation is a pattern of flow and change. And we may change in turn. The result of a really attuned or mutually empathetic relationship is a flexible co-creation of the relationship. It is certainly creative, original, and meaningful. It becomes a beautiful dance, as we hear, respond, change, and reach new awarenesses.

Some people think creativity has little to do with the interpersonal realm or assign it a separate "intelligence" (Gardner, 1983). But whatever one's position, we are talking about creative capabilities we all need in life. All the more if we give new emphasis to creativity within groups, across cultures, and even globally. We must get along if we want to co-create and work together. How nice if we get along marvelously.

Note that we are talking about complex cognitive and affective capabilities. As Jordan (1991) said, "Empathy ... is a complex process, relying on a high level of psychological development and ego strength. Indeed it may provide a good index of both ... " (p. 29).

Empathetic capacities also go hand in hand with multiperspective thinking, as well as with feeling and nondiscursive forms of knowing (Richards, 2007). They very much fit with the *respectful mind* proposed by Gardner (2007). Buber's (1970) "I-Thou" relationship shows this relational creativity to an extreme. One can only imagine the implications for our mirror neurons, never mind for our deeper selves. Higher paths of personal and spiritual development can also proceed from this deeper interpersonal knowing and creative awareness (Hanh, 1997; Tulku, 1978).

Recommendation: A Greater Valuing and Conscious Development of...
VII. KNOWING THE JOY – Perhaps we do not need the question, "Why be creative anyway?" But it is still worth stressing the joy – both to ourselves and to our students. Along with some of the more joyous (and sometimes surprising?) experiences.

We have considered the joy of flow, of true involvement, the use of one's potential, the pride and empowerment borne of achievement, the increases in well being, psychological and physical, even in immune function, from opening to what's valid and true, in oneself and the world, integrating one's experience, and accepting creative challenges. It is about truly being alive. Consider too the therapeutic benefits of art, dance, music therapy, expressive arts, among others (e.g., Richards, 2007d; Rogers, 1993), benefits that are not well enough known, or thoroughly enough studied at all, considering their potential importance.

Why aren't kids learning the self-regulation and self-healing that creativity can offer, and as part of their everyday activity? Why do we denigrate play, which aside from being fun (is that a problem?), carries many of these advantages (Golinkoff, Hirsh-Pasek, & Singer, 2006). Why, in eras of medical cost cutting, do we sometimes overlook our best resources – which are ever-present, universal, even free – in our everyday creativity. Why are creative activities not used more in adult education, senior centers, hospitals, as well as the public schools? And why are they seen as enrichment, and less essential, after the early elementary years. Doesn't a "fourth grade slump" of creativity (Runco, 1999) in some populations tell us something?

Creativity can also be an entrée to more expansive realms of possibility, whether or not one considers this a "spiritual" experience. A walk by the ocean; a breathtaking sunset. Some people turn to creativity for active mediation, as in Frederick Franck's *Zen of Seeing* (Franck, 1973); one Zen master said such active creative activity could approach "positive samadhi" (Master Sekida, cited in Richards, 2007c).

Relationship can invoke higher creativity as noted (Richards, 2007c, 2007e), and the profound joy that can come from relating deeply with another – as well as the fellowship, mutual understanding, peacemaking, and other good things. One can go much further with deep understanding, arriving at loving kindness, compassion, and sympathetic joy, three of the "four immeasure-ables" of Buddhism – plus, the fourth, which is equanimity, meaning in this case that we care for all without exception (Wallace, 1999). Need this be about Buddhism? Certainly not. It is also consistent with many traditions or none. Is this about creativity? It surely could be.

Continuing with a greater good, let us recall that the ethical (and also caring) mind is the fifth of Gardner's (2007) "five minds for the future." Consider altruism and joy. Some think altruism should hurt, but that is anything but true. How curious that Kant saw our concern for another, our compassion, as a misguided sentiment, "Such benevolence is called soft-heartedness and should not occur at all among human beings" (Kant, cited by Keltner, 2004, p. 6). To Kant, our altruism should be much more severe. Should it hurt?

In fact, we seem to be intrinsically altruistic (Keltner, 2004; Kohn, 1990), and can get joy from helping others. Should we not pass on these values in our schools, and outward to our troubled world? Are we held back at all by the fuller ways of knowing required, including gentler and more caring feelings? Do such delicate sensitivities seem less appropriate to the strong professional? It might be of interest that subtle affective "savoring" represents an extremely high form of personal cultivation in traditional Chinese culture, arts, and literature (Sundararajan & Averill, 2007c). Are we Westerners still putting ourselves on a rack of expectations and gender stereotypes? It is interesting that, in Scandinavia, where such roles are less rigid, there are more gender-neutral and family-friendly advantages such as paternity leave, less domestic violence (big boys *can* cry), and interesting patterns such as females comprising 40% of the legislatures (Eisler, 2007). Why did Darwin (Loye, 2007) see some of these caring traits as higher in evolution?

Our everyday creativity is our birthright, survival capacity, and much more. It can bring joy to others, and to us. We can use our creativity for numerous purposes and do some helping along the way. More and more interesting, one finds once again advantages for personal health, in giving to something greater than oneself (Miller, 1999). This does tell us something. We speak here of *caring, collaboration,* and our personal and societal *developing* (Table 10.2) – even as Maslow's (1971) self-actualizers evolved into more dedicated and caring and principled human beings, whose later work, as it turned out, often was toward a greater goal or truth.

Did you know that people witnessing good deeds often feel better and more hopeful about humankind? And it makes them want to be a better person (Haidt, 2005). Consider the reaction of one individual fellow in a study of what was termed "elevation" (the opposite of "disgust") when seeing someone act with courage or compassion. He reported how he and three friends from his church were going home after volunteering at the Salvation Army. It had been snowing and a thick blanket was on the ground when they saw an elderly woman in her driveway with a shovel. He did not think much of it when one person asked to be let off there. But later, when circling around and this guy was seen helping with the shoveling, one woman in the car wrote about her reaction (p. 7):

> I felt like jumping out of the car and hugging this guy.
> I felt like singing and running, or skipping and laughing.
> Just being active. . . . Playing in the snow like a child.

The response was interpreted in terms of a desire to be with, love, and help other people. The torch was passed on.

CONCLUSION

We have looked at ways to open ourselves, and our students, to both outer and inner space (Suggestions 1 and 2). We have considered ways to be brave within ourselves and out in the world (Suggestions 3 and 4). We have seen (Suggestions 5, 6, and 7) ways to cherish creativity, and each other, and to know the true joy of opening to greater creative possibilities, both individually and together. It is a broader program than one sometimes sees suggested for schools.

As desirable as this may seem, it is not necessarily easy. Here our talented, creative teachers and administrators can make all the difference. Creative students – to be sure, all of us, as we continue to develop – need space and opportunity, tolerance, patience, resources, and warm support. The seeds of creative innovation, and the cognitive styles, attitudes and behaviors, that facilitate creative modes of living must be carefully cultivated.

Returning to our original example of the light bulb experiment, with kids shrieking in joy, and an abashed classroom teacher making apologies, we can add several things, looking at the earlier list.

- That teachers and curriculum specialists need to see current educational value systems and develop strategies to help these evolve organically.
- That behavioral patterns of creative kids need to be better understood, and even more than that, that some of these behaviors should be encouraged in now quiet and compliant kids!
- That obstacles to creativity need identification and attention – including school patterns that inhibit innovation.
- That distinctions need to be studied such that creative young people are not punished for their enthusiasm or divergence, while still setting the limits that classrooms require for order and progress.
- That bravery and risk-taking required for creativity be identified and rewarded.
- That curriculum planning and evaluation schemes work synergistically toward creative development.
- That programs for parents and the community pick up these themes while creating subculture change in the broader educational environment.
- That interpersonal creativity, too, be valued and cultivated.
- That group creativity be encouraged, guided, and rewarded, which also includes many challenges to group process, potentially amplified by certain creative behaviors and attitudes.
- That teachers and administrators who encourage these changes be amply applauded, encouraged in their development, and rewarded.

There is much work to be done. But one sees that creative ways of approaching life can work for us individually, can work for us together, and even take us to new places in our minds and in our world. Far from being about the "lone genius" (Richards, 1996), creativity, long viewed by some as an individual activity, only for certain special talented individuals, is really – and quite appropriately – viewed as source of life, human development, and group and cultural evolution. Our everyday creativity pertains to all of our lives and activities, at work and at leisure, and can even take us to new and self-actualizing places we humans might not yet even imagine. Our creativity is, hopefully, a big part of our future in an endangered age. Here is a major creative challenge for educators – to help unleash our highest human possibilities.

REFERENCES

Abraham, F. (1996). The dynamics of creativity and the courage to be. In W. Sulis & A. Combs (Eds.), *Nonlinear dynamics in human behavior*, Vol. 5 (pp. 364–400). Singapore: World Scientific.

Albert, R. S., & Runco, M. A. (1986). The achievement of eminence. In R. J. Sternberg & J. E. Davidson (Eds.), *Conceptions of giftedness* (pp. 332–357). New York: Cambridge University Press.

Amabile, T. (1996). *Creativity in context*. New York: Westview/Perseus.

Andreasen, N. (1987). Creativity and mental illness: Prevalence in writers and their first-degree relatives. *American Journal of Psychiatry*, **144**, 1288–1292.

Barron, F. (1969). *Creative person and creative process*. New York: Holt, Rinehart, & Winston.

Barron, F. (1995). *No rootless flower: An ecology of creativity*. Creskill, NJ: Hampton Press.

Barron, F., & Harrington, D. (1981). Creativity, intelligence, and personality. *Annual Review of Psychology*, **32**, 439–476.

Becker, G. (1978). The mad genius controversy. Beverly Hills, CA: Sage.

Beghetto, R. (2005). Does assessment kill student creativity? *The Educational Forum*, **69**, 254–263.

Beghetto, R., & Kaufman, J. (2007). Toward a broader conception of creativity: A case for "mini-c" creativity. *Psychology of Aesthetics, Creativity, and the Arts*, **1**(2), 73–79.

Bem, S. (1993). *The lenses of gender*. New Haven, CT: Yale University Press.

Brewer, M. (2007). The importance of being "we": Human nature and intergroup relations. *American Psychologist*, **62**(8), 728–738.

Bruffee, K. A. (1993). *Collaborative learning*. Baltimore, MD: Johns Hopkins University Press.

Buber, M. (1970). *I and thou*. New York: Touchstone.

Clark, H. (2002). Prime Minister's statement to Parliament. Retrieved February 11, 2005, from http://www.executive.govt.nz/minister/clark/innovate/speech.htm.

Combs, A., & Krippner, S. (2007). Structures of consciousness and creativity: Opening the doors of perception. In R. Richards (Ed.), *Everyday creativity and new views of human nature: Psychological, social, and spiritual perspectives* (pp. 131–149). Washington, DC: American Psychological Association.

Costa, P. T., & Widiger, T. A. (1994). *Personality disorders and the five-factor model of personality*. Washington, DC: American Psychological Association.

Cramond, B. (2005). *Fostering creativity in gifted students*. Waco, TX: Prufrock Press.

Cropley, A. J. (1992). *More ways than one: Fostering creativity*. Norwood, NJ: Ablex.

Csikszentmihalyi, M. (1990). *Flow: The psychology of optimal experience*. New York: Harper Perennial.

Dalai Lama, His Holiness. (1999). *Ethics for a new millennium*. New York: Riverhead Books.

Eisler, R. (2007). Our great creative challenge: Rethinking human nature, and recreating society. In R. Richards (Ed.), *Everyday creativity and new views of human nature: Psychological, social, and spiritual perspectives* (pp. 261–285). Washington, DC: American Psychological Association.

Feinstein, D., & Krippner, S. (1997). *The mythic path*. New York: Tarcher.

Florida, R. (2005). *Flight of the creative class*. New York: Basic Books.

Franck, F. (1973). *The Zen of seeing: Seeing/drawing as meditation*. New York: Knopf.

Gardner, H. (1983). *Frames of mind*. New York: Basic Books.

Gardner, H. (2007). *Five minds for the future.* Boston, MA: Harvard Business School Press.

Goerner, S. (2007). A "knowledge ecology" view of creativity: How integral science recasts collective creativity as a basis of large-scale learning. In R. Richards (Ed.), *Everyday creativity and new views of human nature: Psychological, social, and spiritual perspectives* (pp. 221–239). Washington, DC: American Psychological Association.

Goleman, D. (1988, September 13). A new index illuminates the creative life. *The New York Times,* Tuesday Science News Section, pp. C1, C9.

Goleman, D. (2006). *Social intelligence.* New York: Bantam.

Golinkoff, R., Hirsh-Pasek, K., & Singer, D. G. (2006). Why play = learning: A challenge for parents and educators. In D. G. Singer, R. Golinkoff, & K. Hirsh-Pasek (Eds.), *Play = learning: How play motivates and enhances children's cognitive and social-emotional growth.* New York: Oxford University Press.

Gruber, H., & Barrett, P. (1981). *Darwin on man: A psychological study of scientific creativity* (2nd ed.). Chicago: University of Chicago Press.

Guilford, J. P. (1968). *Intelligence, creativity, and their educational implications.* San Diego, CA: Knapp.

Haidt, J. (2005). Wired to be inspired. *Greater Good,* 2(1), 6–9.

Hanh, T. N. (1997). *Teachings on love.* Berkeley, CA: Parallax Press.

Helson, R. (1971). Women mathematicians and the creative personality. *Journal of Consulting and Clinical Psychology,* 36, 210–220.

Jamison, K.R. (1993). *Touched with fire.* New York: Free Press.

Jordan, J., Kaplan, A., Miller, J. B., Stiver, I. P., & Surrey, J. L. (1991). *Women's growth in connection.* New York: Guilford.

Kaufman, J., & Beghetto, R. (in press). *Beyond big and little: The four-C model of creativity.*

Kaufman, J., & Sexton, J.D. (2006). Why doesn't the writing cure help poets? *Review of General Psychology,* 10(3), 268–282.

Keltner, D. 2004). The compassionate instinct. *Greater Good,* 1(1), 6–9.

Kinney, D. K., Richards, R., & Southam, M. (in press). Everyday creativity, its assessment, and The Lifetime Creativity Scales. In M. Runco (Ed.), *The handbook of creativity.* Creskill, NJ: Hampton Press.

Kohn, A. (1990). *The brighter side of human nature: Altruism and empathy in everyday life.* New York: Basic Books.

Krippner, S. (1999). Altered and transitional states. In M. A. Runco & S. R. Pritzker (Eds.), *Encyclopedia of creativity* (Vol. 1, pp. 45–52). San Diego, CA: Academic Press.

Lepore, S. J., & Smyth, J. M. (Eds.). (2002). *The writing cure: How expressive writing promotes health and emotional well-being.* Washington, DC: American Psychological Association.

Loye, D. (2007). Telling the new story: Darwin, evolution, and creativity versus conformity in science. In R. Richards (Ed.), *Everyday creativity and new views of human nature: Psychological, social, and spiritual perspectives* (pp. 153–173). Washington, DC: American Psychological Association.

Ludwig, A. (1995). *The price of greatness.* New York: Guilford Press.

Martindale, C. (1999). Biological bases of creativity. In R. Sternberg (Ed.), *Handbook of creativity* (pp. 137–152). New York: Cambridge University Press.

Maslow, A. (1968). *Toward a psychology of being.* New York: Van Nostrand Reinhold.

Maslow, A. (1971). *The farther reaches of human nature.* New York: Penguin.

Mednick, S. (1962). The associative basis of the creative process. *Psychological Review,* 69(3), 220–232.

Miller, W. R. (1999). *Integrating spirituality into treatment. Resources for practitioners.* Washington, DC: American Psychological Association.

Milne, J. (2007). *GO! The art of change.* Wellington, New Zealand: Steele Roberts.

Montuori, A., Combs, A., & Richards, R. (2004). Creativity, consciousness, and the direction for human development. In D. Loye (Ed.), *The great adventure: Toward a fully human theory of evolution* (pp. 197–236). Albany, NY: SUNY Press.

Montuori, A., & Purser, R. (1999). *Social creativity* (Vol. 1). Creskill, NJ: Hampton Press.

Morrison, D., & Morrison, S.L. (2006). *Memories of loss and dreams of perfection: Unsuccessful childhood grieving and adult creativity.* Amityville, NY: Baywood.

Nachmanovitch, S. (1990). *Free play: Improvisation in life and art.* New York: Tarcher.

Pennebaker, J., Kiecolt-Glaser, J., & Glaser, R. (1988). Disclosure of trauma and immune function: Health implications for psychotherapy. *Journal of Consulting and Clinical Psychology,* **56,** 239–245.

Plucker, J. A., & Beghetto, R. A. (2004). Why creativity is domain general, why it looks domain specific, and why the distinction does not matter. In R. Sternberg, E. Grigorenko, & J. Singer (Eds.), *Creativity: From potential to realization* (pp. 153–167). Washington, DC: American Psychological Association.

Pritzker, S. (2007). Audience flow: Creativity in television watching with applications to teletherapy. In R. Richards (Ed.), *Everyday creativity and new views of human nature: Psychological, social, and spiritual perspectives* (pp. 109–129). Washington, DC: American Psychological Association.

Rhodes, M. (1961, April). An analysis of creativity. *Phi Delta Kappan,* 305–310.

Richards, R. (1981). Relationships between creativity and psychopathology: An evaluation and interpretation of the evidence. *Genetic Psychology Monographs,* **103,** 251–324.

Richards, R. (1996). Does the lone genius ride again? Chaos, creativity, and community. *Journal of Humanistic Psychology,* **36**(2), 44–60.

Richards, R. (1998). When illness yields creativity. In M. Runco & R. Richards (Eds.), *Eminent creativity, everyday creativity, and health* (pp. 485–540). Greenwich, CT: Ablex Publ. Corp.

Richards, R. (2000–2001). Millennium as opportunity: Chaos, creativity, and J.P. Guilford's Structure-of-Intellect model. *Creativity Research Journal,* 13(3/4), 249–265.

Richards, R. (2001). A new aesthetic for environmental awareness: Chaos theory, the natural world, and our broader humanistic identity. *Journal of Humanistic Psychology,* **41,** 59–95.

Richards, R. (2006). Frank Barron and the study of creativity: A voice that lives on. *Journal of Humanistic Psychology,* **46,** 352–370.

Richards, R. (2007a). *Everyday creativity and new views of human nature: Psychological, social, and spiritual perspectives.* Washington, DC: American Psychological Association.

Richards, R. (2007b). Everyday creativity: Our hidden potential. In R. Richards (Ed.), *Everyday creativity and new views of human nature: Psychological, social, and spiritual perspectives* (pp. 25–53). Washington, DC: American Psychological Association.

Richards, R. (2007c). Twelve potential benefits of living more creatively. In R. Richards (Ed.), *Everyday creativity and new views of human nature: Psychological, social, and spiritual perspectives* (pp. 289–319). Washington, DC: American Psychological Association.

Richards, R. (2007d). Everyday creativity and the arts. *World Futures,* **63,** 500–525.

Richards, R. (2007e). Relational creativity and healing potential: The power of Eastern thought in Western clinical settings. In, J. Pappas, B. Smythe, & A. Baydala (Eds.), *Cultural healing and belief systems*. Calgary, Alberta: Detselig Enterprises.

Richards, R., & Kinney, D. K. (1989). Creativity and manic-depressive illness (letter). *Comprehensive Psychiatry*, **30**, 272–273.

Richards, R., Kinney, D. K., Benet, M., & Merzel, A (1988a). Assessing everyday creativity: Characteristics of the Lifetime Creativity Scales and validation with three large samples. *Journal of Personality and Social Psychology*, **54**, 476–485.

Richards, R., Kinney, D. K., Lunde, I., Benet, M., & Merzel, A. (1988b). Creativity in manic-depressives, cyclothymes, their normal relatives, and control subjects. *Journal of Abnormal Psychology*, **97**, 281–288.

Rogers, N. (1993). *The creative connection: Expressive arts as healing*. Palo Alto, CA: Science and Behavioral Books.

Rosenberg, M. B. (2005). *Speak peace in a world of conflict: What you say next will change your world*. Encinitas, CA: Puddle Dancer Press.

Runco, M. (1999). The fourth grade slump. In M. Runco & S. Pritzker (Eds.), *Encyclopedia of Creativity* (pp. 743–744). San Diego, CA: Academic Press.

Runco, M. (2007). To understand is to create: An epistemological perspective on human nature and personal creativity. In R. Richards (Ed.), *Everyday creativity and new views of human nature: Psychological, social, and spiritual perspectives* (pp. 91–107). Washington, DC: American Psychological Association.

Runco, M., & Richards, R. (Eds.). (1998). *Eminent creativity, everyday creativity, and health*. Greenwich, CT: Ablex.

Russ, S. (Ed.) (1999). *Affect, creative experience, and psychological adjustment*. Philadelphia, PA: Brunner/Mazel.

Sass, L. (2000–2001). Schizophrenia, modernism, and the "creative imagination": On creativity and psychopathology. *Creativity Research Journal*, **13**(1), 55–74.

Sawyer, K. (2007). *The creative power of collaboration*. New York: Basic Books.

Schneider, K. J. (2004). *Rediscovery of awe: Splendor, mystery, and the fluid center of life*. St. Paul, MN: Paragon House.

Schuldberg, D. (1990). Schizotypal and hypomanic traits, creativity, and psychological health. *Creativity Research Journal*, **3**, 218–230.

Schuldberg, D. (2000–2001). Six subclinical "spectrum traits" in "normal" creativity. *Creativity Research Journal*, **13**(1), 5–16.

Shansis, F., Fleck, M., Richards, R., Kinney, D., Izquierdo, I., Mattevi, B., et al. (2003). Desenvolvimento da versao para o Portugues das Escalas de Criatividade ao Longo da Vida (ECLV). (Development of the Portuguese language version of the Lifetime Creativity Scales.). *Revista de Psiquiatria do Rio Grande do Sul*, **25**(2), 284–296.

Singer, J. (1990). *Repression and dissociation*. Chicago: University of Chicago Press.

Smith, J. K., Smith, L. F., & DeLisi, R. (2001). *Natural classroom assessment: Designing seamless instruction and assessment*. Thousand Oaks, CA: Corwin Press/Sage.

Sternberg, R., Grigorenko, E., & Singer, J. (Eds.). (2004). *Creativity: From potential to realization*. Washington, DC: American Psychological Association.

Storr, A. (1992). *Music and the mind*. New York: Ballantine.

Sundararajan, L. L., & Averill, J. (2007). Creativity in the everyday: Culture, self, and emotions. In R. Richards (Ed.), *Everyday creativity and new views of human nature: Psychological, social, and spiritual perspectives* (pp. 195–220). Washington, DC: American Psychological Association.

Torrance, E. P. (1965). *Rewarding creative behavior: Experiments in classroom creativity*. Englewood Cliffs, NJ: Prentice-Hall.

Torrance, E. P. (1966). *Torrance Tests of Creative Thinking: Norms-technical manual.* Princeton, NJ: Personnel Press.

Torrance, E. P. (2004). Great expectations: Creative achievements of the Sociometric Stars in a 30-year study. *Journal of Secondary Gifted Education,* **16**(1), 5–13.

Tulku, T. (1978). *Openness mind.* Berkeley, CA: Dharma Publishing.

Wallace, B. A. (1999). *The four immeasureables.* Ithaca, NY: Snow Lion.

Wallach, M., & Kogan, N. (1965). *Modes of thinking in young children: A study of the creativity-intelligence distinction.* New York: Holt, Rinehart, & Winston.

Westby, V. L., & Dawson, E. L. (1995). Creativity: Assets or burden in the traditional classroom? *Creativity Research Journal,* **8**, 1–10.

Winner, E. (1996). *Gifted children: Myths and realities.* New York: Basic Books.

Zausner, T. (2007). Artist and audience: Everyday creativity and visual art. In R. Richards (Ed.), *Everyday creativity and new views of human nature: Psychological, social, and spiritual perspectives* (pp. 75–89). Washington, DC: American Psychological Association.

Zimbardo, P., Johnson, R. L., & Weber, A. (2006). *Psychology* (6th ed.). Boston, MA: Allyn and Bacon.

11

Education Based on a Parsimonious
Theory of Creativity

MARK A. RUNCO

The best education is grounded in good science. It is not based on opinion, tradition, or speculation but instead is drawn directly from the reliable information of empirical studies and the logical theories that take into account the empirical data. I have often told my students (many of whom are planning to teach) that it is their ethical responsibility to develop curriculum and follow pedagogy that has been tested and verified.

Fortunately, there is no lack of good information about creativity. This means that educators should have plenty of data and reliable theory to apply in the classroom. There is also quite a bit of bad information about creativity, but if opinion, tradition, and speculation are used to identify untrustworthy sources, it is not that difficult to separate the wheat from the chaff.

Indeed, there may be too much information about creativity. There are different perspectives on various aspects of the creative process (e.g., Simonton, 2007; Weisberg, 2007), which can make it difficult to focus. Many of the differences can be explained by the fact that creativity is a *syndrome* (MacKinnon, 1965; Mumford & Gustafson, 1988), which is affected by quite a few different influences. Additionally, it takes various forms depending on the creator's age (Runco & Charles, 1997) and the domain (Albert, 1980; Gardner, 1983). Age and domain are especially relevant to education because they indicate that certain things may be best for the creativity of a preschool- or elementary school–aged student, but other things may be best for an adolescent or a young adult. Similarly, children with notable creative potential in the arts may flourish under educational conditions that are different from those best suited to a child with creative potential in mathematics, music, or some other domain.

It could be difficult to identify the best education to fulfill creative potentials if in fact there is too much literature, with too many suggestions, many of which conflict because of age, domain, or other similar differences. Yet I believe that creative studies are about to enter into a period of distillation. I say this for the following reasons:

First, two extensive reviews of the creativity literature (Runco, 2004, 2007) suggested that there are in fact subtle commonalities among theories and findings. It is as if creative studies have, for the past 50 years, thrown a very wide net and tackled an enormous range of topics, but now the net is being pulled in and is getting smaller – the wheat is being separated from the chaff.

The second part of my argument is an old idea, but it applies well to creative studies. It is usually worded something like *practice what is preached*, meaning that we should be learning from creative studies and applying what is learned to further creative studies. My first attempt at this involved *questioning assumptions*. That is a widely recognized tactic for creative thinking (Adams, 1980; Runco, 1999) and has been used successfully by many eminent creators (Root-Bernstein, 1987). I took this to heart in an attempt to practice what we are preaching in creative studies. In particular, I questioned the idea that creativity is a complex, as is sometimes implied by, for example, *creativity syndrome* or *multilevel theory*, but the crux is that creativity can take various forms and is influenced by many things. However, the idea of a syndrome has been in existence since at least the work of MacKinnon ([1960] 1983), and I decided to question it.

Not only did I question the assumption that creativity is complex; I also used another tactic, namely *consider the opposite*. Sometimes worded as "turn it on its head," this leads directly to the idea that creativity is simple instead of complex. That would be a highly attractive theory for scientific studies of creativity because it fits so nicely into the principles of *parsimony* and Ockham's razor. Parsimony is one of the most central tenants of the scientific method. Put briefly, it means that, all other things being equal, a simple explanation is preferable to a complex one. The idea that creativity is simple rather than complex would clearly be parsimonious.

Of course, parsimony is not the only criterion of good science. A theory must also be consistent with reliable data. How would the simple theory be tested? What is at the heart of creativity, if it is truly simple? There are clear indications of an answer to these questions in the existing literature – the commonalities mentioned as follows. In the remainder of this chapter, I (1) identify the commonalities among the large number of seemingly disparate research findings and theories of creativity and (2) explore some implications of this parsimonious theory of creativity for education.

Before turning to the critical commonalities among theories, a second guiding principle should be cited, to go along with parsimony. This principle can be summarized by the word *optimization*, but it is better explained with the phrase, *moderation in all things*. Elsewhere, I collected a large number of examples of how that principle fits with what is known about creativity (Runco & Sakamoto, 1996; Runco, 1996). Summarizing, it seems to be true that although divergent thinking can facilitate creative problem solving, too much divergence is not good for creativity. Wild and weird ideas will result and they will not have the effectiveness, fit, or aesthetic appeal that is necessary for something to be truly creative. Divergence should be optimal. The same principle applies to influences on creative individuals and their development. Parents should, for example, provide their children with independence but not to the extreme. Children who have opportunities to explore will discover many things for themselves, but they will have more confidence exploring if they know that the parents are available. The parents are not totally out of the picture, just optimally removed. This same idea of optimization will be very useful as we attempt to identify the crux of simple creativity.

CREATIVITY: WHAT IT IS NOT

There is no need to consider every possible correlate of creativity or every possible topic under study in the past fifty years of creativity research. The field can be narrowed before commonalities are identified. There are two ways to narrow the field. Several correlates of creativity can, for instance, be eliminated. This will ensure that the focus of the parsimonious theory is in fact on creativity and not on anything that merely overlaps with creativity.

General intelligence (the "g" factor) overlaps with creativity. The degree of overlap depends on (1) the measures used to assess each and (2) the level of ability within the sample or demonstrated by the individual. The latter is often called the *threshold theory* because is it based on data that show creativity and intelligence are related but only below some threshold of general ability. Above that level, separation, or *discriminant validity*, is obvious. Creativity is independent of general intelligence.

Creativity also overlaps with, but is not the same thing as, originality. Originality requires novelty, uniqueness, unconventionality, or at least unusualness. The more unusual something is, the more original it is. Creativity certainly requires originality but it requires something else as well – a kind of effectiveness or fit. Sometimes it is aesthetic, as in creative artwork that is both original and meaningful. Originality is, then, necessary but not sufficient for creativity. You might say that creative things are not maximally original but are optimally original instead.

The same conclusion applies to adaptability. Research demonstrating that creative people are adaptive (Flach, 1990; Runco, 1994) implies that adaptability is an expression of creativity – or vice versa. This conclusion may also tie creativity to human evolution (Albert, in press). Of course, creativity must be a result of biological and cultural evolution, but care should be taken so as to not slide into the point of view that creative thinking is merely a kind of adaptive thinking. That would certainly make sense in that adaptation is so valuable phylogenically (I finally am able to cite Darwin, 1869, in one of my papers) and in ontogeny (Piaget, 1976). Yet, creative thinking is not just adaptive thinking. Creative thinking can, for example, be maladaptive. Additionally, creative thinking can be proactive.

Creativity is not always a kind of problem solving. Sometimes creativity occurs in advance of problem solving and is involved in problem finding, problem identification, or problem definition (Mumford, 1994; Runco, 1994). Another way to support the separation with problem solving is to look to the arts, but this is not clear cut. On the one hand, art may be self-expressive rather than an attempt to solve a problem. But problems can be quite personal and are not always articulated, even to the artist. It may be that problems are solved by creating art: The artist may have something to express but is not yet sure how to express it – that could be the problem. Even so, this leaves the possibility that not all art is problem solving. It would be difficult to describe art that is done for fun or created by a self-actualized individual, just for the heck of it, as problem solving, yet it may be creative. It may also help to think about problem solving as a reaction to a problem and about creativity that is not problem solving. This is not far from the idea that creativity may occur in advance of problem solving.

The same logic allows a separation of creativity from ingenuity. Consider in this regard the construction of the Panama Canal. McCullough (1977, pp. 613–614) wrote:

> The creation of a water passage across Panama was one of the supreme human achievements of all time, the culmination of a heroic dream of 400 years and more than 20 years of phenomenal effort and sacrifice. The 50 miles between the two oceans were among the hardest ever won by human effort and ingenuity, and no statistics on tonnage or tolls can begin to convey the grandeur of what was accomplished. Primarily the canal is an expression of that old and noble desire to bridge the divide, to bring people together. It is a work of civilization.

The Panama Canal was constructed, and it was effective, and its grandeur implies a kind of aesthetic appeal. Yet, the Panama Canal seems to be entirely reactive, and thus a kind of problem solving. Moreover, it involved solving *presented* – rather than *discovered* – *problems*. France and then the United States wanted a shortcut around the Horn (the canal saves 8000 nautical miles). There was ingenuity, but how much originality was involved? The locks, for instance, had been used earlier in several canals. For McCullough, the unique thing about the Panama Canal was its magnitude, not the innovative engineering or even conception of the plan.

Discovery per se is probably the easiest process to separate from creativity, because it implies that something is out there, already in existence, and the individual or team finds or identifies it. X-rays were discovered, not created, to give one of many examples. Of course, discovery (and problem solving, adaptability, and ingenuity) may overlap with creativity! The point is merely that they are extricable and not always vital in the creative process.

This point may be most true of the last process to be explored, namely *innovation*. Quite a few definitions of innovation have been presented, with a large amount of variation among them, but they tend to emphasize results, if not products. This provides a useful distinction between creativity and innovation. Creativity involves both originality and effectiveness, as does innovation, but the latter emphasizes the effectiveness as objectively defined more than the former (Runco, 2007a). A child may express himself or herself creatively in imaginative play, but the conversation in the imaginative play may not be entirely consistent with standard English. It may be more original than effective, although still minimally effective. Such play does not qualify as innovation, however, because from the social (and often industrial) perspective, it is not highly effective, not objectively effective.

A HIERARCHY OF DEFINITIONS

Innovation was discussed last in the previous section because of its emphasis is usually on products. The second way we can narrow the field before really focusing on a parsimonious creativity is to consider the relationship of products and creativity in some detail. Many theories of creativity emphasize creativity or even define creativity as a kind of productivity. For years, the *product approach* represented one of the major approaches to the study of creativity. It was one of the four "strands" first identified by Rhodes (1961) after a review of the research up to that point in time. The other strands were *person, process,* and *place.* Simonton (1995) suggested that *persuasion* should be added to that list, the idea being that creative people and things change the way others think. They are in that sense persuasive.

Not long ago I attempted to simplify this alliterative framework (Runco, 2007a). The result of this effect was the hierarchy presented in Figure 11.1. It is a simple hierarchy with two categories at the most general level. One includes definitions and theories that focus on *potential* and the other on actual *performance.* As is apparent in Figure 11.1, some of the original categories in the alliterative framework fit under *potential,* and others fit under *performance.* Hence the hierarchy.

The sixth and newest P is rarely noted explicitly but is implicit in a great deal of research, including that on development, education, enhancement, and personal creativity (Runco, 1996). The central idea is that individuals – and perhaps organizations, cultures, and other units, groupings, and levels – are not performing at their maximum potential and in fact may not be performing in any creative fashion whatsoever. They may not be producing original and

Creative Potential   **Creative Performance**

Person   **Products**
    Personality Traits, Idiosyncrasies, &   Inventions, Patents, Publications
    Characteristics   Ideas

Process   **Persuasion**
    Cognitive   Systems
    Social   Individual-Field-Domain
    Historical

                                                 Interactions
Press   Person X Environment (PxE)
  Distal   State X Trait
      Evolution
      Zeitgeist
      Culture
  Immediate
      Places & Environments

Figure 11.1. Hierarchical framework for the study of creativity.

useful products or collecting achievements that are ambiguously creative. They may, then, appear to be uncreative. They do, however, have the potential to be creative.

Runco (2003) suggested that this may be a most important area for research and the critical educational and enhancement objective because there is likely to be the largest payoff. It is that old cliché about getting "the most bang for your buck." That is because we might be able to help individuals and groups go from a very low level of creative productivity, or perhaps from a complete lack of creative expression, to something much greater. That something will of course vary depending on the exact potential of the group or individual. It is in some ways the opposite of marginal returns, in which increased investments lead to smaller and smaller increments and benefit (Rubenson & Runco, 1992). When you take an individual with mere potential, and provide the tactics, motivations, and opportunities for creative expression, you will have something much greater than marginal returns. In fact there may be maximal returns on the investment if it is directed at creative potential and not directed at highly creative individuals who require very little to maintain their already creative behavior and performances. Individuals and organizations that are already moderately or highly creative are the ones that will show only marginal returns on investments in creativity.

The research that falls under the category of potential is very different from that which has been described in the other categories. Clearly, creative potential is different from creative productivity and the assumptions underlying research on creative potential differ dramatically from the assumptions of research on creative products. Research on creative products assumes that we can look at the end result and concrete objects, and understand creativity. While this is of course sometimes true and the research on productivity and products is interesting and useful, it does not help us to understand and fulfill creative potentials. That is because potentials are not always fulfilled, so it is not reasonable to look at the end result and assume that details can be applied to instances of mere potential. That would be like suggesting that every novice golfer should swing the golf club just like Tiger Woods. Some novices may not have the balance, the finger length, the eyesight, and so on. Many novices are the most likely to fulfill their potentials by playing golf in the manner that suits their own idiosyncrasies.

The research on creative potential is different from that on the creative personality and person, especially when the persons involved in the research have been selected for their manifest creativity. They would of course not have mere potential but already have at least some of the tactics, motivations, resources, and opportunities that are ambiguous or lacking in individuals who are not yet creative or at least not creative to the maximum levels of their potentials. Another difference is suggested by the definition of a personality *trait*. Personality research very frequently focuses on traits, and these are by definition stable characteristics. Although there is some debate about exactly how stable they are if you take a life span perspective, traits are distinct from opinions and attitudes in their stability. Attitudes, for example, may change very quickly. Attitudes are good targets for educational and enhancement research precisely because they can be changed fairly quickly and easily and they have an impact on creative performances (Davis, 1999; Runco & Basadur, 1993). But the point is that personality research tends to focus on stable traits, and the idea of stability is somewhat at odds with the assumption that individuals who have potential can make certain changes and fulfill that potential.

The research on creative potential is dramatically different from that on persuasion as a category of research. Recall here that research falling into the persuasion category assumes that creative individuals share their insights and change the way that other people think (Simonton, 1990). This is very different from individuals who may have potential or are just beginning to fill that potential and are not yet ready to share their ideas, or perhaps are only producing ideas and insights that are creative in a personal sense and not in any social way or in comparison to any larger social norms. Additionally, the research using persuasion as criterion is similar to the creative products research in that it focuses on individuals who are already performing at high levels. Simonton (1990, 1999, 2007) for example, has written extensively about creativity as persuasion, and his studies tend to focus on historically significant figures, including Picasso, Shakespeare, and similar highly eminent persons.

This is a fascinating and robust research, but its focus on high-level and productive creativity suggests that it may not be the best way to understand the fulfillment of potential. Granted, certain inferences can be drawn if we look at eminently creative individuals and then look at their pasts, but that will not inform us about individuals who had potential but did not have opportunities and never fulfilled the potential. In other words, it will not help us to prevent the loss of talent and the failure to recognize creative potential.

As is indicated by Figure 11.1, research on the creative place or press is not necessarily incompatible with the research on creative potential. In fact, it may be that potentials can sometimes be fulfilled by ensuring that the environment and various press factors are conducive to precisely that. One example is what Wallach and Kogan (1965) called the *permissive classroom environment*, where students feel comfortable thinking divergently and sharing original ideas. Another example involves brainstorming and similar team or group work, as outlined by Rubenson and Runco (1995). The basic idea was to minimize the risk placed on individuals so they would be more likely to share original ideas, which are by definition somewhat risky because of their unconventionality and originality. So again, research on creative places and presses is compatible with research on creative potentials but not redundant. The former focuses on environments and settings, whereas the latter focuses on individuals. Sometimes environments and settings can facilitate the transition from potential to actual performance. That of course is one objective of education designed for creative achievement.

Research on the creative process is also not necessarily incompatible with that on creative potential. It may even be that the creative process can be outlined for certain individuals, at least if they are metacognitively ready, and they can then use this information in some sort of systematic fashion, along with various tactics for creativity (Runco, 1999), to exercise and develop their creative potentials. There is, however, much more to creative potential than just a cognitive process. In fact, recall what was said earlier about attitude: It may be one of the most dramatic influences on the fulfillment of potential. Ego strength is also extracognitive and perhaps vital for creative behavior. Runco (2003, 2007a) went so far as to suggest that it is the most important target for enhancement and education. The provocative premise behind this is that everyone has the cognitive resources that are necessary for original thinking but many people do not look to original ideas because they are afraid of the costs. Ego strength allows the individual to have confidence in one's own ideas and may allow someone to stick with his or her originality even in the face of pressures to conform or behave more conventionally.

This does not assume that everyone has the same level of potential. Creative potentials are probably like most other potentials in that there is a range of reaction. The range of possibilities is determined by genetic makeup, and the actual reaction or manifest performance is determined by experiences that fulfill some or all of those genetic potentials. It is fair to say, from a behavioral genetic point of view, that very likely everyone has the potential to be creative, just not the same level of potential.

SIMPLE CREATIVITY

The discussion about *what creativity is and what it is not* was included in this chapter because it indicates that creativity is not the same as general intelligence, nor originality, nor problem solving, nor ingenuity or innovation. In particular, it appears that creativity is unique in that it requires originality (unlike some problem solving and much of general intelligence) but not too much originality. Creativity may be proactive and, unlike maximal originality, it is always effective. Often the connection to a problem or obstacle is less obvious than when the intent is innovation or problem solving. The tie to problem solving can be difficult because it depends to some extent on how you define a problem.

The *hierarchy of definitions* was presented because it also helps us to narrow the field in this effort at identifying a parsimonious creativity. It does this in part by separating influences on creativity from the actual processes used for creative behavior. Features of the place or environment, for example, may be strong influences on creative efforts, but it does not make sense to say that they are a part of the creative process. They are usually static and nothing more than external *influences*. The hierarchy also underscores the need for a definition of creativity that applies to everyone, not just to the famous or highly productive creator. Not quite as obvious but very important, given the interest here in following the scientific method, is that some categories in the hierarchy do not represent research that actually explains creativity. Good science is not just descriptive; it is explanatory. To that end, causes and effects must be isolated and understood. This in turn indicates that several of the categories, such as products and (when focused on famous creators) the person approach, are lacking. They focus on the end result – the effects – and require that the causes be inferred. The process approach, in contrast, offers a way to pinpoint what causes (or leads directly to) creative behavior.

We are now very close to identifying what is at the heart of a simple theory of creativity. To do so we must determine what is common among the correlates of creative behavior. These correlates are quite varied but all point to one fundamental capacity or tendency. Why are they all correlated? What process underlies the correlates of creativity? Here are examples of how the multitude of correlates of creativity can each be tied to some central capacity.

Autonomy

Autonomy will allow an individual to stand up for what he or she believes. It is usually viewed as a personality trait and can be related to creativity in that an autonomous person will be likely to be interested in and comfortable with unconventional ideas and actions. Exactly the same thing can be said about the tendency of creative individuals to value and practice independence (Runco & Albert, 1985). Note also that an independent and autonomous individual will not mind exploring a risky or unconventional line of thought. This person will, then, be the most likely to find remote associates and to invest in what others think are questionable ideas and directions of thought. Yet, that is one way to find original ideas.

Courage

This is sometimes called *ego-strength* (Barron, 1995; Runco, 1996) or simply courage (May, [1975] 1994), but whatever the label, it is easy to connect it to the optimal originality seen in creative behavior. Humans are social animals, but culture exerts enormous pressures on each of us, every day, to fit in. Conformity is sometimes a good thing (e.g., while driving, it is good to stay between the yellow lines, just like everyone else) but it can inhibit original thinking. Often courage is needed to resist the pressures to conform. There are many costs to being creative. Some are psychic, as is the case if someone has a creative idea but worries about what others will think, but most costs have a basis in expectations and other cultural impositions. If this brief discussion of courage sounds much like the brief discussion of autonomy, that is because both are in fact suggestive of the crux of creativity and thus the parsimonious view. Indeed, there is no need to cover another common correlate of creativity, namely *nonconformity*, because it fits neatly into what has just been said about autonomy and courage. It, too, is typical of creative individuals, probably because it allows them to explore unconventional ideas, express original actions, and pursue unusual interests or projects.

Wide Interests

These relate to creativity in several ways. First, a person with wide interests is likely to have a broad knowledge base. In Epstein's (1990) terms, the individual will have a large number of "previously learned responses," which can later be integrated into new combinations and insights. This particular view is quite important and is discussed later.

Wide interests are also indicative of an open mind and one that will consider different things. In fact, wide interests may be tied to the flexibility that is an important part of creativity. After all, how can someone consider a wide array of perspectives without a flexible attitude? And that takes us to yet another bridge between creativity and wide interests, which is *perspective*. The capacity to shift perspectives and take different perspectives into account often benefits creative thinking. This is implied by the interdisciplinary approaches used in the creative theories of Freud (who used neurology to understand the psyche), Darwin (who used geology to understand biological evolution), and Piaget (who used his training in biology to explain human development). It is also quite clear in the research on incubation (which may help creative thinking by allowing the individual to forget a line of thought that has led to only certain kinds of ideas, and to approach problems from new lines of thought). Runco (1999) suggested that changing one's perspective is the most general and potentially powerful tactic for creative thinking.

Openness

This is sometimes operationalized as openness to experience, probably because that is one of the "big five" personality traits that are fairly widely respected. (The other traits are neuroticism, extraversion/introversion, conscientiousness, and agreeableness). Openness to experience is an adequate label as long as "experience" is understood to be personal and abstract as well as social, environmental, and concrete. In other words, creative thinking may be supported or facilitated by an openness to different things, whether ideas or objective events. It must be required for creative ideas because all creativity is original, and original things are by definition *different.* They are new or somehow novel. A person who is only comfortable with tradition and the way things have been done before will not appreciate new and novel things. The individual must be open to ideas which are different and therefore might be creative. (Note the wording, "might be creative." Originality is, it must be emphasized, necessary but not sufficient for creativity.)

Tolerance

See *openness.* Further support is apparent in descriptions of the intrapersonal and interpersonal supports for creative behavior (Florida, 2002; Runco, 2007a). In the classroom, for example, the most creative child may be quite a nonconformist. No one would want nonconformity all of the time, but one hopes there will be opportunities for students to explore unpredictable ideas and insights. It is unreasonable to think that developing a curriculum that supports creativity would be an easy thing to do. After all, how do you make plans for a school day when original ideas by definition cannot be planned and predicted? Educators should, some of the time, tolerate children's input even when it is contrary to plans or expectations. This is another example of moderation and optimization. Children must also learn that, just as originality is often a useful thing, so too must they sometimes conform and do what it takes to fit in or get along with others – including the teacher.

Authenticity

This is probably more commonly subsumed under the label of *self-actualization.* Authenticity is, however, only one manifestation of self-actualization. Spontaneity and self-acceptance are also integral aspects of self-actualization. Maslow (1968) and Rogers (1959) both thought that creativity was an integral part of self-actualization, the latter going as far as to describe self-actualization and creativity as inextricable.

Authenticity and self-actualization can be related to creativity in several ways. Self-actualized individuals are honest in an intrapersonal sense, for example, which means that they are unlikely to inhibit or censor unconventional ideas. Their spontaneity will allow them to try new things and explore fresh lines of thought.

Risk Taking

It can be risky to be creative. Rubenson and Runco (1992, 1995) explained the risks that may occur if an individual has a creative idea, which is by definition unusual and unconventional, in a social setting. There is little risk having unconventional ideas if no one knows about them, but in a group, there is a chance that others will react in an unfavorable manner. This is one reason brainstorming often leads to a large quantity of ideas but few highly original ideas (Rickards & DeCock, in press). Like so many of the characteristics explored earlier, a tolerance of risks is likely to make it easy to find and consider a wide range of ideas, even if some of them are quite marginal and dubious. Many creative individuals not only tolerate risk, they seek out situations that are ambiguous and complex (Barron, 1995).

Contraindicative Traits

Support for the simple theory of creativity can also be found by looking at *contraindicative traits*, which are negatively related to creative behavior. This is often easy to do because many contraindicative traits are simply antonyms of the indicative correlates listed earlier. Rigidity, for example, is a contraindicative trait, but it can be defined as *inflexibility*, and as such can be explained by inverting what was said about flexibility. Conformity and conventionality are much the same; they can be explained by inverting what was said about nonconformity and unconventional tendencies.

OPTIMAL FREEDOM OF THOUGHT

At this point a tentative label for what is at the crux of creativity can be hypothesized. Consider it, at least for now, a *judicious freedom of thought*. That touches each of the traits and correlates listed earlier and could easily describe the process used when thinking and behaving creatively. The use of this provides an answer to questions such as, "How can humans be creative?" The same answer may be given when someone asks, "How did they do that?" after observing an unambiguously creative performance or hearing about creative solutions to some problem. How did they do it? With a judicious freedom of thought.

Before considering educational implications of this parsimonious view, it can be revised. Consider, for example, the criticism to it that creative persons are not always judicious. Some are blatant contrarians, some even criminal (Brower, 1999; Eisenman, 1999). True, but it may be that they were less than judicious in their freedom of thought. After all, not everyone will have just the right balance of realism and originality. We might use the idea of optima yet again and revise the theory so it is an optimal freedom of thought. That works well because it implies that there are two directions of nonoptimalization. One reflects an imbalance in favor of originality, at the cost of realism, with the result being ineffective originality and, sometimes, inappropriately contrarian behavior. The other reflects the opposite imbalance, in the direction of control and realism, and is reflected in thought and action that is always conventional, usually conforming, and never creative.

The concept of optimization is attractive behavior it allows simplicity and parsimony. It allows us to focus on one capacity rather than two. Two processes might be involved if creativity were defined as (1) capacity for originality and (2) capacity to be judicious. Only one is needed if the focus is on freedom of thought (that allows originality), which creative people use but only to optimal levels. Very likely, in searching for the mechanism that allows optimal freedom of thought, it will be necessary to look deep into consciousness and cognition, where intellect and affect are blended.

The issue about two processes or one has been asked many times in the creativity literature. Most of the time, it is not viewed as an issue or a question but is instead just an assumption. In brainstorming, for example, the assumption is that our capacity to generate ideas is separate from our judgments. That is what allows the participants to postpone judgment and focus on quantity of ideas rather than quality. Similarly, all stages of theories of creativity (e.g., Basadur, 1994; Runco & Chand, 1995; Wallas, 1926) assume that evaluation or verification occurs after ideas are generated. Very likely the view that there are separate processes at work is more widely accepted than the alternative, that there is one unitary process that generates only what is consistent with judgments of values and effectiveness.

CONCLUSIONS AND EDUCATIONAL IMPLICATIONS

This chapter opened with brief praise for two tactics – *questioning assumptions* and *consider the opposite*. Before closing I wish to try one more tactic. This one was suggested by Gruber (1995) in his case study of Jean Piaget. Apparently Piaget was quite tactical. He always had a pencil handy, no doubt to "capture the fleeting" (Epstein, 2000). Piaget also took long walks, probably to incubate. Of most relevance was his practice of bouncing his ideas off of a devil's advocate. That is what I wish to try. And the advocate's criticism could easily be, "You are only describing processes that allow people to have ideas, some of which are original." Stated in that fashion, I would only remove the word "only." I do think that the production of ideas (and insights, solutions, and so on) is at the heart of all creative work. This will make the most sense if you keep in mind (no pun intended) that ideas and insights need not be verbal. They may be kinesthetic, as in the case of a dancer or athlete, for example, or visual rather than verbal. I also put originality at the heart of creativity. This does not equate creativity and originality. Several reasons for this were given earlier. Also recall that the idea of optimization was given earlier. That is what allows the simple theory of creativity to be parsimonious. By acknowledging that originality, when used creatively, is optimized rather than maximized, and by acknowledging that creativity results from a single process that can uncover or construct original ideas but is under control such that the resulting ideas are also effective, we can at least tentatively focus on one process. I expect less hypothetical critics to have questions, but I will use that as a working hypothesis and now explore educational implications of this simple theory of creativity.

Several of these have already been articulated in this chapter. Summarizing them, the theory in this chapter suggests that educators must have tolerance, at least some of the time, for imaginative and even wild ideas. They should reward the attitudes that seem to contribute significantly to creative efforts (Basadur, 1994; Davis, 1999) and the ego-strength that will allow children to share or at least think about things that their peers may not appreciate. The impact of the educational setting was also mentioned (Wallach & Kogan, 1965). Two of the overarching ideas in the simple theory of creativity are that the creative process is more important (in education and in research) than actual creative products but that in every case, regardless of the correlate of creativity, optimization is likely to lead to the best result. The best example of this last point is originality, which is a vital part of creativity, but only in optimal amounts.

Some time ago I proposed that educators should do several things: (a) provide models, both immediate and remote, of creative behavior; (b) provide regular opportunities for students to practice creative thinking; and (c) appropriately reinforce creative thinking and behavior. The last of these is qualified with "appropriately" because of the possibility of the overjustification which may undermine intrinsic interest in original thinking and self-expression (Amabile, 1990). The first suggestion, about modeling, actually has two benefits: (1) children may imitate creative behaviors but will also see that (2) the teacher or model clearly values originality, self-expression, and creativity. Students will often internalize the values demonstrated by people they respect. There is no reason why it would not be possible to direct each of these three suggestions (modeling, opportunities, rewards) to each of the correlates mentioned above such that children have all three for autonomy, for courage, for problem solving, and so on.

The most arguable aspect of the simple theory is that it focuses on a process, which it assumes is related to both manifest creative action and the potential for manifest creative action. The argument is that process is only indicative of potential, and there is no guarantee that potential will be fulfilled or even used. That view can be refuted in two ways. First, everyone has potential, so any educational program that targets the potential for optimal freedom of thought, and thereby creativity, will benefit everyone. Some may benefit a great deal, and some not so much, but everyone will benefit. As will society! Imagine what the world could be if everyone made even the slightest gain in their creative potentials. The total impact would be enormous and amazing.

The second point is that, even if there is no guarantee, it is worth trying. Look at it this way: Which possible mistake is preferable? One option is that you try to enhance potential and fail some of the time. The other is that you do not focus on potential and direct theory and enhancement efforts only toward those students who have manifested their talents. In the second case I am sure to make a mistake. I will miss students who have potential that is still hidden. All students deserve education that will help them to develop an optimal freedom of mind.

REFERENCES

Adams, J. (1979). *Conceptual blockbusting* (2nd ed.). New York: Norton.

Albert, R. S. (1980). Family position and the attainment of eminence: A study of special family positions and special family experiences. *Gifted Child Quarterly*, **24**, 87–95.

Albert, R. S. (in press). The Achievement of Eminence as an Evolutionary Strategy. In M. A. Runco (Ed.), *Creativity research handbook* (Vol. **3**). Cresskill, NJ: Hampton Press.

Amabile, T. M. (1990). Within you, without you: The social psychology of creativity, and beyond. In M. A. Runco & R. S. Albert (Eds.), *Theories of creativity* (pp. 61–91). Newbury Park, CA: Sage.

Barron, F. (1995). *No rootless flower: An ecology of creativity*. Cresskill, NJ: Hampton Press.

Basadur, M. (1994). Managing the creative process. In M. A. Runco (Ed.), *Problem finding, problem solving, and creativity*. Norwood, NJ: Ablex.

Basadur, M. (in press). Managing the creative process. In M. A. Runco (Ed.), *Problem finding, problem solving, and creativity*. Norwood, NJ: Ablex.

Brower (1999). Dangerous minds: Eminently creative people who spent time in jail. *Creativity Research Journal*, **12**, 3–13.

Darwin, C. ([1859] 1964). *On the origin of species*. Cambridge, MA: Harvard University Press.

Davis, G. (1999). Barriers to creativity and creative attitudes. In M. A. Runco & S. Pritzker (Eds.), *Encyclopedia of creativity* (pp. 165–174). San Diego, CA: Academic Press.

Eisenman, R. (1999). Creative prisoners: Do they exist? *Creativity Research Journal*, **12**, 205–210.

Epstein, R. (1990). Generativity theory. In M. A. Runco & R. S. Albert (Eds.), *Theories of creativity* (pp. 116–140). Newbury Park, CA: Sage.

Epstein, R. (2000) How to get a great idea. In N. R. Epstein (Ed.), *Creativity, cognition, and behavior*. New York: Praeger.

Flach, F. (1990). Disorders of the pathways involved in the creative process. *Creativity Research Journal*, **3**, 158–165.

Florida, R. (2002). *The rise of the creative class*. New York: basic Books.

Gardner, H. (1983). *Frames of mind: The theory of multiple intelligences*. New York: Basic Books.

Gruber, H. E. (1981). On the relation between 'a ha' experiences and the construction of ideas. *History of Science*, **19**, 41–59.

Gruber, H. E. (1988). The evolving systems approach to creative work. *Creativity Research Journal,* **1**, 27–51.

Gruber, H. (1996). The life space of a scientist: The visionary function and other aspects of Jean Piaget's thinking. *Creativity Research Journal,* **9**, 251–265.

MacKinnon, D. W. (1962). The nature and nurture of creative talent. *American Psychologist,* **17**, 484–495.

MacKinnon, D. ([1960] 1983). The highly effective individual. In R. S. Albert (Ed.), *Genius and eminence: A social psychology of creativity and exceptional achievement* (pp. 114–127). Oxford: Pergamon.

Maslow, A. (1968). Creativity in self-actualizing people. In *Toward a psychology of being* (pp. 135–145). New York: Van Nostrand Reinhold.

May, R. ([1975] 1994). *The courage to create.* New York: Norton.

McCullough, D. (1977). *The path between the seas: The creation of the Panama Canal 1870–1914.* New York: Simon & Schuster.

Mumford, M. D. (1994). In M. A. Runco (Ed.), Problem finding, problem solving, and creativity. Norwood, NJ: Ablex.

Mumford, M. D., & Gustafson, S. B. (1988). Creativity syndrome: Integration, application, and innovation. *Psychological Bulletin,* **103**, 27–43.

Piaget, J. (1976). *To understand is to invent.* New York: Penguin.

Piaget, J. (1981). *Foreword.* In H. Gruber, *Darwin on man: A psychological study of scientific creativity.* Chicago, IL: Chicago University Press.

Rhodes, M. (1961). An analysis of creativity. *Phi Delta Kappan,* **42**, 305–310.

Rickards T, & deCock, C. (in press). Understanding organizational creativity: Toward a multi-paradigmatic approach. In M. A. Runco (Ed.), *Creativity research handbook* (Vol. **2**). Cresskill, NJ: Hampton Press.

Rogers, C. R. (1954/1959). Toward a theory of creativity. In H. H. Anderson (Ed.), *Creativity and its cultivation: Addresses presented at the interdisciplinary symposia on creativity* (pp. 69–82). New York: Harper & Row.

Root-Bernstein, R. S. (1987). Tools for thought: Designing an integrated curriculum for lifelong learners. *Roeper Review,* **10**, 17–21.

Rubenson, D. L., & Runco, M. A. (1992). The psychoeconomic approach to creativity. *New Ideas in Psychology,* **10**, 131–147.

Rubenson, D. L., & Runco, M. A. (1995). The psychoeconomic view of creative work in groups and organizations. *Creativity and Innovation Management,* **4**, 232–241.

Runco, M. A. (1994). (Ed.), *Problem finding, problem solving, and creativity.* Norwood, NJ: Ablex.

Runco, M. A. (1996). Personal creativity: Definition and developmental issues. *New Directions for Child Development,* **72**(Summer), 3–30.

Runco, M. A. (1999). Tactics and strategies for creativity. In M. A. Runco & S. Pritzker (Eds.), *Encyclopedia of creativity* (pp. 611–615). San Diego, CA: Academic Press.

Runco, M. A. (2003). Education for creative potential. *Scandinavian Journal of Education,* **47**, 317–324.

Runco, M. A. (2004). Creativity. *Annual Review of Psychology,* **55**, 657–687.

Runco, M. A. (2007a). *Creativity: Theories and themes: Research, development, and practice.* San Diego, CA: Academic Press.

Runco, M. A. (2007b). A hierarchical framework for the study of creativity. *New Horizons in Education,* **55**(1), 1–9.

Runco, M. A., & Albert, R. S. (1985). The reliability and validity of ideational originality in the divergent thinking of academically gifted and nongifted children. *Educational and Psychological Measurement,* **45**, 483–501.

Runco, M. A., & Basadur, M. (1993). Assessing ideational and evaluative skills and creative styles and attitudes. *Creativity and Innovation Management*, 2, 166–173.

Runco, M. A., & Chand, I. (1995). Cognition and creativity. *Educational Psychology Review*, 7, 243–267.

Runco, M. A., & Charles, R. (1997). Developmental trends in creativity. In M. A. Runco (Ed.), *Creativity research handbook* (Vol. 1, pp. 113–150). Cresskill, NJ: Hampton.

Runco, M. A., & Sakamoto, S. O. (1996). Optimization as a guiding principle in research on creative problem solving. In T. Helstrup, G. Kaufmann, G., & K. H. Teigen (Eds.), *Problem solving and cognitive processes: Essays in honor of Kjell Raaheim* (pp. 119–144). Bergen, Norway: Fagbokforlaget Vigmostad & Bjorke.

Simonton, D. K. (1990). In M. A. Runco & R. S. Albert (Eds.), *Theories of creativity*. Newbury Park, CA: Sage.

Simonton, D. K. (1995). Exceptional personal influence: An integrative paradigm. *Creativity Research Journal*, 8, 371–376.

Simonton, D. K. (2007). The creative process in Picasso's Guernica sketches: Monotonic improvements versus nonmonotonic variants. *Creativity Research Journal*, 19, 329–344.

Wallach, M. A., & Kogan, N. (1965). *Modes of thinking in young children.* New York: Holt, Rinehart and Winston.

Wallas, G. (1926). *The art of thought.* New York: Harcourt Brace.

Weisberg, R. (2007). We are all partly right: Comment on Simonton. *Creativity Research Journal*, 19, 345–360.

12

Roads Not Taken, New Roads to Take: Looking for Creativity in the Classroom

THOMAS SKIBA, MEI TAN, ROBERT J. STERNBERG,
AND ELENA L. GRIGORENKO

A river runs through a village somewhere. And for many years, it is just a river, feeding the rice paddies, carrying away waste, silt, pebbles, and the occasional dog or cat. But one day, without even consciously trying, someone realizes that it is a road, a way out. And later that someone wonders why he or she didn't see it before – that the river is a road and that the road can be a river – even though it had been there all along.

And so we are beginning to realize with creativity that it has always been in the classroom but hidden in plain sight. It is not that creative behavior, creative thinking, and creative learning never existed before in classrooms. A colleague recalls once proposing an unconventional subject of study for a senior project in high school. While his classmates took up the ubiquitous topics of various sports, medicine, feminism, and other well-recycled subjects, he decided to review the history and legitimacy of parapsychology. His topic was firmly rejected. However, being a persistent fellow, he undertook it anyway, approached it seriously, and presented an interesting and worthy paper in the end that earned a high mark. But why was his innovation and unconventional thinking not recognized initially as a form of creativity?

In this chapter, we examine the evolving and exploratory relationship between teachers and creativity in the classroom. Our emphasis in the chapter is that teachers' implicit theories of creativity are often at variance with explicit theories of creativity – that is, what the teachers may value as creative behaviors are actually noncreative, and what they devalue as not creative behaviors may be creative. As a result, teachers may think they are developing creativity when, in fact, they are suppressing it. In the hands and minds of researchers and theoreticians, creativity has been viewed through many lenses and explored in a variety of lights for the last 60 years. But what effect has this had on teaching in the classroom? And has it helped teachers identify and nurture

---

This work, in part, was supported by a generous gift from Karen Jensen Neff and Charlie Neff.

creative behavior in the context of school? In the pages that follow, we will consider the importance of creativity in education, why it warrants a place in the classroom. We will then summarize the various definitions and perspectives on creativity, specifically with respect to how they fit approaches to teaching. Teachers' various understandings (or misunderstandings) of creativity will then be examined, by comparing and contrasting them to researchers' views, and implementations of teaching and assessment strategies will be briefly summarized. We will then discuss the practical aspects of fitting theoretical notions from research into classroom practice. How can creativity research fruitfully and effectively inform lessons and learning? Finally, we will propose for consideration some tools and strategies based on the theory of successful intelligence (Sternberg, 1999) and its accompanying investment theory of creativity (Sternberg & Lubart, 1991).

WHY DOES CREATIVITY MATTER IN SCHOOLS?

In Western society, the public fascination with creativity dates back to iconic artists of the sixteenth century, such as Leonardo da Vinci and Michelangelo (Abuhamdeh & Csikszentmihalyi, 2004). This fascination continued to expand through the Enlightenment and into the inception of cognitive science in the mid-twentieth century, exalting romantic ideals and artistic geniuses who were depicted as conjuring up their creative inner spirits to create imaginative and remarkable works of art (Coyne, 1997). In part as a result of the pioneering work of Guilford (1950) and Torrance (1962), scientists began to rationalize creativity – to study it in its various manifestations – and to develop ways of assessing it and cultivating it in classrooms. Yet, despite this long history of valuing creativity, it is only in recent years that developing creative thinking in all people has been discussed as a necessity in the classroom (Henderson, 2004).

This change in educational values is related to the expansion of telecom-munications and technology in the 1990s, which changed global marketplaces and put a special emphasis on innovation and thus increased international attention on the ineffectiveness of traditional pedagogies in preparing stu-dents for the demands of the next century (Hartley, 2003; Henderson, 2004). The economies of countries like the United States have, over the years, become knowledge and innovation based, reducing the emphasis on their industrial foundations and relying on the invention of products and technologies that provide desirable services for an increasingly technologically advancing soci-ety (Florida, 2003). Hence, there is a recent demand for creative employ-ees who can, while being constantly immersed in new information, display mental flexibility, innovation, complex problem-solving abilities, and pro-ductive collaborations with others (Schoen & Fusarelli, 2008). However, it is important to note that the attention being paid to the economic incentives of fostering creativity in students by policy makers (Craft, 2006) is only part of a more general understanding that creativity has many distinct and pronounced benefits for people's personal lives as well as for society as a whole (for reviews, see Plucker, Beghetto, & Dow, 2004; Runco, 2004). For example, the use of creative abilities to solve relevant problems in one's life can contribute to one's overall success, both personal and financial (Sternberg & Lubart, 1999). Yet, often these general realizations contradict the reality of the accountability-oriented No Child Left Behind–driven classrooms of U.S. public schools.

DEFINING CREATIVITY: AN EMBARRASSMENT OF RICHES

There is a saying that one can have too much of a good thing. Many might debate this, but it would seem to be the case right now with conceptions of creativity. That is, as one begins to work on a new frontier of research, one is compelled to explore, speculate, hypothesize, experiment, and create theories. However, when it comes to applying the research to useful practice, one realizes the need to sort, classify, collapse together, and even possibly discard or at least put to the side some theories that cannot be applied. Conceptions of creativity direct people's approaches to creativity. For example, researchers' varying perspectives and definitions of creativity affect the selection of participants and behaviors for their studies, as well as their research methodology and data analytical techniques (Fishkin & Johnson, 1998). Similarly, educators hold different implicit views of creativity, which they should then be aware of when they choose assessment and teaching tools (Fishkin & Johnson, 1998). The numerous definitions, conceptions, and theories of creativity appropriately reflect the complexity of the construct, but they can also blur one's vision with their myriad views.

It has been noted by more than one researcher that creativity has four major facets or avenues of approach: personality, process, press (situation), and product (MacKinnon, 1961). That is, in studying creativity, one can focus on creative people, their personality, motivation, or cognitive abilities; or the creative process, the stepwise progress that results in the making of something new; or the mental or environmental conditions that facilitate the creation of new things. Or, finally, in studying creativity, one may examine creative products – the actual physical outcomes, such as works of art or inventions, or the nonphysical outcomes, like ideas – pondering their qualities such as originality, relevance to the situation or problem at hand, or their aesthetics. Yet, when following any of these roads, one inevitably finds that they cross each other at multiple junctions. And so it seems that it is the interplay between two or more of these four facets, either explicitly or implicitly stated, that has shaped many subsequent definitions over the years (see, for example, Murdock & Puccion, 1993; Rhodes, [1961] 1987). At a more recent intersection, the study of personality and process in creativity has led to the development of theories of creative styles, such as problem-solving styles with respect to creative problem solving, turning the major question from *How much creativity?* to *How was it accomplished?* (Treffinger, Selby, & Isaksen, 2008). All of these aspects of creativity research have been fruitful and of interest, but what do they all add up to?

One systematic survey of the research literature (Plucker et al., 2004) has charted the extent to which researchers' explicit definitions of creativity varied, and found that clear definitions of creativity are rarely consistent. Definitions ranged from things such as "openness to ideas" (Edwards, 2001, p. 222) to "the ability to form remote ideational associations to generate original and useful solutions" (Atchley, Keeney, & Burgess, 1999, p. 485) to "the bringing into existence of something new" (Hasse, 2001, p. 200). This lack of consensus has two recognized drawbacks. First, when it comes to understanding the field as a whole, one finds oneself attempting to juggle a basket of different "fruits," comparing apples to oranges and bananas to avocados. Second, without a clear definition, those who are most interested in understanding the construct of creativity and conveying it to others (i.e., educators and other practitioners) are left confused or discouraged by the conflicting views. It has been noted that one of the factors limiting the progress of educational implementation of creative thinking lessons and assessment is the lack of a coherent definition of creativity that can be agreed on widely (Plucker, et al., 2004).

WHICH DEFINITIONS OF CREATIVITY ARE MOST USEFUL FOR THE CLASSROOM?

Having considered the problems of multiple definitions of creativity, we turn our attention to issues of definition pertaining specifically to creativity in the classroom, including teachers' implicit views and the definitions that have been based on or have shaped creativity assessment in schools. Our purpose here is to hone in on the importance of focusing on the demands of educational settings and considering a definition that works within the activities of the general classroom.

An initial dichotomy that has improved the clarity and utility of definitions has been the distinction between "Big-C" and "little-c" creativity. Big-C, or eminent creativity, involves the study of famous contributors to society (e.g., Charles Darwin and Toni Morrison) and the factors that led to their achievement (Simonton, 1994, 2004). The Big-C approach is not optimal for developing a theory for educational practice because of the low number of samples and high level of subjectivity regarding the products being evaluated, such as notes, journal entries, and creative products (Beghetto & Kaufman, 2007). Studies and theories based on little-c creativity investigate everyday creativity, including implicit definitions held by people and cognitive processes involved in ordinary people's creative thinking and behaviors (for a review, see

Sternberg, Grigorenko, & Singer, 2004). Little-c creativity can be empirically tested in large samples and applied to the general population. Consequently, a theory of creativity that will work in the classroom requires a little-c approach. [Further models of creativity involving "mini-c" and "Pro-c" have also been proposed (Kaufman & Beghetto, 2009), but Big-C versus little-c is an adequate distinction for the scope of this article.]

Furthermore, the debate between domain-specific and domain-general creativity has complicated the discussion of translating creativity theory into practice. This is because both perspectives, if applied, have very limiting educational implications. It has been stated (Plucker et al., 2004) that domain-specific approaches discourage students' openness to applying their creative abilities to solving problems in all areas of their life when enhancement of creative abilities are closely linked to particular areas of expertise. Conversely, domain-general approaches ignore task-specific growth and interests, which may in fact provide the most effective ways for students to develop creativity. Consequently, it would seem that defining creative approaches that allow flexibility across domains and encouragement of both domain-general and domain-specific creative skills, thinking, or problem solving is best for the classroom setting.

A definition of creativity that is grounded in little-c observable characteristics, that can be evaluated across domains and in all students, and that can be differentiated from other abilities appears to be the most pragmatic solution. When synthesized, elements of many recurring definitions fit these requirements and generally suggest that creativity is an interaction of one's aptitudes, processes, and environment, resulting in a relevant, novel, and useful product (Plucker, et al., 2004). Developing a working definition with specific goals is a necessary step in effectively translating creativity theory into educational practice. Without a comprehensive and precise definition, creativity remains a soft construct, susceptible to pervasive myths related to the obsessive romanticism of Big-C creativity and creative eccentrics, rather than an important facet of education and our everyday lives.

BENDING THE RULES

As if it were not difficult enough to extract a working definition of creativity from theorists, the next step, injecting it into the classroom, has its own complexities. As the intricacies of systematically changing school pedagogies and policy are too broad for this chapter, we are concerned here instead with the demands that creativity education places on individual teachers. How do teachers view creativity, and what challenges must educational psychologists and educators be aware of to properly implement and assess creativity education or education for creativity?

For educational psychologists, preparing teachers to enhance and assess creative thinking skills across many subjects involves both theoretical and pragmatic challenges. Despite the value placed on creativity and a half-century's worth of research, there remains a significant lack of public interest in teachers and curricula that emphasize creative thinking, and there is a dearth of pragmatic approaches for encouraging creativity and integrating theory into education (Makel, 2009). Hence, without proper training, teachers interested in creativity may feel left with only intuitive approaches to enhancing creativity that have not been empirically validated. Also, teachers who are uncomfortable with novel approaches to learning or thinking may inhibit creative thinking and discourage creativity in students. Therefore, consideration of preexisting teacher perceptions of creativity and potential challenges/biases that may hinder effective teaching and accurate assessment is warranted. Yet we must make a brief acknowledgment of the systemic and traditional demands that may conflict with a teacher who would like to incorporate creativity into his or her class.

PRIORITIES AND WEIGHING HIGH-STAKES ASSESSMENTS: CREATIVITY GETS IN LINE

First, teachers have incentives to promote student conformity in the classroom, both to reduce disruption and to focus on fulfilling the demands of standardized assessment (Kim, 2008). The traditional classroom environment is goal oriented and mainly evaluates students' analytical and memory skills. Creativity is suppressed in traditional classrooms in part as a result of lack of opportunity and encouragement based on this narrow approach (Sternberg, 2006). Students may even experience punishment for displaying creativity in the classroom (Guncer & Oral, 1993).

Educators' reluctance to teach for creativity is reinforced by high-stakes standardized testing, which has promoted narrow and well-defined standards for achievement (Beghetto, 2005; Kim, 2008). Typical standardized tests that are used to set standards of accountability for schools and teachers encourage identification of the "right answer," which diminishes the value of divergent approaches to problem solving (Sternberg, 2006). For highly creative students whose preference for novel approaches to learning and thinking may be perceived as inappropriate, negative responses by teachers may lead to discouragement, underachievement, and even dropping out of school (Kim, 2008).

Consequently, teachers play an instrumental role in moderating the effects of traditional practices and standardized assessments on limiting creative thinking in the classroom (Beghetto, 2005). Yet, the literature argues that teachers currently lack the training and incentives needed to promote and assess creative thinking (Beghetto, 2005). Teachers interested in the development of creative thinking in their students often rely on intuitive approaches or assume that creative thinking can be most effectively nurtured in a handful of subjects, such as visual arts, music, and creative writing. Thus, often, there is an attitude of promoting creativity in "artsy" classes and "getting serious about the work" in classes on subjects for which the knowledge mastered may be assessed with standardized tests. And then, amid standardized test scores, creativity can appear irrelevant (Kaufman & Sternberg, 2007).

TEACHER PERCEPTIONS OF CREATIVITY

Given the apparent conflicts of integrating creativity into an educational system that emphasizes traditional standards of behavior, teaching approaches, and assessment, developing an accurate understanding of teacher perceptions of creativity is important before considering how creativity might best be incorporated into the classroom environment. Although education has historically ignored or even undermined creative thinking, most teachers claim to value creative students and a creative classroom atmosphere (Runco & Johnson, 2002). The discrepancy between teachers' claims of valuing creativity and the realities of the classroom can be explained by one or all of the following phenomena:

(1) Teachers are not aware that their behaviors in the classroom actually inhibit creativity (Dawson, Andrea, Affinito, & Westby, 1999). Occupational pressures may overwhelm even well-intentioned teachers, who feel compelled to fall back on traditional authoritarian teaching methods (Besançon & Lubart, 2008) to preserve order and efficiency in the classroom.
(2) It is socially desirable for teachers to claim they value creativity in the classroom even if they do not (Runco & Johnson, 2002).
(3) Teachers' implicit definitions of creativity and creative behavior are uniquely different from the behaviors exhibited by students whom experts would define as creative (Dawson et al., 1999).

To understand the discrepancy between the value placed on creativity and its role in classroom environments, teachers' definitions of creativity needed to be gauged. Parents' and teacher's perceptions of what characteristics describe creative and uncreative children were collected from a set of 300 adjectives (Runco & Johnson, 1993). There was a high level of agreement (67%) between parents and teachers over creative traits. The differentiating traits for teachers' preferences were adjectives describing socially desirable characteristics (e.g., *cheerful, friendly*, and *easy-going*). Parents mentioned more personality-driven traits (e.g., *industrious, impulsive*, and *self-confident*). The rest of the definitions were as expected and described typical favorable traits that illustrate creative children.

For a more in-depth understanding of teachers' perceptions of creative children, teachers were asked to rate their favorite and least favorite student according to twenty terms – ten of the most and ten of the least prototypical characteristics of creative children (Westby & Dawson, 1995). The teachers were also asked to rate which of the twenty characteristics described creative and uncreative children. The traits describing the teachers' favorite students were negatively correlated with the creative traits; as expected, the least favorite students were positively correlated with the creativity prototype. But more telling was the finding that teachers only agreed with 45% of the adjectives defining creative/uncreative characteristics in previous literature. Several of the traits (i.e., *good-natured, reliable,* and *sincere*) unique to teachers' perception of creative students were also socially desirable characteristics; this finding resonates with the finding of a previous study (Runco & Johnson, 1993). Also, teachers rated "nonconformist" as one of the least creative traits, in contrast to almost every expert definition of creativity (Westby & Dawson, 1995).

Thus, although teachers may support the idea of creativity in the classroom (Runco & Johnson, 2002), they appear to prefer students who exhibit socially desirable traits, which they then label as creative. At the same time, they hold negative views of students displaying creative traits (Westby & Dawson, 1995). Furthering our understanding of this complex teacher-student dynamic, another study (Scott, 1999) evaluated college students' ($n = 133$) and teachers' ($n = 144$) assumptions about the potential disruptiveness of students based on four fictitious profiles that gave information about age, grade, and reading, language, and math proficiency, as well as scores on divergent thinking and creative tasks. Each participant rated the four student profiles, which differed in creative aptitude, according to twenty-one characteristics teachers may observe in students that define disruptiveness and creativity. Teacher predictions of behaviors for highly creative students were positively correlated with disruptive characteristics. The teachers' ratings also indicated that they viewed creative students as more disruptive than did the college students' ratings. Furthermore, ratings differed according to sex, suggesting that gender bias plays a role in teacher perceptions of creativity.

Consider the in-class dynamics that may result from teachers' perceptions of creative students. A mixed-method study of prospective middle and high school teachers' preferences toward unique and unexpected comments during class discussion (Beghetto, 2007) demonstrated that most teachers, especially math and high school teachers, perceived the comments as potentially disruptive. In written responses, teachers did express their desire to facilitate unique discussions to make lessons engaging but preferred relevant comments. They expressed the need to maintain relevance to start a conversation topic and feared unique comments might result in the class's getting "off task." The preference of math teachers for strictly relevant comments suggests that teachers who deal with certain subjects may have more difficulty adopting creativity-enhancing practices. Another study (Beghetto, 2008) also concluded that prospective teachers believe that in the primary school grades, memorization should be emphasized over imaginative thinking to establish a necessary foundation for future learning. The preference of memorization was also linked to the view that unique comments are disruptive. These studies help to identify how teachers' educational approaches influence their preferences for specific uncreative classroom behaviors.

In addition to research in the United States, several studies (Chan & Chan, 1999; Diakidoy & Kanari, 1999; Guncer & Oral, 1993; Kwang & Smith, 2004; Lee & Seo, 2006; Runco & Johnson, 2002; Seo, Lee, & Kim, 2005) that have been conducted in other countries illustrate cross-cultural differences in implicit views of creativity and approaches to teaching for creativity. Runco and Johnson (2002) repeated their study on parent versus teacher implicit views of creativity (1993, see earlier) with samples from the United States and India. Similar to the previous U.S.-based study, parent and teacher views did not differ significantly but there was a significant difference between the two cultures' definitions of *creativity* and ratings of the desirability for certain creative traits, showing that cross-cultural differences do exist. Specifically, the U.S. sample significantly favored the two clusters of attitudinal (e.g., *humorous, dreamy*, and *independent*) and intellectual (e.g., *imaginative* and *clever*) definitions of creativity compared to the Indian sample. The desirability ratings of creativity did not suggest a significant cross-cultural difference overall. In a Chinese study, researchers (Chan & Chan, 1999) asked teachers to identify creative traits and differed from the U.S. studies (Runco & Johnson, 1993, 2002) in identifying creative traits as socially undesirable (e.g., nonconformity) but related to high intellectual ability. Korean teachers have also been found to hold similar perceptions about the social undesirability of creativity due to cultural emphases on conformity, while also holding the view that creativity is related to high intellectual abilities (Seo et al., 2005).

At the University of Cyprus, researchers (Diakidoy & Kanari, 1999) analyzed the beliefs of forty-nine prospective teachers regarding their perceptions of creativity. The student teachers defined creativity as a process leading to novel outcomes and that it is a general characteristic that can be fostered in anyone. However, they did not believe creative products necessarily demanded task appropriateness, which contradicts most definitions of creativity (Sternberg & Lubart, 1999). Creativity was seen as being more relevant to artistic and literary work (i.e., domain-specific). The participants also emphasized knowledge acquisition in school as the primary reason for the lack of creativity in education. Thus, traditional methods of education are seen as inhibitors of creativity in other countries. So, while the previous studies are clearly not a summation of the international perspectives on creativity, it is important to understand that creativity exists largely in the context of a specific culture (see Kaufman & Sternberg, 2006, for further review).

It has been important for researchers to establish evidence that teachers hold a variety of views toward creativity, including negative perceptions toward creative students. These negative perceptions suggest that teachers may commonly fail to identify and then value creative students. To highlight this point, researchers (Dawson, et al., 1999) tested third- and fourth-grade teachers' predictions of student creativity via ratings for traditional concepts of creativity (Sternberg, 1985) and teacher concepts of creativity (Westby & Dawson, 1995). The predictions were compared with the students' performance on verbal and figural creativity tasks. Students who were identified as highly creative by teachers and fit the teachers' concepts of creativity received high scores for the verbal creativity task and low scores for the figural task but did not display high levels of traditional creative personality traits. Conversely, students who were rated less creative by teachers had high scores on the figural creativity task and closely reflected traditional creative personality traits. While the findings display some of the limitations in performance assessment of creativity (i.e., lack of correlation between figural and verbal creativity tasks), the researchers noted that teachers continued to favor students with creative abilities related to social domains (Dawson et al., 1999).

Research also suggests that teachers not only have differing views of creativity (Dawson et al., 1999; Runco & Johnson, 1993, 2002; Westby & Dawson, 1995) but also show some biases in favor of uncreative behavior in the classroom (Beghetto, 2007). Psychologists have provided evidence of the current barriers to the display of creativity in the classroom. While education policy and teacher training will need to be developed, providing an adequate definition and set of assessments for creativity represents important first steps in promoting classrooms that will enhance creative thinking. Suggestions for a useful theoretical foundation for teaching and classroom assessment are discussed in the following sections.

TEACHING AND ASSESSING CREATIVITY IN THE CLASSROOM

There are a number of papers that provide comprehensive overviews of ways of nurturing creativity and types of creativity assessment (Esquivel, 1995; Feldhusen & Goh, 1995; Houtz & Krug, 1995). Here, we only briefly summarize them before describing a new approach that attempts to integrate the practice of creativity into classroom curricula.

Based on the research findings on the elements of creativity, a survey of approaches can be based on the so-called Four P model, focusing on people, processes, press, and products. First, there are several proposed models for teaching creativity in the classroom, and these tend to incorporate the development of personality factors (e.g., tolerance of ambiguity, flexibility, risk-taking, persistence, and motivation) and cognitive skills (e.g., problem defining, original thinking, elaboration, finding new connections) with process. Esquivel focuses on three examples of such teaching models that emphasize creative process enrichment, problem solving, and productivity: Torrance's Incubation Model of Teaching, Renzulli's Enrichment Triad Model, and Treffinger's Creative Problem-Solving Model. These models describe systematic, research-based approaches that promote creativity in individuals in a stepwise fashion at various developmental stages.

The Torrance Incubation Model of Teaching (Torrance & Safter, 1990) is a generally applied three-stage model that creates opportunities for creativity in any area of learning by encouraging the mental states that seem to lead to creative thinking – such as being motivated and imaginative, desiring to pursue ideas or knowledge, and being persistent in this pursuit. Renzulli's Enrichment Triad Model (Renzulli, 1977) presents three progressive stages of activities or exercises that can develop creative thinking processes. Type I activities involve general exploratory exercises, which may be field trips or other open-ended experiences that invite exploration. Type II activities emphasize training in particular thinking skills, such as reflective thinking, divergent thinking, and problem solving. They involve such specific activities as brainstorming, elaboration, the practice of flexibility, fluency, and originality. Type III activities involve work with real problems. Treffinger's model describes three levels of instruction toward building creative problem-solving skills (Treffinger, 1991). Level 1 teaches the basic tools for creative and critical thinking. Level 2 promotes extending the basic tools to learning and practicing systematic approaches to problem solving. Level 3 involves applying creative problem-solving processes to real-life problems. In this model, the learning process and the application of systematic efforts toward creative solutions and ideas (the products) are emphasized. These models illustrate how many elements of creativity can be systematically developed within the classroom setting in long-term curriculum-based projects.

Other proposed models are classroom-atmosphere–based, such as establishing a sense of openness, fun, and a safe environment for personal expression (Amabile, 1989), or activity based, such as teaching creativity explicitly and using various instructional activities, media, and teaching methods (Feldheusen & Treffinger, 1977), or they focus on teaching styles, such as not always lecturing, taking into account students' interests, encouraging questions and opinions, and soliciting students' ideas (McGreevy, 1990). Teachers who enhance student creativity are more humanistic in their approach to students – that is, they value interpersonal relationships, want to understand individual students, are open-minded and flexible, have a sense of humor, and can be spontaneous in the classroom (Esquivel, 1995).

In addition to these more generally formulated models, there is another approach that integrates creativity as a skill that can be practiced as part of learning a given curriculum (Grigorenko, Jarvin, Tan, & Sternberg, 2008; Grigorenko & Tan, 2009). Building on the distinction between Big-C and little-c creativity, the authors define *little-c creativity* as a skill that may be used in approaching and successfully addressing novel problems and situations, generally requiring abilities such as imagining, designing, inventing, and dealing with unfamiliar contexts. As a skill, it can then be developed to a level of competency within any number of academic domains. The authors then present a study in which reading comprehension is assessed using traditional means (asking the student to use analytical and memory-based skills) versus creative means (asking the student to use creative skills). These results showed the presence of content/comprehension in both sets of answers but reflected the exertion of two very different sets of skills, both of which can be developed with practice. The value of this view of creativity in the classroom is that it allows for the integration of creative thinking and its exercise and assessment in multiple domains of a curriculum – that is, it can be practiced and developed in the course of teaching content.

BUT WHAT ABOUT FORMAL ASSESSMENT IN THE CLASSROOM?

Under the purview of research, hundreds of tests have been developed to consider the many aspects of creativity (Houtz & Krug, 1995). The more well known of these are The Torrance Tests of Creative Thinking (Torrance, [1966] 1974), Guilford's Alternative Uses Test (Guilford, 1967), Flanagan's Ingenuity Test (Flanagan, 1976), and the Remote Associates Test (Mednick, 1967). These consider mostly the creative components of cognitive ability, such as flexibility and fluency, as well as creative production, such as originality and novelty, and problem-solving skills. In addition to these tests, lists of personality traits and rubrics for judging creative products (artwork or writings) have been developed as useful tools for looking at certain aspects of creativity (associated personalities, behaviors, and productive outcomes) (see Houtz & Krug, 1995, for a comprehensive survey). However, the need for practical applications and teacher assessment tools to consider creativity specifically within the classroom begs the question of what is a viable and useful view of creativity so that it may be recognized, addressed, and nurtured within the context of schooling. That is, what is the most useful way for teachers to view creativity in the classroom so that it can be nurtured productively within that particular context, and what are some appropriate tools for assessing creativity within the classroom that can inform teachers and help them shape their teaching of creativity?

One specific classroom-based example is given by Proctor and Burnett, who developed a Creativity Checklist (2004) for teachers to use within the classroom. Based on the collective literature on the personal characteristics of creative individuals, the list comprises nine items that describe various behaviors characteristic of creative individuals. It is designed to be used as an observational tool by teachers to focus on the creative personality traits displayed by students as they are engaged in a creative endeavor. These are traits such as "A fluent thinker," "An original thinker," and "An intrinsically motivated student," combining both personal dispositional and cognitive traits. This set of traits reflects one type of tool for teachers in the classroom, useful for identifying and characterizing the creative individual. However, other tools have been developed to be integrated directly into the curriculum. These rely on even more generally applicable definitions of creativity. What follows is a description of a theory of intelligence and creativity that has formed the basis for developing a classroom assessment of creativity.

INTEGRATING THEORY AND CLASSROOM ASSESSMENT

Robert Sternberg proposed a theory of intelligence (1996, 1999) that explicitly incorporates creativity as one of the three main abilities that make up intelligence. This theory of intelligence, called the theory of successful intelligence (or triarchic theory of successful intelligence), combines three sub-theories that address the meta-components, performance components, and knowledge acquisition components of conventional intelligence (i.e., analytical intelligence), an experiential component of intelligence (i.e., creative intelligence), and a contextual component of intelligence (i.e., practical intelligence). Summed up, the theory puts forth that intelligence is the ability to achieve one's goals in life, whatever one's context, by adapting to, shaping of, or selecting of one's environment, through a balance in the use of one's analytical, creative, and practical abilities. Within this theory, creative abilities are described through active verbs, such as *imagining, designing, finding new solutions,* and *inventing.* This verbal anchoring in everyday activities keeps the theory close to the observable classroom behaviors that may be exhibited in the course of class work. But a further elaboration on this view of creativity provides an even broader foundation for applications in the classroom.

Sternberg and Lubart (1991, 1995) then conceived the so-called "investment theory of creativity" to capture the nature of creativity as an act of conscious decision making – generally speaking, the decision to buy low and sell high in the realm of ideas. According to their conception, creativity depends on a confluence of six resources: intellectual skills, knowledge, styles of thinking, personality, motivation, and environment (Sternberg, 2006). Each of these resources presents an individual with choices concerning whether to act creatively: whether to use one's intellectual skills to pursue unpopular ideas; whether to build on or be limited by one's set of knowledge; whether to view situations globally rather than locally; whether to take risks or to tolerate ambiguity; whether to seek out creativity motivating factors in a situation; whether to seek out environments that support one's ideas; and whether to defy the challenges the environment may pose against acting creatively. In other words, the power to be creative rests largely within the individual. Creativity, this theory implies, can be activated by providing more encouraging and supportive environments that reward rather than punish the choice to be creative. Creativity can also be nurtured and developed within these environments. Another useful aspect of this view is that it focuses on creativity as something that happens in the real world, in the classroom and in the course of everyday life. This view can be built on in the classroom setting.

One tool that measures creativity as such is currently under construction (Aurora-*r*) is part of an assessment battery for intelligence in students aged 9 to 12 (The Aurora Project) that is based on Sternberg's theory (Sternberg, 1996, 1999). Aurora-*r* is a rating scale designed for teachers to rate an individual student's abilities in these areas, as well as in memory. The scale was developed specifically to tap into teachers' observations of their students executing typical classroom activities, for example, approaching their work in differentiated ways, asking questions, solving problems, and socializing. Using Aurora-*r*, teachers rate their students on a five-point scale – almost always, often, sometimes, rarely, never – responding to questions such as, "This child retains/remembers for long periods of time the following types of information . . . " (memory); "In the course of class discussion, this child asks questions that are . . . " (analytical abilities); and, "This child is able to persuade others of his/her opinion points of view . . . " (practical abilities). The creative portion of this rating scale asks teachers to focus on how often the child comes up with new or unique ideas to solve problems, whether the child responds to open-ended situations by creating new things, whether the child exhibits independence in completing a task, and how the child responds to new materials or methods for doing things. These questions presuppose that the teacher provides opportunities for these behaviors to occur; however, even if they are not occurring, the scale provides the opportunity to think about each student with respect to these behaviors.

In a small study, teachers whose students had taken both Aurora's paper-and-pencil test, which looks at analytical, practical, and creative abilities, and the CogAT (Lohman & Hagen, 2001), a general cognitive abilities test that focuses primarily on analytical thinking, filled out Aurora's rating scales on these same students. Correlations indicated that teachers' ratings of their students' analytical, practical, and creative abilities matched more closely the students' performance on the CogAT than an indication of students' respective skill levels on Aurora-*a*, a maximum-performance assessment of student's analytical, practical, and creative abilities. Why would this be?

One explanation is that teachers have been taught to look for conventional indicators of abilities. That is, they tend to highly rate students that they perceive as "high performing" in general, according to conventional practices of assessment, no matter what a given rating scale asks them to do. Thus, they demonstrate a halo effect in their ratings. Also of note in the results was a marked negative correlation between teachers' ratings of students' creative abilities with students' performance on the creative subtests of Aurora-*a*: four open-ended productive tasks generally calling for the student to generate original answers to novel stimuli, and one multiple-choice receptive task asking a student to respond appropriately to unusual uses of language. That is, students who did well on Aurora-*a*'s creative subtests were not rated as exhibiting creative behaviors by teachers according to Aurora-*r*'s teacher rating scale. This result could indicate that students who perform creatively on a test do not (or are not encouraged to) behave creatively within the general context of the classroom – in discussions, in open-ended activities, in novel problem-solving situations. Or they are not often given these opportunities. Another explanation is that the teachers might not have a clear understanding of what creativity in classrooms might be like. Clearly, if they do not know what it is, they cannot teach it or teach for it.

What all of this underlines is the importance of approaching the assessment of creativity in multiple ways. What one assessment may miss (e.g., a maximum performance test or even a one on one exercise), another may capture. What one context discourages may be elicited in another. A child who finds it difficult to concentrate on her studies in the classroom may go home and immerse herself in writing stories or plays – all of which she dreamed up while staring out of the window during class time. Thus, a parent's input might be important to discover a creative child's engagement in such an activity. At the same time, creative behavior that may be observed by an educator may be missed by a parent. Or something a student may keenly realize about himself may be overlooked by both adults, arguing the usefulness of self-scales. And yet, assessment is only a focal point in a much larger, more important, and more varied picture that has to do with possibility and promise: If creativity (or its seed) exists in everyone, can it be nurtured and grown? And further, can it be developed in the context of the classroom?

CONCLUSION

We must respond emphatically "yes" – creativity can be developed in the context of the classroom! But first, clarity must be established as to what does and does not constitute creative skills and competencies as well as creative behavior in the classroom. We have argued that the most useful definition of creativity for the classroom describes cognitive skills that can be identified in everyday school activities, while mastering literacy, numeracy, and science. However, equally valid classroom methods for teaching and assessing creativity may be developed based on yet to be agreed-on terms between researchers and practitioners concerning the observable and measurable indicators, such as personality traits and classroom products (e.g., ideas, discussion offerings, written and figural products), that truly indicate creative potentials. Views of creativity need to be merged and refocused. For teachers, a proper definition, training, and assessment strategy should help. They need guidance in understanding what creativity is, why this skill is important in the new emergent global economy, and how it can be taught. Concepts such as little-c creativity, creativity as a skill, and the universal possibilities for creativity in almost any context or subject matter can and should support creativity in the classroom.

Building on these concepts and ongoing creativity research, teachers can create tools to implement creative thinking systematically, even within the curriculum requirements established by standardized assessment.

REFERENCES

Abuhamdeh, S., & Csikszentmihalyi, M. (2004). The artistic personality: a systems perspective. In R. J. Sternberg, E. L. Grigorenko & J. L. Singer (Eds.), *Creativity: From potential to realization* (pp. 31–42). Washington, DC: APA.

Amabile, T. (1989). *Growing up creative: Nurturing a lifetime of creativity*. New York, NY: Crown.

Atchley, R. A., Keeney, M., & Burgess, C. (1999). Cerebral hemispheric mechanisms linking ambiguous word meaning retrieval and creativity. *Brain & Cognition*, **40**, 479–499.

Beghetto, R. A. (2005). Does assessment kill student creativity? *The Educational Forum*, **69**, 254–263.

Beghetto, R. A. (2007). Does creativity have a place in the classroom? Prospective teachers' response preferences. *Thinking skills and creativity*, **2**, 1–9.

Beghetto, R. A. (2008). Prospective teachers' beliefs about imaginative thinking in K-12 schooling. *Thinking Skills and Creativity*, **3**, 134–142.

Beghetto, R. A., & Kaufman, J. C. (2007). Toward a broader conception of creativity: A case for "mini-c" creativity. *Psychology of Aesthetics, Creativity, and the Arts*, **1**, 73–79.

Besançon, M., & Lubart, T. I. (2008). Differences in the development of creative competencies in children schooled in diverse learning environments. *Learning and Individual Differences*, **18**, 381–389.

Chan, D. W., & Chan, L. (1999). Implicit theories of creativity: Teachers' perception of student characteristics in Hong Kong. *Creativity Research Journal*, **12**, 185–195.

Coyne, R. (1997). Creativity as commonplace. *Design Studies*, **18**, 135–141.

Craft, A. (2006). Fostering creativity with wisdom. *Cambridge Journal of Education*, **36**, 337–350.

Dawson, V. L. D., Andrea, T., Affinito, R., & Westby, E. L. (1999). Predicting creative behavior: A reexamination of the divergence between traditional and teacher-defined concepts of creativity. *Creativity Research Journal*, **12**, 57–66.

Diakidoy, I. N., & Kanari, E. (1999). Student teachers' beliefs about creativity. *British Educational Research Journal*, **25**, 225–244.

Edwards, S. M. (2001). The technology paradox: Efficiency versus creativity. *Creativity Research Journal*, **13**, 221–228.

Esquivel, G. B. (1995). Teacher behaviors that foster creativity. *Educational Psychology Review*, **7**, 185–202.

Feldhusen, J. F., & Goh, B. E. (1995). Assessing and accessing creativity: An integrative review of theory, research and development. *Creativity Research Journal*, **8**, 231–247.

Feldheusen, J. F., & Treffinger, D. T. (1977). *Teaching creative thinking and problem solving*. Dubuque: Kendall/Hunt.

Fishkin, A. S., & Johnson, A. S. (1998). Who is creative? Identifying children's creative abilities. *Roeper Review*, **21**, 40–46.

Flanagan, J. C. (1976). *Flanagan Aptitude Classification Tests/Ingenuity (FACT Battery)*. Chicago, IL: Science Research Associates.

Florida, R. (2003). *The rise of the creative class: And how it's transforming work, leisure, community and everyday life*. New York: Basic Books.

Grigorenko, E. L., Jarvin, L., Tan, M., & Sternberg, R. J. (2008). Something new in the garden: assessing creativity in academic domains. *Psychology Science Quarterly*, **50**, 295–307.

Grigorenko, E. L., & Tan, M. (2009). Teaching creativity as a demand-led competency. In O. S. Tan, D. M. McInerney, A. D. Liem, & A.-G. Tan (Eds.), *What the West can learn from the East: Asian perspectives on the psychology of learning and motivation* (pp. 11–29). Vol. **7** in Research on multicultural education and international perspectives series (Series eds.: F. Salili & R. Hoosain). Greenwich, CT: Information Age Press (IAP).

Guilford, J. P. (1950). Creativity. *American Psychologist*, **5**, 444–454.

Guilford, J. P. (1967). *The nature of human intelligence*. New York: McGraw-Hill.

Guncer, B., & Oral, G. (1993). Relationship between creativity and nonconformity to school discipline as perceived by teachers. *Journal of Instruction Psychology*, **20**, 7.

Hartley, D. (2003). New economy, new pedagogy? *Oxford Review of Education*, **29**, 81–94.

Hasse, C. (2001). Institutional creativity: The relational zone of proximal development. *Culture & Psychology*, **7**, 199–221.

Henderson, S. J. (2004). Inventors: The ordinary genius next door. In R. J. Sternberg, E. L. Grigorenko & J. L. Singer (Eds.), *Creativity: From potential to realization* (pp. 103–126). Washington, DC: APA.

Houtz, J. C., & Krug, D. (1995). Assessment of creativity: Resolving a mid-life crisis. *Educational Psychology Review*, **7**, 269–300.

Kaufman, J. C., & Beghetto, R. A. (2009). Beyond big and little: The four c model of creativity. *Review of General Psychology*, **13**, 1–12.

Kaufman, J. C., & Sternberg, R. J. (2007). Creativity. *Change*, **39**, 55–58.

Kaufman, J. C., & Sternberg, R. J. (Eds.). (2006). *The international handbook of creativity*. New York: Cambridge University Press.

Kim, K. H. (2008). Underachievement and creativity: Are gifted underachievers highly creative? *Creativity Research Journal*, **20**, 234–242.

Kwang, N. A., & Smith, I. (2004). The paradox of promoting creativity in the Asian classroom: An empirical investigation. *Genetic, Social, and General Psychology Monographs*, **130**, 307–330.

Lee, E. A., & Seo, H. (2006). Understanding of creativity by Korean elementary school teachers in gifted education. *Creativity Research Journal*, **18**, 237–242.

Lohman, D. F., & Hagen, E. P. (2001). *Cognitive Abilities Test (CogAT)*. Rolling Meadows, IL: Riverside Publishing.

MacKinnon, D. W. (1961). The study of creativity. In D. W. MacKinnon (Ed.), *The creative person* (pp. 1-1–1-15). Berkeley, CA: Institute of Personality Assessment Research, University of California.

Makel, M. C. (2009). Help us creativity researchers, you're our only hope. *Psychology of Aesthetics, Creativity and the Arts*, **3**, 38–42.

McGreevy, A. (1990). Tracking the creative teacher. *Momentum*, **21**, 57–59.

Mednick, S. A. (1967). *The Remote Associates Test*. Boston, MA: Houghton-Mifflin.

Murdock, M. C., & Puccion, G. J. (1993). A contextual organizer for conducting creativity research. In S. G. Isaksen, M. C. Murdock, R. L. Firestien & J. D. Treffinger (Eds.), *Understanding and recognizing creativity: The emergence of a discipline* (pp. 249–280). Norwood, NJ: Ablex.

Plucker, J. A., Beghetto, R. A., & Dow, G. T. (2004). Why isn't creativity more important to educational psychologists? Potentials, pitfalls, and future directions in creativity research. *Educational Psychologist*, **39**, 83–96.

Proctor, R. M. J., & Burnett, P. C. (2004). Measuring cognitive and dispositional characteristics of creativity in elementary students. *Creativity Research Journal,* **16,** 421–429.

Renzulli, J. S. (1977). *The enrichment triad model: A guide for developing defensible programs for the gifted and talented.* Wethersfield, CT: Creative Learning Press.

Rhodes, M. (1961/1987). An analysis of creativity. In S. G. Isaksen (Ed.), *Frontiers of creativity research: Beyond the basics* (pp. 216–222). Buffalo, NY: Bearly Limited.

Runco, M. A. (2004). Creativity. *Annual Review of Psychology,* **55,** 657–587.

Runco, M. A., & Johnson, D. J. (1993). Parents' and teachers' implicit theories on children's creativity. *Child Study Journal,* **23,** 91–109.

Runco, M. A., & Johnson, D. J. (2002). Parents' and teachers' implicit theories of children's creativity: A cross-cultural perspective. *Creativity Research Journal,* **14,** 427–438.

Schoen, L., & Fusarelli, L. D. (2008). Innovation, NCLB, and the fear factor. *Educational Policy,* **22,** 181–203.

Scott, L. C. (1999). Teachers' biases toward creative children. *Creativity Research Journal,* **12,** 321–328.

Seo, H., Lee, E., & Kim, K. H. (2005). Korean Science teachers' understand of creativity in gifted education. *Journal of Secondary Gifted Education,* **2,** 98–105.

Simonton, D. K. (1994). *Greatness: Who makes history and why.* New York: Guilford Press.

Simonton, D. K. (2004). *Creativity in science: Change, logic, genius, and zeitgeist.* New York: Cambridge University Press.

Sternberg, R. J. (1985). Implicit theories of intelligence, creativity, and wisdom. *Journal of Personality and Social Psychology,* **49,** 607–627.

Sternberg, R. J. (1996). *Successful intelligence.* New York: Simon & Schuster.

Sternberg, R. J. (1999). The theory of successful intelligence. *Review of General Psychology,* **3,** 292–316.

Sternberg, R. J. (2006). The nature of creativity. *Creativity Research Journal,* **18,** 87–98.

Sternberg, R. J., Grigorenko, E. L., & Singer, J. L. (Eds.). (2004). *Creativity: From potential to realization.* Washington, DC: APA.

Sternberg, R. J., & Lubart, T. I. (1991). An investment theory of creativity and its development. *Human Development,* **34,** 1–31.

Sternberg, R. J., & Lubart, T. I. (1995). *Defying the crowd.* New York: Free Press.

Sternberg, R. J., & Lubart, T. I. (1999). The concept of creativity: prospects and paradigms. In R. J. Sternberg (Ed.), *Handbook of Creativity.* New York: Cambridge University Press.

Torrance, E. P. (1962). *Guiding creative talent.* Englewood Cliffs, NJ: Prentice Hall.

Torrance, E. P. (1966/1974). *The Torrance tests of creative thinking.* Bensenville, IL: Scholastic Test Services.

Torrance, E. P., & Safter, H. T. (1990). *The incubation model of teaching.* Buffalo, NY: Bearly.

Treffinger, D. J. (1991). Creative productivity: Understanding its sources and nurture. *Illinois Council for the Gifted Journal,* **10,** 6–9.

Treffinger, D. J., Selby, E. C., & Isaksen, S. G. (2008). Understanding individual problem-solving style: A key to learning and applying creative problem solving. *Learning and Individual Differences,* **18,** 390–401.

Westby, E. L., & Dawson, V. L. (1995). Creativity: Asset or burden in the classroom? *Creativity Research Journal,* **8,** 1–10.

13

Creativity in Mathematics Teaching:
A Chinese Perspective

WEIHUA NIU AND ZHENG ZHOU

A few years ago, the second author attended a parent-teacher conference in an elementary school located in Manhattan's Upper Westside. She noticed an interesting survey posted outside the classroom of a first-grade class about the students' preferences with regard to the subjects they learn in school. All the students were blind-folded as they raised their hands and responded to the question, "How many people like mathematics/science/reading/social studies/gym?" The survey results charted on the poster indicated that most first-graders liked mathematics. Coincidentally, two years later, when the author made another visit to the same school, she noticed a similar survey and discovered that mathematics had dropped to the third most favored subject among the third-graders.

Mathematics in China, on the other hand, is consistently regarded as an enjoyable subject to learn by many students from elementary school to high school. It is viewed by most Chinese students as a subject that "makes them smart" (Zhang, 2007). A popular belief in China is that learning mathematics well helps people earn a good living. In a survey of 3,371 students of all grades in ten Chinese provinces, Sun, Zheng, and Kang ([1999] 2001) found that more students consistently rated mathematics as "their most favorite subject" in elementary and middle schools than any other subjects. In high school, mathematics was rated as the second most favorite subject, only topped by foreign languages.

There are a considerable number of studies in the past few decades demonstrating that, compared with students from Eastern Asian countries (e.g., China, Japan, Korean, and Singapore), students from the United States not only fall behind in their basic knowledge and skills in mathematics across all age levels but also show less interest in learning and appreciating the

---

The authors equally contributed to this chapter. Correspondence should be addressed to Weihua Niu at wniu@pace.edu or Zheng Zhou at zhouz@stjohns.edu.

subject (Stevenson, Lee, Chen, Lummis, Stigler, Liu, et al., 1990; Stevenson & Stigler, 1992; U.S. Department of Education, 1996). The results of some large-scale cross-national comparative studies on mathematics achievement, such as the International Association for Evaluation of Educational Achievement (IEA) studies, the Third International Mathematics and Science Study (TIMSS) studies, and the Organization for Economic Cooperation and Development (OECD) studies (Fan & Zhu, 2004), also suggest that mathematics education programs in the United States are uninspiring compared to those of other industrial countries.

How can this gap in mathematics achievement and students' attitudes toward learning mathematics be explained? Why is it that Chinese students consistently regard mathematics as their favorite subject, whereas U.S. students show reduced interest in learning mathematics with schooling? There seems to be no straightforward answer to these questions, especially when examining the Chinese mathematics classrooms from a Western perspective. The average class size in China (40 to 50 students) is almost twice as large as the average class size in the United States (Cortazzi & Jin, 2001). Moreover, Chinese teachers widely adopt expository and explanatory pedagogy and use norm-referenced assessments to assist their teaching and ensure student learning. Nevertheless, this apparent counterproductive pedagogy does not seem to prevent Chinese students from acquiring a deeper, more meaningful, problem-solving–oriented approach to learning. Chinese students also seem to develop higher levels of understanding of mathematics and show increased levels of intrinsic motivation toward learning mathematics compared to their U.S. counterparts. These phenomena were captured and examined by Watkins and Biggs (1996, 2001) as the "paradox of the Chinese learners."

To understand the paradox of Chinese learners, it is important to examine the effectiveness of the Chinese method of teaching mathematics. This chapter focuses on examining the Chinese approach to mathematics instruction from a creative teaching perspective. We purport that teaching mathematics in Chinese classrooms is like engaging in the performing arts. As in any other type of performing art, the creative products – the mathematics lessons in this case – are often carefully crafted and executed by Chinese teachers. During this process, the teachers are also frequently observed and critiqued formally and informally by colleagues to achieve perfection in teaching. Paine (1990) describes this method of teaching as the "virtuoso model" in which teachers take center stage, providing lectures and leading students in various activities.

Using Amabile's Componential Framework of Creativity, we analyze how Chinese teachers achieve high levels of creativity in their teaching by focusing on the analyses of the critical components in the framework. These components are observed in Chinese teachers' teaching of mathematics: (1) developing domain-specific knowledge, (2) promoting creative-related processes by developing strategies of teaching with variation, and (3) nurturing intrinsic motivation to learn mathematics by providing well-crafted, interesting, and meaningful activities. In this chapter, we first present Amabile's componential framework and a discussion of how such a framework coincides with the Chinese conception of good teaching, supported by examples of how Chinese teachers facilitate creative problem-solving strategies in teaching mathematics. We will then discuss how Chinese teachers acquire creative teaching techniques through the three approaches discussed previously. Then, we discuss how creative teaching is consistent with the Chinese cultural ideas regarding good teachers and introduce the Chinese teacher-training model and the concept of the model lesson. Finally, we conclude with a discussion of the implications of learning Chinese approaches to the teaching of mathematics.

THEORETICAL FRAMEWORK OF CREATIVE TEACHING

The theoretical consideration of creative teaching is based on Amabile's Componential Framework of Creativity. The theory was first proposed in 1983 and has since been revised many times. According to Amabile (1996), three major components are necessary and sufficient for individuals to produce creative productions in any domain. These components include (1) domain-relevant skills (i.e., factual knowledge about the domain, technical skills, and special domain-relevant talents); (2) creativity-related processes (i.e., cognitive styles, personality characteristics, implicit and explicit knowledge of heuristics for generating novel ideas, and conducive working styles); and (3) task motivation (i.e., attitude toward the task and perceptions of one's own motivation for undertaking the task). We generalize this model of creativity to mathematics instruction. In essence, to creatively teach mathematics, a teacher must have in-depth background knowledge in the subject area of mathematics as well as skills in and knowledge about mathematics instruction. He or she also needs to develop creative processes in the area of mathematics teaching. Last, a teacher must enjoy teaching and know how to motivate his or her students to learn mathematics. All three of these aspects are important in achieving a high level of creative teaching in mathematics.

The core features of creativity in teaching mathematics in Chinese classrooms are embedded in a set of cultural beliefs and manifested in the cultural practice. These beliefs are an integral part that guides teaching behaviors in the Chinese mathematics classrooms. The Chinese sayings of "Famous master brings out excellent apprentice" (*Ming shi chu gao tu*, or 名师出高徒) and "One problem solved with three variations" (*Ju yi fan san*, or "举一反三") highlight the characteristics of a good teacher. The purpose of such teaching is to instill a passion for learning. This cultural model of teaching (consisting of a knowledgeable teacher, creative teaching, and ability to stimulate passion for learning) coincides with Amabile's (1996) componential framework of creativity: domain-relevant knowledge, creativity-related process, and task motivation. Discussions with regard to these three elements supplemented with teaching examples are presented in the following sections.

DOMAIN-RELEVANT KNOWLEDGE

There is very little cross-cultural research on teacher expertise in mathematics that addresses the question of whether Asian teachers are more knowledgeable and skilled in teaching mathematics than are U.S. teachers. Shulman (1986, 1987) proposed that expertise in teaching is based in the development of three knowledge bases: subject matter knowledge (SMK – ideas, facts, and concepts of the field, as well as their relationships), pedagogical content knowledge (PCK – the ways of representing and formulating the subject that makes it comprehensible to others), and general pedagogical knowledge (GPK – psychological and pedagogical aspects of teaching and learning). Guided by Shulman's theoretical framework, Zhou, Peverly, and Xin (2006) compared 162 U.S. and Chinese third-grade mathematics teachers' expertise in teaching fractions. Results show that U.S. teachers lag significantly behind Chinese teachers in SMK (concepts, computations, and word problems) and in some areas of PCK (such as identifying important points of teaching the fraction concepts and how to ensure students' understanding). Findings from the Zhou et al. (2006) study revealed deficits in U.S. teachers' knowledge of fractions (SMK) and their ability to communicate their fraction knowledge to students (PCK). These deficits could underlie a "teaching gap" (Stigler & Hiebert, 1999) between U.S. and Chinese teachers that parallels the "learning gap" in mathematics. Thus, it is likely that U.S. mathematics teachers' domain knowledge and their teaching of fractions (and possibly of other mathematical topics) are not sufficient for the purposes of developing a deep understanding of these concepts in their students. Similarly, Ma (1999) compared U.S. and Chinese elementary school teachers' knowledge of mathematics (SMK) in four areas: subtraction with regrouping, multidigit multiplication, division by fractions, and the relationship between perimeter and area. She found that Chinese teachers had a significantly deeper understanding of these concepts than did U.S. teachers.

How do Chinese mathematics teachers develop solid subject knowledge and pedagogical content knowledge? The within-cultural research in China compared the effectiveness of teachers trained in Teaching-Regulated Ability (TRA) to a control group of teachers not trained in this model (Lin, 1992; Shen & Xin, 1996; Xin, Shen, & Lin, 2000). The results indicated that students taught by TRA-trained teachers showed greater competence in mathematical thinking and learning than did students taught by teachers who use more traditional drill and memorization methods.

In TRA, teachers are trained by experts from Beijing Normal University (BNU) in TRA theory and by expert teachers, selected from schools in the same school district to (1) construct lesson plans, (2) evaluate their own teaching, (3) modify their activities based on their self-evaluations and the evaluations of BNU experts and expert teachers, and (4) develop students' thinking using Lin's Five Traits of Thinking model (Lin, 1992). The latter includes instruction that promotes depth (i.e., analysis and synthesis of relationships between number and quantity), flexibility (i.e., divergent thinking), creativity (i.e., creating unique solutions to existing problems), self-criticism (i.e., evaluating arguments and proofs), and fluency (i.e., speed and accuracy in using the most efficient problem solutions).

More specifically, new teachers are placed in a teaching apprenticeship with a more experienced teacher who regularly conducts observations of the novice's teaching. Novice teachers give demonstration lessons, observe model teachers' teaching, and discuss teaching methods, among other activities. Novice teachers are taught how to evaluate themselves and also are given feedback by their mentors. In TRA training, new teachers meet once every two weeks for three years. Trainees give demonstration lessons, observe each other teaching, and discuss teaching methods. Trainees are taught how to evaluate themselves and are given feedback by experts, students, and colleagues verbally and through video case studies and tests. For several years thereafter, teachers' skills are periodically evaluated to ensure that the quality of their implementation of the TRA principles continues to be high. This "cognitive apprenticeship" is described by Stevenson and Stigler (1992): "Asian [Japanese and Chinese] lessons are so well crafted that one can notice a very systematic effort to pass on the accumulated wisdom of teaching practice to each new generation of teachers and to keep perfecting that practice by providing teachers the opportunities to continually learn from one another" (p. 46). In comparison, U.S. teachers are rarely offered opportunities for collaborative deliberations and can teach for many years without having the opportunity to deepen their understanding of the content they teach (Fullan, 1991; Ma, 1999). A detailed TRA training cycle with descriptions of purposes and activities is presented in Table 13.1.

CREATIVITY-RELATED LEARNING PROCESS

Contrary to the Westerners' perception of Chinese learners' "rote-drill" style of passive learning, systematic and in-depth observations (e.g., Lopez-Real, Mok, Leung, & Marton, 2004, p. 382) have revealed a picture strikingly different from this stereotypical image of how mathematics is learned and taught in China. For the past two decades, Chinese mathematics education reform has been emphasizing children's development of mathematical abilities. Commensurate with the child's cognitive structure, the core feature of the development of children's mathematical thinking centers on cultivating children's understanding of mathematical problem structures, logical thinking, flexibility in

Table 13.1. *Teaching Regulated Ability (TRA) Training Cycle*

TRA Cycle	Objective	Joint Activity between Expert and Teacher

Lesson study	Develop coherent lesson plans based on teacher's understanding of the curriculum content and knowledge of student thinking to facilitate conceptual understanding among students of the topics being taught.	1. Develop an overarching goal to achieve with students.
		2. Identify the gaps between students' knowledge.
		  – Discuss weaknesses they see in their students.
		  – Look at past test scores.
		  – Conduct informal assessments to determine student weaknesses.
		3. Set specific goals for each lesson based on knowledge of students' prior learning.
		4. Review teacher's instructional guide to clarify the goals of the lesson, formulate ideas about how to teach the lesson, consider how this particular lesson relates to other lessons, and locate where this lesson fits within the entire unit of lessons to be taught.
		5. Develop teaching-learning activities for each lesson in four domains.
		  a. Grasping the problem setting (sequence of tasks and key questions planned to ask)
		  b. Expected student reactions
		  c. Teacher response to student reactions (how she relates responses to the ideas she wants children to think about/things to remember (why a question is included/what teachers are working toward)
		  d. Evaluation for determining the success of each step in the lesson

Implementation and observation	Observe whether the intended goals are successfully implemented; assess the strengths and weaknesses during instruction.	Observations by expert teachers, peers, and researchers:
		  a. Use the lesson plan with extra space as a ready.
		  b. Make tool to record observations as the lesson unfolds.
		  c. Observe students' understanding and solution process by recording their strategies and questions asked.
		  d. Observe teacher's responses to students questions and his/her evaluation of students' strategies in problem solving.

(continued)

Table 13.1 (continued)

TRA Cycle	Objective	Joint Activity between Expert and Teacher
Reflection and improvement	Improve teaching strategies and principles that can carry over into their everyday lessons.	1. Have a follow-up meeting on the same day to keep memory fresh. 2. Videotape of the lesson is used for analysis. 3. Teacher who taught begins with his/her own reflection on the lesson. 4. Observers follow discussion with comments. 5. Teacher can accept or reject suggestions. 6. Teacher takes notes and asks questions in order to facilitate lesson improvement. 7. Lesson plan will be revised and the necessary instructional materials will be prepared.
Reflective reports	Create a record of deep and grounded reflection about the complex activities of teaching that can then be shared and discussed with other members of the profession.	Lesson plans developed during the TRA cycle are filed away along with comments recorded during the post-lesson discussions.

thinking, and ability to analyze and synthesize mathematical information. A learning process such as this nurtures creativity in mathematics learning.

Creativity can be illustrated by the teachers' use of multiple methods to solve a problem. Students approach the problem from various angles, using different methods to analyze the problem situation and to find solutions to the problem. The purpose is to facilitate students in their flexible integration of the desired mathematical knowledge with depth and breadth, thus cultivating their mathematical creativity. The following is an example given by a master teacher guiding her third-grade students through solving one multistep word problem involving distance, time, and speed.

The main purposes of the lesson are to (1) actively engage students in mathematical thinking to promote their ability to synthesize what they have learned in the past and to apply the acquired knowledge in solving a novel problem, (2) facilitate students' flexibility in thinking, and (3) expand their breadth of thinking and guide them in connecting prior knowledge across domains to promote creativity in problem solving. The practice of solving one problem with many variations is illustrated in the following example. The teacher encourages her students to come up with as many solutions as possible in solving multiple problems based on the following scenario:

Problem: The distance of a railway between the south and north sides of a city is 357 kilometers. An express train starts from the north; simultaneously, a local train starts from the south. The two trains run toward each other. In three hours, the two trains met. The speed of the express train is 79 kilometers per hour. How many kilometers less does the local train travel per hour than the express train on average?

Student 1: $[357 - (79 \times 3)] \div 3]$

$$= [357 - 237] \div 3$$
$$= 120 \div 3$$
$$= 40 \text{ (km)}$$

The local train travels 40 km/hour. We already know that the express train travels 79 km/hour; therefore,

$$79 - 40 = 39 \text{ (km)}$$

The local train travels 39 km less per hour on average than the express train.

Student 2: $79 - (357 \div 3 - 79)$

$$= 79 - (119 - 79)$$
$$= 79 - 40$$
$$= 39 \text{ (km)}$$

Student 3: Suppose the local train travels x km per hour,

$$79 \times 3 + 3x = 357$$
$$3x = 120$$
$$x = 40$$
$$79 - 40 = 39 \text{ (km)}$$

Student 4: Suppose the local train travels x km per hour,

$$(79 + x) \times 3 = 357$$
$$237 + 3x = 357$$
$$3x = 357 - 237$$
$$3x = 120$$
$$x = 40 \text{ (km)}$$
$$79 - 40 = 39 \text{ (km)}$$

Student 5: Suppose the local train travels x km per hour,

$$3x = 357 - 79 \times 3$$

. . . .

Student 6: Suppose the local train travels x km per hour,

$$359 - 3x = 79 \times 3$$

. . . .

Student 7: Suppose the local train travels x km per hour,

$$79 + x = 357 \div 3$$

. . . .

Student 8: Suppose the local train travels x km per hour,

$$357 \div 3 - x = 79$$

. . . .

Student 9: Suppose the local train travels x km less than the express train per hour,

$$(79 - x) \times 3 + 79 \times 3 = 357$$
$$474 - 3x = 357$$
$$3x = 117$$
$$x = 39 \ (km)$$

Student 10: Suppose the local train travels x km less than the express train per hour,

$$(79 - x + 79) \times 3 = 357$$

. . . .

Student 11: Suppose the local train travels x km less than the express train per hour,

$$(79 - x) \times 3 = 357 - 79 \times 3$$

. . . .

Student 12: Suppose the local train travels x km less than the express train per hour,

$$357 - (79 - x) \times 3 = 79 \times 3$$

Student 13: Suppose the local train travels x km less than the express train per hour,

$$79 + (79 - x) = 357 \div 3$$

Student 14: Suppose the local train travels x km less than the express train per hour,

$$357 \div 3 - (79 - x) = 79$$

. . . .

Student 15: Suppose the local train travels x km less than the express train per hour,

$$79 - x = 357 \div 3 - 79$$

An interview with this master mathematics teacher reveals her view of how to cultivate students' mathematical creativity. According to the teacher, the purpose of solving problems with variations is not just learning to solve the problem. It is a way of promoting students' flexibility in thinking and broadening their logical reasoning skills. Encouraging students to think of all possible ways to solve a problem deepens their understanding of mathematical knowledge structures within and across domains. Solid foundation and skills in mathematics are indispensable to the development of mathematical creativity. If there is no mastery of relevant knowledge and skills, there will be no flexibility, depth, or speed in problem solving.

From this example, it is apparent that to understand or appreciate students' problem solving with variations, the teacher must have a solid understanding of the subject matter. Sternberg and Horvath (1995) identified three differences between expert and novice teachers. Expert teachers' knowledge is more extensive, accessible, and readily organized for use in teaching than that of novice teachers. Expert teachers solve problems more efficiently within their domain of expertise and do so with little or no cognitive effort. They engage more readily in high-order meta-cognitive or executive processes, such as planning, monitoring, and evaluating ongoing efforts at problem solving. Finally, expert teachers have more insight. They are more likely to identify information that is relevant to the solution of problems and are able to reorganize domain knowledge to reformulate problem representations. Often the solutions they arrive at are both novel and appropriate. Wilson, Shulman, and Rickert (1987) observed that teachers who had more subject matter knowledge were more likely to detect misconceptions, deal effectively with general class difficulties in the content area, and correctly interpret students' insightful comments.

Another determining factor in teaching mathematics creatively is the teacher's knowledge of the "longitudinal coherence" (Ma, 1999). Zhou et al. (2006) showed that in comparison to their U.S. counterparts, Chinese mathematics teachers demonstrated a better understanding of their students' prior mathematics knowledge relevant to learning new fraction concepts (i.e., dividing a whole into equal parts, part–whole relationships, knowledge of geometric shapes relevant to understanding fractions). This information is a necessary prerequisite to determining what teaching strategies to use to facilitate students' deeper understanding of these concepts. In addition, the Chinese teachers' responses suggested that their knowledge was not limited to the grade they were teaching. Rather, it seems that they knew when each piece of knowledge is introduced in the overall elementary mathematics curriculum and its relationship with knowledge taught in previous and future grades. In other words, from what we observed, it appeared likely that they knew what students would be taught in later grades that would build on what they were teaching now. Our observations are consistent with Ma's (1999) notion of "longitudinal coherence," the term she used to describe Chinese mathematics teachers' curricular knowledge. Ma observed that Chinese teachers "are ready at any time to exploit an opportunity to review crucial concepts that students have studied previously. They also know what students are going to learn later, and take opportunities to lay the foundation for it" (p. 122). Furthermore, the Chinese teachers' performances we observed were similar to those of the teachers observed by Ma – they all seemed to have a "knowledge package," a network of procedural and conceptual topics supporting or supported by the learning of the topic in question. In comparison, the U.S. teachers in Zhou et al.'s study rarely displayed "longitudinal coherence" or the "knowledge package" so readily articulated by the Chinese teachers.

TASK MOTIVATION

Task motivation includes both intrinsic and extrinsic motivation. Whereas intrinsic motivation refers to motivation that comes from inside an individual, such as a genuine enjoyment for or interest in an activity, extrinsic motivation is motivation based on an external consequence, such as receiving grades or earning money. The difference between the two lies in the sense of agency of an individual when engaging in an activity. The relationship between the two types of motivation – intrinsic and extrinsic – and creativity is the key element in the componential framework of creativity. In two decades of research, Amabile demonstrated that an "intrinsically motivated state is conducive to creativity, whereas an extrinsically motivated state is detrimental" (1996, p. 107). In essence, any outside incentives, such as deadlines, peer-pressure in the classroom, expecting to be evaluated or rewarded, and surveillance, would cause decreases in one's intrinsic motivation and subsequent decreases in creativity (Amabile, 1996; Amabile, Hennessey, & Grossman, 1986; Baer, 1997b, 1998; Hennessey, 2001).

Chinese teachers regard intrinsic motivation as the core of academic learning. They believe that if students demonstrate intrinsic interest in the subject matter, they will be more actively involved in the learning process that enhances observation, thinking, reasoning, and memory. For example, in the elementary school, mathematical games are often used to stimulate young children's interest in mathematical learning. The games often have specific focus on the development of particular mathematical concepts. In teaching the first-grade students geometric shapes, the teacher puts various shapes of different sizes and materials into a bag. The students are divided into two groups. When the teacher calls out a particular shape, one student from each group will compete to grab the correct shape as fast as he or she can. The group that gets the most shapes correct with speed wins the game. To perform the tasks with accuracy and speed, the students need to ignore the irrelevant features of the objects (i.e., size and materials) and focus on the critical features of the shape.

In addition to the games, another method that Chinese teachers use to stimulate students' motivation and interest in learning mathematics is to arouse curiosity among the students so that they are eager to figure out problems. This is achieved through solving mathematical riddles and finding solutions to intricate mathematical scenarios. The following story is presented to a third-grade class when the concept of "rounding up and rounding down" (四舍五入) is introduced.

> A long time ago, there was a miser named Li who loved to eat eggs. On the market, 10 eggs weighed about 500 kg, which cost ¥1.54. Li came up with an idea that he thought would save him money. He gave his servant ¥1.50 and insisted that he buy 500 kg of eggs. If the servant did not bring back 500 kg of eggs, Li would keep his salary. Can you think of a way to help the servant?

This problem stimulates a great deal of interest and curiosity among the students. After much discussion among the students, a solution is born: "The servant will buy one egg at a time for ten times. Each egg costs ¥0.154. By applying the "rounding down" principle, each egg costs ¥0.15 and therefore 500 kg of eggs (10 eggs) costs a total of ¥1.50."

The Chinese believe that motivation in learning is developed from the constant resolution of conflicts entailed in mathematical problems. The teacher's role is to deliberately and carefully present the critical elements in the mathematical problems to challenge students' thinking through discovery and exploration of various solutions. As Amabile (1996) put it, "The intrinsically motivational state is conducive to creativity . . . " (p. 107). As such, the mathematical problem just presented exemplifies the Chinese way of motivating students to learn by effectively controlling the students' attention and stimulating interest, curiosity, and satisfaction during problem solving.

The relationship between some forms of extrinsic motivation and creativity has been examined extensively, and it has been shown that some extrinsically motivated activities can actually enhance an individual's creativity. These forms of extrinsically motivated activities include a direct instruction to be creative (Chen, Kasof, Himsel, Dmitrieva, Dong, & Xue, 2005; Chen, Kasof, Himsel, Greenberger, Dong, & Xue, 2002; Niu & Liu, in press; Niu & Sternberg, 2001, 2003; O'Hara & Sternberg, 2000–2001; Runco, Illies, & Eisenman, 2005) and performance-contingent rewards (Eisenberger & Armeli, 1997; Eisenberger, Armeli, & Pretz, 1998; Eisenberger & Cameron, 1996; Horelik, 2007). For example, contrary to common belief, in a study to examine different types of instructions on creativity, Niu & Liu (in press) showed that Chinese students showed more creativity when given instructions explicitly detailing how to be creative rather than merely reminding the students to be creative. Such a result may suggest that, at least in Chinese classrooms, teachers' explicit instructions may have beneficial effects on student creativity. It may also reflect the fact that, in Chinese classrooms, a significant number of activities are teacher led; it is therefore important for Chinese teachers to be able to design activities to promote individuals' task motivation to learn mathematics, both intrinsically and extrinsically.

What motivates Chinese teachers to devote so much time to developing their creativity in teaching mathematics? We believe that this practice is attributable to two main factors: (1) the Chinese conception of a good teacher and good teaching; (2) the Chinese school system and Chinese teacher training model.

CREATIVITY AND "GOOD TEACHER AND EFFECTIVE TEACHING" IN THE CHINESE CULTURE

In the Chinese culture, there is a longstanding history of honoring "a good teacher" and a belief that only good teachers produce good students. The original Chinese character of "to learn" is actually the same as "to teach." Therefore, to teach is the process of pursuing learning and a good teacher must be a role model to his or her students, someone who enjoys learning and is able to bring out the good nature of his or her students through teaching and self-cultivation (Shim, 2008). Teachers have historically received an eminent social status in Chinese societies (except during the time of the "Cultural Revolution"). The relationship between a teacher and a student is often regarded to be as important and close as the relationship between a father and a son. The title of "good teacher" is very special in Chinese societies and can be a lifelong goal for literati to achieve. Confucius (551–479 B.C.), whose theories and philosophy have profoundly influenced how people view the world not only in Chinese societies but also in neighboring countries such as Korea, Japan, and Vietnam, was a teacher and is regarded as "the teacher of ten generations." In his life, Confucius accepted more than three thousand students. Of these, seventy-two became outstanding scholars. Confucius was vocal in his interaction with his students about the true meaning of teaching and learning and what makes a good teacher. For example, in *Analects*, Book VII, Section 2, Confucius said to his students, "Pleasure is not a means but the goal in itself, so that 'to learn is pleasure.'" In this passage, Confucius emphasized the importance of intrinsic motivation in one's learning. He also believed and demonstrated through his own life the importance of self-cultivation and the ability to continue to learn in teaching. In *Analects*, Book II, Section 1, it was recorded that Confucius once said, "A man is worthy of being a teacher who gets to know what is new by keeping fresh in his mind what he is already familiar with" (Lao, 1983). In this passage, Confucius gives a high status of being a "teacher," someone who possesses good qualities and can be a role model to others. He also illustrates the importance of acquiring old knowledge when developing new skills. Therefore, being a good teacher is not easy according to his model, as Confucius believed everyone possesses a tremendous amount of potential, and it is the teacher's responsibility and privilege to bring out this potential.

The importance of good teachers in the development of students' learning is also recognized by Western scholars. John Baer, for example, in *Creative Teachers, Creative Students* (Baer, 1997a), says it is important to develop teachers' creativity in the domain of teaching to promote students' creative potential in that subject area.

How do modern Chinese teachers view good teachers and effective teaching? In a study comparing Chinese and U.S. views of effective mathematics teaching, Cai and Wang (2007) examined Chinese and U.S. teachers' cultural beliefs concerning what constitutes good teachers and effective mathematics teaching. In this study, Cai and Wang interviewed nine Chinese and eleven U.S. distinguished mathematics teachers and found that one striking difference between the Chinese and U.S. views of good teachers is that Chinese teachers emphasize the teachers' strong mathematics knowledge, especially a thorough understanding of the pedagogy, whereas U.S. teachers pay more attention to the teachers' personal traits such as a sense of humor and an enthusiasm about mathematics. Chinese teachers also stress the ability to provide clear and precise mathematics information to students, but the U.S. teachers stress the ability to listen to students and adjust teaching for individual student needs. They also found there is a fundamental difference between Chinese and U.S. teachers' beliefs about what constitutes effective mathematics teaching. Whereas U.S. mathematics classrooms are student centered, mathematics instruction is more content based in Chinese classrooms. Such a difference may explain why Chinese teachers spend a great deal of time in preparation before each class.

THE CHINESE SCHOOL SYSTEM AND ITS TEACHER TRAINING MODEL

Unlike in the United States, teachers in most Chinese schools only teach one (sometimes two) subject areas from the level of elementary school up to high school, and they teach significantly fewer lessons per week than do their U.S. counterparts (Cortazzi & Jin, 2001). Chinese school administrators also put more effort into helping their teachers to improve their classroom teaching skills and put more emphasis on teachers' continuing education compared to their U.S. counterparts (Cavanagh, 2007). An important mechanism that Chinese schools adopt in helping their teachers to develop expertise in one subject area is called the "model lesson" (*guan mo ke*, or 观摩课). It is a special form of peer observation of a classroom lesson. Typically, when a teacher is asked to teach a model lesson, he or she will be required to first come up with a detailed lesson plan, and the actual delivery of the lesson will be observed and evaluated by a group of colleagues at various levels, such as school, district, city, province, or even nation level. The number of audience members can therefore range between several and hundreds of people. The model lesson is a popular form of research for teaching in China with regard to teachers' training, and it can heavily affect decisions about promotion. A good model lesson can help a teacher to improve his or her teaching, secure a promotion, and even achieve fame. Those who teach excellent model lessons to large audiences may go on to become distinguished teachers, who enjoy superstar status at teachers' conferences and whose model lessons are sought not only by other teachers but also by parents and students as extra learning material.

The mechanism of the model lesson makes teaching mathematics in Chinese schools more like a performing art, such as dancing. Teachers pursue excellent teaching in their classrooms much like a dancer pursues a flawless performance on stage. In this pursuit, Chinese teachers strive to develop all three components illustrated by Amabile (1996) that are necessary to the development of creative teaching abilities illustrated previously.

CONCLUSIONS

Guided by Amabile's Componential Framework of Creativity, we discussed how creativity is cultivated in mathematics classrooms in China. We began by introducing the fact that Chinese students not only achieve well in mathematics by any international standard, they also demonstrate a greater level of interest in learning the subject than their U.S. counterparts. We also introduced the "paradox of the Chinese learners" coined by Watkins and Biggs (2001) – that is, the paradox that some seemingly uninspiring instructional practices such as large class sizes and content-based, teacher-centered teaching strategies adopted by Chinese schools could actually produce higher achievers in mathematics in China. We examined these issues from a creative teaching perspective. We argued that contrary to what most people believe, that Chinese mathematics teachers adopt many counterproductive activities such as having their students to engage in rote-learning, drills, and studying exam-related materials, Chinese teachers actually spend a great deal of effort developing their solid knowledge in mathematics and content-based creative teaching. Using the examples of instructional mathematical problem solving, this chapter also showed the three major approaches Chinese teachers have adopted in developing their creative teaching skills, which included (1) developing profound understanding of the domain knowledge in mathematics and learning how to teach mathematics effectively, (2) promoting their creative-related processes through developing strategies of teaching with variation, and (3) nurturing intrinsic motivation to learn mathematics in both themselves and their students by providing well-crafted, interesting and meaningful activities. The Chinese approach to mathematics instruction coincides with modern creativity theories such as Amabile's componential framework of creativity.

There are at least two reasons why teaching creatively in mathematics is a desirable goal for many Chinese teachers. First, it is a longstanding cultural belief that a good teacher is someone who is knowledgeable, flexible in using various teaching skills, and able to stimulate student interest to learn, a belief that is consistent with modern theories of creativity such as the componential framework of creativity that emphasizes the importance of knowledge, creativity-related processes and task motivation. Second, the Chinese teacher training model and system of promotion encourage teachers to learn from the collective wisdom of their peers with regards to creative teaching strategies. More specifically, the system of exercising the "model lesson" makes Chinese teachers treat classroom teaching as a performing art, and it is both socially and economically desirable for novice teachers to learn and exercise to become an artist in teaching mathematics.

We outline three implications of studying the Chinese approach to mathematics instruction in the United States. First, the "cognitive apprenticeship" that the Chinese mathematics teachers receive in their teaching career is critical in delivery effective instructional practices. In this chapter we elaborated how this process is carried out. For example, the mechanism of the model lesson allows distinguished teachers to showcase their creative teaching abilities and novice teachers to learn first-hand how seemingly abstract concepts are effectively taught in a way that will stimulate student interest in learning.

The second implication is the practice of having specialization in a teaching subject area. The system of having teachers concentrate on just one or two subject areas, even at the elementary school level, allows teachers to develop a high level of expertise. In the Chinese concept of creativity, knowledge is the key element; therefore, Chinese schools exert a great deal of effort to make sure their teachers are well equipped with subject matter knowledge and pedagogical content knowledge.

The final implication is at the societal level. U.S. schools are not producing the excellence in mathematics that is needed for global economic leadership and homeland security in the twenty-first century. The lack of access to quality education, and more specifically a quality mathematics education, has the possibility of limiting human potential and individual economic opportunity. In many other countries, including the United States, knowledge of mathematics acts as an academic passport for entry into virtually every avenue of the labor market and higher education. As the global market moves forward, the pressure to advance the mathematical skills of workers across the world will increase. If the United States hopes to remain competitive in the world economy, the mathematics education of its future generation must be taken seriously and must be addressed early in a student's academic life.

REFERENCES

Amabile, T. M. (1996). *Creativity in context: Update to the social psychology of creativity.* Boulder, CO: Westview Press.

Amabile, T. M., Hennessey, B. A., & Grossman, B. S. (1986). Social influences on creativity: The effects of contracted-for reward. *Journal of Personality and Social Psychology,* **50,** 15–23.

Baer, J. (1997a). *Creative teachers, creative students.* Needham Heights, MA: Allyn & Bacon.

Baer, J. (1997b). Gender differences in the effects of anticipated evaluation on creativity. *Creativity Research Journal,* **10,** 25–31.

Baer, J. (1998). Gender differences in the effects of extrinsic motivation on creativity. *Journal of Creative Behavior,* **32,** 18–37.

Cai, J., & Wang, T. (2007, April). *Conceptions of effective mathematics teaching within a cultural context: Perspectives of teachers from China and the United States.* Presented at the annual meeting of the American Educational Research Association, Chicago, IL.

Cavanagh, S. (2007). Asian equation. *Education Week,* **26,** 22–26.

Chen, C., Kasof, J., Himsel, A., Dmitrieva, J., Dong, Q., & Xie, Q. (2005). Effects of explicit instruction to "be creative" across domains and cultures. *Journal of Creative Behavior,* **39**(2), 89–110.

Chen, C., Kasof, J., Himsel, A., Greenberger, E., Dong, Q., & Xie, Q. (2002). Creativity in drawings of geometric shapes: A cross-cultural examination with the consensual assessment technique. *Journal of Cross-Cultural Psychology,* **33,** 171–187.

Cortazzi, M., & Jin, L. (2001). Large classes in China: "Good" teachers and interaction. In D. A. Watkins & J. B. Biggs (Eds.), *Teaching the Chinese learners: Psychological and pedagogical perspectives* (pp. 115–134). Hong Kong: Comparative Education Research Centre/Victoria, Australia: The Australian Council for Educational Research.

Eisenberger, R., & Armeli, S. (1997). Can salient reward increase creative performance without reducing intrinsic creative interest? *Journal of Personality & Social Psychology,* **72,** 652–663.

Eisenberger, R., & Cameron, J. (1996). Detrimental effects of reward: Reality or myth? *American Psychologist,* **51**(11), 1153–1166.

Eisenberger, R., Armeli, S., & Pretz, J. (1998). Can the promise of reward increase creativity? *Journal of Personality and Social Psychology,* **74,** 702–714.

Fan, L., & Zhu, Y. (2004). How have Chinese students performed in mathematics? A perspective from large-scale international mathematics comparisons. In L. Fan, N.-Y. Wong, J. Cai, & S. Li (Eds.), *How Chinese learn mathematics: Perspectives from insiders* [Series on Mathematics Education] (Vol. 1, pp. 3–26). Hackensack, NJ: World Scientific.

Fullan, M. G. (1991). *The new meaning of educational change.* New York: Teachers College Press.

Hennessey, B. A. (2001). The social psychology of creativity: Effects of evaluation on intrinsic motivation and creativity of performance. In S. Harkins (Ed.), *Multiple perspectives on the effects of evaluation on performance: Toward an integration* (pp. 47–75). Norwell, MA: Kluwer Academic Publishers.

Horelik, I. K. (2007). Rewards and creativity: Building a bridge between two theories. Unpublished doctoral dissertation, Pace University, New York.

Lao, D.C. (1983). *Confucius: The analects.* London: Penguin Putnam.

Lin, C. (1992). *Xuexi yu fazhan* [*Learning and developing*]. Beijing: Beijing Education Publisher.

Lopez-Real, F., Mok, A. C. I., Leung, K. S. F., & Marton, F. (2004). Identifying a pattern of teaching: An analysis of a Shanghai teacher's lessons. In L. Fan, N.-Y. Wong, J. Cai, & S. Li (Eds.), *How Chinese learn mathematics: Perspectives from insiders* [Series on Mathematics Education] (Vol. 1, pp. 382–410). Hackensack, NJ: World Scientific.

Ma, L.-P. (1999). *Knowing and teaching mathematics: Teachers' understanding of fundamental mathematics in China and the United States.* Mahwah, NJ: Erlbaum.

Niu, W., & Liu, D. (2009). The effect of indicative instruction on creativity. *Psychology of Aesthetics, Creativity, and the Arts*, **3**, 93–98.

Niu, W., & Sternberg, R. J. (2001). Cultural influences on artistic creativity and its evaluation. *International Journal of Psychology*, **36**(4), 225–241.

Niu, W., & Sternberg, R. J. (2003). Societal and school influence on students' creativity. *Psychology in the Schools*, **40**, 103–114.

O'Hara, L. A., & Sternberg, R. J. (2000–2001). It doesn't hurt to ask: Effects of instructions to be creative, practical, or analytical on essay-writing performance and their interaction with students' thinking styles. *Creativity Research Journal*, **13**, 197–210.

Runco, M. A., Illies, J. J., & Eisenman, R. (2005). Creativity, originality, and appropriateness: What do explicit instructions tell us about their relationship? *Journal of Creative Behavior*, **39**(2), 137–148.

Paine, L. W. (1990). The teachers as virtuoso: A Chinese model for teaching. *Teachers College Record*, **92**(1), 49–81.

Shen, J., & Xin, T. (1998). Luen Jiaoshi de jiankong nenli [On teachers' teaching-regulated ability]. *Keti Yianjiou Tongxun Zhuan Kang*, 38–46.

Shim, S. H. (2008). A philosophical investigation of the role of teachers: A synthesis of Plato, Confucius, Buber, and Freire. *Teaching and Teacher Education*, **24**, 515–535.

Shulman, L. S. (1986). Those who understand: Knowledge growth in teaching. *Educational Researcher*, **15**, 4–14.

Shulman, L. S. (1987). Knowledge and teaching: Foundations of the new reform. *Harvard Educational Review*, **57**(1), 1–22.

Sternberg, R. J., & Horvath, J. A. (1995). A prototype view of expert teaching. *Educational Researcher*, **24**(6), 9–17.

Stevenson, H. W., Lee, S., Chen, C., Lummis, M., Stigler, J. W., Liu, F., et al. (1990). Mathematics achievement of children in China and the United States. *Child Development*, **61**, 1053–1066.

Stevenson, H. W., & Stigler, J. W. (1992). Mathematics classrooms in Japan, Taiwan, and the United States. *Child Development*, **58**, 1272–1285.

Stigler, J. W., & Hiebert, J. (1999). *The teaching gap: Best ideas from the world's teachers for improving education in the classroom.* New York: The Free Press.

Sun, Y., Zheng, X., & Kang, L. ([1999] 2001). Zhongxiaoxue Xuexi Yu Fazhan de ershi ge Faxian. [Twenty discoveries of public school students' learning and development] [electronic version]. *China Education and Research Network*, May 15; Retrieved from http://www.edu.cn/20010827/208598.shtml.

Xin, T., Shen, J.-L., & Lin, C.-D. (2000). Renwu zhixiangxin ganyu shoduan duai xiaoshijiaxue jiankong nenli de jinxian [The effect of task-oriented intervention on teachers' teaching regulated ability]. *Xinli Kexue*, **23**(2), 129–132.

U.S. Department of Education, National Center for Education Statistics. (1996). *Pursuing excellence: A study of U.S. eighth-grade mathematics teaching and learning* (pp. 127–146). New York: Macmillan.

Watkins, D. A., & Biggs, J. B. (Eds.) (1996). *The Chinese learner: Cultural, psychological and contextual influences.* Hong Kong: Comparative Education Research Centre/Victoria, Australia: The Australian Council for the Educational Research.

Watkins, D. A., & Biggs, J. B. (Eds.) (2001). *Teaching the Chinese learner: Psychological and pedagogical perspectives.* Hong Kong: Comparative Education Research Centre/Victoria, Australia: The Australian Council for the Educational Research.

Wilson, S. M., Shulman, L. S., & Richert, A. E. (1987). "150 Different ways" of knowing: Representations of knowledge in teaching. In J. Calderhead (Ed.), *Exploring teachers' thinking* (pp. 104–124). London: Cassell Educational Limited.

Zhang, M. (2007). *Xinli Zhisheng: Yiwei Xinlixuejia de Jiaoyu Faxian* [*Achieving psychological success: The educational discovery of a psychologist*]. Beijing: Sinopec Press.

Zhou, Z., Peverly, S. T., & Xin, T. (2006). Knowing and teaching fractions: A cross-cultural study of American and Chinese mathematics teachers. *Contemporary Educational Psychology, 31*, 438–457.

14

Possibility Thinking and Wise Creativity: Educational Futures in England?

ANNA CRAFT

INTRODUCTION: CREATIVITY IN THE ENGLISH CLASSROOM

Since the latter years of the twentieth century, creativity has been recognized by policy makers as increasingly important in the education process. At a global level, it has been argued that such policies, whether focused on the youngest learners or those engaged in higher education, are imbued with a "universalized" perspective (Jeffrey & Craft, 2001), which implies that creativity is involved in almost all activities and that all human beings are to some degree capable of creative engagement. In England, Banaji, Burn, and Buckingham (2006) identified nine distinct rhetorics that underpin distinct yet overlapping approaches to creativity in the English classroom. Some are more prevalent than others and each has an age focus, but all are visible in both policy and practice:

- *Creative genius rhetoric* – With its roots in the European Enlightenment, this post-Romantic perspective emphasizes the fostering of extraordinary creativity in a range of domains.
- *Democratic and political rhetoric* – With its roots in the Romantic era, this perspective views creativity as offering empowerment.
- *The notion of creativity as ubiquitous* – This idea views creativity as pervasive.
- *Creativity as a social good* – This concept emphasizes social and individual regeneration, with a focus on inclusion and multiculturalism.
- *Emphasis on the economic imperative* – This rhetoric emphasizes the neoliberal discourse regarding the economic program thus developing a rationale for fostering creativity in the classroom as necessary to developing economic competitiveness.
- *Approaches that emphasize play* – With roots again in Romantic thought, this perspective sees childhood play as the origin of adult creative thought.
- *Approaches focusing on creativity and cognition* – These stem from twentieth-century Piagetian and Vygotskian work; this perspective

289

emphasizes cognitive processing; depending on the root influence, such approaches span individual and collective perspectives on cognition.

- *A discourse around creativity and new technologies* – This emphasizes the affordances of these in relation to creativity.
- *The creative classroom* – This discourse in particular draws connections between spirituality, knowledge, skills, and pedagogy.

These multiple discourses represent varied and extensive classroom practices. The range and reach of foci and activities are perhaps indicators of the extent to which creativity in education has become a vehicle by which a range of other values may be currently promulgated in schools. Creativity has become increasingly significant in education, and it has been argued (Craft & Jeffrey, 2008) that there are three "drivers" of this shift in emphasis.

First, a "democratic" view emerged toward the end of the twentieth century of creativity as inherent in human behavior as an everyday capability (National Advisory Committee on Creative and Cultural Education [NACCCE], 1999), lifewide and domainwide, and necessary as a response to rapid social, technological, economic, and environmental change (Claxton, 2006; Craft, 2005). This discourse values "everyday," or "little-c," creativity and contrasts with the earlier interest in the extraordinary "Big-C," or "high," creativity (Craft, 2001).

Second, the British Government has drawn increasingly strong links between the economy and creativity across the four nations of the United Kingdom (England, Northern Ireland, Scotland and Wales), as reflected in England, for example, in the recent *Creative Economy Strategy Document* (DCMS et al., 2008). The business rhetoric for twenty-first century capitalism, where creativity through risk taking, practical learning, etc., is valued, feeds perspectives on labor that emphasize the need for creativity (Buckingham & Jones, 2001).

Third, in the United Kingdom, creative and cultural development have been elided at policy level since the government-commissioned report of the NACCCE (1999), which argued for a powerful relationship between creative and cultural education and recommended a core role for creativity in terms of both learning and pedagogy. From this report and closely on the heels of a second paper, *Culture and Creativity: The Next Ten Years* (DCMS, 2001), stemmed a large-scale program in England of curriculum development, Creative Partnerships, which invested in education projects involving community artists of all types to both generate creative learners and cultural cohesion. This was extended to a five-hour-a-week "Cultural Offer" piloted from 2008 in ten regions (Creative Partnerships, 2008), to encourage young people's participation as producers of, participants in, and spectators of culture and overseen by a Youth Culture Trust (Creative Partnerships, 2008), enabling young people, through partnership, to "find their talent." This policy presaged the re-interpretation of the Creative Partnerships program as one focusing on "cultural learning" (McMaster, 2008). The conflation of creativity with culture in education is exemplified by the government report – *Nurturing Creativity in Young People* (DCMS, 2006a) and the government's response (DCMS, 2006b). The mixed creative and cultural program recommended by Roberts was also reflected in the findings of a subsequent Parliamentary Select Committee (2007) and taken forward by the government (House of Commons Children, Schools and Families Committee, 2008).

The creativity (and cultural) agenda, then, has been an expanding one at policy level and has encompassed a notion of creativity as everyday and lifewide (Craft, 2005) and as a response to rapidly changing global economic, political, technological, social, and environmental conditions. Yet, the proliferation of creativity and related policies has been paralleled by an expansion of high performativity, in which the government has established a powerful accountability and performance-orientated culture focused on raising standards and achievement nationally. Consequently, teachers and other staff in schools are subject to close regulation, target setting, testing, inspection, rewards, and sanctions where, through league tables and other means, judgment, comparisons, and displays are used as ways of incentivizing, controlling, and changing teaching and learning – a "performative" approach (Ball, 2003). The tensions between these two sets of policies – creativity policies (often focused on encouraging collaborative engagement) and those that focus on standards (usually individualized) – play out at multiple levels including the classroom (Boyd, 2005; Craft, 2008a; Jeffrey & Woods, 1998, 2003). Concern has been expressed by some commentators about the associated decline in opportunities for extended learner engagement and creativity (Spendlove & Wyse, 2008). The near-impossible tensions produced for many teachers (Jeffrey & Woods, 1998) were the subject of a collection of articles in a special issue of the *British Educational Research Journal*, edited by Craft and Jeffrey (2008). Although there is evidence that some are able, particularly through working in partnership with the creative and cultural sector, to maintain and even to meld the two tracks (Arts Council and Creative Partnerships, 2005; Jeffery, 2005; Jeffrey & Woods, 2003), it is argued by others that living with the dual policies of creativity and performativity in a culture of accountability continues to create marked tensions and dilemmas for teachers, who, if they are to embrace more creative and transformative approaches in teaching and learning, also must be able to take risks and support their learners in doing so (Cochrane & Cockett, 2007; Cochrane et al., 2008).

A significant aspect of the early twenty-first century policy context in United Kingdom and particularly in England, which this chapter is concerned with, is the attention increasingly paid to educational futures – that is, systems for the future (Craft, Gardner, & Claxton, 2008) and futures education (Sandford & Facer, 2008). This is in part a response to the challenge laid down by Postman (1996), who argued in his text titled *The End of Education* for the need for narratives to inform education in the future (for Postman, these were moral guidance, a sense of continuity, and understanding of the past, present, and future). In a digitalized world, the World Wide Web reaches far into the homes and lives of children and young people (Craft, forthcoming). Content generation, social networking, and gaming reaching far beyond the geographically immediate community all form an increasingly significant part of lived experience (Furedi, 2009). This digitized global village is accompanied by rapidly changing conceptions of identity, culture, citizenship, rights, and responsibilities and raises deep questions about how education should be conceptualized. Debates about the nature, scope, and goals of education tread a tension between perspectives that see the child or young person as being at risk (Frechette, 2006) and those that emphasize a view of children and young people as empowered (Buckingham, 2007).

The creativity agenda can be seen as being associated in particular with the empowerment perspective as played out face to face in the classroom. In taking forward creativity in education, the Qualifications and Curriculum Authority (QCA) devised a four-year creativity research and development program (QCA, 2005, 2008a) entitled *Creativity: Find It! Promote It!* This program resulted in a creativity policy framework (QCA, 2005, 2008a), to be taught through the early years curriculum (at that stage for ages 3 to 5 years) (DfEE/QCA, 2000) – later rewritten and reissued (Department for Children, Schools and Families [DCSF], 2008; Department for Education and Skills [DES], 2007) and the National Curriculum (DES, 2000) for pupils aged 5 to 16 years replacing the earlier ones which gave much less emphasis to creativity(DfEE,1999a, DfEE, 1999b). The QCA work resulted in a framework that characterizes creativity in education as involving (QCA, 2005, 2008):

- Posing questions
- Making connections
- Being imaginative
- Exploring options
- Engaging in critical reflection/evaluation

The QCA framework also lists the kinds of pedagogical approaches that it perceives enable creativity, including (QCA, 2005, 2008a):

- Establishing criteria for success
- Capitalizing on the unexpected without losing sight of the original objective
- Asking open questions
- Encouraging openness to ideas and critical reflection
- Regularly reviewing work in progress

Creativity has provided a consistent focus in curriculum reform, with the statutory ages-0-to-5 curriculum revised in 2007 to reinforce creativity and creative development and the ages-11-to-14 curriculum revised the same year to include "personal, learning and thinking skills," one of which was critical and creative thinking (QCA, 2008b). By 2008 (at time of writing*), a full-scale review of the primary curriculum was also under way, with creativity likely to play a key role in this, too. In these curriculum reforms, creativity was sometimes portrayed as an individual phenomenon, sometimes as a collective one; it was also sometimes seen as embedded in domain areas, and at other times portrayed as a generalized phenomenon (Craft, 2008b).

The QCA framework, however, was seen as relevant across each conceptualization of curriculum and included the core element of imagination – imagining what might be – which could be termed "possibility thinking" (Craft, 2002), and it is this aspect of creativity that the Possibility Thinking Study at the Open University began to investigate in 2004. Now located also at the University of Exeter, the study seeks to examine the nature of possibility thinking, along with developing an understanding of pedagogy that fosters possibility thinking.

POSSIBILITY THINKING: AT THE HEART OF EVERYDAY CREATIVITY?

Emerging initially from conceptual work (Craft, 1999, 2000, 2001, 2002), Possibility Thinking is posited as being at the core of everyday lifewide creativity, individual or collective (Craft, 2007; Craft, Burnard, Cremin, & Chappell, 2008; Craft, Cremin, Burnard, & Chappell, 2008; Jeffrey & Craft, 2004). At its most fundamental, it involves posing, in many different ways, the question "What if?" – and therefore involves the shift from "What is this and what does it do?" to "What can I do with this?" It was proposed as involving questioning, imagination, and combinatory play in its early formulations (Craft, 1999, 2000). Implicit within possibility thinking, then, is engagement with problems (Jeffrey, 2006), although empirical work with children aged 3 to 11 has demonstrated how this is often embodied, nonverbal engagement (Craft & Chappell, 2007; Craft & Chappell, 2009; Chappell et al., 2008a, 2008b). It involves finding and honing problems as well as solving them, a distinction explored through studies in primary classrooms (Jeffrey, 2006; Jeffrey & Craft, 2004).

The interinstitutional empirical work has been undertaken in the interpretive tradition using qualitative methodology representing epistemological and ontological underpinnings grounded in collaborative team members' shared values, seeking to co-construct meaning so as to gain an "insider" perspective from participants in the setting. A central concern has therefore been to establish co-participative ways of working empirically in early years and primary classrooms, working with children aged 4 to 11 and their teachers, to

---

* By 2010 as this chapter was at proof stage, the government-commissioned independent review of the primary curriculum was complete and preparations under way for a new curriculum for implementation in 2011. Creativity plays a significant role in the new curriculum in terms of behaviors, skills, and habits of mind that contribute to the "essentials for learning and life" informing all curriculum areas, including the arts (Rose, 2009).

characterize possibility thinking in children, and the pedagogical and other strategies that seem to nurture it.

The Possibility Thinking Study has involved several overlapping and focused stages of work. As of October 2008 when this chapter was written, Stages 1 and 2 were complete and Stage 3 continued, with Stage 4 (overlapping with Stage 3) having begun in mid 2008.

Stage 1: Possibility Thinking and Pedagogy (3- to 7-Year-Olds)

Stage 1 (2002 to 2006) involved three early years settings (focusing on children aged 3 to 7). The settings were selected with a professional development rationale (the teachers were engaged in enquiry-based development of their practice) and a policy rationale (each of these settings had been recognized at a national level by the QCA as excellent in nurturing children's creativity [2005, 2008]). This part of the study involved very close collaboration with teachers and support staff in the three settings, each adopted as a case study of classroom interaction. The research questions focused on what constitutes possibility thinking in young children's learning experiences and pedagogical strategies that foster possibility thinking. The data sources and methods included interviews, video (using critical incident charting and video-stimulated review with both the QCA material and additional material collected specifically for this project), and participant and nonparticipant observation. The enquiry process combined co-participative inductive analysis of the data thus collected (undertaken in whole-group critical analytical data surgeries involving and in close paired analysis between researchers and teaching staff), with deductive theory building, leading to the development of the original proposition and conceptualization of possibility thinking (Craft, 2000).

Findings from Stage 1, then, identified a number of distinct but interlinked features of children's and teachers' engagement with possibility thinking that were valued and fostered in the context of an enabling environment – the confirmation of *posing questions* as being a driving element, with other elements including play, immersion, innovation, being imaginative, self-determination, and risk taking (Figure 14.1) (Burnard, Craft, & Cremin, 2006). Stage 1 also reported on the operational elements of possibility thinking and pedagogy, which manifested in the practices of standing back, profiling learner agency, and creating time and space for creative learning as shown in Figure 14.2 (see Cremin, Burnard, & Craft, 2006, for further details).

Stage 2: Focusing on Question Posing in Possibility Thinking (5- to 7-Year-Olds)

Stage 2 (2006 to 2007) involved additional data from the same three settings but, following one of the outcomes of Stage 1, focused tightly on "question posing" and its role in possibility thinking, with the focus on the transition

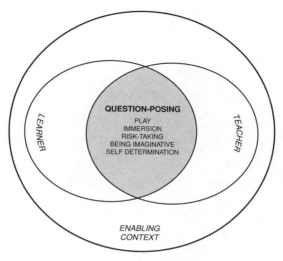

Figure 14.1. Stage 1 model of possibility thinking.

from "what is" to "what might be" in a range of playful, immersive contexts. For this purpose, further systematic video-gathering was undertaken, representing a range of play focusing on child-centered activity representing naturalistic episodes of immersive classroom interaction involving individual, paired, and group activity with a gender balance (Burnard, Craft, & Cremin, 2006). This approach reflected a long tradition in England of observation in making sense of classroom interaction (example.g., Alexander, 2001; Croll, 1986; Galton et al., 1999; Wragg, 1994). A sample of the resultant sequences related across

Figure 14.2. Stage 1 model of pedagogy and possibility thinking. (From Cremin, Craft, & Burnard, 2006.)

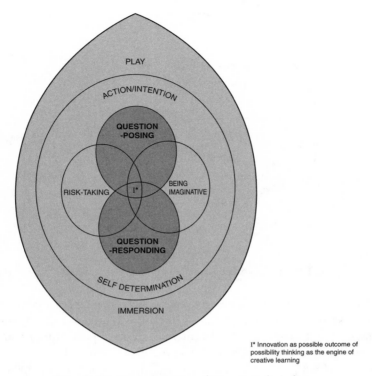

I* Innovation as possible outcome of
possibility thinking as the engine of
creative learning

Figure 14.3. Representation of Stage 2 analysis focus.

a unit of work were subject to fine-grained systematic microanalysis using
an *event record* or *event sampling* of detailed transcription. This approach
made explicit the microlevel of each of the actions, nonverbal and verbal,
used by children in a variety of contexts, to "possibility think." The *activity
record*, as described by Werner and Schoepfle (1987), was used to document
specific actions and make activities explicit. Sampling criteria for an event were
defined as *fluid action, no apparent hesitation*, and *intentional activity*. Both the
visual and verbal data of each episode were transcribed, so that co-occurring
verbal and nonverbal behaviors could be considered together. The *unit of
analysis* was one single discernable action, with each change of action signaling
a new unit, such as putting one brick on top of another, rubbing eyes, or
running away. Interpretive commentaries for each transcript allowed further
elaboration of the analysis, leading to analytical findings from each episode,
working both inductively and deductively as in Stage 1.

Figure 14.3 shows how Stage 2 analysis led to the categorization of *play* and
immersion as the context for PT (made visible by specific behaviors) – hence
their repositioning around the diagram edges. Analysis also indicated that
action/intention (taking intentional action) and *self-determination* (autonomy
and agency) were better described as permeating through possibility thinking

Figure 14.4. Question-posing and question-responding in relation to one another.

rather than being core components. Being *imaginative, risk taking, question posing,* and *question responding* were therefore identified during early Stage 2 as the core components of possibility thinking. *Innovation* was conceptualized as a possible outcome of "possibility thinking" and thus, potentially, a condition for attributing creative learning (Burnard et al., 2008).

The Stage 2 analysis also resulted in a taxonomy of question posing and question responding (Chappell et al., 2008a, 2008b), showing the dynamic relationship between the two (Figure 14.4).

The analysis of Stage 2 also enabled this fine-grained taxonomy of question posing and question responding to be situated within the wider conceptual constellation for possibility thinking emergent from Stage 1, as summarized in Figure 14.5.

Stage 3: Possibility Thinking and Pedagogy (9- to 11-Year-Olds)

Having confirmed the significance of questioning in the overall conceptual structure of possibility thinking at the conclusion of Stage 2, Stage 3 (2007–) has sought to extend the focus to older students, in upper primary education in two new sites in England, returning to the two original research questions in this

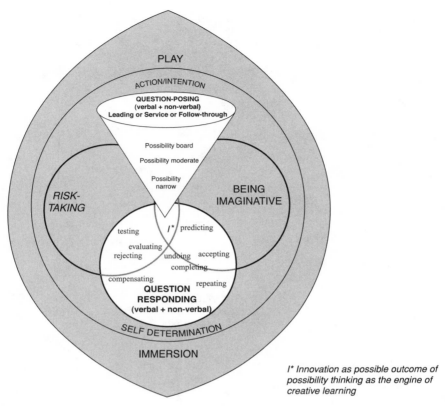

Figure 14.5. Question-posing and question-responding within possibility thinking.

older age-range context, characterizing possibility thinking and pedagogical strategies in relation to possibility thinking.

Stage 3 mirrors Stage 1 in being established as a naturalistic, collaborative inquiry again involving co-participation in three (different classrooms) in sites located in east and southwest England. Data have been collected through videographic observation of classroom activity, interviews, and reflection in and on action (Schon, 1983). At the time of writing (October 2008), the team had triangulated analysis of eight episodes from each site with detailed analysis of two focus episodes in each site against the possibility thinking features.

The analysis to date has resulted in a refinement of the conceptual structure of possibility thinking in relation to these older children, recognizing that immersion at both an individual and a collaborative level provides a context to the other elements, as shown in Figure 14.6, which illustrates the significant role of playful engagement for these older children, at a level more elaborated than the contextual level observed in the studies involving younger children yet lacking evidence of risk taking in these contexts.

As of October 2008, the analysis of Stage 3 was still in progress.

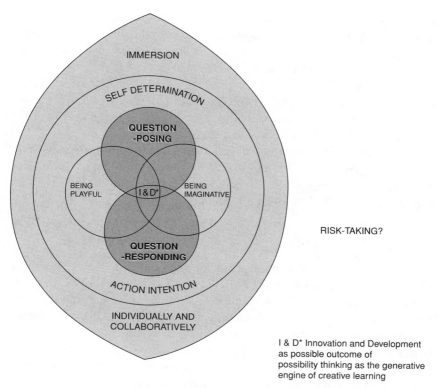

Figure 14.6. Emergent possibility thinking framework, Stage 3 analysis. (From Craft et al., 2008.)

Stage 4: Possibility Thinking and School Aspiration (5- to 18-Year-Olds)

Stage 4 of possibility thinking launched mid 2008 and is situated within the student-led school transformation development and research project named Aspire, also based at the University of Exeter in collaboration with the Open University. Based on a pilot originally located at the Open University (Craft, Twining, & Chappell, 2008), this program involves students aged 4 to 18, in eight schools in the southwest of England, together with their teachers and some parents, in exploring educational futures in their own schools. In practice, the school communities are engaged in exploring and nurturing aspiration and evaluating their own steps toward future education systems.

Stage 4, like all of the previous stages, is situated in an interpretivist frame, the approach taken naturalistic, recognizing the situatedness of activity, in terms of space, time, culture, and social engagement. Of the eight schools involved in Aspire, a smaller sample will be selected for focused data collection and analysis, adopting the case study approach used in the previous stages.

The research questions in relation to possibility thinking in Stage 4 focus on characterizing possibility thinking in the aspiring activity of these schools, and on how it is enabled. In practice, this involves collecting contextualized data as part of the ongoing process of engagement by the students and members of the project team (including the teachers and students). The data set thus includes images, learner artifacts, reflective diaries, field notes written by core team members, schools' own Aspire reports, and documentation in relation to the Aspire framework. We also have audio recordings of semistructured interviews with teachers and students, collected during site visits and at each of the two pupil-focused conferences held by the team so far.

At the time of writing, analysis has just begun; however, the hope is that the Aspire program begins to allow some insight into how the transition from "what is" to "what might be" is experienced and is enabled both individually and collectively in both primary and secondary schools.

POSSIBILITY THINKING AND CREATIVITY IN THE CLASSROOM

The work on possibility thinking seeks, through its naturalistic approach, to understand how creativity in the English classroom is manifest and nurtured. Numerous linked doctoral and postdoctoral studies are under way within the CREATE research group and are looking at possibility thinking in a variety of age groups, from 3 to 18 years, in specific domain contexts, including dance (Craft & Chappell, in press; Chappell & Craft, 2007) mathematics, science, and visual art, in relation to pupil engagement and behavior, as well as in other national contexts, including Iceland, Macau, and Taiwan. At a time when creativity is increasingly valued by educational systems in both the developed and the developing world, this work seeks to contribute insights into nurturing creativity in the classroom.

In England, policy and practice in nurturing creativity in the classroom have coalesced in recent years around a discourse of "creative learning." This term, "creative learning," was appropriated from the work of Woods and Jeffrey (1996), who suggested in their qualitative empirical work in primary schools in England (i.e., schools teaching children aged 3 to 11) that "creative learning" flows from "creative teaching" and is characterized by a sense of ownership, relevance, control, and innovation.

Following the work of Woods and Jeffrey, some writers sought to tighten the distinction between "teaching creatively" and "fostering pupil creativity," arguing that these are actually quite distinct (Craft, 1997; Harland et al., 1998).

In 1999, the publication of the hugely influential government policy paper by the specially commissioned NACCCE (1999) underlined this distinction and, drawing on a range of literature on creativity as well as the experience and advice of many highly creative people both beyond and within education, sought to offer a definition of "creativity in education" as "imaginative activity fashioned so as to produce outcomes that are original and of value" (ibid, p. 29). As noted earlier in the chapter, it was a democratic vision, in that it was argued that all can be creative, and closely connected creativity with the development of culture – an association that has expanded over time, as indicated earlier.

The NACCCE report made at least two large contributions to teaching and learning in English schools. First, it accepted and promulgated a view of creativity as an "everyday" phenomenon. Second, in linking creativity with culture, it recommended the establishment of sustained partnerships between schools and creative agents outside of schools. It was responsible for the establishment in 2002 of a large-scale program, Creative Partnerships, across England, operating in over thirty regions across England; by early 2008, Creative Partnerships had worked with one third of all schools in the country.

This initiative valued the development of multiple models of partnership and encouraged the development of imagination at the heart of creativity, through enquiry-based practice and co-exploration between practitioners from beyond school and those based within. Research has suggested that 5- to 16-year-olds involved in Creative Partnerships outperform those who are not involved (NFER, 2006). Inspection evidence from the Office for Standards in Education (Ofsted, 2006) suggests that the projects:

- Provide rich inspiration for learners
- Foster creative skills such as risk taking, improvisation, resilience, and collaboration
- Contribute to raised confidence and aspirations

At the heart of Creative Partnerships is a focus on the development of *creative learning*, which is significant as it is seen as altering pedagogy in highlighting innovation and as having the potential to prompt change within schools, across the curriculum, and within the wider community. The Creative Partnerships program seeks to build partnership capacity in both schools and creative and cultural sectors in working effectively together and to evidence and disseminate methodologies for creative learning, but the meaning of creative learning itself is still evolving.

Studies exploring creative learning have on the whole been informed by social constructivist models of meaning making, some of them drawing on creative partnerships activity (e.g., Spendlove & Wyse, 2008 which focuses on work being undertaken in the national project, Creative Partnerships, itself). Yet many are situated in a learning context free of the partnership model. These include in-depth studies of how single schools operate to nurture creative learning (e.g., Jeffrey & Woods, 2003) and studies conducted across a much larger number of sites with the same research objective (Hobbs, 2007). It has been argued that "creative learning" can be understood as a "middle ground" between creative teaching and teaching for creativity (Jeffrey & Craft, 2006), combining, as it does, creativity and learning (Jeffrey et al., 2006). Several definitions rely on the concept of imagination in relation to experience in distinguishing "creative learning" from "learning" (e.g., Craft et al., 2006; Hobbs,

2007; Spendlove et al., 2005). Of these, two overlapping groups of researchers have worked from qualitative empirical studies undertaken in several regions of England to develop definitions that emphasize the evaluation of creativity (drawing on Amabile's work on consensual assessment [1988, 1996]) and the role of the domain. An early definition was offered by Spendlove et al. (2005) in suggestion "creative learning develops a capacity for imaginative activity, leading to outcomes judged by appropriate observers to be original and of value." A later definition drawing on work undertaken on how creative learning is fostered in musical and written composition (Craft et al., 2006; Craft, Burnard, Cremin, & Chappell, 2008; Craft, Cremin, Burnard, & Chappell, 2008), suggested a definition of creative learning "as significant imaginative achievement as evidenced in the creation of new knowledge as determined by the imaginative insight of the person or persons responsible and judged by appropriate observers to be both original and of value as situated in different domain contexts" (Craft et al., 2006, p. 77). This latter attempt to locate creative learning in specific contexts for learning is significant especially given the government tendency to situate creativity in relation to culture.

The role of imagination in creative learning seems undisputed and it is in understanding how the seed of imagination is manifest in practice in the classroom, that the Possibility Thinking Study seeks to make a contribution (Craft et al., 2008). It does so by examining how this seed comes to fruition in classroom engagement as discussed above, with increasing attention over time to the social context. For a further feature of researcher stances on creative learning is that some take a collaborative emphasis (e.g., Miell & Littleton, 2004) and others an individualized one (e.g., Eglinton, 2003). While the early conceptual work on possibility thinking (Craft, 1997, 1999, 2000, 2001, 2002) and some of the later work (e.g., Jeffrey & Craft, 2006) focused on the individual, the later empirical work has increasingly moved, through the microanalysis of Stage 2 exploring question posing and question responding, to a focus on social context and engagement (Chappell et al., 2008) to the extent that the social is recognized in the model as indicated above in Figure 14.6 (Craft, Chappell, Cremin, Burnard, & Dragovic, 2008).

QUESTIONING THE MARKETIZED CONTEXT FOR CREATIVITY IN THE CLASSROOM

Although possibility thinking may offer a means of understanding complexities in classroom interactions where the imaginative core of creative learning is concerned, it is important to acknowledge the wider, marketized policy motivations surrounding the emphasis on creativity in the classroom. In England, the twenty-first century policy discourse harnesses creativity (and culture) to the global marketplace as a powerful rationale (Craft, 2005, 2008a, 2008b), reflecting a global trend, as discussed earlier in the chapter. Although the drivers of creativity in education can be seen as involving economic, social, technological, and ecological rationales, the economic rationale is cast as the most significant. The bald argument is that a successful twenty-first century economy is increasingly a creative one, where knowledge is transformed into social and economic assets (Florida, 2002, 2005a, 2005b). It is contended that because thriving twenty-first century economies value highly creative behaviors, creativity is an increasing necessity in the classroom (McWilliam, 2007), with new ways of thinking and learning required (Pink, 2005).

Such arguments are premised on the assumptions that wealth creation and the acquisition of material resources are themselves of high value, that new is consistently better, and that the globe is capable of sustaining such growth indefinitely. Yet, recent commentaries have begun to highlight tensions and dilemmas inherent in this marketized approach to creativity in education (Craft, Gardner, & Claxton, 2008a; Gardner, 2008), claiming that educators, wherever they are located, shoulder a responsibility of nurturing individual and collective generative potential in ways that are both wise and rewarding.

The argument for wise creativity is born of skepticism in the shaping role of the economy. Although Leadbeater and Wilsdon (2007) highlight distinguishing features of specific economies (putting forth, too, that the leading edges of the global economy are Asian), it can nevertheless be claimed that the underpinning value is the mantra of market supremacy inherent in Western capitalism (Craft, 2005, 2008; Leadbeater & Wilsdon, 2007). A feature of Western capitalism is its reification of the individual (Craft, 2005). This stands in contrast to the longer-standing collectivistic culture more typically found in the East (Ng, 2003; Nisbett, 2003). The underpinning view of the market as the pervasive force in nurturing creativity is problematic not only in its "culture blindness" but also in its ecologically destructive and thus ethically questionable (Craft et al., 2008). Seeking to redress such imbalances begs questions about collective responsibility and thus about the nature of trusteeship in the twenty-first century, especially for professionals – teachers included (Gardner, 2008). A challenging task, given the evidence emerging, at least in the United States, from the GoodWork project based at Harvard, Stanford, and Chicago universities, that the societal trustee is declining (ibid).

But perhaps most significant is the argument that education, as essentially an adaptive ecological mechanism (Dillon, 2008), plays a key role in inspiring and influencing the future in relation to the social and the ecological and not purely the economic and the technological. For there are significant problems inherent in Western capitalist individualism. A globalized economic model as primary driver to creativity in education leads to a culture-blind and therefore culturally insensitive model of "development" and "progress." This, imbued with the attitude of "neophilia" – is good (Booker, 1992) – and may manifest as both an ethically and environmentally unwise activity, leading to likely collapse at multiple levels, from the personal to the global. From the perspective of both

Broad	---- mega	--- societal
	---- midi	--- interactions
Narrow	---- mini	--- intra

Figure 14.7. Degrees of wise creativity. (From Claxton et al., 2008.)

culture and environment, then, it is argued that just any creativity will not do; rather, it is *wise* creativity that is needed in the classroom. This is a challenge for, as Sternberg notes, although wise thought involves creativity, creativity does not necessarily involve wisdom (Sternberg, 2003).

WISING UP – A WIDER DRIVING FRAME FOR POSSIBILITY THINKING

As the study of possibility thinking progresses, an emergent concern is how it may offer insight into possibly broader cognitive models that may recognize the connectedness between the subpersonal, and wider culture and ecology with regard to creativity, where creativity and wisdom may be understood as two sides of the same coin (Knoop, 2008).

Such an approach to wise creativity is proposed by Claxton, Craft, and Gardner (2008), suggesting that it is necessary to revisit the Cartesian dualism that tends to drive approaches to educational provision. Drawing on contributions from Knoop (2008), Trotman (2008), and Rowson (2008) in particular, Claxton et al. (2008) challenge the reification of conscious deliberations in favor of an approach to cognition that represents a holistic systems-orientated position encompassing a spectrum of subpersonal (microlevel, neuronal and cellular) and the suprapersonal (macrolevel, social and cultural), summarized in Figure 14.7. One challenge for possibility thinking, then, is to explore how the transition from what is to what might be occurs at this mix of levels. This may, ultimately, involve studies that explore the combination of biology, sociology, and psychology, incorporating the biological neuroscientific exploration of mind, brain, and behavior in relation to possibility thinking, with the phenomenological, interpretive studies that draw on both sociological and psychological traditions.

Underpinning this multilevel challenge is the particular desire to explore how possibility thinking contributes to the manifesting of the special characteristics of wise creativity. According to Claxton, wise creativity demands a tolerance for complexity and uncertainty and uncertainty, assumption questioning, perspective taking, independence, and courage, with a commitment to doing "what seems to be right" even where it may challenge received opinion. For Claxton (2008), there are two conditions to this multilevel-wise creativity. The first is a focus on complexity. The second is a (temporary) allocentric (i.e., not egocentric) de-centred perspective on action (i.e., a concern to recognize and appreciate the good of all rather than being driven by narrow, ego-centric self-interest and thus a capacity to take responsibility for creative actions).

What Claxton's work highlights for the possibility thinking research team is that it is not only complex, a point that is already manifest by the studies undertaken so far, but that it is also socially situated. In other words, although it is a "driver" of imaginative activity, it is also necessarily "driven," being situated in the social and cultural contexts of the classroom and the wider environment, as well as being situated in the microlevel of those engaged in classroom interaction. This social dimension is already visible, particularly through the Stage 2 analysis, and taking the analytical work to the next level demands a focus on the interaction of the creative impulse and the social harnessing of that generative potential. The spectrum of activity this could involve the research group in looking at, includes exploring how social context enhances or diminishes possibility thinking (e.g., investigating the thesis advanced by psychiatrist Andreason [2005], that creativity is enhanced by creative engagement with others).

But, and perhaps more significantly, it could also include investigation of the qualities involved in wise creativity, or wise possibility thinking, which by its nature must involve attention to impact of ideas, and thus implies "trusteeship" (the stewardship of emergent possibilities). Claxton et al (2008) suggest that wise creativity involves honest, detailed perception, patience, a disposition to seek below the surface, intuition, and sensitive and systemic sensibility. These qualities suggest what might be understood as an "orchestral perception" enabling the complex navigation of the unknown in that transition from "what is" to "what might be." As English researchers, policy makers, and practitioners begin to grapple with what lies beyond the current horizons in developing dynamic, inspirational, and appropriate educational provision, the question of trusteeship or stewardship, and especially collective aspects of this, becomes increasingly relevant.

At the time of writing, then, the possibility thinking research team is currently considering how we might position our empirical investigations to enable and explore the development of a "wise creativity" in the context of collective trusteeship. With a particular interest in the agency of the learner in relation to the surrounding adults, Stage 4 of the possibility thinking study therefore adopts as its context an educational transformation project, Aspire, which is focused on the future of learning in eight sites as discussed earlier in the chapter. Drawing on the view of childhood and youth as empowered and effectively moving beyond adult control (Buckingham, 2007; Newburn, 1996) while also acknowledging the contrasting perspective which portrays the child at risk (Frechette, 2006) where adults' roles are to protect, this fourth stage of the study seeks to explore the role of young people's possibility thinking in relation to that of their parents and teachers, in bringing into existence creative educational futures.

CONCLUDING THOUGHTS: BEYOND ENGLISH BORDERS

Although this work has been undertaken in an English context, it is proposed that the conceptualization of possibility thinking nested within the development of wise, creative trusteeship may be equally applicable in other nations and cultural contexts, from west to east, north to south. There is one major reason why wise, creative trusteeship seems relevant beyond England's borders; this turns on the proposition that the neoliberal drive to economic prosperity through inexorable development is questionable.

For, as this chapter has suggested, the neoliberal perspective on creativity in education focuses on the economic benefits of an education that stimulates and expects creativity (Gertler et al., 2002, Leadbeater, 2000, Seltzer & Bentley, 1999). The influences of such discourses are visible in educational policy making and practices in England.

Yet, at the time of writing, the near-collapse of the banking system underpinning the global economy (October 2008) and challenges to the unregulated free market economy perhaps underline the necessity of challenging this discourse. Critique is necessary at the level of whether creativity harnessed to the capitalist economy actually works in practice, as Livingstone and Scholtz (2005) have done in examining the realities of the creative workforce in Canada, as Pope (2005) has done in challenging assumptions put forward by Seltzer and Bentley (1999), and as critics of Florida's (2002, 2005a, 2005b) views on the creative class have done (Malanga, 2004; Scott, 2005). But challenging the predominantly neoliberal rationale for creativity in education is also necessary as a point of principle (Claxton et al., 2008). Framing creativity enhancement as primarily or even entirely an economic imperative promulgates a high-consumption approach that is environmentally, culturally, and spiritually blind (Craft, 2005) and that may ultimately fail to see beyond current horizons to ways of living harmoniously while rising to the challenge of decreasing resources, increasing populations, rising fundamentalist belief–based conflict, rapid environmental degradation, and so on.

Our classrooms need to support students and teachers in applying their capacity for possibility thinking to the question of how to develop wise, creative trusteeship, and they need to support the development of expectations for progression – becoming more skillful – in being wise, creative trustees (Craft et al., 2006) with reference to the stance brought by each involved in the process (Craft et al., 2007). As participants in the educational process, each of us carries some responsibility to ensure that the infrastructure and values of the classroom and its wider educational processes are sufficiently open, flexible, critical, aspirational, and transformational to enable this.

REFERENCES

Alexander, R. J. (2001). *Culture and pedagogy: International comparisons in primary education.* Oxford/Boston: Blackwell.

Amabile, T. M. (1988). A model of creativity and innovation in organizations. In B. M. Staw & L. L. Cunnings (Eds.), *Research in organizational behavior.* Greenwich, CT: JAI.

Amabile, T. M. (1996). *Creativity in context: Update to the social psychology of creativity.* Boulder, CO: Westview Press.

Andreason, N. C. (2005). *The creating brain: The neuroscience of genius.* Washington, DC: The Dana Press.

Arts Council and Creative Partnerships. (2005). *First findings: Policy, practice and progress: A review of creative learning.* London: Creative Partnerships.

Ball, S. J. (2003). The teacher's soul and the terrors of performativity. *Journal of Education Policy* **18**(2), 215–228.

Banaji, S., Burn, A., & Buckingham, D. (2006). *The rhetorics of creativity: A review of the literature.* London: Arts Council England.

Booker, C. 1992. *The neophiliacs.* London: Pimlico.

Boyd, B. (2005). Caught in the headlights. Presented at ESRC Seminar "Documenting Creative Learning," Strathclyde University, October 2005. Retrieved from http://opencreativity.open.ac.uk/recent.htm#previous_papers.

Buckingham, D. (2007). *Beyond technology. Children's learning in the age of digital culture.* London: Polity Press.

Buckingham, D., & Jones, K. (2001). New Labour's cultural turn: Some tensions in contemporary educational and cultural policy. *Journal of Education Policy,* **16**(1), 1–14.

Burnard, P., with Craft, A., Cremin, T., & Chappell, K. (2008). Developing methodology for exploring 'Creative Learning' and 'Possibility Thinking.' Presented at annual meeting *of* American Educational Research Association, New York, March 2008.

Burnard, P., Craft, A., Grainger, T., et al. (2006). Possibility thinking. *International Journal of Early Years Education,* **14**(3), 243–262.

Chappell, K., & Craft, A. (2007). How does developing creative movement change the ways we teach and how we feel about our teaching? In *Project Report and Resource for Broadway Junior School.* Durham: Durham and Sunderland Creative Partnerships Region, December 2007.

Chappell, K., Craft, A., Burnard, P., & Cremin, T. (2008a). Features of 'possibility thinking' in fostering creative learning. Presented at annual meeting of American Educational Research Association, New York, April 2008.

Chappell, K., Craft, A., Burnard, P., & Cremin, T (2008b). Question-posing and question-responding: The heart of 'possibility thinking' in the early years. *Early Years,* **28**(3), 267–286.

Claxton, G. (2006). Creative glide space. In C. Bannerman, J. Sofaer, & J. Watt (Eds.), *Navigating the unknown.* London: Middlesex University Press.

Claxton, G. (2008). Wisdom: Advanced creativity? In A. Craft, H. Gardner, & G. Claxton (Eds.), *Creativity, wisdom, and trusteeship: Exploring the role of education.* Thousand Oaks, CA: Corwin Press.

Claxton, G., Craft, A., & Gardner, H. (2008). Good thinking: Education for wise creativity. In A. Craft, H. Gardner, & G. Claxton (Eds.), *Creativity, wisdom, and trusteeship: Exploring the role of education.* Thousand Oaks, CA: Corwin Press.

Cochrane, P., & Cockett, M. (2007). *Building a creative school: A dynamic approach to school development.* Stoke-on-Trent, UK: Trentham.

Cochrane, P., Craft, A., & Jeffery, G. (2008), Mixed messages or permissions and opportunities? Reflections on current policy perspectives on creativity in education. In Sefton-Green, J. (Ed.), *Creative learning*. London: Creative Partnerships.

Craft, A. (1997). *Can you teach creativity?* Nottingham, UK: Education Now.

Craft, A. (1999). Creative development in the early years: Some implications of policy for practice. *Curriculum Journal*, **10**(1), 135–150.

Craft, A. (2000). *Creativity across the primary curriculum: Framing and developing practice*. London: Routledge.

Craft, A. (2001). Little c creativity. In A. Craft, B. Jeffrey, & M. Leibling (Eds.), *Creativity in education* (pp. 45–61). London: Continuum.

Craft, A. (2002). *Creativity and early years education: A lifewide foundation*. London: Continuum.

Craft, A. (2005). *Creativity in schools: Tensions and dilemmas*. London: Routledge.

Craft, A. (2007). Possibility thinking in the early years and primary classroom. In A. G. Tan (Ed.), *Singapore handbook of creativity*. Singapore: World Scientific Publishing.

Craft, A. (2008a). Tensions in creativity and education: Enter wisdom and trusteeship? In A. Craft, H. Gardner, & G. Claxton (Eds.), *Creativity, wisdom, and trusteeship: Exploring the role of education*. Thousand Oaks, CA: Corwin Press.

Craft, A. (2008b). Approaches to assessing creativity in fostering personalisation. Prepared for discussion at DCSF Seminar "Assessing the Development of Creativity: Is It Possible, and If So What Approaches Could Be Adopted?" London: Wallacespace, October 2008.

Craft, A. (forthcoming). *Creativity and education futures*. Stoke on Trent: Trentham Books.

Craft, A., with Burnard, P., Cremin, T., & Chappell, K. (2008). Creative learning and possibility thinking. Presented at annual meeting of American Educational Research Association, New York, March 2008.

Craft, A., Burnard, P., Grainger, T., & Chappell, K. with Ball, A., Bettridge, A., Blake, P., Burns, D., Draper, V., James, D., & Keene, J. (2006), Progression in creative learning: Final report to creative partnerships. Milton Keynes: The Open University.

Craft, A. & Chappell, K. (2007). Fostering possibility through creative movement. Paper given at *Imaginative Education Research Group International Research Seminar*, Vancouver, July 2007.

Craft, A., & Chappell, K. (2009). Fostering possibility through co-researching creative movement with 7–11 year olds. In S. Blenkinsop (Ed.), *The imagination in education: Extending the boundaries of theory and practice*. Cambridge, UK: Cambridge Scholars Publishing.

Craft, A., Chappell, K., Burnard, P., Cremin, T., & Dragovic, T. (2008). Possibility thinking. Presented at British Educational Research Association Conference, Edinburgh, September 2008.

Craft, A., Cremin, T., Burnard, P., & Chappell, K. (2007). Teacher stance in creative learning: A study of progression. *Thinking Skills and Creativity*, **2**(2), 136–147.

Craft, A., Cremin, T., Burnard, P., & Chappell, K. (2008). Possibility thinking. In A. Craft, T. Cremin, & P. Burnard (Eds.), *Creative learning 3–11 and how we document it*. Stoke-on-Trent: Trentham Books.

Craft, A., Gardner, H., & Claxton, G. (2008). *Creativity, wisdom and trusteeship: Exploring the role of education*. Thousand Oaks, CA: Corwin Press.

Craft, A., & Jeffrey, B. (2008). Creativity and performativity in teaching and learning: tensions, dilemmas, constraints, accommodations and synthesis. *British Educational Research Journal*, **34**(5), 577–584.

Craft, A., Twining, P., & Chappell, K. (2008). Learners reconceptualising education: Widening participation through creative engagement? *Innovations In Education & Teaching International,* **45**(3), 235–245.

Creative Partnerships. (2008). Five hours a week of quality arts and culture, for every child. Retrieved from http://www.creative-partnerships.com/offer.

Cremin, T., Burnard, P., & Craft, A. (2006). Pedagogy and possibility thinking in the early years. *Thinking Skills and Creativity,* **1**(2), 108–119.

Croll, P. (1986). *Systematic classroom observation.* Lewes, Sussex, UK: The Falmer Press.

Department for Children, Schools and Families (DCSF). (2007). *The children's plan.* London: Her Majesty's Stationery Office.

Department for Children, Schools and Families (DCSF). (2008). *Practice guidance for the early years foundation stage.* Nottingham, UK: DCSF Publications.

Department for Culture, Media and Sport (DCMS). (2001). Creativity and culture: The next ten years. London: Her Majesty's Stationery Office. Retrieved from http://www.culture.gov.uk/reference_library/publications/4634.aspx.

Department for Culture, Media and Sport. (Feb 2008). Joint DCMS/DCSF press release on the cultural offer, February 13, 2008.

Department for Culture Media and Sport (DCMS) and Department for Education and Skills (DES). (2006a). *Nurturing creativity and young people.* London: Her Majesty's Stationery Office.

Department for Culture, Media and Sport (DCMS) and Department for Education and Skills (DES). (2006b). *Government response to nurturing creativity and young people.* London: Her Majesty's Stationery Office.

Department for Culture, Media and Sport (DCMS). Department for Business, Enterprise and Regulatory Reform (BERR) & Department for Innovation, Universities and Skills (DIUS). (2008). *Creative Britain: New talents for the creative economy.* London: DCMS.

Department for Education and Employment (DEE) and Qualifications and Curriculum Authority (QCA). (1999a). *The national curriculum handbook for teachers in key stages 1 and 2.* London: QCA.

Department for Education and Employment (DEE) and Qualifications and Curriculum Authority (QCA). (1999b). *The national curriculum handbook for teachers in key stages 3 and 4.* London: QCA.

Department for Education and Employment (DEE) and Qualifications and Curriculum Authority (QCA). (2000). *Curriculum guidance for the foundation stage.* London: QCA.

Department for Education and Skills (DES). (2007). *Statutory framework for the early years foundation stage.* Nottingham, UK: DES.

Dillon, P. (2008). Creativity, wisdom, and trusteeship: Niches of cultural production. In A. Craft, H. Gardner, & G. Claxton (Eds.), *Creativity, wisdom, and trusteeship: Exploring the role of education.* Thousand Oaks, CA: Corwin Press.

Eglinton, K. A. (2003). *Art in the early years.* London: Routledge Falmer.

Florida, R. (2002). *The rise of the creative class and how it's transforming work, leisure and everyday life.* New York: Basic Books.

Florida, R. (2005a). *The flight of the creative class. The new global competition for talent.* New York: HarperBusiness, HarperCollins.

Florida, R. (2005b). *Cities and the creative class.* London: Routledge.

Frechette, J. (2006). Cyber-censorship or cyber-literacy? Envisioning cyber-learning through media education. In D. Buckingham & R. Willett (Eds.), *Digital generations: Children, young people and new media* (pp. 149–171). Mahwah, NJ: Lawrence Erlbaum.

Furedi, F. (2009). *Why education isn't educating*. London: Continuum.

Galton, M., Hargreaves, L., Comber, C., & Wall, D. (1999). *Inside the primary classroom: 20 Years on.* London: Routledge.

Gardner, H. (2008). Creativity, wisdom, and trusteeship. In A. Craft, H. Gardner, & G. Claxton (Eds.). *Creativity, wisdom, and trusteeship: Exploring the role of education.* Thousand Oaks, CA: Corwin Press.

Gertler, M. S., Florida, R. Gates, G., & Vinodrai, T. (2002). *Competing on creativity: Placing Ontario's cities in North American context.* Report prepared for the Ontario Ministry of Enterprise, Opportunity and Innovation and the Institute of Competitiveness and Prosperity. Ontario, Canada.

Harland, J., Kinder, K., Haynes, J., & Schagen, I. (1998). *The effects and effectiveness of arts education in schools: Interim report 1.* Slough, Berkshire, UK: National Foundation for Educational Research.

Hobbs, J. (2007). Why is creative learning so important? London: Specialist Schools and Academies Trust.

House of Commons Children, Schools and Families Committee. (2008). *Creative partnerships and the curriculum: Government response to the eleventh report from the Education and Skills Committee, session 2006–07.* London: The Stationery Office Limited.

House of Commons Education and Skills Committee. (2007). *Creative partnerships and the curriculum. Eleventh Report of Session 2006–07.* Report, together with formal minutes, oral and written evidence. London: The Stationery Office Limited.

Jeffrey, B. (2003). Countering student instrumentalism: A creative response. *British Educational Research Journal,* **29**(4), 489–504.

Jeffrey, B. (Ed.) (2006). *Creative learning practices: European experiences.* London: Tufnell.

Jeffrey, B., & Craft, A. (2001). The universalization of creativity. In A. Craft, B. Jeffrey, & M. Leibling (Eds.), *Creativity in education* (pp. 1–13). London: Continuum.

Jeffrey, B., & Craft, A. (2004). Teaching creatively and teaching for creativity: distinctions and relationships. *Educational Studies,* **30**(1), 77–87.

Jeffrey, B., & Craft, A. (2006). Creative learning and possibility thinking. In B. Jeffrey (Ed.), *Creative learning practices: European experiences* (pp. 73–91). London: The Tufnell Press.

Jeffrey, B., & Woods, P. (1998). *Testing teachers: The effects of school inspections on primary teachers.* London: Routledge/Falmer.

Jeffrey, B., & Woods, P. (2003). *The creative school: A framework for success, quality and effectiveness.* London: Routledge/Falmer.

Jeffery, G. (Ed.) (2005). *The creative college.* Stoke-on-Trent: Trentham Books.

Knoop, H. H. (2008). Wise creativity and creative wisdom. In A. Craft, H. Gardner, & G. Claxton (Eds.), *Creativity, wisdom, and trusteeship: Exploring the role of education.* Thousand Oaks, CA: Corwin Press.

Leadbeater, C. (2000). *Living on thin air: The new economy with a blueprint for the 21st century.* London: Penguin.

Leadbeater, C., & Wilsdon, J. (2007). *The atlas of ideas: How Asian innovation can benefit us all.* London: Demos.

Malanga, S. (2004). The curse of the creative class. *The Wall Street Journal,* January 19, 2004. Retrieved from http://www.opinionjournal.com/extra/?id=110004573.

McMaster, Sir B. (2008). *Supporting excellence in the arts: From measurement to judgement.* London: Department for Culture, Media and Sport.

McWilliam, E. (2007). From 'Made in China' to 'Created in China': Changing our education systems for the 21st century. Speech for the 10th China Beijing International High-tech Expo, Beijing, May 25, 2007.

Miell, D., & Littleton, K. S. (Eds.) (2004). *Collaborative creativity*. London, Free Association Books.

National Advisory Committee on Creative and Cultural Education (NACCCE). (1999). *All our futures: Creativity, culture and education*. London: Department for Education and Employment.

National Foundation for Educational Research (NFER). (2006). The longer term impact of creative partnerships on the attainment of young people. Slough: NFER.

Newburn, T. (1996). Back to the future? Youth crime, youth justice and the rediscovery of 'authoritarian populism.' In J. Pilcher & S. Wagg (Eds.), *Thatcher's children? Politics, childhood and society in the 1980s and 1990s*. London: Falmer.

Ng, A. K. (2003). A cultural model of creative and conforming behaviour. *Creativity Research Journal*, **15**(2 & 3), 223–233.

Nisbett, R. E. (2003). *The geography of thought*. New York: The Free Press.

Ofsted. (2006). *Ofsted inspection of creative partnerships*. Retrieved from http://www.creative-partnerships.com/research-resources/resources/ofsted-report-creative-partnerships-initiative-and-impact,94,ART.html.

Pink, D. H. (2005). *A whole new mind: Moving from the information age to the conceptual age*. New York: Riverhead Books.

Pope, R. (2005). *Creativity: Theory, history, practice*. London/New York: Routledge.

Postman, N. (1996). The end of education: Redefining the value of school. New York: Knopf.

Qualifications and Curriculum Authority (QCA). (2005). *Creativity: Find it, promote It! – Promoting pupils' creative thinking and behaviour across the curriculum at key stages 1, 2 and 3 – practical materials for schools*. London: QCA.

Qualifications and Curriculum Authority (QCA). (2008a). Retrieved from http://www.ncaction.org.uk/creativity/.

Qualifications and Curriculum Authority (QCA). (2008b). *The new secondary curriculum: Personal, learning and thinking skills – supporting successful learners, confident individuals and responsible citizens*. London: QCA.

Rowson, J. (2008). How are we disposed to be creative? In A. Craft, H. Gardner, & G. Claxton (Eds.), *Creativity, wisdom, and trusteeship: Exploring the role of education*. Thousand Oaks, CA: Corwin Press.

Sandford, R., & Facer, K. (2008). *Beyond current horizons*. London: Department for Children, Schools and Families.

Scholtz, A., & Livingstone, D. W. (2005). Knowledge workers and the 'new economy' in Canada: 1983–2004. Presented at third annual Work and Life Long Learning (WALL) conference, Toronto, Canada, June 20th-22nd 2005.

Schön, D. (1983) *The Reflective Practitioner. How professionals think in action*, London: Temple Smith.

Scott, A. J. (2006). Creative cities: Conceptual issues and policy questions. *Journal of Urban Affairs*, **28**, 1–17.

Seltzer, K., & Bentley, T. (1999). *The creative age: Knowledge and skills for the new economy*. London: Demos.

Spendlove, D., Wyse, D., Craft, A. and Hallgarten, J. (2005) Creative Learning. *Creative Learning Definition: work in progress*. Private correspondence emerging from Documenting Creative Learning International Symposium held at the University of Cambridge, April 2005.

Spendlove, D., & Wyse, D. (2008). Creative learning: Definitions and barriers. In A. Craft, T. Cremin, & P. Burnard (Eds.), *Creative learning 3–11 and how we document it*. Stoke-on-Trent, UK: Trentham Books.

Sternberg, R. (2003). *Wisdom, intelligence and creativity synthesised*. Cambridge, UK: Cambridge University Press.

Troman, G., Jeffrey, B., & Raggl, A. (2007). Creativity and performativity policies in primary school cultures? *Journal of Education Policy*, **22**(5), 549–572.

Trotman, D. (2008). Liberating the Wise Educator: Cultivating professional judgment in educational practice. In A. Craft, H. Gardner, & G. Claxton (Eds.), *Creativity, wisdom, and trusteeship: Exploring the role of education*. Thousand Oaks, CA: Corwin Press.

Wallace, D., & Gruber, H. (1989), *Creative people at work: Twelve cognitive case studies*. Oxford: Oxford University Press.

Werner, O., & Schoepfle, G. (1987). *Systematic fieldwork: Vol. 1, Foundations of ethnography and interviewing*. Newbury Park, CA: Sage.

Woods, P. (2007). Academy schools and entrepreneurialism in education. *Journal of Education Policy*, **22**(2), 237–259.

Woods, P., & Jeffrey, B. (1996). *Teachable moments: The art of creative teaching in primary schools*. Buckingham, UK: Open University Press.

Wragg, E. C. (1994). *An introduction to classroom observation*. London: Routledge.

15

When Intensity Goes to School: Overexcitabilities, Creativity, and the Gifted Child

SUSAN DANIELS AND MICHAEL M. PIECHOWSKI

A teacher called the child's mother to show her a large sheet with a drawing of large squares on it. The mother was puzzled, so the teacher explained: "Like all other children, your daughter was asked to draw chickens in the barnyard. She drew the wire mesh. This is very disturbing." A creative child will see things in a new way – instead of following the rules, a creative child will change them, will shift perspective. This child took the chicken's perspective. She grew up to be a world famous pianist. From an early age, she asserted with great intensity her way of approaching things and has the following remembrance (Grimaud, 2006, pp. 1–2):

> "She is never satisfied!"
> As a small child, I heard these words a thousand times.... Long before I understood what these words meant, I made them into a family, much like my stuffed animals. Their family name was "Un." They were the "Uns," and each of them had the same ability to put a surprised or worried look on my mother's face.... I created a family tree for them. The great-grandfather of the words was Uncontrollable.
> After Uncontrollable, there came quite often Unsatisfied. Then Unmanageable. Or Impossible, Undisciplined. Insatiable. Insubordinate... Unadaptable. Unpredictable.

Hélène Grimaud's memoir of her growing-up years, *Wild Harmonies: A Life of Music and Wolves*, offers profound insight into the rocky path of a highly gifted, creative, and passionate person growing up in a world that does not always understand or appreciate such energy, intensity, and passion.

Gifted, talented, and creative people are known to be energetic, enthusiastic, intensely absorbed in their pursuits, endowed with vivid imagination, and strongly sensual, but they are also often emotionally vulnerable. They tend to react strongly to aesthetic, intellectual, emotional, sensual, and other stimuli. Because of this intensity, creative people may be perceived as particularly difficult or challenging. At the same time, this intensity provides the energy behind the drive to create (Daniels & Piechowski, 2009).

One theory is particularly useful in understanding the connections between intensity of personality and creativity. Kazimierz Dabrowski's Theory of Positive Disintegration specifically addresses the psychological development of the gifted, talented, and creative. This theory is presented along with specific applications of the theory for nurturing the personal development and creativity of students within the regular classroom setting.

KAZIMIERZ DABROWSKI

Kazimierz Dabrowski (1902–1980), a Polish psychiatrist and psychologist, studied the development of creatively, artistically, and intellectually gifted youth. He took the intensity of their emotions, their sensitivity and tendency toward emotional extremes, as part and parcel of their growth and development. In their intensified manner of experiencing, feeling, thinking, and imagining, he perceived the potential for further growth (Dabrowski, 1967, 1972). He saw inner forces at work generating overstimulation, conflict, and pain but also a search for a way out of the pain, strife, and disharmony. He devoted his life's work to developing insight into and supporting the development of those individuals with unique potential who – being open to greater possibilities and realities – might also be vulnerable in certain contexts and situations.

In his clinical practice, Dabrowski specialized in working with talented artists, writers, actors, musicians, and intellectually, artistically, and creatively gifted children. He found that those whose considerable emotional richness and creative vision brought them insights and experiences of an unusual nature were easily labeled as abnormal, immature, neurotic, or even delusional and psychotic (Piechowski, 2002). Yet, Dabrowski saw in them, instead, the potential for advanced development.

Dabrowski's concept of developmental potential includes talents, specific abilities, and intelligence, plus five primary aspects of personality (psychomotor, sensual, imaginational, intellectual, and emotional), of heightened excitability or a capacity to become superstimulated. These five overexcitabilities are listed in Table 15.1.

Dabrowski explained the sensitivity and intensity experienced by many creatively gifted individuals in terms of these overexcitabilities – characterized by a greater capacity to be stimulated by and to respond to external and internal stimuli. Overexcitability permeates a creatively gifted person's existence. Whether it is through music, language, physical sensing, kinesthetic activity, imagination, or an intellectual drive, an overexcitability orients and focuses experience. Overexcitability gives energy to intelligence and talents. It shapes personality.

Table 15.1. *Forms and expressions of overexcitability*

Psychomotor
Surplus of energy
Psychomotor expression of emotional tension

Sensual
Enhanced sensory and aesthetic pleasure
Sensual expression of emotional tension

Intellectual
Intensified activity of the mind
Penchant for probing questions and problem solving
Reflective thought

Imaginational
Free play of the imagination
Capacity for living in a world of fantasy
Spontaneous imagery as an expression of emotional tension
Low tolerance of boredom; need for novelty

Emotional
Feelings and emotions intensified; awareness of emotions in self and others
Strong somatic expressions
Strong affective expressions
Capacity for strong attachments, deep relationships
Well-differentiated feelings toward self, inner dialogue and self-reflection

OVEREXCITABILITY

The five overexcitabilities may be likened to color filters or channels through which the world is perceived and felt. An overexcitability is a lens that opens, widens, and deepens perspective. These lenses can be wide open, narrow, or operating at a bare minimum. They are assumed to be part of a person's constitution and to be more or less independent of each other. If more than one of these lenses has a wide aperture, then the depth and breadth of feeling, thought, imagery, and sensation may well lead to dissonance, discomfort, and tension. Consequently, experience becomes multidimensional – enriching, expanding, and intensifying the individual's emotional development, although at times the resulting inner tensions and conflicts may be overwhelming.

Table 15.1 presents an overview of the behaviors and characteristics associated with each overexcitability. In the following sections, examples of how each of the overexcitabilities is manifest for gifted, creative, and talented individuals are described, followed by suggestions of how adults may respond to children's overexcitabilities in a positive way. Suggestions are provided so teachers, counselors, and other educators can help children learn strategies to *modulate* the expression of their overexcitabilities, varying by circumstance and the child's needs.

To *modulate* means (1) to regulate or adjust, (2) to alter or adapt according to circumstance, or (3) to change or vary the pitch. We have observed that all too often children are asked, or expected, to completely quiet or squelch expression of their overexcitabilities. This can be damaging to the child's creative – and overall – development. Instead, we hope that adults have new insights and gain tools to help the child discover choices and options for how and when a child expresses an overexcitability. Please keep in mind that a child may have one, several, or all of the overexcitabilities and that each overexcitability may imbue both advantages and challenges for the child. Generally, the brighter, the more inquisitive, and the more creative the child, the more likely it is that the child's overexcitabilities and related behaviors and needs will permeate and influence daily behaviors. It is helpful to remember that each overexcitability, in some way, likely provides the energy or fuel that contributes to the development of a young person's talent along with the advantages and challenges that fundamentally shape their ultimate development (Daniels & Meckstroth, 2009).

PSYCHOMOTOR OVEREXCITABILITY

Psychomotor overexcitability is significantly correlated with high intelligence (Ackerman, 1993). Intellectually gifted and creative children characteristically exhibit a high energy level. This energy may find expression in myriad ways. Children with heightened psychomotor intensity can appear very busy and restless. In young gifted children, we hear rapid, seemingly excessive, almost compulsive speech. They may explain things until you beg them to stop! They may gesture with their entire body, much beyond punctuating hand gestures. Some gifted children have a voracious appetite for activity; they're "antsy," always moving.

The higher energy level of creative people has been widely documented (Piechowski, 1999; Silverman, 1993), although it is not universal. Some creators were highly spirited and energetic when they were young but were not so in their adult years. Antoine de Saint-Exupéry, Sergie Rachmaninoff, and Thomas Alva Edison are a few of the examples of the many creators who as children were impetuous, hard-to-control bundles of energy. Saint-Exupéry as a boy had wild energy and acted without fear. He was particularly fond of aggressive games and tyrannized his friends. Edison was always getting into scrapes because of his relentless curiosity. Once, he attached wires to two large cats and then attempted to produce electricity by rubbing them vigorously against each other. The resulting scratches and claw marks were deep and long lasting. Rachmaninoff's favorite sport was to jump on and off horse-driven streetcars, a pastime he particularly enjoyed in winter on icy pavement (Piechowski, 2002). Today such highly creative and highly charged children are often mistakenly labeled as hyperactive or as having attention-deficit/hyperactivity disorder (ADHD).

This concept of psychomotor overexcitability has extensive implications for teachers. It is essential that teachers and other school personnel aim to integrate creatively gifted children's often intense, highly active physical needs within the day's confines. These intense children need to have appropriate outlets for their energies and need to learn appropriate and effective ways of self-management.

Psychomotor overexcitability may or may not find expression and release in sports. However released, physical activity is necessary for optimal self-expression and release of physical energy. For some, psychomotor overexcitability is an outward expression of inner emotional tension. In this case, the children have a need to move as a release for their emotional tension. Such pent-up tension can be very difficult for a child to contain in situations where much sitting is required – for instance, in the classroom or during long bus rides to or from school. In anticipation of this, providing plenty of opportunities for movement before, during, and after will help a great deal.

Often, preschool and other early childhood school experiences focus on "socializing" young students. "Rugtime" or circle times are often cornerstones of sharing time, yet they may become excruciatingly constricting to small bodies brimming with energy and urging to move about. Sometimes, for students who have a great deal of psychomotor overexcitability, rugtime compliance becomes an educational goal. Paradoxically, encouraging these children to move about – as long as others are not disrupted – can facilitate their learning because they stop focusing on their aggravating constrictions (Daniels & Meckstroth, 2009).

Although some adults might prefer to entirely dampen or cease the outward expression of this inner energy, such an approach is typically counterproductive. Rather than defying and fighting it, educators can accommodate their students' needs to be on the move and harness this energy in constructive ways. Children do not have to sit down to read; instead let them stand up. Twiddling with a soft and silent plaything is one unobtrusive way to release energy while listening in a group. If children with psychomotor overexcitability are not expected, allowed, and encouraged to move, they may be on a collision course in the classroom.

Another common characteristic and outlet for psychomotor overexcitability is rapid speech. Some children show evidence of psychomotor overexcitability through their abundant verbalizations, literally exploding or "running off" with their mouths. In workshops we have given for teachers, counselors, and educators, when asked, "Can you imagine having Jim Carrey, Whoopi Goldberg, and Robin Williams – intense, verbally expressive stand-up comedians – as children and all in the same third-grade classroom or at the same dinner table?" an audible sigh, and sometimes a collective groan, inevitably follows. Yet this is what these children are like. A classroom teacher might manage blurting or excessive interrupting questions by providing "IQ sheets."

These are photocopied sheets with an 'I' for Interesting Ideas on one side and a 'Q' for Questions on the other. Thus, intense ideas and urgent questions have a waiting place, or parking lot, if you will, to be saved for later exploration at a more opportune time.

Another helpful strategy to facilitate these children's participation is to teach them relaxation techniques. Some teachers have found listening to music or recorded stories particularly calming for their children. If impulsiveness interferes with classroom performance, halting or quieting techniques (take a deep breath; count to 10; smile) can gently intercede and promote self-monitoring and control.

The following suggestions will help to nurture constructive expression of psychomotor overexcitability and related social, physical, intellectual, and emotional development.

Psychomotor Overexcitability: Related Needs and Recommendations

Children with high psychomotor excitabilities need to hear the following:

- You have wonderful enthusiasm and energy.
- Your intensity can help you do many things.
- I wish I had your energy.
- You put your whole body into your learning.
- You like to be able to move and don't really like to sit still.
- Sometimes, our bodies need to relax.

Strategies to encourage modulation of psychomotor overexcitability include the following:

- Discuss the positive aspects of psychomotor overexcitability.
- Avoid activities that require sitting for a long time.
- Plan for movement opportunities before and after a long period of stillness.
- Provide for reasonable movement in a variety of settings.
- Involve them in a physical task; send them on an errand.
- Help the child notice signs of exhaustion or need for quiet time.
- Provide for and model activities that soothe and calm.
- Teach that time-out can be a choice, not a punishment.
- Teach relaxation techniques.
- Consider physical or occupational therapy as needed.

SENSUAL OVEREXCITABILITY

In sensual overexcitability, the pleasures and delights of the senses as well as multisensory experiences become enhanced. Sensual overexcitability gives children heightened experiences of seeing, smelling, tasting, touching, and hearing, too, as well as at times providing irritating experiences through these senses. As our sensually overexcitable children seek and receive heightened pleasure through their senses, they can also experience intense irritation and frustration from sensory overload. Smells and tastes are more pungent to them. Sounds seem to have more depth and character. Those with sensual overexcitability have heightened sensory awareness and with it, often, enhanced aesthetic appreciation.

It is as if these children see through a different pair of glasses than do most of their age peers: their perception is acute and exquisite. Such exceptionally sensitive children seem to view the world as if they are looking through a microscope compared with normal vision. They sometimes see what others cannot even imagine. They catch details and may, for example, be captivated by the beauty of a glistening drop of oil floating and swirling across a rain puddle. The sight of a sunset over water may bring a tear to the eye and hold a sensually and aesthetically aware child captivated until the last sliver or speck of sunlight disappears over the horizon. Some children love color as an entity unto itself and experience the range of tonal palette such that they can veritably hear, feel, and smell the colors as well. Many gifted artists have reflected on the intensity of their perceptions and their cross-modal experiences. For example, they can be deluged with visual, auditory, emotional, and concept impressions that virtually demand to be represented through a single piece of sculpture, music, or poem.

Smells and aromas may hold deep emotional connections for them – such as the aroma of fresh baked bread triggering an instant replay of the last family holiday gathering. Conversely, these children can have intense negative reactions to certain odors. The same sensual sensitivity that could contribute to a later love of fine dining may present in the form of a finicky eater in the early years. Our experiences with families suggest that many gifted children are "picky eaters." Some eat no "mushy" vegetables; others eat only pizza, bread, and peanut butter. Finding creative ways to broaden acceptable food choices to include more variety may prove to be a challenge (Heinigk, 2008).

Some gifted youth crave certain music as others may crave certain foods, listening to Scheherazade or another beloved piece of music until they feel every note and measure completely. Others can gain real comfort from the sound of waves, birds, wind in the trees, or even just their parents' breathing while being tucked in at night. Some sounds, however, become excruciatingly invasive to these children. They may have extreme reactions to the smack of gum chewing or the din on the playground or in the school cafeteria.

As understanding and supportive adults, we can help these children learn to mediate and modulate their experiences. We can help them develop a menu of options to cope with things that irritate and annoy them, and we can also encourage them to seek what gives them pleasure. We can let them make suitable choices and be responsible for adjusting their environment as much as is possible and appropriate – thus giving them opportunities to manage their own needs effectively. Our goal is to promote self-efficacy in these concerns. We can best support them by encouraging self-management and by modeling some important coping skills.

Sensual Overexcitability: Related Needs and Recommendations

Children with high sensual excitabilities need to hear the following:

- You take such delight in beautiful sights, sounds, and feelings.
- You like _____ sound/textures, etc.
- But I notice that ____ noises/textures, etc. bother you.
- I think you know what you like and what feels good to you.
- Sometimes, it's good to try new things. Would you like to try _____?

Strategies to encourage modulation of sensual overexcitability include the following:

- Discuss the positive aspects of sensual overexcitability.
- Provide environments that limit offensive stimuli and maximize comforting stimuli.
- Provide opportunities to dwell in delight. Take time to smell the roses; watch the sunset.
- Co-create a pleasing and comfortable aesthetic environment.
- As much as possible, foster control of the child's own space.

Intellectual Overexcitability

Intellectual overexcitability is seen in intensified activity of the mind, thirst for knowledge, curiosity, capacity for concentration and sustained intellectual effort, avid reading, and precision in observation, recall, and careful planning. Questioning is the hallmark of intellectual overexcitability in the search for knowledge, understanding, and truth. Solving problems, finding it difficult to let go of a problem, and finding new problems to solve are typical. Another trait associated with intellectual overexcitability is reflective thought, exemplified by watching one's own thought processes – or *meta-cognition*, delighting in analyses and theoretical thought – even at very young ages, preoccupation with logic, moral thinking, and introspection.

Children with intellectual overexcitability have a voracious appetite and capacity for intellectual effort and stimulation. Mental activity in these children is usually intensified and accelerated. Driven by wide and deep interests, they relentlessly probe the unknown. Incredibly tenacious and persistent at problem solving, their seemingly endless "why" questions sometimes become annoying and tiresome to parents and teachers, who think, "Don't you ever stop and take a break?" One teacher who attended a workshop on overexcitabilities referred to this as "the perpetual toddler syndrome." While the streaming questions can fuel ongoing intellectual pursuits, they become a challenge for a teacher with thirty-four students to teach in a class period of forty-five to fifty minutes. One teacher instituted a system of question rationing. Although it might sound harsh, the approach had many positive aspects. The teacher would announce "OK, today we'll take four questions" or three or ten, varying with each given day. Some children might display creative problem solving here and invest a great deal of thought in how to phrase his one question to encompass many ideas.

Daydreaming in the classroom is another way highly excitable children engage their imaginations to fuel their voracious appetite for intellectual stimulation: "what if" questions dance in their head. Yet when called on, they may be quite aware of the topic and activity in the classroom. This capacity for multitasking and focusing will come in quite handy over the course of a student's lifetime. Yet a student who is prone to concurrently creating an alternative scenario in her mind may not be appropriately challenged and may need a more highly differentiated curriculum to fuel her ravenous intelligence.

Highly excitable gifted children are already aware of what is still new information for most of their classmates. The U.S. Department of Education's (1993) report *National Excellence: The Case for Developing America's Talent* acknowledged, "Gifted and talented elementary school students have mastered from 35 to 50 percent of the curriculum to be offered in the five basic subjects before they begin the school year" (p. 2). How is this possible? They seem to absorb knowledge from just being in the world, picking up information from adult conversations and various forms of media. Schools have yet to recognize that these children come to school already knowing a great deal. Acknowledging these children's intellectual capabilities and accommodating their particular learning needs have enormous implications for the children, their families, and society. If we take the intellectual needs of these children seriously, providing them with new information and differentiated educational experiences will be essential for their overall development and for nurturing their creative potential.

Intellectual Overexcitability: Related Needs and Recommendations

Children with high intellectual excitabilities need to hear the following:

- Your curiosity fuels your intelligence.
- You have wide and (or) deep interests.
- You have great potential to learn new things and to make changes.
- You really stick to projects that interest you.
- You defend your ideas and are open to learning different information.

Strategies to encourage modulation of intellectual overexcitability include the following:

- Discuss the positive aspects of intellectual overexcitability.
- Honor the need to seek understanding and truth, regardless of the child's age.
- Accept and provide for sustained effort – compacting the regular curriculum to allow for independent project work is one option.
- Help the child find answers to her own questions.
- Teach inquiry methods and communication skills.
- Allow children to develop their own projects based on individual interests.
- Help children to develop goals and engage in self-reflection based on steps toward these goals.
- Seek opportunities to provide interaction with intellectual peers, not necessarily age peers (chess club, multigrade extracurricular offerings or enrichment classes).
- Incorporate multimodal explorations and mind-body integration of experience whenever possible.

Imaginational Overexcitability

Piechowski (2008), writing about imagination and creativity, once said, "Tigers might have **no** imagination, but imaginary tigers can be made of flames," a novel thought, and somewhat quirky, some might say. Yet, this is the way of the imagination. With imagination, anything is possible. Imagination is key to creativity, from everyday creativity to the creativity of eminent individuals. When we ask, "What would I like to do today?" and think of possibilities, our imagination is engaged. When we plan a unique menu for a dinner party and think of a novel color scheme and flower arrangements, our imagination and creativity are involved. And, if one has an imagination like J. K. Rowling, an entire feast hall with floating candelabras, wizards, and dragons can result.

Creative children are closely in touch with this capacity for fantasy and less constrained by notions related to the concrete world. In the imagination, one can travel from a stormy day in the midwestern United States to a land where scarecrows dance, lions sing, and magic red shoes transport and protect you. Imagination turns a sheet draped over two chairs into a fort, a castle, or a cave. Imagination gives birth to creating fairy tales, science fiction, poetry, murals, and amazing structures made from pasta and shaving cream.

Imagination works and plays in the everyday and contributes to daily joy and reverie as well as to great discovery and invention. Einstein said, "Imagination is more important than knowledge." He also said, "It is a miracle that curiosity survives formal education." Picasso reflected that he spent the first half of his career learning to paint and the second half learning to be a child again; he said, "Everything you can imagine is real." The childlike quality of creative people and the imagination that comes with it are essential aspects of their personalities and essential cognitive tools for their work (and play!).

In the vast variety of traits and backgrounds of creative people who later became eminent, one common childhood experience is having an imaginary companion (Singer & Singer, 1990; Taylor, 1999). This is disclosed in the retrospective stories, biographies, and autobiographies of creative writers, artists, performers, inventors, and innovators across domains. At least one political figure has acknowledged the significance of imaginary companions. Princess Margaret of Great Britain directed blame toward her imaginary companion. When her nanny found that little Margaret had done something wrong, she would say, "It wasn't me; it was Cousin Halifax" (Taylor, 1999).

Imagination creates imaginary friends, a hallmark of creativity in children and an antecedent of adult creativity. Even so, imaginary companions make some adults uncomfortable, concerned that the child may be out of touch with the real world. It may comfort these adults to know that children tend to know the difference between the contents of their imaginings and what constitutes our shared sense of what is real.

If there is concern over a child's depth of imagination, exploration in fantasy, and close relationship with imaginary companions, we typically ask concerned adults to consider what kinds of relationships the child has with family, teachers, or other children. Maintaining positive relations with family, teachers, or a close friend provides a reality check that indicates balance and healthy development with others, while fantasy gives our children mental practice in relating to others. In general, as long as a child can give and receive affection and can relate to others, imaginary playmates are unlikely to indicate anything other than brightness, creativity, and imaginational overexcitability.

Children involved in make believe play may well know that their play comes from their imagination (Singer & Singer, 1990). Yet, at other times, children's imaginal experience is real to them (also to imaginative adolescents and adults). Fairies, gnomes, angels, and other little, or giant, folk often appear quite real to the imaginative child.

If an adult suspects that a child is describing some event from his imaginings as if it were actual experience, you might help him discern the difference while still honoring his imagination. This can usually be accomplished with gentle questions: "Is this a story?" or "You have such a great imagination, don't you?" Whatever the imaginary events might be, children's accompanying feelings are real. Accepting the child's feelings and respecting their experience, whatever the source, can help maintain essential trust.

Rich imagination, fantasy play, daydreaming, and imaginary friends are sources of reverie and delight for gifted and creative children. Many who teach and counsel gifted and creative children have had the opportunity to meet a wide assortment of imaginary companions, as well as their pets, friends, and families. One way we can help children to maintain and nurture the development of their imaginations is to help them record or otherwise "save" their creative thoughts and ideas, perhaps in the classroom, where a wall of creative ideas might be posted for community sharing. Where imagination is honored, creativity will flourish.

Imaginational Overexcitability: Related Needs and Recommendations

Children with high imaginational overexcitability need to hear the following:

- You have a rich imagination.
- You view the world in a different way.
- You think of and tell great stories.
- You make the mundane extraordinary.

Strategies to nurture and encourage modulation of imaginational overexcitability include the following:

- Discuss the positive aspects of imaginational overexcitability.
- Model and share examples of creative and imaginational expression.
- Encourage children to share imaginings; tell stories, draw images of imagined friends, pets, buildings, creatures, and worlds. "How would this story be told if it took place in another country or time period or world?" "Would you like to make a picture book about an imaginary pet?"
- Provide opportunities for design and invention. "What do you think cars may look like and be able to do in 2020?" "What are some possible interesting uses for recycled cardboard?"
- Provide opportunities for relaxation and channeling imagination with stories and guided imagery.
- Help children to distinguish between the imaginary and the real world. For example, it is quite fine to refer to one's imaginary friend "Cousin Halifax" as an imaginary friend. It's good to discuss imagination even with very young children and also to highlight that some experiences are very concrete, tangible and mutually experienced.
- Provide outlets for creative pursuits – experimenting, writing, drawing, acting, dancing, designing, inventing, building, etc.
- Include opportunities for both individual and group involvement to validate and honor imaginational activities.
- Help children to use imagination to solve problems and cope with challenges.
- Offer open-ended activities.
- Record imaginative content and ideas in a journal or classroom bulletin board.

Emotional Overexcitability

Of the five overexcitabilities that Dabrowski identified, the expressions of emotional overexcitability are the most extensive (Piechowski, 1979). Intense feelings manifest themselves in extreme, complex, positive, and sometimes negative ways. Deep feelings, affects, and emotion – positive and negative – are part and parcel of the creative personality and are essential aspects of both creative processes and the development of products (Runco, 1994; Russ, 1999).

Such endowment is often regarded as maladjustment and an interference when it comes to a productive, rational life. However, emotional overexcitability can be recognized as a form of giftedness, a finely tuned awareness. For Dabrowski, emotional overexcitability is the most important aspect of human development. It is a significant, logical component of developing a person's potential. Emotions keep people in touch with themselves and their own needs for change as well as connecting them to the larger world and the social fabric of humanity. Conversely, low emotional excitability seriously hampers people from developing their enriching affective possibilities (Piechowski, 1979). Emotion and affect are fertile ground for nurturing creative ideas, processes, and products (Piechowski, 1999).

Intensely emotional children may be bearing enormous loads of feelings that accumulate from various fears and anxieties, concern about death, love, loneliness, deep caring for others, and excruciating self-scrutiny. They are exhilarated in joy and affection and also know great sadness, compassion, ecstasy, and despair. When they are joyous, their radiance lights up the room! When they are sad or disappointed, the weight of the world is on their shoulders.

Their feelings can be complex, and ambivalent. They can simultaneously experience an entire range of contradictory reactions. They may be riveted in an approach–avoidance dilemma. Excitement may draw them toward a person, project, or idea; anxiety may simultaneously create a tug of avoidance or withdrawal.

Sometimes emotional overexcitability inhibits children. They feel so much that they are almost paralyzed to act for fear that they might act wrongly or get a negative reaction from someone. Sometimes, emotional overexcitability is the catalyst for a burst of creative activity.

Emotional Overexcitability: Related Needs and Recommendations

Children with high emotional overexcitability need to hear the following:

- You are sensitive to others' feelings.
- You care very deeply and have deep feelings.
- You are very loyal to those you care about.

- You are very aware of joy, frustration, sadness, love, anger, and a whole world of feelings.
- Your deep feelings can add to many of your creative activities.

Strategies to encourage modulation of emotional overexcitability include the following:

- Accept feelings and their intensity.
- Teach the child to share her emotions and feelings with others in positive and productive ways – verbally or through movement, art, journaling, or music.
- Teach children to be respectful of others' feelings or seeming lack thereof.
- Develop a feeling vocabulary – include a wide range of feeling words. How many ways can we describe feeling "bad"? (Examples include "annoyed," "irritated," "frustrated," "aggravated," "uneasy," "anxious," "uncomfortable," "bored," "concerned," "sad," etc.) How many ways can you describe being "happy"? (Examples include "content," "glad," "joyful," "blessed," "ecstatic," "buoyant," and so on.)
- Learn listening and responding skills. A section is devoted to the importance of listening and responding in *"Mellow Out," They Say*, by Michael Piechowski (2006).
- Teach children to anticipate physical and emotional experiences and to rehearse responses and strategies.
- Teach, model, and share relaxation techniques, including deep breathing, stretching, and two minutes of quiet (a personal time-out).
- Use journaling to express feelings; writing from a place of deep personal feeling may lead to other forms of creative expression.
- Provide art materials and other media for visual expression of feeling states.
- Integrate emotions and affective material within literature or social studies curriculum through creative movement or dramatic activity.

CONCLUSION

The overexcitabilities, according to Dabrowski's theory, are fundamental attributes of a creative personality. Without them, creative talent lacks richness and power. This model of developmental potential offers a way of examining the range of expressions and categories of any given overexcitability in the context of development as the palette of each overexcitability changes its spectrum from individual to individual. An understanding of the potential conveyed through a highly excitable nature affords a framework for approaching the intensities and sensitivities of creative children within a positive developmental perspective.

Psychomotor overexcitability imparts a high level of energy and drive. Sensual overexcitability contributes a richer and more vivid sensory experience frequently in conjunction with emotional overexcitability. Intellectual intensity generates relentless questioning and searching for truth and understanding. Enhanced imagination brings the power to envisage undreamed of possibilities, to create new realities. Emotional overexcitability endows one with greater intensity and complexity of feeling in all dimensions, providing material that holds great possibilities for creative expression – whether through the arts, scientific explorations, invention, or social action. Understanding that overexcitability and creativity often go hand-in-hand provides teachers, counselors, and other educators with insights and strategies for creating opportunities to nurture both the positive expression of overexcitabilities and creativity within our students, within our classrooms, and perhaps throughout the greater school culture.

REFERENCES

Ackerman, C. M. (1993). *Investigating an alternative method of identifying gifted students.* Unpublished master's thesis, University of Calgary, Calgary, Alberta.

Dabrowski, K. (1967). *Personality-shaping through positive disintegration.* Boston: Little, Brown.

Dabrowski, K. (1972). *Psychoneurosis is not an illness.* London: Gryf.

Daniels, S., & Meckstroth, E. (2009). Nurturing the sensitivity, intensity and developmental potential of young gifted children. In S. Daniels & M. Piechowski (Eds.), *Living with intensity: Understanding the sensitivity, excitability, and emotional development of gifted children, adolescents, and adults* (pp. 33–56). Scottsdale, AZ: Great Potential Press.

Daniels, S., & Piechowski, M. (2009). Embracing intensity: Overexcitability, sensitivity, and the developmental potential of the gifted. In S. Daniels & M. Piechowski (Eds.), *Living with intensity: Understanding the sensitivity, excitability, and emotional development of gifted children, adolescents, and adults* (pp. 3–18). Scottsdale, AZ: Great Potential Press.

Grimaud, H. (2006). *Wild harmonies: A life of music and wolves.* New York: Riverhead Books.

Heinigk, P. (2008, June). Soothing overexcitabilities with food. *Parenting for High Potential*, 20–22.

Piechowski, M. (1979). Developmental potential. In N. Colangelo & R. T. Zaffrann (Eds.), *New voices in counseling the gifted* (pp. 25–27). Dubuque, IA: Kendall/Hunt.

Piechowski, M. (1999). Overexcitabilities. In M. Runco & S. Pritzker (Eds.), *Encyclopedia of creativity* (Vol. 2, pp. 325–334). New York: Academic Press.

Piechowski, M. (2002). Experiencing in a higher key: Dabrowski's theory of and for the gifted. *Gifted Education Communicator, 33*(1), 28–31, 35–36.

Piechowski, M. (2006). *"Mellow out," they say. If only I could: Intensities and sensitivities of the young and bright.* Madison, WI: Yunasa Books.

Piechowski, M. (2008). Discovering Dabrowski's theory. In S. Mendaglio (Ed.), *Dabrowski's theory of positive disintegration* (pp. 41–77). Scottsdale, AZ: Great Potential Press.

Runco, M. A. (1994). Creativity and its discontents. In M. Shaw & M. A. Runco (Eds.), *Creativity and affect* (pp. 102–123). Norwood, NJ: Ablex.

Russ, S. W. (1993). *Affect and creativity: The role of affect and play in the creative process.* Hillsdale, NJ: Erlbaum.

Russ, S. W. (Ed.) (1999). *Affect, creative experience and psychological adjustment.* Philadelphia: Brunner Mazel.

Silverman, L. (Ed.), (1993). *Counseling the gifted and talented.* Denver, CO: Love.

Singer, D. G., & Singer, J. L. (1990). *The house of make-believe: Children's play and the development of imagination.* Cambridge, MA: Harvard University Press.

Taylor, M. (1999). *Imaginary companions and the children who create them.* New York: Oxford University Press.

16

Intrinsic Motivation and Creativity in the Classroom: Have We Come Full Circle?

BETH A. HENNESSEY

As I sat down to organize my ideas in preparation for writing this chapter, I came to realize that my thinking and my research efforts have come full circle – or at the very least, that circle is closer than ever before to becoming closed. Almost thirty years ago, I moved to Denver, Colorado, to begin my career as a fledgling teacher. My experiences in my mixed-age classroom filled with 5-, 6-, and 7-year-olds kindled within me a deep interest in motivation and creativity of performance. My concerns about what our educational system was *not* doing to promote student growth in these areas became so great that I eventually left my elementary classroom to return to school myself. I was convinced that it was the field of psychology, and more specifically the study of the social psychology of creativity, that could best provide the answers I was looking for. As a graduate student and later as a professor of psychology, I have been almost single-minded in my attempts to answer empirically the question of how best to structure classrooms so that they are most conducive to student motivation and creativity. Over the past thirty-five years, researchers have contributed literally hundreds of investigations to the psychological and educational psychology literatures; for my own part, in the last few years, I have even been bold enough to end a few chapters or monographs with a "laundry list" of what teachers should and should not do if student intrinsic motivation and creativity are the goal.

Our research has lead to the establishment of a number of models of the intersection between intrinsic motivation and creativity of performance (Amabile, 1996; Hennessey, 2003; Hennessey & Amabile, 1988) that are now widely accepted by researchers in the areas of social psychology and related specialties; and the so-called Intrinsic Motivation Principle of Creativity (Amabile, 1996; Hennessey, 2003) has even been the subject of heated professional debate (Eisenberger, 2003; Eisenberger, Armeli, & Pretz, 1998; Eisenberger & Cameron, 1996, 1998; Eisenberger, Pierce, & Cameron, 1999; Hennessey & Amabile, 1998) – the sincerest form of flattery, as only established theories garner sufficient criticism and ire to be considered controversial. In other words, the academic community has sat up and taken notice. We now understand a great deal about the impact of the environment (classroom and workplace) on creative performance. Yet that question that so haunted me as a young teacher – that question as to how our schools may be undermining the creativity and motivation of students – for me, looms larger than ever. Our world community faces seemingly intractable crises that can only be met with ground-breaking, yet to be imagined, creative solutions: global warming; AIDS and the threat of other equally devastating pandemics; poverty; starvation; water shortages; food shortages; tribal, cultural, and nationalistic strife. The task of finding answers to these and other equally pressing problems rests on the shoulders of young scientists, researchers, and policy makers . . . and on the next generation of professionals who will be entering the work force in the years to come. The promotion of creativity in our schools is now much more than an idealistic nicety or frill. It is essential for our very survival.

But can our laboratory and field study demonstrations as to how to pro-mote creativity be translated into practical educational reforms? What are the applied implications of our work? Over the years, a number of teach-ers have emailed me or approached me at professional conferences or after a presentation I have made to groups of professional educators or parents to say that our research findings have directly affected the way they think about their own classroom process. And practicing teachers continue to con-tact me to inquire about how they might get a copy of the intrinsic moti-vation training tapes I used in a series of "Immunization" studies published in 1989 and 1993 (Hennessey, Amabile, & Martinage, 1989; Hennessey & Zbikowski, 1993). But for me, the most important question is, "What would an entire school filled with classrooms modeled after our research findings look like?" Would students' intrinsic motivation and creativity be anywhere near the levels our laboratory-based and field studies would lead us to predict? Would it be possible and practical for teachers to implement our recom-mendations on a daily basis? Would faculty, students, and staff be able to sustain an excitement for learning and an atmosphere that promotes creative performance?

A few researchers focusing on related areas of psychology have, in fact, been able to explore directly similar questions in conjunction with their own research. Howard Gardner's seminal work on Multiple Intelligences (Chen & Gardner, 2005; Gardner, 1983, 1989, 1991, 1993, 1999; Kornhaber & Gardner, 2006), for example, has had a profound impact on educational practice worldwide. Teachers are now almost routinely asking "*How* are my students smart?" And entire schools have been named for and constructed according to Gardner's now eight-part model of Multiple Intelligences (see, for example, http://www.howardgardnerschool.com/; http://www.thehowardgardnerschool. org/). Similarly, Kurt Fischer and colleagues involved in the so-called Brain and Education Movement (Fischer & Immordino-Yang, 2008; Hanna, 2005;

Posner & Rothbart, 2006) have recently had the opportunity to investigate the real-world implications of their own pioneering studies connecting biology and cognitive science to education in an ever-growing number of what have come to be called "brain-based" schools (see, for example, http://www .allkindsofminds.org/sa/ and http://www.scilearn.com/). These schools and other examples like them have been purposefully patterned after the work of researchers in the fields of psychology, neuroscience, and related areas. To the best of my knowledge, my own research and the work of other investigators in the area of the social psychology of creativity have not directly led to the construction of specific curricula or educational approaches. But what has happened is that a small but growing number of schools have independently arrived at virtually the same conclusions we have. Apparently, at least in many cases, without benefit of our research findings and theorizing, they have come to structure their classrooms and teaching in precisely the ways that our investigations would recommend.

In short, we have available a valuable naturalistic experiment: Individual classroom teachers and in some cases entire schools implementing our research recommendations without any risk of experimenter bias or related pitfalls. Before describing these educational programs and their outcomes, it is first important to set the stage with an explanation of the social psychology of creativity – its roots and major contributions to the field.

THE SOCIAL PSYCHOLOGY OF CREATIVITY

Investigations into what has come to be termed the social psychology of creativity were begun in the mid 1970s. Before this time, theoretical and empirical investigations of creativity were almost entirely restricted to questions of the "creative personality" and the individual difference variables that distinguish highly creative persons from the rest of their peers. Gradually, a small group of social psychologists began to focus their research attention on the impact of situational factors on creative performance, and over time, there emerged the dual understanding that our motivational orientation directly affects the creativity of our behavior and that motivation is largely determined by the social environment in which we find ourselves.

Pioneering this new investigative direction were Lepper, Greene, and Nisbett, who in 1973 investigated the effect of expected reward on young children's motivation and artistic performance. These researchers selected into their study only preschoolers who displayed an especially high level of intrinsic interest in drawing with magic markers. Children met individually with the experimenter and were randomly assigned to either a constraint or no-constraint condition. Children in the expected reward group were told that if they made a drawing, they would be awarded a "Good Player Certificate." Children in the control/no-reward and unexpected reward groups made their drawings without any expectation of reward. The quality of these products was later assessed, as was the motivational orientation of the preschoolers.

Results revealed that working for an expected "Good Player Award" significantly decreased these preschoolers' interest in and enjoyment of the marker task. When compared with the unexpected reward group and the control (no reward) group, the children who had made drawings for the experimenters in order to receive a Good Player Award spent significantly less time using the markers during subsequent free-play periods than did their nonrewarded peers. Moreover, this undermining of interest persisted for at least a week beyond the initial experimental session. Because Lepper and colleagues had set out to examine the impact of expected reward on task motivation, they had not originally planned to code or systematically examine the overall quality of the pictures produced. But a casual examination of the products made by preschoolers in the two experimental conditions showed what these researchers believed were important between-group differences. And a subsequent systematic assessment of the globally assessed "quality" of the drawings confirmed this view. Products produced under expected reward conditions was found to be of significantly lower quality than products made by the unexpected reward or control groups. How was it that this simple, one-time offer of a Good Player Award could serve to undermine the motivation and performance of preschoolers who were passionate about using magic markers? It is precisely this research question that captured my attention as I wrestled with questions of student motivation and creativity in my own elementary school classroom.

It was 1980 and I was in my second year of what I had thought would be a lengthy career as an elementary school teacher. My classroom housed a mixed-age group of 5-, 6-, and 7-year-olds. The idea was that children would stay with me for three years. I would get to know them very well; they would get to know me; older students would help to "teach" and serve as an example for younger students; and the entire learning experience would be enhanced. My first few years of teaching, although supremely challenging, went fairly smoothly. My students were learning to read and write and manipulate numbers, and parents and administrators were pleased with my accomplishments. But after some time, I found that the same nagging problem kept coming back to worry me. While my students may have been gaining essential skills, what was not developing the way I had hoped was their motivation and creativity. Because I had kindergartners and first- and second-graders in this one classroom, it was all too apparent that over time, my kids were actually losing their excitement about learning as well as their willingness to experiment, take risks, and exercise their creativity. Kindergartners arrived at the start of the school year bursting with enthusiasm. They were ready and willing to tackle almost any challenge, and their energy and excitement knew no bounds. They were eager to share wild and fanciful ideas, and their artwork and stories were fantastic. But by the time these same children reached second grade, many had lost their excitement about learning and were reticent to take a chance or try something new. Fairly quickly, my worries as a teacher began to shift from issues of neat handwriting, or the mastery of multiplication tables and reading fluency to the realization that my students' motivation and creativity were dying right before my eyes. Was it something I was doing? Or was this progression inevitable?[1] I decided that I would not be satisfied until I found the answer to one fundamental question: How can teachers structure their classroom routines and curriculum so as to keep students' motivation and creativity alive?

Initially at least, I was confident that I would find the answers I was looking for. I assumed that there were a number of experts working on this problem. But the more I talked with other teachers and administrators and the more I read, the more discouraged I became. I began to realize that while virtually everyone seemed to think that the promotion of student motivation and creativity was extremely important, no one seemed to have any concrete suggestions as to how teachers could accomplish this goal. Eventually, I came across research spearheaded by McGraw and colleagues (McGraw, 1978; McGraw & McCullers, 1979) suggesting that in the classroom, intrinsic motivation is almost always preferable to an extrinsic motivational orientation. I found research evidence showing that intrinsic motivation leads to better problem solving and a deeper level of conceptual understanding and learned that, in the classroom, extrinsic motivation will consistently lead to better performance only on tasks requiring rote recitation, precise performance under strong time pressure, and the completion of familiar, repetitive procedures. Research psychologists and educational experts speculated that school environments fraught with rewards, competition, and frequent evaluation do not offer the best situations for students' overall learning. And the studies I found also suggested that classrooms incorporating these extrinsic constraints might not be the best environments for promoting students' creativity.

Researching further, I soon learned that there were at least a handful of investigators and theorists who were actively pursuing work on the link between motivation and creativity of performance. Unlike the majority of creativity researchers, this group had chosen not to concentrate their efforts on issues of creative personality or process. Instead, they were attempting to take a social psychological approach that focused on the impact of various environmental constraints and motivators placed on students. The same question that I was asking as an elementary school teacher also guided their work: What kind of classroom setting is most conducive to student motivation and creative

---

[1]   My familiarity with the research literature now tells me that I was not the only teacher who observed my students losing motivation and excitement about learning. Working in a variety of settings and using a wide range of measures, a number of investigators have found children's reported intrinsic motivation in school to decrease steadily over time (e.g., Anderman & Maehr, 1994; Harter, 1981; Lepper, Sethi, Dialdin & Drake, 1997).

performance? This research direction was new and exciting, and I was hooked. I left the elementary school classroom and returned to graduate school.

THE PICTURE-TAKING STUDY

A few years later, in 1986, I co-authored a paper (Amabile, Hennessey, & Grossman, 1986, Study 1) that outlined what was to become a prototypical paradigm for my own research program. Unlike the Lepper, Greene, and Nisbett (1973) "Magic Marker Study," in this investigation, the reward offered to elementary school children was not a tangible gift to be delivered afterward. Instead, it was an activity – the chance to play with a camera – that was to be completed before engaging in the target experimental task. Importantly, this opportunity to play with a camera had been found in pretesting to be especially exciting and attractive to this group of children. Study participants assigned to the reward condition signed a contract and promised to tell a story later in order to first have a chance to use the camera. Children in the no-reward condition were simply allowed to use the camera and then were presented with the story-telling instructions; there was no contingency established between the two tasks.

To examine the impact of reward expectation on children's verbal creativity, the children in this study were asked to tell a story into a tape recorder to accompany a set of illustrations in a book with no words (see Hennessey & Amabile, 1988). Elementary school teachers familiar with writing done by students in this age group later rated the stories relative to one another on creativity and a variety of other dimensions. A high level of interrater reliability was reached, and results indicated that, overall, stories produced by children in the no-reward condition were judged to be more creative than were stories produced by children in the reward condition. This main effect of reward was, in fact, statistically significant. Importantly, all children taking part in this investigation took pictures with the camera. The only difference in the experience of the rewarded and nonrewarded children in this paradigm was their *perception* of the picture-taking reward as contingent or not contingent on the target story-telling activity.

A FOCUS ON REAL-WORLD, "EVERY-DAY" CREATIVITY

In the investigation just described, the creativity of elementary school students was assessed based on their performance on a story-telling task not all that different from other language art activities being carried out in their classroom. Rather than concentrate on creative genius and persons at the forefront of their respective fields, our investigations have always been driven by the belief that every individual has some degree of creative potential, and it is our goal to find ways to help them to reach that potential. Toward this end, we do not administer a paper-and-pencil creativity assessment, such as the Torrance Tests of Creative Thinking (Torrance, 1974). Instead, we ask participants in our studies to produce some sort of real-world product. While the Torrance tests and related measures may, in fact, accurately tap one or more creative abilities or predispositions, we believe that a test that captures the full range of creativity components has yet to be developed. Investigators like ourselves have come to rely on the consensual assessment of experts as we set out to determine whether products produced under one set of circumstances are more or less creative than products produced under other, very different conditions.

This Consensual Assessment Technique (CAT) (Amabile, 1982b; Hennessey & Amabile, 1999) is based on the assumption that a panel of independent expert raters, persons who have not had the opportunity to talk with one another or with the researcher about possible hallmarks of product creativity, are best able to make such judgments. Research conducted over the past twenty years has, in fact, clearly established that product creativity can be reliably and validly assessed based on the consensus of experts. Moreover, this approach has proved to be especially well suited to investigations of classroom environmental influences on creativity. Researchers, like myself, who take a social-psychological approach must control for and, as much as possible, eliminate within-group variability in their dependent measures so that they might detect more global between-group differences produced by their direct experimental manipulations of social and environmental factors. This is clearly a different approach from research into personality variables in which individual differences, not experimental condition differences, are the main focus.

In our investigations, in other words, individual differences constitute error variance. We are not interested in whether a particular child is likely to consistently evidence greater levels of creativity than the majority of her peers. We are interested in creativity not as a relatively enduring and stable *trait*, but as the result of a fleeting and delicate motivational *state*, a state very much influenced by environmental factors such as the presence or absence of reward. What we need is a measurement tool that deemphasizes individual differences between study participants, and this measure must also allow for considerable flexibility and novelty of response without depending heavily upon the level of a child's skills or the range of her experience. The CAT fills each of these criteria.

Our elementary school teacher-raters in the 1986 (Amabile, Hennessey & Grossman, 1986, Study 1) investigation did not know one another, and they were not permitted to confer with one another before or during the rating process. Using 7-point scales and guided only by their own, subjective definitions of creativity, these judges were asked to rate the transcripts of the stories relative to one another rather than against some abstract norm. As has almost always been the case in our research program, in this investigation, interrater reliability for story creativity was high, and a sum of the ratings made by our three judges was computed for each product. Finally, these calculations were then used as the dependent measure of product creativity in the remainder of the analyses.

"KILLERS" OF CREATIVITY

Like the investigation just described, the majority of early studies designed to explore the impact of environmental constraints on motivation and performance were focused on the effects of expected reward (e.g., Deci, 1971, 1972; Garbarino, 1975; Greene & Lepper, 1974; Kernoodle-Loveland & Olley, 1979; Kruglanski, Friedman, & Zeevi, 1971; Lepper, Greene, & Nisbett, 1973; McGraw & McCullers, 1979; Pittman, Emery, & Boggiano, 1982; Shapira, 1976). In more recent years, experimental approaches have become increasingly complex, but the basic findings have remained the same. Hundreds of published investigations reveal that the promise of a reward made contingent on task engagement often serves to undermine intrinsic task motivation and qualitative aspects of performance, including creativity (for a more complete review of the literature, see Amabile, 1996; Hennessey, 2000; Hennessey & Amabile, 1988). This effect is so robust that it has been found to occur across the entire life span, with preschoolers and seasoned professionals experiencing the same negative consequences.

Investigators have also expanded their scope to uncover the deleterious impact of a variety of other environmental constraints, such as deadlines, surveillance, and competition (e.g., Amabile, 1982a; Amabile, Goldfarb, & Brackfield, 1990). And there is a good deal of research evidence to show that the expectation that one's work will be judged by others may well be the most deleterious extrinsic constraint of all. Perhaps because situations of evaluation often combine aspects of each of the other "killers" of motivation and creativity, the promise of an evaluation has been shown to undermine severely the task interest and performance of individuals from all walks of life, from preschoolers to professionals whose very livelihood depends on the creativity of their work.

As is the case with the reward literature, studies of the impact of expected evaluation have also become increasingly finely tuned over the years. Researchers now have a much more sophisticated understanding of evaluation effects and are quick to point out that not all evaluative contingencies can be expected to have the same deleterious impact. Theorists now understand that the type of task presented to study participants can, in large part, drive their experimental results; and recent studies reveal that under certain specific conditions, both the delivery of a competence-affirming evaluation and the expectation of an impending evaluation can sometimes increase levels of extrinsic motivation without having any negative impact on intrinsic motivation or performance. In fact, some forms of evaluation expectation can actually enhance creativity of performance. These complex effects of expected evaluation are reviewed in several comprehensive publications (e.g., Harackiewicz, Abrahams, & Wageman, 1987; Jussim, Soffin, & Brown, 1992).

THE INTRINSIC MOTIVATION PRINCIPLE OF CREATIVITY

Studies from this research tradition as just outlined distinguish between two types of motivation. Intrinsic motivation is the motivation to do something for its own sake, for the sheer pleasure and enjoyment of the task itself. Extrinsic motivation, on the other hand, is the motivation to do something for some external goal. More than 30 years of exploration into the role played by motivational orientation in the creative process have led my colleagues and me to the Intrinsic Motivation Principle of Creativity – intrinsic motivation is conducive to creativity, and extrinsic motivation is usually detrimental (Amabile, 1983, 1996). In its earlier incarnations, this proposed relation between motivational orientation and creativity of performance was advanced as a tentative research hypothesis. But investigators working within this tradition have now gathered so much unequivocal research evidence that this proposition has been elevated to the status of an undisputed principle. Importantly, while the work of Eisenberger (1996), Cameron and Pierce (1994), and a handful of other behaviorally trained psychologists (e.g., Eisenberger, 2003; Eisenberger, Armeli, & Pretz, 1998; Eisenberger & Cameron, 1998; Eisenberger, Pierce, & Cameron, 1999) appears to demonstrate that the promise of a reward can, under very specific conditions, have either no impact or even a positive impact on task interest and qualitative aspects of performance, the fact remains that for the majority of persons in the majority of circumstances, intrinsic motivation and creativity are bound to suffer in the face of an expected reward (see Hennessey, 2000, 2002, 2003; Hennessey & Amabile, 1998).

THE REST OF THE STORY – THE CREATIVE INTERSECTION

The Intrinsic Motivation Principle of Creativity and investigations like the Magic Marker and Picture-Taking studies described earlier focus on the individual's motivational orientation and its impact on creative performance. But intrinsic motivation is not the only essential ingredient for creative behavior. Amabile and colleagues, myself included, have long argued that it is a mistake to stop at the individual level of analysis – the person doing the creating (see Amabile, 1996; Hennessey, 2003; Hennessey & Amabile, 1988). And, in fact, even the additional attention paid by social psychologists to aspects of the environment that may impact motivational orientation does not tell

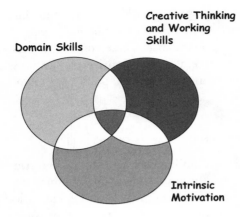

Domain Skills

Creative Thinking
and Working
Skills

Intrinsic
Motivation

Figure 16.1. Amabile's creative intersection.

The Creativity Intersection

the whole story. In our work, we emphasize the fact that the confluence of
a variety of environmental and person variables is necessary for creativity.
More formally, our research is built on a three-part conceptualization of creative performance. For a creative solution to be found or a creative idea or
product to be generated, an individual must approach a problem with the
appropriate *domain skills* (background knowledge and expertise in a given
discipline or area), *creativity skills* (willingness to take risks, experiment,
play with idea), and *task motivation*. Under ideal circumstances, the coming
together of these three factors forms what Amabile (1997) terms the "creative
intersection."

From the perspective of a teacher hoping to promote her students' creativity, the motivational component of this componential model can prove to be
the most problematic. It is certainly possible to provide students with domain
skills such as facility with a paint brush or knowledge of chemistry, physics,
or engineering. In fact, most educators would argue that this is what school
is all about. And even creativity skills, such as the ability to "think outside
the box," brainstorm ideas, or temporarily suspend judgment, are taught in
some schools and corporate environments. Motivational orientation, on the
other hand, is much more ephemeral. In other words, while creativity skills
or domain skills may be fairly stable, motivational state is highly variable and
largely situation dependent. Each of us finds some activities more interesting
or enjoyable than we do others. No one approaches every task with the same
degree of excitement; to a large degree, our level of enthusiasm and task commitment is determined by the specific circumstances we find ourselves in. If the
classroom environment or the overall atmosphere of a school is not conducive
to intrinsic motivation, then all the domain knowledge and creativity skills in
the world will not make up for this detriment.

RECIPE FOR THE TYPICAL AMERICAN CLASSROOM

Expected reward, expected evaluation, competition, deadlines, surveillance – this list of killers of intrinsic motivation reads very much like the blueprint for the typical American school. I know that when I was setting up my own elementary-level classroom I built a wide variety of rewards and incentives, some subtle and some not so subtle, into the school day. Charts bearing gold, silver, and blue stars next to children's names lined my classroom walls. Students who completed high-quality work before the deadline were rewarded with extra recess time, and everyone hoped that their short story, poem, or most recent artwork would be chosen as one of the "best" to be displayed on the bulletin board in the hall. My intentions were good. I was trying my best to boost the children's motivation by loading on the incentives. But now, three decades later, I know better.

What I and other researchers have come to learn is that most of us are not all that in touch with our own motivations. We do not always know why it is that we do the things we do. Almost as if we were outside observers of our own actions, we seem to use essentially the same rubrics for explaining our own behaviors as we do for explaining why others behave in the ways that they do. In situations where both a plausible internal and a plausible external (intrinsic and extrinsic) cause of behavior are present, we tend to *discount* the internal cause in favor of the external cause. For example, a preschooler in the Magic Marker study (Lepper et al., 1973) thinks to herself: "I must be making this picture not because it's fun and I love using markers but because this man has told me that I will get a Good Player Award."

When multiple explanations for their behavior are available, young and old alike have been found to discount their own intrinsic interest in favor of a purely external explanation for task engagement. Researching motivation in the 1970s, one group of social psychologists came to refer to this process as the "discounting principle" (e.g., Kelley, 1973). Other theorists proposed a related explanation termed the "overjustification" hypothesis, a formulation derived from the attribution theories of Bem (1972), Kelley (1967, 1973), and deCharms (1968). According to this model, when a behavior is overjustified (when there exists both a possible internal and external cause for one's own or another's behavior), each of us will tend to overlook the internal cause (the presence of intrinsic task motivation) in favor of the external cause (a reward or evaluation was at stake). In effect, we discount the excess justification for explaining why we did something.

Offering a similar but more contemporary and nuanced view, Deci and Ryan (1985a, 1985b) have attempted to expand on these formulations with a consideration of individual differences. The focus of their theorizing is on causality orientations, or characteristic ways that each of us develops for understanding and orienting to inputs. More specifically, they hypothesize

that individuals vary in the degree to which they exhibit three such orientations ("autonomy," "control," and "impersonal"), and they argue that these
individual differences have important implications for a variety of motiva-
tionally involved processes, including creativity. At the core of what they term
their Self-Determination Theory (SDT) (Ryan & Deci, 2000a, 2000b) is the
consideration of innate psychological needs and the degree to which persons
are able to satisfy these basic needs as they pursue and attain their valued goals.
Within this SDT framework, extrinsic motivation is not seen as the simple
absence of intrinsic motivation. Instead, motivational orientation is viewed as
a highly complicated and multilayered continuum.

In short, when teachers promise their students a reward or impose some
other form of extrinsic constraint in the classroom, they set into motion a
complex sequence of events that run the risk of doing far more harm than
good. It is easy to understand why teachers (as well as parents and managers in
the workplace) are drawn to rewards and other complex systems of evaluation
and behavioral control. Extrinsic incentives really do help to ensure that work
will get done and that it will be completed on time. If every task required
of students were straightforward and algorithmic – with one "right" answer
and one best, most straightforward path to solution – extrinsic incentives
would make sense. The difficulty, of course, is that much of the work that
teachers assign calls for open-ended approaches to problems, far-reaching
thinking, a willingness to take risks and deep stores of intrinsic motivation and
excitement about learning that will allow students to persist with challenging
tasks.

The impact of expected reward, expected evaluation, and competition
on task interest and creativity of performance is significant and complicated.
And research shows that teachers would be advised to avoid the use of these
constraints as they set out to motivate their students. But what are educators to
do? Most teachers, no matter how committed they might be to promoting their
students' intrinsic motivation, creativity, and excitement about learning, find
themselves stewards of a system that makes these goals virtually impossible to
reach. For a wide variety of reasons, some intentional and other accidents of
history, we have somehow managed to structure educational environments in
such a way that intrinsic motivation and creativity are bound to suffer, if not be
completely destroyed. The all-important question that needs to be addressed is
how this situation can be turned around. One solution would be for educators
at all levels, preschool through university, to eliminate from their classrooms
all task-contingent rewards, competitive elements, and controlling systems of
evaluation. But old habits die hard, and it is clear these fundamental changes
in the way that students are taught will not come easily. In fact, in this age
of high-stakes testing, teacher accountability, and national "one size fits all"
educational mandates like No Child Left Behind, such reforms may literally be
impossible.

The work of Seymour Sarason speaks eloquently to this problem of effecting change within the schools; in fact, his seminal book on this subject is titled *The Culture of School and the Problem of Change* (1971, revised 1996). In his research and theorizing, Sarason demonstrates how longstanding educational structures and practices, both at the institutional level and within individual classrooms, stifle reform efforts. The notion that students must be *controlled* via grades, rewards, and other extrinsic constraints is endemic to the school culture. Moreover, Sarason points out that reasoned arguments for the abandonment of these control systems have been met in the past and will continue to be met with strong protests from various groups (classroom teachers, administrators, unions) who believe they must defend their power.

Sarason (1996) doubts whether the unilateral definition and exercise of power are desirable for the development of children, and he argues that the sense of powerlessness that schools engender in students frequently breeds reduced task interest and excitement about learning. Apparently one need not be a researcher interested in creativity to be struck by the fact that our schools are fraught with killers of motivation. Yet in his research, Sarason repeatedly found that it had never occurred to the majority of teachers (or administrators) to question the rules and practices that govern this country's classrooms. Were he to poll teachers in 2008, he might well find that the situation has changed. There is a growing movement in this country among teachers and administrators to question and fight against what many professionals have come to believe is the abuse of standardized testing (and children). National organizations like FairTest (see http://www.fairtest.org/organizations-and-experts-opposed-high-stakes-test) and the NEA are partnering with teachers' associations and parents' groups to call for a broad re-examination of state and federal educational policies. Fortunately for our nation's children, Sarason and many other experts like him continue to work to make their message heard: Schools should and must exist to serve students, yet the external pressure on students (and teachers) to perform according to standards is immense. The gulf between what students are interested in and the ways they best learn and what their teachers are told they must teach and how they must teach is growing ever wider and must be bridged. Perhaps the time will come when curricular reforms imposed from afar, "teaching to the test," and high-stakes evaluations are things of the past. Until that day, a less desirable but certainly more feasible alternative to transforming classroom practice would be to change the way students react to situations of competition or to the promise of an upcoming reward or evaluation.

THE IMMUNIZATION STUDIES

In a series of three related investigations, my colleagues and I set out to study whether creativity and motivation might be maintained even in the face of reward. In our design of these experiments, we were guided by a medical metaphor. We decided to look at the extrinsic constraint of an expected reward as a kind of germ or virus and wondered whether it might be possible to "immunize" children against its usually negative effects on intrinsic motivation and creativity. Again drawing on a biological analogy, our goal was two-fold: (1) to strengthen intrinsic motivation and (2) to provide antibodies (techniques) for fighting the negative effects of extrinsic motivation.

In the first of these research attempts (Hennessey, Amabile, & Martinage, 1989, Study 1), elementary school students (ages 7 to 11 years) were randomly assigned to intrinsic motivation focus or control groups and met with an experimenter over two consecutive days for the purpose of viewing videos and engaging in directed discussion. The tapes shown to students in the intrinsic motivation focus condition depicted two 11-year-olds talking with an adult about various aspects of their schoolwork. Scripts for this condition were constructed so as to help children focus on the intrinsically interesting, fun, and playful aspects of a task. Ways to make even the most routine assignment exciting were suggested, and participants were helped to distance themselves from socially imposed extrinsic constraints, such as rewards. Tapes shown to students in the control condition featured the same two young actors talking about some of their favorite things, including foods, music groups, movies, and seasons.

Following this training procedure, all students met individually with a second adult for testing. As in the previous study described above, half the children in each of the training conditions were told that they could take two pictures with an instant camera only if they promised to tell a story later for the experimenter. For children in the no-reward conditions, this picture taking was presented simply as the first in a series of "things to do." In this 2 × 2 factorial design, presentation of reward was crossed with type of training received. It was expected that only those participants who had been specifically instructed in ways to overcome the usual deleterious effects of extrinsic constraints would maintain baseline levels of intrinsic motivation and creativity in situations of expected reward (i.e., they would be immunized against the negative effects of extrinsic constraints). The data from this initial investigation not only confirmed these expectations but gave us reason to believe that our intervention had much more of an impact than we had expected. Intrinsic motivation-trained children tended to report higher levels of intrinsic motivation on a paper-and-pencil assessment than did children in the control (no-training) condition; in addition, we found that the offer of reward actually augmented the creativity of the trained group. This additive effect of intrinsic and extrinsic motivation was quite robust. In fact, the creativity of children who received intrinsic motivation training and expected a reward was significantly higher than that of any other design group.

In our initial discussion of these immunization study results, we conjectured that children who entered the creativity testing situation after having undergone intrinsic motivation training would have a much more acute awareness of their own intrinsic interest in school-type tasks. Thus, the reward may have served to heighten their already positive feelings about the tasks they were doing. In an effort to test these hypotheses, two follow-up investigations of our intrinsic motivation focus techniques (Hennessey, Amabile, & Martinage, 1989, Study 2; Hennessey & Zbikowski, 1993) were subsequently carried out. Each was designed as a conceptual replication of Study 1. Essentially the same experimental design was used, and it was again the children who had received immunization training and who were expecting a reward who produced the most creative products. Yet, in these subsequent two studies, the effect of training was far less dramatic. Taken together, the results of Studies 2 and 3 indicate that we cannot expect that children exposed to our intrinsic motivation training and offered a reward for their performance will demonstrate unusually high levels of creativity. Nevertheless, we can expect that these children will be able to maintain baseline levels of intrinsic motivation and creativity under reward conditions.

What is it about our immunization procedures that allow students to maintain their creativity even when they expect a reward? It appears that our efforts to help them learn to deemphasize the importance of extrinsic incentives and concentrate instead on their own intrinsic interest and task enjoyment paid off. Even in the face of reward, the children were able to maintain a positive, intrinsically motivated approach. They brought to our experimental tasks a playfulness and a willingness to take risks that many researchers believe are crucial to creativity (Amabile, 1983, 1996; Barron, 1968; Campbell, 1960; Crutchfield, 1962; Dansky & Silverman, 1975; Lieberman, 1965; Stein, 1974).

Evidence from nonexperimental studies coupled with observations of and interviews with artists and other persons who rely on their creativity for their life's work echo our "immunization" results. While all of the "killers" of motivation and creativity that have been isolated experimentally have also been found to be detrimental in the "real world" of work, these negative effects have not proved to be universal. For some people, certain extrinsic motivators have been shown to have either no effects or even a positive effect on task interest and creativity of performance. For example, in a study of commissioned and noncommissioned works done by professional artists, the extrinsic incentive of a commission was seen by some artists as a highly controlling constraint, and the creativity of their work plummeted. Yet for those who looked at the commission as an opportunity to achieve recognition or a confirmation of their competence by respected others, creativity was enhanced (Amabile, Phillips, & Collins, 1994).

How can these individual differences be explained? Our data on these professional artists and the children taking part in our immunization studies parallel nicely earlier work exploring the relevance of self-perception processes to the overjustification effect. In a 1981 investigation carried out by Fazio, the negative impact of expected reward was also mitigated in young children for whom initial intrinsic interest in the target activity had been made salient. In other words, it may not be the expectation of reward per se that undermines intrinsic motivation, rather it may be the individual's interpretation of that reward and his or her role in the reward process that in large part determines whether task motivation will be undermined, enhanced, or remain unchanged.

TRICKLE DOWN

In the twenty-five years that I have been engaged in the research process, I have spoken with thousands of parents, classroom teachers, and school administrators about the undeniable link between intrinsic motivation and creativity of performance and the killers of motivation that are intentionally and routinely built into the school day. My audiences, most especially the teachers, nod their heads in agreement as I outline the seriously negative impact of reward systems and a variety of other extrinsic constraints. They know in their heart of hearts that the research findings I present make sense, but they feel overwhelmed by the prospect of trying to fight an educational system entrenched in tradition and driven by the notion that "if it was good enough for me and my peers, it's good enough for this next generation."

The major impetus behind the immunization studies was, in fact, the overwhelming and paralyzing sense of hopelessness that so many classroom teachers have expressed to me over the years. In my experience as a researcher, it has always been far easier to demonstrate how to kill intrinsic motivation and creativity than it has been to show how motivation and creative behavior might be maintained or even promoted. Intrinsic motivation is an especially delicate and fleeting entity. But I was tired of presenting such a negative message, tired of telling teachers and administrators what they were doing wrong. The immunization research allowed me to offer a concrete list of changes that did not necessitate sweeping curricular or policy reform – changes that teachers interested in preserving the intrinsic motivation and creativity of students could implement in their own classrooms. It has now been almost two decades since the first intrinsic motivation training study results were published. In the past twenty years, I have spoken to numerous educational groups and have heard from a number of teachers about their successful implementation of immunization techniques in their own classrooms. The effectiveness of our admittedly amateurish research video tapes and follow-up scripted conversations conducted by an unfamiliar adult cannot begin to compare to the positive impact of naturalistic teacher-driven discussions built into the school day, conversations about ways students might put grades or test scores into perspective and think less about competing with peers and more about what really interests and excites them.

RECIPE FOR CLASSROOM REFORM

In consideration of our research findings, what exactly would a classroom designed to promote student motivation and creativity look like? In my talks with educators and my more recent publications, I have offered a number of practical suggestions for change. For example, a recent monograph written as part of the NAEG Senior Scholar Series (Hennessey, 2004) concludes with the following suggested steps:

- Teachers must work diligently to create an interpersonal atmosphere which allows students to feel in control of their learning process.
- Students should be helped to feel like "origins" rather than "pawns." In other words, the classroom should be a place in which student behavior is self-determined. There is no room in the classroom for intimidation or coercion.
- Teachers and administrators must step back and critically review the incentive systems that are currently in place.
- When presenting lessons and subject matter that are inherently interesting to students, teachers should work to use tangible rewards as little as possible; they also must avoid setting up situations that encourage students to compare their progress to that of others in the classroom. Performance on in-class and statewide "high stakes" tests must not be driven by a sense of competition and teachers must work to deemphasize the extrinsic incentives built into the myriad of citywide, statewide, or nationwide competitions available to students.
- In situations where extrinsic incentives are in place, students must be helped to distance themselves from those constraints as much as possible.
- We must remember that each of us will be most creative when we enjoy what we are doing. Every effort should be made to encourage students to take risks, to experiment, and to have fun with projects and assignments. Students must be given the opportunity to take pride in what they have already accomplished and to dream of what lies ahead. And at all times, teacher evaluation and surveillance of student work must be kept to a minimum.
- Students must be helped to become more proficient at recognizing their own strengths and weaknesses.

All students, including the most gifted and talented children, must be helped to identify the subject areas that give them the most pleasure and ignite their passion. Since the publication of the results of our own three attempts at immunization and intrinsic motivation training (Hennessey, Amabile, & Martinage, 1989; Hennessey & Zbikowski, 1993), a small number of research psychologists as well as practicing classroom teachers have experimented with our immunization techniques and replicated our results (e.g., Gerrard,

Poteat, & Ironsmith, 1996). These investigators have consistently underscored the unexpected benefits accrued to students who are explicitly asked to consider and talk about their favorite subjects and activities in school.

Intrinsic motivation must be made a regular focus of class discussion because when left to their own devices, students engage in such conversations far too infrequently. Students must be helped to recognize their own excitement for learning. Rather than relying on the feedback of teachers, they must be taught to monitor their own progress; and, whenever possible, they must be given choices about what they will do and how they will accomplish their goals. They must be encouraged to become active, independent learners, confident in their ability to take control of their own learning process.

REAL-WORLD APPLICATIONS

These are the data-driven recommendations coming from academe. But what exactly would an actual classroom (or an entire school) that has been built on this rubric look like? In many respects, our research findings call for a return to the open classroom model. The "open" terminology has traditionally been used to describe a student-centered classroom design made popular in the United States in the 1970s. This educational innovation originated in the British public elementary ("infant") schools after World War II and spread slowly via American educators who visited Great Britain's primary schools during the late 1960s. These teachers encountered classrooms where informal, unstructured approaches dominated both the teaching and learning process and they came away convinced that open classrooms were the answer to our own nation's education ills. For more than a decade, U.S. schools had been attacked from all sides and blamed for producing only unimaginative and unmotivated students who lacked the scientific and other skills necessary to win the Cold War or tackle the growing challenges posed by the Civil Rights Movement and other sweeping societal changes.

The fundamental building block of the open classroom of the 1970s was individualized, hands-on learning, and this approach gave new hope to critics who had long argued that America's formal, teacher-dominated classrooms were crushing students' creativity. Rather than present one-size-fits-all lessons, teachers trained in open classroom techniques were encouraged to abandon detailed, preestablished whole-class lesson plans in favor of an ever-changing and entirely flexible curriculum tailor-made to build on the strengths and interests of each individual child. In the classic open classroom environment, students moved freely and at their own pace from "station" to "station" – exploring reading skills, hands-on science experiments, mathematical manipulatives, and art materials.

My teacher training took place at the Shady Hill School in Cambridge, Massachusetts. Shady Hill was, in fact, the first U.S. school to adopt the British

Infant model. I was well versed, or so I thought, in every aspect of the open classroom approach, and the "Integrated Day" environment (another buzzword of the 1970s) that I constructed when I took my first teaching position in Denver certainly *looked* like the classrooms portrayed in C.E. Silberman's extremely influential and powerful 1973 book *The Open Classroom Reader*. What I did not understand at that time was that a classroom, not to mention an entire educational philosophy, is much, much more than its physical layout or daily routines.

Unfortunately, I, like many other American teachers and administrators who set out to duplicate the highly successful British educational innovation, concentrated almost entirely on the *visible* hallmarks of the open classroom approach. Instead of individual desks for students and teacher, my classroom was populated by a series of work stations offering a wide variety of materials with which children were invited to engage. In a constant flow of activity, my kindergarten and first- and second-grade students traveled either alone or in small, often multiage, groups from space to space – enlisting, when necessary, my help or the help of my co-teacher. I was taught to view my role as more similar to that of a coach or a facilitator than a traditional teacher. Like many other schools across the country, over time, my own school's quest for openness was even extended to the physical layout of the school building itself. An architectural firm was brought in to design "a school without walls," with the idea that children and their teachers needed freedom from the constraints of an arbitrarily restrictive and isolating age-graded system.

Ironically, it was in this open environment, this classroom that I had created for the express purpose of boosting children's confidence, building upon their interests and promoting their creativity, that my concerns about what teachers, myself included, were doing to kill student motivation and creativity took root. Like many other "open" educators across the country, I had failed to see the forest for the trees. I had become almost entirely caught up in the physical trappings and other unique aspects of the open classroom approach. I rightfully took pride in the fact that even my youngest students had become masters at making a contract about how they would spend their time and following through with their plan. They learned how to work together, teach one another, negotiate disagreements and solve interpersonal problems. They learned how to read, write, and manipulate numbers, and along the way they also built some amazing marble chutes and gained some sophisticated understandings about the development of a chick embryo, the ecology of a sea-island farm, and how the rotation of our planet impacts the change of seasons.

According to the yardsticks of standardized testing, administrative approval, or parental satisfaction, my open classroom was a resounding success. What I came to realize over time, however, is that I failed to drive home the most fundamental lessons of all – lessons about the importance of finding joy in learning, of taking intellectual risks, of identifying and then following one's passions, and of being driven by genuine curiosity rather than the promise of reward, the threat of evaluation, or the fear of making mistakes in front of one's peers. And I was not alone in these failings. As more and more districts moved toward the schools without walls approach, a growing number of educational theorists began to worry that America's attempt at open education had missed the mark. As Silberman warned as early as 1973:

> Creating large open spaces does not, by itself, constitute open education. Replacing desks and chairs with "interest areas" does not, by itself, constitute open education. Filling the interest areas with concrete materials that children can manipulate and use does not, by itself, constitute open education. Individualizing instruction does not, by itself, constitute open education. All these techniques, it should be emphasized, can be useful, and some may be essential, in creating and running an open classroom. Technique *is* important; without a mastery of technique, all the understanding in the world can leave a teacher helpless when he or she comes face to face with thirty or forty children. But method alone, without serious, sustained, and systematic thought about education, will turn a teacher into a mere technician with a bag of sterile tricks. No technique should be used unless a teacher has thought about why it is being used, what he or she hopes to accomplish with it, and how it will affect the children in question. (Silberman, 1973, p. xxi)

For my own part, I left elementary education in 1981 to pursue graduate study – in an attempt to figure out once and for all how to construct classrooms that would boost student motivation and creativity. Over time, many other educators and entire school systems also came to question and eventually move away from the open classroom approach, with the result that today in the United States, open classrooms are fairly rare. Classrooms that are physically open have become a rarity, as the majority of schools "without walls" have long ago constructed permanent partitions in an attempt to control noise and reduce distractions. This return to a more traditional school space, this architectural backlash, has been accompanied by a nationwide call for the abandonment of student-centered learning and a return to more traditional teacher-centered approaches, standards-based curricula, and test-based accountability.

A review of the development of American public education across the last two hundred years reveals that sweeping changes in educational policy and theorizing, like the open classroom movement, have taken hold on a number of occasions. Throughout U.S. history, educational decision making has tended to mirror the social and political trends of the time. But was the open education movement in the United States just another misguided and fleeting fancy – a byproduct of the flower child generation or dissatisfaction with the Vietnam Conflict? To discount open classrooms as merely another ideological fad would negate the deeper message of the Open Education Movement. Children really do learn best when they are genuinely interested in and see the importance of what they are doing, and their creativity is dependent on this intrinsic interest as well. Educators did not get things exactly right in the 1970s. But the message rings as true today as it did some three decades ago.

THE IMPORTANCE OF INTRINSIC MOTIVATION FOR LONG-LASTING LEARNING

As outlined earlier, intrinsic motivation is described in the literature as the motivation to do something for its own sake – for the sheer pleasure and enjoyment of the task itself rather than for some external goal. Malone and Lepper (1987) define *intrinsic motivation* simply as "what people will do without external inducement." While almost every educator (and student) would prefer that their classroom be filled with engaged and happy learners, the importance of intrinsic motivation for learning and creativity reaches far beyond affective considerations. Researchers have demonstrated that an intrinsically motivated state is characterized by deeply focused attention, enhanced cognitive functioning, and increased and persistent activity (Alexander & Murphy, 1994; Maehr & Meyer, 1997). Simply stated, intrinsic motivation leads to deeper, more long-lasting learning.

Empirical data supporting this contention come from a variety of sources. As early as 1913, Dewey identified the link between student interest or curiosity and effort expended in the classroom and, in 1967, Simon empirically demonstrated that learners driven by intrinsic motivation and curiosity try harder and exert consistent effort to reach their learning goals.

Several studies found in the reading literature demonstrate that personally interesting text segments and passages written on high-interest topics facilitate children's, as well as college students', comprehension, inferencing, and retention. For example, Guthrie, Wigfield, Metsala, and Cox (1999) reported that intrinsically motivated young readers read more and showed significantly higher levels of reading comprehension and recall than did students who were not excited by or engaged in the reading process. In addition to increasing the amount of recall, student interest also seems to have a substantial effect on the quality of learning. In a variety of investigations, interest has also been reported to lead to more elaborate and deeper processing of texts. In 2000, McDaniel, Waddill, Finstad, and Bourg found that readers asked to engage with uninteresting narratives focused on individual text elements, such as extracting proposition-specific content, whereas readers of interesting texts tended to engage in organizational processing of information. This research suggests that student interest (or lack of interest) in the text being read may affect the degree to which processing strategies benefit memory performance.

Corroborating these findings, Conti, Amabile, and Pollak (1995) reported that college students who approached a learning task with intrinsic motivation demonstrated superior long-term retention of information compared to their extrinsically motivated peers. And a large number of related investigations also demonstrate that when students approach new concepts with high levels of curiosity and interest, information is better learned and remembered (e.g., Flink, Boggiano, & Main, 1992; Gottfried 1985, 1990; Harter & Jackson, 1992; Hidi, 1990; Lepper & Cordova, 1992; Malone, 1981; Malone & Lepper, 1987; Renninger, Hidi, & Krapp, 1992; Schank, 1979; Tobias, 1994). Moreover, when students are given a choice of problems to be solved or learning and performance goals to be reached, intrinsically motivated learners are likely to take risks and explore solutions to problems that represent for them a moderate level of difficulty and challenge. Extrinsically motivated students, on the other hand, will tend to choose the easiest possible problems (Condry & Chambers, 1978; Harter, 1978; Pittman, Emory, & Boggiano, 1982).

A variety of explanations have been offered for this well-documented link between intrinsic motivation and deep, long-lasting learning. Students who are intrinsically motivated have been found to put more effort into studying and use deeper, more logical, efficient, and effective strategies (Condry & Chambers, 1978; Nolen, 1988). Some theorists argue that the harnessing of student interest and curiosity serves to activate learners' prior knowledge, which in turn allows them to make better connections with new material (Alexander, Kulikowich, & Jetton, 1994; Brophy, 1999; Deci, 1992; Thomas & Oldfather, 1997). And another prominent cognitively based view (Malone & Lepper, 1987) explains the link between intrinsic motivation and learning with a "spreading interest" model of curiosity. According to this formulation, people will be interested in new material to the extent that it relates to other topics that are already of interest to them. In other words, intrinsic task motivation may fan out along links between nodes of differing interest values, much like the process suggested by "spreading activation" theories of memory (Collins & Loftus, 1975).

Others point to the intensity and prolonged duration of intrinsically motivated learning activities (Pintrich, Roeser, & DeGroot, 1994; Vollmeyer & Rheinberg, 2000). Csikzentmihalyi's (1993, 1997) studies of the phenomenon he calls "flow" echo this emphasis. Csikzentmihalyi used the term "flow" because in his earliest investigations, several persons described their experience as being carried along by a current. Since that time, research reveals that nearly all individuals occasionally reach an intensely intrinsically motivated and pleasurable state of "optimal experience." While in flow, one's sense of time becomes distorted and all feelings of self-consciousness slip away. For the majority of persons, flow is not an everyday occurrence; and some persons experience it more than others. But when flow does come, it is characterized by feelings of intense concentration and enjoyment... feelings that transport the individual into a new reality to "previously undreamed-of states of consciousness" (Csikszentmihalyi, 1990, p. 74).

WHAT'S A TEACHER TO DO?

Clearly, intrinsic motivation is a crucial ingredient both for students' deep, long-lasting learning and for the creativity of their performance. In terms of the practical, classroom-based implications of the intrinsic motivation research just reviewed, teachers would do well to capitalize on students' existing interests as they construct lesson plans and present new material. In addition, as outlined earlier, there is a great deal of empirical data to suggest that extrinsic constraints such as expected reward, expected evaluation, and restricted choice should be avoided whenever possible.

Combining these two investigative areas, research conducted by Cordova and Lepper (1996) argues for the construction of classroom situations that allow for the provision of student choice coupled with the contextualization and personalization of lessons. Individualized or small-group instruction tailored to build on students' existing areas of interest and incorporating elements of choice in terms of what to learn and how to learn lead not only to increased levels of intrinsic motivation in students but also to deeper levels of engagement in learning and increased amounts of material learned in a fixed time period. Does this mean that schools wishing to promote student intrinsic motivation and creativity of performance must return to the open classroom approach? And would such a return even be possible in this age of budget cuts, high-stakes testing, No Child Left Behind legislation, and accountability? All across this country, decision making in schools is now dominated by the political rhetoric of "standards-based" reform. While the intentions of most policy makers may be good, their mandates are based on the unproved and arguably faulty assumption that standardized instruction and standardized tests will serve to raise intellectual standards and student achievement. More than any other time in our nation's history, teachers and administrators find that both their own job security and their schools' very survival are dependent on student test scores. Deep-seated educational reform would appear to be an impossibility in this current climate. And yet a small but growing number of schools at the elementary and secondary levels have set out to do just that – to rethink the teaching/learning process and devise what appears to be a workable and highly successful solution to the dilemma faced by educators wishing to combine individualized and personalized instruction with increasing assessment and other requirements mandated at the state and national levels.

Spearheading this movement is a core group of educators and theorists committed to integrated curricula, performance-based assessments (as opposed to standardized tests), and smaller schools. One of the more vocal and visible leaders in this initiative is teacher, activist, and noted educational reformer Deborah Meier, who helped to orchestrate ground-breaking changes first at New York's Central Park East (CPE) Schools and later in Boston at the

Mission Hill School. The founding of the first CPE school came in 1974, just as the open classroom movement was falling into disfavor and being blamed for the failings of the nation's teachers to educate our children. For over thirty years, educational reforms at Meier's schools in Harlem and Boston have taken shape to construct a learning environment designed to explore specific reproducible ways of redesigning classroom life and curricula so as to promote individualized instruction and student excitement about learning. Although I doubt that they are aware of research carried out by myself and my colleagues, teachers, and students at CPE and Mission Hill have, in fact, incorporated many of the recommendations we make in our monographs, chapters, and empirical journal articles.

In the city of Boston, right in my own backyard, there is a full-scale naturalistic experiment being carried out. Unbiased by the literature or expectations that classroom data will support university laboratory findings, Mission Hill teachers, children, and parents are testing the conclusions made by psychologists like myself as to how teachers can promote student intrinsic motivation and creativity in the classroom. In sharp contrast to my own lament that "old habits die hard," teachers at Mission Hill demonstrate a true optimism about the possibility of making fundamental and dramatic changes in the ways schools operate, teachers teach, and children learn. One of eighteen pilot schools in the Boston Public School System, Mission Hill serves approximately one hundred seventy urban students in grades K through 8. This intentionally small school employs one principal, eleven lead teachers, one assistant, and a variety of support staff. Children learn in multiage groups of no more than twenty students and typically spend two years with the same lead teacher. Mission Hill classrooms are a combination of art gallery, museum, library, and scientific laboratory. Activities at all grade levels reflect the current schoolwide curriculum theme (e.g., Ancient Africa and the African American Experience, Physical Science, Ancient China and the World of Work, Life Science, Ancient Greece and Democracy), which changes each trimester. Themes are presented over a four-year rotation, with children in kindergarten through third grade getting initial exposure to these topics and then revisiting them again in fourth grade through seventh grade. Eighth-grade students study the effects of media in society and prepare for their portfolio requirements necessary for graduation.

The majority of classrooms at all levels start and end each day with student-led meetings designed to set the classroom agenda and evaluate progress. Most work is done either individually or in small groups and about half the day is devoted to thematic work, which can incorporate reading, writing, research, mathematical computation, art, or the engineering of constructions. At all times, emphasis is placed on depth over breadth learning: Students are helped to master a few areas well, rather than spend their time studying a variety of topics with little understanding. At the core of the Mission Hill curriculum are the Mission Hill Five Habits of Mind,[2] a rubric to guide teachers' and students' approaches to both the traditional academic disciplines and the demands of everyday life.

1. **Evidence:** How do we know what's true and false? What evidence counts? How sure can we be? What makes it credible to us? This includes using the scientific method, and more.
2. **Viewpoint:** How might this look if we stepped into other shoes? If we were looking at it from a different direction? If we had a different history or expectation? This requires the exercise of informed "empathy" and imagination. It requires flexibility of mind.
3. **Connections/Cause and Effect:** Is there a pattern? Have we seen something like this before? What are the possible consequences?
4. **Conjecture: Could it have been otherwise?** Supposing that...? What if...? This habit requires use of the imagination as well as knowledge of alternative possibilities. It includes the habits described above.
5. **Relevance: Does it matter? Who cares?** Knowing "how-to" is no substitute for having good habits. Who cares if you could drive well, if you're not in the habit of doing so? Who cares if you could be on time, if you never are? The Mission Hill Habits of Mind are supplemented by Habits of Work: Habits that include meeting deadlines, being on time, sticking to a task, not getting frustrated quickly, and really hearing out what others have to say.

Mission Hill teachers use a variety of methods to gage student progress in acquiring knowledge, skills, and the habits of work and mind. Every day, they make written observations about children's progress. They observe and carefully document both evidence of growth and sticking points and use these notes to guide their plans for the type of individualized instruction that will come next. Students, too, have many opportunities to voice their own ideas about and evaluations of themselves as learners. These include journal entries, conversations with peers and teachers, and more formal interviews. Tests and quizzes are also a part of the assessment process, but they are heavily supplemented by portfolios and other methods (e.g., research papers, schoolwide presentations, "on demand" essays) devised to give children an opportunity to showcase their accomplishments. The portfolio approach has long been recommended by Theodore Sizer and others affiliated with the Coalition of Essential Schools, of which Mission Hill is a member. In their final eighth-grade year, as part of Mission Hill's competency-based graduation requirements, students are expected to prepare and present tangible demonstrations of their knowledge

---

[2] This list of habits was taken almost verbatim from materials published by the Mission Hill School in Boston, Massachusetts. For a more in-depth description of the Mission Hill philosophy and approach, go to http://www.missionhillschool.org/mhs/Habits_of_Mind.html

and skills in literature, science, art, and mathematics. Finally, because it is a public school in the city of Boston, Mission Hill is required to administer the Massachusetts Comprehensive Assessment System (MCAS) to all students. This battery of "high-stakes" tests includes assessments of reading comprehension, composition, mathematics, social science, history, science, and technology/engineering administered at set points from grades 3 to 10. All students in the state must pass the grade 10 tests in English Language Arts (ELA) and Mathematics to be eligible to receive a high school diploma (in addition to fulfilling local requirements).

While it is clear that the majority of Mission Hill staff and students would prefer that the MCAS not be a requirement, teachers report that they have been quite successful in their attempt to incorporate these evaluations into their curriculum and are diligent about maintaining a range of alternative, authentic objective measures such as biannual tape-recorded reading interviews, scored samples of student writing, and one-on-one math interviews. The challenges faced by educators at Mission Hill and other schools serving an especially diverse, low-income student body are many. But, for the most part, Mission Hill is meeting its target goals. They do very little test prepping, yet in comparison with other schools in the city of Boston, students score exceptionally well in language arts, and by the time they graduate to high school, virtually 100% pass the math MCAS necessary for graduation, most on their first try.

Principal Ayla Gavins works diligently to assist her teaching staff as they implement the recommendations of Deborah Meier and other progressive educators committed to challenging students' curiosity and promoting their creativity. As Meier (1995) explains, the current emphasis on standards-based assessments mandates that material be broken down into a series of discrete skills (to be tested) and makes it unlikely, if not impossible, that teachers will spend their time and effort introducing strong conceptual subject matter with which students can become fully engaged. In the view of noted learning theorist Eleanor Duckworth, our schools are preventing students from the "having of wonderful ideas" (Duckworth, 1996). Multiple-choice tests are no substitute for authentic and meaningful performance.

In many respects, the concerns that drove me out of my Integrated Day classroom are the same concerns that prompted Meier to establish her ground-breaking schools in Harlem and Boston. As I watched my students lose their creativity and intrinsic motivation as they moved from kindergarten through second grade, I wrestled with the question of how to keep alive children's playfulness, willingness to take intellectual risks, and excitement about learning. Meier (1995) also talks about the importance of keeping the spirit of kindergarten alive – of constructing school environments that allow students of all ages to become as deeply involved and absorbed in their "work" as kindergarteners are in their "play."

Under the present U.S. public education system, teachers are expected to work diligently to wean students *away* from their natural tendency to play with objects and ideas. In the eyes of most contemporary educators, books and standardized exams must replace the student-driven learning approach offered to kindergarteners if older students are to excel and reap maximal benefits from the teaching and learning process. As they move through the grades, students are given less and less control over their own learning. Open-ended curricula and opportunities for discovery are replaced with artificial 45-minute periods offering "one size fits all" lessons driving home the messages that learning is a passive activity and that knowledge really can and should be divided into neatly packaged units. Courses in science, mathematics, language arts, social studies, and history are presented in isolation and rarely, if ever, are attempts made to meld these disciplines. Yet it does not have to be this way. Even middle school and high school students can benefit enormously from the discovery-based integrated learning techniques we have come to reserve only for the kindergarten classroom.

A large body of recent research shows, in fact, that hands-on, open-ended learning that allows for true engagement with the curriculum significantly boosts both the interest and performance of older students (Marks, 2000; Mitchell, 1993; Shernoff, Csikszentmihalyi, Schneider, & Shernoff, 2003; Shernoff & Hoogstra, 2001; Shernoff, Knauth, & Makris, 2000; Shernoff, Schneider, & Csikszentmihalyi, 2001; Stipek, 1996; Yair, 2000). As Meier rightly points out, "expertise in early childhood development is a good foundation for starting a school for adolescents" (1995, p. 47).

So what has changed? How is it that I abandoned my own attempts at teaching in an environment dedicated to students' hands-on exploration and the integration of subject matter only to come back years later to a research program that calls for a revival of the "open" education approach? What I, along with a growing group of other researchers and teachers at schools like Mission Hill, now realize is that a classroom is much more than its physical trappings. The substitution of learning stations for desks is all well and good, but what is fundamentally important is that attention be paid to students' motivational orientation. Teachers and their students must remain mindful of the fundamental purpose behind education and of what it means to be an active, engaged, and self-determined learner. And schools and the curricula they offer must be constructed in such a way that the development and maintenance of this mindfulness is possible. Students and teachers at all grade levels must engage in frequent directed and explicit discussion about issues of motivation and the pressures that come with testing and other evaluative or competitive educational trappings. While it would be wrong to assume that there is only one right way, one single path that must be taken to accomplish this goal, it would also be a mistake to assume that the habits of mind practiced at Mission

Hill and a handful of other sites across the country are out of the reach of most schools in this nation.

Yes, intrinsic motivation and creativity have been driven out of the majority of U.S. classrooms with the imposition of increased curricular standards, high-stakes testing, No Child Left Behind legislation, and other accountability mandates. But careful experimental investigation coupled with real-world application of research findings in classroom settings demonstrates that it is possible for teachers who value creativity to nurture students' creative development and expression without drifting into curricular and assessment chaos. In short, the myriad constraints faced by today's teachers need not lead to choosing conformity over creativity or extrinsic motivation over intrinsic motivation. Educational reform has never been and never will be easy. But reform *is* possible. And reform *is* essential. The time has come for teachers at all levels to institute fundamental changes at the grass-roots/individual classroom level.

REFERENCES

Alexander, P. A., & Murphy, P. K. (1994, April). *The research base for APA's learner-centered principles.* Presented at the annual meeting of the American Educational Research Association, New Orleans, LA.

Alexander, P. A., Kulikowich, J. M., & Jetton, T. L. (1994). The role of subject matter knowledge and interest in the processing of linear and non-linear texts. *Review of Educational Research,* **64,** 201–252.

Anderman, E. M., & Maehr, M. L. (1994). Motivation and schooling in the middle grades. *Review of Educational Research,* **64,** 287–309.

Amabile, T. M. (1982a). Children's artistic creativity: Detrimental effects of competition in a field setting. *Personality and Social Psychology Bulletin,* **8,** 573–578.

Amabile, T. M. (1982b). Social psychology of creativity: A consensual assessment technique. *Journal of Personality and Social Psychology,* **43,** 997–1013.

Amabile, T. M. (1983). *The social psychology of creativity.* New York: Springer-Verlag.

Amabile, T. M. (1996). *Creativity in context.* Boulder, CO: Westview.

Amabile, T. M. (1997). Motivating creativity in organizations: On doing what you love and loving what you do. *California Management Review,* **40,** 39–58.

Amabile, T. M., Goldfarb, P., & Brackfield, S. C. (1990). Social influences on creativity: Evaluation, coaction and surveillance. *Creativity Research Journal,* **3,** 6–21.

Amabile, T. M., Hennessey, B. A., & Grossman, B. (1986). Social influences on creativity: The effects of contracted-for reward. *Journal of Personality and Social Psychology,* **50,** 14–23.

Amabile, T. M., Phillips, E. D., Collins, M. A. (1994). *Creativity by contract: Social influences on the creativity of professional artists.* Unpublished manuscript, Brandeis University.

Barron, F. (1968). *Creativity and personal freedom.* New York: Van Nostrand.

Bem, D. (1972). Self-perception theory. In L. Berkowitz (Ed.), *Advances in experimental social psychology* (Vol. **6**). New York: Academic Press.

Brophy, J. (1999). Toward a model of the value aspects of motivation in education: Developing appreciation for particular learning domains and activities. *Educational Psychologist,* **34,** 75–85.

Cameron, J., & Pierce, W. D. (1994). Reinforcement, reward, and intrinsic motivation: A meta-analysis. *Review of Educational Research*, **64**, 363–423.

Campbell, D. (1960). Blind variation and selective retention in creative thought as in other knowledge processes. *Psychological Review*, **67**, 380–400.

Chen, J.-O., & Gardner, H. (2005). Assessment based on multiple-intelligences theory. In D. P. Flanagan & P. L. Harrison (Eds.), *Contemporary intellectual assessment: Theories, tests, and issues* (pp. 77–102). New York: Guilford.

Collins, A. M., & Loftus, E. F. (1975). A spreading-activation theory of semantic processing. *Psychological Review*, **82**, 407–428.

Condry, J., & Chambers, J. (1978). Intrinsic motivation and the process of learning. In M. R. Lepper & D. Greene (Eds.), *The hidden costs of reward* (pp. 61–84). Hillsdale, NJ: Lawrence Earlbaum.

Conti, R., Amabile, T. M., & Pollak, S. (1995). The positive impact of creative activity: Effects of creative task engagement and motivational focus on college students' learning. *Personality and Social Psychology Bulletin*, **21**, 1107–1116.

Cordova, D. L., & Lepper, M. R. (1996). Intrinsic motivation and the process of learning: Beneficial effects of contextualization, personalization and choice. *Journal of Educational Psychology*, **88**, 715–730.

Crutchfield, R. (1962). Conformity and creative thinking. In H. Gruber, G. Terrell, & M. Wertheimer (Eds.), *Contemporary approaches to creative thinking* (pp. 120–140). New York: Atherton Press.

Csikszenthihalyi, M. (1990). The domain of creativity. In M. Runco & A. S. Robert (Eds.), *Theories of creativity* (pp. 190–212). Thousand Oaks, CA: Sage.

Csikszentmihalyi, M. (1993). *Flow.* New York: Harper Collins.

Csikszentmihalyi, M. (1997). *Creativity: Flow and the psychology of discovery and invention.* New York: HarperCollins.

Dansky, J., & Silverman, I. (1975). Play: A general facilitator of fluency. *Developmental Psychology*, **11**, 104.

deCharms, R. (1968). *Personal causation.* New York: Academic Press.

Deci, E. L. (1971). Effects of externally mediated rewards on intrinsic motivation. *Journal of Personality and Social Psychology*, **18**, 105–115.

Deci, E. L. (1972). The effects of contingent and noncontingent rewards and controls on intrinsic motivation. *Organizational Behavior and Human Performance*, **8**, 217–229.

Deci, E. L. (1992). The relation of interest to the motivation of behavior: A self-determination theory perspective. In K. A. Renninger, S. Hidi, & A. Krapp (Eds.), *The role of interest in learning and development* (pp. 43–70). Hillsdale, NJ: Lawrence Erlbaum.

Deci, E. L., & Ryan, R. M. (1985a). The general causality orientations scale: Self-determination in personality. *Journal of Personality and Social Psychology*, **19**, 109–134.

Deci, E. L., & Ryan, R. M. (1985b). *Intrinsic motivation and self-determination in human behavior.* New York: Plenum.

Dewey, J. (1913). *Interest and effort in education.* Boston: Houghton Mifflin.

Duckworth, E. (1996). *"The having of wonderful ideas" and other essays on teaching and learning.* New York: Teachers College Press.

Eisenberger, R. (1996). Reward, intrinsic interest and creativity: New findings. *American Psychologist*, **53**, 676–679.

Eisenberger, R. (2003). Rewards, intrinsic motivation and creativity: A case study of conceptual and methodological isolation. *Creativity Research Journal*, **15**, 121–130.

Eisenberger, R., Armeli, S., & Pretz, J. (1998). Can the promise of reward increase creativity? *Journal of Personality and Social Psychology*, **74**, 704–714.

Eisenberger, R., & Cameron, J. (1996). Detrimental effects of reward: Reality or myth? *American Psychologist*, **51**, 1153–1166.

Eisenberger, R., & Cameron, J. (1998). Reward, intrinsic interest, and creativity: New findings. *American Psychologist*, **53**, 676–679.

Eisenberger, R., Pierce, W. D., & Cameron, J. (1999). Effects of reward on intrinsic motivation – Negative, neutral, and positive: Comment on Deci, Koestner, and Ryan. *Psychological Bulletin*, **125**, 677–691.

Fazio, R. H. (1981). On the self-perception explanation of the overjustification effect: The role of salience of initial attitude. *Journal of Experimental Social Psychology*, **17**, 417–426.

Fischer, K. W., & Immordino-Yang, M. H. (2008). The fundamental importance of the brain and learning for education. In *The Jossey-Bass reader on the brain and learning* (pp. xvii–xi). San Francisco: Jossey-Bass.

Flink, C., Boggiano, A. K., & Main, D. S. (1992). Children's achievement-related behaviors: The role of extrinsic and intrinsic motivational orientations. In A. K. Boggiano, & T. S. Pittman (Eds.), *Achievement and motivation: A social-developmental perspective* (pp. 189–214). New York: Cambridge University Press

Garbarino, J. (1975). The impact of anticipated reward upon cross-age tutoring. *Journal of Personality and Social Psychology*, **32**, 421–428.

Gardner, H. ([1983] 1993). *Frames of mind: The theory of multiple intelligences*. New York: Basic Books.

Gardner, H. (1989). *To open minds: Chinese clues to the dilemma of contemporary education*. New York: Basic Books.

Gardner, H. (1991). *The unschooled mind: How children think and how schools should teach*. New York: Basic Books.

Gardner, H. (1999). *Intelligence reframed. Multiple intelligences for the 21st century*. New York: Basic Books.

Gerrard, L. E., Poteat, G. M., & Ironsmith, M. (1996). Promoting children's creativity: Effects of competition, self-esteem, and immunization. *Creativity Research Journal*, **9**, 339–346.

Gottfried, A. E. (1985). Academic intrinsic motivation in elementary and junior high school children. *Journal of Educational Psychology*, **77**, 631–645.

Gottfried, A. E. (1990). Academic intrinsic motivation in young elementary children. *Journal of Educational Psychology*, **82**, 525–538.

Greene, D., & Lepper, M. R. (1974). Intrinsic motivation: How to turn play into work. *Psychology Today*, **8**, 49–54.

Guthrie, J. T., Wigfield, A., Metsala, J. L., & Cox, K. E. (1999). Motivational and cognitive predictors of text comprehension and reading amount. *Scientific Studies of Reading*, **3**, 231–256.

Hanna, J. (2005). Mind, brain, & education: Linking biology, neuroscience, & educational practice. *Harvard Graduate School of Education News* (1 June). Retrieved May 12, 2008, from /www.gse.harvard.edu/news/features/mbe06012005.html.

Harackiewic, J. M., Abrahams, S., & Wageman, R. (1987). Performance evaluation and intrinsic motivation: The effects of evaluative focus, rewards, and achievement orientation. *Journal of Personality and Social Psychology*, **53**, 1015–1023.

Harter, S. (1981). A new self-report scale of intrinsic versus extrinsic orientation in the classroom: Motivational and informational components. *Developmental Psychology*, **17**, 300–312.

Harter, S., & Jackson, B. K. (1992). Trait vs. nontrait conceptualizations of intrinsic/extrinsic motivational orientation. *Motivation and Emotion, 16*, 209–230.

Hennessey, B. A. (2000). Rewards and creativity. In C. Sansone & J. Harackiewicz (Eds.), *Intrinsic and extrinsic motivation: The search for optimal motivation and performance* (pp. 55–78). New York: Academic Press.

Hennessey, B. A. (2002). The social psychology of creativity in the schools. *Research in the Schools, 9*, 23–33.

Hennessey, B. A. (2003). The social psychology of creativity. *Scandinavian Journal of Educational Psychology, 47*, 253–271.

Hennessey, B. A. (2004). *Developing creativity in gifted children: The central importance of motivation and classroom climate* (RM04202). The National Research Center on the Gifted and Talented Senior Scholar Series. Storrs, CT: NRCG/T, University of Connecticut.

Hennessey, B. A., & Amabile, T. M. (1988). The conditions of creativity. In R. Sternberg (Ed.), *The nature of creativity* (pp. 11–38). New York: Cambridge University Press.

Hennessey, B. A., & Amabile, T. M. (1998). Reward, intrinsic motivation, and creativity. *American Psychologist, 53*, 674–675.

Hennessey, B. A., & Amabile, T. M. (1999). Consensual assessment. In M. Runco & S. Pritzker (Eds.), *Encyclopedia of creativity* (pp. 347–359). New York: Academic Press.

Hennessey, B. A., Amabile, T. M., & Martinage, M. (1989). Immunizing children against the negative effects of reward. *Contemporary Educational Psychology, 14*, 212–227.

Hennessey, B. A., & Zbikowski, S. M. (1993). Immunizing children against the negative effects of reward: A further examination of intrinsic motivation training techniques. *Creativity Research Journal, 6*, 297–307.

Hidi, S. (1990). Interest and its contribution as a mental resource for learning. *Review of Educational Research, 60*, 549–571.

Jussim, L., Soffin, S., & Brown, R. (1992). Understanding reactions to feedback by integrating ideas from symbolic interactionism and cognitive evaluation theory. *Journal of Personality and Social Psychology, 62*, 402–421.

Kelley, H. (1967). Attribution theory in social psychology. In D. Levine (Ed.), *Nebraska symposium on motivation*, Vol. 15. Lincoln: University of Nebraska

Kelley, H. (1973). The processes of causal attribution. *American Psychologist, 28*, 107–128.

Kernoodle-Loveland, K., & Olley, J. G. (1979). The effect of external reward on interest and quality of task performance in children of high and low intrinsic motivation. *Child Development, 50*, 1207–1210.

Kornhaber, M. L., & Gardner, H. (2006). Multiple intelligences: Developments in implementation and theory. In M. A. Constas & R. J. Sternberg (Eds.), *Translating theory and research into educational practice: Developments in content domains, large-scale reform, and intellectual capacity* (pp. 255–276). Mahwah, NJ: Erlbaum.

Kruglanski, A. W., Friedman, I., & Zeevi, G. (1971). The effects of extrinsic incentive on some qualitative aspects of task performance. *Journal of Personality, 39*, 606–617.

Lepper, M. R., & Cordova, D. I. (1992). A desire to be taught: Instructional consequences of intrinsic motivation. *Motivation and Emotion, 16*, 187–208.

Lepper, M. R., Greene, D., & Nisbett, R. E. (1973). Undermining children's intrinsic interest with extrinsic rewards: A test of the overjustification hypothesis. *Journal of Personality and Social Psychology, 28*, 129–137.

Lepper, M. R., Sethi, S., Dialdin, D., & Drake, M. (1997). Intrinsic and extrinsic motivation: A developmental perspective. In S. S. Luthar, J. Burack, D. Cicchetti, &

J. R. Weisz (Eds.), *Developmental psychopathology: Perspectives on adjustment, risk and disorder* (pp. 23–50). New York: Cambridge University Press.

Lieberman, J. N. (1965). Playfulness and divergent thinking: An investigation of their relationship at the kindergarten level. *Journal of Genetic Psychology, 107,* 219–224.

Maehr, M. L., & Meyer, H. A. (1997). Understanding motivation and schooling: Where we've been, where we are, and where we need to go. *Educational Psychology Review,* **9,** 371–409.

Malone, T. W. (1981). Toward a theory of intrinsically motivating instruction. *Cognitive Science,* **4,** 333–369.

Malone, T. W., & Lepper, M. R. (1987). Making learning fun: A taxonomy of intrinsic motivations for learning. In R. E. Snow & M. J. Farr (Eds.), *Aptitude, learning and instruction: III. Cognitive and affective process analyses* (pp. 223–253). Hillsdale, NJ: Erlbaum.

Marks, H. M. (2000). Student engagement in instructional activity: Patterns in the elementary, middle and high school years. *American Educational Research Journal,* **37,** 153–184.

McDaniel, M. A., Finstad, K., Waddill, P. J., & Bourg, T. (2000). The effects of text-based interest on attention and recall. *Journal of Educational Psychology,* **92,** 492–502.

McGraw, K. O. (1978). The detrimental effects of reward on performance: A literature review and a prediction model. In M. Lepper & D. Greene (Eds.), *The hidden costs of reward* (pp. 33–60). Hillsdale, NJ: Erlbaum.

McGraw, K. O., & McCullers, J. (1979). Evidence of a detrimental effect of extrinsic incentives on breaking a mental set. *Journal of Experimental Social Psychology,* **15,** 285–294.

Meier, D. (1995). *The power of their ideas: Lessons for America from a small school in Harlem.* Boston: Beacon Press.

Meier, D. (2002). *In schools we trust: Creating communities of learning in an era of testing and standardization.* Boston: Beacon Press.

Mitchell, M. (1993). Situational interest: Its multifaceted structure in the secondary school mathematics classroom. *Journal of Educational Psychology,* **85,** 424–436.

Nolen, S. B. (1988). Reasons for studying: Motivational orientations and study strategies. *Cognition and Instruction,* **5,** 269–287.

Pintrich, P. R., Roeser, R., & DeGrot, E. (1994). Classroom and individual differences in early adolescents' motivation self-regulated learning. *Journal of Early Adolescence,* **14,** 139–161.

Pittman, T. S., Emery, J., & Boggiano, A. K. (1982). Intrinsic and extrinsic motivational orientations: Reward-induced changes in preference for complexity. *Journal of Pesronality and Social Psychology,* **42,** 789–797.

Posner, M., & Rothbart, M. K. (2006). *Educating the human brain.* Washington, DC: American Psychological Association.

Renninger, K. A., Hidi, S., & Krapp, A. (1992). *The role of interest in learning and development.* Hillsdale, NJ: Erlbaum.

Ryan, R. M., & Deci, E. L. (2000a). Self-determination theory and the facilitation of intrinsic motivation, social development, and well-being. *American-Psychologist,* **55,** 68–78.

Ryan, R. M., & Deci, E. L. (2000b). When rewards compete with nature: The undermining of intrinsic motivation and self-regulation. In C. Sansone & J.M. Harackiewicz, (Eds), (*Intrinsic and extrinsic motivation: The search for optimal motivation and performance.* San Diego, CA: Academic, pp. 13–54.

Sarason, S. (1971, revised 1996). *Revisiting "The Culture of school and the problem of change."* New York: Teachers College Press.

Sarason, S. (1996). Power relationships in the classroom. In R. L. Fried (Ed.), *The skeptical visionary: A Seymour Sarason education reader* (pp. 46–57). Philadelphia, PA: Temple University Press.

Schank, R. C. (1979). Interestingness: Controlling inferences. *Artificial Intelligence*, **12**, 273–297.

Shapira, Z. (1976). Expectancy determinants of intrinsically motivated behavior. *Journal of Personality and Social Psychology*, **34**, 1235–1244.

Shernoff, D. J., Csikszentmihalyi, M., Schneider, B, & Shernoff, E. S. (2003). Student engagement in high school classrooms from the perspective of flow theory. *School Psychology Quarterly*, **18**, 158–176.

Shernoff, D. J., & Hoogstra, L. (2001). Continuing motivation beyond the high school classroom. *New Directions in Child and Adolescent Development*, **93**, 73–87.

Shernoff, D. J., Knauth, S., & Makris, E. (2000). The quality of classroom experiences. In M. Csikszentmihalyi & B. Schneider (coauthors), *Becoming adult* (pp. 122–145). New York: Basic Books.

Shernoff, D. J., Schneider, B., & Csikszentmihalyi, M. (2001). *Assessing multiple influences on student engagement in high school classrooms.* Presented at the Annual Meeting of the American Educational Research Association, Seattle, WA.

Silberman, C. E. (Ed.) (1973). *The open classroom reader.* New York: Vintage.

Simon, H. A. (1967). Motivational and emotional controls of cognition. *Psychological Review*, **74**, 29–39.

Stein, M. I. (1974). *Stimulating creativity* (Vols. 1 and 2). New York: Academic Press.

Stipek, D. J. (1996). Motivation and instruction. In D. C. Berliner & R. Calfee (Eds.), *Handbook of educational psychology* (pp. 85–113). New York: Simon & Schuster Macmillan.

Thomas, S., & Oldfather, P. (1997). Intrinsic motivations, literacy, and assessment practices: "That's my grade. That's me." *Educational Psychologist*, **32**, 107–123.

Tobias, S. (1994). Interest, prior knowledge and learning. *Review of Educational Research*, **64**, 37–54.

Torrance, E. P. (1974). *Torrance Tests of Creative Thinking.* Bensenville, IL: Scholastic Testing Service.

Vollmeyer, R., & Rheinberg, F. (2000). Does motivation affect performance via persistence? *Learning and Instruction*, **10**, 293–309.

Yair, G. (2000). Educational battlefields in America: The tug-of-war over students' engagement with instruction. *Sociology of Education*, **73**, 247–269.

17

Attitude Change as the Precursor to Creativity Enhancement

JONATHAN A. PLUCKER AND GAYLE T. DOW

ATTITUDE CHANGE AS THE PRECURSOR
TO CREATIVITY ENHANCEMENT

Schemas develop from interconnections of ideas and grow into complex, organized mental structures of information (Anderson, 1977; Piaget, 1926). The growth of schemata may occur over a series of experiences and often become engrained in our implicit cognitive processing. Although schema development may be flexible, it is very difficult to completely change them, even in light of contradictory evidence (see Palmer, 1981; Wheatley & Wegner, 2001). This causes particular concern among educational psychologists because many schemata may be inaccurate or based on partially incorrect information. The result can be a mental framework firmly rooted in misinformation.

Creativity is not immune from inaccurate schema representations. *Creativity*, which is defined as "the interaction among *aptitude, process, and environment* by which an individual or group produces a *perceptible product* that is both *novel and useful* as defined within a *social context*" (Plucker, Beghetto, & Dow, 2004, p. 90, emphasis in original), is plagued by implicit myths that, in our view, have led to inaccurate schemata on a mass scale.

These schemata are problematic because there appears to be no shortage of areas in which creativity can be applied constructively to improve people's lives and, perhaps more important, areas in which people can use creativity to improve their own lives. However, few educators address divergent thinking, creativity, and innovation in primary, secondary, or postsecondary education,

The authors wish to thank the many students who took the course described in this chapter for their participation and forthrightness. We also acknowledge the considerable input provided by Michael Slavkin at the University of Southern Indiana and Ron Beghetto at the University of Oregon, who provided valuable insight and suggestions about the course design and greatly assisted in the teaching of the course. Finally, we appreciate the assistance of the staff of the Indiana University Human Subjects Committee, who worked with us to find ways to evaluate and improve the course in a way that met all ethical standards and guidelines.

areas that are generally considered to be ripe for helping students develop schema. For example, primary and secondary classrooms rarely support or encourage creativity, instead emphasizing a traditional structured curriculum and standardized tests (Paige, Hickok, & Neuman, 2002). Furthermore, when creativity is addressed in K-12 classrooms, it is too often viewed as restricted to the arts and music (Diakidoy & Phtiaka, 2001; Olton & Johnson, 1976). We strongly believe that these problems are primarily due to myths and stereotypes about creativity and innovation that are, at best, loosely related to research in this field.

EXAMPLES OF SOME UNHELPFUL MYTHS

Plucker, Beghetto, and Dow (2004) identified four of the main prevailing myths that lead to the development of incorrect schemata of creativity. Many, if not all, of the myths and stereotypes are widespread both in practice and in the research literature (Isaksen, 1987; Treffinger, Isaksen, & Dorval, 1996). Common themes that run throughout the myths are their pervasiveness, even among creativity scholars, and their exclusionary undertones (i.e., their role in reinforcing who is *not* creative). The myth that *people are born creative or uncreative* yields an inaccurate conclusion that creativity is an innate quality resilient to improvement (Treffinger et al., 1996). If this myth is adopted, any attempt to increase one's creative output would be abandoned as a fruitless task. This myth continues to flourish in light of ample evidence to refute it. For example, research on creativity training and environmental techniques that foster creative thinking have been well established (Amabile, 1983, 1996; Fontenot, 1993; Hennessey & Amabile, 1988; Osborn, 1963; Parnes, 1962; Pyryt, 1999; Sternberg & Lubart, 1992; Torrance, 1962, 1972a, 1987; Westberg, 1996, Dow & Mayer, 2004).

The myth that *creativity is a negative attribute* evokes the image of a mad genius with neurotic tendencies (Isaksen, 1987). Such stereotypes are fostered by media portrayals of crazy scientists (e.g., Dr. Frankenstein) and exocentric artists and poets such as Edgar Allen Poe, who directly addressed the topic of his madness in the quote below.

> Men have called me mad, but the question is not yet settled whether madness is or is not the loftiest intelligence – whether all that is profound – does not spring from disease of thought, from moods of mind exalted at the expenses of the general intellect. (Poe, 2005, p. 468)

However, deviant behavior is not a preceding necessity of creativity; instead, it is possible that novelty, which is found in both creativity and deviate behavior (Isaksen, 1987; Plucker & Runco, 1999), or latent inhibition, the capacity to filter irrelevant information, is the underlying connection between creativity and deviance (Carson, Peterson, & Higgins, 2003). In other words, correlation does not necessarily imply causation.

Another myth is that *creativity is a fuzzy, soft construct* limited to shamans, crystal ball mystics, and tea-leaf readers (an exaggeration, but only a little one). This stereotype leads people to believe that creative behavior resides in the world of pop psychology and is not deemed worthy of scientific scrutiny or empirical driven interventions that enhance creativity. However, a large quantity of creativity research is conceptually and empirically rigorous, with a large body of work focused on cutting-edge topics such as complex cognition and neuropsychology (e.g., Dow & Mayer, 2004; Smith, Ward, & Finke, 1995; Ward, Smith, & Vaid, 1997).

The myth that *creativity is enhanced within a group* stems from the business community. This myth has grown from the belief that quantity of ideas equates to greater creativity – thus, the more people working together, the more ideas will be produced, and the greater will be the creativity. However, this myth does not take into account group dynamics that can hinder creative potential. For example, fear of negative evaluation from other group members can hinder idea production, certain group members may dominate the discussion, or the group may fall prey to group-think and agree, wholeheartedly, without giving each idea careful consideration and thought (Dacey & Lennon, 1998; Kurtzberg, 1998; Williams & Yang, 1999). Diehl and Strobe (1986), Finke, Ward, and Smith (1992), and Thornburg (1991), among many others, have found that brainstorming, or generating lists of ideas for a given problem or situation, will result in more ideas if completed in solitude followed by pooling the ideas (see Rickards, 1999).

The impact of these myths is far reaching because creativity can be applied to many domains, both personal (e.g., the development of one's unique talents) and external (e.g., the enhancement of creativity in the education and the business communities). Given that the field of education is specifically geared toward helping students develop schemata, a logical first step is preventing the development of these myths. Unfortunately, the environments in primary and secondary classrooms rarely support or encourage creativity; rather, they tend to opt for traditional structured curriculum with standardized testing (Paige, Hickok, & Neuman, 2002). Even when creativity is addressed in primary and secondary classrooms, it is too often restricted to the arts and music (Diakidoy & Phtiaka, 2001; Olton & Johnson, 1976).

A NEW MODEL OF INNOVATION ENHANCEMENT

Our team is working on the development of a new model of creativity enhancement. The goal of this work is not to generate a model of creativity per se but rather to design a model that seeks to explain how creativity, as defined earlier, can be effectively and efficiently enhanced. We believe that a model of creativity enhancement needs to (1) focus on schema change, (2) help people identify their strengths, and (3) emphasize both personal and external factors related to creativity.

Based on the prevalence of the previously stated myths, the necessity of schema correction forms the foundation of the model. The roots of these myths have grown very deep, to the point that many of them are still widely held despite recent theoretical and empirical advances in the field and the often overwhelming evidence of the misperceptions' fallibility (Plucker et al., 2004; Treffinger et al., 1996). To address these myths at the source, a three-prong approach was adopted based on affective changes through direct experiences with creativity, on behavioral changes through altering the students' actions regarding creativity, and on cognitive changes through highlighting inconsistencies in current beliefs (Olson & Zanna, 1993; Weber & Crocker, 1983). Without a personal analysis of these myths, most creativity enhancement efforts are short-term patches. Throughout the course, changing the students' schemata was addressed by focusing explicitly on identifying the students' affect (e.g., "I *feel* that a person is more often born with creativity"), behavior (e.g., "Creativity is *doing* something in a way that is not the standard"), and cognitive processing ("I *believe* that creativity would be impaired by mental disorders"). This approach was used with the hope that incorrect schemata can be brought to the surface and then reduced or eliminated.

The next component of the model is to help people determine which creativity strategies work best for them. These strategies can be conceptualized in a variety of ways: We have used the traditional Five P approach (i.e., process, product, person, press, and persuasion; Albert & Runco, 1990), and we have used an approach we call CPSEE (i.e., identifying Cognitive, Political, Social, Environmental, and Emotional strengths and preferences). Regardless of the approach, the emphasis is on respecting individual differences in abilities, interests, and preferences.

The third component of the model is the balance in emphasis on external and personal factors in creativity. Highly influential research encourages practitioners to be aware of external or environmental factors when fostering creativity (e.g., Amabile, 1983; Baer, 1997, 1998), but we believe the cautions have often been oversold. When we focus exclusively on external factors (which is how we often see this research applied to education), we remove the responsibility for creativity from the individual. Rather, practitioners should promote a more balanced perspective, one in which students learn to interact successfully with their environment when attempting to solve problems creatively.

UNDERGRADUATE COURSEWORK BASED ON THE MODEL

The goal of our program in creativity enhancement at Indiana University is to help undergraduates enhance their long-term creativity using methods based

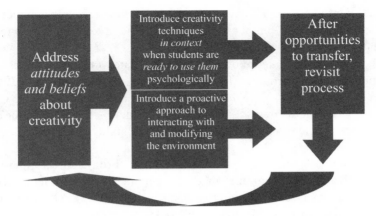

Figure 17.1. Proposed model of creativity enhancement. (© 2008 Jonathan Plucker.)

on this model. To this end, we created a two-stage set of courses: an entry-level course, "Debunking Myths and Enhancing Innovation," and a capstone, "Applied Creativity Seminar," for upper-level undergraduates.

Many of the students who begin a class on creativity bring with them several of the above-mentioned myths and stereotypes about creativity. The purpose of this course in creativity was to identify those myths and to debunk them. The preliminary course has been taught seven times over a five-year period. The capstone seminar has been taught once, when the first groups of students to take the preliminary course became seniors. The sequence of these courses is based on the model – specifically, the premise that creativity cannot be enhanced long-term until myths and stereotypes are examined on a personal level.

In the introductory course, students actively explore contemporary thought and research by investigating the numerous myths about creativity. The major goal of this course was to provide students with the necessary tools for enhancing creatively in other courses. Students are required to participate in discussions, individual and group projects, and class presentations in an effort to obtain a better understanding of creativity; learn techniques for stimulating creativity; discover ways to stimulate the creativity of others; learn to avoid common blocks to creativity; and explore the campus and its numerous resources. The basic approach to the course is depicted in Figure 17.1. The majority of class activities revolve around problem-based learning.[1]

Participants consisted of undergraduate students enrolled in seven sections of the first creativity course. Students came from a wide range of majors, including education, psychology, business, sociology, political science, interior design, chemistry, premed, and prelaw, among many others. Most students

---

[1]   Space limitations do not permit a more detailed description of course activities. Interested readers should contact the first author for this information.

took the course during their first and second years of college, but juniors and seniors also participated. Instructors included the first author of this chapter and an advanced doctoral student with two years of college teaching experience and multiple teaching awards.

In the following section, information from the course is identified and compared in relation to some of the most important myths. This list is not exhaustive, and it is worth noting that the last group of students to take the course identified additional areas of interest that were worked into the semester.

EVALUATING THE APPLICATION OF THE MODEL

Data were collected via a precourse and postcourse version of a demographic worksheet, the Creativity Questionnaire, an Observational Note List, group and individual interviews, and document analysis of the textbook and syllabus used for coursework.

Creativity Questionnaire

Participants completed copies of a creativity questionnaire to assess precourse and postcourse beliefs about creativity. The questionnaire contained the following ten questions regarding the nature of creativity and its implications on the participants' lives:

1. How do you define "creativity"?
2. Can we increase creativity, or are you just born with or without it?
3. How is creativity related to mental illness, drug abuse, and other disorders and negative behaviors?
4. Are individuals or groups more creative when working on a project?
5. Are people creative in many areas or only in a few specific content areas or tasks? In other words, does creativity generalize?
6. How does evaluation influence creativity? For example, how do grades influence your creativity?
7. What is the relationship between constraints and creativity?
8. Is it important to market your creativity? In other words, is it important to get others to accept your creativity? Why or why not?
9. What is the relationship between age and creativity? Consider "age" to represent the entire life span, birth through death.
10. How effective are creativity techniques, such as brainstorming, SCAMPER, etc.?

Observations

Throughout the course, naturalistic recording methods were used to review (1) participants' experiences engaging in creativity coursework and (2) participants' experiences engaging in problem-based curricular experiences. The

Observational Note List was designed in accordance with assessment methods defined by Bechtel (1977) and Krasner (1980). It consisted of notes of participants engaging in activities during coursework.

Group and Individual Interviews

Some participants were randomly selected to participate in group and individual interviews. Interviews were of a semistructured nature and lasted approximately fifteen to twenty minutes. Group interviews occurred following individual interviews. Specific questions were asked regarding (1) their perspectives on the course under study, (2) their beliefs regarding creativity curriculums, and (3) their perspectives on students' and teachers' roles during class activities.

Document Analysis

Document analysis was performed to gain information about the curriculum used during the course. Document analysis was performed on the following items: (1) the textbooks used for coursework, (2) the products created during course activities, (3) the course syllabi, and (4) the lesson plans and other documents used by the course instructors. Information taken from the textbook was used in confirming statements that participants made regarding their coursework and their perceptions of creativity.

Triangulation of Data Sources

Triangulation of data sources was critical in gaining a holistic picture as to the efficacy of creativity coursework in improving student innovation. Triangulation included triangulation by observer, with two observers performing field observations. Triangulation of interpretation also was important as information on the course was reviewed.

Two-Step Member Checking Process

Forty-four students who participated in the study were consulted as to the accuracy of field observations, interview information, and the completed paper. These consultations were performed to assess the validity of records and the accuracy of the results in describing how problem-based learning projects affected creativity-related beliefs and behaviors.

Procedure

All initial data collection took place during the creativity class experience. Participants were observed as they completed a number of hands-on, in-class activities that required both individual and group work.

The creativity questionnaire was administered to the participants in a group by the researcher following one day of coursework. Participants completed the same questionnaire at the end of the last session of the course. Group and individual interviews occurred throughout the course – but in balance primarily toward the end of each semester.

SOME PRELIMINARY EVIDENCE

Seventy-seven participants completed both the precourse and postcourse versions of the creativity questionnaire. Initial data analysis suggests that the myths and stereotypes that plague creativity also inhibit the opportunities of undergraduate students to increase their innovation. Students' responses to the course followed three patterns: (1) deconstructing the myths surrounding creativity takes hands-on work to help students experiment with alternatives, (2) the coursework is difficult for students but "not because it is hard," and (3) improvements in students' creativity and innovation are not necessarily immediate.

Findings Related to Belief and Attitude Change

The stereotypes that were commonly identified by both practitioners and researchers (Isaksen, 1987; Plucker et al., 2004; Treffinger et al., 1996) also were pervasive in the beliefs of students. Their exclusionary undertones dominated the first weeks of the class with such statements as, "I am not a creative individual" "You have to be born creative" "You can't increase creativity through experience" "You only are creative if you are an artist or a musician," and so forth (course observations, multiple students).

Myth 1: People are born creative or uncreative. By asking students "Can we increase creativity, or are you just born with or without it," we are able to tap into the strongest held myth – that creativity is an innate characteristic and that you will never be creative if you are not "born with creativity." For example, Anne, a junior psychology major, was frustrated by the idea that everyone could be taught to be creative:

> Beauty is in the eye of the beholder they say. With this statement comes the implication that beauty is a subjective unit that only can be identified by the people looking at it; there is no objective definition of it. In class we came up with many examples of people that one person thought was creative and another did not. I finally had to move beyond the objective and just admit that a creative person was one who used common elements in an uncommon way. I [realized] that we can increase creativity by allowing ourselves to think outside of the lines. By trying to see another's point of view or not letting limitations defeat you, an individual's creativity will always be able to be increased (Amy, creativity postcourse questionnaire).

Although the majority (69%) of students began to believe that creativity can be increased, 52% of those who believed you were born with it changed their minds by the end of the semester to say that you could increase creativity, whereas only 9% of students changed their minds in the opposite direction.

Of those students who continued to hold the myth that creativity is an innate characteristic, their views tended to soften over the semester. For example, at the beginning of the course, Samantha wrote that, "I think that you either have [creativity] or you don't. You can't force a person to be creative." At the time of the postcourse questionnaire, although she still held onto the myth that creativity is innate, she was beginning to recognize that creativity can be enhanced: "I still believe you are born with or without [creativity], although I think some activities may enhance creativity." Similarly, Carrie noted at the beginning of the course that, "A person is more often born with creativity rather than taught it." Yet by the end of the course, she, too, had softened her view: "I believe that some are born very creative and others are not. But I also feel that if one is born with it, then it can be increased and built upon."

We noted that, at the end of the course, many students claimed to have changed their view of creativity *in others* but not necessarily *in themselves*. For example, Kim shared that:

> Throughout the course of this class, my own personal creativity has not changed as much as my perceptions of other people's creativity have. I am definitely more appreciative of a good movie or an amazing song or a fantastic book. In short, I can now contemplate how creative someone has become through experience instead of just saying "Wow, that's cool" and moving on. I have witnessed how others, through thinking and practicing and challenging themselves, have moved beyond what might be innate or what might have been an earlier socializing agent . . . parents, school, television . . . which is especially damaging to creativity.

In a similar vein, when asked at the end of the course about the effectiveness of creativity techniques such as brainstorming, Catherine wrote that, "For me they aren't effective because I see them as restrictions and criteria I have to meet. For others they provide ideas to build upon."

These results suggest that the goal of completely removing this particular myth may be unrealistic. A more reasonable goal may be to moderate the extreme you-have-to-be-born-with-it perspective.

Myth 2: There is a limited time to be creative. By asking students "What is the relationship between age and creativity?" we were able to assess a myth that paralleled the idea that creativity was an innate gift – that creativity was a gift of the young. Those holding this belief tend to think that if you have reached age 30 without a major creative contribution, you will never achieve one. This belief, outlined in the peak-and-decline model, claims that creativity reaches its peak in young adulthood and begins to decline with dramatic losses in older adulthood. Although there is evidence to suggest that creativity does decline with advanced age (Alpaugh, Parham, Cole, & Birren, 1982; Dennis, 1966; Lehman, 1953; Lindauer, 1993; Simonton, 1999), there is also evidence to suggest that the accumulated knowledge that comes with advancing age can be a positive contribution to one's creativity.

In our questionnaire, students' beliefs regarding the influence of age on creativity fell into four categories. The first category of belief was that children are more creative due to their lack of pressure to adapt to social norms (precourse = 27, postcourse = 32). The perspective is exemplified by Beth, who noted at the beginning of the course that, "As people get older they become less creative, as they are inhibited by what others might think of them. Kids could care less, so they try many more options."

The second category of beliefs was that adults are more creative and that creativity increases with age due to the building of experiences (precourse = 17, postcourse = 13). The third belief was that creativity peaks twice, once in children and again during retirement. The drop during adulthood was explained as caused by social constraints that are rare in childhood, surge in adulthood, and are again absent in retirement (precourse = 6, postcourse = 5). This category is represented by Beth's postcourse comments, in which she said that, "Children, being less inhibited, tend to be more creative.... As one matures, your personal environment and past experiences with sharing innovation can make or break your creativity for life."

The fourth category of beliefs was that all ages are creative but the manner of expression changes form (precourse = 22, postcourse = 25). Although there was movement across categories, in general there was little change in beliefs about the relationship between age and creativity over the course of the semester.

Myth 3: Creativity does not generalize. By asking students "Are people creative in many areas or only in a few specific content areas or tasks? In other words, does creativity generalize?" we were able to determine if they believed that creativity is limited to one area (e.g., art) or is a general thinking pattern that can be applied to many areas. In reality, there is both general ability and specific content areas of creativity (Blicbau & Steiner, 1998; Innamorato, 1998; Kaufman & Baer, 2005; Plucker & Beghetto, 2004).

At the onset of the course, the majority of students believed that creativity is a general (n = 41) rather than specific (n = 29) or combined (n = 7) trait. At the end of the semester, the students' beliefs were more balanced (n: specific = 31, general = 30, both = 14). A typical belief transformation was that of Jenna, who stated at the start of the course that, "People can be creative in many areas. Some are more interested in specific things and may put more time and ability in that area. But I don't think it's generalized." Four months later, however, she expressed a more balanced conception: "I think people have a specific area they are very creative with. But I think it can go further than that.

Table 17.1. *Precourse, postcourse, and change questionnaire results
for "How do you define creativity?"*

Components	Precourse	Postcourse	Change
New/novel/unique	28	28	0
Original	14	10	−4
Thinking outside the box/going beyond the norm	7	8	1
Looking at things differently	4	4	0
Problem solving/finding solutions	6	24	18
Risk taking	1	2	1
Self-expression	7	3	−4
Intelligence	3	0	−3
Art/writing	7	0	−7
Innovative/ invention	8	11	3
Happy/humor	2	0	−2
Create/creation	11	10	−1
Imagination	6	3	−3
Thought/idea/process	25	20	−5
Product/thing	29	38	9

That area may be their strong point, but that creative ability can spill over to other areas."

Myth 4: Creativity is a fuzzy, soft construct. Often, creativity is viewed as a "fuzzy, soft" construct rather than a coherent topic warranting empirical investigations. This stereotype is not limited to undergraduate students; often psychologists and researchers tend to be biased in their thinking that creativity is "soft psychology" even though intelligence, problem solving, and other related topics are not prone to this bias.

Fifteen main components emerged when students were asked, "How do you define creativity?" (Table 17.1). The main difference between precourse and postcourse responses was that problem solving was rarely identified as a component in the precourse questionnaire responses (n = 6), whereas it was a reoccurring theme in the postcourse questionnaire responses (n = 24). Additionally, although several students, at the start of the course, identified the need to have a final product (n = 29), a greater number believed this was a contributing factor at the end of the course (n = 38). It is interesting to note that associating art or writing with creativity was present on the precourse questionnaire (n = 7) but not the postcourse questionnaire.

Myth 5: Creativity is enhanced within a group. By asking "Are individuals or groups more creative when working on a project?" we are able to assess the degree that students support the myth that creativity is enhanced within a group. The majority of students believed that working in a group as opposed to individually enhances creative productivity (n: group = 45, individual = 12, both =19). However, although this myth was still supported at the end of the semester, there was a decrease in the number of students stating that groups enhance creativity (n: group = 34) and an increase in the view that both individual and group contexts can foster creativity (n: both = 25).

A few students elaborated on this idea, suggesting that they are more creative when they are able to work alone initially and then interact with others after a period of time. Still others disliked group work and challenged that their college careers had been plagued by courses where "the quality of the class suffers because not every student invests a sufficient amount of effort in it." Students believed that the group experiences only worked when a substantial number of those participating were invested in the experience.

The students who held onto the myth that creativity is enhanced when working in a group tended to slightly modify this stance and began to accept alternative views. For example, Chris, on the precourse questionnaire, believed that creativity is enhanced in a group: "Groups are more creative than individuals because they possess the energy, experience, and unique perceptive of an individual multiplied several times over." At the time of the postcourse questionnaire, although he still held onto the myth that the creativity is enhanced in a group, he was recognizing the possibility of alternative views: "Generally speaking, a group will be more creative because there are more minds to contribute information, energy, and perspective; however, individuals in complete control of a project have free reign and are not inhibited at all by any close-working group members. It can go either way."

Myth 6: Constraints hinder creativity. One goal of the course is to help students understand that constraints can both help and hinder creativity, depending on one's approach to the constraints they face in a given context. On the precourse questionnaire, the majority of students (n = 43) believed that constraints hinder creativity: Nathan noted that, "Constraints put limits on creativity, which should never have them." Far fewer students believed that constraints helped creativity (n = 12) or both helped and inhibited creativity (n = 11).

However, we observed substantial shifts in attitudes about constraints by the end of the course. Of the 43 students who believed that constraints hinder creativity, 37% maintained that belief at the end of the semester, 23% changed their belief to state that creativity is helped by constraints, and 33% changed their belief to say that constraints can both help and hinder. This resulted in an almost even division in beliefs between constraints inhibiting creativity (n = 25), helping creativity (n = 23), or both helping and hurting (n = 24). Nathan exemplified this somewhat dramatic change in beliefs by observing that "Constraints to a point are positive guidelines to get you on the right track," a very different sentiment than he shared at the start of the semester. Similar thoughts were shared by Tara when she wrote that, "Some constraints are useful to most people, just in putting some sort of framework to a task that needs to be accomplished. Too many guidelines/rules, however, can be stifling to some."

Several students who held onto the belief that creativity is always hindered by evaluation or constraints tended to modify this belief slightly. For example, Amy wrote on the precourse questionnaire that, "When constraints are applied, creativity diminished. People no longer have limitless directions, in which they can go off in any direction. They now have limitations." However, by the end of the course, she recognized the validity of different perspectives on this issue: "Constraints make people less creative, although sometimes it gives people a starting point because it points people away from things that are restricted."

Additional Observations: Creativity Coursework Is Difficult for Students, But "Not Because It Is Hard"

In both precourse and postcourse questionnaires, students indicated that being creative is a difficult enterprise. An overwhelming majority of students shared that the coursework gave them greater insight into themselves and their abilities to tap into unappreciated and underutilized aspects of self. They rarely described their struggles in the class as being "hard," yet many clearly struggled to confront their misconceptions. Interviews provided evidence that the students considered a course to be hard if there is a lot of reading and writing – yet they did not see a course that made them think a lot as being "hard!" The students reported that this newfound growth carried over into other classes, into the workplace, and into their personal relationships (also see Anderson, 1977; King & Pope, 1999; Livingston, 1999; Russ, 1998; Torrance, 1972b, 1987; Zelinger, 1990).

Even more interesting, students suggested that involvement in the class improved their leadership abilities (also see Tierney, Farmer, & Graen, 1999). Students at this large, midwestern university also shared that it was the only class they had taken in college where they knew everyone, were able to learn from each other, and were given the opportunity to form cohesive groups and a sense of community (see Bowman & Boone, 1998; Malekoff, 1987).

Improving Students' Creativity and Innovation

Improvements in students' creativity and innovation are not necessarily immediate. A few students are not ready to think in different ways, to challenge their beliefs and worldviews. These students become very frustrated. Despite frustrations with the experience, Kelly stated:

> Reflecting back, I definitely believe my views on creativity and my own innovation have changed for the better. There are more things about myself that I recognize as creative which never would have struck me as such before this class. My worldview is certainly creative. The way I live my life is also. Probably the least creative thing about me is my job,

which is pretty routine and simple. But there is a lot of down time for me at work, so I am trying to devise something creative to do besides just twiddling my thumbs.

Students who had seen themselves as creative prior to the class began to see others sharing similar abilities in other areas, which caused them to question just how strong their creativity was. In an interview, Martina, an elementary art preservice teacher, asserted

> I found [this class] very interesting and enlightening. When the semester started I was not really sure what to expect. But I have learned a lot and feel that my creativity has grown in many ways. I feel that I am more creative . . . because I am now able to come up with ideas that I would not have seen without this class. I think that changing my definition of what creativity is altered my ideas of my own strengths. When I go places now, I look for creative things. I see creativity much more easily than I had previously, and I appreciate it more. I have a much broader definition of what creativity is.

Other students had been told by teachers and family members that they were not creative, and they had to overcome the myths surrounding their own ineptitude at being original and innovative. However, by the end of the semester, most of these students appeared to benefit from the course, showing greater self-efficacy and improved ability to identify and express the creativity within themselves.

Changing Incorrect Creativity Schemata

To reduce or eliminate students' misconceptions regarding creativity, not only must the misconception be identified but also further components such as the affective, behavioral, and cognitive aspects that underlie this misconception must be targeted for elimination (Halloran, 1967). The result is a three-pronged approach that, once put in place, can aid in the identification and modification of their incorrect schemata (Olson & Zanna, 1993). The first step entails correctly identifying any affectively based misconceptions that are often in direct conflict with logical reasoning or scientific evidence; the second step involves targeting any active behaviors that are propagating the misconception; and the third step requires the modification of thoughts regarding the misconception. By targeting all three components, we believe that changing an incorrect creativity schema is possible.

Furthermore, by explicitly providing students with the correction creativity schema that stems from a body of scientific research, students are more likely to begin to identify and relinquish any of their incorrect views and to slowly begin to change their attitudes toward creativity. Through creativity courses, such as the one outlined here, we hope to begin a course of action in misconception identification and a movement toward schema correction regarding creativity.

MOVING FORWARD

The evidence presented in this chapter is obviously preliminary in nature, but our analyses suggest that the proposed model has potential and should be explored further. The activities do seem to change student perceptions – more effectively in some areas (e.g., nature versus nurture, defining creativity, the role of constraints) than in others (e.g., the impact of age, generality versus specificity, group versus individual work). However, we did observe change in the beliefs and behaviors of individual students regarding all of the targeted myths and stereotypes, suggesting that the model allowed students to create significant change at the individual level.

We see several "next steps" in this line of work, with two areas of activity being the most important. First, more rigorous experimental evaluations should be conducted, ideally comparing students participating in classes based on our model with students participating in other types of creativity training. The difficulties in designing and implementing such a study are profound: tremendous cost, numerous logistical issues, problems of scale, the probability of teacher/instructor effects, the need to focus on both short- and long-term outcomes, etc. Given the tremendous financial costs of an experimental evaluation, external funding will almost certainly be necessary – external funding from a very patient funder, given the long-term nature of the targeted student outcomes.

Second, we plan to seek additional institutions at which the course can be taught and evaluated. We plan to teach the course at one or more U.S. universities, with an emphasis on selecting institutions that are different from the major research university at which the course has thus far been taught. In addition, initial discussions with major universities in China and South Korea provide reason for optimism about the possibilities of adapting and applying the course in other cultural contexts, especially because many educators in these countries believe that the lack of observed creativity among their students is largely cultural and attitudinal.

REFERENCES

Albert, M. A. and Runco, R. S. (1990). *Theories of creativity*. London: Sage.
Alpaugh, P. K., Parham, I. A., Cole, K. D., & Birren J. E. (1982). Creativity in adulthood and old age: An exploratory study. *Educational Gerontology*, **8**, 101–116.
Amabile, T. M. (1983). *The social psychology of creativity*. New York: Springer Verlag.
Amabile, T. M. (1996). *Creativity in context*. Boulder, CO: Westview Press.
Anderson, R. (1977). The notion of schemata and the educational enterprise: General discussion of the conference. In R. C. Anderson, R. J. Spiro, and W. E. Montague (Eds.), *Schooling and the acquisition of knowledge*, Hillsdale, NJ: Erlbaum.

Baer, J. (1997). Gender differences in the effects of anticipated evaluation on creativity. *Creativity Research Journal,* **10**, 25–31.

Baer, J. (1998). Gender differences in the effects of extrinsic motivation on creativity. *Journal of Creative Behavior,* **32**, 18–37.

Barron, F. (1969). *Creative person and creative process.* New York: Holt.

Blicbau, A. S., & Steiner, J. M. (1998). Fostering creativity through engineering projects. *European Journal of Engineering Education,* **23**, 55–65.

Bowman, V. E., & Boone, R. K. (1998). Enhancing the experience of community: Creativity in group work. *Journal for Specialists in Group Work,* **23**, 388–410.

Carson, S., Peterson, J. B. & Higgins, D. M. (2003). Latent inhibition and creative achievement in a high-achieving normative population. *Journal of Personality and Social Psychology,* **89**, 499–506.

Dacey, J. S., & Lennon, K. H. (1998). *Understanding creativity: The interplay of biological psychological and social factors.* San Francisco, CA: Jossey-Bass.

Davis, G. A. (1999). *Creativity is forever* (4th ed., revised). Dubuque, IA: Kendall/Hunt.

Davis, G. A., & Subkoviak, M. J. (1978). Multidimensional analysis of a personality-based test of creative potential. *Journal of Educational Measurement,* **12**, 37–43.

Dennis, W. (1966). Creative productivity between the ages of 20 and 80 years. *Journal of Gerontology,* **21**, 1–8.

Diakidoy, I. N., & Phtiaka, H. (2001). Teachers' beliefs about creativity. In S. Nagel (Ed.), *The handbook of policy creativity: Creativity from diverse perspectives* (Vol. **3**, pp. 12–32). Huntington, NY: Nova Science Publishers.

Diehle, M., & Stroebe, W. (1986). Productivity loss in brainstorming: Toward the solution of a riddle. *Journal of Personality and Social Psychology,* **53**, 497–509.

Domino, G. (1970). Identification of potentially creative persons from the Adjective Check List. *Journal of Consulting and Clinical Psychology,* **35**, 48–51.

Dow, G. T. & Mayer, R. E. (2004). Teaching students to solve insight problems. Evidence for domain specificity in training. *Creativity Research Journal,* **16**, 389–402.

Finke, R. A., Ward, T. B. & Smith, S. M. (1992). *Creative cognition: Theory, research and applications.* Cambridge MA: Bradford/MIT Press.

Fontenot, N. A. (1993). Effects of training in creativity and creative problem finding upon business people. *The Journal of Social Psychology,* **133**, 11–22.

Gardner, H. (1993). *Creating minds.* New York: Basic Books.

Halloran, J. D. (1967). *Attitude formation and change.* London: Leicester University Press.

Halpern, D. F. (1996). *Thought and knowledge: An introduction to critical thinking* (3rd ed.). Mahwah, NJ: Lawrence Erlbaum Associates.

Hennessey, B. A., & Amabile, T. M. (1988). The conditions of creativity. In R. J. Sternberg (Ed.), *The nature of creativity: Contemporary psychological perspectives* (pp. 11–38). New York: Cambridge University Press.

Innamorato, G. (1998). Creativity in the development of scientific giftedness: Educational implications. *Roeper Review,* **21**, 54–59.

Isaksen, S. G. (1987). Introduction: An orientation to the frontiers of creativity research. In S. G. Isaksen (Ed.), *Frontiers of creativity research* (pp. 1–26). Buffalo, NY: Bearly Limited.

Kaufman, J. C. (2001). The Sylvia Plath effect: Mental illness in eminent creative writers. *The Journal of Creative Behavior,* **35**(1), 37–50.

Kaufman, J. C., & Baer, J. (2005). The amusement park theory of creativity. In J. C. Kaufman & J. Baer (Eds.), *Creativity across domains: Faces of the muse* (pp. 321–328). Hillsdale, NJ: Lawrence Erlbaum Associates.

King, B. J., & Pope, B. (1999). Creativity as a factor in psychological assessment and healthy psychological functioning. *Journal of Personality Assessment, 72*, 200–207.

Kurtzberg, T. R. (1998). Creative thinking cognitive aptitude and integrative joint gain: A study of negotiator creativity, *Creativity Research Journal, 11*, 283–293.

Lehman, H. C. (1953). *Age and achievement.* Princeton, NJ: Princeton University Press.

Lindauer, M. S. (1993). The old-age style and its artists. *Empirical Studies of the Arts, 11*, 135–114.

Livingston, J. A. (1999). Something old and something new: Love, creativity and the enduring relationship. *Bulletin of the Menniger Clinic, 63*, 40–52.

Malekoff, A. (1987). The preadolescent prerogative: Creative blends of discussion and activity in group treatment. *Social Work with Groups, 10*(4), 61–81.

Olson, J. M., & Zanna, M. P. (1993). Attitudes and attitude change. *Annual Review of Psychology, 44*, 117–154.

Olton, R. M., & Johnson, D. M. (1976). Mechanisms of incubation in creative problem. *American Journal of Psychology, 89*, 617–630.

Osborn, A. (1963). *Applied imagination: Principles and procedures of creative problem-solving* (3rd ed.). New York: Charles Scribner and Sons.

Paige, R, Hickok, E., & Neuman, S. (2002). *No child left behind: A desktop reference.* Jessup, MD: Education Publications Center, U.S. Department of Education.

Palmer, W. S. (1981). Research: Reading theories and research: A search for similarities, *The English Journal, 70*(8), 63–66.

Parnes, S. J. (1962). Can creativity be increased? In S. J. Parnes & H. F. Harding (Eds.), *A source book for creative thinking* (pp. 185–191). New York: Scribner's Publishing.

Piaget, J. (1926). *The language and thought of the child.* New York: Harcourt, Brace.

Plucker, J., & Beghetto, R. (2004). Why creativity is domain general, why it looks domain specific, and why the distinction does not matter. In R. J. Sternberg, E. L. Grigorenko, & J. L. Singer (Eds.), *Creativity: From potential to realization* (pp. 153–167). Washington, DC: American Psychological Association.

Plucker, J. A., & Beghetto, R. A. (2003). Why not be creative when we enhance creativity? In J. H. Borland (Ed.), *Rethinking gifted education.* New York: Teachers College Press.

Plucker, J. A., Beghetto, R. A., & Dow, G. T. (2004). Why isn't creativity more important to educational psychologists? Potential, pitfalls, and future directions in creativity research. *Educational Psychologist, 39*, 83–97.

Plucker, J. A., & Dana, R. Q. (1999). Drugs and creativity. In M. A. Runco & S. Pritzker (Eds.), *Encyclopedia of creativity* (Vol. 1, pp. 607–611). San Diego, CA: Academic Press.

Plucker, J., & Runco, M. (1999). Deviance. In M. A. Runco & S. Pritzker (Eds.), *Encyclopedia of creativity* (pp. 541–545). San Diego, CA: Academic Press.

Poe, E. A. (1996). *Tales of mystery and imagination.* Consett, UK: Wordsworth Classics.

Poe, E. A. (2005). *Tales of mystery and imagination.* Whitefish, MT: Kessinger Publishing.

Pyryt, M. C. (1999). Effectiveness of training children's divergent thinking: A meta-analytic review. In A. S. Fishkin, B. Cramond, & P. Olszewski-Kubilius (Eds.), *Investigating creativity in youth: Research and methods* (pp. 351–365). Cresskill, NJ: Hampton Press.

Rickards, T. (1999). Brainstorming. In M. A. Runco & S. Pritzker (Eds.), *Encyclopedia of creativity* (pp. 219–227). San Diego, CA: Academic Press.

Russ, S. (1993). Affect and creativity: The role of affect and play in the creative process. Hillsdale, NJ: Lawrence Erlbaum Associates.

Simonton, D. K. (1999). Creativity from a historiometric perspective. In R. J. Sternberg (Ed.), *Handbook of creativity* (pp. 116–133). New York: Cambridge University Press.

Smith, S. M., Ward, T. B., & Finke, R. A. (Eds.), (1995). *The creative cognition approach.* Cambridge, MA: MIT Press.

Stein, M. I. (1974). Stimulating creativity. *Individual procedures.* New York: Academic Press.

Sternberg, R. J., & Lubart, T. I. (1992). Buy low and sell high: An investment approach to creativity. *Current Directions in Psychological Science,* 1, 1–5.

Sternberg, R. J., & Lubart, T. I. (1999). The concept of creativity: Prospects and paradigms. In R. J. Sternberg (Ed.), *Handbook of creativity* (pp. 3–15). New York: Cambridge University Press.

Thornburg, T. (1991). Group size and member diversity influence on creative performance. *Journal of Creative Behavior,* 25, 324–333.

Tierney, P., Farmer, S. M., & Graen, G. B. (1999). An examination of leadership and employee creativity: The relevance of traits and relationships. *Personnel Psychology,* 52, 591–620.

Torrance, E. P. (1962). *Guiding creative talent.* Englewood Cliffs, NJ: Prentice-Hall.

Torrance, E. P. (1972a). Can we teach children to think creatively? *The Journal of Creative Behavior,* 6, 114–143.

Torrance, E. P. (1972b). Career patterns and peak creative achievements of creative high school students 12 years later. *Gifted Child Quarterly,* 16, 75–88.

Torrance, E. P. (1987). Recent trends in teaching children and adults to think creatively. In S. G. Isaksen (Ed.), *Frontiers of creativity research: Beyond the basics* (pp. 204–215). Buffalo, NY: Bearly Limited.

Treffinger, D. J., Isaksen, S. G., & Dorval, B. K. (1996). Creative problem solving: An overview. In M. A. Runco (Ed.), *Problem finding, problem solving, and creativity* (pp. 223–235). Norwood, NJ: Ablex.

Ward, T. B., Smith, S. M., & Vaid, J. (1997). *Creative thought: An investigation of conceptual structures and processes.* Washington, DC: American Psychological Association.

Weber, R., & Crocker, J. (1983). Cognitive processes in the revision of stereotypic beliefs. *Journal of Personality and Social Psychology,* 45, 961–977.

Westberg, K. L. (1996). The effects of teaching students how to invent. *Journal of Creative Behavior,* 30, 249–267.

Wheatley, T., & Wegner, D. M. (2001). Psychology of automaticity of action. In N. J. Smelser & P. B. Baltes (Eds.), *International encyclopedia of the social and behavioral sciences,* (pp. 991–993). Oxford, UK: Elsevier Science Limited.

Williams, W. M., & Yang, L. T. (1999). Organizational creativity. In R. J. Sternberg (Ed.), *Handbook of creativity* (pp. 373–391). New York: Cambridge University Press.

Zelinger, J. (1990). Charting the creative process. *British Journal of Projective Psychology,* 35, 78–96.

18

Creativity in College Classrooms

DIANE F. HALPERN

There is a long history of teaching for creative thinking but, unfortunately, it is not a glorious one; few, if any, studies used rigorous experimental designs, and the inconsistent use of measures of creativity across published studies makes it difficult to compare results from different studies. In this chapter, I consider how the mandate to assess learning outcomes in postsecondary education could have positive effects that help students develop their abilities to think critically and creatively. I discuss the similarities and differences in these two ways of thinking about thinking and provide examples of new ways of teaching that offer the possibility of creating more creative learners. As a way of linking how we could be enhancing creativity in university classrooms with what actually occurs, I describe an informal survey of what is occurring in higher education throughout North America as determined from a sample of exemplary course syllabi. Unfortunately, there appears to be a wide gap between what could be and what is. I end this chapter with a description of a multiyear project that requires a creative product.

THE MANDATE TO ASSESS STUDENT LEARNING OUTCOMES IS CAUSING COLLEGES TO RETHINK THE "WHY" QUESTION FOR HIGHER EDUCATION

Every college and university in the United States must assess student learning outcomes as part of their periodic review for regional accreditation. Unlike its K-12 counterpart, which mandated learning assessments as part of the No Child Left Behind legislation, the assessment of learning in higher education has not received much attention by the general public. There has been considerable grumbling in the higher education community about the requirement that

---

The author thanks Patrick Brandon Williams at Claremont Graduate University for his assistance in reviewing online syllabi for this chapter.

colleges specify what they want their graduates to know and be able to do when they graduate. The grumbling is symptomatic of a strong reluctance to actually collect data to determine if the performance of college graduates matches what that might reasonably be expected of a college-educated person. But, despite this reluctance and considerable foot-dragging, colleges and universities are complying because regional accreditation is a prerequisite for the receipt of federal funding.

The specification of student learning outcomes has been an interesting exercise as every discipline and interdisciplinary major defines what students should know and be able to do when they graduate. This exercise has caused multiple stakeholders in the academic community to come together to consider their response to the implicit question about why students need higher education. What should students gain from attending college that will help in their life out of the classroom and after graduation? In psychology, for example, a taskforce assembled by the American Psychological Association (APA, 2007) divided student learning outcomes into two categories: (1) those that are more specific to a major in psychology, which they described as "knowledge, skills and values consistent with the science and application of psychology," and (2) those that are part of a general education, which they described as "knowledge, skills and values consistent with a liberal arts education that are further developed in psychology." Critical thinking is listed as the third goal in the science and application of psychology section, along with understanding psychological theories and research methods, developing values, and being able to apply what is learned.

The Association of American Colleges and Universities (www.aacu.org/advocacy/leap/vision.cfm) has a list of "essential learning outcomes," which are broadly applicable regardless of a student's major area of study. These outcomes include "critical and creative thinking." Similar lists were drafted by virtually all of the academic disciplinary societies in the United States and in many other countries around the world. Most lists of desirable learning outcome include the idea that students should be better thinkers.

The good news is that the focus on what colleges and universities want their students to know and to be able to do has created a new emphasis on teaching and learning for thinking. But so far, there are few data showing what practices produce better thinkers or how well higher education has achieved this goal. The enhancement of critical and creative thinking is still more of a desirable vision than an empirical outcome.

CRITICAL AND CREATIVE THINKING

Are critical and creative thinking two different types of thinking? This is a question about definitions and which definitions are closer to the way most people think or should think about these topics. There is good agreement on the definition of creative thinking. Virtually all definitions include two necessary components – that the product of creative thinking be (a) unusual and (b) appropriate (e.g., Barron, 1955; Stein, 1953). There is also considerable overlap in most definitions of critical thinking. Jones and his colleagues (Jones, Dougherty, Fantaske, & Hoffman, 1997; Jones, Hoffman, Moore, Ratcliff, Tibbetts, & Click, 1995) obtained consensus from among 500 policy makers, employers, and educators, who agreed that *critical thinking* is a broad term that describes reasoning in an open-ended manner and with an unlimited number of solutions. It involves constructing a situation and supporting the reasoning that went into a conclusion. In a recent study of the effect of creative work on health, the authors define *creative work* as "varied, challenging, nonroutine, and engaging activity directed toward the production or accomplishment of something" (Mirowsky & Ross, 2007). This definition could also be used to describe work that requires critical thinking, which shows the considerable overlap in these two constructs.

Here is a simple definition of *critical thinking* that captures the main concepts: "Critical thinking is the use of those cognitive skills or strategies that increase the probability of a desirable outcome. It is used to describe thinking that is purposeful, reasoned, and goal directed – the kind of thinking involved in solving problems, formulating inferences, calculating likelihoods, and making decisions, when the thinker is using skills that are thoughtful and effective for the particular context and type of thinking task." Critical thinking is more than merely thinking about your own thinking or making judgments and solving problems – it is using skills and strategies that will make "desirable outcomes" more likely (Halpern, 2003).

As seen in the definitions for creative and critical thinking, the end product of both types of thinking has to be appropriate. The only distinction between these terms is that the response or product needs to be novel for the thinking to be defined as creative. The response or product of critical thinking may be novel, but it is not a necessary part of the definition. Thus, given these commonly agreed-on definitions, it seems that creative thinking is a subset of critical thinking. In fact, many textbooks on critical thinking treat it this way and have a chapter on thinking creatively.

DUAL-PROCESS THINKING

There is considerable evidence that there are two processes that underlie thinking (Kahneman, 2003; Stanovich & West, 2000). The first process occurs rapidly, effortlessly, without conscious awareness, and within a second of encountering a problem or a situation in the environment. This process responds to a variety of stimuli, which can include making rapid judgments about a person walking toward you, responding to the smell of smoke, or an immediate response to a problem. The second process is more deliberate, usually requiring conscious thought and effort, and it is slow. Kahenman (2003) calls the first system "intuition" and the second system "reasoning." Howard-Jones (2002) used the distinction between these two thinking systems to propose that creative thought operates in the faster and unconscious system and critical thought is a property of the slower and more conscious second system. I disagree with this distinction that links creative and critical thinking with different processes for several reasons. Creative thinking can be enhanced with the use of deliberate strategies such as using a creative ideas checklist (Davis & Roweton, 1968), which asks people to think about ways of physically changing something (e.g., add or subtract something, rearrange the parts, change design or style) and strategies that people can learn to use when thinking about research (McGuire, 1997; e.g., provide a counterexample, reverse causal direction, push an example to an extreme). Another problem with the idea that creative thinking is part of a rapid unconscious thinking system is that this notion suggests that creative thinking is relatively immune to educational interventions, yet we know that environmental factors, including a teacher's openness to creative responses from students, can have a large effect on the creativity of students (Esquivel, 1995). Thus, creative and critical thinking are not qualitatively different processes, as Howard-Jones (2002) has suggested.

Here, I assume the "nothing special" view of creativity, which is the idea that creative processes are similar to those used in everyday thinking and that everyone is capable of creative thinking (Wan & Chiu, 2002; Weisberg, 1993). By definition, creativity involves the generation of novel responses and a willingness to be nonconforming and independent, and everyone can create something novel and act independently, at least some of the time and under some supporting circumstances (Simonton, 2003). Educational environments that support independent thinking will foster creative thinking and, similarly, an educational environment that only permits students to retell the insights of others will not foster creative thinking. An encouraging environment – in this context, a learning environment – has led scientists who study creativity to suggest that the most fundamental question in nurturing creativity is "Where is creativity?" instead of "What is creativity?" (Csikszentmihalyi, 1988).

There is a variety of evidence that supports the conclusion that creative thinking can be improved with conscious instruction designed for this purpose. But, there is a large gap between what "can be" and what "is." In his presidential address to the American Psychological Association, Guilford (1950) remarked on the lack of correlation between creative thinking and educational practices. Although this admonition has remained largely true over the intervening half-century, recent developments suggest that we may be on the cusp of real changes, with the rapid increase in creative teaching designed to foster creative thinking taking place in higher education.

TECHNOLOGY IS CHANGING HOW AND WHAT WE TEACH AND LEARN

There is a "perfect storm" brewing in higher education. Four powerful forces are coming together to alter how we think about college-level teaching and learning. In the words of an "observer" of this situation, the four forces are "emerging technologies, enormous learner demand, enhanced pedagogies, and erased budgets" (Bonk, 2004, p. 1). e-Learning, which is defined as "instructional content delivered or enabled by electronic technology" (p. 3), is becoming a standard mode of instruction in higher education, sometimes as the sole delivery system for coursework, and other times it is used along with in-class learning. Of course, instruction via electronic means can be as creative or as mind-numbing as instruction delivered in a classroom with a live professor. One recent critique of teaching with technology is that it tends to be constructed in rigid and linear terms (Selwyn, 2007). There is nothing inherent in electronic instruction that would foster creativity, but there are reasons to believe that such instruction will permit more creative learning activities that would foster creativity in students. First, it is a new way to provide instruction; thus, it is inherently novel, which means that the adaptation of traditional classroom instruction to an electronic model will require creativity on the part of the instructor because there are no ready-made guidelines to follow, at least not yet. Some instructors may decide to toss the more traditional model of presenting information to passive student learners and, instead of putting a "talking head" on a computer screen or video, they may rethink the purpose of education and how students learn best and try new ways of engaging students. There is some evidence that this is indeed happening.

LONG-DISTANCE AND CROSS-CULTURAL LEARNING GROUPS

Distance learning is one type of e-learning. Students can be anywhere in the world (or beyond, a possible future scenario). The traditional concept of a class of students breaks down if learners can enter and leave the e-learning environment at different points in time and collaborate electronically with other student learners around the world. New types of cross-cultural learning are possible as students from different parts of the world share assignments, critique each other's work, recognize their own cultural assumptions and biases, and bring vastly different backgrounds and perceptions to the solution of problems. Recent studies show gains in creativity as a result of multicultural experiences. The theoretical basis for these findings is that multicultural experiences provide access to novel ideas from other cultures, which can "destabilize routinized knowledge structures," in turn fostering the synthesis of seemingly incompatible ideas (Leung, Maddux, Galinsky, & Chiu, 2008). In a test of the benefit of multicultural experiences, researchers compared the probability that students would be able to solve the Duncker candle problem (Duncker, 1945) as a function of how long they lived abroad. They found that students who lived in other countries were more likely to solve the problem than were those who did not (60% compared to 42%) and the length of time the students lived in other countries predicted creative solutions. Given that living abroad as opposed to visiting abroad was a critical distinction in this assessment of creative thinking, it is possible that the prolonged interactions with people from multiple countries made possible in multicultural learning experiences via the Internet will also result in enhanced creativity for students. This positive view of the use of e-learning has yet to be realized, and there is much research needed to determine if more novel and appropriate thinking will result from cross-cultural collaboration, but it is an intriguing and hopeful possibility for the future.

PRIVATE TUTORS, WITH ENDLESS PATIENCE, FOR EVERY LEARNER

Peter Drucker, a visionary business leader, often talked about the future of education. He predicted that someday every student will have a personal tutor. Actually, Drucker may have been short-sighted in this particular view of the future because it is already here. In a series of computer-assisted learning program, Art Graesser and his colleagues (Graesser, Person, Lu, Jeon, & McDaniel, 2005) have been using avatars (computer-animated figures) to act as teachers and fellow students who guide learners through a range of scientific content areas. These programs use "latent semantic analysis" so that learners can respond in their natural language (as far as I know these programs are only available to English-language speakers, but that is likely to change soon).

When "learning while holding a conversation with a computer" (Graesser et al., 2005, p. 143), the teaching avatar poses challenging questions to the learner, and the learner can question that teaching avatar as well. When students do not respond correctly, the teaching avatar provides hints and prompts to help the student grasp the concept. In this way, the learning experience is tailored to each student. These programs go far beyond the more usual posting of books and other static content on the Internet – they actively engage the learner with the goal of encouraging deeper levels of understanding. Early studies support the goal of deeper understanding, although no studies of creative thinking per se have been conducted with online tutoring systems. We have ample reason to be optimistic that deeper learning will produce more creative responding because each learner will have more ideas related in conceptually meaningful ways. Like the other new ways of teaching and learning, there is a promise and potential for enhanced creative outcomes, but it will take years before we have sufficient data to determine if the potential is realized.

VIRTUAL WORLDS WHERE ALMOST ANYTHING IS POSSIBLE

It is literally a whole new world out there – one where virtually anything is possible. There are commercially popular sites like *Second Life* where individuals can engage in a world of avatars powered by people from just about any geographical area of the world. A large number of educational programs have been established on private islands in this imaginary world. In a recent view of learning in virtual worlds, Nelson and Ketelhut (2007) found that such environments can support interactive scientific inquiry. Of course, like the real world, virtual ones need to have carefully designed learning environments and activities. Others have suggested that virtual worlds can be especially effective for students with special needs such as those with oral communication disorders. Students with limited skills in social interaction can be provided with various social scenarios in which they can practice appropriate responding (Cobb, 2007). In this regard, they would be learning new ways to handle social problems. Like the other programs, these have not been tested for their effect on creative responding, but the need to design one's own avatar and navigate imaginary world seems to fit the idea of creative thinking. Virtual environments can allow every learner to go "where no man has ever gone before," which was the tag-line for the very popular science fiction series, *Star Trek*. Captain Kirk and his hearty cross-species crew often engaged in creative thinking when they faced novel problems. In *Star Trek, The Next Generation*, the crew would often enter something called the "Holodeck," which was, in essence, a fully immersive virtual reality where they could do everything from playing sports to reliving Sherlock Holmes mysteries. Virtual worlds provide the rest of us with this possibility without having to negotiate distant galaxies.

SERIOUS LEARNING GAMES

Well-designed video games can advance learning and thinking (Gee, 2003). Serious games have a great deal in common with the complex topics encountered in academics and in life – they take a long time to master; they are difficult to learn; and they have a high level of complexity (Gee; http://psyc.memphis. edu/learning). Unlike college and life, serious games are written to ensure there are few to no learning failures, because if a large number of people failed to learn the material needed for success in the game, the gaming companies would go broke. The most popular games have the principles of learning built into them. They start with an identity of what the learner will be if she or he masters the game and then guides the learner through the steps to achieve the goal. Only a small portion of what has to be learned is conveyed in text. For the most part, people have to discover the rules on their own by observing and imitating the actions of others, much in the way we all learned our first language.

An important design of serious games is that most decisions and choices are left up to the learners, who must actively engage in selecting information and deciding how to proceed given the information they just received. Problems are ordered so learners can build on a solid base of knowledge. All serious games use a cycle of learning and discovering in which learners are given a challenge that they must learn how to overcome; they then practice what they learned, and then discover that the solution that has been working no longer works in a new situation. They need to learn new principles, which starts another learning cycle. Complex games, like *Civilization*, have hundreds of facts that must be learned to play well. The learner needs to be able to recognize when a particular fact can be used – in other words, how and when to apply something they learned. Like real life, all serious games evoke emotional responses in their player, who need to learn when an emotion is beneficial or detrimental to play.

Players of serious games need to rethink their goals in a world full of risky options. *World of Warcraft* is a very popular game in which cross-functional teams learn to work together. Like other massively multiplayer games, each player has a different set of skills, so every player needs to master his or her own skills and also understand each other's areas of specialization, and then use this knowledge to work cooperatively toward a common goal. The designer of these games makes people "smart" by giving them smart tools with which to accomplish their task. Many of the same tools would be useful for anyone who wants to major in urban planning, accounting, law, and other areas. Gee (2003) argues that we do not need to put serious games in school, but we need to put the principles used by serious game makers in every school. For example, there is no reason why the same principles could not be used in all science laboratories. Serious games also come with instructions that allow users to remake the game from the ground up if they do not like the game they bought. Game players will be familiar with this concept, known as "mod'ing," which stands for *modifying*. With this capability, every play can design changes in the games. By analogy, if the basic principles were used in higher education, students could redesign their own curriculum. According to Gee, Hull, and Lankshear (1996), serious games teach players to explore a variety of options and to "think laterally not just linearly." This is the language of creative thinking and the language of serious games. Like other innovations in teaching and learning, we have a great deal to learn about the role of serious games in promoting creative thinking, but the groundwork in designing creative environments is already in place.

"Time on task" is almost always a critical variable in determining whether a problem solver will come up with a creative (or even noncreative) solution. The incubation effect is a well-documented extension of this principle. It seems that sometimes, at least when problem solvers are "stuck," they continue to return to the same dead-end path in their hunt for a solution. By taking time away from the task, they are able to move from the "thinking rut" and thus can explore other and better paths for success. Some researchers have suggested that people continue to work on the unsolved problem during the incubation period so it is not clear whether that additional time should count as time on task. We do know that some people become so involved in serious games and other online activities that they will do little else. When time seems to fly, a state called "flow" by cognitive psychologist Cziksentmihalyi (1996), people are so engrossed in the task that they do not want to leave this enjoyable state in which the level of difficulty is optimal. Thus, time on task and the positive affective component of playing serious games contribute to the learning and enhance the probability of a creative outcome.

VISUALIZATION SOFTWARE

There are many software programs that allow learners to convert language-based concepts and information into visual displays. There is a long tradition in the creativity literature that links the critical role of imagery. An image is a picture-like representation in the mind. Images need not be visual; one can image a taste or a sound, but visual images are most often linked with creative thinking. Gonzalez, Campos, and Perez (1997) examined the relationship between imagery and creativity. They gave high school students several tests of imagery and the Torrance Tests of Creative Thinking. They found positive relationships between imagery and creativity, which were stronger for the students with higher intelligence quotients (IQs) than for students who scored within the average range on intelligence tests. Good images should allow thinkers to "see" problems from different perspectives and to visualize a solution to a problem that eluded them when thinking with words.

Many mathematical reasoning tasks, including those that require novel solutions, are easier to solve when the problem solver can draw a visual representation of the information in the problem. High-level visuospatial abilities have been associated with problem solving in engineering, architecture, physics, and surgery (e.g., Sorby & Baartsmans, 2000). We do not know how or if the use of visualization software will affect creative problem solving, especially in fields in which the cognitive demands can be reduced by transforming complex data into a visual display. Based on the literature linking visualization to creativity, it is reasonable to expect that as more people become proficient in converting text-based information to visual displays, they will be better able to see novel solutions.

OPEN INNOVATION

InnoCentive Open Innovation is an online community of people who are working to "solve some of the toughest problems facing the world today" (http://www.innocentive.com/about-us-open-innovation.php). The idea was the brainchild of Mark Bent, a former diplomat from the United States who recognized a critical problem – the dire lack of artificial light in many countries in Africa. Because many countries have little or no electricity, they have no light at night, which means their citizens need to gather more wood, which threatens the environment, and in many places this practice leaves women vulnerable to attack. Women do most of the wood gathering in Africa and this practice means that they need to obtain wood from places far from their home, often in places that are not safe. In addition, all reading and studying must cease at night and people can do little during the dark portions of the day. Bend invented small flashlights that work on stored solar power, but he could not overcome the design problems associated with making a light bright enough to light up a whole room. He turned to the Internet and found funding partners with several nonprofit agencies who were willing to pay cash awards for creative solutions to many important problems in life, such as the one faced by Bent. As one of the cofounders noted, "We don't have an energy crisis; we have an imagination crisis" (cited in Walsh, 2008).

Problems are posted to this Web site, and a community of 14,000 people, from all walks of life, have registered as problem solvers. The problems are discussed over the Internet, revised, and in many cases solved. Creative thinking is modeled for anyone who wants to log on and watch problem solving in action. Many of the solutions are truly "out of the box," a phrase used to describe a novel approach to a problem. As this community grows, interest in creative problem solving will grow with it. This Web site could easily be used in conjunction with a college-level course. Again, this practice should advance creative thinking, but thus far there has been no research to support this hypothesis.

With so many exciting new ways of enhancing teaching and learning, I turn to a sample of exemplary syllabi for college-level courses to see what faculty members are doing in their classes.

A REVIEW OF EXEMPLARY SYLLABI

The Society for the Teaching of Psychology is a professional organization dedicated, as its name implies, to improving teaching and learning in psychology. One of its many services is an online array of teaching resources, including Project Syllabus. Individual faculty members submit copies of what they consider to be exemplary syllabi. The syllabi are reviewed by a committee, and those that are found to be outstanding are posted to the society's Web site. There are several hundred syllabi for a wide range of courses available on the Internet at any time. Patrick Williams, a graduate student assistant, reviewed every syllabus that was posted online during spring semester 2008. He looked for any mention of creative assignments or other evidence that students were expected to produce something novel and appropriate. The majority of courses required some sort of writing assignment, but it was difficult to find any course syllabi that specifically indicated that a creative response or product was desired or expected. Although I recognize that writing can be a creative act, the usual writing assignments were to review a book, respond to questions posed by the instructor, explain a research report, compare two theoretical approaches, and so on. Admittedly, there is some creative thinking necessary in these tasks, but for the most part the desired response is an accurate retelling of other people's thinking. I do not mean to denigrate these tasks because they can be an important part of learning, but they seem to require little in the way of creative thinking.

A PERSONAL EXPERIMENT

Over the last several years I have deliberately written creative assignments into the syllabus and planning for every course that I teach. Students are told that they are expected to produce a creative product related to their class. The assignment is due approximately one month after we talk about critical and creative thinking in class, so students have the same working definition of a creative product in mind as I do and have sufficient time after learning what creativity is to produce a creative product relevant to the course. Not surprisingly, some students complain that this is an assignment with no "right" answer. I respond that there are better answers and that is what I am looking for. The assignment is worth a relatively small number of points toward the final grade. I leave the points low so that students can feel free to take some risk with this assignment. I am also mindful of Amabile's (1996; Hennessey & Amabile, 1998) oft-cited findings regarding environments that support creativity. She found that instructors need to make creative activities compatible with intrinsic motivation, so I attempted to reduce (but not eliminate) the extrinsic rewards for this assignment. Many students come to my office to discuss their creative ideas. As expected, some need more guidance than others. I found that if I provided a few examples, such as making a game that is relevant to the class topic, almost one-third of the class will turn in a variety of games, with most being a variation on a "move around the board" theme with movement on the board allowed by responding correctly to a question. Students seem proud of these games and often tell me how much they enjoyed creating them, but there is a sameness to them that seems to fall short of a creative product.

At least a few students create something quite special when they are encouraged to be creative. For example, one student used a concept we had studied early in the semester in a cognitive psychology class. We discussed a strange cognitive disorder known as Capgras syndrome, in which a person believes that a loved one, usually as parent, child, or spouse, is actually an imposter. We consider the possible brain basis for this bizarre disorder and how our understanding of cognition and the underlying brain processes have changed how we think about mental disorders. As the instructor, I thought this was a short discussion that would introduce some basic concepts, but for the students it was a fascinating case study that they continued to ponder. For his creative project, one student wrote a play in Old English in which a king falls prey to this disorder and accuses his son, who returned home from battle, of being an imposter son. The various members of the king's court try to intervene and correct the king's failure to realize that the young man standing before him really is his true son. I hate to give the plot away, but someone who is young loses his head, literally, in this play. It was so well done that it was hard for me to believe that the less-than-stellar student, who obtained mediocre scores on his exams, created such a fine piece of fiction based on a mental disorder we briefly discussed in class.

In an introduction to psychology course, a student wrote and sang an original song about theories of homosexuality. The student had a beautiful voice and her lyrics were well written. Another musical example came from a student who dropped out of college at the end of his sophomore year to pursue a career in music. He created a prototypical song – the most average song that could be used to represent all contemporary songs. Another student created a video for a memory device, and yet another produced an album of photographs that depicted adolescent development. Thus, although the assignment did not show high levels of creative potential in all of my students, a substantial minority produced stellar products. It became clear to me that if we tell our students that we expect creativity in our courses, we will get more of it than if we silently hope that it will occur. Students need permission to be creative and, in some cases, direction as well, so that they understand the bounds of being novel and appropriate.

WHY SHOULD WE CARE ABOUT CREATIVITY?

The pace of change has been constantly accelerating over the past several decades and seems to be nowhere near a plateau. Solutions that worked for old problems no longer work as the problems we are facing continue to change at a rapid rate. The world is increasingly flat; globalization is a reality; and lifelong learning is a necessity for anyone who wants to stay in place in the workplace and in their personal lives. There are decided health benefits to creative work. Mirowsky and Ross (2007) found that employees who work at jobs that allow them to be creative in their work enjoy substantially better health – effects that go beyond the effects associated with education and income.

There are many exciting developments in how we should be teaching and learning that have the potential to enhance student creativity. So far, the possibility of helping college students become more creative remains a promise that needs to be developed and evaluated. Personal experiences with telling students that they are expected to be creative and helping them understand what that means has provided anecdotal evidence that creativity in college classrooms can be enhanced simply by making it known that it is expected. Of course, like the scarcity of data on new methods of teaching and learning, personal anecdotes are not scientific evidence. But, they form the basis for designing studies to determine how and how much we can help students become more creative thinkers. With so many new possibilities and an ever-growing need for creative solutions to old and new problems, we cannot afford to leave the development of creative potential to chance.

REFERENCES

Amabile, T. M. (1996). *Creativity in context.* Boulder, CO: Westview Press.

American Psychological Association. (2007). *APA guidelines for the undergraduate psychology major.* Washington, DC: Author. Retrieved April 30, 2008, from www.apa.org/ed/resources.html.

Association of American Colleges and Universities. (2008). Essential learning outcomes. Retrieved April 30, 2008, from http://www.aacu.org/advocacy/leap/vision.cfm.

Barron, F. (1955). The disposition toward originality. *Journal of Abnormal and Social Psychology,* **51,** 478–485.

Bonk, C. J. (2004, June). The perfect e-storm: Emerging technology, enormous learner demand, enhanced pedagogy, and erased budgets. Report from The Observatory on Borderless Education. Retrieved April 30, 2008, from http://www.obge.ac.uk.

Cobb, S. V. G. (2007). Virtual environments supporting learning and communication in special needs education. *Topics in Language Disorders,* **27,** 211–225.

Csikszentmihalyi, M. (1988). Society, culture, and person: A system view of creativity. In R. J. Sternberg (Ed.), *The nature of creativity* (pp. 325–339). New York: Cambridge.

Csikszentmihalyi, M. (1996). *Creativity: Flow and the psychology of discovery and invention.* New York: HarperCollins.

Davis, G. A., & Roweton, W. (1968). Using idea checklists with college students: Overcoming resistence. *Journal of Psychology,* **70,** 221–226.

Duncker, K. (1945). On problem solving. *Psychological Monographs,* **58**(5, Whole No. 270).

Esquivel, G. B. (1995). Teacher behaviors that foster creativity. *Educational Psychology Review,* 7, 185–202.

Gee, J. P. (2003). *What video games have to teach us about learning and literacy.* New York: Palgrave/Macmillan.

Gee, J. P., Hull, G., & Lankshear, C. (1996). *The new work order: Behind the language of the new capitalism.* Boulder, CO: Westview.

Graesser, A. C., Person, N., Lu, Z., Jeon, M. G., & McDaniel, B. (2005). Learning while holding a conversation with a computer. In *Technology-based education: Bringing researchers and practitioners together* (pp. 143–167). Information Age Publishing.

Guilford, J. P. (1950). Creativity. *American Psychologist,* 5, 444–445.

Halpern, D. F. (2003). *Thought and knowledge: An introduction to critical thinking* (4th ed.). Mahwah, NJ: Erlbaum.

Hennessey, B. A., & Amabile, T. M. (1998). Reward, intrinsic motivation, and creativity. *American Psychologist,* **53,** 674–675.

Howard-Jones, P. A. (2002). A dual-state model of creative cognition for supporting strategies that foster creativity in the classroom. *International Journal of Technology and Design Education,* 12, 215–226.

Jones, E. A., Dougherty, C., Fantaske, P., & Hoffman, S. (1997). *Essential skills in reading and problem solving: Perspectives of faculty, employers, and policymakers. Project summary.* University Park, PA: The Pennsylvania State University, Center for the Study of Higher Education, National Center on Postsecondary Teaching, Learning, and Assessment.

Jones, E. A., Hoffman, S., Moore, L. M., Ratcliff, G., Tibbetts, S., & Click, B. A. (1995). *National assessment of college student learning: Identifying college graduates' essential skills in writing, speech and listening, and critical thinking.* NCES 95–001. Washington, DC: U.S. Government Printing Office.

Kahneman, D. (2003). A perspective on judgment and choice: Mapping bounded rationality. *American Psychologist*, **58**, 697–720.

Leung, A. K., Maddux, W. W., Galinsky, A. D., & Chiu, C. (2008). Multicultural experience enhances creativity: The when and how. *American Psychologist*, **63**, 160–181.

McGuire, W. J. (1997). Creative hypothesis generating in psychology: Some useful heuristics. *Annual Reviews of Psychology*, **48**, 1–30.

Mirowsky, J., & Ross, C. E. (2007). Creative work and health. *Journal of Health and Social Behavior*, **48**, 385–403.

Nelson, B. C., & Ketelhut, D. J. (2007). Scientific inquiry in educational multi-user virtual environments. *Educational Psychology Review*, **19**, 265–283.

Selwyn, N. (2007). The use of computer technology in university teaching and learning: A critical perspective. *Journal of Computer Assisted Learning*, **23**, 83–94.

Simonton, D. K. (2003). Scientific creativity as constrained stochastic behavior: The integration of product, person, and process perspectives. *Psychological Bulletin*, **129**, 475–494.

Sorby, S.A., and Baartmans, B. J. (2000). The development and assessment of a course for enhancing the 3-D spatial skills of first year engineering students. *Journal of Engineering Education*, **89**, 301–307.

Stanovich, K. E., & West, R. F. (2000). Individual differences in reasoning: Implications for the rationality debate.. *Behavioral and Brain Sciences*, **23**, 645–665.

Stein, M. I. (1953). Creativity and culture. *Journal of Psychology*, **36**, 311–322.

Walsh, B. (2008, March 10). How many people does it take to make a new light bulb? Retrieved May 4, 2008, from http://www.time.com/time/health/article/0,8599,1721082,00.html.

Wan, W., & Chiu, C.-y. (2002). Effects of novel conceptual combination on creativity. *Journal of Creative Behavior*, **36**, 227–241.

Weisberg, R. W. (1993). *Creativity: Beyond the myth of genius.* New York: W. H. Freeman.

19

Teaching for Creativity

ROBERT J. STERNBERG

WHAT IS CREATIVITY?

Creativity is a habit (Sternberg, 2006; Tharp, 2005). The problem is that schools sometimes treat it as a bad habit. And the world of conventional standardized tests we have invented does just that (Sternberg, 1997b). If students try being creative on standardized tests, they will get slapped down just as soon as they get their score. That will teach them not to do it again.

Oddly enough, a distinguished psychometric tester, J. P. Guilford, was one of the first to try to incorporate creativity into the school curriculum, but his efforts show little fruit today (Guilford, 1950). Disciples of Guilford such as McKinnon (1962) and Torrance (1962) had some, but not a great deal more success.

It may sound paradoxical that creativity – a novel response – is a habit, a routine response. But creative people are creative in large part not as a result of any particular inborn trait but rather through an attitude toward life (Maslow, 1967; Schank, 1988): They habitually respond to problems in fresh and novel ways, rather than allowing themselves to respond mindlessly and automatically (Sternberg & Lubart, 1995a, 1995b, 1995c).

Like any habit, creativity can either be encouraged or discouraged. The main things that promote the habit are (1) opportunities to engage in it, (2) encouragement when people avail themselves of these opportunities, and (3) rewards when people respond to such encouragement and think and behave creatively. You need all three. Take away the opportunities, encouragement, or rewards, and you will take away the creativity. In this respect, creativity is no different from any other habit, good or bad.

Suppose, for example, you want to encourage good eating habits. You can do so by (1) providing opportunities for students to eat well in school and at home, (2) encouraging students to avail themselves of these opportunities, and then (3) praising young people who do in fact use the opportunities to eat well. Or suppose you want to discourage smoking. You can do so by (1) taking away opportunities for engaging in it (e.g., by prohibiting it in various places or by making prices of cigarettes so high one can scarcely afford to buy them), (2) discouraging smoking (e.g., advertisements showing how smoking kills), and (3) rewarding people who do not smoke (e.g., with praise or even preferred rates for health and life insurance policies).

This may sound too simple. It is not. Creative people routinely approach problems in novel ways (Albert & Runco, 1999; Baer & Kaufman, 2006). Creative people habitually (1) look for ways to see problems that other people do not look for, (2) take risks that other people are afraid to take, (3) have the courage to defy the crowd and to stand up for their own beliefs, and (4) seek to overcome obstacles and challenges to their views that other people give in to, among other things (Sternberg & Lubart, 1995b, 1995c; see also Sternberg, 1999; Sternberg & Grigorenko, 2007).

Educational practices that seem to promote learning may inadvertently suppress creativity, for the same reasons that environmental circumstances can suppress any habit (Sternberg & Williams, 1996). These practices often take away the opportunities for, encouragement of, and rewards for creativity. The increasingly massive and far-reaching use of conventional standardized tests is one of the most effective, if unintentional, vehicles this country has created for suppressing creativity. I say "conventional" because the problem is not with standardized tests per se but, rather, with the kinds of tests we use. And teacher-made tests can be just as much of a problem.

Conventional standardized tests encourage a certain kind of learning and thinking – in particular, the kind of learning and thinking for which there is a right answer and many wrong answers (Gardner, 1983, 1991, 1993, 2006; Sternberg, 1997b, 2003). To create a multiple-choice or short-answer test, you need a right answer and many wrong ones. Problems that do not fit into the right answer–wrong answer format do not well lend themselves to multiple-choice and short-answer testing. Put another way, problems that require divergent thinking are inadvertently devalued by the use of standardized tests. This is not to say knowledge is unimportant. On the contrary, one cannot think creatively with knowledge unless one has the knowledge with which to think creatively. Creativity represents a balance between knowledge and freeing oneself of that knowledge (Johnson-Laird, 1988). Knowledge is a necessary but in no way sufficient condition for creativity (Sternberg & Lubart, 1995a). The problem is that schooling often stops short of encouraging, being content if students have the knowledge.

Examples are legion (see Sternberg & Grigorenko, 2007). If one is studying history, one might take the opportunity to think creatively about how we can learn from the mistakes of the past to do better in the future. Or one might think creatively about what would have happened had a certain historical event not come to pass (e.g., the winning of the Allies against the Nazis in World War II). But there is no one "right" answer to such questions, so they are not likely to appear on conventional standardized test. In science, one can design an experiment, but again, designing an experiment does not neatly fit into a multiple-choice format. In literature, one can imagine alternative endings to stories, or what the stories would be like if they took place in a different era. In mathematics, students can invent and think with novel number systems. In foreign language, students can invent dialogues with people from other cultures. But the emphasis in most tests is on the display of knowledge, and often, inert knowledge that may sit in students' heads but may at the same time be inaccessible for actual use.

Essay tests might seem to provide a solution to such problems, and they might, but as they are typically used, they do not. Increasingly, essay tests can be and are scored by machine. Often, human raters of essays provide ratings that correlate more highly with machine-grading than with the grading of other humans. Why? Because they are scored against one or more implicit prototypes, or models of what a "correct" answer should be. The more the essay conforms to one or more prototypes, the higher is the grade. Machines can detect conformity to prototypes better than can humans, so essay graders of the kind being used today succeed in a limited form of essay evaluation. Thus, the essays that students are being given often do not encourage creativity – rather, they discourage creativity in favor of model answers that conform to one or more prototypes. In the end, essay tests can end up rewarding uncreative students, who spit back facts as well as creative students do (Sternberg, 1994).

Oddly enough, then, "accountability" movements that are being promoted as fostering solid education are, in at least one crucial respect, doing the opposite (Sternberg, 2004): It is discouraging creativity at the expense of conformity. The problem is the very narrow notion of accountability involved. But proponents of this notion of accountability often make it sound as though those who oppose them oppose any accountability, whereas, in fact, they instead may oppose only the narrow form of accountability conventional tests generate. The tests are not "bad" or "wrong," per se; they are just limited in what they assess. But they are treated as though they assess broader ranges of skills than they actually do assess. Curiously, governments may have a stake in such narrow, but not broad, forms accountability.

Governments often wish to encourage conformity – after all, they see themselves as promoting order, usually order with respect to themselves – and so they inadvertently may prefer an educational agenda that promotes a model of an educated person that minimizes or excludes creative (i.e., nonconforming) thinking. Their goal is not necessarily to punish creativity but rather to ensure their own stability and longevity. The punishment and extinction of creativity are merely byproducts. Thus, they may promote education but not a kind of education that fosters creative thinking. They may also fail to promote active critical thinking, which also potentially puts their longevity at risk. Sometimes, they will allow creative or critical thinking, so long as it is not applied to their own policies. It is easy for a government or other powerful organization to slip into the view that critics are "traitors" who must be ridiculed or punished. Inert knowledge is much safer to stability, because it gives the appearance of education without most of the substance.

Creativity is socialized through thousands upon thousands of acts of teachers, parents, and other authority figures. So is conformity. If people have been socialized over the years to think in conforming ways, and if they have been rewarded for conforming, no single school or government initiative is likely to change the way people think and act. Conformity may be so much a part of the social fabric that people give it up only reluctantly.

Whereas creativity is seen as departure from a mean, conformity is seen as adherence to that mean. Societies often speak of the "tall-poppy" phenomenon, whereby tall poppies – those that stick out – are cut down to size. If one grows up in a society that cuts down the tall poppies, or does what it can to ensure that the poppies never grow tall in the first place, it will be difficult to generate creative behavior. People in such societies will be so afraid of departure from the mean that they will be unwilling to be creative, whatever their creative abilities might be. They may also think that being creative is the province of the mentally ill. Although there are associations between creativity and mental illness (Kaufman, 2001a, 2001b), the overwhelming majority of creative people are mentally well, not ill!

Why is creativity even important? It is important because the world is changing at a far greater pace than it ever has before, and people need constantly to cope with novel kinds of tasks and situations. Learning in this era must be lifelong, and people constantly need to be thinking in new ways (Sternberg, 1997a). The problems we confront, whether in our families, communities, or nations, are novel and difficult, and we need to think creatively and divergently to solve these problems. The technologies, social customs, and tools available to us in our lives are replaced almost as quickly as they are introduced. We need to think creatively to thrive and, at times, even to survive.

But this often is not how we are teaching students to think – quite the contrary. So we may end up with "walking encyclopedias" who show all the creativity of an encyclopedia. As recounted in a recent bestselling book, a man decided to become the smartest person in the world by reading an encyclopedia cover to cover. The fact that the book sold so well is a testament to how skewed our conception has become of what it means to be smart. Someone could memorize that or any other encyclopedia but not be able to solve even the smallest novel problem in his or her life.

If we want to encourage creativity, we need to promote the creativity habit. That means we have to stop treating it as a bad habit. We have to resist efforts to promote a conception of accountability that encourages students to accumulate inert knowledge with which they learn to think neither creatively nor critically.

THE INVESTMENT THEORY OF CREATIVITY

Together with Todd Lubart, I have proposed an Investment Theory of Creativity as a means of understanding the nature of creativity (Sternberg & Lubart, 1991, 1995a, 1995b). According to this theory, creative people are ones who are willing and able to "buy low and sell high" in the realm of ideas. Buying low means pursuing ideas that are unknown or out of favor but that have growth potential. Often, when these ideas are first presented, they encounter resistance. The creative individual persists in the face of this resistance, and eventually sells high, moving on to the next new, or unpopular idea.

According to the investment theory, creativity requires a confluence of six distinct but interrelated resources – intellectual abilities, knowledge, styles of thinking, personality, motivation, and environment. Although levels of these resources are sources of individual differences, often the decision to use the resources is the more important source of individual differences. Ultimately, creativity is not about one thing but rather about a system of things (Csikszentmihalyi, 1988, 1990, 1996, 1999).

Intellectual Abilities
Intellectual abilities are generally acknowledged to be necessary but not sufficient for creativity (Renzulli, 1986). Three intellectual skills are particularly important: (1) the synthetic ability to see problems in new ways and to escape the bounds of conventional thinking, (2) the analytical ability to recognize which of one's ideas are worth pursuing and which are not, and (3) the practical-contextual ability to know how to persuade others of – to sell other people on – the value of one's ideas. The confluence of these three abilities is also important. Analytical ability used in the absence of the other two abilities results in powerful critical, but not creative, thinking. Synthetic ability in the absence of the other two abilities results in new ideas that are not subjected to the scrutiny required to make them work. And practical-contextual ability in the absence of the other two abilities may result in the transmittal of ideas not because the ideas are good but, rather, because the ideas have been well and powerfully presented. To be creative, one must first *decide* to generate new ideas, analyze these ideas, and sell the ideas to others.

Knowledge
Concerning knowledge, on the one hand, one needs to know enough about a field to move it forward. One cannot move beyond a field if one does not know where it is. On the other hand, knowledge about a field can result in a closed and entrenched perspective, resulting in a person's not moving beyond the way in which he or she has seen problems in the past (Frensch & Sternberg, 1989). Thus, one needs to decide to use one's past knowledge but also to decide not to let the knowledge become a hindrance rather than a help.

Thinking Styles

Thinking styles are related to creativity (Kogan, 1973). With regard to thinking styles, a legislative style is particularly important for creativity – that is, a preference for thinking and a decision to think in new ways (Sternberg, 1997c). This preference needs to be distinguished from the ability to think creatively: Someone may like to think along new lines but does not think well, or vice versa. It also helps, to become a major creative thinker, if one is able to think globally as well as locally, distinguishing the forest from the trees and thereby recognizing which questions are important and which ones are not.

Personality

Numerous research investigations have supported the importance of certain personality attributes for creative functioning (Barron, 1969, 1988). These attributes include, but are not limited to, willingness to overcome obstacles, willingness to take sensible risks, willingness to tolerate ambiguity, and self-efficacy. In particular, buying low and selling high typically means defying the crowd, so that one has to be willing to stand up to conventions if one wants to think and act in creative ways. Note that none of these attributes are fixed. One can *decide* to overcome obstacles, take sensible risks, and so forth.

Motivation

Intrinsic, task-focused motivation is also essential to creativity. The research of Teresa Amabile (1996, 1999) and others has shown the importance of such motivation for creative work and has suggested that people rarely do truly creative work in an area unless they really love what they are doing and focus on the work rather than the potential rewards. Motivation is not something inherent in a person: One decides to be motivated by one thing or another.

Environment

Finally, one needs an environment that is supportive and rewarding of creative ideas (Sternberg & Lubart, 1995a; Sternberg & Williams, 1996). One could have all of the internal resources needed to think creatively but, lacking some environmental support (e.g., as a forum for proposing those ideas), the creativity that a person has within him or her might never be displayed.

Confluence

Concerning the confluence of components, creativity is hypothesized to involve more than a simple sum of a person's level on each component (Sternberg & Lubart, 1991). First, there may be thresholds for some components (e.g., knowledge) below which creativity is not possible regardless of the levels on other components. Second, partial compensation may occur in which a strength on one component (e.g., motivation) counteracts a weakness on another component (e.g., environment). Third, interactions may also occur between components, such as intelligence and motivation, in which high levels on both components could multiplicatively enhance creativity.

Creative ideas are both novel and valuable, but they are often rejected because the creative innovator stands up to vested interests and defies the crowd. The crowd does not maliciously or willfully reject creative notions. Rather, it does not realize, and often does not want to realize, that the proposed idea represents a valid and advanced way of thinking. Society generally perceives opposition to the status quo as annoying, offensive, and reason enough to ignore innovative ideas.

Evidence abounds that creative ideas are often rejected. Initial reviews of major works of literature and art are often negative. Toni Morrison's *Tar Baby* received negative reviews when it was first published, as did Sylvia Plath's *The Bell Jar*. The first exhibition in Munich of the work of Norwegian painter Edvard Munch opened and closed the same day because of the strong negative response from the critics. Some of the greatest scientific papers have been rejected not just by one but rather by several journals before being published. For example, John Garcia, a distinguished biopsychologist, was immediately denounced (see Garcia, 1981) when he first proposed that a form of learning called classical conditioning could be produced in a single trial of learning (Garcia & Koelling, 1966).

From the investment view, then, the creative person buys low by presenting a unique idea and then attempting to convince other people of its value. After convincing others that the idea is valuable, which increases the perceived value of the investment, the creative person sells high by leaving the idea to others and moving on to another idea. People typically want others to love their ideas, but immediate universal applause for an idea usually indicates that it is not particularly creative (Sternberg & Lubart, 1995a).

RESEARCH SUPPORTING THE INVESTMENT THEORY

Research within the investment framework has yielded support for this model (Lubart & Sternberg, 1995). This research has used tasks such as (1) writing short-stories using unusual titles (e.g., "The Octopus' Sneakers"), (2) drawing pictures with unusual themes (e.g., the earth from an insect's point of view), (3) devising creative advertisements for boring products (e.g., cufflinks), and (4) solving unusual scientific problems (e.g., How can we tell if someone had been on the moon within the past month?). This research showed creative performance to be moderately domain-specific and to be predicted by the combination of resources specified by the theory.

In another study, creativity was measured using open-ended measures (Sternberg & The Rainbow Project Collaborators, 2005, 2006). These performance tasks were expected to tap an important aspect of creativity that might not be measured using multiple-choice items alone, because open-ended measures require more spontaneous and free-form responses.

For each of the tasks, participants were given a choice of topic or stimuli on which to base their creative stories or cartoon captions. Each of the creativity performance tasks were rated on criteria that were determined a priori as indicators of creativity.

Participants were given five cartoons, minus their captions, purchased from the archives of *The New Yorker*. The participants' task was to choose three cartoons and to provide a caption for each cartoon. Two trained judges rated all the cartoons for cleverness, humor, originality, and task appropriateness on 5-point scales. A combined creativity score was formed by summing the individual ratings on each dimension except task appropriateness, which, theoretically, is not a pure measure of creativity per se.

Participants were further asked to write two stories, spending about fifteen minutes on each, choosing from the following titles: "A Fifth Chance," "2983," "Beyond the Edge," "The Octopus' Sneakers," "It's Moving Backwards," and "Not Enough Time" (Lubart & Sternberg, 1995; Sternberg & Lubart, 1995a). A team of six judges was trained to rate the stories. Each judge rated the stories for originality, complexity, emotional evocativeness, and descriptiveness on 5-point scales.

Participants also were presented with five sheets of paper, each containing a set of eleven to thirteen images linked by a common theme (keys, money, travel, animals playing music, and humans playing music). There were no restrictions on the minimum or maximum number of images that needed to be incorporated into the stories. After choosing one of the pages, the participant was given fifteen minutes to formulate a short story and dictate it into a cassette recorder.

Six judges were trained to rate the stories. As with the written stories, each judge rated the stories for originality, complexity, emotional evocativeness, and descriptiveness on 5-point scales.

Rasch reliability indices for the composite person ability estimates for the written and oral stories were very good (0.79 and 0.80, respectively). The judges for both the written and oral stories varied greatly in terms of their severity of ratings for the stories. For the written stories, the judges also ranged in their fit to the model, although the reliability was still sound (rater reliability = 0.94). For the oral stories, all the judges fit the model very well, so their differences could be reliably modeled (rater reliability = 0.97).

Creativity-based performance tests formed a unique factor in a factor analysis. Furthermore, the creativity tests significantly and substantially increased prediction of first-year college grade-point averages for over 700 highly diverse students from thirteen colleges and universities across the United States that varied widely in quality and geographic location. The tests also substantially decreased ethnic-group differences. The reason is that different groups are socialized to be intelligent in different ways. For example, Native Americans performed relatively poorly in comparison with other ethnic groups on the analytical measure of the battery but had the highest scores on oral story telling.

Teaching creatively means encouraging students to (1) create, (2) invent, (3) discover, (4) imagine if . . . , (5) suppose that . . . , and (6) predict. Teaching for creativity requires teachers not only to support and encourage creativity, but also to role-model it and to reward it when it is displayed (Sternberg & Grigorenko, 2007; Sternberg & Lubart, 1995; Sternberg & Williams, 1996). In other words, teachers need not only to "talk the talk" but also to "walk the walk." Consider some examples of instructional or assessment activities that encourage students to think creatively.

1. *Create* an alternative ending to the short story you just read that represents a different way things might have gone for the main characters in the story. [Literature]
2. *Invent* a dialogue between an American tourist in Paris and a French man he encounters on the street from whom he is asking directions on how to get to the Rue Pigalle. [French]
3. *Discover* the fundamental physical principle that underlies all of the following problems, each of which differs from the others in the "surface structure" of the problem but not in its "deep structure. . . . " [Physics]
4. *Imagine if* the government of China keeps evolving over the course of the next 20 years in much the same way it has been evolving. What do you believe the government of China will be like in twenty years? [Government/Political Science]
5. *Suppose that* you were to design one additional instrument to be played in a symphony orchestra for future compositions. What might that instrument be like, and why? [Music]
6. *Predict* changes that are likely to occur in the vocabulary or grammar of spoken Spanish in the border areas of the Rio Grande over the next 100 years as a result of continuous interactions between Spanish and English speakers. [Linguistics]

Consider twelve keys for developing the creativity habit in students (see also Sternberg & Grigorenko, 2007; Sternberg & Williams, 1996).

Redefine Problems

Redefining a problem means taking a problem and turning it on its head. Many times in life, individuals have a problem and they just do not see how to solve it. They are stuck in a box. Redefining a problem essentially means extricating oneself from the box. This process is the synthetic part of creative thinking.

There are many ways teachers and parents can encourage students to define and redefine problems for themselves, rather than – as is so often the case – doing it for them. Teachers and parents can promote creative performance by encouraging their students to define and redefine *their own* problems and projects. Adults can encourage creative thinking by having students choose their own topics for papers or presentations, choose their own ways of solving problems, and sometimes having them choose again if they discover that their selection was a mistake. Teachers and parents should also allow their students to pick their own topics, subject to the adults' approval, on projects the students do. Approval ensures that the topic is relevant to the lesson and has a chance of leading to a successful project.

Adults cannot always offer students choices, but giving choices is the only way for students to learn how to choose. Giving students latitude in making choices helps them to develop taste and good judgment, both of which are essential elements of creativity.

At some point everyone makes a mistake in choosing a project or in the method they select to complete it. Teachers and parents should remember that an important part of creativity is the analytical part – learning to recognize a mistake – and give students the chance and the opportunity to redefine their choices.

Question and Analyze Assumptions

Everyone has assumptions. Often one does not know he or she has these assumptions because they are widely shared. Creative people question assumptions and eventually lead others to do the same. Questioning assumptions is part of the analytical thinking involved in creativity. When Copernicus suggested that Earth revolves around the sun, the suggestion was viewed as preposterous because everyone could see that the sun revolves around Earth. Galileo's ideas, including the relative rates of falling objects, caused him to be banned as a heretic.

Sometimes it is not until many years later that society realizes the limitations or errors of their assumptions and the value of the creative person's thoughts. The impetus of those who question assumptions allows for cultural, technological, and other forms of advancement.

Teachers can be role models for questioning assumptions by showing students that what they assume they know, they really do not know. Of course, students should not question every assumption. There are times to question and try to reshape the environment, and there are times to adapt to it. Some creative people question so many things so often that others stop taking them seriously. Everyone must learn which assumptions are worth questioning and which battles are worth fighting. Sometimes it is better for individuals to leave the inconsequential assumptions alone so that they have an audience when they find something worth the effort.

Teachers and parents can help students develop this talent by making questioning a part of the daily exchange. It is more important for students to learn what questions to ask – and how to ask them – than it is to learn the answers. Adults can help students evaluate their questions by discouraging the idea that the adults ask questions and the students simply answer them. Adults need to avoid perpetuating the belief that their role is to teach students the facts, and instead they should help students understand that what matters is the students' ability to use facts. This can help students learn how to formulate good questions and how to answer questions.

Society tends to make a pedagogical mistake by emphasizing the answering and not the asking of questions. The good student is perceived as the one who rapidly furnishes the right answers. The expert in a field thus becomes the extension of the expert student – the one who knows and can recite a lot of information. As John Dewey recognized, how one thinks is often more important than what one thinks. Schools need to teach students how to ask the right questions (i.e., questions that are good, thought provoking, and interesting) and lessen the emphasis on rote learning.

Do Not Assume that Creative Ideas Sell Themselves

Everyone would like to assume that their wonderful, creative ideas will sell themselves. But as Galileo, Edvard Munch, Toni Morrison, Sylvia Plath, and millions of others have discovered, they do not. On the contrary, creative ideas are usually viewed with suspicion and distrust. Moreover, those who propose such ideas may be viewed with suspicion and distrust as well. Because people are comfortable with the ways they already think, and because they probably have a vested interest in their existing way of thinking, it can be extremely difficult to dislodge them from their current way of thinking.

Thus, students need to learn how to persuade other people of the value of their ideas. This selling is part of the practical aspect of creative thinking. If students create a science project, it is a good idea for them present it and demonstrate why it makes an important contribution. If they create a piece of artwork, they should be prepared to describe why they think it has value. If they develop a plan for a new form of government, they should explain why it is better than the existing form of government. At times, teachers may find themselves having to justify their ideas about teaching to their principal. They should prepare their students for the same kind of experience.

Encourage Idea Generation

As mentioned earlier, creative people demonstrate a "legislative" style of thinking: They like to generate ideas. The environment for generating ideas can be constructively critical, but it must not be harshly or destructively critical.

Students need to acknowledge that some ideas are better than others. Adults and students should collaborate to identify and encourage any creative aspects of ideas that are presented. When suggested ideas do not seem to have much value, teachers should not just criticize. Rather, they should suggest new approaches, preferably ones that incorporate at least some aspects of the previous ideas that seemed in themselves not to have much value. Students should be praised for generating ideas, regardless of whether some are silly or unrelated, while being encouraged to identify and develop their best ideas into high-quality projects.

Recognize that Knowledge Is a Double-Edged Sword and Act Accordingly

On the one hand, one cannot be creative without knowledge. Quite simply, one cannot go beyond the existing state of knowledge if one does not know what that state is. Many students have ideas that are creative with respect to themselves but not with respect to the field because others have had the same ideas earlier. Those with a greater knowledge base can be creative in ways that those who are still learning about the basics of the field cannot be.

At the same time, those who have an expert level of knowledge can experience tunnel vision, narrow thinking, and entrenchment (Adelson, 1984; Frensch & Sternberg, 1989). Experts can become so stuck in a way of thinking that they become unable to extricate themselves from it. When a person believes that he or she knows everything there is to know, he or she is unlikely to ever show truly meaningful creativity again.

The upshot of this is that I tell students and my own students that the teaching–learning process is a two-way process. I have as much to learn from my students as they have to learn from me. I have knowledge they do not have, but they have flexibility I do not have – precisely because they do not know as much as I do. By learning from, as well as teaching to, one's students, one opens up channels for creativity that otherwise would remain closed.

Encourage Students to Identify and Surmount Obstacles

Buying low and selling high means defying the crowd. And people who defy the crowd – people who think creatively – almost inevitably encounter resistance. The question is not whether one will encounter obstacles; that obstacles will be encountered is a fact. The question is whether the creative thinker has the fortitude to persevere and to go against the crowd (Simonton, 1976, 1984, 1988, 1994). I have often wondered why so many people start off their careers doing creative work and then vanish from the radar screen. I think I know at least one reason why: Sooner or later, they decide that being creative is not worth the resistance and punishment. The truly creative thinkers pay the short-term price because they recognize that they can make a difference in the long term. But often it is a long while before the value of creative ideas is recognized and appreciated.

Teachers can prepare students for these types of experiences by describing obstacles that they, their friends, and well-known figures in society have faced while trying to be creative; otherwise, students may think that they are the only ones confronted by obstacles. Teachers should include stories about people who were not supportive, about bad grades for unwelcome ideas, and about frosty receptions to what they may have thought were their best ideas. To help students deal with obstacles, teachers can remind them of the many creative people whose ideas were initially shunned and help them to develop an inner sense of awe of the creative act. Suggesting that students reduce their concern over what others think is also valuable. However, it is often difficult for students to lessen their dependence on the opinions of their peers.

When students attempt to surmount an obstacle, they should be praised for the effort, whether or not they were entirely successful. Teachers and parents alike can point out aspects of the students' attack that were successful and why, and they can suggest other ways to confront similar obstacles. Having the class brainstorm about ways to confront a given obstacle can get them thinking about the many strategies people can use to confront problems. Some obstacles are within oneself, such as performance anxiety. Other obstacles are external, such as others' bad opinions of one's actions. Whether internal or external, obstacles must be overcome.

Encourage Sensible Risk-Taking

When creative people defy the crowd by buying low and selling high, they take risks in much the same way as do people who invest. Some such investments simply may not pan out. Moreover, defying the crowd means risking the crowd's wrath. But there are levels of sensibility to keep in mind when defying the crowd. Creative people take sensible risks and produce ideas that others ultimately admire and respect as trend-setting. In taking these risks, creative people sometimes make mistakes, fail, and fall flat on their faces.

I emphasize the importance of sensible risk-taking because I am not talking about risking life and limb for creativity. To help students learn to take sensible risks, adults can encourage them to take some intellectual risks with courses, with activities, and with what they say to adults – to develop a sense of how to assess risks.

Nearly every major discovery or invention entailed some risk. When a movie theater was the only place to see a movie, someone created the idea of the home video machine. Skeptics questioned if anyone would want to see videos on a small screen. Another initially risky idea was the home computer. Many wondered if anyone would have enough use for a home computer to justify the cost. These ideas were once risks that are now ingrained in our society.

Few students are willing to take many risks in school, because they learn that taking risks can be costly. Perfect test scores and papers receive praise and open up future possibilities. Failure to attain a certain academic standard is perceived as deriving from a lack of ability and motivation and may lead to scorn and lessened opportunities. Why risk taking hard courses or saying things that teachers may not like when that may lead to low grades or even failure? Teachers may inadvertently advocate students to only learn to "play it safe" when they give assignments without choices and allow only particular answers to questions. Thus, teachers need not only to encourage sensible risk-taking, but also to reward it.

Encourage Tolerance of Ambiguity

People often like things to be in black and white. People like to think that a country is good or bad (i.e., ally or enemy) or that a given idea in education works or does not work. The problem is that there are a lot of grays in creative work. Artists working on new paintings and writers working on new books often report feeling scattered and unsure in their thoughts. They often need to figure out whether they are even on the right track. Scientists often are not sure whether the theory they have developed is exactly correct. These creative thinkers need to tolerate the ambiguity and uncertainty until they get the idea just right.

A creative idea tends to come in bits and pieces and develops over time. However, the period in which the idea is developing tends to be uncomfortable. Without time or the ability to tolerate ambiguity, many may jump to a less than optimal solution. When a student has almost the right topic for a paper or almost the right science project, it is tempting for teachers to accept the near miss. To help students become creative, teachers need to encourage them to accept and extend the period in which their ideas do not quite converge. Students need to be taught that uncertainty and discomfort are a part of living a creative life. Ultimately, they will benefit from their tolerance of ambiguity by coming up with better ideas.

Help Students Build Self-efficacy

Many people often reach a point where they feel as if no one believes in them. I reach this point frequently, feeling that no one values or even appreciates what I am doing. Because creative work often does not get a warm reception, it is extremely important that the creative people believe in the value of what they are doing. This is not to say that individuals should believe that every idea they have is a good idea. Rather, individuals need to believe that, ultimately, they have the ability to make a difference.

The main limitation on what students can do is what they think they can do. All students have the capacity to be creators and to experience the joy associated with making something new, but first they must be given a strong base for creativity. Sometimes teachers and parents unintentionally limit what students can do by sending messages that express or imply limits on students' potential accomplishments. Instead, these adults need to help students believe in their own ability to be creative.

I have found that probably the best predictor of success among my students is not their ability but rather their belief in their ability to succeed. If students are encouraged to succeed and to believe in their own ability to succeed, they very likely will find the success that otherwise would elude them.

Help Students Find What They Love to Do

Teachers must help students find what excites them to unleash their students' best creative performances. Teachers need to remember that this may not be what really excites them. People who truly excel creatively in a pursuit, whether vocational or avocational, almost always genuinely love what they do.

Helping students find what they really love to do is often hard and frustrating work. Yet, sharing the frustration with them now is better than leaving them to face it alone later. To help students uncover their true interests, teachers can ask them to demonstrate a special talent or ability for the class, and explain that it does not matter what they do (within reason), only that they love the activity.

In working with my students and my students, I try to help them find what interests *them*, whether or not it particularly interests me. Often, their enthusiasm is infectious, and I find myself drawn into new areas of pursuit simply because I allow myself to follow my students rather than always expecting them to follow me.

I often meet students who are pursuing a certain career interest not because it is what they want to do, but because it is what their parents or other authority figures expect them to do. I always feel sorry for such students, because I know that although they may do good work in that field, they almost certainly will not do great work. It is hard for people to do great work in a field that simply does not interest them.

Teach Students the Importance of Delaying Gratification

Part of being creative means being able to work on a project or task for a long time without immediate or interim rewards. Students must learn that rewards are not always immediate and that there are benefits to delaying gratification (Mischel, Shoda, & Rodriguez, 1989). The fact of the matter is that, in the short term, people are often ignored when they do creative work or even punished for doing it.

Many people believe that they should reward students immediately for good performance, and that students should expect rewards. This style of teaching and parenting emphasizes the here and now and often comes at the expense of what is best in the long term.

An important lesson in life – and one that is intimately related to developing the discipline to do creative work – is to learn to wait for rewards (Mischel, Shoda, & Rodriguez, 1989). The greatest rewards are often those that are delayed. Teachers can give their students examples of delayed gratification in their lives and in the lives of creative individuals and help them apply these examples to their own lives.

Hard work often does not bring immediate rewards. Students do not immediately become expert baseball players, dancers, musicians, or sculptors. And the reward of becoming an expert can seem very far away. Students often succumb to the temptations of the moment, such as watching television or playing video games. The people who make the most of their abilities are those who wait for a reward and recognize that few serious challenges can be met in a moment. Students may not see the benefits of hard work, but the advantages of a solid academic performance will be obvious when they apply to college.

The short-term focus of most school assignments does little to teach students the value of delaying gratification. Projects are clearly superior in meeting this goal, but it is difficult for teachers to assign home projects if they are not confident of parental involvement and support. By working on a task for many weeks or months, students learn the value of making incremental efforts for long-term gains.

Provide an Environment that Fosters Creativity

There are many ways teachers can provide an environment that fosters creativity. The most powerful way for teachers to develop creativity in students is to *role model creativity*. Students develop creativity not when they are told to, but when they are shown how (Amabile, 1996).

The teachers most people probably remember from their school days are not those who crammed the most content into their lectures. The teachers most people remember are those teachers whose thoughts and actions served as a role model. Most likely they balanced teaching content with teaching students how to think with and about that content.

Occasionally, I will teach a workshop on developing creativity and someone will ask exactly what he or she should do to develop creativity. Bad start. A person cannot be a role model for creativity unless he or she thinks and teaches creatively himself or herself. Teachers need to think carefully about their values, goals, and ideas about creativity and to show them in their actions.

Teachers also can stimulate creativity by helping students *to cross-fertilize in their thinking* to think across subjects and disciplines. The traditional school environment often has separate classrooms and classmates for different subjects and seems to influence students into thinking that learning occurs in discrete boxes – the math box, the social studies box, and the science box. However, creative ideas and insights often result from integrating material across subject areas, not from memorizing and reciting material.

Teaching students to cross-fertilize draws on their skills, interests, and abilities, regardless of the subject. If students are having trouble understanding math, teachers might ask them to draft test questions related to their special interests. For example, teachers might ask the baseball fan to devise geometry problems based on a game. The context may spur creative ideas because the student finds the topic (baseball) enjoyable and it may counteract some of the anxiety caused by geometry. Cross-fertilization motivates students who are not interested in subjects taught in the abstract.

One way teachers can enact cross-fertilization in the classroom is to ask students to identify their best and worst academic areas. Students can then be asked to come up with project ideas in their weak area based on ideas borrowed from one of their strongest areas. For example, teachers can explain to students that they can apply their interest in science to social studies by analyzing the scientific aspects of trends in national politics.

Teachers also need to *allow students the time to think creatively*. This society is a society in a hurry. People eat fast food, rush from one place to another, and value quickness. Indeed, one way to say someone is smart is to say that the person is *quick*, a clear indication of our emphasis on time. This is also indicated by the format of the standardized tests used – lots of multiple-choice problems squeezed into a brief time slot.

Most creative insights do not happen in a rush. People need time to understand a problem and to toss it around. If students are asked to think creatively, they need time to do it well. If teachers stuff questions into their tests or give their students more homework than they can complete, they are not allowing them time to think creatively.

Teachers also should *instruct and assess for creativity*. If teachers give only multiple-choice tests, students quickly learn the type of thinking that teachers value, no matter what they say. If teachers want to encourage creativity, they need to include at least some opportunities for creative thought in assignments and tests. Questions that require factual recall, analytical thinking, and creative thinking should be asked. For example, students might be asked to learn about a law, analyze the law, and then think about how the law might be improved.

Teachers also need *to reward creativity*. It is not enough to talk about the value of creativity. Students are used to authority figures who say one thing and do another. They are exquisitely sensitive to what teachers value when it comes to the bottom line – namely, the grade or evaluation.

Creative efforts also should be rewarded. For example, teachers can assign a project and remind students that they are looking for them to demonstrate their knowledge, analytical and writing skills, and creativity. Teachers should let students know that creativity does not depend on the teacher's agreement with what students write, but rather with ideas they express that represent a synthesis between existing ideas and their own thoughts. Teachers need to care only that the ideas are creative from the student's perspective, not necessarily creative with regard to the state-of-the-art findings in the field. Students may generate an idea that someone else has already had, but if the idea is an original to the student, the student has been creative.

Teachers also need *to allow mistakes*. Buying low and selling high carries a risk. Many ideas are unpopular simply because they are not good. People often think a certain way because that way works better than other ways. But once in a while, a great thinker comes along – a Freud, a Piaget, a Chomsky, or an Einstein – and shows us a new way to think. These thinkers made contributions because they allowed themselves and their collaborators to take risks and make mistakes.

Although being successful often involves making mistakes along the way, schools are often unforgiving of mistakes. Errors on schoolwork are often marked with a large and pronounced X. When a student responds to a question with an incorrect answer, some teachers pounce on the student for not having read or understood the material, which results in classmates snickering. In hundreds of ways and in thousands of instances over the course of a school career, students learn that it is not acceptable to make mistakes. The result is that they become afraid to risk the independent and the sometimes-flawed thinking that leads to creativity.

When students make mistakes, teachers should ask them to analyze and discuss these mistakes. Often, mistakes or weak ideas contain the germ of correct answers or good ideas. In Japan, teachers spend entire class periods asking students to analyze the mistakes in their mathematical thinking. For the teacher who wants to make a difference, exploring mistakes can be an opportunity for learning and growing. Another aspect of teaching students to be creative is teaching them *to take responsibility for both successes and failures*. Teaching students how to take responsibility means teaching students to (1) understand their creative process, (2) criticize themselves, and (3) take pride in their best creative work. Unfortunately, many teachers and parents look for – or allow students to look for – an outside enemy responsible for failures.

It sounds trite to say that teachers should teach students to take responsibility for themselves, but sometimes there is a gap between what people know and how they translate thought into action. In practice, people differ widely in the extent to which they take responsibility for the causes and consequences of their actions. Creative people need to take responsibility for themselves and for their ideas.

Teachers also can work *to encourage creative collaboration*. Creative performance often is viewed as a solitary occupation. We may picture the writer writing alone in a studio, the artist painting in a solitary loft, or the musician practicing endlessly in a small music room. In reality, people often work in groups. Collaboration can spur creativity. Teachers can encourage students to learn by example by collaborating with creative people.

Students also need to learn how *to imagine things from other viewpoints.* An essential aspect of working with other people and getting the most out of collaborative creative activity is to imagine oneself in other people's shoes. Individuals can broaden their perspective by learning to see the world from different points of view. Teachers and parents should encourage their students to see the importance of understanding, respecting, and responding to other people's points of view. This is important, as many bright and potentially creative students never achieve success because they do not develop practical intelligence. They may do well in school and on tests, but they may never learn how to get along with others or to see things and themselves as others see them.

Teachers also need to help students recognize person-environment fit. What is judged as creative is an interaction between a person and the environment. The very same product that is rewarded as creative in one time or place may be scorned in another.

By building a constant appreciation of the importance of person-environment fit, teachers prepare their students for choosing environments that are conducive to their creative success. Encourage students to examine environments to help them learn to select and match environments with their skills.

Creativity, then, is in large part a habit that adults can encourage in students or in themselves. It remains only for teachers to help foster this habit.

CONCLUSION

Creativity is as much a habit in and an attitude toward life as it is a matter of ability. Creativity is often obvious in young students, but it may be harder to find in older students and adults because their creative potential has been suppressed by a society that encourages intellectual conformity. Yet, anyone can decide to adopt the creativity habit. Start right now!

REFERENCES

Adelson, B. (1984). When novices surpass experts: The difficulty of a task may increase with expertise. *Journal of Experimental Psychology: Learning, Memory, and Cognition,* **10**(3), 483–495.

Albert, R. S., & Runco, M. A. (1999). A history of research on creativity. In R. J. Sternberg (Ed.), *Handbook of creativity* (pp. 16–31). New York: Cambridge University Press.

Amabile, T. M. (1996). *Creativity in context.* Boulder, CO: Westview.

Amabile, T. M. (1999). How to kill creativity. In *Harvard Business Review on breakthrough thinking* (pp. 1–28). Boston, MA: Harvard Business School Press.

Baer, J., & Kaufman, J. C. (2006). Creativity research in English-speaking countries. In J. C. Kaufman, & R. J. Sternberg (Eds.), *The international handbook of creativity* (pp. 10–38). New York: Cambridge University Press.

Barron, F. (1969). *Creative person and creative process.* New York: Holt, Rinehart & Winston.

Barron, F. (1988). Putting creativity to work. In R. J. Sternberg (Ed.), *The nature of creativity* (pp. 76–98). New York: Cambridge University Press.

Csikszentmihalyi, M. (1988). Society, culture, and person: A systems view of creativity. In R. J. Sternberg (Ed.), *The nature of creativity* (pp. 325–339). New York: Cambridge University Press.

Csikszentmihalyi, M. (1990). The domain of creativity. In M. A. Runco & R. S. Albert (Eds.), *Theories of creativity* (pp. 190–212). Newbury Park, CA: Sage.

Csikszentmihalyi, M. (1996). *Creativity: Flow and the psychology of discovery and invention.* New York: HarperCollins.

Csikszentmihalyi, M. (1999). Implications of a systems perspective for the study of creativity. In R. J. Sternberg (Ed.), *Handbook of creativity* (pp. 313–335). New York: Cambridge University Press.

Frensch, P. A., & Sternberg, R. J. (1989). Expertise and intelligent thinking: When is it worse to know better? In R. J. Sternberg (Ed.), *Advances in the psychology of human intelligence* (Vol. 5, pp. 157–188). Hillsdale, NJ: Lawrence Erlbaum Associates.

Garcia, J. (1981). Tilting at the paper mills of academe. *American Psychologist, 36*(2), 149–158.

Garcia, J., & Koelling, R. A. (1966). The relation of cue to consequence in avoidance learning. *Psychonomic Science, 4,* 123–124.

Gardner, H. (1983). *Frames of mind: The theory of multiple intelligences.* New York: Basic Books.

Gardner, H. (1991). *The unschooled mind.* New York: Basic Books.

Gardner, H. (1993). *Creating minds.* New York: Basic Books.

Gardner, H. (2006). *Multiple intelligences: New horizons.* New York: Perseus.

Guilford, J. P. (1950). Creativity. *American Psychologist, 5,* 444–454.

Johnson-Laird, P. N. (1988). Freedom and constraint in creativity. In R. J. Sternberg (Ed.), *The nature of creativity* (pp. 202–219). New York: Cambridge University Press.

Kaufman, J. C. (2001a). Genius, lunatics, and poets: Mental illness in prize-winning authors. *Imagination, Cognition, and Personality, 20*(4), 305–314.

Kaufman, J. C. (2001b). The Sylvia Plath effect: Mental illness in eminent creative writers. *Journal of Creative Behavior, 35*(1), 37–50.

Kogan, N. (1973). Creativity and cognitive style: A life-span perspective. In P. B. Baltes, & K. W. Schaie (Eds.), *Life-span developmental psychology: Personality and socialization* (pp. 145–178). New York: Academic Press.

Lubart, T. I., & Sternberg, R. J. (1995). An investment approach to creativity: Theory and data. In S. M. Smith, T. B. Ward, & R. A. Finke (Eds.), *The creative cognition approach* (pp. 269–302). Cambridge, MA: MIT Press.

Maslow, A. (1967). The creative attitude. In R. L. Mooney & T. A. Rasik (Eds.), *Explorations in creativity* (pp. 43–57). New York: Harper & Row.

Mischel, W., Shoda, Y., & Rodriguez, M. L. (1989). Delay of gratification in children. *Science, 244,* 933–938.

Renzulli, J. S. (1986). The three-ring conception of giftedness: a developmental model for creative productivity. In R. J. Sternberg & J. E. Davidson (Eds.), *Conceptions of giftedness* (pp. 53–92). New York: Cambridge University Press.

Schank, R. C. (1988). *The creative attitude.* New York: Macmillan.

Simonton, D. K. (1976). Biographical determinants of achieved eminence: A multivariate approach to the Cox data. *Journal of Personality and Social Psychology, 33,* 218–226.

Simonton, D. K. (1984). *Genius, creativity, and leadership.* Cambridge, MA: Harvard University Press.

Simonton, D. K. (1988). Age and outstanding achievement: What do we know after a century of research? *Psychological Bulletin,* **104,** 251–267.

Simonton, D. K. (1988). *Scientific genius.* New York: Cambridge University Press.

Simonton, D. K. (1994). *Greatness: Who makes history and why?* New York: Guilford.

Sternberg, R. J. (1994). Allowing for thinking styles. *Educational Leadership,* **52**(3), 36–40.

Sternberg, R. J. (1997a). The concept of intelligence and its role in lifelong learning and success. *American Psychologist,* **52,** 1030–1037.

Sternberg, R. J. (1997b). *Successful intelligence.* New York: Plume.

Sternberg, R. J. (1997c). *Thinking styles.* New York: Cambridge University Press.

Sternberg, R. J. (Ed.). (1999). *Handbook of creativity.* New York: Cambridge University Press.

Sternberg, R. J. (2003). Teaching for successful intelligence: Principles, practices, and outcomes. *Educational and Child Psychology,* **20**(2), 6–18.

Sternberg, R. J. (2004). Good intentions, bad results: A dozen reasons why the No Child Left Behind (NCLB) Act is failing our nation's schools. *Education Week,* **24**(9), 42, 56.

Sternberg, R. J. (2006). Creativity is a habit. *Education Week,* **25**(24), 47–64.

Sternberg, R. J., & Grigorenko, E. L. (2004). Successful intelligence in the classroom. *Theory into Practice,* **43**(4), 274–280.

Sternberg, R. J., & Grigorenko, E. L. (2007). *Teaching for successful intelligence* (2nd ed.). Thousand Oaks, CA: Corwin.

Sternberg, R. J., & Lubart, T. I. (1991). An investment theory of creativity and its development. *Human Development,* **34**(1), 1–31.

Sternberg, R. J., & Lubart, T. I. (1995a). *Defying the crowd: Cultivating creativity in a culture of conformity.* New York: Free Press.

Sternberg, R. J., & Lubart, T. I. (1995b). Ten keys to creative innovation. *R & D Innovator,* **4**(3), 8–11.

Sternberg, R. J., & Lubart, T. I. (1995c). Ten tips toward creativity in the workplace. In C. M. Ford & D. A. Gioia (Eds.), *Creative action in organizations: Ivory tower visions and real world voices* (pp. 173–180). Newbury Park, CA: Sage Publications.

Sternberg, R. J., & The Rainbow Project Collaborators. (2005). Augmenting the SAT through assessments of analytical, practical, and creative skills. In W. Camara & E. Kimmel (Eds.), *Choosing students: Higher education admission tools for the 21st century* (pp. 159–176). Mahwah, NJ: Lawrence Erlbaum Associates.

Sternberg, R. J., & The Rainbow Project Collaborators. (2006). The Rainbow Project: Enhancing the SAT through assessments of analytical, practical and creative skills. *Intelligence,* **34**(4), 321–350.

Sternberg, R. J., & Williams, W. M. (1996). *How to develop student creativity.* Alexandria, VA: Association for Supervision and Curriculum Development.

Tharp, T. (2005). *The creative habit: Learn it and use it for life.* New York: Simon & Schuster.

Torrance, E. P. (1962). *Guiding creative talent.* Englewood Cliffs, NJ: Prentice-Hall.

Creativity in the Classroom Coda: Twenty Key Points and Other Insights

JAMES C. KAUFMAN AND RONALD A. BEGHETTO

As you have seen, chapter authors approached the assignment in several different ways. Some of them (such as Baldwin; Hennessey; Piirto; and Richards) talked about their personal journey in discovering creativity in the classrooms. Others used specific, concrete examples of creativity-nurturing curriculum and activities (such as Craft; Fairweather & Cramond; Niu & Zhou; Skiba; Tan, Sternberg, & Grigorenko; and Stokes). Some discussed actually teaching courses on creativity or developing programs to encourage creativity (such as Halpern; Piirto; Plucker & Dow; and Renzulli & de Wet).

One recurring theme in the book is the list of numerous (often unintentional) ways in which creativity can be (and has been) discouraged in the classroom. Nickerson offers a marvelously engaging tongue-in-cheek recipe for how the classroom can be a creativity stifling experience – in a way, his chapter serves as a synthesis of key points from the past literature. Our authors proposed a series of specific ideas and practices that can be used to increase student creativity. These range from tips for good practice to cautions to advice on how to use available resources for your advantage. We now offer our own synthesis of twenty key points that personally resonated with us as educators. We then highlight some other important themes and ideas that recur in these chapters.

Our list of the twenty key points:

1. The benefits of keeping up with amazing advances that are happening every month in technology that can help in supporting creativity, specifically discussed by Halpern as she talks about the prevalence of virtual worlds in which people learn in vastly unique settings from a wide array of "teachers." These technologies also include video games specifically designed to enhance learning and thinking, software that promotes the use of visual imagery, and online communities that foster the sharing of creative ideas (see also Baldwin and Renzulli & de Wet).

2. The power of being able to learn and share classroom ideas with other cultures. One example of this, from Niu and Zhou, is China's concept of

the "Good Teacher" in which the teacher occupies a high place in society and is given societal support and confirmation of the importance of his or her work (see also Halpern and Stokes).

3. The necessity of being aware of limiting and creativity stifling myths and misconceptions. The chapters by Plucker and Dow and Richards highlight (and dispel) several false myths pertaining to creativity being inextricably linked to madness or the view that there is a necessarily disruptive or dangerous component to being creative (see also Beghetto & Kaufman).

4. Baldwin's argument that nurturing creativity is particularly urgent for underserved and marginalized groups, such as students from minority and low socioeconomic backgrounds. This argument is particularly important given the trend of high-poverty "underperforming" schools, which typically serve minority students, turning to increasingly narrow and even scripted curricula. All students deserve opportunities to express and develop their creativity as part of the regular curriculum (see also Beghetto & Kaufman).

5. The importance of developing domain-specific knowledge, as Baer and Garret argue, as a means to prepare students to be creative in that specific area – rather than use general creativity techniques and tactics (see also Niu & Zhou and Stokes).

6. Hennessey writes of the benefits of supporting students' intrinsic motivation and enjoyment while learning and highlights the potential negative effect of rewards on student creativity (see also Niu & Zhou; Piirto; Renzulli & De Wet; and Sternberg). Baer and Garrett also consider how the need to give feedback and rewards can be balanced with the need to enhance intrinsic student motivation.

7. The importance of acknowledging everyday creativity. Both Richards and Beghetto and Kaufman say that most people and activities can be creative, not simply the elect or elite (see also Craft and Plucker & Dow), and argue for the inclusion of creativity in the everyday curriculum.

8. Just as improvisation enhances ensemble musical comedy or theatrical performances, Sawyer argues, so too will creative classroom teaching come from the allowance of unplanned and seemingly tangential thoughts and ideas (see also Baldwin, Piirto).

9. Craft discusses the need to view creativity from a wisdom-oriented perspective in which there is a focus on creativity and wisdom working together to link personal concerns with cultural and ecological priorities that is essential to incorporate into our educational system (see also Richards and Sternberg).

10. Runco outlines the tactics of challenging assumptions and considering opposite possibilities (see also Daniels & Piechowski), including the importance of (1) providing immediate and remote models of creative behavior, (2) regular opportunities for students to practice creative

thinking, and (3) appropriately reinforcing creative thinking and behavior (see also Piirto).

11. Both Sternberg and Richards write of the importance of supportive mentors and environment. Renzulli and de Wet say that one way to encourage creativity is by finding students a wide variety of resources – including mentors who will connect them to potentially meaningful subjects or topics and offering a chance for students' creative ideas to reach an audience.

12. Broadening conceptions of creativity in classroom by exploring potentially limiting self-beliefs about the nature of creativity is particularly important for prospective and practicing teachers, students and parents (Beghetto & Kaufman). This point is in alignment with Plucker and Dow's idea that examining one's own beliefs about creativity (and identifying misconceptions) is a necessary first step toward creating conditions for creativity enhancement.

13. Stokes discusses the value of constraints for creativity. Rather than thinking of constraints placed on classroom tasks as merely a limitation that undermines creativity, Stokes argues that such constraints can actually supports students to think in novel ways – often in ways opposite to what they are accustomed (see also Plucker & Dow).

14. Hennessey says that at a time when it may be especially difficult for teachers to highlight creativity, it is even more important for individual teachers to support creativity at a "grass-roots level" (see also Beghetto & Kaufman; Richards; and Sawyer).

15. When assessing academic and creative ability/potential, Sternberg writes, educators need to be very careful to use the best possible assessments – many of the most commonly used assessments are not the best ones available (see also Baer & Garrett and Sawyer). Skiba, Tan, Sternberg, and Grigorenko underscore this idea by stressing the importance of approaching the assessment of creativity in multiple ways (highlighting several compelling and cutting edge examples of creativity assessment).

16. Daniels and Piechowski discuss the importance for educators to understand *overexcitability* in relation to some students' experience of creativity. Overexcitability is a multidimensional and often overwhelming perception of the world that can be manifested via psychomotor, sensual, intellectual, imaginational, or emotional ways (see also Richards' views on the behavior of some gifted and creative students).

17. Piirto argues for the need to help students develop strong self-discipline, which can both increase creative productivity and enhance persistence in following a creative idea (see also Sternberg). Piirto also stresses the important point that nurturing creativity in the classroom results from a partnership between educators and their students – helping to ensure that creativity becomes a meaningful part of students' and teachers' lives.

18. Sawyer proposes that creativity should go beyond arts education and be present in all types of curriculum (including math and science) via the fostering of learning environments that emphasize active learning and knowledge building (see also Fairweather & Cramond).

19. Skiba, Tan, Sternberg, and Grigorenko stress the importance of teachers' developing a clear understanding of what creativity is, why it is important, and how it can be taught. This involves identifying potential barriers posed by implicit theories of creativity and, as Beghetto & Kaufman also discuss, the universal possibility for students' creativity to be nurtured in almost any context and subject area.

20. Fairweather and Cramond write about how to weave critical and creative thinking skills in the classroom by using a variety of engagement and problem solving techniques (see also Baer & Garrett and Halpern).

Many other themes can be found throughout these pages, such as discipline and methodological diversity (Craft and Niu & Zhou), the importance of imagination and exploring possibilities (Baldwin; Craft, Daniels & Piechowski; Piirto; and Sternberg), the need to specifically tell your students that you want and encourage creative behavior and be ready for that to happen (Halpern), the use of games (Niu & Zhou), creative potential (Beghetto & Kaufman; Runco; and Skiba, Tan, Sternberg, & Grigorenko), the importance of using examples (Runco), the importance of telling students exactly what is expected of them (Fairweather & Cramond and Stokes) and emphasizing that creativity is important and is welcome in the classroom (Beghetto & Kaufman, Richards, and Sternberg), the need to tolerate unique or wild ideas (Daniels & Piechowski and Runco), the multiple ways to teach, learn, and assess creativity (Renzulli & De Wet; and Skiba, Tan, Sternberg, & Grigorenko), the importance of curricular reform (Baldwin; Craft; and Hennessey), and the sad truth that most educational systems do not like change (Hennessey).

We hope that this book was as enjoyable, provocative, and fun to read for you as it has been for us to edit. We would also love to hear stories of teachers coming up with new ways to be creative in the classroom (and, indeed, we are working on a future volume filled with best creative practices) – feel free to e-mail us at beghetto@uoregon.edu or jkaufman@csusb.edu.

INDEX